EDUCATIONAL PSYCHOLOGY

EDUCATIONAL PSYCHOLOGY

A Cognitive Approach

RICHARD E. MAYER
University of California, Santa Barbara

LITTLE, BROWN AND COMPANY
Boston   Toronto

Library of Congress Cataloging-in-Publication Data

Mayer, Richard E., 1947–
  Educational psychology.

  Includes index.
  1. Educational psychology. I. Title.
LB1051.M39 1987   370.15   86-27842
ISBN 0-316-55151-1

Copyright © 1987 by Richard E. Mayer

Library of Congress Catalog Card Number 86-27842

ISBN 0-673-39187-6

9 8 7 6 5 4 3 2

MV

Printed in the United States of America

Credits and Acknowledgments

Figures 2–5 and 2–6: Adapted from R. Gelman (1969) "Conservation acquisition: a problem of learning to attend to relevant attributes." *Journal of Experimental Child Psychology*, 7, 167–186. Reprinted by permission of Academic Press and the author.

Figure 3–2: Adapted from "Knowledge structures and memory development" by M. L. Chi, 1978, in R. S. Siegler (Ed.), *Children's Thinking: What Develops?*, p. 83. Copyright 1978 by Lawrence Erlbaum Associates, Inc. Reprinted by permission.

Table 3–2: Adapted from "Intellectual development from birth to adulthood: a neo-Piagetian interpretation" by R. Case, 1978, in R. S. Siegler (Ed.), *Children's Thinking: What Develops?*, p. 38. Copyright by Lawrence Erlbaum Associates, Inc. Reprinted by permission.

Figure 3–5: From "The origins of scientific thinking" by R. S. Siegler, 1978, in R. S. Siegler (Ed.) *Children's Thinking: What Develops?*, p. 113. Copyright 1978 by Lawrence Erlbaum Associates, Inc. Reprinted by permission.

Figure 3–6: From R. Case (1978), "Implications of developmental psychology for the design of effective instruction" *Cognitive Psychology and Instruction*, edited by A. M. Lesgold, J. W. Pellegrino, S. D. Fokkema & R. Glaser, published by Plenum Publishing Corporation. Reprinted by permission.

(Continued on p. 563)

Dedicated to
my first teachers,
James and Bernis Mayer

Preface

Between the ages of 5 and 18, the average child spends about 12,000 hours in school. For these students, schools become a central focus of their lives, and schooling becomes their dominant activity. During this time something quite amazing happens. The five-year-old who enters the kindergarten classroom for the first time on an autumn morning is quite a different person from the young adult who files through the June graduation ceremony 13 years later. Anyone who has had the ongoing privilege of working with children cannot help but be struck by the changes that occur. Teachers have the opportunity to witness an extremely interesting, and, for our species, extremely important phenomenon—the growth of human beings.

Education is an attempt to create environments that promote and nurture changes in human beings—changes in what people do, in what they know, and in what they feel. The goal of education is growth, including intellectual and personal growth. Educational psychology is the scientific study of these changes, focusing particularly on how the process of instruction influences changes in students.

If you are interested in understanding the process of education, this book is for you. This book is intended as an introductory textbook for courses in educational psychology or related courses, and assumes that you have had no prior coursework in psychology or education.

Educational Psychology: A Cognitive Approach is written to help you understand educational psychology. To better demonstrate the nature of this book let me first explain what it is not about. This book is not an encyclopedia of every study that has ever been done in educational psychology. Instead, the book carefully presents examples of representative studies so that you can understand the main ideas. Second, this is not a "how to do it" book that tells you how to handle every possible classroom problem or tries to replace the many useful "methods" courses offered for teachers. Instead, the book provides you with an understanding of the teaching/learning process so that you can make informed judgments about the implementation of various instructional techniques. For each educational issue, this book carefully explains representative research and always includes a section on instructional implications to help you see how research relates to educational practice. Third, this is not a "watered-down" course in introductory psychology. Instead the book focuses specifically on the domain of educational psychology, including the study of how instructional manipulations influence a student's learning process and outcome. Fourth, this book is not built solely upon the behaviorist psychology of the first half of this century nor is it built upon no theory at all. Instead, this book is built upon the cognitive theme that has dominated the educational research of the 1970s and 1980s—namely, that learning is an active process in which the outcome of learning depends on how the learner processes incoming information. Thus, *Educational Psychology: A Cognitive Approach* provides you with an understanding of the main ideas, research findings, and instructional implications of modern educational psychology.

This text makes use of several pedagogic devices. Each chapter is organized in a similar way: it begins with an outline and abstract, then an introductory activity or example is given, then a manageable number of topics are covered each under its own heading, and finally the chapter ends with a summary. The book makes use of concrete examples in order to help you relate new ideas to what you already know. It is written in modular fashion so that each chapter could make sense on its own; yet, at the same time, the book has a unifying theme—that instructional procedures can be related to cognitive processes and knowledge within the learner. When research is presented, you are given enough information to understand what was done and what was found; each subsection on research is accompanied by a companion subsection on instructional implications so that you can see the relation between research and practice.

The book is divided into several main sections. Chapter 1 gives an organizing introduction to educational psychology. Chapters 2, 3, and 4 constitute the "development" section of the book, with a special focus on the nature of the learner. Chapters 5, 6, 7, 8, and 9 make up the "instruction" section of the book, with special focus on techniques for making learning more meaningful. Chapters 10, 11, 12, 13, and 14 are the "curriculum" section of the book, with special focus on the learning/instruction process within the domains of reading, writing, arithmetic, and science. Chapters 15, 16, and 17 constitute the "measurement" section, with focus on evaluating what students know and on how instruction can be adjusted to the individual needs of students. Chapter 18 on "classroom processes" shows how the learning/instruction process takes place within the rich context of the classroom.

Lastly, to help make the book more useable, an *Instructor's Manual* with a *Test Bank* has been created. In addition to including suggestions for enriching the course, a number of objective test questions for each chapter have been prepared.

Now, how should we proceed in our study of educational psychology? We could begin by analyzing the information we want students to learn and by describing techniques to insure that students acquire this information. This is the traditional approach to education—what Dewey (1902, p. 8) called curriculum centered: "Subdivide each topic into studies; each study into lessons; each lesson into specific facts and formulae. Let the child proceed step by step to master each one of these separate parts, and at last he will have covered the entire ground." The subject matter of this approach is information, i.e., the material that is presented for students to acquire. The theoretical view of this approach is that of the "passive learner" (Dewey, 1902, p. 8): "The child is simply the immature being who is to be matured; he is the superficial being who is to be deepened . . . It is his to receive, to accept." Such a view is consistent with the behaviorism that dominated psychology from Dewey's time up until the 1950s, and which is the basis for many current educational practices.

In contrast, we could begin by trying to understand the learner: the existing knowledge and skills that the learner brings to the learning situation, the process by which knowledge grows in the learner, the nature of the learning outcome in the learner's mind. This could be called a "child-centered" approach (Dewey, 1902, p. 9) because: "The child is the starting-point, the center, and the end. His development, his growth is the ideal." The subject matter of this approach is knowledge—what changes occur in the student's mind. The theoretical view of this approach could be called "the active learner" (Dewey, 1902, p. 9): "Learning is active. It involves reaching out of the mind. It involves organic assimilation starting from within." Modern cognitive psychology, which began in the 1950s and has evolved into the dominant approach to psychology, is consistent with several of the emphases of the child-centered approach.

In summary, on one side we have the "curriculum-centered" approach which views the instructional material as the main subject matter of educational psychology, passive learning as the theoretical basis, and behaviorism as the psychological benefactor; on the other side we have the "child-based" approach which views changes in the child's mind as the main subject matter of educational psychology, active learning as the theoretical basis, and cognitive psychology as the benefactor. This book shares Dewey's (1913, p. viii) bias for a "child-centered" approach to the study of educational psychology: "A child's character, knowledge, and skill are not reconstructed by sitting in a room where events happen. Events must *happen to him* . . ." The cognitive approach pursued in this book represents educational psychology's most current and powerful attempt to fulfill Dewey's vision—to understand how events that happen to a student affect the growth of the student's mind.

Acknowledgments

Writing *Educational Psychology: A Cognitive Approach* has been a labor of love for me. As an educational psychologist who has spent the last 15 years of his life immersed in researching how instructional methods influence learning, I have been writing this book in my head for most of those 15 years. As a teacher and author, I have looked with desperation for ideas on how to improve my students' learning. As a parent of children in the public school system, I have come to recognize the urgent need for a useful educational psychology.

Finally, as a member of this society and as a member of my community's local school board, I have hoped that what we know about educational psychology could be used productively by the extremely dedicated and skilled teachers of our children. Thus, with all these roles motivating me, it has been a pleasure to work on this book. My main wish is that you enjoy reading this book as much as I have enjoyed writing it.

I owe thanks to many people. I appreciate the support of Mylan Jaixen and the staff of Little, Brown and Company, including Barbara Breese who managed the production of this book. Similarly, this book has benefited from Ardyth Behn's copyediting skills as well as Nancy Fraser and Teddi Potter's typing skills. I am grateful for the comments of reviewers who read several drafts of the manuscript: Karen Block, University of Pittsburgh; Theodore Coladarci, University of Maine at Orono; Sylvia Franham-Diggory, University of Delaware; Charles H. Gregg, The University of Utah; David S. Lane, Jr., Oklahoma State University; Sharon Nodie Oja, University of New Hampshire; John Rickards, The University of Connecticut; and M. C. Wittrock, University of California, Los Angeles. While these reviewers cannot be held responsible for any remaining shortcomings, they are responsible for many improvements. I owe a large debt to Jim Greeno, who introduced me to many of the issues in educational psychology. I also appreciated the graduate training that I received at The University of Michigan, including chances to learn from Bill McKeachie, Art Melton and others. My first job at Indiana University provided me with the chance to learn from Frank Restle as well as many others. The cognitive group here at the University of California, Santa Barbara, has provided me with colleagues who have been supportive and stimulating, including Bobby Klatzky, Russ Revlin, John Cotton, Prentice Starkey, Alice Klein, Jim Pellegrino, Susan Goldman, Tracy Kendler, and Priscilla Drum. I also benefited from chances to interact with colleagues during my sabbatical leaves at the Learning Research and Development Center (University of Pittsburgh) and at the Center for the Study of Reading (University of Illinois). These colleagues and teachers have helped me to become interested in educational psychology, and have also helped me to see that there is much more to be learned. My parents, James and Bernis Mayer, and my brothers, Bob and Bernie Mayer, have provided encouragement. Finally, I wish to thank my wife, Beverly, and my children, Kenny, David, and Sarah, for their understanding and support while I worked on this project.

Richard E. Mayer
Santa Barbara, California
September 1986

Brief Contents

Contents

Part II LEARNING AND INSTRUCTION

Part III   CURRICULUM

Part IV MEASUREMENT

Part V CLASSROOM PROCESSES

EDUCATIONAL PSYCHOLOGY

1 Introduction to Educational Psychology

Chapter Outline

Wild Boy
What Is Educational Psychology?
A Closer Look at the Cognitive Approach
Conclusion

This chapter defines educational psychology, analyzes the main components in the teaching/learning process, and explains how the cognitive approach can be used to answer questions about educational practice. It also provides an organization for the rest of the book.

WILD BOY

Suppose a child was freed completely of all social interaction with other humans. Suppose this child was allowed to develop without any social contact with other people. This experiment could be viewed as providing a child with the ultimate in educational freedom. What would happen to such a child? What would the child be like? Is society needed in order to help children develop to their fullest potential as human beings? Take a moment to provide some predictions in Box 1–1.

These questions were at the heart of an historic educational experiment that began in 1800 in Paris. The experiment involved only one student, an adolescent boy named Victor, and his teacher, a physician named Dr. Jean-Marc Itard. Victor had been discovered living in the forests of Aveyron in France. Apparently, the boy had grown up in the forest, without any human contact. When captured, the boy was completely naked, dirty, and inarticulate. He seemed insensitive to temperature and pain, and was incapable of maintaining attention. He ate his food raw, using only his hands. Although physically

BOX 1–1   What Would It Be Like for a Child to Grow Up Without Any Human Contact?

Suppose that a child grew up from birth to age twelve in a forest, without any human contact. What do you think the child would be like at age twelve? Place one check mark for each pair of attributes.

_____ physically weak and unhealthy	_____ physically strong and healthy
_____ attentive to stimuli	_____ unattentive to stimuli
_____ responsive to pain	_____ unresponsive to pain
_____ responsive to temperature	_____ unresponsive to temperature
_____ interested in other people	_____ uninterested in other people
_____ enjoyed broad variety of food tastes	_____ restricted to a very few food tastes
_____ had developed a form of oral language	_____ hadn't developed a form of oral language
_____ had developed a form of gesturing language	_____ hadn't developed a form of gesturing language
_____ had developed a form of written language	_____ hadn't developed a form of written language
_____ had developed basic arithmetic skills	_____ hadn't developed basic arithmetic skills
_____ had invented many useful tools	_____ hadn't invented useful tools
_____ was well mannered with people	_____ wasn't well mannered with people
_____ longed for human affection	_____ was not interested in human affection
_____ would be able to learn basic social skills swiftly	_____ wouldn't be able to learn basic social skills swiftly
_____ would be able to learn basic language skills swiftly	_____ wouldn't be able to learn basic language skills swiftly

healthy, he was totally unsocialized. The public showed great interest in the boy, and he become popularly known as the *enfant sauvage de l'Aveyron*—that is, the wild boy of Aveyron. Dr. Itard was convinced that the boy, who he named Victor, could be taught to become a civilized member of French society. For the next five years, Dr. Itard worked with his student, often having to develop new materials and instructional techniques.

Dr. Itard's educational program was based on several principles. First, he believed that the needs and characteristics of the student should dictate the educational program. Instead of letting the curriculum determine what students would learn, in lock-step fashion, the teacher must be free to shape instruction to suit the needs of the student. Second, he believed that education depends on the student having had certain experiences (i.e., most educational programs assume that the child has acquired "readiness skills" through natural interactions with the physical and social environment). For example, a student needs experiences with objects before learning the language names for them. If a student lacks appropriate sensory experiences, then these experiences must be provided as prerequisites to more academic components of an educational program. Third, he believed that the student had to be motivated to learn. According to Dr. Itard, Victor had successfully learned to cope in the wild because his survival depended on it. Now, Dr. Itard introduced new needs for Victor so that Victor would be motivated to learn social skills. Finally, Dr. Itard believed that instruction often requires the development of new instructional devices and techniques. Many of the materials and techniques of behavior modification that Dr. Itard developed became the basis for subsequent programs to teach deaf and retarded students.

How far did Victor progress during the five years of instruction? He learned basic social skills, such as dressing himself, sleeping in bed without wetting, and eating with utensils. He learned to make use of his senses including sight, sound, and taste. He learned to show affection and to try to please others. Although he never learned to speak effectively, he did learn to communicate using written language. However, Victor did not reach full self-sufficiency, and spent the rest of his life under the supervision of a caretaker. The lack of complete success has been attributed to many causes including the lack of appropriate stimulation during critical periods of development, the limitations of Itard's methods (including his insistence than Victor use spoken rather than sign language), and the possibility that Victor was born mentally retarded. Thus, you would have been correct in your predictions in Box 1–1 if you had checked each of the attributes on the right-hand side and none on the left side of Box 1–1.

As we leave the "wild boy," let's consider what we have learned about the nature of education. Some of the broader educational issues addressed by Itard were (Lane, 1976, p. 129): (1) Society (including formal instruction) is crucial for human development. "The moral superiority said to be natural to man is only the result of civilization . . . [and without society, man] pitifully hangs on without intelligence and without feelings, a precarious life reduced to bare animal functions." (2) People learn in order to satisfy their needs. "In the most isolated savage as in the most highly civilized man, there exists a constant relation between ideas and needs." (3) Instructional programs should be based on science. "The progress of education can and ought to be illuminated by the light of modern medicine, which of all the natural sciences can help most powerfully toward the perfection of the human species." (4) Instructional programs should take into account the individual characteristics of each student. "[Progress will be made] by detecting the organic and intellectual peculiarities of each individual and determining therefrom what education ought to do for him."

The conclusions of Itard, written in the early 1800s, can serve as a starting point for this book on educational psychology. This book shares many of the biases expressed by Itard's conclusions: that education can be a positive force in the development of human potential; that the motivation to learn comes from the personal, social, and intellectual needs of the learner; that educational techniques and materials can be informed by results of scientific research; that an understanding of the entering characteristics of the learner can help in the creation of an effective educational program. The remainder of this chapter explores some of the basic issues in educational psychology.

WHAT IS EDUCATIONAL PSYCHOLOGY?

What is educational psychology? Although this seems like a straightforward question, you are not likely to find total agreement among educational psychologists concerning the answer. There are two quite different approaches to educational psychology: behaviorist and cognitive.

Behaviorist Versus Cognitive Approaches to Educational Psychology

A behaviorist approach to educational psychology is summarized in the top of Figure 1–1. As you can see, the behaviorist approach involves determining the relationships between two factors—instructional manipulations and outcome performance. Both correspond to externally observable events: instructional manipulations refer to the nature of the stimulus that is presented to the learner while outcome performance refers to the nature of the response that the learner gives on tests. According to this approach, the goal of educational psychology is to determine how instructional manipulations affect changes in behavior. Thus the main question here is: What is the relationship between instructional manipulations and outcome performance?

In contrast, a cognitive approach to educational psychology is summarized in the bottom of Figure 1–1. As you can see, the cognitive approach involves determining the relationships among external factors (e.g., instructional manipulations and outcome performance) and internal factors (e.g., learning pro-

FIGURE 1–1 Two Approaches to Educational Psychology

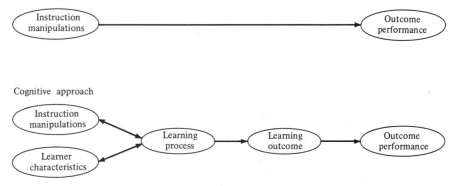

cesses, learning outcomes, and the existing knowledge and skill of the learner). The cognitive approach attempts to understand how instructional manipulations affect internal cognitive processes such as paying attention, encoding, retrieving; how these processes result in the acquisition of new knowledge; and how new knowledge influences performance, such as on tests. According to the cognitive approach, the goal of educational psychology is to explain the relation between *stimulus* (i.e., instructional manipulation) and *response* (i.e., outcome performance) by describing the intervening cognitive processes and structures. Thus, the main question here is: What are the internal cognitive processes and states that allow us to understand the relationship between instructional manipulations and outcome performance?

The distinction between these two approaches to educational psychology is certainly not new. For example, in his classic book, *The Nature of Intelligence*, Thurstone (1924, p. 165) argued against behaviorist approaches to education:

> A brand of educational psychology is being taught to prospective teachers in which they are drilled in the jargon of establishing "bonds" between stimuli and the desired behavior. It would be more appropriate to describe the normal impulses of children, and the methods by which children may be induced to express these impulses in ways that are profitable.

In essence, Thurstone points out that there is more to learning than helping students build stimulus-response (S-R) connections; indeed, the internal processes of the learner play a central role in the education process.

Thurstone's complaint, and those of modern cognitive educational psychologists, have had little impact on educational practice until fairly recently. During the past twenty years, there has been an explosion of research and theory concerning how the human mind works (see Mayer, 1981). One useful product of this cognitive revolution has been the development of a framework for describing the cognitive factors underlying the instruction/learning process.

This book is concerned with a cognitive approach to educational psychology. Some of the reasons for this approach are:

1. Useful.   If we find out that instructional method A results in more learning that instructional method B, it is useful to also know why method A seems to be better than method B. This information will help in determining when to use the methods, how to modify the methods, and so on.
2. Current.   The cognitive approach is a more recent approach that serves to enhance and interpret earlier behaviorist work. Thus the cognitive — approach represents what is new in educational psychology.
3. Widespread.   The cognitive approach has come to dominate most fields of psychology, including the study of how we perceive, learn, remember, think, etc. Thus the cognitive approach that is already dominant in most fields of psychology can also be applied successfully to educational psychology.

By using a cognitive approach, this book will provide you with an integrated approach to educational psychology that is useful, current, and widely accepted.

Factors in the Instruction/Learning Process

Table 1–1 summarizes some examples of factors that might be involved in the cognitive approach to educational psychology. The factors are as follows:

Instructional manipulations: the sequence of environmental (i.e., external) events including the organization and content of instructional materials and behaviors of the teacher. The instructional manipulations include both what is taught and how it is taught, and depend on the characteristics of the teacher and on the curriculum.

Learner characteristics: the learner's existing knowledge, including facts,

TABLE 1–1   Examples of Factors in Educational Psychology

Instructional Manipulations	Learner Characteristics	Learning Processes	Learning Outcome	Outcome Performance
Repeating a lesson	Existing knowledge	Paying attention	Acquisition of information	Retention
Providing an example	Existing modes and capacities of memory representation	Identifying relevant existing knowledge	Understanding of information	Transfer
Asking the learner to put an idea in his/her own words		Integrating new information with old		

Adapted from Mayer (1984)

> procedures, and strategies that may be required in the learning situation, and the nature of the learner's memory system, including capacity and mode of representation in memory.
>
> *Learning processes:*   the learner's internal cognitive processes during learning, such as how the learner selects, organizes, and integrates new information with existing knowledge.
>
> *Learning outcome:*   the cognitive changes in the learner's knowledge or memory system, including the newly acquired facts, procedures, and strategies.
>
> *Outcome performance:*   the learner's performance (i.e., behavior) on tests, such as retention or transfer to new learning tasks.

As you can see, the cognitive approach involves several factors that are internal to the learner—learner characteristics, learning processes, learning outcomes. Since these factors are not directly observable, they can only be inferred from the learner's behavior. Thus a major challenge of the cognitive approach is to devise methods of study that allow us to make correct inferences about internal processes and states in the learner.

Definition of Educational Psychology

Now that we have selected the cognitive approach to educational psychology, we can return to our original question: What is educational psychology? Educational psychology is a branch of psychology concerned with understanding how the instructional environment and the characteristics of the learner interact to produce cognitive growth in the learner. In particular, educational psychology focuses on the scientific study of techniques for manipulating human cognitive processes and knowledge states. There are three major components in this definition:

1. Educational psychology is a science, namely a branch of psychology.
2. Educational psychology investigates the instructor's manipulation of the environment.
3. Educational psychology investigates resulting changes in the learner's cognitive processes and knowledge structures.

Educational psychology stands between teaching and learning (i.e., between the instructional manipulations provided by the teacher and the changes in knowledge and behavior created in the learner). Teaching refers to the teacher's construction of experiences for the student, where such experiences are intended to foster changes in the learner's knowledge and behavior. For example, Gagné (1974, p. vii) defines instruction as "the arrangement of external events to activate and support the internal processes of learning." Learning refers to changes in the learner's knowledge, where such changes are due to experience. In his classic textbook, *Principles of Teaching*, E. L. Thorndike (1913, p. 1) recognized that the central theme in education is an externally manipulated change in the learner:

> The word education is used with many meanings, but in all its usages it refers to changes. No one is educated who stays as he was. We do not educate anybody if we do nothing that makes any difference or change in anybody. . . . In studying education, then, one studies always the existence, nature, causation or value of change of some sort.

In summary, teaching and learning are inevitably connected processes that involve the fostering of change within the learner.

In his provocative little book *Experience & Education*, John Dewey (1938, p. 25) described the relationship between teaching—providing students with useful experiences—and learning—the acquisition of knowledge. "All genuine education comes about through experience," Dewey argued. However, he added an important warning that "all experiences are not genuinely or equally educative." Unfortunately, many instructional manipulations are what Dewey calls "mis-educative":

> Some experiences are mis-educative. Any experience is mis-educative that has the effect of arresting or distorting the growth of further experiences. . . . Every experience lives on in further experiences. Hence the central problem of an education based on experience is to select the kind of present experiences that live fruitfully and creatively in subsequent experiences.

In summary, instructional manipulations result in changes in the learner's knowledge. Since all learning involves connecting new information to existing knowledge, it is crucial to help students develop knowledge structures that can support the acquisition of useful new information. If students have not acquired knowledge, then information cannot be successfully connected with it.

Organization of Educational Psychology

There are several "actors" in the drama of the teaching/learning process, as summarized below:

The Learner.   We begin with a learner who comes to the learning situation with an existing storehouse of knowledge, skills, and other characteristics. The nature of the learner is explored in the first section of this book, Development. Chapter 2 provides a general overview of cognitive development; Chapter 3 provides a summary of research on individual differences in memory capacity; and Chapter 4 summarizes research on individual differences in learning styles and strategies.

The Teacher.   We add a teacher who provides experiences that are intended to influence the growth of knowledge in the learner. The role of instructional manipulations is explored in the second section of this book, Learning and Instruction. Chapter 5 provides an overview of basic learning and motivational processes, with focus on learning of simple responses. Chapter 6 provides a summary of research on learning from prose, and Chapter 7 summarizes research on learning from tutorials. Chapter 8 explores teaching of learning strategies and Chapter 9 explores teaching of thinking strategies.

The Curricuium.   We also add the subject matter to be acquired by the learner (i.e., a description of the proposed changes in the learner). The third section of this book, Curriculum, focuses on several representative subject matter areas. Reading is covered in Chapters 10 and 11; writing is covered in Chapter 12; mathematics is dealt with in Chapter 13; and science is the topic of Chapter 14.

The Outcome.   Any study of the teaching/learning process must include the outcome of learning (i.e., a description of the actual changes that took place in the learner). The fourth section of this book, Measurement, presents techniques for evaluating changes in the learner's knowledge. Chapters 15 and 16 summarize how evaluation can play a useful role in a program of instruction; Chapter 17 explores the role of individual differences in determining what is learned.

The Classroom.   Finally, the learning/teaching process often occurs within the social context of a classroom or group of students. The final section of this book, Classroom Process, consists of Chapter 18, which examines the role of classroom processes in education.

In summary, these actors represent the who, how, what, and where of the teaching/learning situation. The learner corresponds to the "who," that is, who we are trying to help change. The teacher corresponds to the "how," that is, how we try to foster changes in the learner. The curriculum and the outcome correspond to the "what," that is, a description of what changes we proposed and actually fostered in the learner. The "where" corresponds to the classroom context of learning.

A CLOSER LOOK AT THE COGNITIVE APPROACH

This book is concerned mainly with the processes by which we can influence the intellectual growth of the learner. More specifically, this book is concerned with understanding how instructional manipulations affect changes in the learner's knowledge, including changes in cognitive strategies and the structure of memory. As you can see, *knowledge* is at the center of the educational process. Changing the learner's knowledge—manifested in changes in academic, motor, social, and personal behavior—is what education is all about.

Kinds of Knowledge

Cognitive psychologists have found it useful to distinguish among several different kinds of knowledge, including the following (Mayer, 1981):

Semantic knowledge refers to a person's factual knowledge about the world, including what Gagne (1974) calls *verbal information*. Examples include being able to answer the questions, What is the capital of California? or How many sides does a square have?

Procedural knowledge refers to an algorithm, or list of steps, that can be used in a specific situation, including what Gagne (1974) calls *intellectual skill*. An example is being able to use the procedure for long division in order to solve the problem, $234234 \div 13 =$ _____. Other examples are being able to classify objects, such as different geometric shapes, into categories, or being able to change a word to plural form using the rule "Add s."

Strategic knowledge refers to a general approach for how to learn or remember or solve problems, including the self-monitoring of progress in the use of the strategy. Gagne (1974) refers to this kind of knowledge as *cognitive strategy*. Examples include being able to design and monitor a plan for how to compose an essay, or being able to decide on a technique for how to memorize a list of definitions.

These kinds of knowledge are summarized in Table 1–2. In subsequent chapters, such as Chapter 12, we explore how each kind of knowledge is related to school tasks. There are other kinds of knowledge that are affective, motoric, personal, or social. However, this book will focus mainly on the kinds of knowledge listed in Table 1–2, because this is the area in which most of the research has been carried out.

Kinds of Memory Stores and Processes

If "knowledge" is at the center of educational psychology, then the "memory system" is the place where the action is! Figure 1–2 presents a typical description of the architecture of the memory system (Mayer, 1981). As you can see, there are three main components indicated as rectangles:

Sensory Memory.   Incoming information is accepted by the sense recep-

TABLE 1–2   Three Kinds of Knowledge

Type of Knowledge	Example
Semantic knowledge	What is the capital of California?
Procedural knowledge	How do you change "dog" into plural form? What is $234234 \div 13$?
Strategic knowledge	How would you go about composing an essay on education?

FIGURE 1–2 An Information-Processing Model of the Memory System

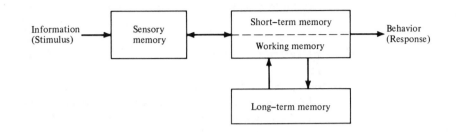

tors and is held very briefly in a sensory memory store. According to the classic model, the capacity of sensory memory is unlimited, the mode of representation is sensory, the duration is very brief (e.g., one half second for visual information), and loss occurs due to time decay.

Short-term Memory. If you pay attention to the incoming information before it decays, you may be able to transfer some of that information to short-term memory. You can think of STM as that part of memory corresponding to your active consciousness or awareness. According to the classic model, the capacity of short-term memory is extremely limited (e.g., you can actively think about only five or so different things at one time), the mode is acoustic or some other modification of the sensory input, the duration is temporary (e.g., items are lost after about 18 seconds unless you actively rehearse), and loss is due to new information displacing the items in STM. In addition, a portion of STM can be used for performing mental manipulations such as mental arithmetic—this portion is referred to as *working memory*.

Long-term Memory. If you encode the information from STM into long-term memory, then some of that information may be retained permanently. Long-term memory has unlimited capacity including the three kinds of knowledge listed above, can retain information for long periods of time, and loses information when other information interferes with retrieving the target information.

In addition to these three components, the arrows in the figure represent processes that are fundamental to the memory system including the basic processes following:

Attention: is involved in transfer of information from SM to STM.
Rehearsal: is involved in keeping information active in consciousness (i.e., keeping information temporarily in STM).
Encoding: involves transfer of information from STM to LTM, including the integration of that information with existing knowledge in LTM.
Searching: involves finding a piece of information in LTM.

In subsequent chapters, such as Chapter 3, we explore how individual differences in these memory stores and processes can be related to differences in how children learn.

Cognitive Conditions of Learning

Now that we have briefly explored the kinds of knowledge and the architecture of the memory system, let's return more closely to the theme of this book—educational psychology. For example, let's suppose that we ask a student to read a short lesson on how radar works. Some people will not remember much from the lesson—these could be called nonlearners. Some people will remember much of the information but will not be able to creatively use the information to solve problems or make explanations—these could be called nonundersanders. Finally, some people might be able to remember information and to use that information creatively in problem solving—these are understanders. Table 1–3 summarizes the differences in the performance among the three learners.

What conditions of learning create each of these kinds of outcomes? Gagne (1974) has made a useful distinction between two kinds of conditions of learning: *internal conditions* refer to the knowledge, processes, and strategies that are involved inside the learner at the time of learning; *external conditions* refer to the instructional events that occur outside of the learner. Since the outcome of learning depends both on the internal and external conditions, Mayer (1975, 1984) has suggested that three major conditions must be met for meaningful learning:

Reception: The to-be-learned material must be received by the student (i.e., the learner must have contact with and pay attention to the target information).

Availability: The learner must possess existing knowledge that is relevant to the new information.

Activation: The learner must actively organize the new information and integrate the new information with the existing knowledge.

These three conditions are presented in Figure 1–3. As you can see, three scenarios can be generated:

Nonlearning: If the first condition is not met, nothing will be learned.

TABLE 1–3   Three Kinds of Learners

Type of Learner	Retention Performance	Transfer Performance
Nonlearner	Poor	Poor
Nonunderstander	Good	Poor
Understander	Good	Good

Adapted from Mayer (1984)

FIGURE 1–3   Some Conditions of Meaningful Learning

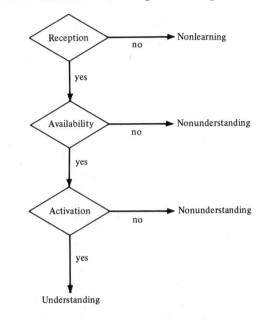

Thus, even when a student may be actively thinking about all he or she knows about radar (presumably involving the second and third conditions), nothing will be learned if the student fails to carefully read the passage.

Nonunderstanding—If the first condition is met, but the second or third condition is not met, then the student will learn in a nonmeaningful way. For example, in reading a passage on radar, if the learner does not possess or activate relevant existing knowledge (e.g., the idea of echoes), then the material will not be well integrated with existing knowledge.

Understanding—If all three conditions are met, then the student will learn in a meaningful way. For example, the new information about radar will be integrated with existing knowledge so that it can be used in transfer situations. Although these distinctions are much too vague to qualify as a theory of instruction, they do provide a framework for describing different kinds of learning situations. The main theme, of course, is that learning depends both on external conditions (e.g., instructional manipulations) and on internal conditions (e.g., the existing knowledge and learning process used by the learner).

CONCLUSION

This chapter presents an example of an early educational experiment, presents a definition of educational psychology, describes the cognitive approach to educational psychology, and gives arguments for why a cognitive approach to education is needed.

The example of the Wild Boy of Aveyron raises issues concerning the role of education in human development. This example suggests that natural experience—everyday interactions with the environment—must be supplemented by manipulated experience—instructional sequences designed by teachers.

The definition of educational psychology requires a distinction between the behaviorist and cognitive approaches. The behaviorist approach focuses on external conditions of learning, such as instructional manipulations and outcome performance. The cognitive approach adds internal conditions of learning such as learner characteristics, learning processes, and learning outcomes. Educational psychology is a branch of psychology, concerned with understanding how the instructional environment and the characteristics of the learner interact to produce cognitive growth in the learner. Thorndike and Dewey both recognized that the central theme in education is an externally manipulated change in the learner. The "actors" in the teaching/learning process are the learner, the teacher, the curriculum, the outcome, and the classroom context.

The cognitive approach is based on the idea that instruction brings about changes in the knowledge of the learner. Three kinds of knowledge are semantic, procedural, and strategic knowledge. The architecture of the memory system includes memory stores—sensory memory, short-term memory, and long-term memory—and memory processes—attention, rehearsal, encoding, and searching. Instructional manipulations may result in no learning, nonunderstanding, or understanding. Understanding, or meaningful learning, requires that the learner pay attention, that the learner possess appropriate prerequisite knowledge, and that the learner actively organize and integrate the new information with existing knowledge.

Educational psychology is concerned with understanding how the external conditions of learning—such as instructional manipulations—and internal conditions of learning—such as the existing knowledge and learning strategy used by the learner—interact to result in intellectual changes in the learner. The remainder of this book attempts to investigate this idea from several different perspectives—the cognitive development of the child (Chapters 2–4), the instructional manipulations of the teacher (Chapters 5–9), the curriculum as a guide to what should be learned (Chapter 10–14), the measurement of what is learned (Chapter 15–17), and the classroom context of learning (Chapter 18).

SUGGESTED READINGS

Ausubel, D. P. (1968). *Educational psychology: A cognitive view*. New York: Holt, Rinehart & Winston. (An early attempt to relate educational psychology to cognitive psychology.)

Dewey, J. (1938). *Experience and education*. New York: Collier. (Provides a dose of Dewey's "child-centered" educational philosophy.)

Gagne, E. (1985). *The cognitive psychology of school learning*. Boston: Little, Brown. (Summarizes modern cognitive research and its relation to the psychology of instruction.)

Gagne, R. M. (1974). *Essentials of learning for instruction*. Hinsdale, Ill.: Dryden Press. (Summarizes the instructional theory of a well-respected educational psychologist.)

Mayer, R. E. (1981). *The promise of cognitive psychology*. New York: Freeman. (Presents an overview of cognitive psychology, with special focus on practical applications.)

PART I

DEVELOPMENT

The three chapters in this section focus on the cognitive development of the learner. Chapter 2 focuses on three major intellectual transitions in how children think and learn—corresponding roughly to the transition from home to preschool, from preschool to elementary school, from elementary school to secondary school. Chapter 3 focuses on the development of memory capacity, while Chapter 4 focuses on the development of learning strategies. Thus, we begin with a focus on the learner—including the cognitive skills, memory capacities, and learning strategies available to children at various levels of development.

The cognitive framework summarized in Figure 1–3 lists three general conditions for meaningful learning—reception of the material to be learned, availability of appropriate knowledge for processing the material, and activation of this knowledge during learning. This section emphasizes the importance of availability (e.g., the availability of general cognitive skills, memory capacities, or learning strategies) and shows how children at different developmental levels learn quite differently. A theme of this section is that the outcome of learning depends both on what is presented and on the learner (i.e., the developmental level of the learner's cognitive processing is as crucial as the material that is presented). A complementary theme is that developmental growth of cognitive skills and capacities can be influenced by appropriate instructional environments.

2 _Cognitive Development_

This chapter focuses on the developmental changes that occur in the way that children represent and think about the world. The chapter provides an overview of Piaget's theory of cognitive development, with special focus on major changes that coincide roughly with the child's transition into preschool, elementary school, and secondary school. Finally, the chapter explores the degree to which cognitive development can be taught and the degree to which teaching must be adjusted to the child's level of cognitive development.

SHELL GAMES

Suppose that I had three shells and a coin, as shown in the top of Figure 2–1. I take the coin and place it under the middle shell, as shown in the figure. Which shell would you lift in order to find the coin? _____

Now, suppose that I move the middle shell to the first position, as shown in Figure 2–1. Which shell would you lift in order to find the coin? _____

These tasks are similar to some used by Piaget in order to determine whether young children could mentally represent objects (e.g., coins) that are not visually present. Children who are still in Piaget's first period of cognitive development—sensorimotor—would be unable to correctly answer the two questions listed above; however, children in Piaget's second period— preoperational—would be able to find the coin. Thus changes in children's

FIGURE 2–1   Some Shell Games

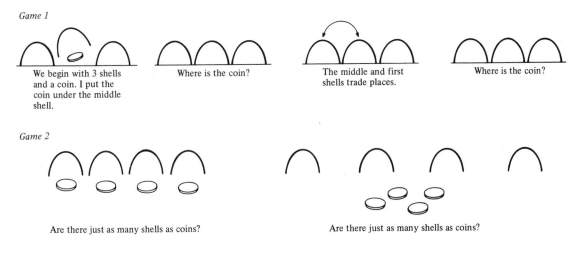

Game 1

We begin with 3 shells and a coin. I put the coin under the middle shell.

Where is the coin?

The middle and first shells trade places.

Where is the coin?

Game 2

Are there just as many shells as coins?

Are there just as many shells as coins?

Game 3

There are coins under 20 of these 40 shells.
If you lifted up 4 shells, how many coins would you find?
If you lifted up 20 shells, how many coins would you find?

ability to perform in tasks like this shell game represent major changes in the way children think (i.e., a transition from the sensorimotor to the pre-operational period).

Now, consider the row of shells and row of coins shown in the middle portion of Figure 2–1. Are there just as many shells in the top row as coins in the bottom row? _____ Good, I'll assume you said, "yes." Now, look at what I am doing. In the middle portion of Figure 2–1 you can see that I am moving the top row apart and the bottom row together. Now, are there just as many shells on top as coins on the bottom? _____

This task is similar to one used by Piaget in order to determine whether children were able to perform logical mental operations on their representations of concrete objects. In this case, the child must be able to rearrange mentally the two sets of objects back into their original configuration of two corresponding rows. Children in Piaget's second period of cognitive development, preoperational, would have trouble with this task; in contrast, children in the third period, concrete operations, would be able to respond correctly. Thus tasks such as this one help to demonstrate another major transition in children's thinking—from preoperational to concrete operational thought. The correct answer, of course, is that the two sets are equal no matter how you arrange the shells.

Finally, let's suppose that we have forty shells, with coins placed under twenty of them, as shown in the bottom of Figure 2–1. We completely mix up the shells, and then we lift up four of them. How many coins will we find? _____ Suppose we lift up twenty of them. How many coins would we find? _____

Again, this task is somewhat similar to tasks used by Piaget in order to evaluate children's concept of probability. Younger children, in Piaget's second and third periods of cognitive development—preoperational or concrete operations—were unable to deal consistently with probability. The very youngest children might predict that all the shells would have coins (or that none would) and would not be surprised if the twenty shells that were lifted each had a coin. Adolescents who were in Piaget's final period of development—formal operations—would be able to recognize that the probability of getting all twenty shells to have coins would be quite remote and that as more shells are lifted the probabilities of finding a coin change. Tasks like this one help to show a major transition in thought from concrete operations to formal operations. The answers to the questions, of course, are not definite: any number of coins from zero to four could be found by lifting four shells but we would expect to find two on the average; similarly, with twenty shells lifted we could get any number of coins from zero to twenty, but we would be very surprised to get an extreme number (like zero or twenty) and more confident about getting a number close to the average of ten.

These three shell games help to illustrate the three major transitions in children's cognitive development as proposed by Jean Piaget. This chapter will explore each of these three transitions, as well as give a brief introduction to Piaget and his theory, and a brief critique of the relevance of his work in education.

PIAGET'S THEORY

Background

Jean Piaget was "one of the most remarkable figures in contemporary behavioral science." So begins Flavell's (1963, p. 1) famous synthesis of Piaget's theory. Indeed, Piaget has produced the world's most comprehensive theory of cognitive development, and his ideas have significantly influenced American education and psychology.

Yet Piaget's background would seem to make him an unlikely candidate for this title. He lived in Switzerland and wrote in French, so his work did not have a direct route to American education and psychology. He was trained as a biologist, not as an educator or psychologist. In fact, he published his first biology paper in a scientific journal at the age of ten, and he had published more than twenty papers in natural science before his twenty-first birthday. His interest was in philosophy. In particular, he was concerned with the philosophical issue of "genetic epistemology"—the study of the growth of knowledge within a person. Thus Piaget considered himself to be primarily a genetic epistemologist rather than primarily an educational or developmental psychologist.

Elkind (1967, p. xviii) has summarized Piaget's background as follows: "He is not fundamentally a child psychologist concerned with the practical issues of child growth and development. He is rather, first and foremost, a genetic epistemologist concerned with the nature of knowledge and with the structures and processes by which it is acquired."

The motivating question for Piaget was, How does a person come to possess knowledge? This could be viewed purely as a philosophical question, and Piaget could have attempted to answer from the comfort of an armchair. Instead, he decided to apply the methods of scientific observation and experimentation (i.e., he decided to collect some empirical information just as he had done earlier for his research in biological science). He used the "clinical method"—carefully observing how children in naturalistic environments responded to small tasks that he created. His early work involved studying the intellectual growth of infants from the first days of life, including intensive study of his own three children. Subsequent work investigated the role of language and logic in cognitive development, as well as the development of abstract, scientific thinking.

Major Features of Piaget's Theory

Although Piaget's theory is complex and massive, you can capture some of its flavor by focusing on the following major features of cognitive growth (i.e., that it is relative, functional, dialectical, intrinsically motivated, and occurs in stages).

Relative. One major theme is that all cognitive growth is relative to existing knowledge. New information is never directly perceived or directly added to memory. Instead, new information is always interpreted in terms of existing knowledge; all learning involves combining what is presented with what the child already knows. In this way, all learning (or perception) is distorted because it is filtered through and mediated by existing knowledge.

Functional. Another major theme is that humans are alive and trying to survive; thus people acquire knowledge in order to function successfully in their environments. Two functional requirements of a person's representation of the world are:

1. *Adaptation*—one's mental representation of the world must correspond to reality.
2. *Organization*—one's mental representation of the world must be consolidated into a coherent and internally consistent structure.

As you can see, these two requirements are at odds with one another: adaptation continually calls for more information from the world, whereas organization continually calls for a reduction in complexity. Building a functional mental representation of the world, however, requires that the knowledge be both relevant (i.e., adaptive) and usable (i.e., organized).

Dialectical. The tension between adaptation and organization suggests a third major feature of Piaget's theory—the idea that all cognitive growth results from the opposing processes (or dialectics) of assimilation and accommodation. These processes are concerned with how new knowledge from the outside world is combined with existing knowledge already in memory. Assimilation refers to the changing of new knowledge so it fits in with existing knowledge; this process is analogous to the restructuring of food that is ingested so that it can be incorporated into the body. Accommodation refers to changing of existing knowledge so that it can incorporate (or accommodate) new incoming information; this process is analogous to altering the structure and composition of existing cells with new material from food that was ingested. As you can see, assimilation and accommodation each requires the other.

The regulating process that balances assimilation and accommodation is equilibration. For example, if there is too much assimilation, this results in a world view that is too different from reality. In contrast, if there is too much accommodation, this results in a world view that lacks coherence, meaning, and direction. The process of equilibration maintains a balance so that new information is acquired (i.e., assimilation) with only small disruption to existing knowledge structures (i.e., accommodation).

Intrinsic. Another theme is that the motivation for cognitive growth is intrinsic to the person. A child will naturally seek out the kind of new information in the environment which is most useful for that child's growth. If the child is exposed to new information that is vastly different from anything he already knows, the child will not be able to take in that information. Hence, there will be no cognitive growth. If the new information is very similar or identical to existing knowledge, the child will be able to take in the information. However, there will be no cognitive growth because nothing new has been brought in. Cognitive growth occurs when the child assimilates information that is just slightly more complex than existing knowledge; the information can be brought into the cognitive system but it also requires some accommodation. Thus the assimilation/accommodation process results in a new cognitive structure that includes both the assimilated information and the existing knowledge to which it was assimilated. This new structure is now capable of assimilating slightly more complex information than the previous structure, and so on.

Stages. A final theme is that cognitive growth can be described as a series of stages. In a sense, each encounter with the environment elicits changes in the way that information is processed by a person. Piaget has used the term *stage* to describe some of the major changes in the way that information is represented and processed. These stages can be thought of as descriptions of information-processing strategies and modes of representation, moving from less powerful strategies and modes in the beginning stage to more powerful strategies and modes in the later stage. The strategies and modes of representation that evolve are "better" than earlier strategies and representations in the sense that the new techniques allow one to better function in the environment.

Table 2–1 shows the four major stages of cognitive development, according to Piaget's theory. Although ages are suggested for each stage, there are often great individual differences among the ages at which children move from one stage to another. However, Piaget argues that the order of the stages is invariant (i.e., children move through the stages in exactly the order indicated). Piaget's stage theory is described more fully in the next sections of this chapter.

In summary, the major idea running through all of these themes is that cognitive development involves the growth of knowledge within the child. Piaget's theory is an attempt to describe the process by which new knowledge is acquired, and the changes in information processing strategies and representations that evolve.

SENSORIMOTOR TO PREOPERATIONAL PERIOD: UP FROM INFANCY

Theory: Changes in the Child's Representation of Objects

Piaget's description of cognitive growth begins with the sensorimotor period, lasting roughly from age zero to two. According to Piaget, the newborn infant does not perceive or represent the world in the same way that adults do. For

TABLE 2–1   Piaget's Stages of Cognitive Development

Four Major Stages	Approximate Ages
Sensorimotor period	0–2 years
Preoperational period	2–7 years
Concrete operations period	7–11 years
Formal operations period	11–adult

Three Major Transitions	Approximate Age	Example Accomplishment
Sensorimotor to preoperational	2	Object permanence (Game 1)
Preoperational to concrete operations	7	Conservation (Game 2)
Concrete operations to formal operations	11	Abstract thought (Game 3)

example, Piaget argues that sensory experience is not coordinated in the newborn—the child must learn to coordinate visual, tactile, auditory, and other sensations into a single concept of space and action. Piaget also argues that during the sensorimotor period, the child tends to represent the world in terms of motor behavior (i.e., how the world responds to the child's actions).

Research on Object Permanence

One of the major accomplishments of the sensorimotor period is the development of the concept of "object permanence"—the idea that objects exist even when they cannot be directly observed. Piaget provides several "experiments" in which an infant behaves as if objects cease to exist once the objects are out of sight. For example, Piaget (1954, p. 39–40) presents his seven-month-old daughter with a toy duck and then, as she watches, he hides it under a sheet:

> Jacqueline tries to grasp a celluloid duck on top of her quilt. She almost catches it, shakes herself, and the duck slides down beside her. It falls very close to her hand but behind a fold in the sheet. Jacqueline's eyes have followed the movement, she has even followed it with her outstretched hand. But as soon as the duck has disappeared—nothing more. It does not occur to her to search behind the fold of the sheet which would be very easy to do. . . . I then take the duck from its hiding-place and place it near her hand three times. All three times she tries to grasp it, but when she is about to touch it I replace it very obviously under the sheet. Jacqueline immediately withdraws her hand and gives up.

After a long series of observations such as the one given above, Piaget (1954, p. 46–47) concludes: "The child's universe is still only a totality of pictures emerging from nothingness at the moment of action, to return to nothingness at the moment when action is finished." Piaget's (1954, p. 51) observation of his daughter at age nine months suggests that she is beginning to develop the concept of object permanence:

> Jacqueline is seated on a sofa and tries to get hold of my watch. I place it under the edge of the coverlet on which the child is seated; Jacqueline immediately pulls the edge of the coverlet, spies the watch, and takes possession of it.

Thus, even though the object has been placed out of sight, the child seems to be able to temporarily represent the object in memory. However, Piaget (1954, p. 56) finds that Jacqueline (at age ten months) fails to perform a slightly more demanding task:

> Jacqueline is seated on a mattress without anything to disturb or distract her. . . . I take her parrot from her hands and hide it twice in succession under the mattress on her left, in A. Both times Jacqueline looks for the object immediately and grabs it.

Then I take it from her hands and move it very slowly before her eyes to the corresponding place on her right, under the mattress, in B. Jacqueline watches this movement very attentively, but at the moment when the parrot disappears in B she turns to her left and looks where it was before in A.

Finally, when Jacqueline is almost eighteen months old, she is able to find an object that has been hidden first in one place (A) and then in another (B).

Jacqueline watches me when I put a coin in my hand, then put my hand under a coverlet. I withdraw my hand closed; Jacqueline opens it, then searches under the coverlet until she finds the object. I take the coin back at once, put it in my hand and then slip my closed hand under a cushion situated on the other side; Jacqueline immediately searches for the object under the cushion. I repeat the experiment by hiding the coin under a jacket; Jacqueline finds it without hesitation.

In this quote from Piaget (1954, p. 68) we see that after a year and a half of progress, Jacqueline seems to have finally mastered the concept of object permanence.

Piaget carefully documents the substages in the development of object permanence: First, there is no active search for a vanished object; second, the child watches the trajectory of an object as it's being hidden but ignores the object once it's out of sight; third, the child actively searches for a hidden object, but only at the point where it vanished; fourth, the child actively searches, taking successive displacements into account; and finally, the child actively searches, even taking invisible displacements into account. From Piaget's observations of his own three children, we are introduced to some fundamental changes that occur during the first two years of life: As sensory experience becomes more integrated, the child is better able to anticipate that one event will cause another; as actions and sensations become more coordinated, the child begins to be able perform successful motions; and as the concept of object permanence develops, the child begins to be able to represent objects mentally. Thus, as the child enters preschool at about age two, he or she has developed capabilities for how to represent and behave successfully in the environment.

Implications: Transition from Home to Preschool

The first transition in Piaget's theory—from sensorimotor to preoperations—corresponds roughly to a major transition in a child's education—from home (or day care) to preschool. This transition does not, of course, mean that the child's home is no longer an educational environment; however, the transition to preschool, which often begins at about age two, represents a milestone in a child's education, namely the formal entry into an institution called school.

The child's first learning environment is simply wherever the child is: his crib, his playpen, his parent's arms, his home. For example, as I write this book, I am watching my infant daughter, who is sitting in a high chair gazing at a tower of blocks I have built for her. She moves her hand near the blocks and accidentally knocks down part of the tower. This causes her to show signs of joy, including much movement and gleeful utterances. She now moves her hands in the same general direction as before, first taking a few high swipes (and missing the tower) and then taking progressively lower swipes that tend to topple the tower systematically row by row. When it is completely destroyed, she looks again at me. Her accomplishment in this episode involved systematically coordinating her hand and eye in order to carry out the demolition of the tower I built.

What have we learned (aside from why it took me three years to write this book)? First, new advances build on previous advances. My daughter's progress in moving towards preoperational thinking was based on prerequisite skills. She already was able to reach out and touch objects that attracted her attention. What was new in her performance was the degree to which she controlled the height of her swipes at the tower, but this accomplishment depended on earlier expertise in hand-eye coordination. Second, learning requires action. My daughter had to act upon the tower I built. Third, the motivation for action came from my daughter and her being placed in an interesting situation. I could have shown her how to take swipes at the tower systematically, but I doubt whether she would have appreciated my tutorial. Instead, the child should be free to participate in environments that are interesting to her.

A child-centered approach to cognitive development, such as Piaget's theory, would recommend that infants be allowed to act upon their environments. Infants need to touch, to pull, to drop, to push, to move, and even suck on objects in their environment. They need an environment that is responsive to their actions and interesting enough to attract their actions. Finally, Piaget's work shows that infant's play is the basis of intellectual growth.

PREOPERATIONAL TO CONCRETE OPERATIONS: TRANSITION INTO CHILDHOOD

Theory: Six Limitations of Preoperational Thought

The world of the preschooler, occurring roughly from ages two to seven, is the world of the preoperational period. Although the child has mastered concepts such as object permanence and movement in space, the child's thinking at this stage is still quite different from that of adults. In particular, the child has not yet developed logical ways of operating on mental representations. Phillips (1969) lists six limitations of preoperational thought:

Concreteness. The child is restricted to thinking about objects that are physically present or associated with the current situation. For example, Piaget (1951) describes how his daughter, Jacqueline at age two years and seven months, is unable to recognize her sister out of context:

> Seeing Lucienne in a new bathing suit, with a cap, Jacqueline asked: "What's the baby's name?" Her mother explained that it was a bathing costume, but J. pointed to Lucienne herself and said, "But what's the name of that?" (indicating Lucienne's face) and repeated the question several times. But as soon as Lucienne had her dress on again, Jacqueline exclaimed very seriously: "It's Lucienne again," as if her sister had changed her identity in changing her clothes.

Irreversibility. The child cannot mentally rearrange objects in a logical way. For example, Phillips (1969) provides an example in which a four-year-old boy is asked, "Do you have a brother?" He answers, "Yes." When asked, "What's his name?" the four-year-old answers, "Jim." However, when asked, "Does Jim have a brother?" the child answers, "No."

Egocentrism. The child behaves as if everyone else knows what he or she knows and perceives exactly what he or she perceives. For example, Piaget (1965) observed schoolchildren playing the game of marbles:

> Not only do they tell us of totally different rules . . . but when they play together they do not watch each other and do not justify their respective rules even for the duration of the game. The fact of the matter is that neither is trying to get the better of the other; each is merely having a game on his own, trying to hit the marbles in the square, that is, trying to win from his point of view.

Centering. The child focuses on only one dimension or aspect of a situation at a time. Piaget (1952) gave children a set of four sticks that varied in length, and asked the child to arrange them in order. The result might be something like this:

Apparently, the child centers on only one dimension—the top of the sticks—and does not simultaneously consider other dimensions, such as the bottom of the sticks.

States Versus Transformations. The child focuses on static perceptual states rather than on the actions that produced the state. For example, Bruner (1964) conducted a study involving two identical beakers filled with identical amounts of liquid. The contents of one of the beakers was poured into another beaker that was wider—resulting in a lower liquid level. When the pouring was conducted behind a screen, so that children could see the pouring but not the liquid levels, many four-year-olds said that the newly poured beaker contained just as much liquid as the original beaker. However, when the screen was removed, and the child could see the lower liquid level, all of the four-year-olds changed their answer—saying that the newly poured beaker did not contain just as much as the original beaker. Apparently, young children are overwhelmed by the perceptual state rather than being able to consider the transformation that created it.

Transductive Reasoning. The child associates objects or events without using deductive or inductive reasoning. Piaget (1951) provides an example from his conversation with his two-year-old daughter:

> Jacqueline wanted a doll dress that was upstairs. She said, "Dress," and when her mother refused to get it, "Daddy get dress." As I also refused, she wanted to go herself "To mommy's room." After several repetitions of this she was told that it was too cold there. There was a long silence, and then: "Not too cold." I asked, "Where?" "In the room." "Why isn't it too cold?" "Get dress."

Research on Conservation

By the time a child enters elementary school at age five or six, a transition is starting to take place—a "great leap" from preoperational to concrete operational thought. For example, the child's cognitive processing changes in several of the six areas just listed. Piaget captures the essence of this transition through a series of what he calls "conservation tasks"—little experiments in which the child is given a demonstration and asked to answer a simple question. As examples, let's consider two types of conservation tasks: conservation of number and conservation of quantity.

Conservation of Number. Figure 2–2 summarizes the procedure for a typical conservation of number experiment, in which Piaget (1965) presents a child with eggcups and eggs. A four-year-old, presumably in the preoperational period, was able to compare the two sets in only a global way (Piaget, 1965, p. 50):

E: "Take just enough eggs for the eggcups, not more and not less, one egg for each cup."
C: (The child made a row the same length but containing far too many eggs.)
E: "Is there the same number of eggs and eggcups?"

FIGURE 2–2   Conservation of Number

Is there the same number of eggs and eggcups?

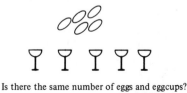

Is there the same number of eggs and eggcups?

Is there the same number of eggs and eggcups?

C: "Yes."
E: "Well, then, put the eggs in, to see whether they're right."
C: (He did so.)
E: "Were they the same?"
C: "No."
E: "Are they the same now?"
C: "Yes." (Removed the extra eggs.)
E: "Now we'll take all the eggs out." (Makes them into a pile in front of the eggcups.) "Are they the same now?"
C: "No."
E: "Why?"
C: "There are more eggcups."
E: "Are there enough eggs for the eggcups?"
C: "I don't know."
E: (The eggcups were put closer together and the eggs spread out.) "Look, now is there the same number of eggs and eggcups?"
C: "No, there are more eggs."
E: "Are there enough eggcups for eggs?"
C: "No, I don't know."

As you can see, the child seems unable to produce a "one-to-one correspondence" between egg and eggcup. Instead, the child seems to base his answers on the perceptual comparison of the lengths of the rows. The child focuses on states rather than actions, is unable to reverse mentally the action of bunching the eggs or eggcups together, and is centered only on one dimension—the length of the row of eggs or eggcups. In contrast, an older child (age five years and eight months) shows characteristics of concrete operations (Piaget, 1965, p. 55):

E: (After laying out one egg for each eggcup, the eggs are grouped together in front of eggcups.) "Is there the same number?"
C: "Yes."
E: "Why?"
C: "Because they're like that." (Gestures to the eggs as grouped together.)
E: "And now?" (Spaces out the eggs and moves eggcups close together.)
C: "Yes."
E: "Why?"
C: "If you spread the eggs out, it's the same number."

The child's last statement suggests a major accomplishment in cognitive development—the ability to reverse an action mentally. Thus the child can perform a "concrete operation"—mentally rearranging the eggs or eggcups. This frees the child from making decisions based solely on the perceptual qualities of visual states. Thus the difference between the first dialogue and second helps to demonstrate the transition from preoperational to concrete operational ways of thinking.

Conservation of Quantity.   Now, let's briefly consider conservation of quantity. In one version of this task, the child is shown two identically shaped glasses (A1 and A2), both filled to the same level with some liquid such as lemonade. In addition, there is an empty glass (B1) that is shorter and wider than the other glasses. Figure 2–3 shows the procedure for a typical experiment. First, the child is asked to verify that the two glasses (A1 and A2) have the same amount of lemonade. Then, as the child watches, the contents of one glass (A2) are poured into another glass (B1). Now, the child is asked whether the glasses (A1) and (B1) contain the same quantity of lemonade. The preoperational child will say that B1 contains less (if he focuses on height) or more (if he focuses on width) than A1. When the liquid is poured back from B1 to A2, the preoperational child will say that there is now the same quantity of lemonade in both glasses. The preoperational child behaves as if there is less (or more) to drink when the lemonade is in a short wide glass than when it is in a tall narrow glass. In contrast, the child who has achieved concrete operations is able to recognize that the two glasses contain equivalent amounts of lemonade. This child is able to *decenter*—that is, deal with more than one dimension at a time. In this case, the child is able to recognize that height and width compensate for one another. This child can mentally pour the lemonade rather than relying solely on the perceptual appearance of the glasses.

What Does Conservation Mean?   Based on the examples given, what does

FIGURE 2–3 Conservation of Quantity

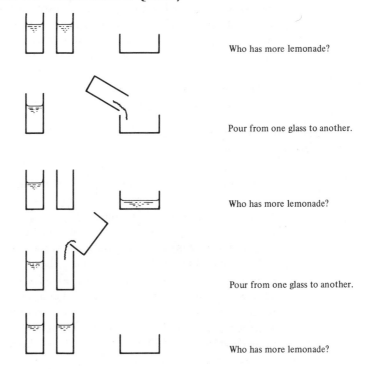

Who has more lemonade?

Pour from one glass to another.

Who has more lemonade?

Pour from one glass to another.

Who has more lemonade?

the conserver know that the nonconserver does not know? The conserver has made progress in overcoming several of the limitations of preoperational thought listed earlier in this section:

Reversibility—The child is able to mentally operate on objects in logical ways. For example, the child can conceive the regrouping of a bunch of objects back into a row or repouring the liquid from one glass back into the original glass.

Decentering—The child is able to deal logically with more than one dimension at a time. For example, the child can see that length and width of a set of objects, or that the height and width of a glass compensate for one another.

Transformations Versus States—The child is no longer overpowered by the perceptual images of states, but rather can think about the transformations that created the states.

Loss of Egocentrism—The child no longer sees every situation from only one point of view, but now is able to take on multiple points of view.

Logical Thinking—The child's thinking shows some signs of appropriate logic in some concrete situations.

A major limitation that still remains is the child's inability to think logically about abstract, hypothetical, or probabilistic situations. In addition, not all of the aspects of concrete operations appear at the same time; when in transition, a child might be able to successfully conserve on some types of conservation tasks but not on others. Thus, as the child enters elementary school, the child may have achieved all or most of the characteristics of concrete operational thought.

Implications: Transition from Preschool to Elementary School

The second major transition in Piaget's theory—from preoperations to concrete operations—corresponds roughly to another major transition in a child's education—from preschool to elementary school. The transition to elementary school, at about age five, represents another milestone in a child's education, namely, the beginning of compulsory education mandated by government.

You can think of preschool as a place where children's minds change, a place where children acquire the thinking skills that allow them to benefit from elementary school. Why do most preschools admit children who are two years of age or older? This age limit, while certainly subject to great individual differences among children, allows preschools to serve children who have reached (or almost reached) preoperational thought and are "working" on the development of concrete operations.

Suppose we were to look into a typical preschool. We might see a physical plant consisting of several classrooms, a large playground, many materials, and much equipment. We might also see several dozen children between ages two and five, and several teachers.

As we look closer, we might focus on a child, named Sarah, sitting on the floor with a bucket of building blocks of various sizes, shapes, and colors. Sarah sifts through the bucket looking for red blocks; each time she finds a red block she takes it out of the bucket and puts it in a pile. This is an example of *classification*—sorting things into groups based on similarities and differences among the things (such as color). Next, Sarah takes some blocks and builds a structure in which the front row consists of little blocks, the middle row consists of middle-sized blocks, and the back row consists of large blocks. This is an example of *seriation*—arranging things in order based on some attribute (such as size). Finally, we see Sarah taking five small square blocks and putting a long block on top of each. This is an example of *one-to-one correspondence*—matching a set of things (such as five square blocks) to another set of things (such as five long blocks) such that one thing in one set corresponds to one thing in the other set.

Are there any implications for education in our observations of a little girl playing with blocks? Although there was no teacher, no curriculum, no assignments, not even any numbers spoken, we have just observed a mathematics lesson. Three implications of Piaget's theory are particularly relevant: First, according to Piaget's theory, the concept of number is based on the child's prerequisite knowledge of concepts such as classification, seriation, and one-to-one correspondence. New concepts should not be imposed on a child who has not yet acquired the underlying, prerequisite concepts. Second, development of concepts such as classification, seriation, and one-to-one correspondence comes from physical experience in manipulating concrete objects (such as blocks). Children need experience with appropriate concrete objects. Third, the motivation to learn comes from the child. Children should not be forced to move lock-step through a series of teacher-imposed learning tasks.

A child-centered approach, based on Piaget's theory, would recommend that the best way to allow a child to develop the concept of number is to give the child chances to actively manipulate concrete objects in a way that the child chooses. Useful materials and activity centers are described by Sharp (1970) and Furth & Wachs (1975). In contrast, a curriculum-centered approach might drill the child on tasks such as counting from one to ten. What's wrong with this approach? Sharp (1970, p. 23–27) warns that understanding comes through self-directed experiences rather than teacher-directed memorization:

> Children can be taught to count, but an understanding of number is something they must develop out of their own experiences. . . . Don't let your child's ability to count mislead you into thinking that numbers mean the same thing to him that they do to you. . . . If arithmetic is imposed on a child before he has developed the necessary prenumber concepts, he merely memorizes, thus storing up trouble for the future.

In summary, our brief look inside a preschool has focused on the example of mathematical ability. We have found that "playing with concrete objects" can be every bit as much a mathematics lesson for preschoolers as deriving equations on a blackboard can be for high school students. In short, self-directed play serves a function at the preschool level that may be more important than teacher-imposed "academics." Similarly, peer social interaction—such as discussing how to determine who gets "the next turn" on a toy—provides the basis for intellectual development such as the loss of egocentrism.

CONCRETE TO FORMAL OPERATIONS: TRANSITION INTO ADOLESCENCE

Theory: Adult Thinking

According to Piaget's theory, there is another major change at about age 11 as the child prepares to enter junior high school or middle school. This change involves the transition from the concrete operations period to the formal operations period. Flavell (1963) has isolated three major aspects of formal operations: hypothetical-deductive thought, abstract thought, and systematic thought.

Hypothetical-Deductive Thought. Hypothetical thought refers to the child's ability to logically deal with the possible as well as with the actual (i.e., with hypothetical situations as well as real situations). For example, Shapiro & O'Brien (1970) asked elementary school children to answer "yes," "no," or "not enough clues" to the question in the following situation:

> If this is room 9, then it is the fourth grade.
> This is not room 9. Is it the fourth grade?

Almost all the children answered "no," although the correct answer is "not enough clues." This task requires hypothetical-deductive thought (i.e., assuming a hypothetical situation and then making logical deductions).

Abstract Thought. Abstract thought refers to the child's ability to think abstractly as well as concretely (i.e., with symbols as well as with actual numbers or objects). In addition, the child can perform operations on abstract propositions, which Piaget calls "second degree operations." For example, the use of random variables in an equation involves abstract thought. Abstract thought is also required in word problems such as, "Find a number such that 8 less than 2 times the number is the same as 2."

Systematic Thought. Systematic thought refers to the child's ability to isolate all relevant variables and all possible combinations of variables. For example, suppose I asked you to list all the possible ways to arrange the letters *ABCD*. There are twenty-four possible arrangements, and several systematic ways of generating them. In addition, systematic thought involves controlling for irrelevant variables in a way such as that required in scientific research.

Research on the Pendulum Problem

As an example of formal operational thought, consider the pendulum problem shown in Figure 2–4. The subject is shown the pendulum and is asked to determine what influences the rate of oscillation (i.e., what influences how fast the pendulum swings). The subject may "experiment" by varying the length of the string, the weight of the suspended object, the height of the released object, and the force with which it is released.

In order to solve this problem, the subject must generate all possible hypotheses. For example, one of the four variables may affect the rate of oscillation. Then, the subject must systematically and logically test each hypothesis. For example, to test the hypothesis that "length of string" is the critical variable, the subject must control for all other variables while manipulating string length; first, a short string can be tested, then a long string can be tested, with identical weight, height, and force in both tests.

Inhelder & Piaget (1958) summarize the performance of a formal operations adolescent (age fifteen) as follows:

FIGURE 2–4   What Determines How Fast the Pendulum Swings?

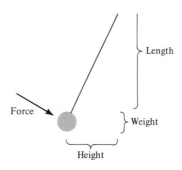

. . . after having selected 100 grams with a long string and a medium length string, then 20 grams with a long and short string, and finally 200 grams with a long and short, concludes, "It's the length of the string that makes it go faster or slower; the weight doesn't play any role." She discounts likewise the height of the drop and the force of her push.

As can be seen, this subject displays each of the characteristics of formal operations—hypothetical-deductive, abstract, and systematic thought.

The pendulum problem helps to demonstrate that formal operational thought is at the heart of scientific inquiry. For example, Lawson (1982) has found a strong correlation ($r = .69$) between tests of formal operations and science achievement in ninth graders. However, Karplus and his colleagues (1979) have found that most junior high school science students do not seem to possess formal operations, in spite of the fact that most science instruction assumes that students are capable of formal operational thought. The relation between formal operations and science instruction is discussed more fully in Chapter 14.

Implications: Transition from Elementary to Secondary School

The third major transition—from concrete to formal operations—corresponds roughly to the third major transition in a child's formal education—from elementary school to junior high school (or middle school). Traditionally, elementary school involves a common curriculum that all students are expected to master, while junior high school involves options concerning which courses to take, how to manage one's time, and so on. Elementary school serves children who are developing the intellectual, social, and personal skills required for success in junior high school.

Why does formal education begin at about age five? Could we move kindergarten down a year, or should we move it up a year? The answer seems to be that children entering elementary school must be ready to benefit from instruction. They need to have the skills required to learn to read and write and compute, for example. The mental skills that come with concrete operations provide the prerequisites upon which the elementary school curriculum is built, and the experiences of the child during this period lay the groundwork for the next transition.

Let's look briefly into an elementary school classroom. David, a fourth grader, is filling out a work sheet on mathematical computation, but he comes to a problem for which he lacks a memorized answer or procedure: "John has 20 marbles to divide among 4 friends. How many will each friend get?" David responds by whispering, "Four, eight, twelve, sixteen, twenty," and simultaneously extending first one, then two, then three, then four, and finally five fingers. Then he looks at his hand, with five extended fingers, and writes "5" as his answer on the worksheet. Apparently, David lacked expertise in carrying out division problems so he changed a division problem into an addition problem. This discovery represents progress in the transition from concrete to formal operations—for David has discovered a general rule that can be applied logically to many problems.

What have we learned from David's discovery? First, intellectual inventions—such as discovering the relationship between division and addition (or counting by fours)—are based on prerequisite knowledge and concepts. David possessed the concept of number, part-whole relations, one-to-one correspondence, and he knew how to carry out the addition procedure effortlessly. Being able to automatically carry out basic procedures—such as addition—can be a prerequisite to creative intellectual invention. Second, the process of intellectual development requires active participation of the learner. Although David did not have to manipulate concrete objects (as the preoperational child), he did actively use his fingers and counting by fours. For example, he used his fingers to represent the five sets of four marbles in the problem. Third, the motivation to invent came from David's interaction with his environment. Had the teacher explicitly shown David how any division problem can be converted into an addition problem, it is unlikely that David would have understood and appreciated the insight. Instead, cognitive growth seems best served through the self-direction of the learner.

A CLOSER LOOK AT EDUCATIONAL IMPLICATIONS OF PIAGET'S THEORY

Child-Centered Versus Curriculum-Centered Education

The hallmark of Piaget's theory is that the intellectual growth of the child depends both on the level of the child's cognitive development and the nature of the child's interaction with the environment. Piaget (1971, p. 166–67) defines two possible views concerning whether cognitive development can be taught:

> IF "the structural variations in the child's thought are determined from within, bound by an immutable order of succession and an unvarying chronology, each stage beginning at its appointed moment and occupying a precisely ordained period of the child's life" THEN "the teacher would be wasting his time and his effort attempting to speed up the development of his students."
>
> IF "the development of reason depended uniquely on individual experience and on the influences wielded by the physical and social environment" THEN "school . . . could very well accelerate that development."

According to Piaget, some schools tend to ignore the role of internal maturation and development, assuming that the child is a miniature adult. These schools may focus solely on the curriculum—viewing schooling as a process in which children acquire specific knowledge and behaviors. Other schools view development as a fixed hereditary process, assuming that all growth depends on time. These schools may focus on a tracking system—viewing schooling as a process in which the more advanced students are separated from the less advanced students.

Piaget (1965, p. 169) offers a compromise: "allowing room for internal structural maturation and also for the influences of experience . . . and environment." Thus a major instructional implication is that schools should provide environments which, when matched to the child's level of development, may serve to stimulate further development. Schooling can be viewed as a process in which children are stimulated to develop useful knowledge, learning skills, and reasoning skills.

A caveat that follows from the Piagetian perspective is that early emphasis on curriculum-centered academics, such as teaching preschoolers to read and compute, forces intellectual growth that would have come naturally later. Stanley (1973, p. 3) summarizes this implication as follows:

> Many nursery school educators believe that spending much of a child's early years systematically teaching him things he or she would probably learn later at home, school, or community may deprive the child of time for other experiences, especially those more directly promoting social and emotional development.

At the same time, the lock-step grade-level organization of schools can result in a failure to provide appropriate instructional experiences for each child, especially those who are most developed. Failing to provide systematic academic instruction to a child who can benefit from such experience is as much a violation of Piagetian theory as prematurely forcing instruction on a child who is not developmentally ready.

Can Cognitive Development Be Taught?

This question has received considerable attention, including laboratory testing and the establishment of school programs.

Laboratory Studies of Conservation Training.   As an example of laboratory studies, let's consider research on training of conservation performance. During the past twenty years there have been hundreds of conservation training studies (Murray, 1978; Beilin, 1974; Brainerd, 1974; Glaser & Resnick, 1972; Goldschmidt, 1971; Kuhn, 1974; Strauss, 1972; Nurss & Hodges, 1982). Conservation training studies begin with children who do not conserve on standard Piagetian conservation tasks. Then the children are given training on how to perform, and finally the children are retested in order to determine whether they have learned to conserve. Although various teaching techniques have been used by different researchers, there is "no longer any doubt that conservation can be taught" (Murray, 1978, p. 421). However, Murray also points out that conservation training is not always successful. The following conditions seem to be characteristics of successful conservation training: The experiment has a well-defined target behavior to be taught; the child is already in transition towards the target behavior; social interaction is involved—such as role playing or allowing a nonconserver to come to a group consensus with conservers.

As an example of conservation training, let's consider a study by Gelman (1969; Gelman & Gallistel, 1978) aimed at teaching conservation of number and conservation of length. Children were given practice on thirty-two problem sets, with six problems in each set. The left side of Figure 2–5 shows a typical problem set for conservation of number; the right side shows a typical

FIGURE 2–5   A Training Trial for Conservation of Number (or Length)

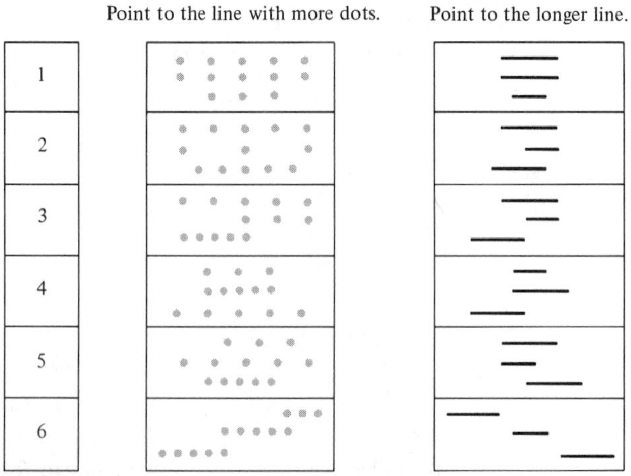

Adapted from Gelman (1969)

problem set for conservation of length. On each problem, the child is shown three sets of dots (or lines) and asked to indicate which one is different. On the first and last problem in each problem set, the dots (or lines) are arranged to elicit a correct response. However, on Problems 2–5, the arrangements include many irrelevant features. The child is given feedback after each problem. According to Gelman, the child must learn to pay attention to the relevant aspects of the stimulus and to ignore the irrelevant aspects. Figure 2–6 shows that the more training a child was given, the better the chances that the child will succeed on a corresponding conservation task. As you can see, with no training, only about 60% of the children conserved, but with training that figure approached 100%.

Piagetian School Programs. It is more difficult to find documented evidence of success in school programs aimed at training in cognitive development. For example, in a recent review Hopper & DeFrain (1980) argue that a "fair evaluation of Piagetian alternative programs" must wait until some school system establishes "an open classroom system" based on Piagetian principles "for the preschool, elementary, and the secondary school years." These authors do, however, summarize the operation of several well-known "Piagetian-inspired" preschool programs: Cognitively Oriented Curriculum (Weikart, Epstein, Schweinhart & Bond, 1978), Piaget for Early Education (Kamii & DeVries, 1977), Thinking Goes to School (Furth & Wachs, 1974), Piagetian Preschool Educational Program Early Childhood Curriculum (Lavatelli, 1970).

For example, the Piagetian Preschool Educational Program (PPEP) was conducted with three- to five-year-olds in Wisconsin. According to Hooper & DeFrain (1980, p. 170): "Children were encouraged to actively manipulate objects, were asked probing questions, and were encouraged to interact openly with their peers, but correct answers were not taught if they had not already

FIGURE 2–6 **Percent Correct on Conservation Task for Various Amounts of Training**

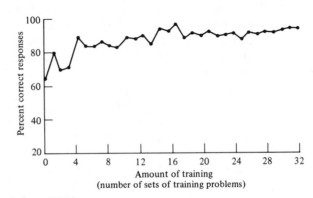

Adapted from Gelman (1969)

developed in the mind of the child." Children attended each day for 150 minutes during the twenty-eight-week school year. An evaluation of children's progress over three years revealed that children in the program did show gains on Piagetian measures of cognitive development; however, similar gains were shown by control children who did not participate in the program, that is, "few of the PPEP versus control group comparisons were significant" (Hooper & DeFrain, 1980, p. 172).

In another study, Weikart et al. (1978) compared a Piagetian "open classroom," a programmed curriculum that involved direct instruction and a traditional "child-centered" curriculum that emphasized social-emotional goals as in most nursery schools. The children were retarded three- and four-year-olds in Michigan. An evaluation of the project found that children in all three kinds of preschools showed gains in cognitive development, but there were no differences among the three programs. Thus the specific curriculum did not seem to have an impact on developmental changes.

These results, coupled with the fact that many programs do not even involve evaluations, do not provide convincing evidence that Piagetian preschool programs are useful. One limitation of this research is the limited number of Piagetian programs that can be tested. A broader issue concerns the effects of "open classrooms." However, in a recent review, Marshall (1981, p. 181) concluded that the term may have outlived its usefulness, since "reviews of research on the effectiveness of open education continue to reveal the inconclusive nature of the results."

Head Start and Title 1 Programs.   One program that has been implemented and evaluated nationally in the United States is the Head Start program. The program was intended to improve intellectual functioning and increase academic achievement among underprivileged children of preschool age. When the program began in 1965, the "results of research concerning the effects of early education on intellectual development were negative" (Caruso, Taylor, & Detterman, 1982, p. 45). After more than a decade of operation and the expenditure of $6.5 billion on Project Head Start, "nothing had changed" (Caruso, Taylor, & Detterman, 1982, p. 45).

According to Caruso et al., in most studies there either are no gains in IQ or the gains are largely lost as the children get older. Stanley (1973, p. 7) summarizes a review of early evaluations by noting that "great expenditures of time and effort have not yet succeeded in permanently elevating IQs of disadvantaged children much. Large gains the first year are common, but tend not to persist through the primary grades." Nurss & Hodges (1982, p. 501) provide a similar summary of research on the effectiveness of compensatory early childhood education programs: "compensatory programs appear to result in immediate . . . gains . . . which are greater for target children than for control children. . . . These broad gains appear to dissipate over time, however, so that scores for control and experimental children approximate both one another and their preintervention scores after a few years in elementary school."

The most massive compensatory education programs for elementary school children have been funded by the U.S. federal government under Title 1 (later changed to Chapter 1). Although more than $40 billion has been spent since 1965, early evaluation studies generally failed to find convincing evidence of lasting positive effects (Wargo, Tallmadge, Michaels, Lipe, & Morris, 1972).

In the most complete study of the effects of Title 1 programs on elementary school children, Carter (1984) collected data on over 100,000 students as they progressed over three successive years. Figure 2–7 shows the standardized mathematics achievement scores at the beginning and end of the first grade for regular students, Title 1 students who began at a fairly high level, and Title 1 students who began at a fairly low level. Regular students received no compensatory education, higher-level Title 1 students received compensatory education for the first year and then were promoted out of the program, and lower-level Title 1 students received compensatory education during each year of the study. As you can see, the higher-level Title 1 students show great improvement during grade 1 and even reach the same level as the regular students; in contrast, the lower-level Title 1 students do not display a strong improvement.

The results in Figure 2–7 indicate that compensatory education has positive short-term effects for the more able students in the program. Can the success of the first year of compensatory education be sustained throughout a student's school career? Unfortunately, the results of Carter's (1984) analysis indicate that the answer is no. First, Carter (1984, p. 7) found that compensatory education "is more effective in the lower grades than in the higher grades." Second, Carter (1984, p. 7) noted that "by the time students reached junior high school there was no evidence of sustained or delayed effects of Title 1."

Laboratory Research Versus School Programs. We are left with a seeming paradox: well-controlled laboratory studies can succeed in improving

FIGURE 2–7 **Compensatory Education Helps Higher-level Students But Not Lower-level Students**

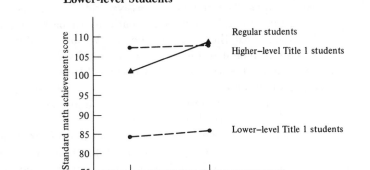

Adapted from Carter (1984)

performance on cognitive tasks, yet large-scale school programs are not over-whelmingly successful. However, the resolution to this paradox may be seen in the way that laboratory research and instructional practice are merged. Many school programs are developed without benefit of developmental research, and may be implemented on a large scale. For example, some of the Head Start and Title 1 programs were not necessarily based on any sound psychological or educational theory. In contrast, Caruso et al. (1982) suggest that intervention programs should begin with a solid research base and that they should begin on a small scale so they can grow into maturity.

A second problem is that early childhood programs are often viewed as "one-shot deals" rather than as the beginning of a continual educational process involving constant contact with the child. This point is graphically made in the following quotation by Ball & Bogatz as cited in Stanley (1973, p. 2):

> We argue that education, like morphine, is not likely to have a long-term "high" (effect) through a one-shot deal. . . . If compensatory education is to have a permanent effect, it must be a constant input (just as living with well-educated parents provides a constant input). In our view, it is unfair to expect 130 hours spread over six months to revolutionize a child's entire life.

Both laboratory studies and school programs can show short-term effects; apparently, long-term effects depend on a continuing educational program aimed at fostering intellectual development.

CONCLUSION

This chapter has explored Piaget's theory of cognitive development, including a summary of the general ideas, a summary of the stages, and examples of some instructional implications. Piaget's theory has been criticized on several grounds: The theory is massive and very difficult to fully understand, the research methods are sometimes questionable, and parts of the theory are so vague that they may not be testable at all. More recent work in cognitive development is aimed at clarifying individual issues rather than at building a massive theory. The following two chapters provide some examples of recent issue-oriented research.

In spite of these criticisms, it is important to have some understanding of Piaget's theory. Piaget's work raises questions that are fundamental to educational psychology—the primary question concerns the role of the child and the role of the school. Piaget's theory has been interpreted as advocating both a "child-centered" and an "environment-centered" education. His theory is child-centered because he emphasizes the importance of the child's cognitive developmental level in any learning situation. The child is not a miniature adult who lacks only great quantities of knowledge. Instead, the child at any stage possesses modes of representing and processing information that are quite different from adult thinking. Thus instructional experiences will be useful only if they are matched to the child's level of cognitive development.

Piaget's theory is "environment-centered" in the sense that all cognitive growth comes as a result of experience in the environment. Through interaction with the environment, the child assimilates and accommodates information, which results in a cognitive change. Especially in preschool and elementary school, experience with appropriate concrete objects is crucial. Thus, although the child is an active participant in the growth process this growth is made possible by providing an environment in which the child can be challenged properly.

As we leave Piaget's theory, we leave with the central theme that any instructional program must take the characteristics of the learner into account. This theme can also be summarized by saying that the intellectual growth of a child depends both on the characteristics of the child at the time of instruction and on the characteristics of the instruction.

SUGGESTED READINGS

Flavell, J. F. (1977). *Cognitive development*. Engelwood Cliffs, N.J.: Prentice-Hall. (Summarizes Piagetian and related theories of cognitive development.)

Furth, H. G. & Wachs, H. (1975). *Thinking goes to school*. New York: Oxford University Press. (Describes how to apply Piaget's theory to the operation of a school.)

Ginsburg, H. & Opper, S. (1969). *Piaget's theory of intellectual development*. Englewood Cliffs, N.J.: Prentice-Hall. (Systematically explains Piaget's theory, using many examples.)

Phillips, J. L. (1979). *The origins of intellect: Piaget's theory*. New York: Freeman. (Systematically explains Piaget's theory, using many examples.)

Piaget, J. (1967). *Six psychological studies*. New York: Random House. (Collection of some of Piaget's papers, organized and introduced by an American psychologist, David Elkind.)

Piaget, J. (1971). *Science of education and the psychology of the child*. New York: Viking Press. (Piaget presents his philosophy of education in very general terms.)

3 Development of Memory Capacity

One of the main lessons of the previous chapter was that effective instruction must be geared to the intellectual capacities and processes of the learner. This chapter takes an in-depth look at one of the best documented characteristics of the human information processing system—namely, that the amount of information you can actively think about in your working memory or hold in your short-term memory at any one time is extremely limited. Moreover, there appears to be a developmental trend in which young children are able to handle less information at one time than older children. The theme of this chapter is that instruction must take into account the extremely limited capacity of children to process information.

THE MEMORY CAPACITY PROBLEM

In a moment I will give you some lists of digits. Your job is to read each digit in the list, at a rapid rate and without looking back. Then try to recite the list in order.

Here is a list: 7 6 3
Now recite the list in order: _____.

Here is another list: 8 3 4 5 1
Now recite the list in order: _____.
Here is another list: 2 7 3 1 8 4 9 6 7 3 1 5
Now recite the list in order: _____.

If you are like most adults, you were able to correctly recall the three-digit list and the five-digit list, but you had trouble with the twelve-digit list. In general, adults make no errors for lists up to 5 or 6 digits long, but do make some errors for longer lists. This task is used to measure the *span of immediate memory* (or memory span)—the longest list that a person can recite back in order without error.

Let's try another task. In a moment, I will show you some dots. Look at them for just one glance, without trying to count them, and then tell me how many there were.

Here are some dots: . . .
How many were there? _____
Here are some dots: . . . . .
How many were there? _____
Here are some dots: . . . .
How many were there? _____

If you are like most people, you recognized that there were three dots in the first set and five dots in the second set, but it was hard to tell exactly how many were in the third set. In general, adults make no errors when there are up to five or six dots, but do make errors for larger sets of dots. Apparently, we can *subitize* for dot sets up to 6 items but we must *estimate* for sets greater than six. This is a task that measures the *span of attention* (i.e., the largest number of items a person can recognize perfectly in one glance).

You have just participated in versions of two classic information processing tasks. In particular, each measures how much information you can think about or work on at one time. Thus these tasks can be seen as ways of measuring the capacity of short-term memory.

Both the dots and digits examples of information-processing capacity evidence the extreme limitations on how much information a person can handle at one time. The limit appears to be between four and eight items, depending on the specific task and the person being tested.

LIMITS ON MEMORY CAPACITY

Holding Capacity of Short-term Memory

The foregoing examples demonstrated that short-term memory seems to be limited. In his famous paper, "The Magic Number Seven Plus or Minus Two:

Some Limits on our Capacity for Processing Information," Miller (1956) argued that our short-term processing of information was limited to about seven chunks of information. More recently, Simon (1974) has shown that our capacity is even more limited. For example, the memory span is closer to five chunks than seven chunks. Thus one conclusion from research on memory span and attention span is that short-term memory can hold only about five chunks of information.

Strategies for Overcoming Limits on Memory Capacity

In short, Miller's (1956) and Simon's (1974) message is that there is both good news and bad news about the capacity of short-term memory. The bad news— just demonstrated—is that humans are able to think actively about only a few chunks of information at any one time. The good news, however, is that people can learn to use efficient chunking strategies so that one chunk can account for a great deal of information. As an example, consider a list of binary digits like: 101000100111001110. Normally, a person can remember about twelve binary digits. However, if you use a recoding strategy, you can group the list into triplets such as, 101–000–100–111–001–110, and then translate each triplet from binary to base 10, such as 504716. By using this recoding strategy for chunking information, people can recall forty binary digits. Box 3–1 summarizes the role of chunking strategies. Miller (1956) provided this example to demonstrate that chunking strategies can allow you to increase the amount of information in each chunk.

As another example of a chunking strategy consider the following list of words: Lincoln, milky, criminal, differential, address, way, lawyer, calculus, Gettysburg. Simon (1974) reports that when he tried to recall this list, he made errors, presumably because the list exceeded his span of six or seven words. However, you can reorganize the list into larger chunks as follows:

BOX 3–1   Chunking Strategy for a List of Binary Digits

Given list	1 0 1 0 0 0 1 0 0 1 1 1 0 0 1 1 1 0	
Grouped list	101 – 000 – 100 – 111 – 001 – 110	
Recoded list	5 0 4 7 1 6	
Grouped recoded list	Fifty Forty-seven Sixteen	

Adapted from Miller (1956)

Lincoln's Gettysburg Address
Milky Way
Criminal lawyer
Differential calculus

With the list organized into larger chunks, Simon had no trouble remembering all of the words. Thus, when you use a chunking strategy you can increase your performance on memory span tests, even though the actual size of your short term memory presumably remains constant.

In response to examples like these, Simon (1974) sought to answer the question, "How big is a chunk?" He made lists consisting of one-syllable words, two-syllable words, three-syllable words, two-word phrases, and eight-word phrases. Figure 3–1 shows that his span was six or seven words when the stimuli were words, and three or four phrases when the stimuli were phrases. However, when he measured his performance in terms of the span for syllables, his span was seven syllables for one-syllable words and twenty-six syllables for eight-word phrases. Apparently, a chunk can range from at least one to twenty-six syllables; with practice in chunking strategies, a chunk can even be larger.

FIGURE 3–1   Span of Immediate Memory for Words and Phrases

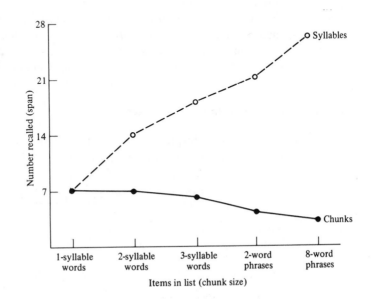

Adapted from Simon (1974)

DEVELOPMENT OF MEMORY CAPACITY

Research on Memory Capacity

Memory Span. There appears to be an interesting developmental progression in the capacity of short-term memory performance as measured by memory span tasks. For example, Table 3–1 shows the typical memory span for digits (i.e., *digit span*) for ages 2½ through adult. These numbers are based on a children's intelligence test in which increased digit span reflects a higher level of intelligence (Woodworth & Schlosberg, 1965). As you can see, the span is two digits for children at age 2½ but rises to about 8 for adults.

Stimulus-Response Game. In order to study the developmental changes in memory capacity, Pascaul-Leone (1970) taught children from ages five to eleven to give different responses for each of several visual cues (e.g., clapping their hands for red color and raising their hands for square shapes). Once they had learned to respond faultlessly to each stimulus, they were given a test on compound stimuli. Each compound stimulus contained more than one cue (e.g., red square) and the subject's job was to make all appropriate responses (e.g., clap *and* raise hands). The results indicated that five-year-olds were able to respond correctly to only two aspects of a compound stimulus while eleven-year-olds were able to respond to as many as five aspects. Apparently, the younger children were able to keep track of only a few visual cues at a time.

Number Series Game. Another demonstration of developmental changes in memory capacity comes from a study by Case (1972). Children of ages six through ten were given a series of numbers in ascending order such as 3, 9, 18 and asked to fit a probe number such as 11 into the series (e.g., 3, 9, 11, 18). The six-year-olds performed well on this task when the series involved no more than two numbers, whereas the ten-year-olds could perform well for a series of up to four numbers. Again, this study suggests that older children are able to hold more pieces of information in memory at one time than younger children.

Theory: Actual Capacity Versus Performance Capacity

One possible interpretation of these patterns is that the capacity of short-term memory increases as children grow (i.e., there is a structural change in the size

TABLE 3–1   Digit Span for Several Age Levels

Age	Digit Span
2½	2
3	3
4½	4
7	5
10	6
Adult	8

Adapted from Woodworth & Schlosberg (1965)

of short-term memory). An alternative interpretation is that the actual capacity of short-term memory remains constant, at least from about age four to adulthood, but that people learn to use more efficient strategies for handling information in short-term memory.

The foregoing has suggested that although our short-term memory capacity may be extremely limited, we can compensate by using efficient chunking strategies. In other words, although the structural characteristics of short-term memory are fixed, our voluntary processing strategies are not fixed. Chi (1978) has distinguished, for example, between *actual capacity* and *performance capacity*. Actual capacity refers to the underlying structural limitation on the number of chunks that can be held in short-term memory, whereas performance capacity refers to how much information we can process using various chunking strategies. With respect to development, an important question is whether observed changes in performance capacity are due to underlying changes in the actual capacity or to changes in the child's chunking strategies.

Implications: Avoid Overloading the Child's Memory

The severe limits on children's short-term memory capacity point to several educational implications. First, when confronted with a task that requires actively holding a long list, the child is likely to fail. For example, if you asked a kindergartener to go into the next room and bring back a piece of paper, she would probably be able to carry out that task. However, if you asked her to bring back a piece of paper, a bottle of paste, a green marker, a paper clip, and a toy block, she probably would not be able to comply. Tasks that require such memory load should be avoided. Second, children are capable of developing strategies for chunking lists that they want to remember. For example, the alphabet can be changed from a string of twenty-six letters to a familiar rhyme and rhythm:

abcd . . . efg . . . hijk . . . lmnop . . . qrs . . . tuv . . . wx . . . yz.

For school tasks that require heavy loads, children must be encouraged to develop useful chunking strategies.

DEVELOPMENT OF CHUNKING STRATEGIES

Research: Memory for Chess

Chi (1978) performed an interesting study to test the idea that age differences in memory span reflect differences in children's familiarity with the material (hence, their chunking strategies) rather than differences in children's memory capacity. Chi asked a group of children and a group of adults to participate in two memory tasks. The children averaged 10.5 years in age, and were experts in chess; the adults were not chess experts. One task was a version of the digit span task: the experimenter read a list of ten digits and the subject was asked to recite the list. As expected, the children's memory for digits was poorer than the adults' memory. Another task was to look for 10 seconds at a chess board that contained approximately 22 pieces. The positions of the pieces on the board were from the middle of an actual game. The recall task was to place the pieces on a blank board in the same positions as they had been in. On this task, the children performed better than the adults. The results are summarized in Figure 3–2.

Theory: Actual Capacity Versus Performance Capacity

Chi concludes that performance on memory span tasks involves both the learner's actual capacity and the chunking strategies that are available to the learner. Since the children were chess experts, they were better able to chunk chess pieces together into configurations. People with less specific experience in chess playing might be more likely to treat each single piece as a separate chunk. In the present example, the children were able to use a "specific strategy" for chunking information, namely, a strategy based on specific experience with the domain of chess. Apparently, at least part of the developmental change in memory span may be due to children acquiring more domain-specific knowledge.

FIGURE 3–2   Recall of Digits and Chess Stimuli for Two Age Groups

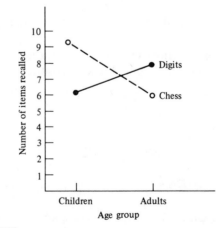

Adapted from Chi (1978)

Implications: Chunking Strategies
Improve with Experience

Chi's results offer two provocative implications for education. First, improvements in a child's memory capacity depend on the accumulation of many hours of experience. For example, through extended experience in using numerals, a child might develop techniques for chunking digit strings. Such experience could help a child see $111 \times 55 = $ _____ as involving two numbers (111 and 55) rather than as five numerals (1, 1, 1, 5, and 5). This chunking frees up some memory capacity to monitor where the child is in carrying out the multiplication. Similarly, through extended experience with reading words, a child might develop techniques for chunking letter strings. Such experience could help a child see a word like *restarted* as *re-* plus *start* plus *ed* rather than as nine separate letters. This chunking frees memory capacity that can be used to build a representation of the meaning of the sentence rather than to just decode each successive word.

Second, memory capacity for a particular domain depends on experience using materials from that domain. For example, having lots of experience with numerals would not likely lead to improvements in memory capacity for processing letters and words, and vice versa. In summary, lots of domain-specific experience is one way of increasing the amount of information a child can process.

DEVELOPMENT OF
PROBLEM-SOLVING STRATEGIES

Theory: The Automaticity Hypothesis

In an earlier chapter on Piaget's theory (Chapter 2), you saw that children's performance on a variety of tasks tends to change by developmental stages. For example, the leap from preoperational to concrete operational thought was demonstrated by changes in performance on conservation tasks; similarly, the shift from concrete operations to formal operations was demonstrated by changes in performance on tasks like the balance beam problem or the bending rods problem. Piaget's theory is based on the idea that the maturing child acquires more powerful information-processing techniques, such as general strategies for operating on information.

A complementary explanation for the change in performance on many Piagetian tasks is based on the idea that the size of working memory is limited (Case 1978a, 1985; Pascaul-Leone, 1970). Since working memory is limited, the problem-solving strategy used at a given developmental level must not exceed the capacity of working memory. Changes in the sophistication of strategies used for solving problems occur because the child becomes more experienced with the basic operations (i.e., the basic operations become automatic). This automaticity allows the child to chunk many operations together into a single one, thus freeing up space in working memory for use of more complex procedures. At first, even a very simple procedure may require much monitoring and thus much space in working memory; however, as a simple procedure becomes automatic, the child is able to add more complexity to it. According to Case (1978a, p. 37): "automaticity at one stage is prerequisite for transition to the next stage."

Research on Automaticity in Problem Solving

Juice Problem.   As a demonstration of the "automaticity hypothesis," consider the *juice problem* shown in Figure 3–3. The child is shown two empty pitchers, with a certain number of containers of orange juice and a certain number of pitchers of water ready to pour into one, and a certain number of containers of orange juice and a certain number of containers of water ready to pour into the other pitcher. The child's job is to predict which pitcher will taste more strongly of orange juice, if the containers were poured in.

Noelting (as reported in Case, 1978a) has identified four distinct developmental levels in children's solution strategy for the juice problem, as summarized in Table 3–2. At age three or four, children use an isolation strategy, looking to see which side has juice. As long as one side has juice and the other does not, the child can solve the problem. This approach requires that at any one time the child hold one piece of information in working memory: whether or not there is an orange juice container for one pitcher.

At ages four to five, children use a unidimensional comparison strategy based on comparing the number of juice containers on the two sides. As long as one side has more juice containers than the other, the child can solve the problem. This approach requires that at any one time the child hold two pieces

FIGURE 3–3   The Juice Problem

Which pitcher tastes more strongly of juice?

This pitcher gets two containers of orange juice and one container of water.

This pitcher gets two containers of orange juice and two containers of water.

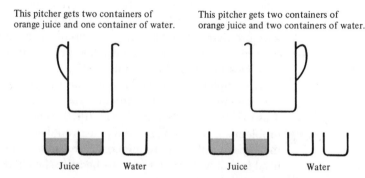

Juice   Water   Juice   Water

TABLE 3–2   Four Solution Strategies for the Juice Problem

Developmental Level	Age of Acquisition	Type of Problem Passed	Strategy	Maximum Memory Load
1	3 to 4	∪ ∪	Isolated centration	1
2	4 to 5	∪∪∪∪∪ ∪∪∪∪∪	Unidimensional comparison	2
3	7 to 8	∪∪∪∪ ∪∪∪∪∪∪∪	Bidimensional comparison	3
4	9 to 10	∪∪∪∪∪ ∪∪∪∪∪∪∪∪	Bidimensional comparison with quantification	4

Adapted from Case (1978)

of information in working memory: the number of orange juice containers for one pitcher and the number of orange juice containers for the other pitcher.

By ages seven to eight, children can use a bidimensional comparison strategy that involves determining whether there are more water containers or more orange containers for each pitcher, and then choosing the pitcher that has an excess of juice containers to water containers. This strategy works unless both pitchers have more juice than water, both have more water than juice, or if both have equal water and juice. Using this strategy requires the ability to hold three items in working memory: whether there is more or less orange juice than water for pitcher A, the number of juice containers for B, the number of water containers for B.

Finally, by ages nine to ten, children begin to use a bidimensional comparison with quantification strategy, based on determining which side has a greater number of excess juice containers or a fewer number of excess water containers. This strategy works on all problems except those that require the use of proportions or ratios. This strategy requires that the child hold four items in memory: whether there are more juice or more water containers for pitcher A, the difference between water and juice containers for pitcher A, whether there are more juice or more water containers for pitcher B, the difference between water and juice containers for pitcher B.

The load on memory for each strategy is summarized in Table 3–2. As you can see, there is a progression from a strategy that requires only one item held in memory to a strategy that requires the child to hold four items in memory at one time. According to Case's "automaticity hypothesis," the child progresses to a more sophisticated strategy when the current strategy becomes so automatic that space in working memory is freed. Case's explanation (1978, p. 58) for the developmental progression in solving these problems is as follows:

The most satisfactory explanation I can think of for this cyclic pattern is the following: (1) There is one central working memory which can serve as a space for storing information or for operating on it . . . (2) the underlying capacity of this working memory does not change with age at least after the age of two . . . (3) the measured increase in capacity within each stage is due to a decrease in the capacity required to execute the operations which are characteristic of that stage.

In short, Case argues that developmental changes occur when the child develops techniques for compensating for the limited capacity of working memory.

Balance Beam Problem.   Siegler (1978) has shown how development involves the acquisition of progressively more complex strategies for solving problems like the balance beam problem in Figure 3–4. In the balance beam problem, as adapted from Inhelder & Piaget (1958), the experimenter puts some weights on both sides of the beam and asks the child to predict which side will go down.

Table 3–3 summarizes four solution strategies for the balance beam problem that were identified by Siegler (1978); Figure 3–5 presents the strategies as flowcharts. By age 4 or 5, children use rule 1, which predicts that the side with the most weights will go down or that the beam will be balanced if both sides have equal weight. This approach works on problems where the weights are located the same distance from the fulcrum on both sides. By age 8 to 10, children may use rule 2, which predicts that the side with the most weights will go down; however, if the number of weights is equal on both sides then the side with the greatest distance from the fulcrum will go down. This approach does not work when there are many weights near the fulcrum versus fewer weights far from the fulcrum. By age thirteen, children use rule 3, which is the same as rule 2 except that when there is a conflict (many weights close to the fulcrum versus fewer weights far from the fulcrum) the child will guess. Finally, with

FIGURE 3–4 The Balance Beam Problem

Here is a balance beam:

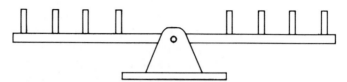

Suppose I put some weights on each side, as shown below:

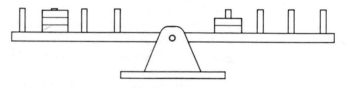

Which side of the balance beam will go down?

TABLE 3–3 Four Solution Strategies for the Balance Beam Problem

Developmental Level	Age of Acquisition	Type of Problem Passed	Strategy
1	4 to 5	(Correct 100%)	Rule 1: Choose side with more weights; if same weight on both sides choose "balanced."
2	8 to 10	(Correct 100%)	Rule 2: Same as rule 1 except if same weight on both sides, choose side with more distance
3	13	(Correct 33%)	Rule 3: Same as rule 2 except if one side has more weight and other side has more distance, guess any answer.
4	Adult (with training)	(Correct 100%)	Rule 4: Same as rule 3 except if one side has more weight and one side has more distance, use cross products.

Adapted from Siegler (1978)

training, some adults can reach the level of rule 4, which involves computing cross products (i.e., weight × distance) for both sides.

Siegler views cognitive development as the acquisition of progressively more complex solution rules. One important aspect of acquiring more complex rules is the ability to encode increasing numbers of variables from the problem. At first, for rule 1, children can encode only one variable (i.e., "which side has more weight"), but eventually the child adds a second variable in rule 2 (i.e., "which side has more distance"); finally, in rule 4 the child encodes four variables (i.e., weight for side A, distance for side A, weight for side B, distance for side B).

Implications: Reduce or Automate Component Skills

The educational implications of the foregoing research are straightforward. Successful execution of complicated problem-solving tasks depends on not letting memory capacity become completely dominated by thinking about the basic components required by the task. There appear to be two instructional techniques that can be used to provide memory capacity needed to monitor complex problem-solving procedures: First, a student should be able to perform basic component skills effortlessly before learning to solve complex problems that require those skills. Alternatively, a student may be freed from the requirements to correctly carry out basic component skills when learning to solve complex problems that require those skills.

As an example, consider the memory load imposed on a student who is writing a composition. The writer must develop a theme and organization, must develop coherence among ideas in the composition, and so on. However,

FIGURE 3–5　Flow Charts of Four Strategies for Solving the Balance Beam Problem

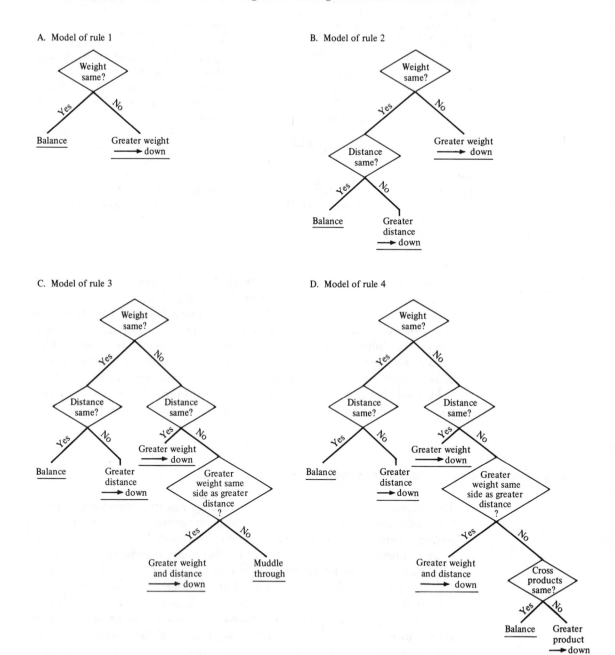

From Siegler (1978)

there are also certain basic components of the task: the writer must know how to form each letter in handwriting, how to spell each word, how to punctuate, how to construct grammatical sentences, and so on. For example, for some children a task like producing the letter S requires consciously thinking of the needed series of actions, and essay writing requires consciously thinking about the correct spelling of each word in the essay. The memory load imposed by these basic components would not leave much memory capacity for higher-level thinking about theme and organization and coherence.

One solution would be to not allow students to write compositions until they attained a high level of automaticity on these basic component skills (i.e., until they could form the letters effortlessly and spell without any trouble). This solution has the unfortunate side-effect of delaying the pleasure of writing until the child has spent many years in school. A second solution, described more fully in Chapter 12, is to free the child from the constraints of proper handwriting, spelling, punctuation, and so on. For example, by using a word processor, a child would be freed from the need to worry about how to form each letter in handwriting and could easily correct spelling and punctuation on a second draft. Assuming the child could type effortlessly, this solution would free memory capacity for attention to the higher-level aspects of the composition.

As another example, consider a child working on a mathematics story problem about the space shuttle that requires the use of long division, such as $35682 \div 141$. In order to solve this problem, a student must keep track of where she is in the procedure, where the next number goes, what the next step is, and so on. In addition, a student needs to carry out basic components of the task such as simple division, multiplication, subtraction, and addition. If the student has not yet reached automaticity on the basic component computations (such as estimating how many times 141 goes into 356, or multiplying 141×2 or subtracting 282 from 356), then there will be very little memory capacity left to monitor the long division solution process.

One solution to this problem is to drill the student on basic computational skills, so the student can carry them out effortlessly before the student is ever asked to solve problems that require long division. A second solution is to allow the child to use a calculator for all of the component computations in the long division problem. This frees the child from concentrating attention on the basic computations and allows memory capacity to be used to think about setting goals and monitoring progress. Chapter 13 discusses mathematical problem solving in more detail.

In summary, the two techniques described each have their own advantages and disadvantages. The "prior automatization" solution is based on an interesting compromise between "memorization" of basic skills and "creativity" in problem solving. This approach is based on the findings that use of complicated creative processing requires that the basic components be well memorized. One disadvantage of this approach is that it does not allow younger students to experience the joy of creative problem solving. The "freedom from constraints" solution is based on the idea that lower-level components can be ignored. The disadvantage of this approach is that children might never learn the basics. A useful compromise would be to employ both techniques—making sure that students eventually become automatic in their use of basic component skills but along the way allowing children to enjoy (sometimes) the freedom of problem solving that is not constrained by having to use the basic component skills properly.

ADAPTING INSTRUCTION TO MINIMIZE MEMORY LOAD

Case (1985) has argued that poor performance on some problem-solving tasks may be attributed to children's difficulty in using procedures that require a heavy memory load on short-term memory. Children may use procedures that are incomplete because the complete procedure requires that the child hold many different pieces of information in memory at one time. Case suggests that instruction should be sensitive to the limited memory capacity of children and should be designed to minimize the load on short-term memory. This section provides two examples of situations in which lightening of memory load can lead to improved conceptual learning: learning to solve missing addend problems and learning to form letter concepts.

Missing Addend Problems

For example, consider the following missing addend problem:

$$4 + [] = 7$$

As an adult, when you look at this problem, it is easy for you to see how the principle of part-whole relation applies in the problem—the two sets on the left must equal the set on the right. You are familiar with the numerals, 4 and 7, and with the symbols + and = and []. The relevant features of the task (the two numerals and three symbols) are comprehensible to you. However, for a kindergartener or first grader who has had very little experience with written numerals and symbols, what to look for is not obvious, and how to apply them to the part-whole concept is not clear. If a kindergartner or first grader were given this problem, a common answer would be 11. In this case, the child pays attention to the 4 and the + and the 7, and applies his knowledge of addition to this representation of the problem.

Why does the child give a wrong answer? According to Case (1978b), the child can understand the part-whole relation involved in the problem, but fails to do so because his memory is overloaded with unfamiliar symbols and numerals. In order to overcome this problem, Case suggests that principles, such as the part-whole concept in the missing addend problem, be taught in familiar contexts using materials that are meaningful to the child.

Figure 3–6 presents materials that Case used to make the task more familiar to the child. The child, presumably, has had more experience with faces and the features of faces than with equations and can learn how to apply the part-whole relation to faces more easily than to equations. First, the child was given an initial addition exercise, as shown at the top of Figure 3–6. Then, the missing addend format was introduced in a subsequent addition exercise, as shown in the bottom of Figure 3–6. This allows the child to become familiar with symbols like + and = and [] in the context of a familiar situation. Finally, a corresponding missing addend problem was presented.

In order to test the effectiveness of the "faces" training, Case compared ten kindergartners who learned using his "faces" procedure to ten kindergartners who spent the same amount of time learning the same problems in the conventional way. On a post-test involving standard missing addend problems, 8% of the problems were answered correctly by the conventionally trained children, but the faces trained children achieved 74% correct.

In summary, Case argues that his procedure helped students learn a principle in a familiar context and then transfer it to mathematical notation. This procedure allows for conceptual learning in children, even when their developmental level severely limits the holding capacity of short-term memory. Case (1978b, p. 459) recommends that this kind of procedure also be used for mentally retarded or remedial students: "By definition a retardate is one whose development lags behind that of his peer group and who reaches a lower terminal level. For such a child, the strategy of waiting for development to take its course is clearly not an advisable one."

Concept Learning Problems

Memory overload may also be a source of difficulty in concept learning tasks. For example, suppose that a kindergartner or first grader was asked to learn to touch his nose when the teacher held up a card with a b and to stand up when the teacher held up a card with a d. To an adult, this is an extremely easy task. Through countless years of experience, you have learned that the main features of letters are lines and curves and that the main distinguishing feature between b and d is the relation between the curve and the line. For a young child, however, the materials are not familiar. The correct relevant feature could be the font, the size, the color, the inflection of the teacher's voice, or so on. The high number of possible features puts an extreme load on memory.

What can be done to allow the child to learn concepts? One technique is to make the relevant features of the materials very obvious (e.g., printing the curves in red ink and the lines in normal black ink). This draws the child's attention away from the many possible irrelevant features and towards the relevant feature. In short, this procedure reduces the load on the child's

FIGURE 3–6   Minimizing Memory Load for Instruction in Missing Addend Problems

First, the student learns what = means in a familiar context.

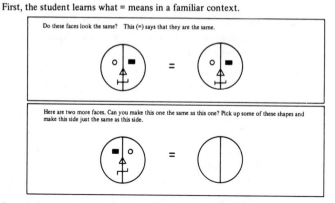

Second, the student learns what + means in a familiar context.

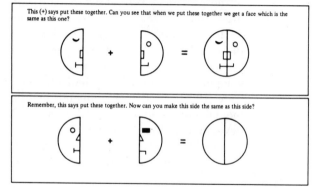

Third, the student learns what a missing addend means in a familiar context.

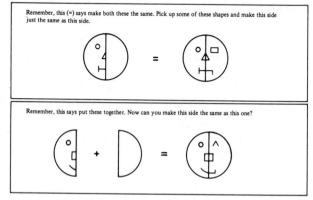

Finally, the student learns to apply this procedure to missing addend problems.

4 + [   ] = 7

Adapted from Case (1978)

memory so that attention can be focused on the process of testing hypotheses until the correct concepts are formed. For example, in a classic study, Zeaman & House (1963) found that when the relevant cue is made obvious, retarded children learn to form concepts as quickly as nonretarded children.

CONCLUSION

This chapter has explored the idea that cognitive development corresponds partly to the child's capacity for processing information (i.e., the child's ability to hold several pieces of information in short-term memory at once). First, the chapter demonstrated some limits on our ability to process information. Then, the chapter introduced evidence for a developmental trend in which memory capacity (such as measured by memory span) appears to increase with age. Then, research was presented which suggests that actual memory capacity may be constant after age four or five, but that children acquire techniques for compensating—such as chunking information or automating a complex procedure. In other words, there seems to be a difference between a child's actual capacity and performance capacity. Finally, some instructional implications of the short-term memory limitations were presented. These included automating basic component skills before teaching complex skills (prior automatization approach) or teaching complex skills in a way that does not require paying attention to component skills (freedom from constraints approach).

SUGGESTED READINGS

Lesgold, A. M., Pellegrino, J. W., Fokkema, S. D. & Glaser, R. (eds). (1978). *Cognitive psychology and instruction*. New York: Plenum Press. (A collection of papers relating cognitive psychology to instruction; the last sections on "cognitive development" and "approaches to instruction" are particularly useful.)

Siegler, R. S. (ed.) (1978). *Children's thinking: What develops?* Hillsdale, N.J.: Erlbaum. (A collection of papers by researchers in developmental psychology.)

Sternberg, R. J. (ed.) (1984). *Mechanisms of cognitive development*. New York: Freeman. (A collection of theoretical papers concerning the cognitive mechanisms underlying development.)

Development of Learning Strategies

4

The premise underlying this chapter is that learning new material depends partly on the information-processing strategies that the child has developed. When confronted with a learning task, the learner must recognize which kinds of learning strategies are needed, must possess these strategies, and must apply them appropriately to the learning situation. The intellectual development of the child includes the development of these strategies and is the focus of this chapter.

THE METAMEMORY PROBLEM

Suppose that I asked you to memorize a list of names of objects. You see a picture of each object for 1 second, and then I ask you to recite the names of the objects in order. What is the longest list that you could remember in order, without error, on an immediate test?

For example, if I showed you three pictures, could you remember them all in order? Could you remember a list of five, or seven, or ten, or twenty? Write your prediction of how many names are in the longest list you can recall: _____.

Now, you can test yourself using the stimuli in Figure 4–1. Cover the list of pictures with your hand, and then move your hand across the page, giving yourself about 1 second for each picture. Stop when you have seen the number of pictures you predicted that you could recall. Then, cover the pictures in Figure 4–1 again, and try to write the names of the objects in order:

Were you successful in predicting your test performance on this task? If you are like most adults, you probably were fairly accurate. For example, in one study the average prediction for memory span was 5.9, and the actual span averaged 5.5 (Yussen & Levy, 1975).

However, if you try a task like this one with children, you are likely to obtain quite different results. For example, Flavell, Friedrichs, & Hoyt (1970) asked children to predict their memory span, using a procedure that was somewhat more complicated than the one you just tried. Figure 4–2 shows the results for children in nursery school, kindergarten, second grade, and fourth grade. As you can see, the youngest children—in nursery school and kindergarten—produced highly inaccurate predictions, tending to grossly overestimate how many items they would recall. In contrast, older children—such as the fourth graders—were far more accurate in predicting their performance on this memory span task. Apparently, the ability to judge how well you can learn changes as children are exposed to more learning tasks. This example is important because learning involves making efficient use of one's learning strategies. If a student cannot assess the nature of the task, the student will not be able to choose adequate learning strategies.

These results should not be taken to mean that children are unable to accurately predict their behavior in all tasks. For example, Markman (1973) found that five-year-old children were highly inaccurate in predicting their memory span (as in the Flavell et al. study), but they were quite accurate in predicting the distance that they could jump. In addition, some five-year-olds

FIGURE 4–1 A Learning Task

Look at each picture for 1 second. Stop when you feel you have learned all you can.
Then, recall the list in order.

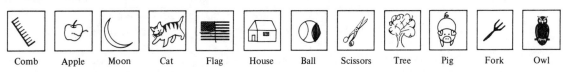

Comb   Apple   Moon   Cat   Flag   House   Ball   Scissors   Tree   Pig   Fork   Owl

showed improvement in predicting their memory span when the experimenter allowed them to practice by giving them many memory span trials. Markman's research suggests that the developmental changes in metamemory (i.e., in knowledge of one's memory capacity) may be due to increased experience in learning tasks.

Some younger children, however, seem to be insensitive to feedback on their memory span performance. For example, Yussen & Levy (1975) conducted a memory span prediction study in which four-year-olds predicted they could remember nine or ten items even though they had seen that could not recall that many in a practice trial. In spite of practice, they still made inaccurate predictions and commented, "If you gave me a different list like that, I could do it" (p. 507).

Flavell (1971; Flavell & Wellman, 1977) coined the term *metamemory* to refer to a person's awareness of his/her own memory capacities and processing. Flavell & Wellman (1977, p. 4) offer an example: "a person has metamemory if he knows some things are easier for him to remember than others." The task of predicting your memory span is a test of metamemory because you are being asked to characterize the nature of your memory capacity. A learner who is able to exercise metamemory skills on a given task is better able to select appropriate learning strategies.

FIGURE 4–2   Predicted and Actual Memory Span for Four Age Groups

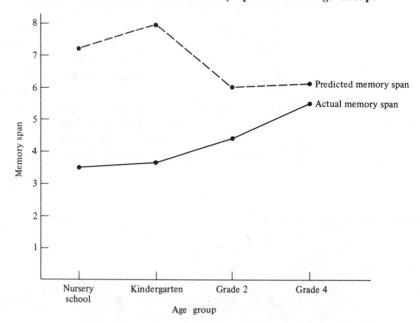

Adapted from Flavell, Friedrichs & Hoyt (1972)

LEARNING STRATEGIES

A learning strategy refers to any activity by a learner that is employed during learning in order to enhance learning. Examples of learning strategies include actively rehearsing the presented material, reorganizing the material into meaningful chunks, and elaborating on the material by generating visual images. As you can see, learning strategies involve the learner's actively manipulating the flow of information in a way that is appropriate for a particular learning goal.

The focus of this chapter is on developmental changes in (1) the availability of useful learning strategies in the learner and (2) the appropriate usage of learning strategies during learning. As you will see, there is evidence that most young children (such as preschoolers) do not spontaneously make use of learning strategies for basic learning tasks while most adults do. The remainder of this chapter focuses on three strategies that emerge during the school years: (1) rehearsal strategies, (2) organizational strategies, and (3) elaboration strategies.

DEVELOPMENT OF
REHEARSAL STRATEGIES

Serial Learning Tasks

Suppose that I gave you a list of fifty items to memorize and then recite to me in order. For example, my list could be the states of the United States in order of their admission to the union: Delaware, Pennsylvania, New Jersey, Georgia, Connecticut, Massachusetts, Maryland, South Carolina, New Hampshire, Virginia, New York, North Carolina, Rhode Island, Vermont, Kentucky, Tennessee, Ohio, Louisiana, Indiana, Mississippi, Illinois, Alabama, Maine, Missouri, Arkansas, Michigan, Florida, Texas, Iowa, Wisconsin, California, Minnesota, Oregon, Kansas, West Virginia, Nevada, Nebraska, Colorado, North Dakota, South Dakota, Montana, Washington, Idaho, Wyoming, Utah, Oklahoma, New Mexico, Arizona, Alaska, Hawaii. Look over the list, one state at a time until you think you know it. Now recite the list in order.

This is an example of serial learning. In a serial learning task, the student is presented with a list and must be able to recall the list in serial order. Since serial learning is a component of some school learning tasks (e.g., learning to count, memorizing the alphabet, reciting the months of the year), it has been subjected to careful research scrutiny.

When you engage in serial learning, several strategies can be used to enhance your encoding of the material. Rehearsal strategies refer to actively stating or repeating the names of the stimuli to be learned. The level of sophistication of rehearsal may vary, including the following strategies:

Cumulative rehearsal—When a stimulus is presented, you repeat the names of all the stimuli you have seen so far, in order. For the states example, when you are given the first item, you say, "Delaware"; when you are given the second item you say, "Delaware, Pennsylvania"; when you are given the third item you say, "Delaware, Pennsylvania, New Jersey"; when you are given the fourth item, you say, "Delaware, Pennsylvania, New Jersey, Georgia"; and so on.

Partial rehearsal—When a stimulus is presented, you repeat the name of at least one stimulus that has been previously presented. For the states example, when given the fifth state, you might say, "Delaware, New Jersey, Connecticut."

Naming—When a stimulus is presented, you name it or repeat its name. For the states example, when given the sixth state, you say, "Massachusetts."

Figure 4–3 gives examples of these three varieties of rehearsal, assuming that the stimuli are presented as a series of pictures.

FIGURE 4–3   Three Ways to Rehearse a Serial List

The list is presented, one picture at a time.

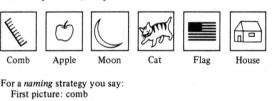

Comb   Apple   Moon   Cat   Flag   House

For a *naming* strategy you say:
First picture: comb
Second picture: apple
Third picture: moon
Fourth picture: cat
Fifth picture: flag
Sixth picture: house

For a *partial rehearsal* strategy you may say:
First picture: comb
Second picture: comb, apple
Third picture: apple, moon
Fourth picture: comb, cat
Fifth picture: comb, apple, flag
Sixth picture: flag, house

For a *cumulative rehearsal* strategy you say:
First picture: comb
Second picture: comb, apple
Third picture: comb, apple, moon
Fourth picture: comb, apple, moon, cat
Fifth picture: comb, apple, moon, cat, flag
Sixth picture : comb, apple, moon, cat, flag, house

Research on Development of Rehearsal Strategies

As you can see, rehearsal strategies involve active verbalization by the learner and are under the learner's voluntary control. Rehearsal strategies seem to be used spontaneously by adults in serial learning tasks and can greatly enhance learning. In this section, we explore the question of whether the use of rehearsal strategies emerges as a child gets older.

Rehearsal During Learning. Flavell, Freidrichs, & Hoyt (1970) have provided evidence that spontaneous use of rehearsal strategies during learning seems to increase with age. For example, in one study, subjects were given a row of windows with a button underneath each, as shown in Figure 4–4. If the

FIGURE 4–4 A Serial Learning Task

Picture stays on for as long as you press the button underneath it:

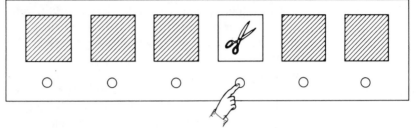

Mean number of responses for four age groups

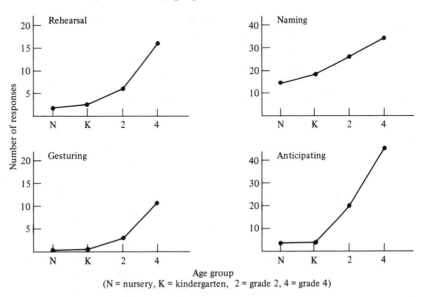

Age group
(N = nursery, K = kindergarten, 2 = grade 2, 4 = grade 4)

Adapted from Flavell, Freidrichs & Hoyt (1970)

subject pressed the button under a window, a light would come on so that the subject could see the picture. The light would stay on as long as the button was pushed, but once the subject stopped, the window would become blank again. The subject's task was to keep pressing buttons, one at a time, for as long and as many times as needed to recall the whole series of pictures.

The subjects were nursery school children, kindergartners, second graders, and fourth graders. The experimenters carefully recorded the childrens' behavior during learning, including the number of times the child *names* a picture (i.e., upon pressing a button and seeing the picture, the subject immediately names the object in the picture), the number of times the child *rehearses* a name other than the object in the picture (i.e., the subject names objects from previous pictures even though they are not presently in view), the number of times the child *anticipates* a picture (i.e., with a finger ready to press a button, the child names the object in the window), and the number of times the child *gestures* (i.e., the child rhythmically points to buttons or finger counts or head nods). The results summarized in the bottom of Figure 4–4 show that younger children tend to engage in far less naming, rehearsing, anticipating, and gesturing during learning than the older children. Apparently, by the time a child moves from nursery school to the fourth grade, the child can make much greater use of rehearsal strategies and related techniques for memorizing new information.

Rehearsal During Retention Interval.   A study by Hagen & Kail (1973) provides more evidence for the idea that younger children are less likely to spontaneously rehearse as compared to older children. The subjects, ages seven and eleven, were shown a series of pictures each on a card. The first picture was shown to the child and then placed facedown. Then the next picture was shown and placed facedown next to the first, and so on. In all, eight pictures were shown and placed facedown in a row in front of the child. Then there was a 15-second retention interval. For the test, the experimenter showed a probe picture that was the same as one of the eight presented pictures. The subject was asked to point to the picture—now facedown—corresponding to the probe. One group of subjects was asked to count aloud during the retention interval in order to block rehearsal; another group was asked to "think about the pictures" during the retention interval. The results indicated that the older children performed much better than the younger children when allowed to think during the retention interval; however, when rehearsal was prevented as in the counting group, both age-groups performed at similarly low levels. These results compliment those given earlier. Since the younger children do not spontaneously rehearse during the retention interval, preventing rehearsal is not as detrimental as it was for the older children.

A related study by Flavell, Beach & Chinsky (1966) investigated the role of rehearsal strategies in five-, seven-, and ten-year-old children. For example, in a typical trial, the subject was shown an array of seven pictures such as apple, comb, flag, etc. The experimenter sequentially pointed out three of these to be remembered in order by the subject. Then there was a 15-second delay during which the subject could not see the array. Finally, the subject was shown an array of the seven pictures and asked to point to the three target pictures in the same order that the experimenter had pointed to them.

During the retention interval, the experimenter carefully noted whether the subject's lips moved (i.e., whether the subject was rehearsing the presented material). The results, shown in Figure 4–5, indicate that almost none of the five-year-olds gave evidence of using the retention interval for rehearsal whereas almost all of the ten-year-olds did show signs of rehearsal as indicated by lip movements. Apparently, the young children do not spontaneously use rehearsal strategies, even though such strategies generally tend to enhance learning.

Training Children to Rehearse. One issue raised by the Flavell et al. (1966) study concerns whether young children lack the ability to label pictures and rehearse those labels. In order to investigate this question, another study was conducted by Kenney, Cannizzo & Flavell (1967). First graders were given the kind of memory task described earlier. Some of the children moved their lips during the retention interval, and thus could be called *rehearsers;* other children did not show signs of rehearsing during the 15-second retention interval, and could be called *nonrehearsers*. As expected, the children who spontaneously rehearsed during the retention interval performed significantly better on the memory test.

In addition, subjects who did not spontaneously rehearse were explicitly instructed that they should name the pictures during the retention interval. This training served to boost performance on the memory test. Similar instructions for the children who spontaneously rehearse did not influence memory performance. These results are summarized in Figure 4–6. However, on

FIGURE 4–5 Spontaneous Use of Rehearsal Strategies for Three Age Groups

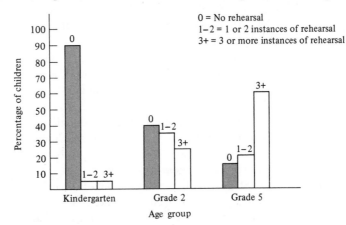

Adapted from Flavell, Beach & Chinsky (1966)

FIGURE 4–6   Effect of Instructions to Rehearse on Two Groups of First Graders

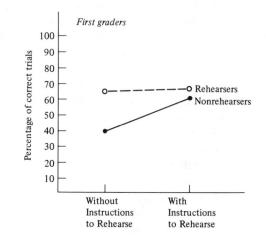

Adapted from Kenney, Cannizzo & Flavell (1967)

subsequent tasks when nonrehearsers were not explicitly reminded to rehearse, they failed to spontaneously rehearse and their memory performance returned to low levels.

Theory of Development of Rehearsal Strategies

Availability Versus Production.   Based on findings like those described above, Flavell (1970; Flavell & Wellman, 1977) argues that some young children have rehearsal strategies *available* to them, but generally fail to *produce* (or apply) them appropriately in learning tasks. A child's failure to rehearse during learning, on a task where rehearsal would be beneficial, can be caused by either of the following two problems:

Availability deficiency—the child does not know how to rehearse.
Production deficiency—the child does not know when to use a rehearsal
strategy.

As you can see, an availability deficiency involves the need for training in learning strategies, as discussed in Chapter 8. In contrast, a production deficiency is a type of metamemory problem (i.e., a lack of awareness about how to use one's rehearsal strategies).

Stages.   These studies suggest that there is a developmental progression in the way that children use rehearsal strategies in simple learning tasks. In the first stage (below five years), children tend not to spontaneously use rehearsal strategies in learning, are not distracted by activities that limit rehearsal, and do not seem to use different approaches to tasks with different requirements.

Thus these children seem to not have rehearsal strategies available to them. In the second stage (usually ages six to seven), children are often able to use rehearsal strategies when explicitly instructed to do so, but may not be able to generate useful strategies spontaneously. These children seem to have rehearsal strategies available, but do not seem to know how to use them. Finally, in the third stage (usually ages eleven or twelve), children tend to spontaneously rehearse during learning, to be distracted by activities that interfere with rehearsal, and to modify their rehearsal behavior in line with the goals of the task. While the rate of progression is influenced by the difficulty of the task and the sophistication of the learner, there does appear to be a distinct change in the way that children use rehearsal.

Implications of the Development of Rehearsal Strategies

The results presented in this section show that success on even simple learning tasks depends on the cognitive processing of the learner. First, many entering elementary school children do not know how to rehearse. Since the elementary school curriculum includes many serial learning tasks, children who lack rehearsal skills will be at an extreme disadvantage. Simple learning tasks should be geared to the developmental level of the child, and should be used to help nonrehearsers acquire skill in rehearsing. Second, some children in the early elementary grades may know how to rehearse but lack the metamemory skills needed for determining when rehearsal is appropriate. Again, simple learning tasks (such as the serial learning tasks described earlier) should be used as a vehicle to help children acquire the metamemory skills appropriate for their developmental level, including when and how much to rehearse.

The idea that teaching of learning strategies—including metamemory skills—should be part of school curriculum is pursued in Chapters 8 and 9. The foregoing research, however, shows that instruction in learning strategies must be sensitive to the student's developmental level. For example, although nonrehearsers can be taught how to rehearse, it is unrealistic to expect that they will simultaneously learn *when* to rehearse. Instruction in metamemory skills such as deciding when to rehearse would not be useful until the child has achieved competence in being able to rehearse when told to do so.

DEVELOPMENT OF ORGANIZATIONAL STRATEGIES

Free Recall Learning Tasks

Suppose that I gave you a list of the fifty states of the United States and asked you to recite the states back to me in any order. For example, my list could be: Alabama, Alaska, Arizona, Arkansas, California, Colorado, Connecticut, Delaware, Florida, Georgia, Hawaii, Idaho, Illinois, Indiana, Iowa, Kansas, Kentucky, Louisiana, Maine, Maryland, Massachusetts, Michigan, Minnesota, Mississippi, Missouri, Montana, Nebraska, Nevada, New Hampshire, New Jersey, New Mexico, New York, North Carolina, North Dakota, Ohio, Oklahoma, Oregon, Pennsylvania, Rhode Island, South Carolina, South Dakota, Tennessee, Texas, Utah, Vermont, Virginia, Washington, West Virginia, Wisconsin, Wyoming. Read over this list until you are ready to recall the states. Then, try to recite the states in any order you like.

This is an example of *free recall learning*. In a free recall task, the subject is given a set of items to remember, and may recall them in any order. Since free recall is commonly found in some school learning tasks, such as the above example, it has been subjected to much research study.

One strategy that you could use for encoding material in free recall tasks is to try to organize the items into groups that are similar. For example, in the foregoing list of states you might organize the states by geographical area such as New England, Northeast, Southeast, Great Lakes, Southwest, Northwest. Alternatively, you might organize the states by size, such as large states, middle-sized states, and small states.

Research on the Development
of Organizational Strategies

As you can see, organizational strategies involve active and voluntary processing by the learner. When a learner uses organizational strategies, the learner actively rearranges the presented material into categories. Adults are likely to spontaneously use organizational strategies based on taxonomic categories when given a free recall task. The focus of this section is on how organizational strategies emerge in children as they get older.

Organizing During Learning.   An interesting free recall study involving five- to eleven-year-olds was conducted by Moely, Olson, Halwes & Flavell (1969). Subjects were given a collection of pictures arranged in a circle, as shown in Box 4–1. The pictures included objects from various categories such as animals, furniture, vehicles, apparel, but no pictures from the same category were adjacent to one another in the presented circle of pictures. The subject was told to memorize the pictures in order to be able to recite them back to the experimenter. In addition, the subject was allowed to rearrange the pictures in the circle.

The experimenter measured how many times a learner rearranged the pictures so that pictures from the categories were adjacent, with a score of 1 meaning all pictures from the same category were placed together and 0 meaning that no two pictures from the same category were adjacent. The results summarized in the bottom of Box 4–1 show that spontaneous use of an organizational strategy is not strong among children in the five- to seven-year-old range but begins to emerge by age eight or nine and is strong among the

BOX 4–1 Children's Use of Organizational Strategies

Learning Task

Okay, now I'm going to leave for a couple of minutes . . . and you study the pictures and try to remember them while I'm gone. You see these pictures are just sitting there loose, and you can move them around any way you want to—you can do anything with the pictures you want to, to help you remember them. Move the pictures a little, so I know you can do it. So you can move them around if you want to. You don't have to, of course, but you can if you want to. Okay, here I go—try hard to learn the pictures.

Amount of Spontaneous Organization in Learning and Recall for Four Age Groups

	Ages 5–6	Ages 6–7	Ages 8–9	Ages 10–11
Proportion of clustering during learning	.04	.12	.16	.58
Proportion of clustering during recall	.30	.30	.34	.68
Overall proportion recalled	.68	.72	.67	.82

Note: Proportion of clustering is the number of times two items from the same category were put next to each other divided by the total number of possible clustered pairs of items.

Adapted from Moely, Olson, Halwes & Flavell (1969)

ten- to eleven-year-old children. Apparently, spontaneous use of organizational strategies does not begin as early as rehearsal strategies, perhaps because organizational strategies are more complicated.

Training Children to Use Organizational Strategies. The failure of the younger children to use organizational strategies during free recall learning may be due either to lack of availability of the strategies (i.e., the younger children do not know how to categorize) or what Flavell (1970) has called a "production deficiency" (i.e., the younger children fail to apply the strategy in appropriate situations). In order to examine these explanations, Moely et al. (1969) conducted an instructional study. Nine-year-old children who were not spontaneously categorizing were trained to rearrange the pictures by adult models. The children were readily able to rearrange the pictures into categories when instructed to do so, indicating that the necessary categorization skills were available to them. In addition, recall performance was enhanced. In short, the younger children could be trained to use organizational strategies like the older children. Again, as with rehearsal strategies, there is evidence for the "production deficiency" idea that some younger children may possess appropriate learning skills but fail to spontaneously apply them during learning.

Types of Organizational Strategies. There is also considerable evidence that children in the preschool years may actually lack skill at categorical organization. For example, Entwistle, Forsythe, & Muuss (1964) gave free association tests to children from age six to ten. The experimenter would present a word such as *man*, and the child's task was to state the first word he or she thought of as going with that word. Entwistle et al. noted a developmental shift in which the youngest children tended to produce sentencelike responses, such as "man-work," whereas by age ten the children were more likely to produce responses using words from the same grammatical category, such as "man-boy." For example, 43% of the responses for six-year-olds were from the same grammatical category, whereas 69% of the responses for eight-year-olds and 76% of the responses for ten-year-olds were from the same grammatical category.

The shift in organizational strategies for words is illustrated in a study by Rossi & Wittrock (1971). The experimenter read a list of twelve words to children in the two- to five-year-old age range and asked for free recall. For example, the children may hear the list: "sun, hand, men, fun, leg, work, hat, apple, dog, fat, peach, bark." Some of the words can be paired based on rhyme e.g., "sun-fun" and "hat-fat"; some can be paired syntactically, e.g., "men-work" and "dog-bark"; some can be paired based on taxonomic category, e.g., "peach-apple" and "leg-hand". As you can see, no two words from a pair were presented next to each other in the presentation list.

The order in which the children recalled the words often showed that words from the same taxonomic, syntactic, or rhyming pair were recalled in sequence. Figure 4–7 shows the proportion of recall showing taxonomic, syntactic, and

FIGURE 4–7   Techniques in Organization of Recall for Four Age Groups

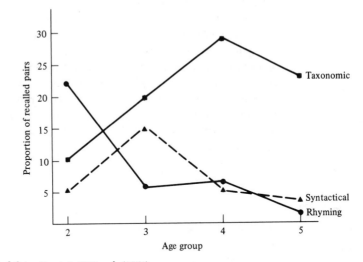

Adapted from Rossi & Wittrock (1971)

rhyming organization. As you can see, the two-year-olds use sound as a basis for organizing items but this way of organizing the words is not strongly evident for older children. Similarly, the three-year-olds show signs of organizing based on syntax, but this type of organization fades for older children. In contrast, the tendency to organize by taxonomic category increases with age, so that by ages four and five, it is clearly the dominant strategy.

Theory of Development of Organizational Strategies

Availability Versus Production.   As with rehearsal strategies, the main problems that children have with organizational strategies are failure to have the strategy available (availability deficiency) or failure to appropriately use the strategy (production deficiency).

Stages.   These studies suggest that there is a developmental progression involved in learning the organizational strategies needed for free recall tasks. In the first stage, preschool children tend not to know how to organize words by taxonomic category. However, there is some evidence that preschoolers can pair words by sound (e.g., rhymes) or syntax (e.g., subject-verb pairs). In the second stage, emerging at about age five or six, the child knows how to organize words by taxonomic category but does not spontaneously do so. In the third stage, emerging at about age ten or eleven, the child spontaneously uses organizational strategies when it is beneficial to do so.

Implications of the Development of Organizational Strategies

The instructional implications for organizational strategies essentially replicate those for rehearsal strategies. First, beginning students need practice in using organizational strategies. Such practice could begin with rhymes, moving during the early elementary years to taxonomic categories for word lists. Second, later in the elementary school years, children need practice in determining how to use organizing strategies productively. Regular school tasks involving free recall list learning can serve as vehicles for promoting the development of organizing strategies.

DEVELOPMENT OF ELABORATION STRATEGIES

Paired-Associate Learning Tasks

Suppose that I gave you some pairs of words and asked that you form associations so that you could tell me the second word whenever I say the first word. For example, the pairs might be the states and their capitals, such as: Alabama—Montgomery, Alaska—Juneau, Arizona—Phoenix, Arkansas—Little Rock, California—Sacramento, Colorado—Denver, Connecticut—Hartford, Delaware—Dover, Florida—Tallahassee, Georgia—Atlanta, Hawaii—Honolulu, Idaho—Boise, Illinois—Springfield, Indiana—Indianapolis, Iowa—Des Moines, Kansas—Topeka, Kentucky—Frankfort, Louisiana—Baton Rouge, Maine—Augusta, Maryland—Annapolis, Massachusetts—Boston, Michigan—Lansing, Minnesota—St. Paul, Mississippi—Jackson, Missouri—Jefferson City, Montana—Helena, Nebraska—Lincoln, Nevada—Carson City, New Hampshire—Concord, New Jersey—Trenton, New Mexico—Santa Fe, New York—Albany, North Carolina—Raleigh, North Dakota—Bismark, Ohio—Columbus, Oklahoma—Oklahoma City, Oregon—Salem, Pennsylvania—Harrisburg, Rhode Island—Providence, South Carolina—Columbia, South Dakota—Pierre, Tennessee—Nashville, Texas—Austin, Utah—Salt Lake City, Vermont—Montpelier, Virginia—Richmond, Washington—Olympia, West Virginia—Charleston, Wisconsin—Madison, Wyoming—Cheyenne. Read over each pair until you have associated the second word (i.e., the capital) with the first word (i.e., the state). When you are ready, take the following test:

Michigan _____, Hawaii _____, New Jersey _____,

Wisconsin _____, Oklahoma _____, Georgia _____,

New Mexico _____, Vermont _____, Oregon _____,

South Carolina _____, Alabama _____, California _____,

North Dakota _____, Wyoming _____, Connecticut _____,

Washington _____, New Hampshire _____, Ohio _____,

Tennessee _____, Kentucky _____, Mississippi _____,

Arizona _____, New York _____, Texas _____,

Utah _____, Virginia _____, Maryland _____,

West Virginia _____, Maine _____, Montana _____,

Rhode Island _____, North Carolina _____, Pennsylvania _____,

South Dakota _____, Arkansas _____, Nevada _____,

Massachusetts _____, Delaware _____, Florida _____,

Colorado _____, Nebraska _____, Missouri _____,

Louisiana _____, Indiana _____, Kansas _____,

Iowa _____, Illinois _____, Alaska _____,

Idaho _____, Minnesota _____.

This is an example of a paired associate learning task. In paired associate learning, the learner is given pairs of items such as two words or two pictures. The learner's job is to associate the two words so that he/she is able to recite the second item of the pair whenever the teacher gives the first item. Paired associate learning occurs in various school learning tasks, ranging from learning the name of each letter in the alphabet to the example just given. Because of this, paired associate learning has been extensively studied in psychological research.

One strategy that you can use for associating items in a paired associate task is to form a visual image uniting the two items. For example, for the pair Illinois—Springfield, you might imagine a spring in a field of very "ill" corn. This approach is called a visual elaboration strategy, because the learner elaborates on the pair of items by forming a visual image. An alternative is a verbal elaboration strategy, such as forming a sentence that unites the items or parts of the items. For example, for the Illinois—Springfield pair you might use the sentence: "I got ill in the spring."

Research on Induced Versus Imposed Imagery

As you can see, elaboration strategies involve active and voluntary processing by the learner during the learning task. When a learner actively elaborates on the material in paired-associate learning, the learner is adding a context that associates the items. The focus of this section is on how children develop the ability to generate and use visual elaboration strategies.

Levin (1976) has distinguished between "experimenter induced" imagery strategies (in which the learner is instructed to generate and use visual imagery to associate the items) and "experimenter imposed" imagery strategies (in which the experimenter provides an image and asks that the learner use that image to associate the two items). In a recent review, Reese (1977) has noted that experimenter-imposed imagery tends to improve performance for kindergartners and first graders, but experimenter-induced imagery is better for sixth graders and adults. Apparently, younger children are not able to generate images independently but are able to use imagery provided by the experimenter; in contrast, older learners who are able to generate their own images may be distracted by the experimenter's imagery.

For example, Wolff & Levin (1972) conducted a paired-associate learning study involving kindergartners and third graders. According to Piagetian theory (Piaget & Inhelder, 1971), the younger children are more likely to use "reproductive imagery" (i.e., a static image that cannot be rearranged by the child) while by age seven or eight children can use "anticipatory imagery" (i.e., a dynamic image that can be mentally manipulated by the child). The stimuli were sixteen pairs of toys, so that the children had to learn to associate one toy with another for each of sixteen pairs.

Some children were given standard instructions (control group). Some children were given instructions to form a mental image (experimenter-induced imagery group); these children were being asked to use "anticipatory imagery." For other subjects, the experimenter provided an image to connect the toys such as putting the wristwatch around the neck of the giraffe (experimenter-imposed imagery group), and for still other subjects the experimenter allowed the subject to physically manipulate the toys (subject-imposed imagery group). The children in these latter two groups had access to actual physical representations and thus could rely on "static imagery."

For the test, subjects were given all sixteen of the response toys. As the experimenter presented a stimulus toy, the child had to select the response toy that went with it. The results are summarized in Figure 4–8. As you can see, imagery instructions did not greatly increase the memory performance of kindergartners, but had a strong positive effect for the third graders. Apparently, the kindergartners had difficulty in generating dynamic images. However,

FIGURE 4–8   Role of Imagery in Learning Paired-Associates for Two Age Groups

The experimenter presents 16 pairs of toys such as,
"Form an image of the toys playing together."

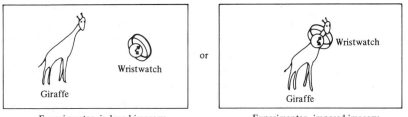

Experimenter–induced imagery   Experimenter–imposed imagery

Percentage correct by treatment group for two age groups

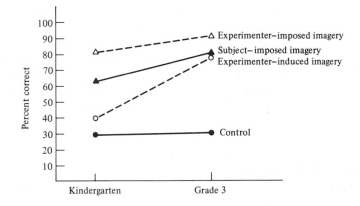

Adapted from Wolff & Levin (1972)

when the toys were placed together into a coherent image either by the experimenter (experimenter-imposed imagery) or by the subject (subject-imposed imagery), memory performance was enhanced for both age groups. Apparently, allowing the young children to physically manipulate the toys enabled them to form useful mental images.

Theory of Development of Elaboration Strategies

Availability Versus Production.   The foregoing research on elaborations is consistent with the distinction between availability versus production deficiencies. For example, students who do not benefit from instructions to form elaborative images apparently do not have elaborative strategies available (i.e., they suffer from an availability deficiency). Students who use imagery when instructed to do so, but fail to use elaborative imagery spontaneously during learning suffer from a production deficiency.

Stages.   The research on elaboration demonstrates stages that parallel those for rehearsal and organizational strategies, except that the elaboration stages tend to develop later. The progression in the ability to use elaborative imagery strategies depends, however, on whether the teacher actually generates the image for the child or just instructs the child to use an image, and also on the concreteness of the materials to be learned (Levin & Kaplan, 1972). In the first stage, beginning elementary school children behave as if they lack the ability to form elaborative images (e.g., benefiting from teacher-provided images for concrete stimuli, but not from instructions to form images). In the second stage, by the later elementary school years, children behave as if they possess the ability to form elaborative images but fail to do so spontaneously (e.g., benefiting from instructions to form images but not from teacher-provided images that conflict with their own imagery). By the third grade, children are able to generate and use imagery strategies when the materials to be learned are concrete objects. When the materials to be learned are pictures, children appear to be able to follow instructions to generate and use imagery instructions by age eleven or twelve. However, when the stimuli are words, imagery instructions do not greatly enhance recall in eleven- and twelve-year-olds, but do enhance recall for adults. Finally, in the third stage, some older students and adults spontaneously use elaboration without instruction. Apparently, this stage is attained much less frequently for elaboration than for rehearsal and organizational strategies.

Implications of the Development
of Elaboration Strategies

Elaboration is perhaps the most powerful of the three learning strategies described in this chapter, and one that can be used in a wide variety of situations beyond paired-associate learning. For example, in Chapter 8, note taking is viewed as an elaborative activity for learning from lectures. Since elaboration strategies frequently are not produced spontaneously, and since they are powerful, it is particularly important to provide instructional experiences that foster elaboration.

Consistent with the previous sections, the research on elaboration suggests two major implications for instruction: First, children need practice in using elaboration strategies. Such practice could begin in early elementary school with the teacher providing images that the child can use to learn to form associations. For example, to help students remember that the letter S makes an "sssss" sound, the letter can be associated with a picture of a punctured tire with air escaping. As children gain more experience in using images, by the later elementary grades, they can be encouraged to create their own images. Second, children need practice in determining when elaboration would be useful and in determining which type of elaboration would be appropriate. For example, in learning foreign language vocabulary, students need to be able to spontaneously form elaborations such as the key-word method described in Chapter 8.

CONCLUSION

This chapter began with an example of the role of metamemory in children's learning. In particular, preschoolers tend to lack the ability to assess their memory and processing capacity, whereas by age eleven or twelve, children can generate accurate predictions of memory performance.

The chapter summarized research concerning the emergence of three basic kinds of learning strategies—rehearsing, organizing, and elaborating. For each strategy, learning progresses in the following three stages.

Early. During the early stage, learning strategies are not available and are not spontaneously used by the learner. This stage seems to occur during the pre-school years for each of the three strategies reviewed in this chapter.

Transitional. During the transition stage, learning strategies may be available to the learner but are not spontaneously used to enhance learning. With explicit instruction from an adult, children at this stage can use learning strategies. This stage seems to occur in the primary school years, but depends on the complexity of strategy.

Late. During the late stage, learning strategies are available and are appropriately used without the need for adult instruction. In addition, children at this stage are able to adjust their strategies to fit with the learning goal for a task. This stage seems to appear between junior high school years and adulthood, depending on the strategy. The progression through these stages is influenced, of course, by the nature of the learning task and the characteristics of the learner.

The major implications for instruction are: First, the development of effective learning strategies should be considered a part of the curriculum; second, the introduction of basic learning tasks should be matched to the level of development of learning strategies in the children. Chapter 8 is devoted to a closer examination of the teaching of learning strategies.

SUGGESTED READINGS

Brown, A. L. (1978). "Knowing when, where, and how to remember: A problem of metacognition." In R. Glaser (ed.), *Advances in Instructional Psychology*. Hillsdale, N.J.: Erlbaum. (A detailed summary of research on the development of memory skills, such as "comprehension monitoring," related to reading.)

Kail, R. (1984). *The development of memory in children*. (Second Edition). New York: Freeman. (An interesting introduction to the development of memory in children, including chapters on mnemonic strategies, metamemory, and individual differences.)

Kail, R. V. & Hagen, J. W. (1977). *Perspectives on the development of memory and cognition*. Hillsdale, N.J.: Erlbaum. (A detailed set of chapters by leading researchers in the field of children's memory development, including chapters on metamemory by Flavell & Wellman, on memory strategies by Hagen & Stanovich, organizational factors by Moely, and imagery by Reese.)

PART II

LEARNING & INSTRUCTION

The five chapters in this section focus on instructional methods. Chapter 5 shows how traditional research on reinforcement theory must be amended when it is applied to educational settings such as classroom management. Chapter 6 focuses on instructional methods for improving the understandability of textbooks, including advance organizers, signaling, and adjunct questions. Chapter 7 focuses on instructional methods for making classroom teaching more meaningful including the use of concrete manipulatives, discovery learning, and inductive learning. Chapter 8 deals with recent research on teaching students how to learn including memory mnemonics, outlining techniques, and note-taking techniques. Chapter 9 deals with recent research on teaching students how to think, including a look at several thinking skills programs. In summary, this section focuses on the teacher—including how instruction is delivered.

The cognitive framework in Figure 1–3 lists three general conditions for meaningful learning—reception, availability, and activation—which require that the learner engage in several cognitive processes during learning. Meeting the "reception" condition requires paying attention to incoming information. Meeting the "availability" condition requires possessing prerequisite knowledge. Meeting the "activation" condition requires building internal connections (i.e., making logical or structural connections among the ideas in the incoming information) and building external connections (i.e., making appropriate connections between ideas in the incoming information and ideas already in memory). As you read these chapters, you should try to keep in mind how each of the instructional methods affects these four cognitive processes. For example, discovery learning focuses mainly on activation (i.e., on the cognitive process of building connections) while using adjunct questions focuses mainly on reception (i.e., on the cognitive process of paying attention).

5 Basic Learning and Motivational Processes

This chapter focuses on the educational implications of Thorndike's famous law of effect, the idea that learning depends on feedback. Since the early part of this century and even continuing on today, classroom instruction has probably been more strongly influenced by the law of effect than by any other idea in the psychology of learning. In order to help you better understand this principle and its relation to instruction, this chapter investigates how the law of effect can be related to classroom management, response learning, and concept learning. For each topic, the chapter contrasts a behaviorist versus cognitive view of the learner and the learning process.

A RESPONSE LEARNING TASK

Let's try a simple motor skill task. You will need about ten pennies (numbered 1 through 10) and a small square of paper (e.g., about 3 inches by 3 inches). Place the square flat on the floor, about 3 feet away from you. Then, sit down with the pennies near you. With your eyes closed, toss each penny toward the square, trying to get the penny as close to the square as possible. After you have tossed ten pennies, take a ruler and measure how many inches each penny landed away from the square. (If a penny landed on the square, its score is 0.) Now, fill in the left portion of Figure 5–1. Put a dot indicating how far away the first penny landed from the target, how far the second penny landed, and so on for all ten pennies. This is your "baseline" performance (i.e., your performance before any training).

Now, let's see if you can teach yourself to be more accurate. Collect the ten pennies, and again sit down where you sat before. With your eyes closed, as before, toss a penny toward the square. Then, open your eyes and measure how far off you were. Close your eyes, and toss the next penny; then, open your eyes and measure how far off you were. Repeat this procedure for 20 tosses. Now, fill in the middle portion of Figure 5–1. Put a dot indicating how far away the first penny landed, and so on for all twenty pennies. This is your "training" performance (i.e., your performance during the training period).

Finally, repeat the procedure you used for the baseline. Sit down and, with your eyes closed, toss each of the ten pennies. Then, measure how far off each one was and fill in the results on the right-hand portion of Figure 5–1. This is your extinction performance (i.e., your performance after training, when feedback is no longer given for each response).

Are you more accurate in tossing pennies during the training period than during the baseline period? If so, we might be tempted to say that you are learning! Why does your performance increase during the training phase? One possible answer is that you have more practice. However, if you conducted the "baseline" part of the task for many tosses, you might find no improvement in your performance. Practice—by itself—might not be enough to enable learning. Thus a second explanation is that you have practice with feedback. The feedback tells you how far away each penny landed from the target. Thus

FIGURE 5–1   Fill in Your Performance on a Simple Motor Learning Task

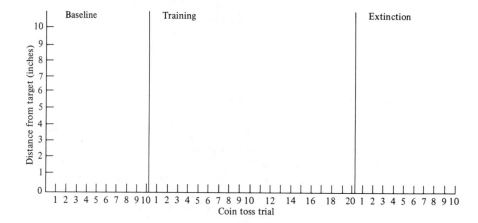

knowing the effects of your behavior seems to be a potent force in helping you to change your behavior.

Does your accuracy decrease during the extinction period? If so, we can say that feedback is needed for you to maintain your performance. If you are able to maintain a high level of accuracy even during the extinction period, we can say that you have learned to provide intrinsic feedback. That is, you have learned to be able to tell whether your performance is accurate without external feedback.

In this chapter, you will learn how feedback affects response learning and concept learning. In response learning, the outcome of learning is a change in a single aspect of the learner's behavior. Examples of response learning include learning to say "six" when you are presented with a flash card that contains 3 + 3, learning to raise your hand before you speak in class, or learning to turn a handle on a water fountain in order to get a drink. In concept learning, the outcome is being able to classify stimuli, such as sorting cards with the letter *a* into one pile and the letter *b* into another pile.

INTRODUCTION TO LEARNING

Definition

What is learning? A typical definition (Mayer, 1982) is: learning is a relatively permanent change in a person's knowledge or behavior due to experience. This definition has three parts: (1) The duration of the change is long-term rather than short-term. (2) The locus of the change is the content and structure of knowledge in memory or the behavior of the learner. (3) The cause of the change is the learner's experience in the environment rather than motivation, fatique, drugs, physical condition, or physiological intervention.

Behaviorist Versus Cognitive Theories

As you can see from this definition, there is a lack of agreement concerning "what is learned." Behaviorist theories of learning focus on changes in behavior whereas cognitive theories focus on changes in knowledge. Thus, in cognitive theories, the effects of learning can be determined only indirectly—by making inferences based on the learner's behavior.

Learning Versus Performance. A distinction must be made between learning and performance, since a person's performance is not always a good indication of what has been learned. Learning refers to the acquisition of knowledge or behavior, whereas performance refers to the actual behavior that a learner produces on a given occasion. For example, performance on a test can be influenced by the location of the test, the stress experienced by the learner, the amount of sleep the learner has had, and many other factors unrelated to what the learner has learned.

Kinds of Learning

There are many different kinds of learning tasks, and the principles that apply to one type of learning may not apply to others (Mayer, 1983). In a classroom, for example, each of the following types of learning may be taking place at any time:

1. *Response learning* refers to the acquisition of a new response, such as tossing a coin so that it lands on a target.
2. *Concept learning* refers to the acquisition of a new classification rule based on experience with instances, such as learning to add *ed* to a verb in order to signify "past tense."
3. *Rote verbal learning* refers to the ability to produce a list of verbal responses (e.g., reciting the alphabet).
4. *Prose learning* refers to the learning of new semantic or procedural knowledge from written or spoken prose (e.g., learning about the "nitrogen cycle" from reading a lesson in a science textbook).

This chapter will focus on response learning and concept learning because they are the most basic kinds of learning; subsequent chapters will deal with the other types of learning.

THE LAW OF EFFECT

Thorndike's Theory

In order to get a better understanding of response learning, let's consider an early study performed by E. L. Thorndike (1898, 1911). Figure 5–2 shows a puzzle box used by Thorndike. As you can see, the puzzle box is a cage containing a door that can be opened from inside the cage. A hungry cat was placed inside the puzzle box, with a dish of food outside. In a typical experiment, the cat had to learn to unlatch the door by pulling a string. The first time the cat was put into the puzzle box, the cat engaged in many behaviors, including scratching the bars, meowing, and pouncing on the floor. Eventually, the cat accidentally pawed at the string; this opened the door and allowed the cat to escape and eat the food in the dish. On subsequent trials, the cat tended to spend less time engaging in irrelevant behaviors such as pouncing and meowing and tended to require less time before pulling the string. After many trials, the cat would immediately pull the string upon being placed in the

FIGURE 5–2   A Puzzle Box

"When put into the box the cat would show evident signs of discomfort and of impulse to escape from confinement. It tries to squeeze through any opening; it claws and bites at the wire; it thrusts its paws out through any opening and claws at everything it reaches. . . . It does not pay very much attention to the food outside but seems simply to strive instinctively to escape from confinement. . . . The cat that is clawing all over the box in her impulsive struggle will probably claw the string or loop or button so as to open the door. And gradually all the other unsuccessful impulses will be stamped out and the particular impulse leading to the successful act will be stamped in by the resulting pleasure, until, after many trials, the cat will, when put in the box, immediately claw the button or loop in a definite way."

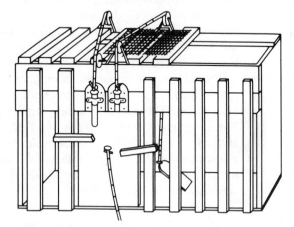

From Thorndike (1898, p. 13)

puzzle box. Figure 5–3 shows the time (in seconds) a cat spent in the puzzle box before pulling the string for each of twenty trials. As you can see, the cat required a minute or more on the first two trials but required just a few seconds by the twentieth trial.

The change in the cat's performance suggests that the cat has learned something. According to Thorndike, the cat learned to form a strong association between the stimulus—being in the puzzle box—and a response—pulling the

FIGURE 5–3   Time Spent in the Puzzle Box on Each Trial

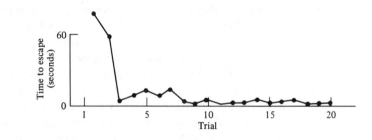

Adapted from Thorndike (1898)

string. At the start of the experiment, the cat had many associations for the stimulus, including pouncing, meowing, scratching, etc. However, each time the cat engaged in one of these behaviors, the result was not positive; thus, according to Thorndike, the association between the stimulus (i.e., being in the puzzle box) and that response (e.g., meowing) was weakened. Similarly, each time the cat pulled the string, the result was positive; thus, according to Thorndike, the association between the stimulus (i.e., being in the puzzle box) and the response (i.e., pulling the string) was strengthened. At first, the conditioned response of pulling the string was very weakly associated with the stimulus of being in the box, but by the end of the experiment the association was strong. At first, several irrelevent behaviors were strongly associated with being in the box, but by the end of the experiment those associations were weaker. Thus, according to Thorndike, learning to make an appropriate response involves strengthening the relevant association and weakening the other associations. The principle underlying this learning is called the "law of effect." The law of effect is the idea that if a behavior is followed by a pleasing state of affairs it is more likely to occur again in the future under the same circumstances, and if a behavior is followed by an unpleasing state of affairs, it is less likely to be given again in the future. Here is how Thorndike (1911, p. 244) summarized the law of effect:

> Of several responses made to the same situation, those which are accompanied or closely followed by satisfaction . . . will, other things being equal, be more firmly connected to the situation, so that, when it recurs, they will be more likely to recur; those which are accompanied or closely followed by discomfort . . . will, other things being equal, have their connections with the situation weakened, so that when it recurs, they will be less likely to occur. The greater the satisfaction or discomfort, the greater the strengthening or weakening of the bond.

Skinner's Theory

Skinner (1938, 1953, 1957, 1968, 1969) has conducted extensive research that served to improve on Thorndike's methodology and modify his theories. For example, with respect to methodology, Skinner developed devices that have been called "Skinner boxes." Figure 5–4 shows a Skinner box for a white laboratory rat. As you can see, the Skinner box consists of a metal cage, a metal grid floor, a bar that can be pressed down, and a food tray that is connected to a machine that delivers food pellets. First, let's put a white lab rat into the Skinner box. The rat will engage in many behaviors but will rarely press the bar. Thus the "baseline" rate of bar pressing is very low, as shown in the left portion of Figure 5–5. Now, let's adjust the food pellet machine so that it delivers a food pellet to the food tray each time that the bar is pressed. At first, the rat—like Thorndike's cat—engages in many irrelevant activities. Eventually, the rat—like Thorndike's cat—will accidentally produce the desired be-

FIGURE 5–4   A Skinner Box

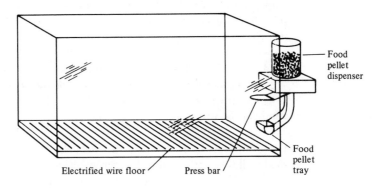

Courtesy of Ralph Gerbrands Co., Arlington, Mass.

havior. As soon as the rat presses the bar, a food pellet appears in the tray and the rat presumably will eat the pellet. Over the course of this "learning" session, the rate of bar pressing will increase dramatically, as shown in the right-hand side of Figure 5–5. As you can see, the Skinner box is an improvement over Thorndike's puzzle box because the animal does not have to be placed back into the box after each successful response.

In order to describe the learning process, Skinner has developed "reinforce-

FIGURE 5–5   Rate of Bar Pressing for Each 10-minute Time Block in the Skinner Box

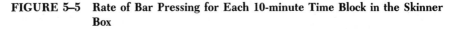

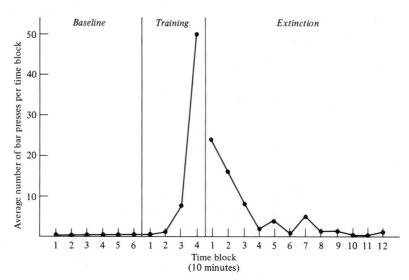

Modified from Skinner (1938)

ment theory." The main idea in reinforcement theory is that reinforcers can control behavior. A reinforcer is any stimulus that, when contingent on a response, serves to increase the rate of responding. As you can see, this definition has two components:

1. *Contingency*—the reinforcer occurrence depends on (e.g., follows immediately upon) the occurrence of the learner's response.
2. *Rate of responding*—the reinforcer serves to change the learner's rate of responding.

For example, the food pellet fits the definition of a reinforcer because: (1) the food pellet is delivered immediately after the bar is pressed (i.e., the delivery of the food pellet is contingent on the learner pressing the bar); (2) the rate of bar pressing increases when bar pressing is reinforced.

Is Reward More Effective Than Punishment?

A reinforcer may be positive or negative. A positive reinforcer is anything that when presented contingent on a response, tends to increase the probability or rate of that response. A negative reinforcer is anything that when taken away contingent on a response, tends to increase the probability or rate of that response. For example, presenting a food pellet to a hungry rat is an example of a positive reinforcer whereas stopping an electrical shock is an example of a negative reinforcer. Thus a response can be reinforced by either presenting a reward or taking away a punishment.

In contrast, there are two kinds of stimuli which may serve to decrease the rate or frequency of responding: (1) presenting an aversive stimulus contingent on a response and (2) taking away a rewarding stimulus contingent on a response. You can consider these to be forms of *punishment*. For example, the rat might decrease its rate of bar pressing if a shock followed each bar press or if pressing a bar caused a machine to stop supplying food pellets for 60 seconds.

Although the original law of effect, as presented in the preceding section, gave equal status to reward and punishment, this version did not survive Thorndike's lifetime. Toward the end of his scientific career, after hundreds of studies, Thorndike (1932, p. 276) felt compelled to revise the law of effect by downplaying the role of punishment in changing behavior:

> In the early statements of the Law of Effect, the influence of satisfying consequences of a connection in the way of strengthening it was paralleled by the influence of annoying consequences in the way of weakening it. . . . I now consider that there is no such complete and exact parallelism. In particular, the strengthening of a connection by satisfying consequences seems, in view of our experiments . . . to be more universal, inevitable, and direct than the weakening of a connection by annoying consequences.

Skinner's later application of reinforcement theory to instruction was also based on the power of rewarding appropriate behavior through positive reinforcement rather than punishing incorrect behavior. Thus the remainder of this chapter will focus mainly on the uses of reward in school-related tasks.

APPLICATIONS OF THE
LAW OF EFFECT

What Is Classroom Management?

As you may have noticed the "law of effect" (or reinforcement theory) suggests many classroom applications. In this section, we will explore some examples of how the law of effect can be applied to the task of classroom management. In the next section, we will explore some limitations of classroom management techniques and relate these techniques to a cognitive theory of learning.

In any classroom, students will exhibit some behaviors that are disruptive and some behaviors that are productive for learning. One goal of a classroom management program is to decrease the frequency of disruptive behaviors and increase the frequency of productive behaviors. As you can see, this situation seems similar to that of Thorndike's puzzle box or the Skinner box because we have some target behavior that we want to increase or decrease. Thus a major question is whether the principles of reinforcement developed from animal research can be applied successfully to humans.

Contingency Contracting

Contingency contracting is one application of reinforcement techniques to a classroom situation. In contingency contracting, the student and teacher make a contract that specifies which student activities will lead to which rewards or punishments. For example, Sulzbacher & Houser (1968) conducted a study in a class of retarded children. The first step was to define the behavior to be changed; in this study, the teacher attempted to decrease the frequency of children making a disruptive gesture referred to as the "naughty finger." The next step was to determine a contingent event that might serve to decrease the rate of responding; in this study, the teacher used a loss of 1 minute of recess time from a 10-minute recess. As you can see, this contingency seems to involve both punishment and reward; for each inappropriate behavior, a rewarding stimulus (1 minute of recess) is taken away but for appropriate behavior no time will be lost from recess. This procedure is called "response cost," because inappropriate behavior costs the student in terms of diminishing a reward. Another frequently used contingency is called "time out"—for each case of inappropriate behavior the child is moved to a quiet place for a short time. These techniques seem to be more useful than traditional types of punishment such as verbal disapproval or threats. Finally, the third step in classroom management is to establish a clear procedure for administering the program, with clearly articulated rules.

For 9 days, the teacher simply kept track of the frequency of occurrence of the "naughty finger." This is the baseline period, and as you can see in Figure 5–6, the rate of responding for the class was about 15 occurrences per day. At the beginning of the tenth day, the teacher began the training period by making the following announcement (Sulzbacher & Houser, 1968, p. 88):

> From now on there will be a special ten minute recess at the end of the day. However, if I see the naughty finger or hear about it I will flip down one of these cards, and you will have one minute less of recess whenever this happens. Remember, every time I flip down one of these cards, all of you lose a minute from your recess.

As you can see in Figure 5–6, the rate of occurrences of the "naughty finger" fell to less than five per day. After 18 days of training, the teacher told the class that the recess policy no longer was in effect. As you can see in the right portion of Figure 5–6, during the first 9 days of this extinction period, the rate of responding increased. By the ninth day, the rate was back up to where it had been before training!

Two aspects of Figure 5–6 merit special attention. First, note that the rate of responding fell dramatically on day 10. This fall cannot be attributed to the training, because training had just begun; instead, the students seem to be able

FIGURE 5–6   Number of Disruptive Behaviors per Day in a Special Education Classroom

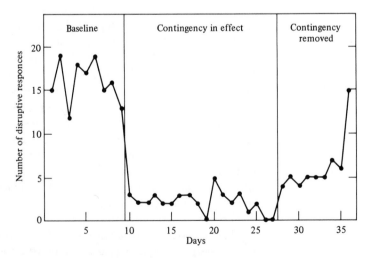

From Sulzbacher & Houser (1968)

to adjust their performance based on the verbal instructions of the teacher. Second, note that the suppression of the disruptive behavior is short-lived. Once the contingencies are removed, the disruptive behavior seems to increase back to its former strength. We will examine these two problems in more detail in the next section.

Token Economies

Token economies are another application of reinforcement theory to a classroom situation. In a token economy, students are given tokens (e.g., check marks by their names on a blackboard) for appropriate (or inappropriate) behaviors, and these tokens can be traded in for prizes or privileges. The first step is to describe clearly the behavior to be changed. For example, suppose a teacher wishes to reduce the amount of disruptive behavior in a classroom. For purposes of our example, let's define disruptive behavior as any one of the following behaviors (O'Leary, Becker, Evans & Saudargas, 1969): (1) motor behaviors (e.g., walking around the room), (2) aggressive behaviors (e.g., hitting or kicking another person), (3) disturbing someone else's property (e.g., grabbing another person's book or tearing another person's paper), (4) making noise (e.g., stamping feet or clapping hands), (5) verbalizations (e.g., blurting out answers or talking out of turn), (6) turning around (e.g., looking to the rear of the class when the teacher is in front of the class), (7) inappropriate tasks (e.g., drawing a picture during a spelling lesson). The second step is to find a contingent stimulus that will serve as an effective reinforcer for the children who produce these behaviors. Weil & Murphy (1982) have suggested three categories of rewards for classroom management:

1. *Social rewards* (e.g., smiles, praise, or hugs).
2. *Material rewards* (e.g., stickers, stars, and awards).
3. *Tokens* (e.g., tickets, passes, or check marks on a chart) that can be redeemed for valued prizes or privileges.

For our example, let's rely on tokens. In our classroom token economy a child receives from 1 to 10 points after each 30-minute lesson for each of four lessons on each afternoon. The points (or tokens) are placed in a small booklet on each child's desk. On redemption days, the child can trade in points for prizes, such as 25 points for a level 1 prize, 35 points for a level 2 prize, and so on. The third step is to implement the program in a clear and consistent way. The rules are made clear to the student. For example, the teacher could write the following rules on the blackboard (O'Leary, Becker, Evans & Saudargas, 1969, p. 5):

We sit in our seats; we raise our hands to talk; we do not talk out of turn; we keep our desks clear; we face the front of the room; we will work very hard; we do not talk in the hall; we do not run; and we do not disturb reading groups.

The teacher reviews the rules regularly. In addition, the teacher puts the token system into effect during short structured activities during the afternoon, such as spelling or science lessons in which the entire class participates. As part of the token economy, the teacher praises appropriate behavior and ignores inappropriate behaviors. Threats, such as "If you're not quiet by the time I count to three . . ." and criticism such as "Sit in your seat" have been eliminated.

The example just outlined is very similar to a token economy program for second graders that was carefully studied by O'Leary et al. (1969). In a classroom of twenty-one students, the teacher identified seven students who tended to frequently produce disruptive behaviors such as those described. As part of the study, observers noted whether each of the seven children was engaged in appropriate or disruptive behavior during various 20-second periods throughout the school day. Figure 5–7 shows the percentage of time that the seven children were engaged in disruptive behaviors at different points in the study. First, there was a baseline period during which no changes were made in the classroom. As you can see, the children were disruptive on more than half of the observations made. A few days later, the teacher introduced the classroom rules and wrote them on the board. As you can see, this did not result in any major change in disruptive behavior. A few days later, the classroom afternoon

FIGURE 5–7   **Percentage of Disruptive Behaviors per Day during the Afternoon in a Second Grade Classroom**

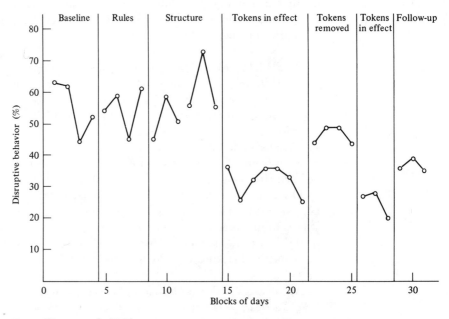

From O'Leary et al. (1969)

structure was changed into easily identifiable 30-minute lessons. As you can see, stucture had no major impact either. A few days later, the teacher began a policy of praising appropriate behavior and ignoring disruptive behavior during the afternoon. The result was a modest increase in disruptive behavior. Finally, a few days later, the teacher began the token economy system of presenting points to each child after each of four 30-minute lessons each afternoon. As can be seen in Figure 5–7, the token economy procedure resulted in a dramatic reduction of disruptive behavior. Then the token system was stopped. Disruptive behavior increased almost back to its original baseline level. However, when the token economy was reestablished, disruptive behavior fell again. Finally, during a follow-up period, the teacher stopped giving tokens, but continued using rules, structured lessons, and praise. In addition, the teacher gave stars for good behavior—with each day beginning with a clean wall chart for each child's stars. As you can see, disruptive behavior increased, but was still maintained at well below the baseline level.

The preceding discussion is based only on performance during the afternoon (i.e., the time when the token economy was in effect). During the morning, no token economy was ever in effect. Did the reduction in disruptive behavior during the afternoon transfer to the morning? Figure 5–8 summarizes

FIGURE 5–8 Percentage of Disruptive Behaviors per Day during Mornings in a Second Grade Classroom

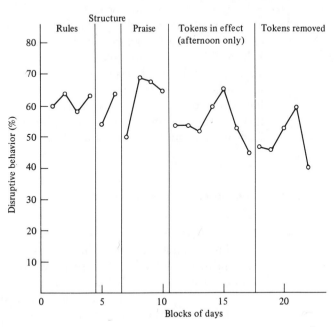

From O'Leary et al. (1969)

the percentage of disruptive behavior during the morning for each phase of the study. As you can see, the token economy procedure does not cause a large change in disruptive behavior during the morning even though there was a large change in disruptive behavior during the afternoon. Apparently, the children are able to discriminate between conditions under which appropriate behavior results in rewards (i.e., afternoon) and conditions during which appropriate behavior does not result in rewards (i.e., mornings).

In a more recent study involving six disruptive ninth graders, Main & Munro (1977) were able to replicate many of the results of the O'Leary et al. study. As in the O'Leary study, providing structured lessons and praising appropriate behavior while ignoring inappropriate behavior had only a slight effect on reducing disruptive behavior. Use of tokens greatly reduced disruptive behaviors; withdrawal of tokens produced an increase in disruptive behavior. During a final follow-up period, the token system was reestablished but tokens were gradually thinned out, leaving a contract system and teacher praise. This follow-up procedure was successful in maintaining a relatively low level of disruption.

From these examples, we can begin to see the characteristics of a successful classroom token economy. First, the systems have clearly stated rules and structure. Students know what is expected of them and what will happen if they behave in certain ways. Second, the systems tend to use reward rather than punishment. For example, Bandura & Walters (1963) have found that when a model (e.g., a teacher) uses punishment on a child, the child is more likely to use aggression as a way of controlling others. Madsen, Becker, & Thomas (1968) found that verbal punishments (e.g., saying, "Stop that!") tend to increase disruptive behaviors. Similarly, ignoring disruptive behavior does not help to reduce it. Third, the systems are administered in a way that always allows for fairly rapid recognition of appropriate behavior. Students receive feedback within a few minutes of their behavior, and prior inappropriate behavior cannot cancel out rewards for current appropriate behavior. In the first example, feedback was given to the entire class; in the second example, feedback was given to each student separately.

Implications of Research on Classroom Management

The limitations of classroom management systems are also clear from the preceding examples. It is very difficult to establish a program that works (i.e., a program that eventually can dispense with constant use of material rewards). Students may come to rely heavily on external rewards as a guide to how they should behave; instead, a goal of many classroom management systems is to help children develop intrinsic or self-motivated methods of behavior control. These limitations—and how they relate to a cognitive theory of learning—are explored in the next section.

UNDERSTANDING CLASSROOM MANAGEMENT: HIDDEN COSTS OF REWARD

Behaviorist Versus Cognitive Theories of Reward

There are many "how-to" books for classroom management. However, in order to effectively use these techniques, it is important to understand the theory of how reinforcers (e.g., tokens) affect behavior. In this section, we will explore two kinds of theories of reinforcement—behaviorist theories and cognitive theories. Behaviorist theories are based on Thorndike's and Skinner's interpretations of the law of effect, namely, the idea that a reinforcer (such as a token) serves to stamp in a response (such as appropriate behavior) and its link with a stimulus (such as the classroom environment). The strength of the stimulus-response association is automatically increased each time the response is reinforced; the process does not require active awareness or interpretation by the learner. In contrast, cognitive theories are based on an alternative interpretation of the law of effect, namely, the idea that the learner actively thinks about and interprets the reinforcer and its relation to the learner's response. Thus the reinforcer in cognitive theory serves as information that the learner uses in building a plan for responding.

Hidden Costs of Contingency Contracting

Let's examine what these two theories predict in a simple reward situation. Suppose we observe a preschool to see how children spend their free time. We find that many of the children spend a large portion of their free time in a drawing activity—using colored marking pens and large sheets of drawing paper. Let's take those children who like to spend free time drawing, and assign them to one of three groups. In the "expected reward condition," we will make a contingency contract with each child: the child agrees to produce some drawings in exchange for an extrinsic reward (i.e., a certificate with a gold seal and ribbon). In the "unexpected reward condition," no contract is made, but the child is given the same reward (i.e., a certificate) after drawing some pictures. However, the child does not know in advance that a reward will be given for drawing. Finally, in the "no reward condition," the child does not receive a reward (i.e., certificate) for engaging in the drawing activity.

In order to see how rewards affect behavior, let's examine how our preschools spend their free time after the rewards are given. Let's come back to the preschool a week or two later and observe the percentage of free time spent in drawing. What do the behaviorist and cognitive theories predict? The behaviorist theory would predict that children in the "expected reward condition" and "unexpected reward condition" should spend more free time drawing because they were rewarded for drawing. In contrast, the cognitive theory predicts that "expected reward condition" children will spend less time drawing as compared to children in the other two groups. One cognitive theory—called "overjustification" (Lepper & Greene, 1978)—states that the children are interpreting or justifying their own behavior and extrinsic rewards. If a child engages in a behavior, that behavior must be justified by the child. Thus children who draw without expecting to receive a reward (no reward and unexpected reward conditions) can justify their behavior by saying they draw because they like to draw; in contrast, children who draw with the expectation of receiving a certificate can justify drawing by saying they draw because they get something for it. When rewards are no longer given, the justification for engaging in that behavior is reduced for these children.

In a classic study, Lepper, Greene & Nisbett (1973) carried out the procedure just described. Figure 5–9 summarizes the percentage of free time spent in the drawing activity for children who had experienced the three treatment conditions. As you can see, the results conflict with the behaviorist theory—which states that the two rewarded groups should behave similarly—but is consistent with the cognitive theory—which states that the "expected reward condition" (or "expected award condition") should spend less time drawing than the other groups. Apparently, when children are rewarded for engaging in a behavior that is already interesting to them, the effect can be to diminish their intrinsic motivation for engaging in that behavior. Lepper & Greene (1975) refer to this process as "turning play into work."

FIGURE 5–9   Some Hidden Costs of Reward for Preschoolers

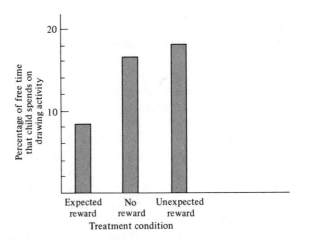

Adapted from Lepper, Greene & Nisbett (1973)

Hidden Costs of Token Economies

As you can see, this research shows that there can be some "hidden costs of reward" (Lepper & Greene, 1978). Based on their findings, Lepper, Greene & Nisbett (1973, p. 136) recommend caution in using token economies, especially when rewards are given out for behaviors that are already intrinsically satisfying to children:

> It has already been recommended by some thoughtful proponents of token economies that their use be limited to circumstances in which less powerful techniques have been tried and found inadequate—in other words, only when they are necessary. . . . The present study provides some empirical evidence of an undesirable consequence of the unnecessary use of extrinsic rewards, supporting the case for the exercise of discretion in their application.

Greene, Sternberg, & Lepper (1976) have obtained similar results in a classroom token economy. Fourth and fifth graders were given rewards for spending time on certain math activities (such as creating geometric designs), some of which were already interesting to the students. Once the reward phase of the study ended, students could spend their math time as they wished. Students tended to spend less time with the previously rewarded activities as compared to a control group that received no rewards. In most cases, students who had been rewarded for engaging in certain math activities spent less than half as much time on those activities during the "withdrawal phase" as they had during the "baseline phase." Again, the hidden cost of reward can be a drop in students' intrinsic motivation for rewarded activities. Similar results have been obtained by Ross (1975), Lepper & Greene (1975), and Deci (1971).

Implications of Research on the Hidden Costs of Reward

The instructional prescription "use positive reinforcement" is one that needs to be applied in light of research on the hidden costs of rewards. Indiscriminate use of rewards to reinforce all desired behaviors can backfire. Students should not be rewarded for doing things that they already enjoy doing. For example, if a student enjoys reading novels and spontaneously does so, it would not always be appropriate to enter into a contingency contract in which the student receives prizes for reading and reporting on a certain number of books. Similarly, in many cases where rewards are used, the ultimate goal should be to encourage the student to develop intrinsic motivation.

HOW DOES FEEDBACK AFFECT RESPONSE LEARNING?

Response Learning in the Classroom

Another major instructional application of Thorndike's work has been an emphasis on drill and practice with feedback. For example, consider the following dialogue:

TEACHER: "How do you spell behavior?"
STUDENT: *"B-e-h-a-v-e-r."*
TEACHER: "No, you have the first two syllables correct, but the last syllable is misspelled."
STUDENT: *"B-e-h-a-v-i-o-r."*
TEACHER: "Right."

In this case, the teacher presents a question (i.e., a stimulus) and the student spells a word (i.e., a response). If the response is correct, the teacher says "right" and if the response is wrong the teacher says "no" and gives a hint.

Behaviorist Versus Cognitive Theories of Response Learning

Let's examine two contrasting interpretations of how feedback affects learning. First, according to a reinforcement interpretation, feedback serves to "reinforce" (or "strengthen") the association between the response and the stimulus. In the spelling example, the reinforcer is "right," and this serves to strengthen the student's tendency to emit the correct spelling for *behavior*. Feedback automatically "stamps in" the correct response without the learner having to actively be aware that learning is taking place. Second, according to a cognitive interpretation, feedback serves as information to the learner. The learner can interpret this information and use it as a key in generating responses. In the spelling example, the feedback concerning where the error was is helpful information that the learner can use in generating a better response. Feedback is actively interpreted by the learner so that its effect depends on how the learner thinks about it. In summary, the controversy concerning how feedback affects learning centers on the question, Does feedback serve as a reinforcer that automatically stamps in a response, or does feedback serve as information that is interpreted by the learner?

Research on Response Learning

Practice with and without Feedback.   Early work by Thorndike (1931) clearly demonstrated that feedback improved response learning in humans. In one study, subjects were seated at a desk with a pencil and a large pad of paper. The subjects were asked to close their eyes and draw a line 4 inches long and to continue trying to draw 4-inch lines keeping their eyes closed throughout. Subjects were asked to perform this task day after day until 3000 lines had been drawn. The results of this tedious study were clear: repetition of the response 3000 times caused no learning. The performance of the subjects at the end of the study was no better than the performance at the start of the study. However, in another experiment, Thorndike gave feedback after each line drawing: "right" if the line was within $\frac{1}{8}$ inch of the target length and "wrong" if it was not. Under these conditions, subjects' performance did improve. After approximately 4000 trials, performance increased from 13% correct to 25% correct. Based on research studies like these, Thorndike concluded that practice alone would not promote learning, but practice with feedback would. His argument was so compelling that it served to change school practices; instead of forcing students to practice without feedback, schools began to make use of praise and reward as techniques for increasing learning. Feedback was viewed as a way of reinforcing correct responses.

Quality of Feedback. Subsequent research has suggested that feedback may serve as information rather than reinforcement. If feedback serves mainly as a reinforcer, then the important aspect of feedback is to tell the learner whether or not the response was correct. If feedback serves mainly as information that is actively interpreted by the learner, then detailed feedback should be more effective than simple "right-wrong" feedback. An early study by Trowbridge & Cason (1932; reported in Adams, 1976) helps to test these predictions. Students were blindfolded and asked to draw one hundred 3-inch lines. Some subjects were told "right" for each line within $\frac{1}{8}$ inch of the target and "wrong" for all other lines ("right-wrong" feedback group); some subjects were told how many eighths of an inch too long or too short each line was ("how much" feedback group); some subjects received no feedback (no feedback group). As you can see in Figure 5–10, the no-feedback group showed no improvement, thus confirming Thorndike's observation that practice alone does not enhance learning. Moreover, (see Figure 5–10), the "right-wrong" group showed some improvement, ending up with an average error of about $\frac{1}{2}$ inch. This result is also consistent with Thorndike's research showing that "right-wrong" feedback aided learning. However, the main new result in Figure 5–10 is that the "how much" feedback group showed dramatic improvement from the start, ending up with an average error of less than $\frac{1}{8}$ inch. Thus the group given detailed feedback learned more rapidly and more completely than the group given only "right-wrong" feedback. This study suggests that learners can use the information in feedback to help revise their plans for how to generate lines. It is interesting to note that the most useful information came on errors; in other words, subjects in the "how much" group seem to have been able to learn from their mistakes. This result conflicts with reinforcement theory's assertion that learning occurs mainly when a correct response is reinforced. In summary, these results are most consistent with the "feedback-

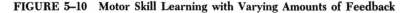

FIGURE 5–10   Motor Skill Learning with Varying Amounts of Feedback

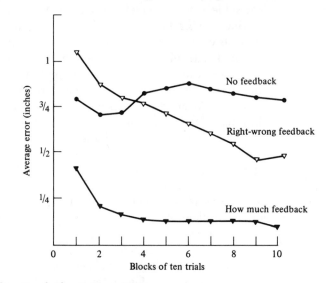

Adapted from Trowbridge & Cason (1932)

as-information" view rather than the "feedback-as-reinforcement" view of response learning.

   Duration of Feedback.   Subsequent research has also provided additional support for the "feedback-as-information" view. For example, let's consider what would happen if you provided feedback for part of the time and then stopped giving feedback. If feedback served mainly as reinforcement, then once the feedback is taken away we can expect extinction (i.e., performance will deteriorate). If feedback serves as information that the learner uses for building an internal plan or procedure, then once a correct plan is learned, feedback is no longer needed. In order to test these conflicting predictions, Newell (1974; described in Adams, 1976) gave subjects seventy-five tries at moving a lever 9.5 inches. Some subjects received feedback after each try (all feedback group); some subjects received feedback after the first fifty-two tries but not the last twenty-three tries (fifty-two-trial feedback group); some subjects received feedback on the first seventeen tries but not on the last fifty-eight trials (seventeen-trial feedback group); some subjects received feedback after just the first two trials (two-trial feedback group). As you can see in Figure 5–11, the group given feedback on all seventy-five trials and the group given feedback on fifty-two trials both performed about the same. Apparently, after fifty-two trials the subjects had acquired an internal procedure for how to generate internal feedback concerning the appropriate response, so that external feedback was no longer needed. However, when feedback was taken away early in the learning (e.g., after two of seventeen trials), performance

FIGURE 5–11 Effects of Withdrawal of Feedback Early Versus Late in Motor Skill Learning

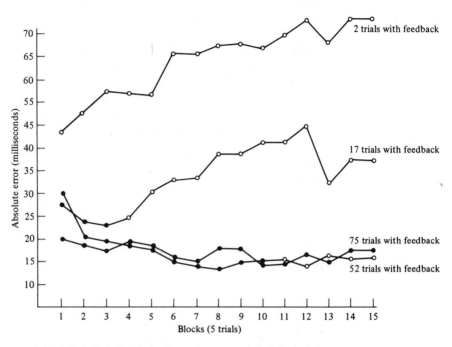

Solid circles indicate that feedback was given; open circles indicate that no feedback was given.

Adapted from Newell (1974)

deteriorated, as would be expected under extinction. Apparently, subjects had not yet developed a way of generating internal feedback, so they were lost once external feedback was taken away. These results suggest that "what is learned" due to feedback is not always just the stamping in of a response; rather, under some conditions, learners can build an internal plan that allows them to generate internal feedback.

Finally, there is growing evidence that practice with feedback causes qualitative differences in what is learned. In Chapter 12 (Mathematics), you will learn that a child's computational skill goes through several stages rather than simply a series of strengthening associations. As responses become "automatized" through practice with feedback, this allows the learner to use those automatized procedures in more complicated tasks. In summary, although feedback can be used to enhance response learning, the effective use of feedback must be based on an understanding of how the learner interprets the information in feedback.

Implications of Research on Response Learning

The research presented in this section highlights the crucial role that feedback plays in children's response learning. However, research presented in this chapter indicates that feedback does not simply stamp in (or reinforce) the response. Instead, students think about the feedback and use the feedback as information to help them interpret their learning. Thus, high-quality feedback is most useful (i.e., children need to be told specifically that what they are doing is correct or incorrect rather than just being told "right" or "wrong"). Furthermore, eventually, children may learn to give themselves feedback on a well-practiced task. Thus, teacher-provided feedback should be withdrawn only when the child has reached a level of automatic internal feedback, an event that may take many trials of practice but that should be the ultimate goal of instruction for response learning.

HOW DOES FEEDBACK AFFECT
CONCEPT LEARNING?

Concept Learning in the Classroom

So far in this chapter you have seen how the law of effect can be related to response learning, such as simple motor behavior or appropriate classroom behavior. Another kind of learning that may be related to the law of effect is concept learning. In concept learning, a person learns to make the same response to an entire set of stimuli. For example, consider the following classroom episode in which the teacher holds up cards portraying various geometric shapes and asks students to name the shape.

TEACHER: Do you know what a geometric shape is? Can you name some geometric shapes?

STUDENT: Ummm . . . circle . . . square . . . triangle . . . rectangle. . . . Is that what you mean?

TEACHER: Yes, that's right. Let's play a game about geometric shapes. It's called, Name That Shape. I am going to hold up some cards. Each card has a shape on it. For example, some cards, like this one, show a square:

Other cards, like this one, show a circle:

Other cards will show other shapes like rectangles, triangles, and so on. Your job is to tell me the name of the shape. Now, let's begin. What is this?

$$\square$$

STUDENT: I don't know.
TEACHER: It's a square. Now what is this?

$$\square$$

STUDENT: Square.
TEACHER: Right, it's a square. Very good. Now, what is this?

$$\square$$

STUDENT: Square.
TEACHER: Sorry, that's not right. Its a rectangle.

In this example of a concept learning task, the teacher presents a series of "instances" one at a time. For each instance, the student must tell which category it belongs to and then the teacher gives feedback, namely, the correct category. In this example, the student seems to classify all four-sided shapes as "squares." Thus the student has acquired a concept of square that is a bit too broad, because it includes rectangles, parallelograms, and so on.

Behaviorist Versus Cognitive Theories of Concept Learning

Concept learning, like response learning, has been studied intensively (Mayer, 1983a). In most concept learning tasks, like the preceding one, students begin by making many errors, but with practice and feedback, they eventually learn to categorize instances without error. In fact, after practice with feedback, students are even able to correctly categorize instances they have not yet seen. For example, in the Name That Shape game students eventually learn to correctly name a certain circle or square even though they have not previously seen the particular circle or square before.

What is the learning process that accounts for concept learning? As in the previous section on response learning, the two fundamental kinds of theories are behaviorist and cognitive. A behaviorist theory of concept learning extends Thorndike's and Skinner's interpretations of the law of effect to the learning of concepts. For each instance that is presented, the learner strengthens the association between each feature of instance and the correct response. For example, for the first instance in the foregoing episode, the learner associates the response "square" with each of the stimulus features, "has four sides," "each side is equal," "sides all right angles," "black ink," "small size," and so on. At the end of the first instance, after the student has been told it's a "square," the following are some of the S-R associations that exist in the learner (with the number of times a stimulus has been associated with a response indicated in parentheses):

Stimulus	Strength of Association	Response
Has four sides	—(1)→	Square
Each side is equal	—(1)→	Square
Sides all right angles	—(1)→	Square
Black ink	—(1)→	Square
Small size	—(1)→	Square

The second instance has several stimulus features that are associated (albeit weakly) with the "square," so the student has a weak tendency to answer "square." After receiving feedback on the second instance, the learner associates the response "square" with the stimulus features, "has four sides," "each side is equal," "sides all right angles," "black ink," "medium size." At the end of this second instance, the following are some of the S-R associations that are accumulating in the learner:

Stimulus	Strength of Association	Response
Has four sides	—(2)→	Square
Each side is equal	—(2)→	Square
Sides all right angles	—(2)→	Square
Black ink	—(2)→	Square
Small size	—(1)→	Square
Medium size	—(1)→	Square

The third instance has some features that are associated with "square," so the student says "square." However, after receiving feedback, the learner associates each feature of the third instance with "rectangle", yielding the following accumulated associations:

Stimulus	Strength of Association	Response
Has four sides	—(2)→	Square
Has four sides	—(1)→	Rectangle
Each side is equal	—(2)→	Square
Only opposite sides equal	—(1)→	Rectangle
Sides right angles	—(2)→	Square
Sides right angles	—(1)→	Rectangle
Black ink	—(2)→	Square
Black ink	—(1)→	Rectangle
Small size	—(1)→	Square
Medium size	—(1)→	Square
Medium size	—(1)→	Rectangle

As you can see, each time the student sees an instance and gets feedback, new S-R connections are established or old ones are strengthened. Concept learning is a process of building connections based on feedback.

In contrast, the cognitive theory rejects the idea that the learner is being passively conditioned by the feedback. Instead, the learner is actively testing a hypothesis. For example, after the first instance, the learner may select the hypothesis: if it has four sides, it's a square. The learner keeps the hypothesis if it generates the correct answer, and selects a new one if it generates an incorrect answer. On the third trial, the hypothesis generates an incorrect answer, for example, so the learner may generate a new hypothesis such as: if it is small, it is a square. In the strictest version of this cognitive (or "hypothesis testing") theory, the learner has no memory for past errors when selecting a new hypothesis.

As you can see, the two theories offer very different interpretations of how feedback promotes concept learning. The behaviorist theory sees the learner as passive; the cognitive theory sees the learner as actively forming hypotheses. The behaviorist theory sees learning as a gradual process of building associations; the cognitive theory sees learning as "all-or-none" (i.e., the student either has the correct hypothesis or not). The behaviorist theory sees learning occurring when feedback is given; the cognitive theory sees learning occurring only after the learner makes an error (i.e., the learner changes hypotheses only after making an error).

Research on Concept Learning

Changing the Rule Prior to Solution. Which theory best accounts for the fact that people learn concepts when they are given feedback? Suppose that you are in a concept learning situation involving stimuli that are complicated drawings and responses that are either "yes" or "no." The teacher presents a stimulus, you give a response, and the teacher tells you the correct answer. Further, let's suppose that partway through the concept learning task, but before you have completely learned the concept, the teacher reverses the rule for classifying the drawings as "yes" or "no." Let's say that you make an error on the twentieth trial, and we reverse the rule for the rest of the task. Instead of saying "yes" for white and "no" for black as in trials 1–20, the teacher now says "yes" for black and "no" for white. The teacher does not tell you that the rule has changed, of course.

What do the behaviorist and cognitive theories predict about our rule reversal task? According to the behaviorist theory, reversing the rule should have a devastating effect on learning—the learner will have to unlearn all the associations that have been building up over the first twenty trials and then form associations in the opposite direction. Thus learners who have the rule reversed before they have finished learning a concept should require many more trials to learn as compared to learners who have had the same rule throughout. According to the cognitive theory, reversing the rule should have no effect on the rate of learning. If a learner has made an error (e.g., on the twentieth trial), that means that the learner has not yet selected the correct hypothesis. After making an error, the learner will simply put the failed hypothesis back in the pool of hypotheses, "stir" the pool of hypotheses, reach in and take out a hypothesis again. Thus each time the learner makes an error, the learner essentially starts over again fresh—changing the rule has no effect because the learner has learned nothing yet!

Bower & Trabasso (1963) conducted a series of experiments like the one already described. As predicted by the cognitive theory, reversing the rule prior to solution did not slow down learning: learners required about the same amount of time and stimuli to learn when the same rule was used throughout as when the rule was reversed after an error during the learning phase. Apparently, the learners in Bower & Trabasso's study did not gradually build up stimulus-response associations but rather seemed to actively form and test hypotheses.

Developmental Differences in Concept Learning.   The Kendlers (Kendler & Kendler, 1962, 1975) also investigated two conflicting theories of concept learning. Figure 5–12 summarizes the experimental method used. The subject was presented with a pair of stimuli consisting of a combination of large black, large white, small black, or small white shapes, and was asked to point to the correct one. First, the subject learned one concept, such as to always point to the large object for each pair of objects that was presented. After the subject could choose the correct object without error on a long string of trials, the rule was changed without telling the subject. For some subjects the rule was changed to a "reversal shift" (also called intradimensional shift); this involved reversing the rule such as changing from "point to large" to "point to small." For other subjects, the rule was changed to a "nonreversal shift" (also called

FIGURE 5–12   The Reversal Shift Task

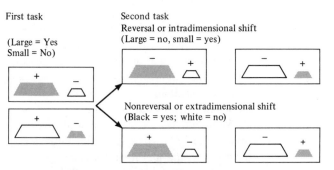

In the example above, the subject learns Task 1 and is given a second task that involves either a reversal or nonreversal shift. The reversal shift uses the same dimension (size), but a nonreversal shift uses a different dimension (color).

Adapted from Kendler & Kendler (1962)

extradimensional shift); this involved basing the rule on a different dimension such as size instead of color. For example, the rule could be changed from "point to large" to "point to black."

Which would be more difficult to learn, a reversal or nonreversal shift? According to "single association theory" (like the behaviorist theories described above), a reversal shift should be harder, because the subject must unlearn four old S-R associations and replace them with four opposite ones. For example, large black was "yes" and now is "no"; large white was "yes" and now is "no"; small black was "no" and now is "yes"; small white was "no" and now is "yes." In contrast, only two new associations need to be learned for the nonreversal shift—large black remains "yes" and small white remains "no" in both parts of the study. According to a "mediational theory" (like our cognitive theories), during the first part of the task the subject learns to pay attention to the relevant dimension (e.g., size is the relevant dimension in the first part of our example), and the subject learns to assign the correct values on that dimension (e.g., large size is "yes" and small size is "no"). A reversal shift involves changing only one aspect of the problem—the dimension is still "size," but the values are changed. In contrast, for a nonreversal shift, two things are changed—both the dimension and the values. Thus, in searching for a new hypothesis, the reversal shift should be easier than the nonreversal shift.

As you can see, the two theories make opposite predictions. The Kendlers found that laboratory animals tended to have more trouble with reversal than nonreversal shifts, suggesting that they learned in a way best described by a behaviorist interpretation. Preschoolers also tended to find the reversal shift more difficult than the nonreversal shift, but older children and adults found the nonreversal shift to be more difficult than the reversal. As the age of the children increased, the tendency for nonreversals to become more difficult than reversal increased. This suggests that as children get older their concept learning changes away from a behaviorist style and toward a more cognitive approach.

Implications of Research on Concept Learning

The behaviorist and cognitive views of concept learning suggest quite different strategies for teaching concepts to students. The behaviorist approach, as promoted in Skinner's (1968) view of programmed instruction, requires asking easy questions so students can give correct answers that will be rewarded. Learning occurs, according to this view, when the student gives a correct response and is rewarded for that response. In contrast, the cognitive approach requires that the student be free to make errors—because it is only after making an error that a student forms a new hypothesis.

The foregoing research suggests that preschool children have a tendency to learn concepts in a way suggested by behaviorist theories. Concept learning at this age should be based on eliciting correct responses that can be rewarded.

However, throughout elementary school, there is an increasing tendency to learn concepts by actively forming hypotheses. Concept learning at these ages should be based on allowing the child to construct hypotheses and test them, and especially, to see how a hypothesis can be falsified. In fact, hypothesis-testing strategies can be productively taught to elementary school children (Olton & Crutchfield, 1969) as described in Chapter 9.

In summary, feedback is effective in teaching concepts. However, these studies show that for most school-age students, feedback influences learning because it provides information relevant to the learner's active search for hypotheses rather than because it stamps in a particular response.

CONCLUSION

This chapter began with a look at Thorndike's famous law of effect, the idea that feedback following a response serves to determine the likelihood that the response will be made again. Then we looked at three situations that seem related to the law of effect: classroom management, response learning, and concept learning.

In each case, we compared two contrasting views of the learner. The behaviorist view is that the learner is passively being conditioned by the feedback; that is, reinforcers serve to automatically stamp in (or stamp out) responses. In contrast, the cognitive view is that the learner is actively interpreting the feedback or reinforcement that is given; that is, reinforcers serve as information that the learner uses in building a learning outcome.

For classroom management, we found that token economies and contingency contracting can serve to increase desired behaviors and decrease undesired behaviors. However, the mechanism underlying the behavior change seems to be best described by a cognitive theory (i.e., by assuming that the learner attempts to interpret or justify the rewards that are given).

For response learning, practice with feedback tended to enable improvements in performance, whereas practice alone did not affect performance. Again, however, the mechanism underlying the behavior change seems best described by a cognitive theory (i.e., by assuming that the learner uses feedback as information).

For concept learning, practice with feedback again served to improve performance. Again, a cognitive theory (i.e., hypothesis testing) seemed to be the best explanation of the behavior change.

In summary, we are left with a sort of irony. The basic findings of Thorndike and Skinner and other behaviorist-oriented researchers seem to be fairly well established—the appropriate use of feedback (or reinforcers) given after the learner's responses can serve to change behavior. However, the processes of response learning and concept learning do not seem to fit the theoretical description given by the behaviorists. Instead, as we have seen in this chapter, the learner appears to be actively involved in trying to interpret the feedback that is given. Any effective use of feedback or reinforcement techniques requires an understanding of the active cognitive processing of the learner. In essence, we leave with a modified view of the law of effect: it is not the feedback or reinforcement which changes behavior, but rather the learner's interpretation and understanding of that feedback or reinforcement.

SUGGESTED READINGS

Kazdin, A. E. (1977). *The token economy: A review and evaluation*. New York: Plenum. (A review of token economy programs.)

Lepper, M. R. & Greene, D. (1978). *The hidden costs of reward*. Hillsdale, N.J.: Erlbaum. (A book of articles concerning people's interpretations about reward.)

Thorndike, E. L. (1913). *Educational psychology*. New York: Columbia University Press. (An historically interesting discussion of Thorndike's theories applied to education.)

6 *Instructional Methods for Prose Learning*

This chapter explores how students learn from prose, and is particularly concerned with instructional techniques that can make prose more understandable. For example, some instructional techniques for improving prose include advance organizers, signaling, and adjunct questions. This chapter considers how each of these techniques affect the student's cognitive processing during learning and the cognitive outcome of learning.

HOW TO IMPROVE A TEXTBOOK LESSON

Sometimes a person can read a new lesson in a textbook and then use the information creatively to solve problems. In other circumstances, a person can read the same information, retaining much of it, without being able to solve problems.

For example Box 6–1 shows a lesson about radar that you might find in a school textbook. Please read the lesson just once, but read carefully.

When you are finished, try to answer the questions in Box 6–2. Be sure to go in order, starting with question 1 and working down. Notice that Box 6–2 contains recall, problem-solving, and verbatim recognition questions.

If you are like most people, you had a hard time in trying to understand the radar lesson. For example, in a recent study (Mayer, 1983), college students who had listened to the radar lesson recalled less than 20% of the information and scored below 30% on problem solving. However, students did seem to learn some specific pieces of information. For example, they scored at about 80% correct on verbatim recognition and they recalled about 50% of the specific facts, such as the speed at which radar travels. Thus, if you are like most people who read this passage, you were able to remember some specific factual details, but you had trouble seeing how it all fit together.

The goal of this chapter is to explore some techniques for increasing the understandability of textbooks. We could pose the question, What can we do to increase the learner's understanding in learning from prose? In particular, this chapter will focus on three techniques: concrete advance organizers, signaling the organization of prose, and adjunct questions. Following a brief cognitive analysis of prose learning, this chapter examines some examples, theories, research, and implications for each of these techniques.

COGNITIVE THEORY OF INSTRUCTION

Observable Versus Cognitive Variables

The traditional approach to instructional research has been to conduct some instructional manipulation (such as presence versus absence of advance organizers) and then measure the performance of students who learned under each method. Thus the goal of research was to determine the effects of some observable manipulation on some observable behavior. In general, the results of such studies may be summarized as "method A is better than method B."

One problem with this approach is that it does not provide an understanding of why or how method A is better than method B. A teacher could make better use of instructional methods by understanding the general principles that mediate between instruction and test performance. The cognitive approach to instruction seeks to determine how instructional procedures influence internal information-processing events and the acquired cognitive structure.

Some of the major types of variables in instructional research are summarized in Table 6–1. As you can see, the table includes two observable variables—the instructional method and test performance. These are the only variables involved in the traditional approach to instruction. However, for the cognitive approach, internal cognitive processes and learning outcomes have been added.

BOX 6–1   The Radar Passage

Radar means the detection and location of remote objects by reflection of radio waves. The phenomena of acoustic echoes is familiar: sound waves reflected from a building or cliff are received back at the observer after a lapse of a short interval. The effect is similar to you shouting in a canyon and seconds later hearing a nearly exact replication of your voice. Radar uses exactly the same principle except that the waves are radio waves, not sound waves. These travel very much faster than sound waves, 186,000 miles per second, and can cover much longer distances. Thus, radar involves simply measuring the time between transmission of the waves and their subsequent return or echo and then converting that to a distance measure.

To send out the radio waves a radio transmitter is connected to a directional antenna which sends out a stream of short pulses of radio waves. This radio pulse that is first transmitted looks very much like the effect of tossing a pebble into a quiet lake. It creates concentric circles of small waves that continue to grow outward. Usually both a transmitter and a receiver are employed separately but it is possible to use only one antenna in which pulse transmission is momentarily suppressed in order to receive echo pulses. One thing to remember, though, is that radar waves travel in fundamentally straight lines and that the curvature of the earth eventually interferes with long-range transmission. When you think about the reception of the returning pulses or echoes you should remember that any object in the path of the transmitted beam reflects some of the energy back to the radio receiver. The problem then becomes transmitting the pulses picked up by the receiver to a display mechanism for visual readout. One mechanism in large use is the cathode-ray tube, a familiar item in airport control towers, which looks somewhat like a television screen.

It is easiest to understand how radar is displayed if you begin with one of the earliest models used around the 1930s. These types of displays were able to focus the broad radar pulse into a single beam of light which proceeded from the left of screen to the right. When no object impedes the traveling radar pulse it continues its travel until lost from the screen on the right. When there is an object present the pulse would strike it and begin to travel back to the receiver. When the object is struck by the radar pulse, it creates a bright spot on the face of the screen and the distance of the object can be measured by the length of the trace coming from the object back to the receiver. With this model, however, you are only able to measure the distance of an object and not its absolute location, since the beam of light on the screen actually represents the entire width of the broader radar pulse.

Models employed today use two simple techniques which make location of objects much easier. First, the transmitter now operates much like the searchlight used in airports. It emits a single beam of radar pulses that make continuous circular sweeps around the area under surveillance.

Secondly, the display screen is adjusted so that its center corresponds to the point where the radar pulses begin. The radar pulse seen on the screen operates like the second hand of a clock, which continually moves. When an object is present, it leaves a bright spot on the face of the screen. An additional feature is that the face of the screen actually shows a maplike picture of the area around the radar giving distance and, of course, location. Thus, it is very easy now to determine the location of objects by noting their location on the screen's map.

Adapted from Clarke (1977)

BOX 6–2 A Test for the Radar Passage

Recall Test
1. Write down all you can remember about the radar passage.

Problem-Solving Test
2. It was pointed out that the curvature of the earth limits the effectiveness of radar beyond a certain distance. One way around this, of course, is to set up radar detection centers at various places on earth such that all areas are covered. Can you think of another way of doing this?

3. If an object remained at a constant distance from the receiver but its location changed with each measurement what form would the object's movement take? Explain and/or diagram.

Verbatim Recognition Test
Each of the following questions contains two statements one of which is taken verbatim from the passage you just read and another which has slight changes. Read each pair of statements carefully and then check the one statement that you think came directly (word for word) from the passage.

4. _____ It is easiest to understand how radar is displayed if you begin with one of the earliest models used around the 1930s.
   _____ It is easiest to understand how radar is displayed if you begin with one of the earliest models used around the 1940s.

5. _____ The phenomena of acoustic echoes is familiar: sound waves reflected from a building or cliff return to the observer after a lapse of a short interval.
   _____ The phenonomena of acoustic echoes is familiar: sound waves reflected from a building or a cliff are received back at the observer after a short interval.

6. _____ When an object is present, it leaves a bright spot on the face of the screen.
   _____ When an object is present, it leaves a lighted area on the face of the screen.

TABLE 6–1   Variables in Instructional Research

Instructional Methods	Cognitive Processes and States	Cognitive Outcomes	Performance
Advance organizers	Possessing prerequisite knowledge	Rote	Retention
	Paying attention	Integrated	Transfer
Signaling	Building internal connections		
Adjunct questions	Building external connections		

Cognitive Processing During Learning

In order to understand these cognitive variables, consider the simple information-processing system shown in Figure 6–1 (as described more fully in Chapter 1). Information from the outside world enters through sense receptors and eventually reaches active consciousness (called "working memory"); at the same time, the learner may possess existing knowledge in "long-term memory" and may search and bring some of this existing knowledge to "working memory." Thus learning may involve actively relating what is presented with existing knowledge; this integration process takes place in working memory, with the result being stored in long-term memory.

Some of the cognitive processes and states that are relevant for a cognitive theory of instruction include:

Possessing Prerequisite Knowledge.   The learner comes to the learning situation with a vast storehouse of knowledge and strategies stored in long-term memory. This state is represented by the "B" in long-term memory.

Paying Attention to Incoming Information.   The learner can influence the amount of information that reaches working memory by changing the amount of

FIGURE 6–1   Learning Processes in an Information-Processing System

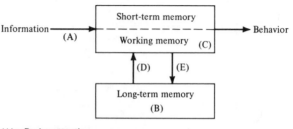

(A) = Paying attention
(B) = Possessing prerequisite knowledge
(C) = Building internal connections
(D) = Building external connections
(E) = Storing outcome in long-term memory

attention that is paid; the learner can influence the type of information that reaches working memory by changing the selectivity of attention. The role of attention—both overall attention and selective attention—is represented by the letter "A" by the arrow from outside into working memory.

Building Internal Connections.   The learner can reorganize the information in working memory so that it is a coherent lesson. For example, the learner can organize the material around the topical outline of the passage. This process is represented by the letter "C" in working memory.

Building External Connections.   The learner can transfer relevant prerequisite knowledge from long-term memory to working memory, as indicated by the letter "D" next to the arrow. Then, the learner can integrate new knowledge with old, such as putting information into her own words.

Cognitive Outcomes of Learning

The cognitive processes and states are involved in building a cognitive structure in working memory that eventually gets stored in long-term memory. This is indicated by the "E" arrow from working memory to long-term memory. Let's consider some of the possible learning outcomes that might be stored in long-term memory.

No Learning.   First, if the learner fails to pay attention to the incoming information, no information will be transferred to working memory and there will be no learning. Thus the amount of attention is related to the overall amount of information learned.

Rote Learning.   Second, suppose that the learner pays attention but that the learner lacks appropriate prerequisite knowledge. In this case, the information to be learned is transferred to working memory, but it cannot be combined with existing knowledge. If there is no building of internal and external connections, the information will be stored in long-term memory in the form in which it was presented. This type of learning should allow the learner to perform well on tests of verbatim retention.

Integrated Learning.   Third, suppose that the learner pays attention and that the learner is able to engage in building of internal and external connections. In this case, the outcome is reorganized and integrated with existing knowledge. This type of learning enables the learner to use the information learned in creative problem solving and in new learning of related material.

The goal of cognitive instructional research is to determine how various instructional methods influence the cognitive processes and outcomes of learning. For example, the following sections will explore the idea that advance organizers enhance the building of external connections and the possessing of prerequisite knowledge, signals foster selective attention and the building of internal connections, and adjunct questions promote overall and selective attention as well as building internal and external connections.

ADVANCE ORGANIZERS

Example of Advance Organizer

What can be done to improve the reader's understanding of the lesson in Box 6–1? Some researchers have suggested presenting a concrete model of the principles to be learned. For example, the main conceptual information in the passage concerns the idea of a radar pulse: a pulse is transmitted, it bounces off a remote object, it travels back to a receiver, the time and angle of the pulse can be converted to measures of distance and location. These ideas are presented in the passage, but most readers fail to remember them. Figure 6–2 presents a diagram that clearly summarizes the principles of radar, as described in the passage. The diagram does not add any information that is not already in the passage, but it does provide a familiar way to organize the passage. If you had seen this diagram for 60 seconds before you read the radar lesson, do you think you would have understood the passage better?

In a recent study (Mayer, 1983b), subjects who were given this diagram for 60 seconds before they listened to the passage performed quite differently on tests than subjects who listened to the same lesson but without the diagram. For example, the diagram subjects recalled 50% more information overall as

FIGURE 6–2   An Advance Organizer for the Radar Passage

There are five steps in radar.

1. Transmission: A pulse travels from an antenna.

2. Reflection: The pulse bounces off a remote object.

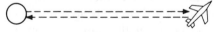

3. Reception: The pulse returns to the receiver.

4. Measurement: The difference between the time out and the time back
   tells the total time traveled.

   Out   Back

5. Conversion: The time can be converted to a measure of distance, since
   the pulse travels at a constant speed.

_____ seconds = _____ miles

From Mayer (1984)

FIGURE 6–3   Effects of Advance Organizer on Retention and Transfer

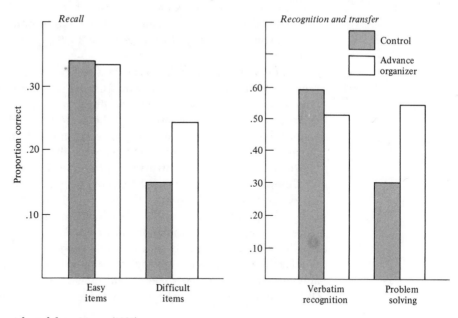

Adapted from Mayer (1983)

compared to the no diagram group; in particular, recall was enhanced for conceptual information in the lesson. In addition, problem-solving scores for the diagram group were twice as high as for the no diagram group. Apparently, the diagram helped learners to reorganize the lesson around the major points of the passage rather than trying to memorize the passage as presented. Not surprisingly, the diagram subjects actually performed worse than the no diagram group on tests of verbatim recognition and factual recall, presumably because the diagram helped learners to put the information into their own words. These results are summarized in Figure 6–3.

Theory: Advance Organizers Provide Prerequisite Knowledge and Foster External Connections

An advance organizer is information that is presented prior to learning and that can be used by the learner to organize and interpret new incoming information. According to Ausubel (1968, p. 148), the function of the organizer is "to provide ideational scaffolding for the stable incorporation and retention of more detailed and differentiated material that follows." Advance organizers may influence cognitive processing in several ways, such as providing prerequisite knowledge (i.e., process "B" in Figure 6–1) or building external connections (i.e., process "D" in Figure 6–1). Advance organizers that serve to make appropriate prerequisite knowledge available to the learner are called "expository organizers"; advance organizers that serve to build external connections with existing knowledge that is relevant to the new information are called "comparative organizers."

Expository Organizers for Prerequisite Knowledge.   First, let's look at an example of an expository organizer. Ausubel (1960) asked college students to read a 2500-word passage about metallurgy after reading either a 500-word expository organizer that presented the underlying concepts or a 500-word historical passage. The advance organizer group performed better on a subsequent test of retention, presumably because the learners were able to tie the information to knowledge structures presented in the organizer.

Comparative Organizers for External Connections.   Second, let's look at an example of a comparative advance organizer. Ausubel & Youssef (1963) asked college students to read a 2500-word passage on Buddhism after reading either a comparative advance organizer that pointed to the relation between Buddhism and Christianity or a nonorganizing historical introduction. Retention for the target passage was higher for the advance organizer group, presumably due to the learners' being encouraged to understand new concepts (Buddhism) in terms of existing knowledge about Christianity.

Research on Advance Organizers

Ausubel (1960, 1968) was the first to systematically study the role of advance organizers in meaningful learning from prose. Over the course of a long series of studies such as those just summarized, Ausubel obtained consistent but small advantages in retention due to advance organizers. Ausubel's work has stimulated a great deal of research on advance organizers during the past twenty years (Mayer, 1979); however, recent reviews (e.g., Barnes & Clawson, 1975) have pointed out that many advance organizer studies fail to yield significant results. Thus there is not a single answer to the question, Do advance organizers facilitate learning? Instead, it may be more fruitful to determine the conditions under which advance organizers are most likely to influence learning. Thus the remainder of this section focuses on the question, Under what conditions do advance organizers foster learning?

Advance Organizers Are More Effective for Unfamiliar Text.   First, advance organizers should be most effective in situations where the learner either does not possess or would not normally use appropriate prerequisite knowledge for organizing incoming information. Advance organizers should be most effective for students who lack prior knowledge, but not as effective for those who already possess prior knowledge. For example, West & Fensham (1976) asked high school students to learn about the principle of equilibrium after presentation of an advance organizer or a control introduction. In addition, all subjects were pretested to determine their background knowledge in the area. Results indicated a pattern of knowledge-by-treatment interaction

(KTI) in which advance organizers significantly increased learning for subjects who scored low in background knowledge, but not for those who scored high. When remedial pretraining was provided to students who scored low in prerequisite knowledge, the effects of advance organizers were eliminated. Similar results have been reported in other studies that measure the amount of background knowledge or domain specific ability (Mayer, 1979).

Advance Organizers Promote Transfer.   Second, the effects of advance organizers should be most visible for tests that involve creative problem solving or transfer to new situations, because the advance organizer allows the learner to organize the material into a coherent structure. For example, in the radar study (Mayer, 1983b) cited earlier in this section, the advance organizer group performed better on creative problem solving but worse on verbatim retention when compared to a control group. Advance organizers could hinder verbatim retention because learners reorganize the material and put it in their own words. The dependent measures used in some advance organizer studies may be more like verbatim retention than creative problem solving; hence, we would not expect to find a strong positive effect for advance organizers in those studies. In a series of studies that measured creative problem solving, Mayer (1979) found consistently strong transfer effects due to advance organizers.

Concrete Models As Advance Organizers.   Third, advance organizers must be correctly designed to be effective. Ausubel called for using abstract advance organizers that are "presented at a higher level of abstraction, generality, and inclusiveness." More recently, Mayer (1979) has suggested that concrete advance organizers may be more effective in serving to provide appropriate prerequisite knowledge. For example, Royer & Cable (1975, 1976) asked subjects to read an abstract passage on the flow of heat through metals or the conduction of electricity after reading a passage that either presented relevant physical analogies or that presented only relevant abstract principles. In their study, a concrete analogy for electricity involved the following: impurities in the conducting wire are like having bulky objects such as a pack of cigarettes in a row of toppling dominoes, because there is an obstacle to the orderly transfer of energy. Results showed that preexposure to the concrete analogies significantly facilitated learning and memory for the second passage.

As another example of a concrete analogy, let's consider the way in which most textbooks present the concept of Ohm's law. In a recent analysis of science textbooks White & Mayer (1980) found that most textbooks include a brief biography of Ohm, a formal statement of the law such as $R = V/I$, a statement of the law in words, definitions of key terms, computational examples of how to derive numerical values, and practical facts about metals. One book provided an analogy of a boy pushing a cart up a steep road: the angle of the slope is analogous to resistance; the boy's push is analogous to voltage; and the actual speed up the hill is analogous to intensity. Mayer (1983b) used another concrete model of an electrical circuit: the amount of congestion in the wire is analogous to resistance; the number of electrons pumped out of the battery per time unit is analogous to voltage; the actual number of electrons passing any point per time unit is analogous to intensity. When students were presented with diagrams for this model prior to reading a passage on Ohm's law, their retention of information was enhanced, especially their retention of conceptual information from the passage (Mayer, 1983b).

Similarly, Mayer (1975a, 1976, 1979) asked nonprogrammers to read a ten-page manual on BASIC-like computer programming. A concrete model of the computer such as is shown in Box 6–3 was presented for 3 minutes either before or after reading the passage. As is shown in Box 6–3, the concrete model represented memory as an eraseable scoreboard, input as a ticket window, output as a note message pad, and executive control as a shopping list with

---

BOX 6–3 An Advance Organizer for a Manual on Basic Computer Programming

For purposes of this manual, let's assume that the computer consists of four main parts:

1. Memory scoreboard. There are several scoreboard boxes, each with a name such as A1, A2, A3 and so on. A number can be written in each box; when a new number is put in, the old number must be erased.
2. Input window. Data numbers waiting to be processed form a queue for the input window. The numbers are processed one at a time in the "in" part of the window; after processing, the data number is moved to the "out" part of the window.
3. Program list and pointer arrow. The computer has a list of things to do. It begins with the first thing on the list. When that is done, it moves to the next thing on the list and so on.
4. Output pad. Messages from the computer to you are written on an output pad, with one message written per line on the pad.

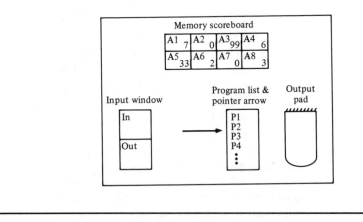

Adapted from Mayer (1975)

pointer arrow. Students who received the model prior to reading the manual performed much better on recall of conceptual information and on creative problem solving (e.g., generating complicated programs), while students who received the model after reading the manual performed better on recall of grammatical details and on solving problems just like those given in the manual. The same pattern was obtained when students were given actual physical models that could be manipulated or pictorial diagrams that could not be manipulated. Apparently, the model served to help the learner understand and organize the information during learning.

Implications of Research on Advance Organizers

These results allow us to predict the conditions under which advance organizers should be used. First, they should be used when students lack the prerequisite knowledge that is necessary for understanding the material to be learned. If no prerequisite knowledge is needed, or if students are likely to already possess and use such knowledge, advance organizers are not needed. Second, advance organizers should be used when the goal of instruction is transfer of learning to new problems. If the goal is verbatim retention of specific information, or performance on problems like those given in instruction, then advance organizers are not needed. Third, advance organizers should be easy for the student to acquire and use and should present an integrated model of the material to be learned. Concrete analogies seem to be particularly useful in meeting these criteria.

SIGNALING

Example of Signaling

Let's return to the radar passage shown in Box 6-1. What else can be done to enhance the learner's understanding of this passage? Some researchers have suggested that we could make the structure of the passage more obvious to the reader. For example, we could outline the passage and place headings in the passage that correspond to the major subdivisions in the passage. Box 6-4 gives an example of how we could revise the radar passage by using signals to the reader concerning the structure of the passage. Notice that the headings show the reader what the major topics are.

Theory: Signaling Fosters Building Internal Connections

Signaling techniques refer to the placement of noncontent words in a passage that serve to emphasize the conceptual structure or organization of the passage. Meyer (1975) has suggested four types of signals:

BOX 6–4   A Signaled Version of the Radar Passage

Definition

Radar involves five basic steps. Once you understand these five steps, you will have a basic knowledge of how radar works. The five steps are:

1. Transmission—A radio pulse is sent out.
2. Reflection—The pulse strikes and bounces off a remote object.
3. Reception—The reflected pulse returns to the source.
4. Measurement—The amount of time between transmission and reception is measured.
5. Conversion—This information can be translated into a measure of distance if we assume the pulse travels at a constant speed.

Thus radar involves the detection and location of remote objects by reflection of radio waves.

Echo Example

In order to see how these five steps of radar relate to one another, let's consider an example. The example is a familiar phenomenon, an acoustic echo.

1. First, you shout in a canyon. This is like transmission of a pulse.
2. Second, the sound waves are reflected from a cliff. This is like reflection of a pulse off a remote object.
3. Third, a nearly exact replication of your voice is received back at the observer. This is like reception of a radar pulse.
4. Fourth, there is a short lapse between shouting and hearing an echo. This corresponds to measurement of time.
5. Fifth, you notice that the further away a cliff is, the longer it takes to receive back an echo. This corresponds to conversion of time to a measure of distance of remote objects.

The same principle is used in radar, except that the waves involved are radio waves, not sound waves. These travel very much faster than sound waves, 186,000 miles per second, and can cover much longer distances.

Devices

Let's consider the actual devices that are used for the five steps of radar.

Transmission.   To send out the radio waves, a radio transmitter is connected to a directional antenna that sends out a stream of short pulses of radio waves. As an example of how the antenna sends out radio waves, think of tossing a pebble into a quiet lake. The pebble creates concentric circles of small waves that continue to grow outward.

Reflection.   Any object in the path of the transmitted beam reflects some of the energy back to the radio receiver.

Reception.   Usually a transmitter and a receiver are employed separately, but it is possible to use only one antenna. In this case, pulse transmission is momentarily suppressed in order to receive echo pulses. One thing to remember about the reception of returning pulses or echoes is that radar waves travel in fundamentally straight lines and that the curvature of the earth eventually interferes with long-range transmission.

Measurement and conversion.   The problem then becomes transmitting the pulses picked up by the receiver to a display for visual readout. One mechanism in large use is the cathode-ray tube, a familiar item in airport control towers which looks somewhat like a television screen.

Early Display System

The earliest display system, used around the 1930s, dealt with the five steps of radar as follows:

To represent transmission, the display system focused the broad radar pulse into a single beam of light, which proceeded from left of the screen to right. When no object impedes the traveling radar pulse, it continues to travel until lost from the screen on the right.

To represent reflection, a bright spot is created on the face of the screen when an object is struck. Thus, when an object is present, the pulse would strike it and begin to travel back to the receiver.

To represent reception, there is a trace on the screen coming from the object back to the receiver.

To represent measurement and conversion, the distance of the object can be measured by the length of the trace. With this system, however, you are only able to measure the distance of object, not its absolute location.

Modern Display Systems

Display models employed today use different techniques for representing the five steps of radar, and thus make location of objects much easier.

For transmission, the transmitter emits a single beam of radar pulses that make continuous circular sweeps around the area under surveillance.

> Thus an example is to think of the transmitter as being like the searchlight used at airports. In addition, the display screen is adjusted so that its center corresponds to the point where the radar pulse begins. As an example, the radar pulse seen on the screen operates like the second hand of a clock, which continually moves.
>
> For reflection, when an object is present it leaves a bright spot on the face of the screen.
>
> For reception, there is a trace coming back from the bright spot to the center of the screen.
>
> For measurement and conversion, the face of the screen actually shows a maplike picture of the area around the radar, giving distance and, of course, location. Thus it is very easy now to determine the location of objects by noting their location on the screen's map.

a. "Specification of the structure of relations," which involves providing cues such as "first," "second," "third," or "the problem is . . ." and "the solution is . . .";

b. "Prematurely" presenting an abstracted or paraphrased statement of key information that is to follow such as "the main ideas discussed in this paper are . . .";

c. "Summary statements," which are like abstracts except that they occur at the end of the passage; and

d. "Pointer words," which indicate the author's perspective or emphasize important information (e.g., by specifying "more important" or "unfortunately").

Signals do not provide any substantive information, but they do make the outline structure of the passage more clear. Thus signals provide a conceptual framework for the reader to use in selecting relevant information (i.e., process A in Figure 6–1) and in organizing the information into a coherent representation (i.e., process C in Figure 6–1).

Research on Signaling

In order to investigate the role of signaling on learning from expository prose, Meyer (1975) asked subjects to read and later to recall passages about breeder reactors, schizophrenia, or parakeets. Signaled passages included all the previously mentioned signals, whereas the nonsignaled passages were created by deleting many of the signal words. Results indicated that signals tended to increase the number of idea units recalled, but the effect was small and not statistically significant. For example, Meyer & Rice (1980) found that the total number of idea units recalled from a passage about supertanks was 33% without signals and 37% with signals.

Although signals have not been shown to have a large overall effect on recall, Meyer (1980) has argued that signals should have a strong effect under certain conditions. Thus the main question addressed in this section is, Under what conditions does signaling influence meaningful learning?

Signals Are More Effective for Less Skilled Readers. First, signaling should be most effective for learners who do not normally use what Meyer (1980) calls, "the structure strategy"—readers who do not normally follow the general outline of the passage. For example, Meyer (1980) asked older and younger adults to read either signaled or nonsignaled passages and then take a twenty-item short answer comprehension test. The results indicated that signaling improved recall more strongly for older adults—who presumably do not normally use the structure strategy—than for younger adults. In addition, Figure 6–4 shows the average number of idea units recalled by good, average, poor, and underachieving readers who learned from either signaled or nonsignaled text (Meyer, Brandt, & Bluth, 1981). As can be seen, signaling did not help the good readers, but did have a strong positive effect for less able readers—who presumably are less likely to structure the material spontaneously. However, when students were tested several days later on a delayed recall test, the effects of signaling were no longer evident, suggesting that signaling may affect only the ease of initial encoding.

Signals Promote Selective Retention and Transfer. Second, signaling is more likely to enhance retention of the conceptually relevant information than lower-level details, and signaling is more likely to improve creative problem solving than verbatim retention of specific facts. This prediction follows from

FIGURE 6–4 Effects of Signaling on Recall

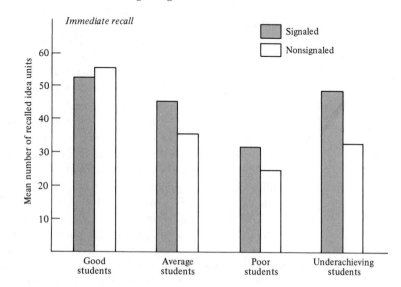

Adapted from Meyer, Brandt, & Bluth (1980)

the idea that signaling helps the reader to reorganize the material into a coherent structure rather than a list of specific propositions. For example, Meyer & Rice (1980) reported that signaling increased recall of logical relations from 49% (without signals) to 59% (with signals), but improved overall recall only by four percentage points. Similarly, Meyer (1980) reported that signaling helped older adults recall more conceptual information (increasing recall of major conceptual ideas from 47 to 67%) but not more details (9% with signals versus 14% without signals).

More recently, Loman & Mayer (1983) asked students to read a passage about red tides either with or without signals. Three types of signals were used: preview sentences to emphasize the structure of the passage, underlined headings to identify each of the major conceptual parts of the passage, and logical connective phrases, such as "because of this," to clarify the cause-and-effect chain within each part. Box 6–5 lists the signaled and nonsignaled version of the red tides passage. Subjects were asked to recall the passage and take both a verbatim recognition test and a problem-solving test with questions such as "How can you prevent red tides?" Figure 6–5 shows that the signaled subjects recalled about 50% more conceptual information than the nonsignaled subjects,

---

BOX 6–5   Signaled and Nonsignaled Versions of the Red Tides Passage

NONSIGNALED VERSION

"The Mystery of the Red Tides"

What makes the sea turn red and causes thousands of fish to die? As far back as anyone could remember the blame was placed on the "red tides."

In 1947, scientists finally traced the condition called the red tides to a microscopic sea organism called the dinoflagellate.

The dinoflagellate is so tiny that 6000 of these organisms may be contained in a single drop of water. It stands on the border between plant and animal in its classification. It manufactures its own food, as plants do. But it moves freely and eats other organisms, as animals do.

Dinoflagellates are normally only one of the many kinds of organisms found in plankton. Plankton is the name given to all very small forms of sea life. However, when the air and water are calm and warm, dinoflagellates multiply or "bloom" with amazing speed. The surface of the water appears to be covered with a red carpet.

The "blooming" dinoflagellates give off a poisonous secretion. Many fish die. Their bodies are washed up on the beach. Beaches are not fit for use. Fish that are not killed may become poisonous to animals or people who eat them. Commercial fishing comes to a halt.

As dinoflagellates exhaust the food and oxygen in an area, they die.

After a time, the sea returns to normal. But when conditions are right, the red tide blooms again.

At least nine times in this century, the west coast of Florida has been plagued by the red tide. In 1957, the Arabian Sea was affected. At different times, the coasts of western Australia and Peru have suffered from this invasion from the sea.

SIGNALED VERSION

"The Mystery of the Red Tides"

What makes the sea turn red and causes thousands of fish to die? As far back as anyone could remember the blame was placed on the "red tide."

In 1947, scientists finally traced the condition called the red tides to a microscopic sea organism called the dinoflagellate.

The purpose of this lesson is to explain the life cycle of dinoflagellates. The dinoflagellate is so tiny that 6000 of these organisms may be contained in single drop of water. It stands on the border between plant and animal in its classification. It manufactures its own food, as plants do. But it moves freely and eats other organisms, as animals do.

There are three main phases in the life cycle of dinoflagellates: dinoflagellates bloom, dinoflagellates secrete poison, and dinoflagellates die.

1. *Dinoflagellates bloom.* Dinoflagellates are normally only one of many kinds of organisms found in plankton. Plankton is the name given to all very small forms of sea life. However, when the air and water are calm and warm, this causes the dinoflagellates to multiply or "bloom" with amazing speed. Because of this, the surface of the water appears to be covered with a red carpet.

2. *Dinoflagellates secrete poison.* The "blooming" dinoflagellates give off a poisonous secretion that causes many fish to die. Their bodies are washed up on the beach. As a result, beaches are not fit for use. Fish that are not killed may become poisonous to animals or people who eat them. Because of this, commercial fishing comes to a halt.

3. *Dinoflagellates die.* As dinoflagellates exhaust the food and oxygen in an area, the result is that they die. After a time, the sea returns to normal. But when conditions are right, the red tide blooms again.

At least nine times in this century, the west coast of Florida has been plagued by the red tide. In 1957, the Arabian Sea was affected. At different times, the coasts of western Australia and Peru have suffered this invasion from the sea.

From Liddle (1977)

but both groups recalled about the same amount of nonconceptual information. Thus there is evidence that signals can direct a reader's attention towards conceptual information. In addition, the signaled subjects generated about 50% more good answers to problem solving questions than the nonsignaled subjects, but the groups did not differ on verbatim recognition. Apparently, signals encouraged learners to organize the material around conceptual information, which is useful for creative problem solving.

Implications of Research on Signaling

Signaling the conceptual structure of a passage can be accomplished by using headings, organizing sentences, and logical connectives. Such techniques will be most effective: (1) for subjects who do not normally pay attention to the outline structure of a passage, and (2) when the goal of instruction is retention of the major conceptual information for creative problem solving. Apparently, signals can influence selective attention and the building of internal connections.

FIGURE 6–5   **Effects of Signaling on "What Is Learned"**

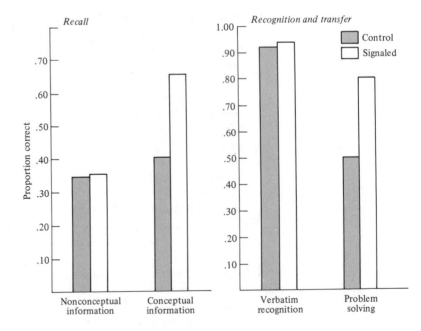

Adapted from Loman & Mayer (1983)

ADJUNCT QUESTIONS

Example of Adjunct Questions

The radar passage in Box 6–1 can also be altered by inserting questions in the text. Box 6–6 suggests some of the kinds of questions that could be inserted after each paragraph.

Theory: Adjunct Questions Guide the Learner's Attention

Adjunct questions may serve several functions, including both "forward" and "backwards" effects. The forward effect refers to the idea that questions inform the reader concerning what to pay attention to in subsequent portions of the text. For example, if the reader sees that all of the questions deal with specific factual statements, the reader will be more likely to focus on this type of information in subsequent sections of the passage. The backwards effect refers to the idea that questions require that the reader go back and review portions of the passage that have already been read. Thus the questions serve to repeat specific portions of the texts allowing *more* exposure to the material. Thus, the forward effect refers to selective attention to the type of information mentioned in the questions whereas the backwards effect refers to the amount of attention being paid to the specific information mentioned in the questions. Presumably, adjunct questions can be used to direct and magnify the reader's attention. In addition, questions about the structure of the passage (e.g., "What is the main idea?") may enhance building of internal connections, whereas questions about applying information to a familiar situation (e.g., "Can you give an example?") may enhance building of external connections.

BOX 6–6 Adjunct Questions for the Radar Passage

After reading this passage, you should be able to answer the following questions:

Radar travels at a rate of _____.
Radar means the detection and location of remote objects by _____.
Radar uses _____ waves.
Radar travels in _____ lines.
The earliest display models were used in _____.
Modern display screens operate like _____.

Research on Adjunct Questions

Modern research on adjunct questions began with studies by Rothkopf and his colleagues (Rothkopf, 1966; Rothkopf & Bisbicos, 1967). For example, in a typical study, students were asked to read a passage about the "Sea Around Us" either with or without adjunct questions. Performance on subsequent retention tests was much higher for subjects who had read passages with adjunct questions. Since this pioneering work, subsequent research has focused on two main issues: where to place questions and what types of questions to use.

Placement of Questions.   First, let's consider the placement of questions. In Rothkopf's (1966) study, some subjects received the questions after the text (postquestion group), some subjects received the questions before the text (prequestion group), and some received no questions at all (read-only group). Figure 6–6 shows the performance on tests for incidental (i.e., previously unquestioned material) and intentional (i.e., previously questioned material) learning. As can be seen, performance on intentional learning is enhanced for both prequestion and post-test question groups, but performance on incidental learning is enhanced mainly for the post-test question group.

In another study, Boker (1974) asked students to read a 250-word lesson on historical geology. The lesson was divided into ten sections, and two factual multiple-choice questions were placed either before each section (prequestion group), after each section (postquestion group), or not at all (read-only group). Subjects then took a forty-item post-test that included the twenty adjunct

FIGURE 6–6   Intentional and Incidental Learning for Three Adjunct Question Groups

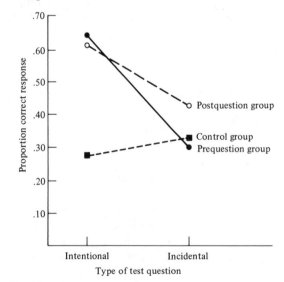

Adapted from Rothkopf (1966)

questions (intentional learning) plus twenty similar questions covering other factual information from the lesson (incidental learning). The test was given both immediately after reading the passage (immediate test) and one week later (delayed test). The students were allowed to read at their own rates, but they were not allowed to go back to previous sections of the text, and they were not allowed to look at the text when they were given adjunct questions to answer. Figure 6–7 summarizes the results. The prequestion and postquestion groups both performed better than the control on intentional learning, presumably because they paid more attention to this information in the passage. However, the postquestion group performed better than the read-only group on incidental learning while the prequestion group performed worse. This pattern suggests that the prequestions may have served to focus the readers' attention on information that was relevant to the questions. The same pattern was obtained on the immediate and delayed tests.

In a review of thirty-five adjunct question studies, Anderson & Biddle (1975) found that while both prequestions and postquestions generally enhance performance on tests of intentional learning, prequestions can often have the effect of inhibiting performance on "new criterion test items." Apparently, questions can serve as cues to readers concerning what to pay attention to.

Types of Questions.   A second major research issue concerns what types of

FIGURE 6–7   Performance on Immediate and Delayed Test for Three Adjunct Question Groups

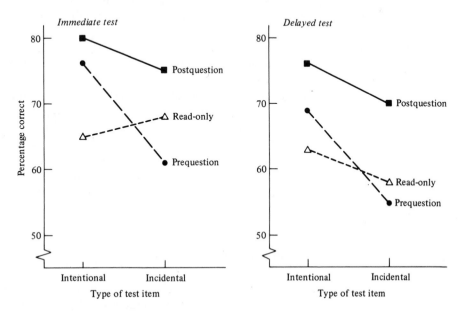

Adapted from Boker (1974)

question to ask. For example, Rickards & DiVesta (1974) asked college students to read an 800-word passage about a fictitious African nation "Mala." One group of subjects had rote questions printed after every two paragraphs, such as "How many inches of rainfall per year in southern Mala?" Another group had meaningful questions printed every two paragraphs, such as, "Why can it be said that southern Mala is a desert?" A control group was given irrelevant questions after every two paragraphs. On a recall test, the meaningful question group recalled about 35 pieces of information compared to about 21 pieces of information for the rote question group, and 15 for the control group. Rickards & DiVesta (1974) suggest that the meaningful questions encouraged learners to organize the material into an outline structure rather than memorize a list of facts.

Although these studies suggest that meaningful questions result in broader learning than rote questions, another important question is whether this is due to forward or backward processing. In order to investigate the effects of question type on forward processing, McConkie & Rayner & Wilson (1973) asked subjects to read a series of six 500-word passages on topics such as set theory, the biosphere, and the Reconstruction Era. After each of the first five passages, subjects received one type of question—such as number questions ("In New York City what _____% of all tetanus cases occurred with addicts?") or structure questions ("Which point did the author make after saying that the slaves who had acquired some education and skills under slavery became Negro leaders?"). After the sixth passage, all subjects received all types of questions. Performance on the test after passage 6 indicated that subjects tended to perform best on the type of question they had received on previous passages; however, in some cases performance was enhanced for other question types as well.

Mayer (1975b) asked students to read six passages on mathematical probability theory, with one type of question printed after each passage. Some subjects were asked to compute numerical values (calculation group), some were asked to recite formal definitions of terms (definition group), some were asked to state principles in terms of concrete models (model group), and some received no questions on the first six passages (control group). After the seventh and eighth passages, all subjects received all three types of questions. Figure 6–8 summarizes the results. Subjects tended to perform best on the type of problem they expected, but the model group performed well on all types. Apparently, the model questions encouraged building of external connections, even on passages 7 and 8.

Implications of Research on Adjunct Questions

The foregoing section has shown that adjunct questions can serve many functions, including helping the learner to pay more attention to the material, focusing the learner's attention on certain types of information, and building

FIGURE 6–8   Percentage Correct for Four Groups on Three Types of Test Items

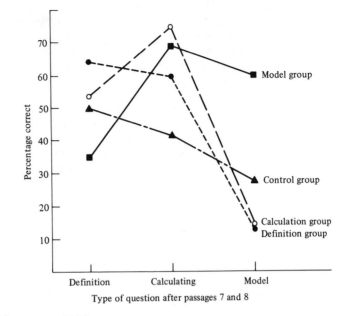

Adapted from Mayer (1975)

internal and external connections. The placement and type of questions are crucial in determining how the learner will process the information. If the goal of instruction is memorization of specific information, then rote questions (both before and after a passage) may be useful. Explicit behavioral objectives (i.e., directing the learner's attention) may serve the same function as prequestions. If the goal of instruction is the ability to apply information in new situations, then meaningful questions should be used (especially *after* a passage).

CONCLUSION

This chapter examines three techniques for improving the understandability of a textbook lesson. In particular, this chapter has provided some examples of how instructional methods influence the learner's processing of information. If the goal is to direct the reader's attention, then signals and prequestions should be used. If the goal is to encourage building of external connections, then advance organizers and certain types of postquestions should be used. If the goal is to encourage building of internal connections, then signaling and certain types of postquestions should be used.

SUGGESTED READINGS

Bransford, J. D. (1979). *Human cognition*. Belmont, C.A.: Wadsworth. (A review of cognitive research on learning, with special focus on learning from prose.)

Britton, B. K. & Black, J. B. (1985). *Understanding expository text: A theoretical and practical handbook for analyzing explanatory text*. Hillsdale, N.J.: Erlbaum. (A collection of papers by authors concerned with how to improve students' reading of expository text.)

Flammer, A. & Kintsch, W. (1982). *Discourse processing*. Amsterdam: North-Holland. (Section on "Instructional Implications" presents eleven brief summaries of research on improving instructional text.)

Meyer, B. J. F. (1975). *The organization of prose and its effects on memory*. Amsterdam: North-Holland. (A detailed description of a research project aimed at understanding how people learn from prose.)

7 Instructional Methods for Tutorial Learning

Chapter Outline

The Parallelogram Problem
Structure-Oriented Methods
Discovery Methods
Inductive Methods
Conclusion

This chapter explores the classic distinction between meaningful and rote learning, and investigates three instructional methods aimed at producing meaningful learning—structure-oriented methods, discovery methods, and inductive methods. For each technique, an example is presented, theoretical concepts are explained, representative research is presented, implications for instruction are suggested, and an application using computers is provided.

THE PARALLELOGRAM PROBLEM

Consider the parallelogram in Figure 7–1. How would you teach children to solve problems like the parallelogram problem in this figure? Let's assume that the children have already learned how to find the area of rectangles, but they have not yet learned about the area of parallelograms.

The Gestalt psychologist, Wertheimer (1959) suggests two distinct methods of instruction for this material. The first method is to teach the child to find the height and the base, and to plug them into the formula, Area = Height × Base. In the example in Figure 7–1, this means the child must find that the height is 5, the base is 11, so the area is 5 × 11 or 55. Wertheimer calls this the "rote method" because the child learns to mechanically apply a formula. The rote method is summarized in the top of Figure 7–2.

FIGURE 7–1   Find the Area of a Parallelogram

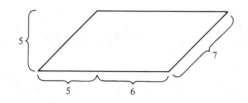

The second method suggested by Wertheimer is to allow the child to have "structural insight" (i.e., to see how a parallelogram can be changed into a rectangle by moving the triangle on one end to the other end). Once the child sees how to restructure the parts of a parallelogram into a rectangle, the child can go ahead using a previously learned method for finding the area of a rectangle. Wertheimer calls this the "meaningful method," because the learner understands how the parts of a parallelogram fit together. The middle of Figure 7–2 summarizes the meaningful method.

FIGURE 7–2   Rote and Meaningful Methods of Instruction for the Parallelogram Problem

Rote method
Drop a perpendicular to find height. Measure a base. Multiply height times base.

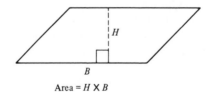

Area = $H \times B$

Meaningful method
Let the child cut the parallelogram into parts and rearrange them into a rectangle.

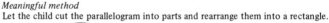

Transfer to novel problems

Why should we be concerned whether a child learns by rote or by understanding? Isn't it enough to teach the child how to use the formula effectively, so that the child can get the right answer on parallelogram problems? Wertheimer's answer to these questions is that "understanding" is important for some instructional objectives but not for others. For example, according to Wertheimer, both methods of instruction lead to good performance on standard problems like those given as examples during instruction. Thus, if the goal of instruction is efficient application of a rule on standard problems, then the meaningful method of instruction is not needed. However, what happens when you present children with unusual problems such as shown in the bottom of Figure 7–2? According to Wertheimer, the children who learned by understanding are able to solve transfer problems whereas the children who learned by rote say, "We haven't had that yet." Thus the payoff for meaningful methods of instruction is not in exact retention of the taught material, but rather in creative transfer to new situations. If the goal of instruction is that the child be able to creatively apply learning in new situations, then meaningful methods of instruction are important.

Wertheimer and other Gestalt psychologists (Katona, 1942; Kohler, 1925) distinguished between learning by rote and learning by understanding. While their work provides many interesting examples of the distinction, the cognitive theory underlying the distinction was not well spelled out. In this chapter, therefore, we investigate several well-known attempts to provide "meaningful" methods of instruction: structure-oriented methods, discovery methods, and inductive methods.

STRUCTURE-ORIENTED METHODS

Example of Structure-oriented Method

One way to make an idea more meaningful is to make it more concrete. For example, in the parallelogram problem, the teacher may make the concept of area more concrete by using 1×1 squares. Figure 7–3 shows how using 1×1 squares can give a concrete way of representing area. These materials are called "concrete manipulatives," because the student can physically move and rearrange them.

Theory: Mapping Concepts to Concrete Models

Why does a concrete representation of the material to be learned influence learning? One explanation comes from Bruner's (1966) theory of cognitive development. According to Bruner, children develop modes of representing information in the following order:

FIGURE 7–3   How Many Unit Squares Are Needed to Cover the Parallelogram?

If we put 1 X 1 unit squares over part of the parallelogram, we need 5 X 6, or 30 squares.

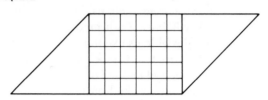

If we move the triangle from one end to the other and cover the triangles with 1 X 1 unit squares, we need 5 X 5 or 25 squares.

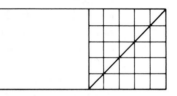

The total number of squares needed to cover the parallelogram is 11 X 5 or 55.

Enactive mode—using actions to represent information, such as tying a shoe.

Iconic mode—using visualization to represent information, such as thinking of a friend's face.

Symbolic mode—using language or other symbols to represent information (e.g., knowing that the circumference of a circle equals pi times the square of the radius).

In learning a new skill, such as arithmetic, several modes of representation may be involved, as shown in Figure 7–4. The enactive mode involves the physical actions of counting aloud with fingers; the iconic mode involves visualizing bundles of sticks that can be grouped by tens; the symbolic mode involves numerals.

The development of understanding must progress through the same stages as representation in intellectual development: first, understanding by doing, then by visualizing, and eventually by symbolic representation. Bruner & Kenney (1966, p. 436) state this idea as follows: "We would suggest that learning mathematics may be viewed as a microcosm of intellectual development. It begins with instrumental activity, a kind of definition of things by doing." Eventually, mathematical operations "become represented . . . in the form of . . . images," and finally, "with the help of symbolic notation, the learner comes to grasp the formal or abstract properties of the things he is dealing with." According to this view, understanding progresses from the level

FIGURE 7–4   Three Ways of Representing a Problem

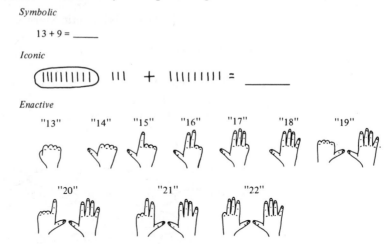

Adapted from Wertheimer (1959)

of active manipulation of objects and images, and eventually leads to symbolic representation. Therefore, instruction that begins with formal symbolic representations, without first allowing the learner to develop an enactive or iconic representation, will lead to rote learning. Concrete manipulatives may be useful in connecting one mode of representation to another.

Research and Development: Concrete Manipulatives in Mathematics

Bundles of Sticks.   Brownell (1935) was one of the first to demonstrate the important pedagogic role of concrete analogies in school learning. For example, Brownell suggested using manipulatives such as bundles of little sticks to concretize the subtraction algorithm. Suppose you wanted to teach children to subtract two-digit numbers such as 65 – 28 = _____. One method of instruction would be to drill the student on the subtraction procedure as shown in the top of Box 7–1. An alternative, which Brownell called the "meaningful method," is to show how the problem can be represented as bundles of sticks, as shown in the bottom of Box 7–1. In this system, place value can be represented by tying each ten sticks together into a bundle.

In a careful research study, Brownell & Moser (1949) taught third graders by the standard method or the meaningful method. On subsequent tests, both groups of children were able to solve two-digit subtraction problems like those given during instruction; however, the children who learned with the concrete analogy performed better than the standard group in learning to solve different

BOX 7–1   How to Make Arithmetic More Concrete

Standard Method

65   I can't take 8 from 5 so I think of 5 as 15.
−28   8 from 15 is 7, and I write 7.
         Since I thought of 5 as 15, I must think of 6 as 5.
         2 from 5 is 3, and I write 3.

Meaningful Method

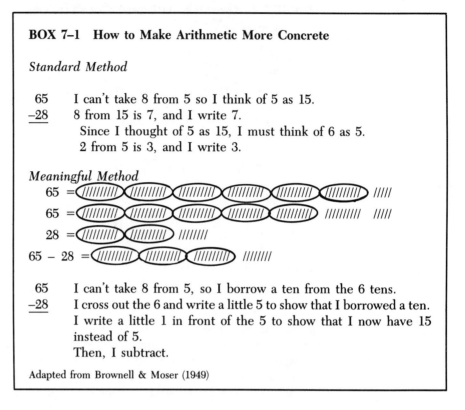

65   I can't take 8 from 5, so I borrow a ten from the 6 tens.
−28   I cross out the 6 and write a little 5 to show that I borrowed a ten.
         I write a little 1 in front of the 5 to show that I now have 15
         instead of 5.
         Then, I subtract.

Adapted from Brownell & Moser (1949)

kinds of problems. Apparently, the advantage of "meaningful learning" comes when the child is asked to transfer to new situations.

According to Brownell (1935, p. 10), a student needs to relate each piece of information together within a meaningful framework: ". . . one needs a fund of meanings, not a myriad of automatic responses." Brownell (p. 19) notes that drill is appropriate only after "ideas and processes already understood are to be practiced to increase efficiency."

Let's suppose that concrete manipulatives such as bundles of sticks can help children to understand the concepts of number, place value, sets, and operations on sets. Is it better to avoid teaching computational procedures until students first understand the concepts, or is it better to present the computational procedures first and then show how they relate to concrete manipulatives? Unfortunately, as Resnick & Ford (1981, p. 110) point out: "This is the sort of question that research has not yet answered."

Montessori Materials.   Montessori (1964) has developed concrete materials that can be used to teach the structure underlying arithmetic. For example, Figure 7–5 shows some Montessori materials that can be used to teach the concept of place value:

FIGURE 7–5   Some Montessori Materials for Numbers

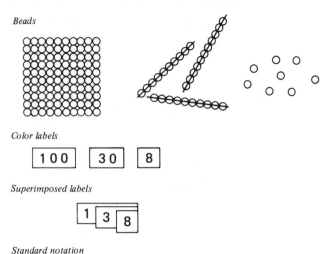

Beads

Color labels

Superimposed labels

Standard notation

1 3 8

Beads—can be used individually to represent units, the beads can be strung
   into lines to represent tens, and the beads can be arranged into a 10 ×
   10 square to represent hundreds.
Colored labels—are printed in green, tens are printed in blue, and hundreds are printed in red.
Superimposed labels—can be combined to produce a single representation.

These materials allow the child to progress from representing numbers as beads
(with units, tens, and hundreds) to expanded notation using the colored labels,
to standard notation using superimposed labels.

To teach computational algorithms, the Montessori materials include wood-
en squares with "1" printed in green, "10" printed in blue, or "100" printed in
red. A problem can be translated from standard notation into colored squares,
such as shown in Box 7–2. Then, a child can learn the procedure of carrying as
trading in ten green unit-squares for one blue 10-square, or trading ten blue
10-squares for one red 100-square. Once the child is proficient at such ex-
changes, the symbolic notation for carrying can be introduced. For example,
the "1" written at the top of the tens column in the standard algorithm
corresponds to exchanging ten units for one ten in color squares.

Dienes Blocks.   Another set of concrete materials was developed by
Dienes (1960, 1963, 1967). For example, place value and computation can be
represented using *multibase arithmetic blocks* (MAB), also known as *Dienes
blocks*, such as shown in Figure 7–6. The blocks come in *units* that are about 1
cubic centimeter; units can be snapped together into lines of 10 called *longs;*
longs can be attached to form 10 × 10 squares called *flats;* flats can be piled
together to form 10 × 10 × 10 cubes called *blocks*.

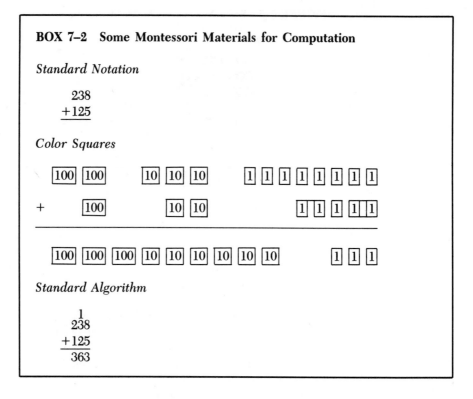

BOX 7–2   Some Montessori Materials for Computation

Standard Notation

$$238$$
$$+125$$

Color Squares

Standard Algorithm

$$\begin{array}{r} 1 \\ 238 \\ +125 \\ \hline 363 \end{array}$$

Bruner & Kenney (1965) have shown how materials adapted from Dienes blocks can be used to teach the underlying structure of factoring quadratic equations. Figure 7–7 shows that materials consisted of units (i.e., 1 by 1 blocks), longs (i.e., blocks that are 1 by X), and flats (i.e., blocks that are X by X). To make a square that is $(X + 1)$ by $(X + 1)$, you need one flat, two longs, and a unit. To make a square that is $(X + 2)$ by $(X + 2)$ you need one flat, four

FIGURE 7–6   Dienes Blocks for Numbers

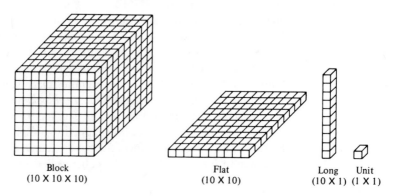

Block
(10 X 10 X 10)

Flat
(10 X 10)

Long
(10 X 1)

Unit
(1 X 1)

FIGURE 7–7   Using Modified Dienes Blocks to Teach Quadratic Factoring

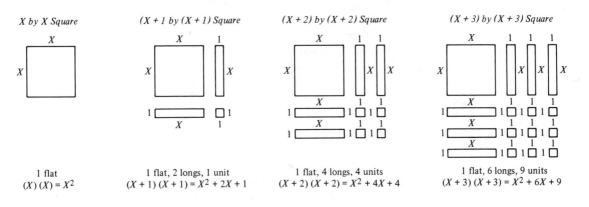

Adapted from Bruner & Kenney (1965)

longs and four units. To make a square that is $(X + 3)$ by $(X + 3)$ you need one flat, six longs, and nine units, and so on. Once the child can represent squares using blocks such as the $(X + 1)$ square, the formal notation can be given such as $(X + 1)^2 = X^2 + 2X + 1$. Bruner & Kenney suggest that instruction should begin by giving children a chance to actively manipulate actual objects and eventually progress towards the symbolic representation of the problem.

Based on his observations of children, Bruner (1960, pp. 7–11) has argued for the importance of teaching the underlying structure of mathematics and science to children: "Grasping the structure of a subject is understanding it in a way that permits many other things to be related to it meaningfully. To learn structure, in short, is to learn how things are related. . . . The teaching and learning of structure, rather than simply the mastery of facts and techniques, is at the center of the classic problem of transfer." For example, the child who learns through manipulating beads or blocks that $7 + 3$ is the same as $6 + 4$ or $2 + 8$, has learned something about how arithmetic "facts" are related to one another.

Implications of Structure-oriented Methods

So far we have sampled some of the commonly used manipulatives in mathematics instruction. Other manipulatives include attribute blocks, Cuisenaire rods, and geoboards. These materials are used in an attempt to present the underlying structures of mathematics in a simple and concrete way to children.

During the 1960s, mathematics curricula were reformed to emphasize the structure-oriented approach and to deemphasize drill and practice. However, in a recent review of manipulatives in mathematics instruction, Resnick & Ford (1981, p. 126) have pointed out that there has been very little research to identify the psychologically important structures that underlie mathematics:

"The structure-oriented methods and materials have not been adequately validated by research, and we know little from school practice about the effects of the curriculum reforms upon the quality of children's mathematical learning." Structure-oriented methods must take into account the intellectual capacity of learners; once a learner "understands," drill and practice may be needed to ensure increased efficiency.

Computer Applications:
Computer Simulations in Science

More recently, advances in educational computing technology have made it possible to allow students to interact with computer simulations of real-world objects and events. For example, White (1984) has created a computer simulation—or "microworld"—for teaching Newton's laws of motion. The computer simulation takes the form of several different games, each involving a spaceship that can be guided through space. The spaceship appears on the screen, and the student uses finger-controlled buttons to fire a rocket (i.e., kick the spaceship) either heading 0, 90, 180, or 270 degrees. Each "kick" is equal in strength.

According to White, creating a game involves creating a microworld based on the following design principles:

1. Encourage the application of relevant knowledge from other domains. To accomplish this, the idea of frictionless space is represented by using the analogy of a spaceship in outer space.
2. Represent the phenomena of the domain clearly. To accomplish this, the spaceship leaves a visible trail and fires rockets at 0, 90, 180, or 270 degrees only.
3. Eliminate irrelevant complexities. To accomplish this, the command options are simplified such that the direction of the rocket's "kick" can be only 0, 90, 180, or 270 degrees (controlled by the left hand) and the firing has only one intensity, but can be repeated (controlled by the right hand).
4. Facilitate better problem-solving heuristics. To give the student time to think, the student has access to a pause button that freezes the motion of the spaceship.
5. Focus students on the aspects of their knowledge that need revising. For example, previous studies, including the misconceptions research cited in Chapter 14, have indicated that many students believe (incorrectly) that an object moves in the direction of the most recently applied force.

Figure 7–8 presents one of the games, CORNER. As shown in the first panel, the spaceship initially faces the right (90 degrees) and has an initial speed of zero. If you could "kick" the ship as many times as you like in any of four directions (0, 90, 180, or 270 degrees), what would you do?

Many high school students began by "kicking" the ship forward (i.e., by pressing the fire rocket button at a heading of 90 degrees); then, when the ship got to the corner, they tried to turn the ship left by "kicking" it with a 0 degree heading. The second panel in Figure 7–8 shows the result: the ship turns only 45 degrees and thus fails to negotiate the corner. This approach reflects the misconception that an object moves in the direction of the most recently applied force (i.e., since the ship was last kicked at a heading of 0 degrees, it should go in that direction). However, from the simulation, students see that the directional effects of forces are additive, so that one kick at 90 degrees and one kick at 0 degrees averages to moving in a direction of 45 degrees—a 45-degree turn occurs instead of the expected 90-degree turn. When students' misconceptions of the law of motion cause them to lose the game, they clearly see that their knowledge needs to be revised.

Eventually many students develop strategies based on Newtonian physics for winning the game of CORNER. One simple strategy is to move the ship towards the corner by pressing the forward rocket button heading 90 degrees and then stop the ship when it gets to the corner by pressing the rocket button

FIGURE 7–8 A Computer Game for Teaching Newton's Laws of Motion

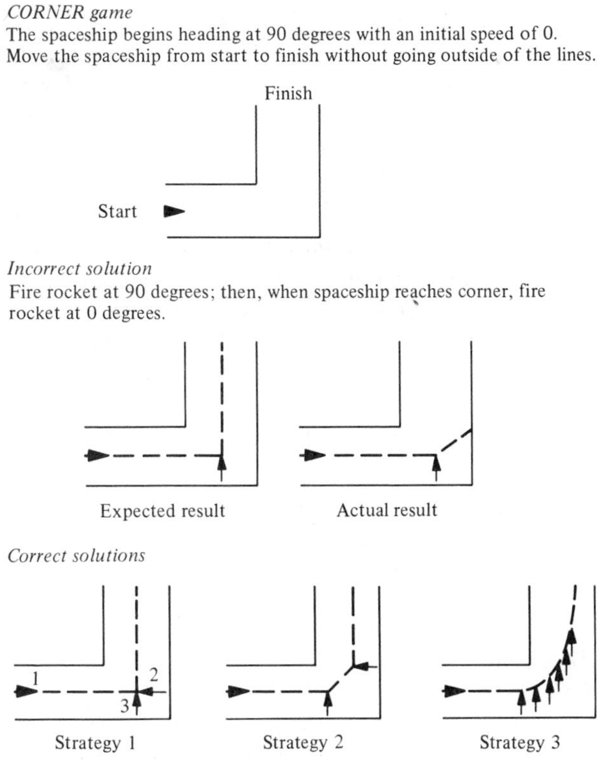

CORNER game
The spaceship begins heading at 90 degrees with an initial speed of 0.
Move the spaceship from start to finish without going outside of the lines.

Finish

Start ▶

Incorrect solution
Fire rocket at 90 degrees; then, when spaceship reaches corner, fire rocket at 0 degrees.

Expected result   Actual result

Correct solutions

Strategy 1   Strategy 2   Strategy 3

Adapted from White (1984)

in the opposite direction (i.e., 270 degrees); then, the ship can be moved left by firing the rocket at 0 degrees. A second strategy is to move the ship towards the corner by pressing the forward rocket button at a 90-degree heading, firing an upward (0-degree) impulse as the ship enters the corner and a backwards (270-degree) impulse as the ship approaches the end of the corner. A third strategy is to move the ship towards the corner by pressing the forward rocket button at a 90-degree heading; as the ship approaches the corner, start pressing the rocket button at a 0 degree heading and keep pressing as needed to avoid hitting the walls as the ship moves around the corner. Each of these strategies is shown in the bottom panels of Figure 7–8.

The strategies needed for winning the game of CORNER, as well as other spaceship games, require that the student replace his or her misconceptions of the laws of motion with correct Newtonian physics. Does a computer simulation like CORNER affect students' knowledge of physics? In order to investigate this question, White (1984) presented application questions about force and motion to high school students who had just studied the physical laws of motion from a well-respected physics textbook. Consistent with other research on students' misconceptions of science summarized in Chapter 14, the students in White's study performed poorly in spite of the efforts of excellent teachers. Some of the students were then given approximately 1 hour of experience with spaceship simulation games such as CORNER. These students showed large improvements in their performance on the force-and-motion questions, while the students who did not play the games did not show large improvements. White's explanation for these results is that the computer games make Newton's laws more concrete. By manipulating "concrete objects" on the computer screen, the student is able to relate general principles to more familiar objects.

These results are promising because they show that "concrete manipulatives" can be moved productively to the computer screen, at least for high school students. The number of commercially available educational computer simulations is increasing, and research such as White's suggests that some simulations may be useful. However, not all computer games are useful instructional tools. What makes a "good" game? The foregoing example suggests that good games are based on appropriate design principles, are presented at a level that is appropriate for students, and are integrated with other parts of the school program.

DISCOVERY METHODS

Example of Discovery Methods

Let's return to the parallelogram problem shown in Figure 7–1. What else can be done to make the rule for finding area more understandable? One suggestion is to encourage the learner to actively try to solve problems before being presented with the rule to be learned. For example, Figure 7–7 presents some parallelogram problems to solve (using concrete objects as suggested in the previous section).

Theory: The Joy of Discovery

Bruner (1961) helped to instigate modern interest in discovery learning in his famous essay, "The Act of Discovery." Bruner's paper distinguished between two modes of instruction: *expository mode*, in which the teacher controls what is presented and the student listens, and *hypothetical mode*, in which the student has some control over the pace and content of instruction and may take on an "as if" attitude. The hypothetical mode allows the learner *to discover* new rules and ideas, rather than simply memorize rules and ideas that the teacher presents. According to Bruner, the discovery of rules results in better learning—because the learner has organized the material in a useful way—and results in the student becoming a better learner and problem solver in general, because the student gets practice in processing information.

Research and Development: Discovery of Rules

Although Bruner is an eloquent proponent of the discovery method and although his suggestions were implemented in some curricular projects (Davis, 1973), you might wonder whether or not there is any empirical evidence that discovery enhances learning. During the 1960s there was a flurry of research concerned with the question of how much guidance a teacher should provide (Shulman & Kresler, 1966). Although the researchers often used terms in different ways, we can define three basic levels of guidance in instruction:

1. *Pure discovery*—the student receives representative problems to solve with minimal teacher guidance;
2. *Guided discovery*—the student receives problems to solve, but the teacher provides hints and directions about how to solve the problem to keep the student on track; and
3. *Expository*—the final answer or rule is presented to the student.

Logical Reasoning. An early study by Craig (1956) was the forerunner of more recent method-of-instruction studies. Students were given training in "finding the word that doesn't belong" in sets of five words. For example, given:

CYCLE   SELDOM   SAWDUST   SAUSAGE   CELLAR

the appropriate answer is to mark CYCLE since it does not share the same initial sound as any of the other words. Items were organized in sets of four, all having the same relational rule (e.g., initial sound) and each training booklet contained several such types of rules.

Two instructional methods were used: a "guided discovery" group was told the relation (e.g., "look for initial sound") at the beginning of each set of four items but was not told the answer per se; the other group, which could be called "pure discovery" was not given any hints. Results indicated that the group given some guidance learned more efficiently, retained more, and transferred just as well as a pure discovery group. This study calls into doubt the emphasis on extreme classroom freedom and independence; some learners simply may not be able to discover the appropriate concepts and rules without some direction from the teacher.

Kittel (1957) reported a study using material similar to Craig's but which involved all three levels of guidance—pure discovery, guided discovery, and expository. The training, like Craig's involved giving the learner a set of five words, such as,

GONE   START   GO   STOP   COME

and asking the learner to mark the word that doesn't belong. In the preceding example, the relational principle is "form two pairs of opposites"; hence, the correct answer is "GONE." In the training booklets, each set of three items had the same principle and there were fifteen such principles in all.

Some subjects were not given any direction (pure discovery); some subjects were told the principle (e.g., "form two pairs of opposites") for each set of problems but were not given the answer (guided discovery); some subjects were told both the principle and the correct answer for each problem (expository). Figure 7–9 summarizes some of the major results of the study. As can be seen, the pure discovery group performed worse than the other two groups on immediate retention, suggesting that pure discovery resulted in less initial learning. On tests of transfer and long-term retention, the guided discovery group outperformed both the pure discovery group and the expository group. Apparently, the pure discovery group did not discover many of the principles during learning; in addition, while the guided discovery and expository groups seem to have learned equal amounts during initial learning, the extra processing and thinking during learning led the guided discovery group to retain the information and transfer the information better than the expository group.

Mathematical Reasoning.   The foregoing results suggest that a major drawback of pure discovery methods is that some students may fail to discover the underlying principle. In order to overcome this problem, Gagne & Brown (1961) conducted a study in which students learned to solve series sums and derive formulas using three different instructional methods. For example, students learned how to compute the sum of "1,3,5,7,9 . . ." and to write a formula for the series. In the pure discovery method students were given problems to solve; however, if they were unable to solve the problem, hints were provided until the correct principle was found. Thus the pure discovery

FIGURE 7–9   How Much Guidance Should Be Given During Learning?

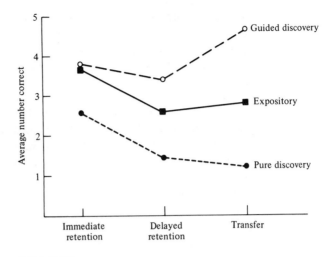

Adapted from Kittel (1957)

method was modified to make it more like guided discovery (i.e., to ensure that the student actually learned). In the guided discovery method, problems were given, along with a systematic succession of questions to aid the student. Thus there was more guidance concerning how to solve the problem. The expository group was given problems along with the solution formula already worked out. All students had to continue working until they were able to master four separate series; thus all students were forced to learn equal amounts.

Table 7–1 shows the amount of time and number of errors in learning under the three methods of instruction, and the amount of time and number of errors on a subsequent transfer test for the three treatment groups. As can be seen, the guided discovery group took the longest amount of time to learn, but performed best on the transfer test. The pure discovery group also performed well on transfer, presumably due to the procedure of ensuring that initial learning actually occurred.

TABLE 7–1   Effects of Discovery Methods on Learning and Transfer

	Pure Discovery	*Guided Discovery*	*Expository*
Learning time (errors)	28(6)	46(17)	41(9)
Transfer time (errors)	20(2)	17(1)	27(6)

Adapted from Gagné & Brown (1961)

Implications of Discovery Methods

Our review of research on discovery identifies the following patterns: (1) Pure discovery methods often require excessive amounts of learning time, result in low levels of initial learning, and inferior performance on transfer and long-term retention. However, when the principle to be learned is obvious or when a strict criterion of initial learning is enforced, pure discovery subjects are likely to behave like guided discovery subjects. Apparently, pure discovery encourages learners to get "cognitively involved" (Anastasiow, Bibley, Leonhardt, & Borish, 1970), but fails to ensure that they will come into contact with the rule or principle to be learned. (2) Guided discovery may require more or less time than expository instruction depending on the task, but tends to result in better long-term retention and transfer as compared to expository instruction. Apparently, guided discovery both encourages learners to search actively for how to apply rules and makes sure that the learner comes into contact with the rule to be learned. (3) Expository instruction may sometimes result in less learning time than other methods and generally results in equivalent levels of initial learning as compared to guided discovery. However, if the goal of instruction is long-term retention and transfer, then expository methods seem inferior to guided discovery. Apparently, expository instruction does not encourage the learner to actively think about the rule, but does ensure that the rule is learned. When the goal of instruction is long-term retention and transfer of learned principles, then the teacher needs to use enough guidance so that the student finds the to-be-learned principle but not so much guidance that the student is discouraged from working actively on understanding how the principle can be applied.

Computer Applications:
Discovery in Computer Programming

Although research in the 1960s tended to argue against the usefulness of pure discovery, the introduction of computers into schools during the 1980s has brought renewed calls for discovery learning. For example, Papert (1980) in his influential book, *Mindstorms*, argues eloquently for two important aspects of computing instruction: (1) "hands-on" discovery in which students are allowed to "learn without being taught," (i.e., students receive unstructured, "hands-on" computer experience that is not tied to any curricular demands), and (2) LOGO environment, in which students work in a powerful and responsive computer environment that is supposedly provided by the programming language LOGO.

In order to understand the LOGO environment, let's focus briefly on "turtle graphics," generally the first aspect of LOGO to be learned by elementary school children. You begin with a "turtle," represented as a triangular cursor on a computer screen, as shown in Figure 7–10. You can turn the

FIGURE 7–10 Some Logo Commands

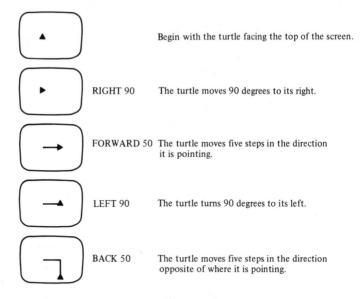

Begin with the turtle facing the top of the screen.

RIGHT 90   The turtle moves 90 degrees to its right.

FORWARD 50   The turtle moves five steps in the direction
             it is pointing.

LEFT 90   The turtle turns 90 degrees to its left.

BACK 50   The turtle moves five steps in the direction
             opposite of where it is pointing.

turtle by issuing commands such as RIGHT _____ or LEFT _____, where each command is followed by a number that indicates how many degrees the turtle will turn. For example, RIGHT 90 means turn the turtle 90 degrees clockwise from its current position and LEFT 90 means turn the turtle 90 degrees counterclockwise from its current position. You can move the turtle by issuing commands such as FORWARD _____ or BACK _____, where each command is followed by a number indicating how many steps the turtle will take. Examples of these four commands are given in Figure 7–10.

Suppose you want to draw a square. What commands would you type into the keyboard? One way to correctly solve this problem would be to type:

```
FORWARD 100
RIGHT 90
FORWARD 100
RIGHT 90
FORWARD 100
RIGHT 90
FORWARD 100
RIGHT 90
```

However, below are the commands (using abbreviations) produced by a child who was trying to draw a square (Papert, 1980):

```
FD 100
RT 100
```

```
FD 100
ERASE 1      (This undoes the previous command.)
RT 10
LT 10
LT 10
FD 100
RT 100
LT 10
RT 100
LT 10
FD 100
RT 40
FD 100
RT 90
FD 100
```

As you can see, the child has a difficult time turning the turtle at right angles, presumably because the child does not know that 90 degrees is a right angle. However, once you have developed a program to draw a square you can name and save the program, such as by naming it SQUARE. Then you can "call" this program at any time within another program simply by typing SQUARE as a command. For example, if you wanted to draw a house (i.e., a square with a triangle on top) you could use the SQUARE command within your program, since drawing a square is a component in drawing a house. Then you could name that new program HOUSE and use it within a larger program and so on.

According to Papert, as children explore LOGO, they develop "powerful ideas" concerning how to solve problems procedurally—including how to modularize a program and call each subprogram when needed. What evidence is there to support Papert's demand for unrestricted, hands-on experience in a LOGO environment and his claim that learning LOGO will transfer to other problem-solving domains? Unfortunately, there is almost no evidence available, and the evidence that is available does not support Papert's claims. Real children in real classrooms generally have difficulty learning even the fundamentals of LOGO programming (Dalbey & Linn, 1985; Gregg, 1973; Pea & Kurland, 1984, 1985; Perkins, 1985; Webb, 1984). For example, Kurland & Pea (1985) tested seven children, ages eleven to twelve, who averaged over fifty hours of hands-on LOGO programming instruction under discovery conditions. Children were given programs and asked to predict the output. The children had little trouble with short, simple programs which involved only commands to move or turn the turtle. However, on transfer problems that involved using fundamental programming concepts, students performed poorly. Through in-depth interviews, Kurland & Pea found that the children had developed incorrect conceptions of how programs operated. Furthermore, while "none of these sources of confusion will be intractable to instruction," in the study under discussion the students learned according to Papert's discovery methods "in the absence of instruction" (Kurland & Pea, 1985, p. 242). Apparently, hands-on experience does not guarantee productive learning of LOGO, and these results suggest that "discovery needs to be mediated within an instructional context" (Kurland & Pea, 1985, p. 242).

Similar difficulties have been observed in students learning BASIC, another "beginner's language" (Bayman & Mayer, 1983; Linn, 1984; Mayer, 1985). For example, in one study (Bayman & Mayer, 1983; Mayer, 1985) low ability college students learned BASIC either through hands-on experience only or through hands-on experience supplemented with direct instruction in the basic programming concepts, such as how data is stored in memory. Students who learned with only hands-on experience exhibited many misconceptions of fundamental programming concepts, such as not knowing how data is stored in memory, not understanding where incoming data comes from, not understanding how the computer determines which command it will follow next, and so on. In contrast, students who were given direct instruction in how these concepts related to each command, displayed many fewer misconceptions, as expected. On programming tests involving transfer, such as writing or interpreting complex programs, the group given added direct instruction performed better than the hands-on only group. Although hands-on experience was not effective for low ability students, complementary studies found that hands-on experience was effective for high ability students. Presumably, the high ability students came to the learning situation with appropriate knowledge they could use to interpret their programming experiences. These results show that hands-on experience does not always lead to meaningful learning of programming concepts, especially when students lack appropriate prerequisite knowledge.

In summary, there is very little evidence to support Papert's eloquent calls for pure discovery as the way of teaching computing to children. Based on the present research, the most productive approach appears to be a mix of teacher-based instruction and student-based exploration. However, students need to be tested frequently in order to determine whether they are acquiring useful programming concepts. If they are not, direct instruction is warranted.

INDUCTIVE METHODS

Example of Inductive Methods

Another issue concerning how to teach students to solve parallelogram area problems—such as in Figure 7–1—concerns when to present the formula or rule. We could begin by stating the rule, area = height × base and then ask students to solve problems. This is a deductive method, because the rule is given first. Alternatively, we could begin by asking the student to solve problems and only after the student has built up some good intuitions, then present the formula. This is an inductive method because the rule is given only after the learner has induced the underlying framework for the rule.

Theory: Assimilation to Existing Knowledge

Ausubel (1968) and Mayer (1975a) have suggested that meaningful learning involves actively connecting new material with existing knowledge. Thus learners must be challenged into thinking about how new principles or laws relate to other ideas in the learners' memory. In inductive methods of instruction, learners are exposed to long periods of mental searching before they can verbalize the rule or what Hendrix (1947, 1961) called "nonverbalized awareness." This period of mental searching helps to activate more of the learner's prior knowledge and enables the learner to actively encode the strategy or concept to be learned into a wider or more meaningful context. In contrast, deductive methods of instruction do not encourage this search, and predispose the learner toward encoding an isolated series of mechanical steps.

Research and Development: Induction of Mathematical Principles

As early as 1913, Winch presented evidence demonstrating the superiority of deductive methods over inductive methods for short-term retention performance, and the superiority of inductive methods for certain types of transfer performance. In a literature review covering the subsequent half century, Hermann (1969) concluded that there still is qualified support for the claim.

Computational Principles. For example, in a well-controlled classroom study, Worthen (1968) used two methods to teach children such concepts as notation, addition and multiplication of integers, the distributive principle of multiplication over addition, and exponential multiplication and division. One group was given inductive instruction: examples were presented for the child to solve followed by verbalization of the required principle or concept. Another group was given inductive instruction: verbalization of the required concept or principle followed by examples for the child to solve. Significant effects due to instructional method were found in measures of learning ease (inductive inferior to deductive), long-term retention (inductive superior to deductive), and transfer (inductive superior to deductive), with no differences in subject attitude.

As a part of a larger study, Roughead & Scandura (1968) used inductive and deductive methods to teach children about series summation. In a deductive method, the rule was given and applied to several problems, then the subject was asked to solve similar problems that were based on the same rule. In the inductive method, subjects were asked to solve some problems, then the rule was given and applied to similar problems. The deductive group learned faster than the inductive group; however, in a transfer task, the inductive group learned to solve the new problems faster than the deductive group. These results are summarized in Figure 7–11.

Statistical Principles.   Another study (Mayer & Greeno, 1972) varied the sequencing in a programmed text for the concept of binomial probability (i.e., the probability of obtaining R successes in N trials). An inductive booklet began by presenting underlying concepts such as "trial," "success," and "probability of success" and gradually put the parts together into a formula by the end of the booklet. A deductive booklet began by presenting the computed formula in symbolic notation and then gradually showed how the component variables figured in using the formula. Although both booklets presented the same basic information and same computational examples, the inductive booklet was sequenced to move from examples to rule, and the deductive booklet was sequenced to move from rule to example. Figure 7–12 summarizes the groups' performance on a subsequent test that included problems just like those given in the booklet (Type F), problems that were slightly modified from those given in the booklet (Type T), problems that were unanswerable (Type U), and questions about when and how to use the formula (Type Q). As can be seen, emphasis on the formula (i.e., deductive training) resulted in better performance on problems like those that the student was trained to solve, but emphasis on underlying concepts resulted in better performance on recognizing when the formula did not apply and on creative question answering. The Mayer &

FIGURE 7–11   Effects of Deductive and Inductive Methods on Learning and Transfer

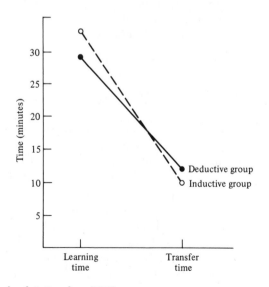

Adapted from Roughead & Scandura (1968)

FIGURE 7–12   Effects of Inductive and Deductive Methods on Problem Solving

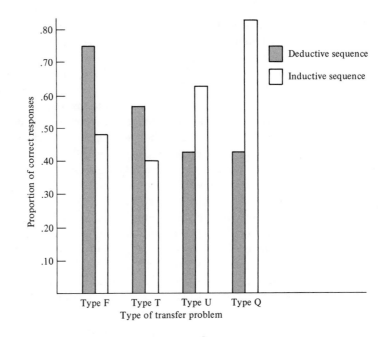

Adapted from Mayer & Greeno (1972)

Greeno study suggests that deductive methods are better for simple retention of a basic rule while inductive methods are better for situations in which the rule must be transferred to new situations.

Implications of Inductive Methods

Research on sequencing of instruction suggests that deductive methods lead to superior performance when there is one single rule to learn or a limited number of problems to be solved. Explicit instruction and practice in applying a specific rule is most effective when the goal of instruction is limited to behaviors that are similar or identical to those being taught. In contrast, the foregoing research demonstrates that inductive methods of instruction are useful when the goal of instruction is the ability to learn how to form rules (rather than learning of a specific rule) or how to transfer to new situations. By encouraging the learner to think actively about how to solve problems during instruction, the learner develops problem-solving strategies that can be applied in many situations.

Computer Applications: Computer Tutors for Science

How would an expert teacher use an inductive method? The most famous example is a dialogue between Socrates and a slave boy named Meno, which forms the basis for the Socratic method of teaching (Plato, 1924). Socrates wanted Meno to induce the geometric principle that a square with sides that are each the square root of 2 is twice as large as a square with sides that are each 1 unit long. Socrates posed examples and asked Meno to make predictions. Then, Socrates helped Meno to see how his hypotheses led to contradictions.

As you can see, expert Socratic tutoring involves providing specific cases for which the student makes predictions. By carefully presenting specific cases, the tutor can help the student to use logical reasoning to induce the causal relationships and principles underlying the cases. Since the time of Socrates, folk wisdom has held that inductive methods of teaching are effective. For example, the case method is used in many schools of law (where the cases are court decisions) and medicine (where the cases are individual patients), although as Collins (1977) points out there is little scientific evidence concerning Socratic tutoring.

Similarly, during the curriculum reform movements of the 1960s, the "inquiry method" was systematically integrated into the science curriculum (Suchman, 1960, 1966). In Suchman's inquiry method, interesting situations or events are presented, and the student is encouraged to develop a cause-and-effect explanation. In one study (Suchman, 1960), children were shown a demonstration in which a heated metal ball would not pass through a ring but when the ball was cooled it would pass through. Box 7–3 gives a typical inquiry dialogue between tutor and student. The student is encouraged to form hypotheses based on the evidence, test the hypotheses, and induce some general laws of science. For Suchman, inquiry training focused as much on teaching scientific principles as on teaching the scientific process of how to ask questions productively. Suchman's dialogues provide a modern day example of how an expert tutor would provide inductive teaching.

More recently, Collins and his associates (Collins, 1977; Collins & Stevens, 1982; Collins, Warnock, Aiello & Miller, 1975; Stevens, Collins & Goldin, 1982) have attempted to develop an intelligent computer tutor that would act like an expert Socratic teacher. For example, suppose that you wanted to teach students about the factors involved in rice growing. You could present a chart such as Figure 7–13 and have students memorize all the causal links in the rice-growing system. According to the foregoing literature review, however, students would not be able to use this information creatively. In contrast, let's suppose you want to teach in a way that fosters transfer—in short, you want to use a Socratic approach.

The first step in developing an expert computer tutor was to carefully observe dialogues between expert teachers and their students. Collins and his colleagues found that good teachers generally have specific goals at each point in a lesson, including teaching facts, teaching rules, and teaching how to derive

---

BOX 7–3   A Tutorial Dialogue Concerning the Concept of Heat

TEACHER: Were the ball and ring at room temperature to begin with?

PUPIL: Yes.

TEACHER: And the ball would go through the ring at first?

PUPIL: Yes.

TEACHER: After the ball was held over the fire it did *not* go through the ring, right?

PUPIL: Yes.

TEACHER: If the ring had been heated instead of the ball, would the results have been the same?

PUPIL: No.

TEACHER: If both had been heated, would the ball have gone through then?

PUPIL: That all depends.

TEACHER: If they had both been heated to the same temperature would the ball have gone through?

PUPIL: Yes.

TEACHER: Would the ball be the same size after it was heated as it was before?

PUPIL: No.

TEACHER: Could the same experiment have been done if the ball and ring were made out of some other metal?

PUPIL: Yes.

From Suchman (1960)

rules. Collins and his colleagues focused on the latter two goals. A careful analysis of the teaching techniques used by good teachers revealed the following strategies:

Systematic variation of cases—Present problems that will highlight specific rules.

Counterexamples and hypothetical cases—When students develop incorrect or incomplete rules, present counterexamples that force the students to notice inconsistencies.

Entrapment strategies—Entrap students into making incorrect predictions so that their misconceptions can become more obvious.

Hypothesis identification strategies—Encourage students to make predictions and generate rules.

Hypothesis evaluation strategies—Encourage students to evaluate whether their predictions or rules are consistent with available facts.

FIGURE 7–13   Some Factors Involved in Growing Rice

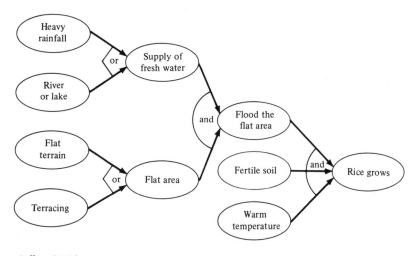

From Collins (1977)

The second step was to develop a data base to which the strategies can be applied. For example, to facilitate learning of the principles summarized in Figure 7–13, a tutor needs to know about many cases of successful and unsuccessful rice growing, such as the factors present in Louisiana that are not present in Washington state. In addition, the data base needs to include the basic kinds of misconceptions that students normally have concerning the subject matter. For example, Stevens, Collins, & Goldin (1982) identified sixteen frequently observed misconceptions concerning the causes of rainfall, such as: cooling by contact (mountains cause condensation because cold land touching air causes condensation); heating by radiation (the sun warms the rising air); and small moisture source (a 12-foot by 12-foot by 10-foot pool is enough to cause rainfall).

Box 7–4 shows how a good teacher applies general instructional strategies to specific knowledge about cases (and misconceptions) to produce a Socratic dialogue. As you can see, in line 1, the tutor begins by asking about a known case. Then, in line 3, the tutor asks for factors, such as the availability of water. Then, in line 5, the tutor shifts to an entrapment strategy by choosing a counterexample that will cause the student to consider factors like climate and terrain in addition to availability of water. In line 7, the tutor asks for factors, so the student will explicitly state that climate and terrain are needed. In line 9, the tutor asks for a prediction about an unknown case.

The third step was to formalize the instructional rules and the data base into a computer program so that a student can sit at a computer terminal and communicate by typing into the keyboard and reading from the screen.

BOX 7–4   A Tutorial On Growing Rice

(1) TUTOR: Where in North America do you think rice might be grown?

(2) STUDENT: Louisiana.

(3) TUTOR: Why there?

(4) STUDENT: Places where there is a lot of water. I think rice requires the ability to selectively flood fields.

(5) TUTOR: OK. Do you think there's a lot of rice in, say, Washington and Oregon?

(6) STUDENT: Aha, I don't think so.

(7) TUTOR: Why?

(8) STUDENT: There's lots of water up there too, but there's two reasons. First, the climate isn't conducive, and second, I don't think the land is flat enough. You've got to have flat land so you can flood a lot of it, unless you terrace it.

(section omitted)

(9) TUTOR: Do you think they might grow rice in Florida?

(10) STUDENT: Yeah, I guess they could, if there were an adequate fresh water supply. Certainly a nice, big, flat area.

Adapted from Collins (1977)

Although the programming principles involved in building such an intelligent tutor are beyond the scope of this book (see Stevens, Collins, & Goldin, 1982), you can see that intelligent computer tutors represent quite an advance over traditional computer-assisted instruction (O'Shea & Self, 1983). Traditional systems typically act as electronic workbooks in which the student answers a question and then gets feedback in lock-step fashion. In contrast, a computer tutor actually carries on a dialogue with the student, in English, using the strategies of expert Socratic teachers.

What effect do computer tutors have on classroom learning? It is simply too early to answer that question. At present, although there are a number of impressive demonstration projects involving computer tutors (Sleeman & Brown, 1982), there are still no commercially available products for use in schools. O'Shea & Self (1983) predict that such programs will be available by the 1990s. In the meanwhile, some benefit results from the act of formally describing how good teachers teach—as a prerequisite for building expert tutoring systems.

CONCLUSION

This chapter has explored three representative techniques for providing meaningful methods of instruction—concrete materials, discovery activities, and inductive sequencing. In each case, there is some laboratory-based evidence that meaningful methods of instruction encourage the learner to become more cognitively involved in the learning task, and thus the outcome of learning allows for better problem-solving transfer.

The major curriculum development efforts of the 1960s attempted to incorporate aspects of meaningful methods of instruction. Since that time, there has been a reaction against developments such as the "new math." In an effort to reestablish the traditional emphasis on "getting the right answer," the pendulum seems to have swung "back to basics" during the 1970s and 1980s. Yet, in the swing, many of the positive features of the "meaningful" approach have been lost.

Will meaningful methods again become an acceptable part of school learning? This chapter has provided current computer applications that may help the pendulum swing again. During the 1970s, teaching machines, including classroom computers, were best adapted for drill and practice on basic skills. However, during the 1980s, as computers became more powerful, they enabled meaningful methods of instruction (e.g., computer simulation games, LOGO environments, and intelligent tutors) aimed at teaching problem-solving skills. Whether or not these advances will rekindle a more lasting and productive interest in meaningful learning remains to be seen.

SUGGESTED READINGS

Bruner, J. S. (1968). *Toward a theory of instruction*. New York: Norton. (Summarizes Bruner's theories of how instructional methods influence what is learned.)

O'Shea, T. & Self, J. (1983). *Learning and teaching with computers*. Brighton, UK: Harvester. (A survey of how computers have been and could be used in schools.)

Wertheimer, M. (1959). *Productive thinking*. New York: Harper & Row. (Presents classic arguments for "meaningful" methods of instruction.)

8 Instruction for Learning Strategies

The model of the instructional/learning process presented in Chapter 6 is based on the idea that learning depends both on the material that is presented and the way that the material is processed by the learner. Based on this model, there are two ways of improving the instructional/learning process: improving the way that material is presented (i.e., instructional methods) or improving the way that students process information (i.e., learning and thinking strategies). Chapters 6 and 7 focused on instructional methods as ways of improving the methods of presentation while Chapters 8 and 9 focus on learning and thinking strategies as ways of improving the student's processing of material. In this chapter, you will learn about three types of learning strategies—mnemonic techniques for rote learning of paired associates and lists, structure training for helping students to build appropriate internal connections among ideas in expository prose, and generative activities for helping students to build external connections between their own knowledge and ideas presented in prose.

HOW TO IMPROVE READING COMPREHENSION TEST SCORES

One of the major learning activities in schools involves asking a student to read a printed passage or listen to a lecture, and later take a test on the material that was presented. For example, read the passage in the top of Box 8–1 and then answer the questions below.

BOX 8–1   A Reading Test

A new kind of star is shining over New York City. It is at the top of a tall, steel tower on an office building. It can be seen from a distance of five miles and tells by changing its color what kind of weather New York City is going to have.

Clear weather is coming if the star is green. Orange means the weather will be cloudy. If the star is flashing orange, New York children wear rubbers and raincoats because rain is on the way. When the star is flashing white, snow is on the way and children get out their sleds. This is the most modern way to predict what the weather is going to be. For a long time radio and newspapers were the principal sources of information concerning the weather. Now a new way has been found.

How would you like to have a star tell you when you can go on your picnic? Maybe the star will tell you the weather is unsuitable and you will have to eat your picnic lunch inside.

A green star shining atop the building means

a. children should wear their boots.
b. snow.   ○
c. clear weather.   ●
d. children should get out their sleds.   ○

What can be seen from a distance of five miles?

a. New York City   ○
b. A steel tower   ○
c. An office building   ○
d. A new kind of star   ●

Adapted from California Assessment Program (1980)

The passage and questions are taken from the reading section of the California Assessment Program (1980) for Grade 6. The CAP is given to all students in grades 3, 6, and 12 in California public schools in order to assess achievement in reading, writing, and mathematics. The passage in Box 8–1 is typical of items found on many other reading comprehension tests. Performance on tests like these seems to be predictive of success in school (i.e., students who are good at reading passages and answering questions on tests also seem to do well, in general, at school).

What does a skilled reader know about how to process this passage that a less skilled reader does not know? A less skilled reader might view this passage as a list of unrelated facts, in which the goal is to carefully "read every word." A more skilled reader may view this passage as an organized body of knowledge that makes sense. Such a reader knows the following:

How to determine the theme of the passage
How to determine which facts are important
How to remember facts that are important

These are examples of "learning strategies." Skills like these seem to be crucial for a student's success in school. While some students acquire these skills without explicit training, other students do not master even the most basic learning strategies. In spite of this problem, until quite recently, there was not much emphasis on teaching students how to learn.

A growing number of psychologists and educators have argued for the importance of teaching children how to learn (i.e., of including learning strategies as part of the curriculum). For example, Norman (1980, p. 97) observes:

It is strange that we expect students to learn yet seldom teach them anything about learning. . . . We sometimes require students to remember a considerable body of material yet seldom teach them the art of memory. It is time that we make up for this lack, time that we developed the applied disciplines of learning . . . and memory. We need to develop the general principles of how to learn, how to remember . . . and then develop applied courses, and then to establish the place of these methods in an academic curriculum.

Norman referred to an emerging discipline of *cognitive engineering*—the development of understanding about how we can manipulate our own cognitive processes. Similarly, Lochhead (1979) has called for the implementation of *cognitive process instruction*—teaching students how to process information.

Can students be taught to be more efficient processors of information? Are there general learning strategies that can be taught to students that will improve their performance on tests like those in Box 8–1? The issue of learning strategies is explored in this chapter. In particular, this chapter investigates: (1) mnemonic techniques for increasing memory of rote information, (2) schema training techniques for recognizing prose schemas or organizations, (3) generative techniques for notetaking and outlining of prose and lecture material.

MNEMONIC TECHNIQUES

Examples of Mnemonic Techniques

Part of school learning involves rote memorization. For example, students are asked to memorize the states and their capitals, and addition facts such as

"2 plus 2 equals 4" and "3 plus 3 equals 6," and so on. In the passage in Box 8–1, one of the "facts" that the reader must remember is that "green means clear." To remember this fact, you could imagine a green traffic light with a clear intersection: *green* means *go*, and you can *go* when the road is *clear*. In this section, we will explore some techniques for more efficient memorization.

Theory: More Associations

Mnemonic strategies are activities which help the learner to remember material. In his book, *The Art of Memory*, Yates (1966) notes that Simonides developed an imagery-based mnemonic system 2500 years ago. Since that time, most work on mnemonics has attempted to develop useful techniques rather than to provide a theory of human memory. In contrast, Paivio (1971) has argued that mnemonic strategies may work for a number of reasons:

> *Dual coding*—Many memory strategies involve using imagery as well as verbal representations. This provides two distinct codings of the same material; hence, there are more ways to find the information in memory.
>
> *Organization*—Many memory strategies provide a coherent context or organization into which new information can be fit. The organization serves to hold the information together rather than as many separate bits.
>
> *Association*—Many memory strategies involving forming strong associations between elements. Stronger associations allow for superior remembering.

Unfortunately, there is still very little information concerning which theory is most accurate. Thus the present section presents a summary of typical mnemonic strategies without emphasis on underlying theory. In all cases, the mnemonic techniques are aimed at getting more information into memory.

Research and Development on Mnemonic Techniques

Key-Word Method for Learning Paired Associates. The modern impetus for educational applications of mnemonic techniques comes from research on the key-word method for teaching foreign language vocabulary by Atkinson & Raugh (Atkinson, 1975; Atkinson & Raugh, 1975; Raugh & Atkinson & Raugh, 1975). For example, in memorizing Spanish-to-English vocabulary such as *carta* means (postal) "letter," the key-word method involves two stages:

> 1. *Acoustic link*—The foreign language word is changed into an easily pronounced English "key word" that sounds like part of the foreign word. For example, *carta* can be converted to "cart."
> 2. *Imagery link*—An interacting image is formed to combine the key-word

FIGURE 8–1   An Image That Links the Key Word "Cart" with "Letter"

Carta means Letter
(cart)

From Pressley & Levin (1978)

and the corresponding English word. For example, the learner could imagine a large postal letter in a shopping cart, such as shown in Figure 8–1. In spite of some advice to the contrary (Lorayne & Lucas, 1974), it is not necessary that the image be unusual or bizarre.

In a typical experiment, Raugh & Atkinson (1975) asked college students to learn sixty Spanish-to-English vocabulary pairs in 15 minutes. Examples (with key words in parentheses) include: *charco* (charcoal) puddle; *gusano* (goose) worm; *nabo* (knob) turnip; *trigo* (tree) wheat. Experimental subjects were given pretraining in use of the key-word method. During learning, the key words were provided but the subjects had to generate their own images. Control subjects were given the same sixty vocabulary pairs including key words, for the same amount of time as the experimental group. These subjects were instructed to rehearse the pairs so they could perform well on the test. On a subsequent test, the experimenter read the Spanish words and asked the subjects to write the corresponding English definition. The experimental group scored 88% correct on this test compared to 28% for the control group. In another study involving Russian vocabulary, students who used the key-word method recalled 72%, compared to 46% for the control group (Atkinson & Raugh, 1975).

Based on these results, it appears that the key-word method is far more effective than other methods, such as rehearsal and recitation. In teaching college students, Raugh & Atkinson (1975) suggested that the key-word method works best when the instructor provides the key word (i.e., a short English word that sounds like part of the foreign language word) and when the learner is allowed to form his/her own image. However, Pressley and his colleagues (Pressley & Levin, 1978; Pressley, 1977; Pressley & Dennis-Rounds, 1980) have found that younger children have difficulty in spontaneously generating useful images even when they are trained to do so. Pressley & Dennis-Rounds (1980) found evidence that children as old as twelve do not spontaneously use the key-word method even when they have had training in how to use it. Thus Levin (1981) and Pressley (1977) suggest that when the subjects are children, the key-word method should be adapted to provide both key words and pictures.

As an example, consider how the key-word method could be adapted to help elementary school children learn English vocabulary. In a typical study (Levin, McCormick, Miller, Berry, & Pressley, 1982), fourth graders learned the definitions of twelve verbs such as: *celebrate, gesture, glisten, harvest, hesitate, intend, introduce, object, orbit, persuade, relate,* and *resolve.* Subjects in the experimental group learned a key word for each vocabulary word; the key word was a familiar word that sounded like a salient part of the vocabulary word, such as the key word "purse" for the vocabulary word *persuade.* Then the experimental subjects were given pictures that showed the key word interacting with the definition of the vocabulary word, such as a woman being *persuaded* to buy a "purse"; at the bottom of the picture was the vocabulary word's formal definition. The top panel of Figure 8–2 provides an example picture. The control subjects were given training in recognizing the words and were given sentences such as, "The lady's friend was trying to persuade her to buy a pocketbook." They also were given the formal definition for each word, in the same words as in the experimental group. Control subjects were given the same amount of time to learn the definitions and were told to use their "own best method." On a subsequent test, the key-word subjects recalled 83% of the definitions compared to 55% for the control subjects.

These results suggest recall is aided by giving children explicit pictures that connect the key word and its definition. However, Levin et al. (1982) also found that pictures that do not explicitly connect the vocabulary word to the key word, such as in the bottom panel of Figure 8–2, do not improve learning. Similarly, in another study (Levin et al., 1982), subjects who learned vocabulary with pictures that gave both the key word and the vocabulary word (e.g., top panel of Figure 8–3) remembered almost twice as many definitions as subjects who learned with pictures that failed to give the key word (e.g., bottom panel of Figure 8–3). These results suggest that pictures or key words alone are not enough to enhance memory in elementary school children; successful key-word techniques in children seem to require pictures showing both the key word and the vocabulary word.

In another series of experiments, Pressley, Levin, & McCormack (1980) used a modified version of the key-word method to teach Spanish-to-English vocabulary to fifth and second graders. All subjects learned the key word for each Spanish word, but unlike previous studies no pictures were used for the experimental group. Instead, the experimental group was instructed: "The Spanish word _____ sounds like _____ (key word) and means _____. Make up a sentence in your head about a _____ (key word) and a _____ (translation) doing something together in order to remember the meaning of _____ (Spanish word)." The control group was told: "The Spanish word _____ means _____. Try hard to remember that the

FIGURE 8–2   Key-Word Pictures for Learning the Definition of *Persuade*

A key-word picture that includes the vocabulary word

PERSUADE (PURSE)   When you talk someone into doing something

A key-word picture that omits the vocabulary word

PERSUADE (PURSE)   When you talk someone into doing something

From Levin, McCormick, Miller, Berry & Pressley (1982)

FIGURE 8–3   Key-Word Pictures for Learning the Definition of *Syrup*

A picture with keyword and vocabulary word

SURPLUS (SYRUP) having some left over, having more than was needed

A picture without keyword and with vocabulary word

SURPLUS having some left over, having more than was needed

From Levin, McCormick, Miller, Berry & Pressley (1982)

Spanish word _____ means _____." Although all subjects learned the same key words and spent the same time learning, the experimental group remembered more than twice as many Spanish-to-English vocabulary items as the control group—72% correct versus 27% correct, respectively.

Levin (1981) has reviewed research studies involving adapting the key-word method to various school tasks. In addition to teaching foreign language vocabulary and English vocabulary as previously described, the key-word method has been successfully applied to memorizing unfamiliar medical terminology, functions of various biochemicals, cities and their products, famous people and their accomplishments, states and capitals, and the U.S. presidents in order of their terms. For example, Jones & Hall (1982) gave eighth graders five 30-minute training sessions on how to use the key-word method for associating definitions with words, as well as other similar tasks. After training, several tests were given in order to see whether students would spontaneously use the memory strategies they had learned. One test involved names and facts such as, "Hamilton—designed the Coca-Cola bottle"; another test involved definitions of medical terms such as, "*duodenitis*—inflammation of the intestines"; a third test involved memory for thirty-six conceptually interrelated sentences; and the final test involved writing an essay. The results are shown in Table 8–1. As can be seen, the trained group performed much better on the tests that involved use of the key-word technique but not on tests that didn't involve the key-word technique as compared to the control group.

Loci, Pegword, and Chunking Methods for Learning Lists.   The key-word method is useful for memorizing paired associates (i.e., memorizing a certain response that goes with a certain stimulus). In addition, Higbee (1977) and Paivio (1971) have suggested several other mnemonic techniques that can be adapted to learning lists of items in order. Some of the more popular techniques for memorizing lists are: method of loci, pegword, and chunking strategies.

The method of loci (or place method) involves dividing a room or some other location into a series of places. For example, any room can be divided into fifty places as shown in Figure 8–4, as suggested by Feinaigle in 1813 (Paivio, 1971). As you can see, each wall contains nine spaces arranged as a tic-tac-toe board, with the entire wall counting as the tenth space. Now suppose you

TABLE 8–1   Proportion Correct on Four Tests for an Experimental and Control Group

	Key-Word Relevant Tests		Key-Word Irrelevant Tests	
Group	Names and Facts	Definitions	Recall	Essay
Experimental group (key-word training)	.89	.73	.44	.71
Control group	.59	.54	.53	.82

Adapted from Jones & Hall (1982)

wanted to memorize a list of fifty historic events in chronological order. During the memorization phase, you mentally associate the first item in the list with the first space on the first wall, the second item goes in the second space on the first wall, and so on. In the remembering phase, you simply look around the room at each space in order, and the items to be remembered will come bouncing back into consciousness.

The pegword method for memorizing a list is to associate the items in the

FIGURE 8–4 How to Find Fifty Memory Locations in a Room

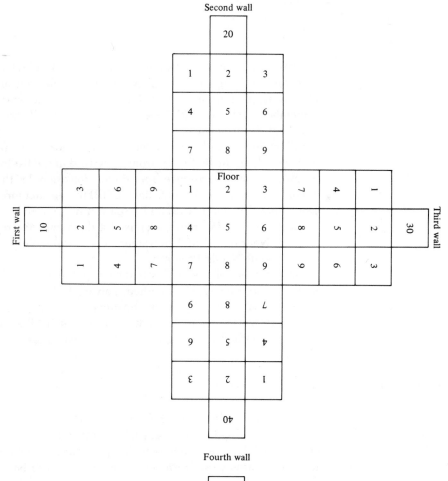

From Paivio (1971)

list with a well-known verbal series. For example, the standard rhyming pegword list is:

one is a bun
two is a shoe
three is a tree
four is a door
five is a hive
six are sticks
seven is heaven
eight is a gate
nine is a line
ten is a hen

Suppose you have a list of names to memorize. The first step is to associate the first word in the list with the pegword, bun, by forming an image involving the two words; then, form an image involving the second word, shoe, and so on. To remember, just start with "one is a bun" and recall the word associated with bun, and so on down the list.

Chunking is another mnemonic technique for remembering lists. Chunking involves taking the first letter from each word in the list to be remembered and forming a word or sentence from them. For example, the music student who needs to remember the staff lines EGBDF can memorize "Every Good Boy Does Fine." As another example, space travelers can remember the bodies in the solar system (Mercury, Venus, Earth, Mars, Asteroids, Jupiter, Saturn, Uranus, Neptune, Pluto) by remembering "Men Very Easily Make All Jobs Serve Useful Needs Promptly."

In a review of the research involving the method of loci, the pegword method, and the chunking method, Paivio (1971) found some support for their effectiveness, especially when the items to be remembered were common words. However, there has not been as much effort as there was for the key-word method in trying to test these techniques in school learning tasks.

Implications of Mnemonic Techniques

Suppose that children are required to learn foreign language vocabulary or definitions of English words as part of the regular instructional program. Some children will have no difficulty with this task and do not need special training in mnemonic strategies. However, some children will have great difficulty and, for them, training in mnemonics holds some promise. For example, this section has shown that learning of paired associates can be improved through explicit instruction in the key-word method.

The work of Pressley and Levin has shown that mnemonic strategies need to be adapted to the needs of the child. For example, in learning the key-word method, some children may not be able to form their own images and may need teacher-provided images. These children can benefit from practice in using teacher-imposed images to remember paired associates. Others may be able to form images on their own, but may need to be told to do so by the teacher. These children can benefit from practice in forming useful images for paired associates. Finally, for students who are proficient at using the key-word method but unsure about when to use it, practice is needed in recognizing paired-associate learning tasks. For various learning tasks, students could be asked, "Will using key words help you learn this material?"

STRUCTURE TRAINING TECHNIQUES

Example of Structure Training Techniques

Let's return to the reading comprehension task shown in Box 8–1. Suppose we wanted to help the reader to effectively organize the information in the passage (i.e., to see how the main ideas are related to one another). The reader could view the passage as a list of separate facts, as shown in the top of Box 8–2 or the reader could outline the material, as shown in the bottom of Box 8–2. In the outlined organization, the passage is broken into three main topics—location of the star, color of the star, and sources of weather prediction information. There are several facts that describe the location; this part of the structure could be called description. There are four colors, each predicting a different weather event; this part could be called collection. Finally, we can compare the star to traditional sources of information; this could be called comparison. Description, collection, and comparison structures are discussed in this section, along with several other ways of describing the organization of prose passages. In addition, this section explores the idea that training subjects to recognize typical prose structures can help them to organize the information more effectively in memory.

Theory: Building Internal Connections

In reading a passage such as the one in Box 8–1, part of your task is to identify the author's organization of the material (i.e., you must find the logical connections among main ideas in the passage). In a previous chapter, we referred to this process as "building internal connections." Students may need training in how to identify key ideas and connect them into a coherent organization.

Graesser (1981) has distinguished between *narrative prose*, such as stories, and *expository prose,* such as explanation of events or objects. This distinction is important, because there is ample evidence that students are better able to organize and remember narrative passages than expository passages that are equally complex (Graesser, Hauft-Smith, Cohen, & Pyles, 1980).

Rumelhart (1975) and Thorndyke (1977) have shown that the organization of stories can be represented using a "story grammar." For example, Thorndyke's (1977) story grammar involves the following rules:

1. A story consists of a setting, theme, plot, and resolution.
2. A setting consists of characters, location, and time.
3. A theme consists of a goal.
4. A plot consists of episodes.
5. A resolution consists of an event or state.
6. An episode consists of events and states.

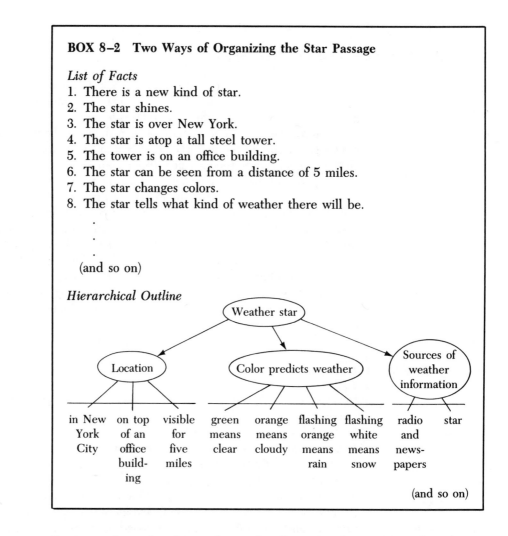

BOX 8–2   Two Ways of Organizing the Star Passage

List of Facts
1. There is a new kind of star.
2. The star shines.
3. The star is over New York.
4. The star is atop a tall steel tower.
5. The tower is on an office building.
6. The star can be seen from a distance of 5 miles.
7. The star changes colors.
8. The star tells what kind of weather there will be.
   .
   .
   .
(and so on)

Hierarchical Outline

Weather star

Location | Color predicts weather | Sources of weather information

in New York City | on top of an office building | visible for five miles | green means clear | orange means cloudy | flashing orange means rain | flashing white means snow | radio and newspapers | star

(and so on)

Stories can be analyzed into a hierarchy of events and states using this system. Several researchers have found that students tend to use story grammars for comprehending stories (see Chapter 11 on Reading Comprehension). Apparently, people have had a great deal of experience with stories and therefore have developed expectations about how events and states in stories can be organized.

In contrast, most people have not had extensive experience in reading expository prose, and therefore are less likely to possess strategies for organizing expository prose. Meyer, Brandt & Bluth (1980) have argued that readers may use a "default strategy" of organizing expository prose as a list of facts. One implication of this lack of experience is that students could profit from explicit training concerning expository prose structures. Successful training would help students to build internal connections among the central ideas in a passage. The outcome of such learning would be manifested in increased memory for the central ideas in a passage (rather than details) and in superior performance of problem-solving tests involving inference.

Research and Development on Structure Training Techniques

Learning to outline textbook material or lecture material is widely recognized in the folk wisdom of our culture as an important study skill. What evidence is there that outlining techniques improve learning, and how do such techniques work? This section explores three research and development efforts that have demonstrated effective techniques for teaching students how to outline—networking, top level structuring, and schema training.

Networking.   Suppose that you were asked to read a passage about wounds from a nursing textbook. To help you organize the material you could try to construct an outline. To do this, you must first identify and summarize each of the ideas in the text (i.e., what you will write on each line of the outline) and then you must determine how they are related to one another (i.e., which ideas are subordinate to which other ideas).

Dansereau and his colleagues (Dansereau, 1978; Dansereau, Collins, McDonald, Holley, Garland, Diekoff & Evans, 1979; Holley, Dansereau, McDonald, Garland & Collins, 1979) have developed a technique called *networking* that trains the student to identify ideas and relations among them. In a typical outline, the only kind of relation is subordination (i.e., one idea is subordinate to another). In order to help the student better understand the relationships among ideas in a passage, Dansereau and his colleagues have identified several kinds of links. As summarized in Table 8–2, the relation between one idea and another can be any of the following: part of, type of, leads to, analogous to, characteristic of, evidence for.

Figure 8–5 shows how the linking analysis can be used to build a network for a passage on wounds from a nursing textbook. As you can see, the discussion of wounds can be broken into two major parts: "types of wounds" and "process of wound healing." The "types of wounds" include "open," "closed," "accidental," and "intentional"; types of "open wounds" include "incision," "abrasion," "puncture," "laceration"; a characteristic of "open wounds" is that

TABLE 8–2   Six Types of Links for Expository Prose

	Hierarchy Structures	

Part (of) Link
 	
   hand
   ↑
   p
   ↓
   finger
	The content in a lower node is part of the object, process, idea, or concept contained in a higher node.	*Key Words*
		is part of
		is a segment of
		is a portion of

Type (of)/Example (of) Link
 	
   school
   ↑
   t
   ↓
   private
	The content in a lower node is a member or example of the class or category of processes, ideas, concepts, or objects contained in a higher node.	*Key Words*
		is a type of
		is in the category
		is an example of
		is a kind of
		Three procedures are

	Chain Structures	

Leads to Link
 	
   practice
   ↑
   1
   ↓
   perfection
	The object, process, idea, or concept in one node leads to or results in the object, process, idea, or concept in another node.	*Key Words*
		leads to
		results in
		causes
		is a tool of
		produces

	Cluster Structures	
Analogy Link ↑ College a factory	The object, idea, process, or concept in one node is analogous to, similar to, corresponds to, or is like the object, idea, process, or concept in another node.	*Key Words* is similar to is analogous to is like corresponds to
Characteristic Link sky c blue	The object, idea, process, or concept in one node is a trait, aspect, quality, feature, attribute, detail, or characteristic of the object, idea, process, or concept in another node.	*Key Words* has is characterized by feature is property is trait is aspect is attribute is
Evidence Link broken e X-ray arm	The object, idea, process, or concept in one node provides evidence, facts, data, support, proof, documentation, confirmation for the object, idea, process, or concept in another node.	*Key Words* indicates illustrated by demonstrated by supports documents is proof of confirms

From Holley et al. (1979)

FIGURE 8–5   A Network of a Chapter from a Nursing Textbook

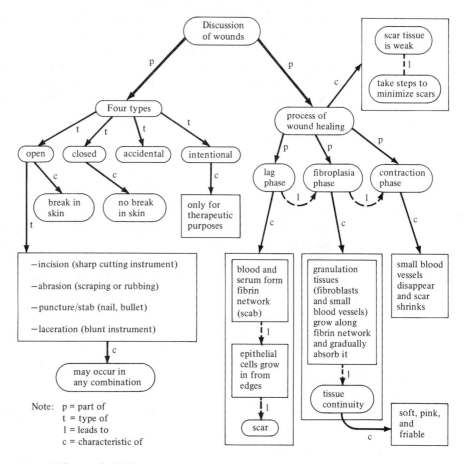

From Holley et al. (1979)

there is a "break in the skin"; and so on. Networking involves breaking a passage into parts (i.e., ideas) and then identifying the linking relations among the parts. The result is a pictorial representation of the passage, that is, a network.

Does networking training affect student learning? In order to test the effectiveness of networking training, Dansereau and his colleagues (Holley, Dansereau, McDonald, Garland, & Collins, 1979) trained college students to recognize types of links (such as in Table 8–2), to apply the networking procedure to sentences, to apply the networking procedure to passages, and, finally, to apply the networking procedure to their own textbooks. Training required approximately five and one half hours spread over four sessions. Networking-trained students and control students who received no training were then asked to study a 3000-word passage from a geology textbook. On subsequent tests including multiple choice, fill-in, short answer, and essay, the networking-trained subjects performed much better than the control subjects in remembering the main ideas but not in remembering the details. In addition, the positive effects of networking seemed to be particularly strong for students with low grade point averages, but not for students with high grade point averages. Apparently, high GPA students already have developed their own techniques for organizing prose material. These results are summarized in Figure 8–6.

In another study, students who took a "learning strategy class" that met for twelve 2-hour sessions were compared to a control group (Dansereau, Collins, McDonald, Holley, Garland, Deikhoff, & Evans, 1979). All students were given a pretest and post-test in which they read a 3000-word textbook passage and answered multiple choice and short-essay questions. Students who had received training in networking showed an improvement from a score of 47 on the pretest to a score of 57 on the post-test, whereas the control subjects averaged a score of 47 on both the pretest and the post-test. Other types of strategy training such as paraphrasing and forming mental images were not as successful as training in networking. Apparently, students can be trained to

FIGURE 8–6   **Proportion Correct on Post-tests for Networking and Control Groups**

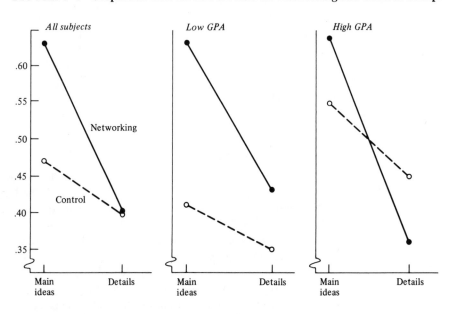

Adapted from Holley et al. (1979)

organize information as they study, and this training is useful for long textbook passages.

As you can see, networking involves using what Holley & Dansereau (1984) call a "spatial learning strategy." Other techniques that involve summarizing the structure of an expository prose passage in a diagram or chart include mapping (Armbruster & Anderson, 1984), schematizing (Camstra & van Bruggen, 1984; Mirande, 1984), and concept structuring (Vaughan, 1984). Although these techniques have not been subjected to as rigorous an empirical study as networking, there is some evidence that these spatial learning strategies are effective, especially for poorer readers and with difficult text (Holley & Dansereau, 1984).

Top-Level Structure Training.   Consider the supertanker passage in Box 8–3. If you were supposed to read this passage as part of a course assignment, you might try to outline it. However, Meyer and her colleagues (Meyer, 1975, 1981; Meyer, Brandt & Bluth, 1980) have found that there are certain basic outline forms, called top-level structures, that correspond to most expository passages, such as the supertanker passage. Five top-level structures are summarized in Table 8–3: covariance, comparison, collection, description, and response.

If a student knows about these kinds of structures, the student will have an easier time outlining the passage. Which structure corresponds to the supertanker passage? According to Meyer, the supertanker passage is based on a

TABLE 8–3   Five Top-Level Structures

Top-Level Structure	Definition	Example
Covariance	Causal relationship between antecedent and consequence.	"Lack of power and steering in supertankers" leads to "oil spills."
Comparison	Similarities and differences between two or more topics.	"Ground control stations for supertankers" are analogous to "control towers for aircraft."
Collection	Several objects or events or ideas belong to the same group or can be sequenced in time or space.	"Three ways to improve supertanker safety" are "training officers," "building safer ships," and "installing group control systems."
Description	General statement along with supporting detail, attribute, explanation, or setting.	"Oil spills kill wildlife" is exemplified by "200,000 seabirds died."
Response	Question and answer, problem and solution, or remark and reply.	"A problem is that supertankers spill oil" and "a solution is to improve their safety."

Adapted From Meyer (1975, 1981)

BOX 8–3   The Supertanker Passage

A PROBLEM OF VITAL CONCERN IS THE PREVENTION OF OIL SPILLS FROM SUPERTANKERS. A typical supertanker carries a half-million tons of oil and is the size of five football fields. A wrecked supertanker spills oil in the ocean; this oil kills animals, birds, and microscopic plant life. *For example,* when a tanker crashed *off the coast of England, more than 200,000 dead seabirds* washed *ashore*. Oil spills also kill microscopic plant life *which provide food for sea life and produce 70 percent of the world's oxygen supply*. Most wrecks RESULT FROM THE LACK of power and steering equipment to handle emergency situations, *such as storms. Supertankers have only one boiler to provide power and one propeller to drive the ship.*

THE SOLUTION TO THE PROBLEM IS NOT TO IMMEDIATELY HALT THE USE OF TANKERS ON THE OCEAN since about 80 percent of the world's oil supply is carried by supertankers. INSTEAD, THE SOLUTION LIES IN THE TRAINING OF OFFICERS OF SUPERTANKERS, BETTER BUILDING OF TANKERS, AND INSTALLING GROUND CONTROL STATIONS TO GUIDE TANKERS NEAR SHORE. First, OFFICERS OF SUPERTANKERS MUST GET top TRAINING in how to run and maneuver their ships. Second, tankers should be BUILT with several propellers *for extra control* and backup boilers *for emergency power*. Third, GROUND CONTROL STATIONS SHOULD BE INSTALLED at places where supertankers come close to shore. These stations would act like airplane control towers, guiding *tankers along busy shipping lanes and through dangerous channels*.

Note: Capitalized = message; lowercase = major details; italics = minor details; underlined = signaling.

From Meyer, Brandt & Bluth (1980)

"response" structure because it states a problem and a solution. Figure 8–7 shows how the supertanker passage can be broken down with "response" as its top-level structure as well as other structures in the lower parts of the passage.

Skill at identifying the top-level structure of a passage is a characteristic of good readers. In a recent study, Meyer, Brandt & Bluth (1980) asked ninth graders to read several passages including the supertanker passage and then take immediate and delayed recall tests. Table 8–4 shows that most good readers (as measured by a standard reading achievement test) recalled the top-level structure of the passage while most poor readers did not. In other

FIGURE 8–7 A Structural Analysis of the Supertanker Passage

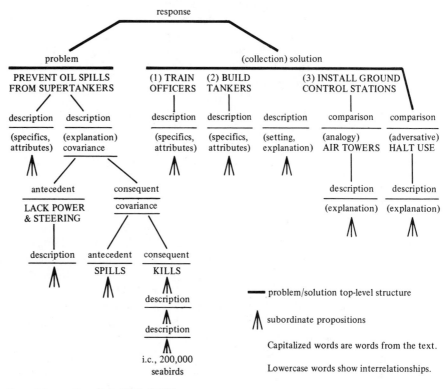

From Meyer, Brandt & Bluth (1980)

TABLE 8–4 Role of Top-Level Structure in Prose Learning

| | *Immediate Recall* | | |
Reading Level	Proportion of Subjects Using Author's Top-Level Structure	Amount Recalled by Subjects with Same Top-Level Structure as Author	Amount Recalled by Subjects with Different Top-Level Structure from Author
Good	.76	59	44
Average	.47	51	34
Poor	.19	48	23
	Delayed Recall		
Good	.49	43	22
Average	.31	38	14
Poor	.09	33	8

From Meyer, Brandt & Bluth (1980)

words, good readers were likely to organize their recall protocol for the super-tanker passage around the problem/solution format while most poor readers tended to organize recall as a list of facts. In addition, Table 8–4 shows that students who used the same top-level structure as the author also tended to recall more information from the passage. Similarly, Taylor (1980) found that use of top-level structure in students' recall was 82% for adults, 47% for good sixth-grade readers, and 12% for good fourth grade readers. Thus there is evidence that younger readers and poorer readers within an age-group do not spontaneously make use of the organizational structure of expository passages.

One implication of this research is that paying attention to a passage's structure is related to recall of information from the passage. Bartlett (1978; reported in Meyer, Brandt, & Bluth, 1980) trained ninth graders to identify four major types of top-level structures and to use the structures to organize recall. Other students (in a control group) received unrelated training from the teacher of the strategy training group. On tests of reading comprehension given before and after training, the strategy trained subjects showed much higher gains than the control group. Apparently, students can be taught to be sensitive to organizational structure of expository material, and using this organization leads to superior learning and memory of the material.

Schema Training.   Cook (1982) has also developed a training procedure called schema training to help students identify prose structures that are found in science textbooks. The five structures are: *generalization, enumeration, sequence, classification,* and *compare/contrast*. Examples and definitions are given in Box 8–4. As you can see, Cook's prose structures are somewhat different from those suggested by Meyer, although some structures are quite similar. One reason for the differences may be that Meyer's structures are based on general expository prose while Cook's structures are based on text-book passages found in chemistry, biology, and physics prose.

As a first step, Cook (1982) conducted a study to determine whether students could be taught to recognize the five structures summarized in Box 8–4. Some college students (structure training group) were given a booklet that described and exemplified the five structures while other subjects (control group) received no training. Then all subjects were given sheets containing twenty science passages (i.e., four passages for each of the five structure types); subjects were asked to sort the passages into five groups based on the structure of the material (rather than content). Results indicated that the structure training group correctly sorted 79% of the passages, compared to 61% correctly sorted passages for the control group. The next step in Cook's (1982) project was to provide an extensive training program to junior college students who were taking a chemistry course. The training involved an initial session in which students learned to recognize three types of prose structures—generalization, enumeration, and sequence. Subsequent training involved asking the student to fill out work sheets such as shown in Box 8–5; the subject filled out three work sheets for each of the three structures, based on nine sections from the students' chemistry textbook. The instructor provided feedback after each work sheet. In contrast, students from another section of the course received no training and served as a control group.

In order to assess the effectiveness of the training, Cook gave a pretest and post-test to all subjects. Each test consisted of reading three passages (i.e., generalization, enumeration, and sequence passages on science material other than chemistry); after reading, subjects were asked to recall each passage and to answer questions about verbatim details (retention questions) and about applying the information to solve a problem (problem-solving questions). Table 8–5 summarizes the results. As can be seen, the structure trained group showed an increase in recall of high-level information but not low-level information, as compared to the control group. Similarly, the structure trained group showed an increase in problem solving but not in retention of facts, as compared to the control group. Apparently, training in general prose structures can be applied to new passages, resulting in more coherent mental organization of the material.

Implications of Structure Training Techniques

Suppose that students are asked to read a chapter in their science textbook. Some students will read the material, and be able to correctly answer questions about the main concepts in the chapter. These students are able to figure out what is important and what is not important; if asked, these students would be able to provide an outline of the passage similar to the author's. These students do not need training in structure strategies.

In contrast, other students will read the material, perhaps even carefully read each word, and still not be able to correctly answer questions about the main ideas in the passage. These students are not aware of the way that sections of science books are organized, such as generalization or sequence or classification, and these students could not produce a coherent outline of the material. These students seem to be excellent candidates for training in structure strategies.

The research presented in this section shows that students can be taught to use effective strategies for organizing expository material. Two central features of successful training systems are: emphasis on specific types of structures (or

TABLE 8–5 Pre-test-to-Post-test Changes for Trained and Control Groups

Group	Recall		Retention of Facts	Problem Solving
	Low Level	High Level		
Trained	–4%	11%	14%	24%
Control	3%	0%	1%	–3%

Adapted from Cook (1982)

BOX 8–4   Five Prose Structures for Science Text

Generalization

1. Passage always has a main idea.
2. Most of the other sentences in the passage try to provide evidence for the main idea by either clarifying or extending.
   a. Explain the main idea by using examples or illustrations. These tend to *clarify* the main idea.
   b. Explain the main idea in more detail; *extend* the main idea.
3. Things to look for: definitions, principles, laws.
4. Reading objectives: Understand the main idea; be able to explain it in your own words, using the supporting evidence.

Example

Irritability is defined as an organism's capacity to respond to conditions outside itself. An organism responds to a stimulus from the environment. The stimulus may be light, temperature, water, sound, the presence of a chemical substance, or a threat to life. The organism's response is the way it reacts to a stimulus.

For example, a plant may have a growth response. This happens when a root pushes toward water or a stem grows unevenly and bends toward light.

Enumeration

1. List of facts one after the other.
2. There are two general kinds of enumeration passages:
   a. Specified—actually lists the facts by numbering them
   b. Unspecified—lists facts in paragraph form, with each fact stated in one or more sentences.
3. It is difficult to produce a single statement that summarizes the information accurately.
4. Reading objectives: Note the general topic; more important, though, is the retention of each subtopic or the individual facts.

Example

There are four general properties of solids:

1. Tenacity is a measure of a solid's resistance to being pulled apart.
2. Hardness is a measure of a substance's ability to scratch another substance.
3. Malleability refers to a solid's ability to be hammered or rolled into thin sheets.
4. Ductility is the ability to be drawn out in the form of wires.

Sequence

1. Describes a continuous and connected series of events or the steps in a process.
2. Examples of sequences include changes as the result of growth, a biological process, steps in an experiment or the evolution of some event.
3. Signal words: "The first step in," "stages," "and then."
4. Reading objectives:

Example

Hearing can be described in five separate stages. First, sound waves are captured by the external portion of the ear. The outer ear's function is to focus or concentrate these sound waves. During the second stage, the sound waves travel down the auditory canal (a tube embedded in the bones of the skull) and strike the tympanic membrane or eardrum. The third stage occurs

a. Be able to describe each step in the sequence.
b. Be able to tell the differences between each stage or step.

when the vibrations of the eardrum begin a series of similar vibrations in several small bones. These vibrations are then transmitted to the inner ear (called the cochlea) during the fourth stage. At this point, the vibrations are turned into neural impulses that are sent to the brain. The fifth and final stage of the hearing process represents the brain's interpretation of the sound patterns.

Classification

1. Groups or segregates material into classes or categories.
2. Develops a classification system to be used in the future to classify items.
3. Signal words: "can be classified," "are grouped," "there are two types of," etc.
4. Reading objectives:
   a. Know and be able to list class or grouping factors.
   b. Understand how the classes differ.
   c. Be able to classify new information.

Example

Experimental variables can be grouped into one of two categories; either a manipulated variable or a controlled variable. A variable that can be acted on directly is called a manipulated variable. The flow of steam into a room is an example of a manipulated variable, as it can be controlled directly. In contrast, a variable that can't be acted on directly is called a controlled variable. The temperature of a room is an example of a controlled variable because it must be achieved through manipulating another variable. In this case, it must be achieved through manipulating the flow of steam.

Compare/Contrast

1. Primary objective is to examine the relationship between two or more things.
2. Compare means to analyze *both* the similarities and differences while contrast focuses *only* on the differences.
3. Signal words include: "in contrast to," "the difference between," etc.
4. Reading objectives: be able to discuss similarities/differences between things.

Example

There are two different hypotheses for the origin of the earth: the nebular hypothesis and the comet-produced hypothesis. The nebular hypothesis maintains that our planet began in an aggregation of interstellar gas and dust. This theory is gaining more and more acceptance. In contrast, the comet-produced hypothesis states that the earth began as a piece of the sun that was ripped out by a comet. The first hypothesis assumes the earth began as small elements which combined into larger ones. The latter hypothesis asserts the earth was essentially already formed when it began taking on its present-day characteristics.

From Cook (1982)

BOX 8–5   Work Sheets for Generalization, Enumeration, and Sequence Passages

Generalization
Step 1:   Identify the generalization (main idea).

List and define key words in the generalization.

Word   Definition

Restate the generalization in your own words.

Step 2:   What kind of support is there for the generalization? Does it use examples, illustrations? Does it extend or clarify the generalization?

Supporting Evidence   Relation to Generalization

Enumeration
Step 1:   What is the general topic?

Step 2:   Identify the subtopics.
A.
B.
C.
D.
•
•
•

Step 3:   Organize and list the details within each subtopic. (Do one subtopic at a time, use your own words.)
A.
B.
C.
D.
•
•
•

Sequence
Step 1:   Identify the topic of the passage.

Step 2:   Take each step, name it, and then outline the details within each:

```
                 Step 1
                 Step 2
                 Step 3
                 Step 4
                   •

                   •

                   •


Step 3:   Discuss (briefly) what is different from one step to the next.
          Step 1 to 2
          Step 2 to 3
          Step 3 to 4
            •

            •

            •
```

From Cook (1982)

schemas) commonly found in expository prose and extensive practice in recognizing and applying these structures when actually reading textbooks.

The initial step in structure training is to define explicitly each of the major prose structures that the student is likely to find in the textbook. This section gave examples of three different systems—networking, top-level structuring, and schema training—but they all begin by teaching the student about a small set of structures. Since different subject matter domains rely on different types of structures (e.g., biology emphasizes classification while chemistry emphasizes sequence), the teacher needs to choose about five basic structures that are most commonly used in the class's textbook. Then, students need practice in recognizing which paragraphs in the textbook correspond to which structures.

The second major step is to help students outline their textbook, based on the underlying prose structure. For example, once a student recognizes that a paragraph is "generalization," then the student should be able to list the main assertion followed by supporting evidence. Feedback from the teacher (or other models) is useful so the student can compare his or her outline to the teacher's.

Structure training is likely to be most useful for less skilled readers—since skilled readers presumably possess organizing skills—and for unfamiliar expository material—since students have more experience with the structure of stories. Unlike the mnemonic techniques discussed in the preceding section, structure training should be used when the goal of instruction is to help the learner determine what is important versus what is unimportant in expository material.

GENERATIVE TECHNIQUES

Example of Generative Techniques

The preceding section explored ways to help the learner to become familiar with specific prose structures such as sequence and generalization. Another approach to learning strategy training is to teach students to use general strategies. For example, in reading the star passage (Box 8–1), we could teach a student to take notes or underline. Box 8–6 shows three different ways of taking notes for the star passage—verbatim copying, outlining the main ideas, and relating the main ideas to existing knowledge.

BOX 8–6 Three Approaches to Note Taking for the Star Passage

Verbatim Copying
A new kind of star
shining over New York
top of a tall steel tower
seen from a distance of five miles
tells by changing its color what kind of weather
    .
    .
    .

Outline
Colors (1) green = clear
       (2) orange = cloudy
       (3) flashing orange = rain
       (4) flashing white = snow
    .
    .
    .

Analogy
weather star is like litmus paper—put it in air and it turns color corresponding to precipitation in air
normal clear air causes no change so it stays green
some clouds cause change to orange
    .
    .
    .

Theory: Manipulating Cognitive Processes

Rothkopf (1970) has coined the term, "mathemagenic activity" to refer to any activity of the learner that "gives birth to knowledge." For example, taking notes, underlining, answering questions, or repeating aloud all are mathemagenic activities. Similarly, Wittrock (1974) has argued that "learning is a generative process," in which the learner must actively generate the relations between ideas. Some activities such as note taking may help some students to engage in generative processing.

Generative or mathemagenic activities such as note taking can have several quite different effects on a learner's cognitive processing in terms of:

Directing attention—Note-taking activities could focus the student's attention on a very limited amount of information.

Building internal connections—Note-taking activities could help the learner to see how one part of the passage is related to another (e.g., could help the reader find the main idea and its supporting evidence).

Building external connections—Note-taking activities could help the learner to relate the information presented to existing knowledge.

The remainder of this section explores these three alternatives.

Research and Development on Generative Techniques

Suppose that students could be freed from the act of taking notes. In lecture classes, for example, students could receive the notes of an expert note taker after each class, such as from note-taking services that are now common on many college campuses. Do students learn differently when they take notes versus when they do not take notes? The results presented in this section show that the answer to this question is "yes"; as you will see, generative activities such as active note taking influence the learning process. The present section explores how the act of note taking can affect three aspects of a student's cognitive processing during learning: paying attention, building internal connections, building external connections.

Note Taking for Guiding Attention. In some cases, note taking could serve to direct the learner's attention towards some material and away from other material. For example, Aiken, Thomas & Sheenum (1975) found that material that was in a learner's notes was twice as likely to be recalled as material that was not in the learner's notes. Similar results have been reported by Howe (1970), by Carrier & Titus (1981), and by Barnett, DiVesta, & Rogozinski (1981), even when students are not allowed to review their notes.

Note taking could serve not only to focus attention, but also could limit the amount of attention available during learning. The limiting effects of note taking are strongest when the presentation rate is fast, when the material is difficult or technical, when the learner is not given a chance to review the notes, or when the learner lacks efficient encoding skills (Aiken, Thomas & Shennum, 1975; Faw & Waller, 1976). For example, Peters (1972) found that note taking resulted in poorer test performance than no note taking; the material was presented at a fast pace with no pauses for review of notes, and the negative effects of note taking were strongest for the poorer students. The detrimental effects of concurrent note taking can be eliminated by allowing learners time to review their notes (Carter & Van Matre, 1975; Crawford, 1925). In studies using slower presentation rates or shorter passages, note taking even without review resulted in superior retention as compared to no note taking (DiVesta & Gray, 1973; Fisher & Harris, 1973). In addition, when students were allowed to read at their own rates, note taking enhanced retention (Kulhavy, Dyer & Silver, 1975; Bretzing & Kulhavy, 1981).

Note Taking for Building Internal Connections.   Note taking can also serve to help the learner organize the material (e.g., by building internal connections). For example, Shimmerlick & Nolan (1976) presented a 1220-word anthropology lesson to students for 9 minutes. One version of the passage was organized by society (i.e., giving the attributes of one society and then the next society, and so on). Another version of the passage was organized by attribute (i.e., telling how each of four societies dealt with one aspect of life, and then how they all dealt with the next aspect of life, and so on.) Some subjects were asked to take sequential notes (i.e., to follow the order of ideas given in the passage). Other subjects were asked to take notes that reorganized the material; for example, if the subject read a version of the passage organized by society, then the notes should use attribute as the main topics.

Figure 8–8 shows that the group who took reorganizing notes recalled more of the passage on an immediate test than the sequential notes group as well as on a delayed test given one week later. In addition, the figure shows that the effects of reorganizing note taking were particularly strong for students who were not above average in verbal ability. Students in the reorganizing group took notes that encouraged active construction of a coherent structure for the passage. Apparently, reorganizing elicited constructive processes that would not otherwise be used by average readers. DiVesta, Schultz, & Dangel (1973) reported similar findings in a study where subjects were trained and instructed to engage in reorganization or sequential organization of material.

Barnett, DiVesta & Rogozinski (1981) asked subjects to listen to an 1800-word passage on the history of roads in America. The passage was presented at a moderately slow rate of 120 words per minute to college students. Note takers were asked to identify the main ideas and to outline them. Thus, in this experiment, subjects in the note-taking group were encouraged to actively organize the material and were given sufficient time to do so. Other subjects were given a printed outline of the material to use during listening to the passage, but were not allowed to take their own notes. Finally, a control group listened to the passage without an outline or notes. The results are summarized in Figure 8–9. As can be seen, subjects who actively organized the lecture into

FIGURE 8–8   Effects of Note Taking on Recall Reorganization

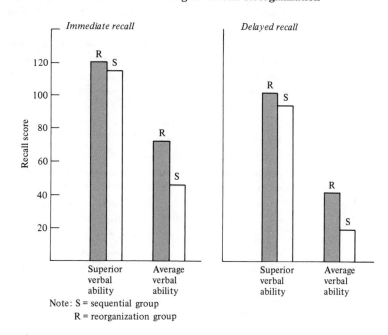

Note: S = sequential group
R = reorganization group

Adapted from Shimmerlick & Nolan (1976)

FIGURE 8–9   Recall Scores for Three Groups

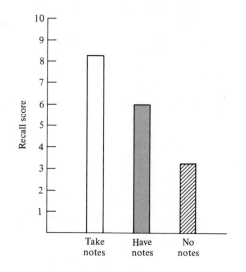

Adapted from Barnett, DiVesta, & Rogozinski (1981)

an outline recalled more than subjects who did not take notes. In addition, if subjects were encouraged to outline the material or elaborate on the material during a subsequent review period, these activities increased the performance of the non-note-taking subjects but not of the note-taking group. Apparently, the note takers had already formed a coherent outline of the material during presentation.

Other ways of encouraging students to identify the internal connections in a passage include summary note taking and underlining. In a summary note-taking study, Doctorow, Wittrock, & Marks (1978) asked elementary school children to read a passage and then recall the passage. Some students were asked to generate a summary sentence that expressed the main idea for each paragraph (summary group); some students were given a two-word heading for each paragraph that summarized the main idea (heading group); some students received both treatments (summary and heading group); and some subjects read the passage without headings or summary note taking.

Figure 8–10 summarizes the results on a subsequent retention test for good readers who were given a 1125-word passage for 20 minutes and for poor readers who were given a 372-word passage for 8 minutes. As can be seen, for both good and poor readers, the summary group retained more than 50% more information as compared to the control group, and this advantage was enhanced when headings were provided for each paragraph.

FIGURE 8–10   Effects of Summary Note Taking and Headings on Prose Comprehension

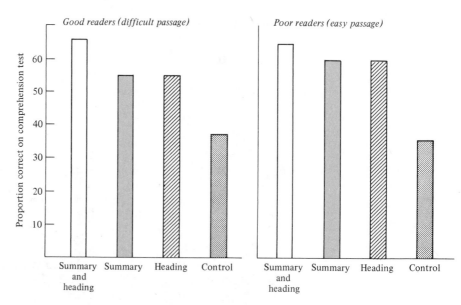

Adapted from Doctorow, Wittrock & Marks (1978)

Wittrock (1974) argues that subjects who write summaries engage in "generative learning"—generating connections among ideas in the passage rather than memorizing specific words. Because the process of generative learning is idiosyncratic, summarizing activities should free the learner to take notes in a way that is best for each individual.

Note Taking for Building External Connections. Finally, under some conditions, note taking may help the learner to build external connections (i.e., to relate the information presented to existing knowledge). The subject may be encouraged to explain an idea in his/her own words or to relate information to a familiar concrete model. For example, Mayer (1980) asked college students to read a manual on computer programming with one programming command described on each page. For some subjects, after each page they were asked to explain the command in their own words and relate it to a concrete familiar situation (elaboration group). Other students read each page without elaborating (non-elaboration group). Subjects in the elaboration group tended to recall more conceptual information from the booklet and to perform better on problem-solving tests that involved applying commands to new tasks as compared to the nonelaboration group. However, the nonelaboration group performed just as well as the elaboration group on recall of details from the manual and on solving problems just like those given in the manual. Apparently, elaborative note taking encouraged readers to relate the presented information to what they already knew.

In a similar series of studies, Peper & Mayer (1978, 1986) asked college and high school students to view a 15-minute videotaped lecture on computer programming or statistics. Some subjects were asked to take notes during the lecture while others were not allowed to take notes. Following the lesson, students were given problem-solving tests that included problems like those given during the lecture (near transfer) and problems that required creative use of the information in new situations (far transfer).

Figure 8–11 shows that for low ability subjects, the note-taking group excelled on far transfer whereas the non-note-taking group excelled on near transfer. For high ability subjects, note taking increases performance by a modest amount on both types of questions. If note-taking served mainly to focus the learner's attention, we would expect superior performance on problems like those given in the lesson; if note taking served mainly to elicit integrative processing (i.e., building external connections), then we would expect better performance on tests of creative transfer. Thus the increase in far transfer performance is most consistent with the idea that note taking in this study resulted in building external connections.

In addition, subsequent recall tests revealed that note takers excelled mainly on recall of conceptual information but not on recall of specific details and that note takers produced more "intrusions" about information that was not in the booklet. If note taking served mainly to focus attention on the main facts in the lesson, we would expect better recall of specific facts. If note taking helped the learner to construct coherent external connections, we would

FIGURE 8–11   Effects of Note Taking on Creative Problem Solving

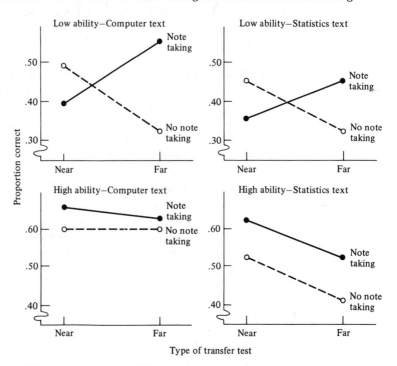

Adapted from Peper & Mayer (1978)

expect better recall of the basic conceptual principles in the passage. These results are consistent with the idea that when appropriate dependent measures are used—such as far transfer or recall of concepts—evidence for integrative processing emerges.

It should be pointed out that some more restricted forms of note taking may not elicit the building of external connections. For example, Mayer & Cook (1980) asked subjects to listen to a passage about how radar works. Some subjects were asked to repeat each phrase verbatim, during pauses in the presentation. Verbatim shadowing of the passage resulted in poorer performance on memory for the conceptual principles and on creative problem solving, as compared to a control group that simply listened to the passage. Thus verbatim copying seems unlikely to lead to the building of external connections even though the learner is being forced to be "active."

Implications of Generative Techniques

Suppose that a class is listening to a lecture on American history. Does this mean that learning must be a passive process, in which the students simply take the teacher's words and put them in their memories? This section has shown that learning—even learning from lecture—can be an active process. The student can control the learning process by using generative techniques such as note taking or summarizing.

When the goal of instruction is verbatim retention of specific facts, then verbatim copying (or underlining in textbooks) guides the learner's attention. When the goal of instruction is long-term retention and transfer, then students need to engage note taking or summarizing procedures that are aimed at building connections among ideas. Note taking can be an exercise that requires the student to determine what is important and what is not important, and a process that requires linking the new information to existing knowledge.

The active cognitive processing elicited by these forms of note taking presumably can be taught. Some students spontaneously take effective notes and do not need generative training. Other students will take effective notes only when told to do so. These students need practice in note taking and in seeing how note taking can improve their test performance. Finally, some students do not know how to take effective notes. These students need practice in taking notes, and in comparing their notes to those of "experts," such as the teacher or other students.

In summary, note taking is not necessarily a mindless chore with no benefit to the learner. On the contrary, in learning to take notes, a student can learn how to control his or her cognitive processes—including guiding attention, finding organization in what is presented, and relating what is presented to what one already knows.

CONCLUSION

This chapter has explored three types of learning strategies—mnemonic strategies aimed at increasing the amount of information learned, structure training aimed at helping students build internal connections, and generative activities aimed at helping students build external connections.

Several mnemonic techniques have been repeatedly shown to be successful, including the key-word method, method of loci, pegword method, and chunking method. However, there are developmental differences in students' ability to learn and spontaneously use some of these strategies.

Structure training has also been successful in helping students to recognize and use expository prose structures, such as cause-and-effect or sequence-of-events. This kind of training seems to have its strongest effects on transfer performance. Chapter 11 (Reading Comprehension) provides some additional examples of classroom research on the development of children's awareness that some pieces of information are more important than others.

Generative activities include note taking, summarizing, and underlining. Many of the more sophisticated generative activities are aimed at building external connections, and show their strongest effects on tests of transfer.

Chapter 11 provides some additional examples of classroom research on helping students learn how to make inferences while reading.

The theme of this chapter is that teaching of learning strategies is an appropriate instructional activity, although in practice very little time is devoted to teaching students how to learn (Weinstein & Mayer, 1985). Teaching a child how to remember information, how to determine what is important, or how to figure out the theme of a passage may be just as important for the child's academic success as teaching a child specific facts and concepts. This chapter has shown how learning strategies can be taught effectively within regular subject matter contexts (i.e., using textbook material that is part of the regular program). In the course of teaching science or history, for example, the teacher can also help the student learn how to effectively read, process, and remember the material in a textbook.

The appropriateness of strategy training also depends on the teacher's goals. When the goal is to help students memorize paired associates as in foreign language vocabulary, then mnemonic techniques are warranted. When the goal is to teach students how to figure out what is important and what is not important in a passage, then structure training techniques are called for. When the goal is to determine the theme of the passage, then generative techniques can be taught. The appropriateness of any strategy training also depends partly on the learner (e.g., whether or not the learner would normally use the strategy). Before strategy training is carried out, each child should be tested to determine whether they know how to use a particular strategy. If a child is already proficient in using a strategy, training is not needed for that child.

SUGGESTED READINGS

Hayes, J. R. (1981). *The complete problem solver*. Philadelphia: Franklin Institute Press. (Part II on "Memory and Knowledge Acquisition" summarizes learning strategies based on psychological research.)

Holley, C. D. & Dansereau, D. F. (1984). *Spatial learning strategies*. New York: Academic Press. (Describes techniques for summarizing the organization of expository passages as visual diagrams or charts.)

O'Neil, H. F. (ed.) (1978). *Learning strategies*. New York: Academic Press. (A collection of papers by leading researchers and developers of learning strategy programs.)

Pressley, M. & Levin, J. R. (eds.) (1983). *Cognitive strategies training and research*. New York: Springer-Verlag. (An integrated review of modern research on learning strategies.)

9

Instruction for Thinking Strategies

Problem solving is a skill that can be learned just like any other skill. This is the premise that is explored in Chapter 9. In particular, this chapter investigates research on teaching problem-solving skills for school tasks.

HOW TO BOOST PERFORMANCE IN PROBLEM SOLVING

In the Spanish language, the article *el* or *la* precedes singular nouns. Here are some examples:

> *el rio*
> *la casa*
> *el camino*
> *la boca*
> *la biblioteca*
> *el libro*

As a test, you can try to fill in the article (*el* or *la*) for the following nouns:

_____ *palabra*
_____ *huevo*
_____ *plaza*

This is an example of an inductive reasoning task. In this case you are given a series of examples, and you must induce a general rule, such as "put *el* with words that end with *o* and put *la* with words that end with *a*." Thus your answers would be: *la, el, la*. In inductive reasoning, your job is to form a rule. Other examples include concept learning and learning of grammar rules.

Suppose that someone made the following assertion, "If you get bitten by a black widow spider that has a red dot on its tummy, then you will get sick." Also suppose that you have four ways of testing this assertion:

1. You get bitten by a black widow spider that has a red dot, and check to see whether or not you get sick.
2. You get bitten by a black widow spider that does not have a red dot, and check to see whether or not you get sick.
3. You get sick from a black widow spider bite, and then check to see whether or not the spider has a red dot on its belly.
4. You do not get sick from a black widow spider bite, and then check to see whether or not the spider has a red dot on its belly.

Which of these four tests do you need to carry out in order to determine whether the "law of red dots" is false?

In order to solve this problem, you must logically compare each of the tests with the "if . . . then" rule. According to Wason (1968; Johnson-Laird & Wason, 1977), who used a different version of this task, the most likely answer is to choose tests 1 and 3; however, the correct answer is to choose tests 1 and 4. In test 1, if you do not get sick, then the rule is wrong. In test 4, if the spider has a red dot, then the rule is wrong. In contrast, tests 2 and 3 cannot conflict with the rule regardless of the outcome, because the rule does not make a prediction concerning whether or not you'll get sick if the spider does *not* have a red dot.

This is an example of a deductive reasoning task. In deductive reasoning, you are given all of the relevant information—called premises—and your job is to use the premises to draw logical conclusions. In short, your job is to logically apply a rule. Other examples of deductive reasoning include solving algebra equations or syllogisms.

Now, let's try one last problem. Suppose that in the future, humans were able to control the weather. What consequences would follow? Write down as many consequences as you can think of in two minutes.

_____

_____

_____

_____

_____

_____

_____

_____

This is an example question that requires creative problem solving according to Olton & Covington (1969). In particular, Guilford (1950, 1959) defined "divergent thinking" problems as those requiring the generation of many alternatives rather than a specific correct answer. To evaluate your answer on a divergent thinking problem, we could use the following measures:

Fluency—how many acceptable answers you were able to generate in a given period of time;

Originality—how many of your answers were different from those suggested by other people, and

Importance—such as ratings by judges of how useful your answers are in solving the problem.

As you can see, your job in a divergent thinking task is not to logically use a rule in order to find the answer, but rather to generate alternatives.

Inductive, deductive, and divergent thinking are three basic types of thinking. Getzels & Jackson (1963) have pointed out that most school problem-solving tasks emphasize deductive and inductive thinking—forming and using rules—rather than divergent thinking—coming up with creative ideas. In addition, although there is a positive correlation between performance on tests of intelligence (as measured mainly by inductive and deductive reasoning) and tests of creativity (as measured mainly by tests of divergent thinking), some students are high in intelligence and low in creativity, and vice versa. Getzels & Jackson (1963) found that teachers seemed to prefer high intelligence students to high creative students, presumably because the high intelligence students were more conventional in their behavior and more responsive to the teacher's authority.

In this chapter we explore the issue of whether we can teach our students to become better thinkers. For example, this chapter investigates whether there are ways to improve students' skills in inductive, deductive, and especially in creative thinking. In addition, this chapter explores the question of how "thinking-strategies training" should be incorporated into the curriculum.

WHAT MAKES AN EFFECTIVE
PROBLEM-SOLVING PROGRAM?

Consider the following scenerio: The country you live in has decided to make a national commitment to improving the intellectual performance of its citizens. The nation's president has appointed you as the first "Minister of State for the Development of Human Intelligence." What can you do to improve the people's problem-solving skills?

Although this may seem like an artificial problem, it is a real problem for Dr. Luis Alberta Machado. Dr. Machado was recently appointed to head the new Ministry for the Development of Human Intelligence in the country of Venezuela, the first such ministry in the world. Minister Machado (1981, pp. 3–4) summarized the rationale for his ministry as follows:

> In the same way that investment of resources and political strategy are planned so should the different nations by means of a common effort, plan the attainment of a higher degree of intelligence in the least time possible by all mankind. . . . When the necessary means are organized to systematically improve the intelligence of all people, mankind will have taken the most important step towards progress.

Similarly, Dominguez (1985, p. 531) notes that "in Venezuela we are attempting to put these ideas about the modifiability of human intelligence to work in the service of mankind." Although the Venezuela project is just beginning, it represents an important effort to teach thinking skills on a massive scale.

If you were in a position like Dr. Machado's, there are several questions you might want to ask concerning the teaching of problem-solving skills. First, what are the teachable aspects of problem solving? Second, how should problem-solving skills be taught? Third, how much transfer to new problem-solving tasks should we expect? Each of these issues is addressed in this section.

What Are the Teachable Aspects of Problem Solving?

Many Cognitive Skills Versus One General Ability.   The first major issue concerns whether there are many smaller skills that together account for a person's intellectual ability (cognitive skills theory) or whether there is one single general intellectual ability (general intelligence theory). Although this topic is addressed more fully in Chapter 16, most theories of intellectual ability correspond to the cognitive skills theory. For example, based on his studies of individual differences among French school students, Binet (1911/1962, p. 150) offered one of the first arguments for the cognitive skills theory:

> . . . intelligence is not a simple indivisible function with a particular essence of its own . . . but, it is formed by the combination of all the minor functions . . . all of which have proved to be plastic and subject to increase. With practice, enthusiasm,

and especially with method, one can succeed in increasing one's attention, memory, and judgment, and in becoming literally more intelligent than before; and this process will go on until one reaches one's limit.

Binet (1911/1962, p. 150) devised a series of exercises that he called "mental orthopedics": "In the same way that physical orthopedics straightens a crooked spine, mental orthopedics strengthens, cultivates, and fortifies attention, memory, perception, judgment, and will."

If you accept Binet's assertions that intellectual performance is based on "small" intellectual skills that can be identified and taught, the next task becomes one of trying to better describe these skills. The cognitive approach to thinking is based on the idea that intellectual performance can be analyzed into component processes (Mayer, 1981), including the following:

> *Representational processes*—for building a coherent and useful internal representation of the problem, and
>
> *Solution processes*—for planning, carrying out, and monitoring a plan.

The specific representational and solution processes may depend on the specific intellectual task.

Using a cognitive approach, for example, Hayes (1981), Wickelgren (1974), and Bransford & Stein (1984) have designed problem-solving courses that teach strategies for representation of problems and searching for solutions. Some suggestions for representational strategies are: relate the problem to a previous problem, restate the problem in other words, draw a picture or diagram, etc. Some suggestions for searching include: work from the goal to the givens, break the problem into subgoals, only make moves that solve a particular subproblem.

Polya's Teaching of Problem Solving. Polya's (1945, 1965) program for teaching problem solving has influenced the development of many more recent programs. For example, Polya's (1965, p. 8) observations of high school mathematics students lead him to emphasize techniques for representing and planning problem solutions:

> I wish to call heuristics . . . the study of the means and methods of problem solving. . . . I am trying, by all means at my disposal, to entice the reader to do problems and to think about the means and methods he uses in doing them. . . . What is presented here are not merely solutions but case histories of solutions. Such a case history describes the sequence of essential steps by which the solution has been eventually discovered, and tries to disclose the motives and attitudes prompting these steps. The aim . . . is to suggest some general advice or pattern which may guide the reader in similar situations.

In short, Polya argues that students should be asked to solve problems and to observe others solve problems, with the emphasis on the process of problem solving rather than on the final answer. Some of the heuristics suggested by

Polya are: find a related problem that you can solve, break the problem down into smaller parts, draw a picture of the problem.

In his classic little book, *How to Solve It,* Polya (1945) offered a four-step general procedure for solving problems, especially mathematics problems. The four steps are:

1. Understand the problem. The problem solver must see what is given, what is unknown, and what operations are allowed. In short, the problem solver must represent the problem.
2. Devise a plan. The problem solver must determine a general course of attack, such as restating the problem so it is more like a familiar problem.
3. Carry out the plan. The problem solver must carry out the computations and other needed operations.
4. Look back. The problem solver looks over the processes he/she went through, trying to see how this experience can be helpful in solving other problems.

Box 9–1 provides an example of how these four steps can be applied to the problem of finding the volume of the frustrum of a right pyramid.

Although Polya's ideas have been highly influential, especially among some mathematics educators, you might wonder whether there is any evidence that problem-solving heuristics (or skills) can be taught. In order to help answer that question, Schoenfeld (1979) taught heuristics for mathematical problem solving to college students. The trained group was given a five-problem pretest, training on how to solve twenty example problems, and then a five-problem post-test. The trained group was given a list and description of heuristics such as partially shown in Box 9–2. Then, in each session all the problems were solvable by the same heuristic and subjects were explicitly told which heuristic to apply to the problems. The control group received the same pretest, the same twenty example problems, and the same post-test as the trained group.

BOX 9–1   Polya's Four Steps in Problem Solving

PROBLEM

Find the volume of the frustrum of a right pyramid with a square base, given the altitude of the frustrum, the length of a side of its upper base, and the length of a side of its lower base.

STEP 1: Understand the Problem.

What is Given?
The altitude, the length of the upper base, the length of the lower base.

What is Unknown?
The volume of the frustrum.

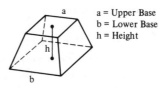

a = Upper Base
b = Lower Base
h = Height

STEP 2: Devise a Plan.

Is There a Related Problem?
The volume of a right pyramid can be obtained as follows:

$$\text{Volume} = \frac{(\text{Base})^2 \times (\text{Height})}{3}$$

Can You Restate the Unknown?
Find the volume of the large pyramid minus the volume of the small pyramid.

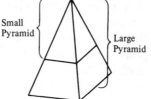

Small Pyramid

Large Pyramid

STEP 3: Carry out the Plan.

Calculate volume of large pyramid.
Calculate volume of small pyramid.
Subtract the second from the first.

STEP 4: Look Back.

This technique can be applied to other problems such as : Find the area of a donut, given the radius to the inside and outside.

Adapted from Polya (1968).

BOX 9–2   Five Problem-Solving Strategies Taught by Schoenfeld

The Five Problem-Solving Strategies
1. Draw a diagram if at all possible.
2. If there is an integer parameter, look for an inductive argument.
3. Consider arguing by *contradiction* or *contrapositive*.
   Contrapositive: Instead of proving the statement "If X is true, then Y is true," you can prove the equivalent statement "If Y is false, then X must be false."
   Contradiction: Assume, for the sake of argument, that the statement you would like to prove is false. Using this assumption, go on to prove either that one of the given conditions in the problem is false, that something you know to be true is false, or that what you wish to prove is true. If you can do any of these, you have proved what you want.
4. Consider a similar problem with fewer variables.
5. Try to establish subgoals.

Adapted from Schoenfeld (1979)

However, the control group was not given a list of heuristics (as in Box 9–2) and the problems in each session were not all solvable by the same heuristic.

The results showed that the trained group increased from an average score of 20% correct on the pretest to 65% on the post-test, whereas the control group averaged 25% correct on both tests. Although the sample size was small in this study, the results suggest that it is possible to identify teachable aspects of problem solving—in this case, some Polya-like heuristics within the domain of mathematics.

Criterion 1: Teach Component Skills.   In summary, problem solving can be broken down into individual representational or solution strategies that can be taught. Training in problem solving involves teaching students the component processes in problem solving. The particular list of problem-solving strategies (or skills) tends to vary depending on the subject matter of the problems to be solved. The implications for the design of a problem-solving program are that the content of the course should be definable skills for representing and solving problems, including skills for planning and monitoring one's plans. In subsequent sections of this chapter, some of the specific content of problem-solving programs will be explored.

How Should Problem-Solving Skills Be Taught?

Process Versus Product.   Once a set of problem-solving skills has been identified, the next issue concerns how to teach these skills to students. "We should be teaching students how to think; instead we are primarily teaching them what to think." So asserts Lochhead (1979, p. 1) in the introduction to the book he wrote with John Clement, *Cognitive Process Instruction*. What Lochhead and others are saying is that teachers are currently emphasizing "product" (i.e., getting the right answer) instead of "process" (i.e., how to go about solving problems).

Bloom & Broder's Teaching of Problem Solving. In one of the first experimental research studies on teaching problem solving, Bloom & Broder (1950) carried out a program to improve the problem-solving performance of college students at the University of Chicago. The university required that students pass a series of comprehensive examinations in subject matter areas. As you might expect, some students (called "model students") performed quite well on the exams. In contrast, other students (called "remedial students") who were just as motivated, studied just as hard, and scored just as high in scholastic aptitude, were unable to pass the exams. Although the model and remedial students seemed equivalent in ability, knowledge, and motivation, the remedial students apparently lacked skills necessary to answer the questions. Thus Bloom & Broder tried to develop a training program to help the remedial students think like the model students for exam questions.

In determining what to teach, Bloom & Broder distinguished between:

Products of problem solving—whether or not the student produced the correct answer, and
Process of problem solving—the thought process that a person engages in.

Box 9–3 shows a problem and the answers given by three students. As you can see, although the students generated the same final answer, their descriptions of how they generated the answer are quite different. Bloom & Broder decided that the training program for remedial students should focus on teaching of useful problem-solving strategies rather than on reinforcing students for emitting correct answers.

In determining how to teach, Bloom & Broder decided to let remedial students compare their solution strategies with those used by the model students. Using a "thinking aloud" procedure, remedial students were asked to describe their thought process for a problem, and model students were asked to describe their thought process for the same problem. Then, the remedial students were asked to find the differences between how they solved the problem and how the model students solved the problem. For example, Box 9–4 shows a list of differences that remedial students found between their strategies and those of model students.

In a typical experiment, remedial students were given 10 to 12 training sessions in which they compared their solution strategies to those of models. Students who were trained tended to score about .50 to .70 grade points higher on the exam and expressed more self-confidence than students of equivalent

BOX 9–3   How Three Students Solved the Inflation Problem

Problem

Some economists feel that there is danger of an extreme inflationary boom after the war. It is the opinion of such economists that the government should control the boom in order to prevent a depression such as the one following the stock-market crash of 1929.

Below are a number of specific suggestions. For each of the following items, determine if it would be *consistent* with the policy of controlling the boom; if it is directly *inconsistent* with the policy.

26. Lower the reserve that banks are required to hold against deposits
27. Reduce taxes considerably
28. Encourage the federal reserve banks to buy securities in the open market

Mary's Answer

Mary W. *(Score 2):* (Read the statements and the directions.)

(Read item 26.) "Look down to see what I'm supposed to do.

(Reread the statements and the directions.) "Not quite sure what I'm doing." (Reread the statements and the directions for the third time.)

(Reread item 26.) "Not sure of this, so on to second one.

(Read item 27.) "Say inconsistent, because if there is inflationary boom, if people make more money, taxes have to keep up with it to take away the money so they can't spend it.

(Read item 28.) "Trying to figure out what bearing that had exactly.

(Reread item 26.) "I'm a time waster, say 26 would be consistent—no, that I know, banks have reserve—idea is to get people to deposit as much as possible—not answer 28.

(Reread item 28.) "Say inconsistent, I feel it is."

Diagnosis: unsystematic, jumps around, uses "feeling" rather than "reasoning," not confident.

James' Answer

James S. *(Score 2):* (Read the statements.) "In other words, the OPA and such.

(Read the directions.) "Take for granted they're going to control the boom.

(Read item 26. Reread item 26.) "That would be inconsistent.

(Read item 27.) "That would be inconsistent, because you can't have too great a boom as long as you have taxes, at least in my interpretation of boom—although if taxes go up, prices go up—no, I'll stick to my answer.

(Read item 28.) "Consistent—however, I think I need more subject-matter background to tell how I thought it out—more of a guess—don't think inconsistent, so put consistent."

Diagnosis: translates problem into something more familiar (OPA), lacks subject-matter knowledge, guesses.

Dora's Answer

Dora Z. (Score 2): (Read the statement and the directions—emphasizing the key words.)

(Read item 26.) "Lower the reserve, raise the amount of money in circulation—if you raise the money in circulation—inconsistent. By raising the money in circulation you don't control a boom.

(Read item 27.) "Also inconsistent for the same reason.

(Read item 28.) "Open market—think what the open market is. This would take money out of circulation, therefore would be consistent."

Diagnosis: focused on key ideas, reduced three items to a single problem, attempted to determine how money supply is affected by each item, attacks problem on basis of single rule or principle, higher-order problem solving.

Adapted from Bloom & Broder (1950)

ability and background who were not given training. Thus Bloom & Broder were able to influence problem-solving performance in subject areas by focusing on process rather than product, and by giving students practice in comparing their strategies to those of models.

Criterion 2: Focus on the Problem-Solving Process. In summary, Bloom & Broder's study suggests that the method for teaching problem solving should focus on "process" rather than "product," and that students need practice in relating their own problem-solving processes to those of models. This technique has become the basis for many of the problem-solving programs discussed in subsequent sections of this chapter.

How Much Can Problem Solving Be Improved?

Specific Versus General Transfer. Once the content and method of instruction are determined, the next step is to determine the expected outcome of learning. Should we expect students to learn general problems-solving techniques that can be applied to a wide variety of tasks, or should we expect students to perform well mainly on applying specific techniques to problems like those given in training? For example, suppose that your goal is to teach students how to break a problem into parts. Should you teach this as a general

BOX 9–4 Students' Lists of Differences between Model and Self

Jean's List

1. I didn't think it necessary to formulate the general rule.
   Generalization too broad.
   Verbalization reversed actually.
2. Lack of understanding of given terms.
   Define and illustrate as alternatives.
   I looked for "true" and "false"—others looked for "best." Didn't interpret directions properly.
   I looked for answer—didn't have an answer before I looked. Higher degree of inaccuracy. (I get this OK with syllogisms.)
3. He associated and brought in intermediary events with dates. I did the same with the second part, but didn't know country.
4. He employed an illustration for proof.
   Should set up criteria for an answer: if not enough, set up illustrations and examples.
5. Didn't get essential terms of what I was looking for before I began reading alternatives.
   Jumped to conclusion without carrying illustrative reasoning through.
   Did read terms thoroughly but didn't keep them in mind; reversed them.
6. Didn't define terms of statements. Got it right through outside example.
7. Should pull out main words. Got it right, though.
8. Didn't establish relations between terms. Got it right, though.
   Careless about selecting right alternative.
   Keeping directions in mind. I think in terms of "true" and "false" instead of "scientific study," etc.

Ralph's List

1. Find rule or formula that applies to problem under consideration.
2. Apply rule and formulate answer, then check with offered answers.
3. Progress into problem by formula that has been generalized through application.
4. Rules should deal with specific problem.
5. Try to read directions clearly the first time.
6. Do not answer by guessing or supposition.
7. Think before the formulation of answer.
8. Direct thought in stream which has been pointed in the direction of the problem at hand.
9. Emphasis on the major ideas in the problem, not all ideas.
10. Box off ideas into main question in the problem.
11. Reason from known knowledge or examples.
12. In graphs, formulate a specific picture.

Adapted from Bloom & Broder (1950)

skill in a separate lesson on "general problem solving," or should you teach how to break down a math problem into parts (during mathematics instruction), how to break a composition into its parts (during language instruction), and so on?

Latin Schools' Teaching of Problem Solving.   The first attempts to teach problem-solving skills in American schools focused on teaching general skills— what were called "good habits of mind." Rippa (1980) points out that as early as 1712 the curriculum of the Boston Latin School required that students learn to read, write, and speak Latin as well as have some knowledge of Greek and mathematics. The premise underlying the Latin School movement was that learning Latin (and to a lesser extent, Greek and mathematics) would foster the traits of mental discipline and logical thinking. For example, the eighteenth century entrance requirements to Harvard College were as follows (Rippa, 1980, p. 41):

> When any scholar is able to read Tully or such like classicall Latine Authour ex temporare, and make and speake true Latin Verse and prose, Suo (ut aiunt Marte), and decline perfectly the paradigms of Nounes and verbes in the Greeke tongue, then may hee bee admitted into the Coledge, nor shall any claim admission before such qualifications.

The Latin School approach, still strong a century ago, has finally given way to a new curriculum based on the practical demands of an emerging technological and democratic society. Yet the fundamental challenge of the Latin school approach remains the same: Is there any evidence that learning of Latin serves to establish "good habits of mind"? In the early part of this century, Thorndike (1913) conducted some studies comparing the school performance of students who learned Latin versus those who did not. Results indicated that learning of Latin did not transfer to other domains, that is, students who learned Latin did not have an advantage over non-Latin students in different school subjects. Based on these results, Thorndike (1913) proposed his "identical elements theory of transfer," which held that transfer was specific rather than general. In essence, Thorndike's theory says that when you learn Latin you learn a lot of specific skills directly related to Latin. If you are given new tasks that do not require those skills, then knowing Latin will be of little value. Rather than studying Latin as a way of improving one's skill on spelling or arithmetic or logic problems, Thorndike argues that it would be better to practice directly on these tasks.

Criterion 3: Expect Specific Transfer.   Thorndike's research is extremely important to the development of instruction for problem solving. He has evidence that it is best to have students practice on tasks that are similar to the tasks they will be expected to perform later. In a recent review of three popular problem-solving programs aimed at teaching general skills, Bransford, Arbitman-Smith, Stein & Vye (1985, p. 202) concluded:

> The idea of developing general skills that permit transfer to a wide variety of domains seems similar to the idea of teaching formal discipline. . . . As far as we can

tell, there is no strong evidence that students in any of these three thinking-skills programs improved in tasks that were dissimiliar to those already explicitly practiced.

In short, the lesson seems to be that if you want students to perform well on certain kinds of problems, teach them problem-solving skills using those kinds of problems. For example, mathematical problem-solving skills should be taught separately from composition writing skills. Yet there may be some very general skills that are conveyed in problem-solving courses, including "meta-cognitive" skills such as telling when a plan isn't working or knowing when something doesn't make sense. Unfortunately, it is very difficult to define or measure these skills, and hence there is, as yet, not much evidence for general transfer. In light of these findings, it makes the most sense to teach problem solving within the specific contexts or domains in which students will eventually be tested.

Implications for Teaching Problem Solving

This brief historical overview helps to provide some tentative answers to our three questions. First, once you choose the kinds of problems that the students need to be able to solve, the intellectual performance required for these problems should be broken into smaller skills that can be taught. Some of these skills involve techniques for representing problems and some involve techniques for planning and monitoring plans. Second, students should learn problem solving by focusing on process rather than product, and should have models to which they can refer. Third, it seems to make the most sense to teach specific problem-solving skills within specific contexts; it may also be possible to teach what appear to be general domain-free strategies, but there is not much evidence that these will transfer beyond the contexts they are taught in.

PROBLEM-SOLVING COURSES

This section explores four widely used problem-solving courses that have been well received in school settings. Each is an independent problem-solving course rather than an attempt to integrate problem solving within subject matter domains. For each program, this section presents the underlying theory, briefly describes the program, and evaluates the changes in students' thinking. The four programs are the Productive Thinking Program, Instrumental Enrichment, CoRT Thinking Program, and Patterns of Problem Solving.

Productive Thinking Program

Background.   During the 1960s several large-scale curriculum development efforts were carried out, including projects that emphasized teaching students in elementary and secondary schools "how to think." Some of the best known curriculum development projects for teaching thinking skills are: *Productive Thinking Program* (Covington, Crutchfield & Davies, 1966; Covington, Crutchfield, Davies & Olton, 1974) which provided practice in solving detective stories in order to teach general problem-solving skills to fifth and sixth graders; *Inquiry Training* (Suchman, 1960, 1966) which asked students to make predictions about filmed or live demonstrations in science; *Thinking Creatively* (Davis & Houtman, 1968) which asked students to answer questions in a workbook that involved a humorous discussion among several cartoon characters; and *Myers-Torrance Idea Books* (Myers & Torrance, 1968), which asked elementary school children to solve creativity problems in a workbook. A summary of creativity training programs for use in schools is contained in Davis (1973).

Let's take a closer look at the *Productive Thinking Program,* since it has been the most thoroughly studied project. Like Bloom & Broder's project, the Productive Thinking Program teaches the *process* of problem solving and uses imitation of *models* as the key instructional method. Unlike Bloom & Broder, the Productive Thinking Program involves a series of printed workbooks (rather than dialogues) that a student can work on alone and is directed at how elementary school children solve detective problems rather than how college students pass comprehensive exams.

Description.   The program consists of fifteen cartoonlike booklets, each about 30 pages in length. Each booklet presents a detective story involving two children, Jim and Lila, as well as Jim's Uncle John and Mr. Search. The story presents clues and asks the reader to answer questions aimed at "restating the problem in his own words," "formulating his own questions," and "generating ideas to explain the mystery" (Covington & Crutchfield, 1965, p. 3). After the reader has generated some ideas, then Jim and Lila give theirs. Thus Jim and Lila serve as "models to be emulated." Like all realistic models, they make some mistakes at first, but with the help of comments from the adults in the booklet, they eventually figure out the mystery.

Box 9–5 gives a few pages from one of the first lessons in the program, "The Riverboat Robbery." As you read the lesson you are given some information and asked to generate some responses. Then, you get feedback by seeing what Jim and Lila do, and how Uncle John critiques their strategies. (If you read the entire booklet very carefully, you will discover that the culprit is Mr. Larkin—the bank manager.) Each lesson is designed to teach some of the strategies listed in Box 9–6; for example, "The Riverboat Robbery" attempts to teach strategies 4, 5, 6, 9, 11, and 15.

Evaluation.   More than a dozen studies have evaluated the effectiveness of

BOX 9–5   Excerpts from "The Riverboat Robbery"

The TV Announcer:
"Following the robbery, things moved quickly. The captain of the boat called the Elmtown police. When the boat docked in Elmtown, the police were already on guard there. No one was allowed on or off the boat except the police and our reporter and TV cameraman."

"Here is the police chief on the boat, telling our reporter what has happened so far:"

1   What persons besides Louie might be the thief?

Before Lila tells her idea, what thoughts do you have about other possible suspects? Use your Reply Notebook to write down all the ideas you can think of.

There are several people besides Louie who might have stolen the money. You may have thought of the steward who called Mr. Burk to the phone, or perhaps you even considered the riverboat captain.

Lila has another possible suspect in mind.

Uncle John is right. You can always think of more ideas. And you should never be afraid to talk about your ideas.

From Covington et al. (1974)

BOX 9–6 Some Problem-Solving Skills Taught in the Productive Thinking Program

1. Take time to reflect on a problem before you begin to work. Decide exactly what the problem is that you are trying to solve.
2. Get all the facts of the problem clearly in mind.
3. Work on the problem in a planful way.
4. Keep an open mind. Don't jump to conclusions about the answer to a problem.
5. Think of many new ideas for solving a problem. Don't stop with just a few.
6. Try to think of unusual ideas.
7. As a way of getting ideas, pick out all the important objects and persons in the problem and think carefully about each one.
8. Think of several general possibilities for a solution and then figure out many particular ideas for each possibility.
9. As you search for ideas, let your mind freely explore things around you. Almost anything can suggest ideas for a solution.
10. Always check each idea with the facts to decide how likely the idea is.
11. If you get stuck on a problem, keep trying. Don't be discouraged.
12. When you run out of ideas, try looking at the problem in a new and different way.
13. Go back and review all the facts of the problem to make sure you have not missed something important.
14. Start with an unlikely idea. Just suppose that it is possible, and figure out how it could be.
15. Be on the lookout for odd or puzzling facts in a problem. Explaining them can lead you to news ideas for solution.
16. When there are several puzzling things in a problem, try to explain them with a single idea that will connect them all together.

Adapted from Covington et al. (1974)

the *Productive Thinking Program* (Mansfield, Busse, & Krepelka, 1978). For example, Olton & Crutchfield (1969) gave training in the Productive Thinking Program to twenty-five fifth graders while an equal number of fifth graders received no training. Box 9–7 gives examples of pretests given before training, post-tests given immediately after training, and delayed post-tests given 6 months after training. Figure 9–1 shows that the trained group and control group scored at about the same level on the pretest, but the trained group outperformed the control group on the immediate and delayed post-test.

BOX 9–7   Some Pretests, Post-tests and Follow-up Tests Given to Study the Effectiveness of the Productive Thinking Program

Pretests

Controlling the weather	Student thinks of various consequences of man's future ability to change the weather.
Project for a village	Student puts himself in the shoes of a Peace Corps volunteer who must first acquaint himself with the customs and mores of a tribal village. Then, without offending such customs, he must figure out ways the inhabitants can earn money for their village needs.

Immediate Post-Tests

Transplanting organs	Student thinks of various consequences of man's future medical ability to transplant bodily organs from one person to another.
"Black House" problem	Student attemps to solve a puzzling mystery problem in which he must make an insightful reorganization of the elements of the problem.

Delayed Post-Tests

The missing jewel problem	Student attempts to solve a puzzling mystery problem in which he must make an insightful reorganization of the elements of the problem.
The nameless tomb	Student works on a hypothetical problem in archeology in which he must discover which of ten possible suspects is buried in a nameless ancient tomb.

In interpreting these results you should note that the test problems were similar to the types of problems given in the booklets, and that factors other than training may account for differences among the groups, such as higher motivation by the trained subjects. In a review of a dozen evaluation studies, Mansfield et al. (1978) concluded that the effects of the Productive Thinking Program are smaller in well-controlled studies and seem limited to problems like those given in the lessons; concerning the issue of transfer of problem-solving strategies to new problems, Mansfield et al. (1978, p. 522) concluded: "it is unclear whether the effects of training are sufficiently generalizable to be

FIGURE 9–1   Effects of Training in Productive Thinking on Creativity

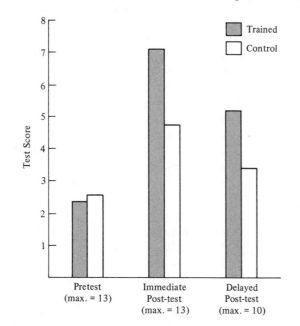

Adapted from Olton & Crutchfield (1969)

useful in real-life problem solving situations." Apparently, it is possible to teach students to perform well on a certain class of problem, but there is not strong evidence that such training transfers to other domains.

Instrumental Enrichment

Background.   Do you remember the Wild Boy of Aveyron from the first chapter of this book? As you might recall, he was an adolescent who grew up in the forest without any human contact. When he was found, he performed quite poorly on most intellectual tasks. If he were a student in today's schools, he would probably be labeled mentally retarded.

Yet, you might be somewhat skeptical of this labeling because the Wild Boy actually showed a great deal of intelligence by surviving on his own in the forest. Some questions you might ask are: Does the boy have potential for a higher level intellectual functioning than he is currently performing? What types of natural experiences would lead to the boy reaching or not reaching his highest potential? If the boy has missed many of the natural experiences needed for intellectual development, can instruction when he is an adolescent help him reach a higher level of intellectual functioning?

These are the kinds of questions addressed by Feuerstein (1979, 1980; Feuerstein, Jensen, Hoffman, & Rand, 1985) based on his work with special education adolescents in Israeli schools. First, if a student performs poorly on academic tasks, Feuerstein prefers to label that child a "retarded performer." Feuerstein found that it is useful to make a distinction between a child's manifested low level of functioning (i.e., retarded performance) and the child's actual potential for intellectual performance. He even developed a test called the "learning potential assessment device" (LPAD) to evaluate how much improvement he could expect for each "retarded performer." Instead of a static mental ability test, the LPAD presents the student with learning tasks and measures the amount of teacher intervention needed to help the student accomplish the tasks.

Second, Feuerstein noticed that students who have trouble learning in schools often came from homes in which parents do not explain, discuss, or interpret events (including their culture) to their children. Feuerstein notes that such children are "mediationally deprived"; that is, the normal events in their lives do not seem to have any meaning or purpose because no one provides any interpretation of them. Mediationally deprived students have trouble responding to new problems or new learning tasks. According to Feuerstein, these children have been denied exposure to what he calls "mediated learning experiences" (MLE). For example, in playing with a typewriter, a child can learn about cause and effect. A parent might say: "When you press the A key, it makes this metal strike the ink and print a letter A on the paper." As another example, a family trip to the beach can be the basis for learning to plan. A parent might say: "Go bring your bucket and shovel in case you want to build sand castles." As another example (Feuerstein et al., 1980, p. 21), a parent can ask a child to go to the store: "Please buy three bottles of milk so that we will have some left over for tomorrow when the shops are closed." This helps show the role of planning much more than the statement, "Please buy three bottles of milk." These are examples of MLEs because the parent helps interpret events, so the child can see the meaning or purpose or intentionality in the surrounding world.

Third, Feuerstein has developed a program called "instrumental enrichment" that is intended to provide low functioning students with the kinds of mediated learning experiences that children normally receive. To compensate for the inadequate MLEs of his students, he provides them with a series of problems—each one different—that serve as the basis for discussion and interpretation with an adult.

Description.   Feuerstein's instructional enrichment (IE) program consists of a series of paper and pencil exercises for low functioning adolescents. The program is intended to be administered as an adjunct to regular academic instruction; for example, IE could occur for 3 to 5 hours per week over a 2-year period, for a total of 200 to 300 hours. The tasks are organized into fifteen instruments, with each instrument focusing on one or more cognitive skills.

Figure 9–2 gives an example exercise from the "Organization of Dots," the

FIGURE 9–2   Example Exercises from the Organization of Dots

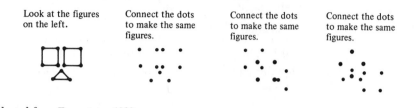

Adapted from Feuerstein, 1980

first instrument in the IE program. The student's job is to connect the dots so that they form the same shapes as on the left (i.e., two squares and a triangle). Each dot can be used only once, and each shape must be the same size as the model on the left. However, the drawn shapes can overlap and be in different orientations than the model shapes on the left are. For each exercise, the teacher introduces the problem and allows for individual work on the problem. Then, there is a class discussion of methods for solving the problems and a summary by the teacher. Thus, students get exposed to many novel problems and learn to compare their approach to the methods used by others. Since each problem is novel, the students cannot memorize answers. Exercises such as these are intended to teach students how to generate and evaluate problem representations and solution strategies. The problems are organized so they increase in difficulty. According to Feuerstein, the Organization of Dots problems teach students the following cognitive skills: breaking a problem into parts, representing a problem, and thinking hypothetically. Other instruments focus on spatial orientation, temporal relations, family relations, numerical progressions, analytic perception, transitive relations, and syllogisms.

Evaluation.   Does the IE program help students to become better able to deal with new problems (i.e., to become better thinkers)? Feuerstein and his colleagues (1980; Feuerstein, 1979) report an evaluation study comparing adolescent special education students who received IE over a 2-year period versus students who received the normal enrichment procedures. Both groups performed at the same level on pretests of cognitive skill but after 2 years, the IE scored higher on tests involving spatial and mathematical reasoning (i.e., tests of spatial relations, figure grouping, number, and addition). Follow-up studies on the same students 2 years later found that the IE group still scored higher than the control group on tests of nonverbal intelligence.

Feuerstein's program seems consistent with the three criteria for a successful program described in the preceding section: First, the program content focuses on a set of "small" cognitive tasks, mainly specific strategies for representing problems and planning solutions. Second, the method involves lots of practice and modeling of the processes used by successful problem solvers. Third, although the program appears to teach general problem-solving skills independent of subject matter area, the skills that are taught actually are quite specific and similar to tasks on nonverbal intelligence tests. Bransford, Arbitman-Smith, Stein, & Vye (1985, p. 201) point out that "there is an emphasis on training students to solve certain types of problems so that they will be able to solve similar problems on their own within each instrument." However, Feuerstein does not assume that learning one instrument will help a student learn another instrument that requires different cognitive skills. Instead, the IE program seems to be providing students with many specific subskills that, taken together, are useful for performance on tests of nonverbal intelligence.

CoRT Thinking Program

Background.   Here are some practical problem-solving exercises not commonly found in a school's curriculum:

What makes a TV or radio show interesting?
Mail services usually lose a lot of money. If you were running these services, what alternatives would you suggest?
A father forbids his thirteen-year-old daughter to smoke. What is his point of view and what is yours?

These are examples of some of the problems that students learn to solve in de Bono's CoRT Thinking Program (de Bono, 1976, 1985), a commerically available problem-solving course currently in use in thousands of classrooms around the world. The goal of CoRT is to provide students with skills needed for solving practical problems.

Description.   The CoRT program is divided into six sections of ten lessons each. Box 9–8 lists the ten lessons for the first section, "Breadth." As you can see, each lesson is well focused on a particular strategy for how to represent or analyze a problem situation. For example, PMI involves listing the good points (i.e., pluses), bad points (i.e., minuses), and interesting points for a given example. For example, in considering the concept of "year round schools," CoRT students would be asked to list all the pluses (e.g., "could cover more material," "would not have to relearn everything forgotten over the summer"), all the minuses (e.g., "would disrupt family vacation plans," "would cost more money") and all the interesting points (e.g., "the historical reason for our current calendar is to let children help on the farms").

Each lesson begins with the teacher briefly explaining the cognitive skill to be learned, such as what PMI is, and giving examples. Then students are given practice problems to work on within small groups. After a few minutes, the groups report on their progress, and the teacher leads a discussion. Most of the examples are practical, real-world problems rather than artificial puzzles or games. Students come away from the CoRT program with an arsenal of strategies for how to analyze problems, plan solutions, and so on.

BOX 9–8   Ten Lessons from the Breadth Section of the CoRT Thinking Program

CoRT I: Breadth
This section is concerned with helping students develop tools and habits for scanning widely around a thinking situation. The following tools are emphasized:

Treatment of ideas (PMI): Deliberately examining ideas for good, bad, or interesting points, instead of immediately accepting or rejecting them.

Factors involved (CAF): Looking as widely as possible at all the factors involved in a situation, instead of only the immediate ones.

Rules: Draws together the first two lessons.

Consequences (C & S): Considering the immediate, short, medium, and long-term consequences of alternative strategies.

Objectives (AGO): Selecting and defining objectives; being clear about one's aims and understanding those of others.

Planning: Draws together the preceding two lessons.

Priorities (FIP): Choosing from a number of different possibilities and alternatives; putting one's priorities in order.

Alternatives (APC): Generating new alternatives and choices instead of feeling confined to the obvious ones.

Decisions: Draws together the preceding two lessons.

Viewpoint (OPV): Considering all the viewpoints involved in a situation.

From de Bono (1985)

Evaluation.   How can you judge the effectiveness of the CoRT program? De Bono offers three major sources of support: longevity, acceptance, and testimonials. First, the CoRT program has been successfully promoted as a problem solving course for the past ten years. Second, according to de Bono (1985), the program is being used in over 5000 classrooms in ten countries, including plans to train over one million children in Venezuela. Third, de Bono (1985, p. 383) claims that he has a "considerable amount of unpublished data" from informal studies as well as a "large number of anecdotal reports from teachers." Unfortunately, none of these kinds of support offers any scientifically acceptable evidence that the CoRT program works.

In reviewing the research evidence concerning the CoRT program, Polson & Jeffries (1985, p. 445) make the following observations:

The most disturbing aspect of the de Bono program is the lack of well-designed evaluation studies such as the excellent research on the Productive Thinking Program. . . . None of the evaluation studies have been published. . . . Experiments that are described are informal studies. . . . The program has been in existence for over 10 years and is claimed to be in wide use both in the British Isles and in Venezuela. Furthermore, de Bono makes strong claims concerning the effectiveness of the CoRT program. Yet, after 10 years of widespread use, we have no adequate evidence concerning those claims and thus no support for the effectiveness of the program or the theoretical assumptions from which it was derived.

Certainly, CoRT seems to be consistent with some of our criteria for a successful program—namely, teaching of discrete problem solving skills by focusing on practice and modeling of correct procedures. Since de Bono's program focuses on solving practical problems, usually within a verbal format, one would expect the program to have its strongest effects for these kinds of problems. However, valid evidence is needed concerning whether CoRT helps students solve CoRT-like problems and whether CoRT training transfers to other school domains such as in science, mathematics, and language.

Patterns of Problem Solving

Background.   Rubinstein (1975, 1980) has developed one of the best known college-level courses on thinking skills. For more than ten years, Rubinstein's course on "Patterns of Problem Solving" has been taught to thousands of students at UCLA. The course provides the student with a varied and pragmatic assortment of specific problem-solving tools, such as how to use a matrix for representing logical premises or how to convert a story problem into an equation.

Description.   The course takes ten weeks and involves many examples of worked-out problems, taken mainly from the fields of engineering and mathematics. The first half of the course teaches general techniques such as how to draw a concrete picture that represents an unfamiliar, formal statement, as shown in Box 9–9. The second half of the course explores some mathematical foundations of problem solving, including probability theory and decision theory. Thus students see lots of examples of the problem-solving process used by experts, and students learn some formal techniques for representing problems.

Evaluation.   Unfortunately, Rubinstein (1980) has not provided a systematic evaluation of the course. The course is extremely popular, however, with an enrollment of 1200 students per quarter, and Rubinstein has accumulated a large number of student testimonials. But as Polson & Jeffries (1985, p. 438) point out, "popularity is not the same as effectiveness." In an unpublished evaluation of a Rubinstein-inspired course at another university, students who took the course increased their scores on IQ tests as compared to a control group (see Rubinstein, 1980). However, in a review of that study, Hayes (1980, p. 144) was forced to conclude: "I simply do not believe the result." The reason

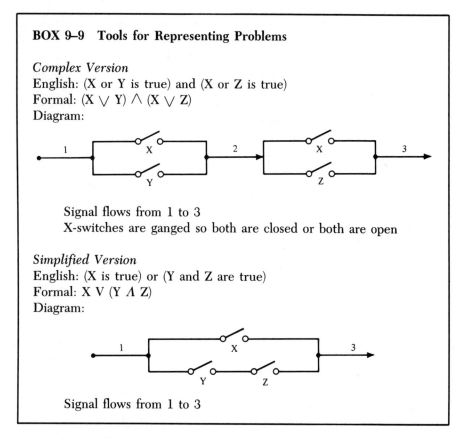

BOX 9–9   Tools for Representing Problems

Complex Version
English: (X or Y is true) and (X or Z is true)
Formal: $(X \lor Y) \land (X \lor Z)$
Diagram:

Signal flows from 1 to 3
X-switches are ganged so both are closed or both are open

Simplified Version
English: (X is true) or (Y and Z are true)
Formal: $X \lor (Y \land Z)$
Diagram:

Signal flows from 1 to 3

Adapted from Rubinstein (1975)

for Hayes' doubts is that almost all other research has indicated that transfer of problem-solving strategies is quite specific. Like de Bono's CoRT program, Rubinstein's Patterns of Problem Solving course has not been subjected to extensive scientific evaluation.

Implications of Problem-Solving Courses

In this section, you have learned about four popular problem-solving courses that have been used in schools. There are, of course, many other problem-solving courses (see Segal, Chipman & Glaser, 1985), but these four are among the most popular and well known. How do the programs reviewed in this section rate on the three criteria for an effective problem-solving program described in the previous section? Consistent with the criteria, each program focuses on a set of specific problem-solving skills, gives students practice in the process of problem-solving (including modeling of good procedures), and seems to show improvement only on tasks like those in the training program. In short, although the specific tasks and target audiences vary from program to program, they seem to share the formula of teaching individual cognitive skills, emphasizing process rather than product, and resulting in specific rather than general transfer.

Thus we are faced, in some respects, with a paradox. Although these problem-solving courses appear to deal with general thinking ability, they actually focus on a series of individual skills that help performance mainly on specific tasks like those used in the program. It follows that a more fruitful approach to teaching of problem solving would be to identify target tasks and then teach the skills required to succeed on those tasks. This is the approach followed in the next section.

COMPONENTIAL TRAINING OF PROBLEM SOLVING

One very specific approach to the training of thinking skills involves *componential analysis*. First, you select a reasoning task such as solving analogies or series completion problems. Second, you analyze the problem into the processes that a person would have to perform in order to solve it. Third, you provide training and practice in each of the major processes required for solving the problem.

As you can see, componential training requires that you know the processes for a given reasoning task. Fortunately, cognitive psychologists have provided cognitive analyses of the standard types of problems that are found on tests of thinking and reasoning.

Series Completion

For example, in a series completion problem such as used by Thurstone & Thurstone's (1941) tests of intelligence, you must fill in the missing letters:

abcmbcdlcdek __ __ __ __

Recently, Simon & Kotovsky (1963) and Kotovsky & Simon (1973) have provided a cognitive analysis of series completion problems that identifies four major processes:

Detection of interletter relations—The problem solver must be aware of relations between letters such as *identify*, *next*, and *backwards next*. An identity relation occurs when letters are the same such as the "x's" in axbxcxdxex; a next relation occurs when letters occur in the same order as in the alphabet such as the first, third, fifth, seventh, and ninth letters in axbxcxdxex; a *backwards next* relation occurs when letters are in the reverse order as the alphabet such as the first, third, fifth, seventh, and ninth letters in exdxcxbxax.

Discovery of periodicity—The problem solver must find the interval at which the relation or a break in the relation occurs. For example, the sequence axbxcxdxex has a period of two, whereas abcmbdelcdek has a period of four.

Pattern description—The problem solver must formulate the rule; for example, the rule for axbxcxdxex could be "every even position is x" and "every odd position requires that you use the next letter."

Extrapolation—The problem solver must apply the rule to the unknown (missing) letters in the problem. For example, the next letter in axbxcxdxex is f.

Holzman, Glaser & Pellegrino (1976) have used the Simon & Kotovsky analysis in order to develop a training program that teaches elementary school children how to solve series completion problems. Table 9–1 shows fifteen problems that the children were asked to solve before training and fifteen equally difficult problems they were asked to solve after training. Children in the training group were given four 30-minute training sessions on detection of relations and discovery of periodicity. For relations training, the students were taught the three relations—identify, next, and backwards next—through a

TABLE 9–1   Some Series Completion Problems

Instructions: List the next four letters for each series.

Pretest	Post-test
cdcdcd	xyxyxy
aaabbbcccdd	hhhiiijjjkk
pononmnmlmlk	dcbcbabaz
rscdstdetuef	efpqfgqrghrs
npaoqapraqsa	acmbdmcemdfm
wxaxybyzczadab	hilijmjknklolm
abmcdmefmghm	ghrijrklrmnr
defgefghfghi	klmnlmnomnop
mabmbcmcdm	aopapqaqra
urtustuttu	mjlmklmllm
qxapxbqxa	tadsaetad
abyabxabwab	hifhiehidhi
atbataatbat	piqpippiqpi
aduacuaeuabuaf	gjagiagkaghagl
jkqrklrslmst	cdjkdekleflm

From Holzman, Glaser & Pellegrino (1976)

series of oddity problems. For example, students had to tell which pair of letters did not belong in a set of four pairs, such as:

cd xy lm mx

Another problem is: aa cc mn vv

A second part of relations training asked students to draw lines connecting letters, based on one of the three relations. For example, students had to draw lines between all letters connected by the "next relation" in a series such as:

z c d f a l m n r s w

For periodicity training, students were given series and asked to place slash marks to indicate the period. For example, one problem was:

a a a x x x m m m

and another problem was:

m k f m t z m b d

Box 9–10 summarizes these training procedures.

Figure 9–3 shows that the performance of the trained children improved

---

BOX 9–10   Componential Training for Series Completion Problems

Relations Training
Circle the odd pair:

cd   xy   lm   mx
aa   cc   mn   vv

Draw lines connecting letters next to each other in the alphabet:

z c d f a l m p n r s w

Periodicity Training
Draw slash marks to indicate period:

a a axxxmmm
mkfmtzmbd

Based on Holzman, Glaser & Pellegrino (1976)

FIGURE 9–3 Effects of Componential Training on Solving Series Completion Problems

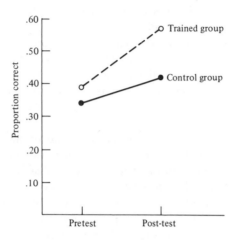

Adapted from Holzman, Glazer & Pellegrino (1976)

greatly from pretest to post-test whereas there was only modest improvement for a control group that received the same tests with no training. In addition, the trained group showed a much greater gain on the difficult problems and on problems involving the next relation as compared to the control group. In a follow-up study, third and fifth graders were given practice in solving many series completion problems—but without any explicit training in the processes involved. The third graders showed no improvement—scoring at about 33% correct at the beginning and end—whereas the fifth graders improved greatly from about 46 to 66% correct at the end. Apparently, explicit training in the specific processes is helpful for younger children and for the difficult problems presumably because the appropriate processing strategies are not otherwise available. In contrast, the older children seemed to have possessed the appropriate processing strategies but needed practice in using them.

Analogical Reasoning

Sternberg & Ketron (1982) trained college students in the processes for solving analogy problems. For example, Figure 9–4 shows some typical problems of the form "A is to B as C is to _____". The problem solver's job is to choose either response 1 or 2 in order to complete the analogy. According to an earlier analysis by Sternberg (1977) there are five major steps in solving these problems:

Encoding—The problem solver must represent the terms A, B, and C in the analogy.

Inference—The problem solver must determine the relation between A and B.

Mapping—The problem solver must relate this relation to the C-D pair.

Application—The problem solver must apply the rule to the C term in order to generate the D term.

Response—The problem solver must press the button corresponding to the answer.

As you can see from the examples in Figure 9–4, many attributes are involved. For the top analogy the attributes are hat color (black versus white), suit pattern (striped versus polka dotted), headgear (suitcase versus umbrella), and footwear (shoes versus boots). For the bottom analogy, the attributes are height (tall versus short), weight (fat versus thin), clothing color (black versus white), and sex (male versus female).

Sternberg & Ketron (1982) trained some subjects to use the following strategy:

1. First, you infer the relation between a single attribute of A (the first analogy term) and a single attribute of B (the second analogy term). The attribute may be any one of the four. This inference requires you to figure out whether the attribute changes in value from A to B, or remains the same.

FIGURE 9–4   Some Analogy Problems

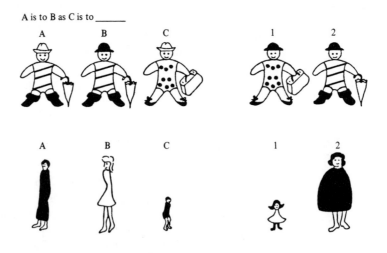

From Sternberg & Ketron (1982)

2. Next, you attempt to apply from C (the third analogy term) to each of the two answer options the relation you inferred from A to B. In doing so, you attempt to apply the attribute of C onto each option. If the attribute you happened to select enables you to distinguish which option is right and which is wrong, go to Step 3. This would be the case if either an attribute that changed from A to B changed from C to one option but not the other, or if an attribute that remained constant from A to B remained constant from C to one option but not the other. If, however, the attribute you chose does not enable you to distinguish the wrong answer from the right answer, you should return to Step 1, selecting a second attribute from the three that remain untested. You then infer and apply this attribute, again attempting to solve the analogy. You continue the process until you have chosen an attribute that enables you to distinguish between options.
3. Finally, you respond with the correct answer option, that which completes the analogy, A : B :: C : D.

Table 9–2 shows the performance of the trained students and control students on an analogy post-test that consisted of several hundred problems. This table shows that students who learned the strategy took longer to solve problems but committed fewer errors than a control group that received no training. Another interesting finding is that scores on a mental ability test (such as general reasoning ability) correlated with performance on analogy post-test for the control group but not for the trained group. Apparently, training in a specific strategy that would not normally be used can be accomplished and tends to minimize the effects of "general reasoning ability."

Implications of Componential Training

In summary, componential training is focused on training people to use processes that are parts of specific types of problems. The foregoing research encourages the idea that specific processes can be taught to students, and that such training does influence performance on the target tasks. Some authors have tried to build problem-solving courses around the componential approach; for example, Whimbey & Lochhead's (1979) *Problem Solving and*

TABLE 9–2   Performance on Analogy Problems by Trained and Untrained Students

Group	Average Solution Time (seconds)	Error Rate (%)
Trained group	7.6	1.0
Untrained group	2.8	2.5

Adapted from Sternberg & Ketron (1982)

Comprehension: A Short Course in Analytic Reasoning tries to provide training in how to solve several types of problems including analogies. One shortcoming of this approach, however, is the lack of evidence that training in solving a specific type of reasoning problem transfers to any other types of problem-solving tasks. In other words, the effects of componential training for a given reasoning task may be narrowly limited.

Suppose that you have identified some problem-solving skills that you want students to learn, such as how to make and test hypotheses. Is it better to use selected parts of a general problem-solving course that focuses on these kinds of skills or to use componential training for these skills? The answer to this question is that both approaches turn out to be quite similar. The main difference between general problem-solving courses and componential training involves the specificity of the problem-solving strategies that are taught.

When your goals are very specific (e.g., students need to be able to solve verbal analogy problems), then a componential approach is warranted. For example, one subskill might be to identify hypotheses that would be relevant to verbal analogies (such as "opposites"). The advantage of the componential approach is that it provides skills that are directly related to success on the task to be learned. The disadvantage of the componential approach is that the effects of instruction are unlikely to transfer to other types of problems.

When your goals are somewhat more general (e.g., students need to be able to generate hypotheses), then selected parts of a general course might be more appropriate. Yet, even a general course is likely to have quite limited transfer. As we have seen, if students are taught how to generate hypotheses concerning verbal problems, there is little reason to suppose that hypothesis-generating skills would generalize to scientific problems or logical reasoning problems.

Since problem-solving skills seem to be learned in a fairly specific way, it makes most sense to define clearly the kinds of problems that students will be expected to solve and then to use a componential approach for teaching the needed skills. One way of trying to foster some general transfer would be to coordinate teaching of the same set of skills simultaneously within several subject areas. For example, hypothesis generation could be taught as part of composition lessons on writing expository essays, as part of mathematics lessons on geometry proofs, and as part of science lessons on the laws of motion.

TRAINING NOVICES TO BECOME EXPERT PROBLEM SOLVERS

The preceding two sections have explored techniques for teaching problem-solving skills such as how to represent a problem or plan a solution strategy. Programs for teaching problem-solving skills involve investments ranging from a few hours to 200 hundred hours. While the programs focus on teaching problem-solving skills, they tend to ignore the role of a person's background knowledge.

Yet, if we look back at Bloom and Broder's famous study concerning teaching of problem-solving skills to college students, we see that becoming a proficient problem solver in a domain (e.g., in economics) requires both problem-solving skills and domain specific knowledge. Bloom & Broder (1950, pp. 76–77) concluded:

> It became clear that some specific knowledge was necessary for the solution of examination problems and that a certain amount of background in the subject was indispensable. It became apparent that methods of problem solving, by themselves could not serve as a substitute for the basic knowledge of the subject area.

This section explores the question of what it takes to become an expert problem solver in some domain. For example, what does an experienced physician know about diagnosing a medical problem that a first-year medical student does not know? What does an experienced physicist know about how to to solve a physics problem that a first-year physics student does not know? What does an experienced mathematician know about how to derive a mathematical proof that a first-year math student doesn't know? What does a master musician know about how to compose a musical score that a beginning music student does not know?

The answer to these questions seems to be that expert problem solvers possess both good problem-solving strategies and a rich bank of knowledge about the domain. This section investigates the idea that building expertise in problem solving requires more than a "quick fix" course on general problem-solving skills. In particular, this section focuses on expert problem solving in science, art, and medicine.

Expert Scientific Problem Solving

This approach to the thinking strategy problem asks: What is needed in order to turn a novice into an expert? Larkin and her colleagues (Larkin, 1979; Larkin, McDermott, Simon & Simon, 1980) have investigated differences between expert (professors and advanced graduate students) and novice (students in an introductory physics class) solvers of physics problems. Figure 9–5 shows a typical problem that might be covered in an early chapter of a physics textbook. Experts and novices were asked to solve problems like the one in Figure 9–5 by thinking aloud—that is, they were asked to describe what they were thinking about as they solved the problem.

The results indicated, not surprisingly, that experts solved the problems in about one-fourth the time required by novices. A second major difference was that experts seemed to organize knowledge, such as physics formulas, into large units; in contrast, novices seemed to organize knowledge in small fragments,

FIGURE 9–5 A Physics Problem

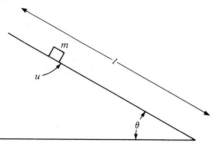

A block of mass m moves from rest down a plane of length l.
If the coefficient of friction between block and plane is u,
what is the block's speed as it reaches the bottom of the plane?

From Larkin et al. (1980)

such as remembering each individual formula. For example, in a problem where you must find the value for C but values are given for A, X, Y, and K, novices behave as if they use small knowledge units such as $C = A + B$, $B = K/L$, $L = X \times Y$, and must substitute one equation into another; in contrast, experts behave as if they can solve the problem using one large formula such as $C = A + K/(X \times Y)$. A third major difference is that novices tend to work backwards from the unknown to the givens, going step by step with a lot of checking; in contrast, experts tend to work forwards, plugging the givens into a large formula and generating the value for the unknown. For example, novices may begin by looking for a way to get a value for C, using the formula $C = A + B$; since B is not given, they must find a formula for B such as $B = K/L$; and since L is not given, they must find a formula for L such as $L = X \times Y$. This generates a value for L which can be used to find a value for B and this can be used to find a value for C. In contrast, experts can simply fill in the values for A, K, X, and Y into the equation $C = A + K/(X \times Y)$.

In summary, experts have had so much experience with problems that they can rapidly recognize what type of problem is presented and then select a solution equation to solve it. As a way of validating these observations, Larkin et al. (1980) produced computer programs to simulate the performance of expert and novice physics problem solvers. The expert program has knowledge stored as large units and solves by working forward; in contrast, the novice program has knowledge stored as individual fragments and works backwards in a step-by-step procedure. The main output of the program is the order in which equations are used. The output of the expert program was consistent with the order in which experts used variables, and the output of the novice program was consistent with the order in which novices used variables. One implication is that expertise results from exposure to many problems, so that a person can learn how to recognize problem types.

Larkin (1981) has developed a way of allowing her "novice program" to learn by solving problems. Each time the "novice program" successfully solves a problem, it adds to its memory the cluster of given variables that allowed it to find the unknown. By working on problems, it adds new "formulas" to memory—formulas that are essentially integrated and larger versions of the simple formulas it began with. Whenever the program encounters another situation with the same cluster of given variables and unknowns as a previous problem, the program can recognize this problem type and use the same procedure. Eventually, through lots of experience in solving problems, the program develops a larger bank of recognizable problem types.

Expert Artistic Problem Solving

The creation of a work of art is another example of expert problem solving. Even a highly gifted artist may require some period of study before making contributions of high quality. In a recent study, Hayes (1985) provides some evidence that it takes at least ten years of concentrated study in music before a composer is able to create a masterpiece. To substantiate this claim, Hayes searched the biographies of all the composers listed in Schonberg's (1970) *The Lives of the Great Composers*. For each of seventy-six composers, Hayes was able to determine the year in which they began intensive study of music, along with a list of the years that each of their works was created. Then, by looking in *Schwann's Record and Tape Guide*, he counted the number of recordings of each work of each of the seventy-six composers.

Figure 9–6 shows the relationship between number of years since starting the study of music and the number of works listed in the Schwann guide,

FIGURE 9–6   Average Number of Masterpieces per Year by Seventy-six Great Composers

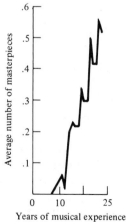

Adapted from Hayes (1985)

summed over all seventy-six composers' careers. As you can see, the Schwann guide lists almost no work by any composer that was created before the composer had spent ten years studying music. Beginning in the tenth year and continuing up to the twenty-fifth year, composers appear to be more able to create masterpieces. Differences in death rates make it difficult to continue past the twenty-fifth year, but Hayes has additional evidence that composers maintain their productivity through their fortieth year but begin to decline by the fiftieth year. Hayes' results can be summarized by saying there is a "ten-year rule" for becoming an expert artist (i.e., even a talented person needs at least ten years of intensive study in art to become a great artist). In a parallel study, Hayes found that the "ten-year rule" seems also to apply to great painters.

What does the ten-year rule mean for teaching problem solving? The findings suggest that to become an expert in any domain, ranging from writing poetry to history to athletics, requires both problem-solving skills and domain-specific knowledge. Hayes (1985, p. 399) warns that "it is unlikely that the use of strategies can circumvent the need to spend large amounts of time acquiring a knowledge base for such skills."

Expert Medical Problem Solving

Another source of information about expertise comes from computer simulations such as INTERNIST (Pople, 1977) which performs medical diagnoses, and MYCIN (Shortliffe, 1976), which diagnoses bacteriological diseases. These systems require a huge amount of very specific information, in addition to some general techniques for manipulating that information. The need for vast amounts of knowledge in order to simulate expertise led Simon (1980, p. 82) to conclude: "There is no such thing as expertness without knowledge—extensive and accessible knowledge."

Implications of Expert Problem Solving

Research on humans and computers seems to suggest that one way to turn a novice problem solver into an expert problem solver is to provide many examples—including problems that are worked out by the instructor (or book) and problems that worked out by the student. The examples must help the learner to see the step-by-step procedure, rather than just the final answer. This work seems to contradict the idea that general thinking skills can be easily taught; in contrast, this work shows that thinking skills are learned within a particular context such as physics or algebra and that becoming an expert problem solver takes a lot of learning. In fact, Simon (1980) and Hayes (1981, 1985) estimate that to become an expert problem solver in a particular subject domain takes at least 50,000 chunks of knowledge, and this learning requires at least ten years.

Advanced training in professional fields such as law, medicine, art, and science involves intensive study of problem solving within those domains. Law students learn how to reason about court decisions; medical students learn how to diagnose patient case histories; scientists learn how to test hypotheses in their particular fields; artists learn the techniques and concepts of their area. Would it be better to teach problem solving as a set of domain-free general skills or to continue our practice of teaching problem solving within professional domains? The research on expertise seems to point clearly to the latter as the proper choice.

Apparently, good thinking skills cannot be learned in a vacuum. Rather, teaching of strategies should be incorporated into subject matter areas. For example, Simon (1980) has pointed out that instruction in algebra often involves drill in the use of basic operations—such as adding the same value to both sides of an equation, distributing a value across parentheses, factoring an equation, and so on—but students are given little practice in judging *when* to use these procedures. Similarly, Greeno (1978) found that students' solutions of geometry problems required "strategic knowledge"—knowledge of how to attack a problem—but that such information was almost never explicitly taught. In conclusion, Greeno (1980, p. 21) summarizes the research as follows: "There is no basis in current scientific knowledge for changing our present policy of intensive disciplined training for individuals who aspire to making creative changes in the domains in which they choose to work."

CONCLUSION

This chapter has investigated techniques for teaching students how to think. Historically, schools began by teaching thinking as if it were a single, general ability; however, systematic research seems to show that problem-solving training is most effective when the material to be taught consists of specific, individual problem-solving skills. Historically, schools began with attempts to teach thinking skills through drill and practice in applying rules; however, systematic research suggests that students also profit from generating and analyzing worked-out examples and comparing their own solution processes to those of experts. Historically, schools have taught thinking skills independent of subject matter domains in hopes that such skills would transfer to many situations; however, systematic research shows that students tend to learn specific skills that can be applied mainly in the same kinds of contexts as the examples used during instruction.

This chapter reviewed four popular problem-solving courses. All share the focus on individual skills (rather than general ability), teaching the process of problem solving (rather than focusing on product), and success on tests of specific transfer (but not general transfer).

Componential training, based on a cognitive analysis of problem-solving tasks, offers a more specific kind of training. Since the effects of training seem to be specific, componential training offers an important avenue for future problem-solving courses.

Finally, this chapter reviewed the characteristics of expert problem solving in the domains of science, art, and medicine. In each case, expert problem solving required both problem-solving skills and a wealth of knowledge about the domain. There is no shortcut to becoming an expert in a professional field, because good strategies alone are not sufficient for success.

SUGGESTED READINGS

Bransford, J. D. & Stein, B. (1984). *The IDEAL problem solver*. New York: Freeman. (A guide to problem solving, based partly on cognitive research.)

Hayes, J. R. (1981). *The complete problem solver*. Philadelphia: Franklin Institute Press. (Another guide to how to solve problems, partly based on cognitive psychological research.)

Rubinstein, M. F. (1975). *Patterns of problem solving*. Englewood Cliffs, N.J.: Prentice-Hall. (A college-level course in problem solving.)

Segal, J. W., Chipman, S. F. & Glaser, R. (eds.) (1985). *Thinking and learning skills, Vol. 1*. Hillsdale, N.J.: Erlbaum. (Presents a collection of papers concerning problem-solving programs.)

Wickelgren, W. A. (1974). *How to solve problems*. New York: Freeman. (Another guide to problem solving, based on cognitive psychological research.)

PART III

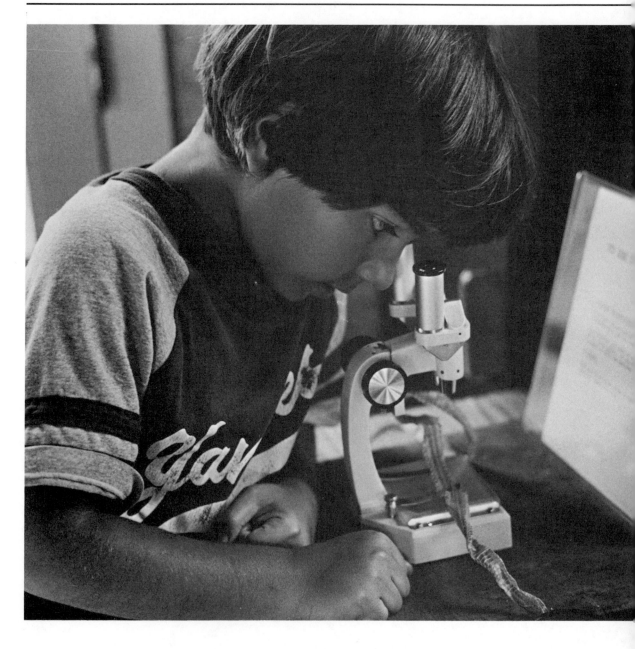

CURRICULUM

The five chapters in this section focus on learning and instruction within subject matter areas. What does a skilled reader know that a less skilled reader does not know? In teaching students how to write, does freeing students from the need to use proper spelling and grammar on the first draft result in better final drafts? Can we teach students to improve their skills in representing problems and planning solution strategies for mathematical problem solving? How do students' existing conceptions of motion and force affect their learning of school physics? These are the kinds of questions addressed here.

In particular, Chapter 10 deals with how students gain fluency in reading, or what could be called "learning to read," including how they learn to decode print into sounds, find the meaning of words in memory, and integrate the words into a meaningful sentence. Chapter 11 deals with reading comprehension, or what could be called "reading to learn," including the role of the reader's prior knowledge about the domain of the passage, the reader's sensitivity to the distinction between important and unimportant information, the reader's tendency to make inferences during reading, and the reader's ability to monitor and assess his own reading process. Chapter 12 covers the process of writing including research on three main phases in writing: planning what to write, translating the plan into actual writing, and reviewing what was written. Chapter 13 explores research on learning mathematics, including four phases in mathematical problem solving: problem translation, problem integration, solution planning, solution execution. Chapter 14 briefly surveys three important issues in science education: What is the role of the learner's existing misconceptions?, Are schoolchildren capable of scientific thinking?, and How do expert scientists think about science problems? In summary, this section focuses on the curriculum in an attempt to see how students attempt to make sense out of what is presented to them.

An issue running through these chapters is the distinction between automatic versus effortful use of basic skills in subject matter areas such as reading, writing, mathematics, or science. Success in each domain requires that the student acquire basic skills, some of which become automatic and some of which may remain effortful. For example, in writing, when skills such as spelling and punctuating become automatic, this frees processing capacity to concentrate on effortful activities such as planning a well-organized composition. Similarly, in reading, when a reader becomes fluent in decoding, this allows the reader to pay more attention to effortful processes such as making inferences during reading or recognizing inconsistencies. Finally, in math or science, developing a useful strategy for solving a problem is easier when the student has automated procedures for computation. Thus, the conditions for meaningful learning that were summarized in Figure 1–3 can be extended to the meaningful learning of basic skills in subject matter areas. Higher level skills such as planning and monitoring one's reading or writing or mathematical/scientific problem solving appear to be facilitated when the student has automated some lower-level skills. You should keep this theme in mind as you read the next five chapters.

10 Reading Fluency

This chapter is concerned with early reading instruction. In particular, this chapter focuses on three skills involved in learning to read: decoding the symbols on the page into pronounced words, accessing the meaning of each word in long-term memory, and integrating the words into a coherent sentence. Research and instructional implications are explored for each of these topics.

THE PROBLEM OF READING A WORD

Let's consider the task of reading words from a printed page as you are doing now. How much time do you think that it takes you to read a typical word? The answer is that competent adult readers can read a word in a fraction of a second, usually less than $\frac{1}{4}$ second (Carpenter & Just, 1981; Just & Carpenter, 1980). The act of reading a word may seem so rapid and so automatic that it could not possibly involve much cognitive processing. However, in this introduction, I will try to convince you that the simple act of reading a word may indeed involve many cognitive processes.

First, can you read aloud the words in Box 10–1? Go ahead and try to pronounce each word.

If you are like most adult readers, you used a variety of strategies in trying to pronounce the words and you made errors on about one-tenth of the words (Baron, 1977). Some possible strategies are sounding out the letters and blending them together, finding a real word that rhymes with the to-be-

---

BOX 10–1   Can You Pronounce These Words?

caws
saif
wight
hought
frish
ait
fign
shud
phrend
blud
nal

Adapted from Baron (1977)

pronounced word, pronouncing some real word that is similar to the to-be-pronounced word.

This word pronunciation task highlights an aspect of reading that is referred to as *decoding*. Decoding is the process of translating printed symbols into sounds.

Now, let's try another task that may be related to reading. You will need a pencil and watch with a second hand. In a moment, I will ask you to look at the words in Box 10–2, and to circle each word that is a member of the category "animal." Note your starting time and ending time, so that you can determine how many seconds this task takes you. Go ahead whenever you are ready.

If you are like most readers, you were able to accomplish this task without too much difficulty. For those of you who like to keep score, there were seven animals in the list, and it takes schoolchildren about 1 second per word to make decisions like the ones you made (Perfetti & Lesgold, 1979).

This word recognition task requires decoding as well as another process that could be called *meaning accessing*. Meaning accessing refers to the process of searching your long-term memory for the meaning of a word.

Let's try one more reading task, using the sentences in Box 10–3. Read each sentence; then, pick the one that is the easiest and the one that is the hardest to read. Sentence one is an excellent candidate for the hardest because it requires moving your eye many times in order to read the words. Sentence 4 is an excellent candidate for the easiest because it is presented in the most familiar format. However, you probably could learn to read sentences presented as words or phrases, such as sentences 2 and 3.

As you can see in this task, reading involves moving your eye across the page to take in information. In addition to using the processes of decoding and meaning access, you must also put all the information in each sentence together. This task helps to demonstrate that the integration process may be easier for presentation formats that allow the eye to take in a lot of information on each glance. We can use the term *sentence integration* to refer to the process of putting all of the words of a sentence together into a coherent idea.

The three tasks you have just tried represent three kinds of processes in reading words: decoding, meaning access, and sentence integration. In this chapter, a brief historical and theoretical overview will be presented, followed by an examination of each of these three kinds of processes.

A MODEL OF READING

What Is Reading?

Any serious discussion of reading must confront the problem that *reading* means different things to different people. For example, Carver (1973), following Spache (1965), has proposed four levels of reading:

1. Decoding words and determining their meaning in a particular sentence.
2. Combining meanings of individual words into a complete understanding of the sentence.
3. Understanding of the paragraph and its implied main idea, as well as cause-and-effect, hypothesis-proof, implications, unstated conclusions, and ideas associated with but tangential to the main idea of a paragraph.
4. Evaluation of ideas, including questions of logic, proof, authenticity, and value judgments.

The first two levels represent basic reading skills in which the developing reader gains increasing automaticity. This chapter (Chapter 10) deals mainly with these reading skills, focusing on decoding, meaning access, and sentence integration. The last two levels represent what Carver calls "reasoning" and what has traditionally been referred to as "reading comprehension." Chapter 11 deals mainly with reading comprehension, focusing on the role of prior knowledge about the subject domain, strategic knowledge about prose structure and inference making, and metacognitive knowledge about comprehension monitoring and reading for purpose.

Let's continue by making another fundamental distinction between *learning to read* and *reading to learn* as suggested by Chall (1979), Singer (1981), Weaver & Resnick (1979), and many others. *Learning to read* involves learning how to translate printed words into another form. Developing automaticity in this translation process is a dominant focus of reading instruction in grades K–3. However, Singer (1981) notes that the mastery of learning to read may be accomplished by the third grade in some children while other children may not have mastered the skill by the end of junior high school. The present chapter

BOX 10–2   Circle Each Animal Word

house
rabbit
tree
shoe
horse
table
mountain
elephant
dog
lamp
bed
shirt
zebra
belt
deer
cloud
basket
mouse

BOX 10–3   Which Sentence Is Easiest and Which Sentence is Hardest to Read?

Sentence 1

R	e	c	e	n	t				
r	e	s	e	a	r	c	h		
h	a	s	s	h	o	w	n		
t	h	a	t	s	a	c	c	a	d	e
l	e	n	g	t	h	i	s		
a	b	o	u	t	o	n	e	o	r
t	w	o	w	o	r	d	s,		
w	h	i	c	h					
c	o	r	r	e	s	p	o	n	d	s
t	o	a	b	o	u	t			
e	i	g	h	t	l	e	t	t	e	r
p	o	s	i	t	i	o	n	s	
p	e	r	f	i	x	a	t	i	o	n.

Sentence 2
One
educational
implication
of
this
work
is
that
students
can
read
faster
if
they
can
be
taught
to
increase
their
saccade
length.

Sentence 3
Training in speed reading
can increase reading rates
from less than 300 words a minute
to more than 900 words a minute.

Sentence 4
However, many research studies have shown that there can also be a corresponding drop in readers' performance on tests of comprehension.

deals with this phase of reading. *Reading to learn* involves the use of reading as a tool for gaining specific knowledge in some subject-matter domain. The acquisition of specific knowledge from reading is a dominant focus of reading instruction in grade 4 and thereafter. Chapter 11 examines techniques for improving students' success in extracting useful knowledge from text, while Chapters 6 and 8 examine variables that influence how skilled readers learn from prose.

History of Reading Research

In the early days of educational psychology, the question of how people learn to read was a fundamental research issue. In his classic book, *The Psychology and Pedagogy of Reading*, Huey (1908/1968, p. 6) summarized the importance of understanding the reading process:

> And so to completely analyze what we do when we read would almost be the acme of a psychologist's achievement, for it would be to describe very many of the most intricate workings of the human mind, as well as to unravel the tangled story of the most remarkable specific performance that civilization has learned in all its history.

In a recent review of early reading research in educational psychology, Tzeng (1981) lists five major experimental studies that were published in the late 1800s, including Cattell's (1886) famous paper, "The Time Taken Up by Cerebral Operations."

Unfortunately, the early enthusiasm for experimental research on reading did not find a comfortable home in the psychology of the early 1900s. The behaviorist movement, which swept across the scene during the first half of the twentieth century, was not consistent with the study of underlying cognitive processes in reading. As Kolers points out in his introduction to a reissued version of Huey's book in 1968, "remarkably little empirical information has been added to what Huey knew" (Huey, 1968, p. xiv.).

The rebirth of cognitive psychology in the 1960s has brought with it a rebirth of interest in the psychological study of reading. During the past decades, many models have been proposed to describe the process by which people understand written language. A review of all of the proposed models is beyond the scope of this book, but we should point out that there are three major classes of models:

> *Bottom-up models*—focus on the perceptual processes of going from the stimulus sensation to some internal representation. For example, visual images of printed words are transformed, through a series of processes, into a meaningful sentence.
>
> *Top-down models*—focus on the cognitive processes of using one's existing knowledge to impose organization on incoming sensations. For example, based on the context, a reader may generate a hypothesis concerning what the next word in the passage will be.
>
> *Interactive models*—focus on both bottom-up perception of visual stimuli and top-down imposition of structure, because both types of processing occur simultaneously and interactively. For example, a reader can use hypotheses such as that a certain word should be a noun and may also extract features from the word in order to build a percept of the letters.

Interactive Processes in Reading

Since a strictly bottom-up or top-down model is not consistent with the research evidence nor with a logical analysis of reading, let's focus more closely on how an interactive model of reading would work. Rumelhart (1977) has described an interactive model in which the reader continuously makes guesses (or hypotheses) about the words on the page and tests these guesses using several different levels of hypothesis testing.

For example, suppose that we presented a student with a page to read and the first words in the first sentence were, "THE CAT." According to the interactive model, the student would engage in some levels of processing based on the physical features of the words such as:

> *Feature level hypothesis testing*—Readers generate and test hypotheses concerning the features of the graphemes, such as whether the first letter contains a vertical straight line. If the reader expects the article THE as the first word, then a feature level analysis should show that there is a vertical straight line in the first position.
> *Letter level hypothesis testing*—Readers generate and test hypotheses about letters, such as guessing that the first letter is T.
> *Letter cluster level hypothesis testing*—Readers generate hypotheses about common groups of letters, such as guessing that the first cluster of letters is TH.

Similarly, the student would also generate other hypotheses based on what the reader knows about grammatical rules and word meanings:

> *Lexical level hypothesis testing*—Readers generate and test hypotheses about words, such as guessing that the first word is THE.
> *Categorical level hypothesis testing*—Readers generate and test hypotheses about parts of speech, such as guessing that the first word is an article.
> *Phrase level hypothesis testing*—Readers generate and test hypotheses about word clusters, such as guessing that the first two words form a noun phrase.

Unlike flowchart models in which a series of processes occur, one after the other, in serial order, Rumelhart's interactive model allows all levels of hypotheses testing to occur interactively, at the same time. The reader is continually making guesses, holding the best guesses until they are either confirmed or rejected at several levels of hypothesis testing. If a hypothesis, such as that the first word is *the*, is consistent with hypotheses testing at several levels, such as "straight vertical line" in feature level testing and "article" in categorical level testing, then reading can proceed smoothly and rapidly. If there are many wrong guesses concerning a word, such as when the hypotheses generated at one level conflict with the testing at another level, then reading time for the particular word will be longer. In this system, all levels of hypotheses testing contribute to the reading of each word. This reading process is summarized in Box 10–4.

As can be seen in Rumelhart's interactive model, some of the processing involves matching the input features to specific letters and letter clusters (as would be required in *decoding*), some of the processing involves matching the letter clusters to actual words in one's vocabulary (as would be required in *accessing meaning*), and some of the processing involves seeing how the words fit into a larger sentence structure (as would be required in *integrating*). Each of these three types of processing is examined in the next three sections.

DECODING

What Is Decoding?

As noted in the first section, decoding refers to the process of translating a printed word into a sound. You may sense that decoding is a rather restricted process: it involves being able to pronounce (or name) printed words rather than being able to tell what they mean. In this section, we explore the long-standing debate concerning how to teach decoding, some major research findings that are related to decoding—word superiority effects (discussed later in this chapter) and pronunciation strategy effects, and modern research on decoding training.

The Great Debate

One of the great debates (Chall, 1967) in the teaching of reading concerns whether to use a "phonics" or a "whole word" approach. The phonics (or "code-emphasis") approach involves teaching children to be able to produce sounds for letters or letter groups and to blend the sounds together to form words. For example, Box 10–5 shows forty-two basic sounds in spoken English

---

BOX 10–4 Six Levels of Hypotheses for the Input String "The Cat"

INPUT:	The cat
FEATURE LEVEL:	The first letter position contains a vertical straight line and a horizontal straight line.
LETTER LEVEL:	The first letter position contains a *t*.
LETTER CLUSTER LEVEL:	The first cluster is *th*.
LEXICAL LEVEL:	The first word is *the*.
CATEGORICAL LEVEL:	The first word is an article.
PHRASE LEVEL:	The two words are a noun phrase.

Adapted from Rumelhart (1977)

BOX 10–5 Common Sound Units for English Words

Character	Common Spellings	Examples
b	b	back
c or k	c, k	cat, kitten
ch	ch, _tch	chief, catch
d	d	dog
f	f, ph	fit, elephant
g	g	give
h	h	help
j	j, _dge, ge, gi, gy	just, fudge, age, giant, gym
l	l	lion
m	m	milk
n	n, kn	no, know
ng	ng	sing
p	p	pot
r	r, wr	right, write
s	s, c	sent, cent
sh	sh, _t_, _c_	shoe, nation, special
t	t	ten
t͟h	th	thin
t̅h̅	th	that
v	v	voice
w	w	way
wh	wh_	white
y	y	yes
z	s, _s	zebra, nose
zh	_s_	vision
a	a, a_e, ai_, -ay, ea, -ey	able, cape, train, day, steak, they
e	e, ee, e_e, ea, _y, _i_	equal, feet, eve, each, baby, babies
i	i, i_e, igh, _y, _ie, ai	I, bite, high, sky, pie, aisle
o	o, o_e, oa, _ow, _oe	go, phone, boat, low, toe
u	u, ue, you, u_e, _ew	using, cue, youth, use, few
a̅	a, au, ai	hat, aunt, plaid
ah	a, al, o	father, calm, on
aw	a, aw, au, o	tall, law, caught, soft
e̅	e, ea	bed, bread
i̅	i, ui, u, ea, ee, ie	sit, build, busy, dear, deer, pierce
u̅	u, o, ou, a, e, o	cup, some, couple, alone, loaded, wagon
oo	oo, u, ew, ue, ou, o	too, rule, new, due, group, do
o̅o̅	oo, u	book, full
oi	oi, -oy	oil, toy
ow	ow, ou	owl, ouch
ar	ar	park, car
ur	ur, ir, er, or, ear	hurt, stir, term, word, earn

Note. This table does not include separate listings for q (as in queen) or for changes in sounds in unaccepted syllables. Pronunciation guides vary in listing from 41 to 45 sounds.

Adapted from Open Court Phonics Kit (1983), Stein (1966), Carrell & Tiffany (1960), Clark & Clark (1977).

BOX 10–6 Phonics Instruction Involves Associating Sounds with Letters or Letter Groups

S   sat
ce   cent
ci   cinder
cy   bicycle

Adapted from *Open Court Phonics Kit* (1979)

and gives examples of letters that correspond to the sounds. Readers learn to associate the appropriate sound to the appropriate letters. Box 10–6 shows a picture of a flat tire (making the "sssss" sound) along with letters that can correspond to this sound.

In contrast, the whole word method involves teaching children to "sight read" words, that is, to be able to pronounce a whole word as a single unit. For example, an early reading program may concentrate on introducing a few hundred words. Figure 10–1 shows some typical "first words" to be learned by beginning readers. With more experience, new words are systematically added to the reader's repertoire. The whole word approach is generally part of a "meaning-emphasis" approach, in which determining the meaning of each word is a major goal.

Singer (1981) provides a fascinating summary of the history of reading instruction in America. In the beginning, during the 1700s, the phonics method was emphasized. The standard textbook was *The New England Primer*, first published in 1690. First, children learned the alphabet; then, they learned to read two-letter combinations (such as "ab, ac, ad, af, . . . uz") and consonant-vowel syllables (ba, da, ca, . . . and so on); then, children were asked to read words containing up to five syllables. Children were drilled on correct pronunciation for each syllable and correct spelling of words until they could spell

FIGURE 10–1 Whole Word Instruction Involves Associating Word Names with Printed Words

Cat   Ball   House

and read short words by sight. Finally, children orally read sentences and stories and afterwards answered comprehension questions.

The phonics tradition was also heavily used up into the early 1800s, when the dominant textbook was *The American Spelling Book*. Published in 1790, this book, like *The New England Primer*, progressed from alphabet to syllables to words. However, where *The New England Primer* focused on religious material, *The American Spelling Book* focused on national loyalty and traditions.

During the middle 1800s, there was a swing to the whole word method. The dominant textbooks were *McGuffey Readers,* which appeared between 1836 and 1844. *McGuffey Readers* systematically introduced new words by letting the student see the word, hear the word, see a picture or sentence referring to the word, and later spell the word (or break it into sounds). Unlike previous books, *McGuffey Readers* were a graded series which allowed for children to be grouped by age and achievement.

By the 1880s emphasis had turned to reading of fine literature and back to the phonics method of instruction. The scientific alphabet was introduced in 1902; it consisted of forty-four phonemes along with forty-four corresponding symbols. Students learned to write sentences phonetically, using the forty-four symbols. Other techniques involved teaching students to sound out words before giving any hints with pictures or sentence context.

By the early 1900s scientific research in education influenced instruction. Emphasis was placed on silent reading rather than oral reading. For example, as an introductory lesson, a teacher might write, "Come here" on the blackboard; students would then carry out the commands that were written. Emphasis was also placed on getting the meaning out of stories; teachers would question children about their experiences before asking them to read a story. Students learned to recognize whole words before they learned how to break them into parts.

Since the end of World War II, the dominant reading textbooks in American schools have been basal readers. Like *McGuffey Readers,* the modern basal readers are an integrated and graded series of reading books and activities, with each successive book in the series requiring more sophisticated and difficult reading skills. Most basal readers employ aspects of the whole word and the phonics approach, but according to many critics (Singer, 1981; Flesch, 1955), the emphasis is on whole-word methods. For example, Flesch's (1955) famous book *Why Johnny Can't Read and What You Can Do About It* called for a shift back to the phonics method of instruction. Chall's (1967) classic book *Learning to Read: The Great Debate* reviewed the research literature and came to the conclusion that children should learn first the relation between sounds and letters before they learn to read for content and meaning.

Chall (1979) notes that her call for a return to "code-emphasis" rather than "meaning-emphasis" for beginning readers has had an impact. For example, she notes that "Sesame Street" and "The Electric Company" opted for a phonics approach as their primary method of early reading instruction. Chall's recommendations are based on the idea of a developmental progression in which children first master decoding skills and later master comprehension skills. Another way to state this transition is to say that children must first learn to read (code-emphasis) before they can successfully read to learn (meaning-emphasis).

As you can see, there have been several swings in American reading instruction between a "phonics method" that progresses from letters to syllables to words to sentences versus a "whole word method" that progresses from meaningful context to words to parts. In a recent review of research on beginning reading instruction, Weaver & Resnick (1979) observed that the "great debate" goes on. What does research have to say about how people read and how to conduct beginning reading instruction? The next section explores research on two important aspects of the great debate about decoding—*word superiority effects* involves research on how people identify letters and *pronunciation strategy effects* involves research on how people put letters together to make words.

Research on Decoding

Word Superiority Effects.   One way to provide information concerning the great debate is to determine how skilled readers, such as normal adults, read letters in words. For example, we might ask: Do people read each letter and put these parts together to form a word, as would be suggested by a phonics approach to reading? Or do people read the whole word first, and then recognize each letter?

The second alternative may strike you as odd, because common sense seems to tell us that you must recognize the parts before you recognize the whole. However, some early research may surprise you. For example, Cattell (1886) found that letters can be perceived more accurately when they are part of a word than when they do not form a word. In experiments, if unrelated letters were flashed on the screen for very brief exposures, people could correctly perceive about three letters; however, if the letters formed simple three-letter words, subjects correctly perceived about six letters. This phenomenon—that people can read letters faster and more accurately when they are parts of words—has been called the *word superiority effect* (Baron, 1978; Kreiger, 1975; Reicher, 1969; Smith & Spoehr, 1974).

The word superiority effect is one of the oldest and best established facts in experimental psychology. As an example of research on the word superiority effect, let's consider an experiment by Johnston (1978, 1981). Subjects were asked to watch a screen, and to be ready to report on letters that were flashed on the screen. Table 10–1 shows that a word (such as COIN), a letter string (such as CPDT), or a letter (such as C) was presented briefly such as for 30 milliseconds; then, a mask (such as **NNNN**) was presented in order to blot out any afterimages; finally, subjects were asked to take a forced choice test concerning

TABLE 10–1 The Word Superiority Effect

Treatment	Example of Stimulus	Mask	Forced Choice Test		Proportion Correct
Word	COIN	NNNN	COIN	JOIN	.845
Letter string	CPDT	NNNN	CPDT	JPDT	.686
Single letter	C	NNNN	C	J	.710

From Johnston (1981)

one of the letters (e.g., was the first letter of the word a "C" or a "J", or was the letter that you saw a "C" or a "J"). Subjects were not told in advance which letter in a word or letter string would be the one they would be tested on. As you can see in Table 10–1, subjects were more accurate on recognizing letters when they were parts of words (such as recognizing the "C" in "COIN") than when they were presented singly (such as recognizing "C" when it is presented alone) or in nonsense strings. In Johnston's experiment, the word superiority effect represents a difference of about 13 to 16% in accuracy.

The word superiority effect has been used as a rationale for teaching reading by the "whole word method" (Singer, 1981), since it seems to imply that readers perceive words more easily than individual letters. However, you need to be suspicious of this conclusion. The word superiority effect is not a theory; it is just a well-established empirical fact. What is needed is a theory of how people read and how they learn to read. Educational practice should be based on our understanding of the reading process (i.e., a unified theory of reading) rather than single facts.

Johnston (1981) has suggested three different ways to interpret the word superiority effect. Theory 1 says that the visual shape of the word provides information that is not present for single letters. However, in contrast to this theory, the word superiority effect still is obtained when the word is presented all in capital letters (such as COIN), in alternating letters (such as CoIn or cOiN), or with irregular spacing (such as CO IN). Theory 2 says that the word provides cues about what the letters can be; for example, if you know that the last three letters of a four-letter word are NOB you can limit your hypotheses concerning the first letter to "S" and "K." However, in contrast to this theory, words that constrain the possible first letters to one of three letters (such as -RIP) do not provide better word superiority effects than words that constrain the possible first letter to one of nine possible letters (such as -ATE). The third theory states that the word allows for better retention through the mask. However, this theory is inadequate because it cannot explain why the code for a word should be easier to remember than the code for a letter. In short, Johnston (1981) concludes that all of the popular theories for the word superiority effect should be rejected.

What causes the word superiority effect? Johnston (1981; Johnston & McClelland, 1980) offer a theory based on the idea that a word is analyzed on several levels. When a word such as "COIN" is presented, the reader begins to form and test hypotheses about the word, on each of the following levels:

Feature detectors—These determine whether the lines are curved or straight and the orientation of lines for each position.
Letter detectors—These determine which letter is present at each position, based partly on information from the feature detectors.
Word detectors—These determine which word is present, based partly on information from the letter detectors.

However, as soon as the mask is presented, the feature and letter detectors are erased. Thus the only level of analysis that survives the mask is the word level. If the stimulus is a letter or a letter string, no word level analysis can take place and thus the mask is more likely to damage performance. Thus Johnston and his colleagues seem to be able to explain the "word superiority effect" by assuming that readers analyze words by their parts; if this theory is correct, then the word superiority effect does not suggest that the whole word method of instruction is better than the phonics method for beginning readers.

Pronunciation Strategy Effects.   As another source of research information, let's return for a moment to the pronunciation task shown in Box 10–1. Barron (1977) presented pronounceable nonsense words like these to adults; subjects were asked to pronounce each word and to tell how they decided on the pronunciation.

The results indicated that Baron's subjects tended to use three distinct strategies. In the *similarity strategy,* subjects pronounced a nonsense word so that it sounded exactly the same as a real word that was familiar to the subject. For example, BLUD was pronounced "blood." In the *analogy strategy* subjects pronounced the word so that it partially rhymed with a real word. For example, ROTION was pronounced in a way so that it rhymed with "motion." In the *corresponding strategy,* subjects used phonetic rules to sound out each part of the word and then blended the sounds together. For example, SHUD was pronounced as *sh* for SH, *ah* for U, and *d* for D, yielding "sh-ah-d."

In Baron's study, the most commonly used strategy was the corresponding strategy (i.e., sounding out the word). This strategy corresponds to the "phonics" method of reading instruction in which students learn the relation between letters and sounds. In contrast, the similarity strategy in Baron's study corresponds somewhat to the "whole word" method of reading instruction. Finally, the analogy approach seems to involve a compromise that deals with sounds of word parts (phonics) and whole words. An analysis of subjects' errors in pronunciation tended to favor the analogy strategy as the most effective.

In order to test the merits of the analogy strategy, Baron (1977) provided explicit training to some subjects in how to use the analogy strategy in pronouncing nonsense words. Subjects given analogy strategy training showed a large improvement in pronunciation performance, with errors dropping from 9 to 4%. Barron also has shown that training in the analogy strategy can be applied successfully to children as young as four years old. For example, students can be taught to pronounce three-letter words ending in "IN" and "AX" such as "TIN" and "TAX" or "PIN" and "WAX," by using rhymes.

The foregoing studies may be criticized on the grounds that they involve skilled readers rather than beginning readers. One important research technique is to compare differences in the reading processes of skilled readers and less skilled readers. In particular, Chall (1967) and others have argued that before one can effectively comprehend written material, one must first develop automatic decoding skills. Perfetti & Lesgold (1979) argue that students who must consciously monitor their decoding process have less attentional capacity for making inferences and otherwise trying to comprehend the passage.

In order to investigate this idea, Perfetti & Hogaboam (1975) selected third and fifth graders who either scored low in standardized tests of reading comprehension (such as below the thirtieth percentile) or scored high in reading comprehension (such as above the sixtieth percentile). Reading comprehension involves being able to "read to learn" (i.e., to answer meaningful questions about a passage that you have just read). Subjects were asked to participate in a pronunciation task like Barron's task. A word was presented on a screen and the subject's job was to say the word as soon as he or she knew what it was. This task requires decoding, but not comprehension.

Some of the words were very common and familiar; as you can see in Figure 10–2, skilled and less skilled readers did not differ greatly in their pronunciation times for familiar words. Some of the words were unfamiliar to the readers: as can be seen in Figure 10–2, the less skilled readers averaged 1 second longer than the skilled readers. One explanation may be that skilled readers are more familiar with the "unfamiliar" words, perhaps because skilled readers spend more time reading more difficult texts. However, Figure 10–2 also shows that the less skilled readers required an average of more than one extra second as compared to the skilled readers for pronouncing pseudowords (i.e., nonsense words that could be pronounced). Apparently, skilled readers employ fast and automatic decoding processes, even for words that have no meaning whereas less skilled readers have great difficulty in decoding words that are not part of their "sight reading" vocabulary. These results are consistent with the idea that well-practiced decoding skills allow the reader to use his or her attentional resources to comprehend the passage. In fact, fluent readers may be so well practiced in decoding that they are unaware of the rules of pronunciation (Calfee, Chapman & Venezky, 1972). Apparently, the learning of efficient decoding skills is a prerequisite for the learning of efficient comprehension skills.

Implications for Instruction: Automaticity Training

The major implication of the research cited is that readers must learn how to recognize letters automatically and sound out letter groups. The main focus of reading instruction during the first few years of school should be to help

FIGURE 10-2   Mean Pronunciation Time for Highly and Less Skilled Readers

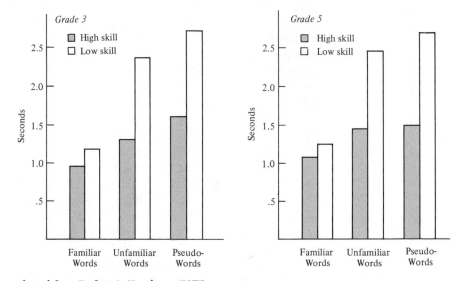

Adapted from Perfetti & Hogaboam (1975)

students develop decoding skills that are automatic (i.e., that do not require extensive conscious effort by the reader). This section focuses on how to provide training for decoding automaticity.

Stanovich (1980) has summarized research on decoding by noting that good readers differ from poor readers mainly on rapid context–free word recognition. The interactive model of reading described earlier in this chapter assumes that reading involves many bottom-up and top-down processes occuring simultaneously. Furthermore, the limited capacity of the memory system requires that if some processes require a great deal of attention, then there will not be attention available for other processes. For example, LaBerge & Samuels (1974) have proposed that fluent readers are able to decode text automatically, leaving attention available for comprehension processes. In contrast, beginning readers' attention must be devoted mainly to decoding, leaving relatively little processing capacity available for comprehension processing. Perfetti & Hogaboam (1975, p. 466) summarize this idea as follows: "To the extent that decoding is a mainly automatic process, it does not make great demands on the readers' higher comprehension processes."

LaBerge & Samuels (1974) have proposed three stages in the development of automaticity:

1. Nonaccurate stage, in which the reader makes errors in word recognition;
2. Accuracy stage, in which the reader can recognize words correctly but it requires great attention to do so; and

3. Automatic stage, in which the reader can recognize words correctly without requiring attention.

How can we teach students to gain automaticity in decoding? Samuels (1979) has suggested a technique called the "method of repeated readings." According to this technique, a student reads a short, easy passage over and over again until a satisfactory level of fluency is reached. Then, this procedure is repeated for another passage, and so on. Figure 10–3 shows the reading and word recognition rate as a student read five different passages using the method of repeated readings. Two findings are particularly interesting. First, for each passage, the fluency improves greatly with repetition. Second, fluency tends to improve from one passage to the next, even though the words are different.

What is the best way to increase word recognition automaticity? Samuels (1967) has proposed the "focal attention hypothesis"—the idea that visual attention should be focused on the printed word rather than the context. Thus word recognition training that relies on context such as pictures and sentences distracts the reader from focusing on the printed word. For example, Ehri & Roberts (1979) asked first graders to learn to read sixteen words, using flash cards. For some students, each card contained just one word; for other students, each card contained a target word within the context of a sentence. As expected, students in the word-only condition could sight read the words faster (averaging 10.9 seconds) than the context condition (averaging 15.7 seconds). Students in the word-only condition, as compared to the context condition,

FIGURE 10–3   Improving Decoding Fluency by Repeated Readings

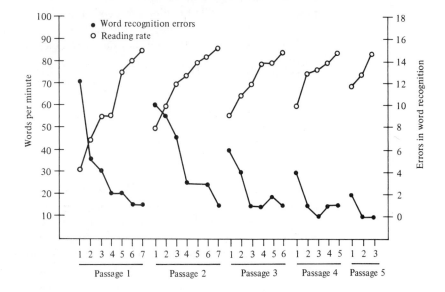

Adapted from Samuels (1979)

remembered more about the orthographic characteristics of the words such as the correct spelling but less of the semantic characteristics of the words needed to generate a sentence using the word. Similarly, Nemko (1984) asked first graders to learn to read sixteen words using flash cards, with each word presented either individually or in the context of a sentence. The test involved reading each word either individually or within a sentence. The best performance was for students who learned and were tested with individual words.

Samuels (1979, p. 405) argues that as readers become more fluent, their comprehension will improve: "as less attention is required for decoding, more attention becomes available for comprehension." Unfortunately, there has not been universal support for the idea that training in decoding automaticity will improve reading comprehension. Fleisher, Jenkins & Pany (1979) gave decoding training to poor readers in the fourth and fifth grades. First, students in the trained group practiced on rapidly reading single words from flash cards while students in the control group received no training. Then, all students took a criterion test in which they were asked to read a list of randomly ordered words (i.e., the words that the trained group had practiced reading). Students in the trained group reached a level of automaticity in which they made nearly no errors and read at least 90 words per minute; in contrast, the control students read at half the rate and made many more errors. Then, all students read two passages—containing the practice words—and took a twelve-item comprehension test. Although the trained group read the passage faster than the control group (i.e., 91 words per minute versus 61 words per minute), there were no significant differences between the groups in comprehension test performance. A reasonable conclusion to draw from this study is that automatic decoding is a necessary but not sufficient condition for improved comprehension. Rapid decoding skill may help to reduce the "bottleneck" (or demands on memory processes), but a skilled reader also needs more. In addition to the opportunity to use comprehension strategies, the reader needs to know *how* to use comprehension strategies. (Comprehension strategies are discussed in the next chapter.)

MEANING ACCESS

What Is Meaning Access?

How does a person read a word? The preceding section showed how bottom-up processing contributes to reading a word. Apparently, word reading involves being able to put all the parts together. However, according to the interactive model of reading discussed earlier in this chapter, bottom-up processing is only half of the story. Readers also make use of their knowledge of semantics (i.e., word meaning) and syntax (i.e., grammatical rules about parts of speech) in trying to understand words found in text. The search for word meaning could be called "meaning access." This section explores some top-down processes involved in reading words, including context effects and vocabulary effects.

Research on Meaning Access

Context Effects. Context effects refer to the idea that the speed and accuracy of word recognition is influenced by the context of the word within a sentence. Tulving & Gold (1963) reported a landmark study concerning the role of sentence context on word meaning. In the experiment, a word was flashed on the screen and the subjects were asked to read the word aloud. Before the word was flashed, subjects were given a cue such as, "The actress received praise for being an outstanding _____." As you can see, this cue provides what Tulving & Gold called an "appropriate context" for the target word *performer,* but an "inappropriate context" for the target word *potato.* The length of the cue given before the target word was zero (i.e., no cue), one, two, four, or eight words. Longer cues, presumably, provide a stronger context for the target word.

Figure 10–4 summarizes the results of the experiment. The experimenters measured the amount of time that a word had to be presented for a subject to be able to read the word. When the target word was presented after an appropriate context, subjects were able to read the word even when the duration of the flash was short. When the target word was presented after an inappropriate context, subjects required that the word be flashed for a longer duration. As you can see in the figure, the time to read a word that followed a

FIGURE 10–4   Time to Perceive a Word in an Appropriate Versus Inappropriate Sentence Context

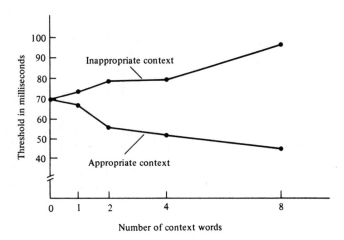

From Tulving and Gold (1963)

long, appropriate cue was about half as much as the time to read a word that followed a long, inappropriate cue. Inappropriate contexts tended to inhibit the subject's ability to read a word, as compared to having no cue; appropriate contexts tended to facilitate the subject's ability to read a word, as compared to having no cue.

These results demonstrate the role of the reader's knowledge of meaning and syntax in word reading. One explanation is that the context provides syntactic cues (i.e., cues about what part of speech should occur) and semantic cues (i.e., cues about the possible meanings of the word). These cues allow the reader to generate specific hypotheses even before the target word is presented. If the hypotheses are correct, less reading time will be required; if the hypotheses are incorrect, more time will be required to generate and test new hypotheses.

Individual Differences in Context Effects. West & Stanovich (1978) extended the Tulving & Gold research method to younger readers. For example, fourth graders, sixth graders, and adults were asked to read words that were presented on a screen. Some target words were preceded by a sentence context that was not congruent with the word; some target words were preceded by a sentence context that was not congruent; and some were preceded only by "the." West & Stanovich measured the amount of time between presentation of the target word, and the subject's pronunciation of the word. Figure 10–5

FIGURE 10–5 Average Time to Pronounce a Word in a Congruous or Non-congruous Context or Preceded Only by "The"

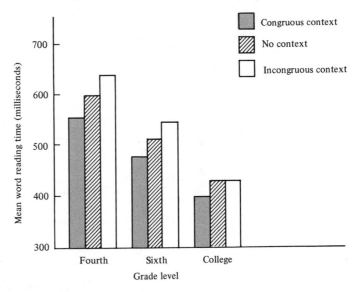

From West & Stanovich (1978)

shows that for all age-groups, performance was better for words in congruous sentences; however, the effects of context appear to weaken for older subjects. Apparently, adults are less reliant on context than children. One implication is that adults search for word meaning in an automatic way while children are more conscious of the context.

In a recent review of research comparing good and poor readers, Spoehr & Schuberth (1981) found that poor readers were more influenced by context cues than good readers. For example, in the West & Stanovich study, poorer readers showed a greater context effect than good readers. Similarly, Schvaneveldt, Ackerman & Semlear (1977) found a developmental trend similar to that obtained by West & Stanovich in which younger readers showed a greater context effect than older readers. These results are consistent with the idea that use of context cues becomes automatic in good readers, while it is more time-consuming and conscious in poorer or younger readers.

Implications for Instruction

The foregoing results show that good readers are more efficient than less skilled readers in finding a word's meaning from memory. Let's suppose that improvements in the speed of meaning access (i.e., the time to find a word's meaning from long-term memory) is a skill that that can be taught. Vocabulary training and sentence structure training are popular techniques for increasing the efficiency of readers' meaning access processes.

Vocabulary Training.   Not surprisingly, children who have better vocabularies (i.e., knowledge of the meanings of more words) perform better on comprehension tests (Anderson & Freebody, 1981). Similarly, changing unfamiliar words in a passage to more familiar synonyms increases children's reading comprehension (Marks, Doctorow & Wittrock, 1974) and word recognition is easier when words are embedded in a familiar rather than unfamiliar context (Wittrock, Marks & Doctorow, 1975). The explanation of these results is that when the words in a passage are unfamiliar, students must focus their attention on the process of meaning access; in contrast, when the words are familiar, students can access the meaning of words automatically and can use their attention for trying to comprehend the passage.

A straightforward implication is that reading comprehension will be enhanced if students are given vocabulary training. However, recent analyses of school reading materials in grades 3–9 found that as many as 88,000 distinct word meanings were required and the average school student acquires about 3000 to 5000 words per year (Nagy & Anderson, 1984; Nagy & Herman, 1984; Nagy, Herman & Anderson, 1985). According to Nagy and his colleagues, direct instruction of vocabulary words would not be able to produce such large vocabulary growth in students. Instead, the bulk of new vocabulary words must be learned from context—that is, from reading or listening to or producing prose. Thus exercises such as silent sustained reading—in which students read books for a certain period of time on a regular basis—may serve as vocabulary training exercises.

In spite of these warnings concerning the limitations of direct vocabulary instruction, there have been many studies aimed at teaching vocabulary to young readers. Many of these studies are successful in teaching vocabulary as measured by multiple choice tests, but not in greatly influencing readers' comprehension (Nagy & Herman, 1985; Pearson & Gallagher, 1983). One reason for the failure of some vocabulary training programs is that much school printed material can be understood with a vocabulary of only 4000 words. Training in new words reaches a point of diminishing returns, since most vocabulary words outside of this basic core of 4000 words occur very rarely in school materials. For example, Nagy & Anderson (1984) found that most of the words in school printed materials occur less than one per million. Learning the meaning of words that occur with such low frequency is unlikely to have a large effect in comprehension.

Vocabulary training programs that are successful in enhancing comprehension tend to be programs that help the reader to embed each word within a rich set of experiences and knowledge and that involve test passages containing the just learned vocabulary words (Kameenui, Carnine & Freschi, 1982). For example, in a series of studies, fourth, fifth, and sixth graders read a passage and then answered test questions about the passage. Some of the subjects received a passage that contained difficult vocabulary words while others received a passage with easier synonyms substituted. The following example is a portion of the passage with difficult words in italics and the easier synonyms indicated in parentheses:

Joe and Ann went to school in Portland. They were *antagonists* (enemies). They saw each other often. They had lots of *altercations* (fights). At the end of high school, Ann *maligned* (said bad things about) Joe. Then Ann moved away. Joe stayed in Portland. He got a job as a *bailiff* (worked for a judge). One day Joe was working, and he saw Ann. Ann did not see Joe. Ann looked *apprehensive* (afraid). She was being *incarcerated* (under arrest).

The test included literal questions such as:
    Joe and Ann saw each other _____ in school.
        (a) never
        (b) not much
        (c) frequently
        (d) often
In addition, the test included inference questions such as:
    Joe works in a _____.

(a) school
(b) hospital
(c) courthouse
(d) university

Figure 10–6 shows the percentage correct for students reading the difficult and easy vocabulary versions of the passage on literal and inferential questions. As you can see, the easy voculary version resulted in slightly better performance on literal questions and greatly enhanced performance on inference questions. Apparently, a reader who understands the words has more opportunity to make meaningful inferences about the story.

The most interesting aspect of the study, however, involved an attempt to train some readers in the meanings of the six difficult vocabulary words before they read the passage. The training involved extensive discussions about each word, such as the following dialogue for *altercations*.

The experimenter presented one index card (containing one vocabulary word and meaning) to the subject. The card was placed on the desk in front of the subject.

FIGURE 10–6   Percentage Correct on Literal and Inferential Questions for Three Vocabulary Treatment Groups

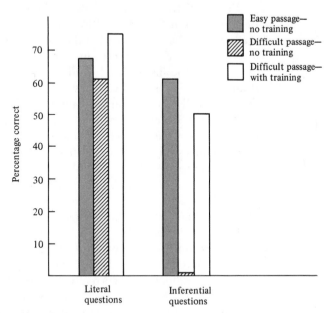

Adapted from Kameenui, Carnine & Freschi (1982)

EXPERIMENTER: "This word is altercations. What word is this?"
CHILD: "Altercations."
EXPERIMENTER: "Correct, altercations. What does altercations mean?"
                 (The experimenter points to meaning given on card.)
CHILD: "Fights."
EXPERIMENTER: "Yes, altercations means fights. Listen, do you have
                 altercations with your teacher?" (Child responds.) "Do
                 you have altercations with a tree?" (Child responds.) "So
                 what does altercations mean?"
CHILD: "Fights."

The new vocabulary word is then integrated with the next one. For example, after the experimenter has gone through the same kind of process for *antagonists*, the experimenter asks: "Listen, do you have any antagonists?" (Child responds.) "Do you have any altercations with your antagonists?" (Child responds.)

Does vocabulary training improve reading comprehension? As you can see in Figure 10–6, students who are given vocabulary training before reading the difficult vocabulary version of the passage tend to excel both in answering literal and inference questions. You should note, however, that the training was for words that were specifically required for the passage and that the training forced the reader to connect the vocabulary words with the reader's prior knowledge and experience.

Beck and her colleagues (Beck, Perfetti & McKeown, 1982; McKeown, Beck, Omanson & Perfetti, 1983) have also developed techniques for helping readers to embed words within their own experiences. Their extensive vocabulary training has been successful in increasing readers' comprehension of texts that contain the just learned words. Again, the success in vocabulary training studies seems to be tied to "knowledge-based training" and tests that involve the specifically taught words (Stahl & Fairbanks, 1986).

Sentence Structure Training.   In addition to vocabulary, readers also use knowledge of syntax, such as how to organize words into a sentence. For example, in a study by Weaver (1979), some third graders were trained on how to solve sentence anagram problems while other third graders received no training. The sentence anagram problems involved giving a list of words that had to be organized into a sentence. The training involved focusing on action words and then asking the "WH questions" (e.g., what, where, when, who, why, how) for each action word. The training also involved rules for how to order word units and how to use "helping words" such as function words and articles. Students practiced for 15 minutes per session and the training continued until a student could correctly solve most of the anagrams in a session. On the average, eighteen sessions were required for each trained student. On a post-test, as expected, the trained group performed better in solving new sentence anagrams than the control group. In addition, the trained group outperformed the control group on several measures of reading comprehension including time to read sentences, prompted verbatim recall, and a cloze test in which the student had to fill in missing words from a passage.

SENTENCE INTEGRATION

What Is Sentence Integration?

The previous sections have shown that reading a word involves both decoding and meaning accessing. However, reading a text also involves fitting the words together into a coherent sentence structure. This process could be called sentence integration, and one way of investigating this process is to observe readers' eyes as they read a passage.

Research on Sentence Integration

Eye Movements During Reading. Let me ask you to introspect about what your eyes are doing as you read the words in a passage, such as this paragraph. Does reading seem to involve a smooth and continuous flow of information from the page into your eyes? Does it seem that your eyes move smoothly across the page, taking in information that is analyzed by your brain? If so, your description corresponds to what has been called a "buffer model" of reading—the idea that your eyes smoothly scan each line from left to right, placing information into a short-term buffer so that the information can be continuously analyzed.

Although this description of reading may be consistent with the "common sense" experiences of skilled readers, it has been subjected to rigorous experimental tests by researchers. One technique that can provide some information is to observe a reader's eye movements during reading. In the late 1800s, researchers such as Javal, working in France, and Erdmann & Dodge, working in Germany, discovered that readers' eyes tended to move in discontinuous jumps rather than in a smooth, continuous flow. In a recent review of the eye movement literature, McConkie (1979) noted that there is clear and consistent evidence for:

Fixations—The eyes focus on a point in the text for an average of 200 to 250 milliseconds.

Fixation span—When the eyes are fixated on some point in the text, the center of the reader's field of vision is about 1 or 2 degrees of visual angle; in normal reading, this corresponds to about eight letter positions. However, readers may have some reduced acuity for letters up to 4 or 5 degrees (i.e., thirty-two to forty letter positions) from the fixation point.

Saccades—The eyes rapidly jump to another point in the text, with the jump lasting about 30 milliseconds; no information can be acquired during the jump.

Saccade lengths—The eyes move from left to right across the page (or return to the beginning of the next lower line) at a rate averaging eight or nine letter positions (or about $1\frac{1}{2}$ words) per move.

The fact that the eyes move in a pattern of fixations and saccades tends to conflict with readers' reports that the information seems to flow smoothly. This experience of smooth processing might result if the eyes moved at a regular rate (i.e., all fixations averaging about the same time) and at a regular distance (i.e., all saccade lengths averaging about the same number of spaces). However, McConkie (1976) has reported that there is great variance within a reader both in the duration of the fixation (ranging from less than 100 milliseconds for simple words to more than 1 second for words at the ends of sentences) and saccade length (ranging from one to fifteen letters, depending on the shape of surrounding words). Thus readers do not sweep their eyes across the page at regular intervals and for regular distances. Instead, eye movements seem to be controlled partially by the text. For example, Rayner & McConkie (1976) observed fewer fixations in the space between sentences than for the rest of the text.

How Much Is Seen in One Fixation?   How can the text control the eye fixations and movements until the reader knows what he or she is reading? In other words, how can you know where to move your eyes until you've looked to see what is ahead? In order to investigate this question, McConkie & Rayner (1975) asked high school students to read a passage that was presented on a computer terminal screen. The computer determined where the reader was fixating on the screen; the computer did not alter the area around the fixation point (called the "window"), but did alter the rest of the text.

On each fixation the size of the window was thirteen, seventeen, twenty-one, twenty-five, thirty-one, twenty-seven, forty-five or one hundred letter positions; this means that if a person was reading the line shown in Box 10–7 with a window of seventeen letters, all would be perfect for the eight letter positions before and the eight letter positions after the fixation point. However, beyond this window, each word would be changed to nonsense letters or X's. For some fixations, the spaces between words was filled in either with other letters or X's, whereas for other fixations the spaces between letters was retained. Box 10–7 shows examples of the "filled" and "spaces" treatments.

Figure 10–7 shows the median saccade length and average reading time for each window size. As can be seen, when the window is artificially restricted, the saccade length drops from about eight letter spaces to six letter spaces and reading rate falls. In addition, filling in spaces between words with letters also tended to reduce the saccade length, with window sizes up to 25. In a subsequent study, Rayner, Well & Pollastek (1980) found that readers are affected only by the size of the window to the right of the fixation point; for example, similar results are obtained for a window of eight letters on either side of the

---

BOX 10–7 Examples of Reading Task Used by McConkie & Rayner

Original Text
Graphology means personality diagnosis from handwriting. This is a

Window Size of 17 with Peripheral Text Filled
Hbfxwysyvoctifdlexiblonality diagnosiscabytewfdnehbemedveee clfw

Window Size of 17 with Peripheral Text Spaced
Hbfxwysyvo tifdl xiblonality diagnosis abyt wfdn hbemedv. Awcl el f

---

Adapted from McConkie & Rayner (1975)

FIGURE 10–7 Median Length of Forward Saccades and Median Reading Rates for Eight Windows

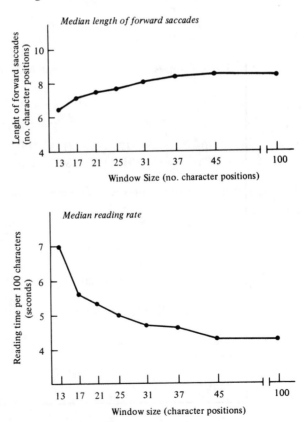

Adapted from McConkie & Rayner (1975)

fixation point as for only eight letters to the right of the fixation point. These results suggest that readers focus on about six to eight letters at a time and can look ahead approximately fifteen letters to determine the appropriate length of the next saccade.

Where Do Readers' Eyes Fixate?   As another example of eye movement research, let's consider the passage shown in Box 10–8. Carpenter & Just (1981) asked a college student to read this passage, while a computer monitored where

---

BOX 10–8   A Reader's Eye Fixations While Reading a Passage on Radioisotopes

The sequence of fixations within each sentence is indicated by the successively numbered fixations above the word being fixated. The duration of each fixation (in milliseconds) is shown immediately below the fixation number.

(4)	(11)
286	466

(1)	(2)	(3)	(5)	(6)	(7)	(8)	(9)
166	200	167	299	217	268	317	399

Radioisotopes have long been valuable tools in scientific and medical

	(16)	
	183	

(10)	(12)	(13)	(14)	(15)	(17)	(18)	(19)	(20)
463	317	250	367	416	333	183	450	650

research. Now, however, four nonradioactive isotopes are being produced.

(24)	(28)
366	183

(21)	(22)	(23)	(25)	(26)	(27)	(29)	(30)	(31)
250	200	367	400	216	233	317	283	100

They are called "icons"—four isotopes of carbon, oxygen, nitrogen, and

(32)	(33)
683	150

sulfur.

From Carpenter & Just (1981)

and how long the reader's eyes fixated on the text. In the box, numbers are given above places in the line that were fixated; the numbers in parentheses indicate the order of fixations and the numbers below them indicate the length of the fixations in milliseconds.

What do Carpenter & Just's observations tell us about the reading process? First, the results demonstrate that fixation points are not randomly or evenly selected. For example, almost all content words are fixated while blank space between sentences is not heavily fixated. You can also see that there is great variability in the length of the jumps from one fixation point to the next, with some saccades spanning just three letters (such as from the twelfth to the thirteenth fixation) and others spanning about ten letters (such as from the twenty-first to the twenty-second fixation).

Second, the results demonstrate that each fixation is not treated equally. For example, there is great variability in the duration of fixations, with some fixations ranging from 100 to 683 milliseconds. You can also see that unfamiliar words, such as *radioisotopes* and *icons*, are fixated for much more time than familiar words. These results are inconsistent with the buffer theory (i.e., the idea that the eye moves at a relatively constant rate taking in information that is analyzed later). Instead, these results suggest that eye movements are guided, in part, by the nature of the text.

A third major discovery is that readers seem to be thinking about what they read during the reading process. For example, fixation durations are generally much longer at the end of a sentence, such as for "medical research" in the first sentence or "being produced" in the second sentence. This result suggests that readers may be trying to integrate the information at sentence or major clause boundaries. Since the fixation seems to be much longer than is required to perceive the word, the long fixations at sentence (and clause) boundaries imply that additional cognitive processing is occurring. Carpenter & Just (1981) call this activity "sentence wrap-up" and suggest that it includes searching for referents, building relations among clauses, drawing inferences, and resolving inconsistencies.

Just & Carpenter (1978) provide an example of how eye fixations may be related to reader's integration of information. In their study, subjects read paragraphs containing two sentences. For example, one paragraph was:

> It was dark and stormy the night the millionaire was murdered. The killer left no clues for the police to trace.

Other readers received a corresponding passage with a slightly different first sentence:

> It was dark and stormy the night the millionaire died. The killer left no clues for the police to trace.

As you can see, the noun "killer" in the second sentence is the agent for the verb "murdered" (or "died") in the first sentence. In reading the second sentence, the reader must make the inference that the killer is responsible for the death of the millionaire. Just & Carpenter found that readers paused an average of 500 milliseconds longer for the second sentence in the second paragraph above than in the first paragraph. The two main places that required extended fixation times were on the word "killer" and at the end of the sentence on the word "trace." Apparently, the integration of information can be observed through careful observation of eye fixations.

Implications for Instruction: Speed Reading

The research described in this section has implications for training in speed reading. Speed reading programs generally attempt to teach students how to increase their fixation span (i.e., how many letters they see in one fixation), to decrease fixation duration (i.e., how long their eyes remain fixated), and to decrease the number of fixations or increase saccade length (i.e., to skim across or down a page). Many speed reading programs claim to be able to increase a person's reading speed without decreasing comprehension. Crowder (1982) observed that the following techniques are often used to accomplish these goals:

1. The student is taught to eliminate subvocal speech so less time is spent on each fixation.
2. The student is taught to use his index finger as a guide that moves down the page, so fewer fixations will be made and each fixation can take in more information.
3. The student is taught to be a more active reader by making inferences during reading.

How does the eye movement research square with these practices and claims? Unfortunately, the research on eye movements would lead us to be cautious in accepting the claims of speed reading advocates. First, the foregoing research shows that pauses in reading (e.g., long fixations at the end of phrases or sentences) may be related to the reader's integrating the information in the phrase or sentence. Thus teaching students to reduce their fixation time could serve to disrupt the integration process. Second, the research cited shows that a reader can usually take in only one or two words per fixation, so increasing the saccade length (or decreasing the number of fixations) means that some words may never be seen.

In order to evaluate the effectiveness of a typical speed reading program, let's consider the following scenario. A school district decides to hire a speed reading company to improve students' reading rates. The company agrees to provide approximately fifty hours of instruction and practice, and guarantees that at least 75% of the students will quintuple their reading rates and increase their comprehension by 10%. Do you think the program will be successful?

A program just like the one in the scenario described above was carried out in a school district in southern California (Crowder, 1982). Students were given reading speed and comprehension tests before and after instruction. The average reading rate rose from 155 words per minute before instruction to 657 words per minute after instruction while comprehension scores fell slightly from 35 to 33% correct.

Should you be happy with these results? Crowder (1982) points out that the company failed to reach its goal since only 13% of the students quintupled their reading rates and increased their comprehension by 10%. In addition, Crowder points out that there was no comparison group, so we do not know how much improvement there would have been over the course of the year if students had not received speed reading instruction. In fact, most standardized tests show that students gain in comprehension each year. Finally, Crowder points out that the reading speed test given after training was easier than the test given before training; thus any gains claimed by the speed reading company cannot be accepted as valid.

In summary, this example points out why you should critically examine any claims that are made concerning speed reading. In a review of evaluation research on speed reading, Crowder (1982) found that reading rates can be increased up to 800 or 900 words per minute (versus less than 300 words per minute in average college students). However, there can also be a corresponding drop in readers' comprehension of the material. For example, Carver's (1971) book, *Sense and Nonsense in Speed Reading,* shows that speed reading courses that teach people to move their eyeballs faster do not often help people to comprehend more text. Apparently, some pauses are needed for readers to make inferences, access meanings of unusual words, and to integrate the information into a coherent message. The positive features of speed reading training are that students may learn how to skim material effectively, and some students may become more automatic in their decoding skills. The negative features are that when the rate of reading is pushed beyond the physical limits of how fast the eye can move, the reader is forced to skip some material and to spend less time integrating the material—which results in less comprehension.

CONCLUSION

A great deal of cognitive processing occurs during the quarter of a second that a reader's eye looks at a word on the printed page. This chapter has explored three related processes: decoding, meaning access, and integration.

Research on reading is notable on several grounds. First, it represents a very old area in psychology that is currently experiencing a welcome revival. Second, there is an extremely large and rapidly growing literature on reading.

Third, there are many different approaches to the study of reading, ranging from pronunciation tasks to eye movement tasks, and many different theoretical approaches, ranging from top-down to bottom-up.

Some of the basic findings concerning decoding have implications for whether to use a whole word or phonics approach in reading instruction. First, there is a word superiority effect in which skilled readers can recognize letters in words more easily than individual letters. Second, skilled readers possess and use pronunciation strategies for combining letters or letter groups into words. This research suggests that skilled readers have automated the processes involved in word decoding, including the use of word context to identify letter sounds and of pronunciation strategies for combining letters. As children's decoding processes become more automatic, the child has more attentional capacity to use for comprehending the material. The current consensus of reading researchers is that the best way to help children acquire automatic decoding process is to rely on the phonics approach.

Some of the research findings concerning meaning access have implications for vocabulary training and sentence structure training. Beginning or younger readers tend to rely on the context of the other words in a sentence in recognizing the meaning of a word; in contrast, older or more skilled readers are able to access word meaning directly. In order to help children become more automatic in their use of sentence context and in understanding unusual words, students can benefit from vocabulary training and sentence structure training. Other direct training includes encouraging children to regularly engage in silent sustained reading and providing an environment where children hear spoken language. The ultimate goal of such training is to help students automate their meaning accessing processes, so that more attention can be devoted to sentence integration and other comprehension processes.

Some of the research findings concerning sentence integration have implications for speed reading training. First, reading involves eye movements, with each fixation requiring a certain amount of time and each fixation able to take in only a small amount of text. Second, long fixations (or pauses) often occur at the end of a phrase or sentence, suggesting that the reader needs time to integrate the material. Speed reading programs that reduce the fixation time may reduce time for integration; similarly, speed reading programs that reduce the number of fixations per page may reduce the amount of information that a reader takes in. Thus, while speed reading training may help students learn how to skim, it may also result in poorer comprehension.

In summary, the implications of psychological research on reading are still far from complete; however, based on the current state of our understanding, instruction in reading should: (1) emphasize phonics in beginning readers as well as meaning approaches for developing readers; (2) emphasize automatic word reading skills through practice; and (3) emphasize increasing reading speed only when a reader does not lose comprehension or when skimming is the goal of reading.

SUGGESTED READINGS

Crowder, R. G. (1982). *The psychology of reading: An introduction*. New York: Oxford University Press. (An excellent textbook that summarizes psychological research on the reading process.)

Lesgold, A. M. & Perfetti, C. A. (eds.) (1981). *Interactive processes in reading*. Hillsdale, N.J.: Erlbaum. (An edited collection of papers that review theory and research on the psychology of reading.)

Resnick, L. B. & Weaver, P. A. (eds.) (1979). *Theory and practice of early reading*. Hillsdale, N.J.: Erlbaum. (An edited set of three volumes containing a wealth of information about early reading including papers by both research psychologists and reading practitioners.)

Tzeng, O. J. L. & Singer, H. (eds.) (1981). *Perception of print: Reading research in experimental psychology*. Hillsdale, N.J.: Erlbaum. (An edited collection of papers that review psychological research on reading, including an interesting history of reading instruction by Singer.)

11   *Reading Comprehension*

This chapter examines techniques for improving students' comprehension of text. Three kinds of knowledge needed for effective reading comprehension are content knowledge, such as having and using prior knowledge; strategic knowledge, such as making inferences during reading and using prose structure to determine important information; and metacognitive knowledge, such as monitoring whether or not one comprehends the material. Finally, this chapter examines reading programs that attempt to teach one or more of these kinds of knowledge.

EFFORT AFTER MEANING

Let me ask you to read the passage in Box 11–1. After you have read over the passage one time, please put it aside and write down all you can remember.

This passage was used by Bartlett (1932) in his famous research on how people learn and remember meaningful prose. Since Bartlett asked British college students to read a folk story from a North American Indian culture, his readers did not have much prior experience with the ideas in the passage. In Bartlett's study, first one person read the passage and then wrote down all he could remember; this version was then read by a second person who wrote down all he could remember; this version was passed on to the next person and so on. By the time the story was read and recalled by the last person, it had

---

BOX 11–1   Original Version of the "War of the Ghosts" Story

The War of the Ghosts

One night two young men from Egulac went down to the river to hunt seals, and while they were there it became foggy and calm. Then they heard war-cries, and they thought: "Maybe this is a war-party." They escaped to the shore, and hid behind a log. Now canoes came up, and they heard the noise of paddles, and they saw one canoe coming up to them. There were five men in the canoe, and they said:

"What do you think? We wish to take you along. We are going up the river to make war on the people."

One of the young men said: "I have no arrows."

"Arrows are in the canoe," they said.

"I will not go along. I might be killed. My relatives do not know where I have gone. But you," he said, turning to the other, "may go with them."

So one of the young men went, but the other returned home.

And the warriors went on up the river to a town on the other side of Kalama. The people came down to the water, and they began to fight, and many were killed. But presently the young man heard one of the warriors say: "Quick, let us go home: that Indian has been hit." Now he thought: "Oh, they are ghosts." He did not feel sick, but they said he had been shot.

So the canoes went back to Egulac, and the young man went ashore to his house, and made a fire. And he told everybody and said: "Behold I accompanied the ghosts, and we went to fight. Many of our fellows were killed, and many of those who attacked us were killed. They said I was hit, and I did not feel sick."

He told it all, and then he became quiet. When the sun rose he fell down. Something black came out of his mouth. His face became contorted. The people jumped up and cried.

He was dead.

From Bartlett (1932)

changed greatly, as you can see in Box 11–2. If you are like the subjects in Bartlett's study, here are some of the changes you made in your recall:

1. *Leveling or flattening*—You left out many of the details such as proper names (Egulac, Kalama). You lost the verbatim writing style of the writer and instead remembered the general "gist" of parts of the story.

2. *Sharpening*—You remembered and maybe even emphasized a few dis-

tinctive details, such as the Indian not being able to go to fight because he had an old mother at home.

3. *Rationalization*—You made the passage more compact and coherent and more consistent with your expectations. For example, if you viewed the passage as a story about a fishing trip or a naval battle, then you would be less likely to remember references to spirits and ghosts.

As you can see, the main point of this demonstration is that people's memories do not work like computer memories. We do not tend to remember information perfectly in verbatim form. We remember some things, but not in the same form as presented. We often add some things that were not given, and we try to organize our memories in a way that makes sense.

According to Bartlett, when we read a meaningful prose passage we are not passively putting the information into our minds; instead, we are actively trying to understand the passage. Bartlett referred to this active comprehension process as "effort after meaning." In reading a text, humans must assimilate the new information to existing knowledge—or what Bartlett called "schemas." What a person learns from reading a text does not correspond directly to what is presented, but rather to a combination of what is presented and the reader's schema to which it is assimilated. Readers change the new information to fit their existing concepts, and in the process, details are lost and the knowledge becomes more coherent for the reader. For the "War of Ghosts" passage, most readers lacked the appropriate schema concerning spirits. Since learning involves assimilating new material to existing concepts, the readers were at a loss. According to Bartlett (1932, p. 172): "Without some general setting or label as we have repeatedly seen, no material can be assimilated or remembered." Since mystical concepts were not a major factor in the readers' culture, the mystical aspects of the story were not well remembered; instead the story was changed into a more common "war story."

Bartlett also proposed that recalling a story involves an active "process of construction" rather than straightforward retrieval. During recall, we use the general schema—such as a "war story"—to help generate details that fit with it.

BOX 11–2   What Do Readers Remember from the "War of the Ghosts" Story?

Version Reproduced by the First Subject

The War of the Ghosts

There were two young Indians who lived in Egulac, and they went down to the sea to hunt for seals. And where they were hunting it was very foggy and very calm. In a little while they heard cries, and they came out of the water and went to hide behind a log. Then they heard the sound of paddles, and they saw five canoes. One canoe came toward them, and there were five men within, who cried to the two Indians, and said: "Come with us up this river, and make war on the people there."

But one of the Indians replied: "We have no arrows."

"There are arrows in the canoe."

"But I might be killed, and my people have need of me. You have no parents," he said to the other, "you can go with them if you wish it so; I shall stay here."

So one of the Indians went, but the other stayed behind and went home. And the canoes went on up the river to the other side of Kalama, and fought the people there. Many of the people were killed, and many of those from the canoes also.

Then one of the warriors called to the young Indian and said: "Go back to the canoe, for you are wounded by an arrow." But the Indian wondered, for he felt not sick.

And when many had fallen on either side they went back to the canoes, and down the river again, and so the young Indian came back to Egulac.

Then he told them how there had been a battle, and how many fell and how the warriors had said he was wounded, and yet he felt not sick. So he told them all the tale, and he became weak. It was near daybreak when he became weak; and when the sun rose he fell down. And he gave a cry, and as he opened his mouth a black thing rushed from it. Then they ran to pick him up, wondering. But when they spoke he answered not.

He was dead.

Version Reproduced by the Tenth Subject

The War of the Ghosts

Two Indians were out fishing for seals in the Bay of Manpapan, when along came five other Indians in a war-canoe. They were going fighting.

"Come with us," said the five to the two, "and fight."

"I cannot come," was the answer of the one, "for I have an old mother at home who is dependent upon me." The other said he could not come, because he had no arms. "That is no difficulty," the others replied, "for we have plenty in the canoe with us"; so he got into the canoe and went with them.

In a fight soon afterwards this Indian received a mortal wound. Finding that his hour was coming, he cried out that he was about to die. "Nonsense," said one of the others, "you will not die." But he did.

From Bartlett (1932)

Memory is not detailed but rather is schematic, that is, based on general impressions. Although recall produces specific details that seem to be correct, many are, in fact, wrong.

Bartlett's work, though more than fifty years old, is concerned with many of the same issues raised by modern cognitive psychologists. Of particular interest is Bartlett's view of the reader as actively engaged in an effort after meaning—that is, that the reader uses his or her existing knowledge to guide reading.

SCHEMA THEORY

What Is a Schema?

Bartlett was one of the first psychologists to address the question of how people learn from meaningful prose. Bartlett's main theoretical idea was the "schema"—a person's existing knowledge which is used both to assimilate new information and to generate recall of information. For example, in reading the "War of the Ghosts" story you must construct an appropriate schema such as "war story," assimilate facts from the story to the schema such as getting mortally wounded, and use the schema for constructing a recall including inferences that are consistent with the theme.

What is a schema? In a sense, answering this question is a major part of the agenda of modern cognitive psychology (Rumelhart, 1980). Although each theorist offers a slightly different view of schema, a general definition would contain the following points (Mayer, 1983):

> General—A schema may be used in a wide variety of situations as a framework for understanding incoming information.
> Knowledge—A schema exists in memory as something that a person knows.
> Structure—A schema is organized around some theme.
> Comprehension—A schema contains "slots" that are filled in by specific information in the passage.

Thus a schema is a reader's general knowledge structure, that serves to select and organize incoming information into an integrated, meaningful framework.

Schemas for Expository Prose. Graesser (1980) and others have pointed out that younger readers often lack appropriate schema for expository prose. Chapter 8 presented several basic kinds of expository prose structures such as process, enumeration, and classification.

Schemas for Narrative Prose. For narrative prose, several authors have proposed "story grammars" that readers might use (Mandler & Johnson, 1977; Rumelhart, 1975; Thorndike, 1977). For example, Mandler & Johnson (1977) have suggested that most folk stories can be divided into two main parts: STORY = SETTING + EPISODE(S). An episode can be divided into two parts: EPISODE = BEGINNING + DEVELOPMENT. The development of an episode contains two parts: DEVELOPMENT = RESPONSE + ENDING. A response can consist of two simple parts: RESPONSE = SIMPLE REACTION + ACTION. Or a response can be more complex: RESPONSE = COMPLEX REACTION + GOAL PATH. A goal path consists of two parts: GOAL PATH = ATTEMPT + OUTCOME. Box 11–3 shows how the "War of the Ghosts" story can be analyzed according to Mandler & Johnson's story grammar. As you can see, the story is broken into a setting and five episodes. Episode 1 is followed by Episode 2, which is followed by Episode 5; Episodes 3 and 4 are subepisodes connected to Episode 2. Within each episode, there is usually a beginning event followed by some reaction that results in some outcome or ending.

When a reader is given a story to read or listen to, the reader will have expectations that the story will have a structure, such as is indicated in Mandler & Johnson's story grammar. For example, readers expect that there will be episodes in which some beginning event is followed by attempts to respond to it that result in an ending. Whaley (1981) found that third graders are far less able than sixth graders to predict what will come next in a story. Presumably, younger readers are not as aware of story grammars as older readers. Thus learning to read involves learning to fill in each general part of the structure (such as the beginning, action, and ending of each episode) with specifics from the story.

What Are the Skills for Reading Comprehension?

This chapter is concerned with the process of reading comprehension, and in particular with understanding the skills that underlie a reader's "effort after meaning." What are these skills? In a recent review of five major basal reading series, Rosenshine (1980) found that all emphasized the following eight skills: locating details, recognizing the main idea, recognizing the sequence of events, drawing conclusions, recognizing cause-and-effect relationships, understanding words in context, making interpretations, and making inferences from the text. However, Rosenshine found no evidence that the basal series taught these skills in the same order and sequence. Although these skills have long been part of reading comprehension programs taught to millions of students, we are just beginning to understand how these skills are related to the process of reading comprehension.

In this chapter, we explore three kinds of knowledge suggested by Brown, Campione & Day (1981) that a reader might use in the process of "effort after meaning":

> *Content knowledge*—refers to information about the subject domain of the passage. This is discussed in the section titled "Using Prior Knowledge."
>
> *Strategic knowledge*—refers to the reader's collection of procedures for

BOX 11–3   Analysis of the "War of the Ghosts" Story Using Story Grammar

Setting   1   One night two young men from Egulac went down to the river to
                                    hunt seals,
                                2   and while they were there it became foggy and calm.

Episode 1

Beginning   3   Then they heard war-cries,
Complex Reaction   4   and they thought, "Maybe this is a war party."
Attempt   5   They escaped to the shore,
                                6   and hid behind a log.
                                7   Now canoes came up,
Ending   8   and they heard the noise of paddles,
                                9   and saw one canoe coming up to them.

Episode 2

Setting   10   There were five men in the canoe,
Beginning   11   and they said, "What do you think? We wish to take you along.
                               12   We are going up the river to make war on the people."
Attempt   13   One of the young men said, "I have no arrows."
Outcome   14   "Arrows are in the canoe," they said.
                               15   "I will not go along.
Attempt   16   I might be killed.
                               17   My relatives do not know where I have gone.
                               18   But you," he said, turning to the other, "may go with them."
Outcome   19   So one of the young men went,
                               20   but the other returned home.
Ending   21   And the warriors went on up the river to a town on the other side
                                    of Kalama.

Episode 3

Beginning   22   The people came down to the water,
                               23   and they began to fight,
                               24   and many were killed.
                               25   But presently the young man heard one of the warriors say, "Quick,
                                    let us go home; that Indian has been hit."
Simple Reaction   26   Now he thought, "Oh, they are ghosts."
                               27   He did not feel sick,
Action   28   but they said he had been shot.
Ending   29   So the canoes went back to Egulac,

Episode 4

Beginning   30   and the young man went ashore to his house and made a fire.
                               31   And he told everybody and said, "Behold I accompanied the ghosts,
                                    and we went to a fight.
                               32   Many of our fellows were killed,
Action   33   and many of those who attacked us were killed.
                               34   And they said I was hit
                               35   and I did not feel sick."
                               36   He told it all,
Ending   37   and then he became quiet.

		Episode 5
Beginning	38	When the sun rose he fell down.
	39	Something black came out of his mouth.
	40	His face became contorted.
Action	41	The people jumped up and cried.
Ending	42	He was dead.

From Mandler & Johnson (1977)

learning more effectively. These are discussed later in the sections titled "Using Prose Structure" and "Making Inferences."

Metacognitive knowledge—refers to the reader's awareness of his/her own cognitive processes and whether he or she is successfully meeting the demands of the task. These skills include comprehension monitoring, self-checking, and adjusting performance for different goals; they are explored in the section titled "Using Metacognitive Knowledge."

USING PRIOR KNOWLEDGE

What Is the Reader's Perspective?

One of the most persistent findings in the adult literature on prose learning is that people's prior knowledge about the topic of a passage influences what they remember from the passage. What is remembered seems to depend both on what is presented in the passage and on what perspective the reader brings to the reading task.

As an example of the role of prior knowledge, consider the passage shown in the top of Box 11–4. Bransford & Johnson (1972) asked college students to read this passage, to rate the passage's comprehensibility (1 is low and 7 is high), and to recall the passage. Some students were given a title ("Washing Clothes") for the passage before they read the passage; some students were given the title after they had read the passage; and some were given no title at all. The bottom of Box 11–4 shows the performance of the three groups on the recall and comprehension rating tasks. As you can see, the title-before group gave a much higher comprehension rating and recalled about twice as much as the other groups. Apparently, giving students the title of the passage allowed them to relate the new information to their prior knowledge about washing clothes; providing the title after reading or not at all left the reader without a way of meaningfully relating the new information to prior knowledge during reading.

Box 11–5 presents another passage for you to read. Suppose I asked you to read the passage from the perspective of a potential homebuyer. Alternatively, suppose I asked you to read from the perspective of a burglar. Would what you

BOX 11–4   The Washing-Clothes Passage

The Passage

The procedure is actually quite simple. First you arrange items into different groups. Of course one pile may be sufficient depending on how much there is to do. If you have to go somewhere else due to lack of facilities that is the next step; otherwise, you are pretty well set. It is important not to overdo things. That is, it is better to do too few things at once than too many. In the short run this may not seem important but complications can easily arise. A mistake can be expensive as well. At first, the whole procedure will seem complicated. Soon, however, it will become just another facet of life. It is difficult to foresee any end to the necessity for this task in the immediate future, but then, one never can tell. After the procedure is completed, one arranges the materials into different groups again. Then they can be put into their appropriate places. Eventually they will be used once more and the whole cycle will then have to be repeated. However, that is part of life.

Comprehension and Recall Scores for the Passage

	No Topic	Topic After	Topic Before	Maximum Score
Comprehension ratings:	2.29	2.12	4.50	7.00
Number of idea units recalled:	2.82	2.65	5.83	18.00

From Bransford and Johnson (1972)

remembered from the passage be influenced by your perspective—homebuyer versus burglar—while reading the passage? Pichert & Anderson (1977) asked subjects to read the house passage from the perspective of a potential home-buyer or burglar or with no perspective instructions. Subjects' recall of details from the passage was greatly influenced by their perspective while reading. For example, details such as where dad keeps the coin collection were better recalled by the subjects with the burglar perspective. Again, these results show that what is learned from reading depends both on the passage and the reader's perspective.

Research on Differences in Children's Prior Knowledge

Differences in the Amount of Prior Knowledge.   More recently, similar results have been obtained in studies using younger readers. Pearson, Hansen

---

BOX 11–5   The House Passage

The two boys ran until they came to the driveway. "See, I told you today was good for skipping school," said Mark. "Mom is never home on Thursday," he added. Tall hedges hid the house from the road so the pair strolled across the finely landscaped yard. "I never knew your place was so big," said Pete. "Yeah, but it's nicer now than it used to be since Dad had the new stone siding put on and added the fireplace."

There were front and back doors and a side door which led to the garage which was empty except for three parked 10-speed bikes. They went in the side door, Mark explaining that it was always open in case his younger sisters got home earlier than their mother.

Pete wanted to see the house so Mark started with the living room. It, like the rest of the downstairs, was newly painted. Mark turned on the stereo, the noise of which worried Pete. "Don't worry, the nearest house is a quarter of a mile away," Mark shouted. Pete felt more comfortable observing that no houses could be seen in any direction beyond the huge yard.

The dining room, with all the china, silver and cut glass, was no place to play so the boys moved into the kitchen, where they made sandwiches. Mark said they wouldn't go to the basement because it had been damp and musty ever since the new plumbing had been installed.

"This is where my Dad keeps his famous paintings and his coin collection," Mark said as they peered into the den. Mark bragged that he could get spending money whenever he needed it since he'd discovered that his Dad kept a lot in the desk drawer.

There were three upstairs bedrooms. Mark showed Pete his mother's closet which was filled with furs and the locked box which held her jewels. His sisters' room was uninteresting except for the color TV, which Mark carried to his room. Mark bragged that the bathroom in the hall was his since one had been added to his sisters' room for their use. The big highlight in his room, though, was a leak in the ceiling where the old roof had finally rotted.

From Pichert and Anderson (1977)

& Gordon (1979) asked second graders to read a modified basal passage on spiders. Although all of the children were classified as "good readers" based on their standardized reading comprehension test scores, half the students knew a lot about spiders and half did not. After reading the spider passage, the children answered text-explicit questions dealing with information specifically presented in the passage such as, "What does Webby bite insects with?" and text-implicit questions, which required inferences such as "What part of Webby's body is nearly the same as part of a snake's body?". Figure 11–1 shows that the high knowledge readers scored almost three times better than the low knowledge readers on questions requiring inference and about 25% better on questions requiring retention of facts. These results are consistent with the idea that good reading skill alone is not the main determinant of what is learned from reading a passage. In addition, the knowledge that the reader brings to the reading situation seems to heavily influence the reader's ability to make inferences about the material.

Marr & Gormley (1982) also found evidence that prior knowledge tends to enhance readers' inference making performance more than simple retention of facts. Fourth graders were asked to read either familiar or unfamiliar passages, and then asked to retell the story and to answer some questions. Examples are given in Box 11–6. Responses were scored as "textual" if they referred to material in the text and "scriptal" if they involved inferences. As you can see in Box 11–6, the differences between the familiar and unfamiliar texts were not great for textual responses on the retell or question-answering tasks; however,

FIGURE 11–1   **Effects of Background Knowledge on Reading Comprehension and Retention**

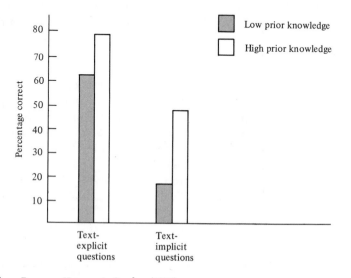

Adapted from Pearson, Hanson & Gordon (1979)

BOX 11–6   **Effects of Familiar and Unfamiliar Passages on Reading Comprehension and Retention**

A Familiar Sports Passage

Baseball is a summer game. Usually it is played outdoors on a field. Baseball is a team sport that has nine players. A baseball has a rubber center that is covered with both string and leather. The pitcher winds up and throws the baseball to the batter. Then the batter tries to hit the ball out of the baseball field. A run is made each time a baseball batter hits the ball, runs all three bases, and touches home plate. A game is won by the team scoring the most runs. This game is an exciting sport.

An Unfamiliar Sports Passage

Curling is a winter game. Usually it is played indoors on the ice. Curling is a team sport that has four players. A curling stone is a round rock that has a handle on the top. The curler slides the stone down the ice toward colored circles. The team captain or skip stands at the end with these circles. A point is scored each time the curling stone is thrown, aimed toward the skip, and stops on a colored circle. A game is won by the team scoring the most points. This game is an unusual sport.

Number of Textual and Scriptal Responses on Two Tests

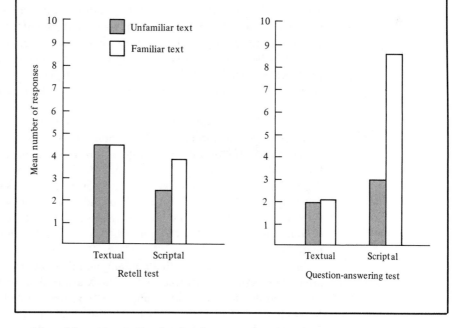

Adapted from Marr & Gormley (1982)

the familiar texts generated considerably more scriptal responses as compared to the unfamiliar text for both retell and question-answering tasks. Again, it appears that prior knowledge has its strongest effects on helping readers make useful inferences rather than on simple retention of facts.

Differences in the Kinds of Prior Knowledge. In a better controlled study, Lipson (1983) varied the background knowledge of readers who all read the same passages. The subjects were Jewish and Catholic students in grades 4, 5, and 6. All were classified as good readers, but they differed in their knowledge of Jewish and Catholic ceremonies. The passages included one entitled, "Bar Mitzvah" and one entitled, "First Communion." Subjects were asked to read and recall the material in the passages. As expected, the Jewish students read the Bar Mitzvah passage faster than the Catholic students while the Catholic students read the First Communion passage faster than the Jewish students. Figure 11–2 summarizes the number of pieces of information correctly recalled (text-explicit recall), the number of correct inferences (inference recall), and the number of errors (error recall). As you can see, readers recalled more text-explicit information, made more inferences, and made fewer errors on passages for which they possessed a large amount of prior knowledge versus passages for which they did not.

Implications for Instruction

The main theme of this section of the chapter is that readers of all ages seem to use their "prior knowledge" to help them understand what they are reading. The foregoing examples demonstrate that a passage may be difficult to comprehend when the reader lacks an appropriate perspective or when the reader's perspective is different from the writer's perspective. In summary, reading comprehension depends partly on the content knowledge that the reader brings to the task.

The implications for instruction include making sure that reading material is appropriate for the interests and experience of the child. This recommendation is particularly important when children are reading either far above or below their grade level. For example, a student who reads books intended for children who are three or four years older may be able to decode each sentence, but may lack the necessary prior knowledge to appreciate the theme of the material. Similarly, a student who is reading books intended for children three or four years younger than him may be bored with the immature theme of the material.

A related implication is that reading should be integrated with other subject areas. For example, if a topic such as the Maya Indians in Mexico is covered in social studies, then it might be appropriate to read a folk story about the life of Maya children. The material learned in the social studies unit could provide the "prior knowledge" students need to appreciate the folk story.

FIGURE 11–2   **How Different Perspectives Affect What Is Remembered from the Same Passage**

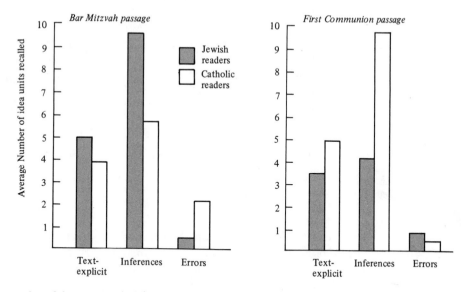

Adapted from Lipson (1983)

Finally, some classroom discussion and activity can provide the "prior knowledge" readers need for comprehending a passage. This kind of prereading activity can help to turn unfamiliar passages into familiar ones.

USING PROSE STRUCTURE

Does the Reader Remember Important Information?

Another persistent finding in the adult literature on learning from prose is that important information from a passage is remembered better than unimportant information (Johnson, 1970; Mayer, 1983; Meyer & McConkie, 1973; Meyer, 1975; Kintsch, 1976). This finding suggests that skilled readers know about the macrostructure of the passage—that is, about how the passage may be broken down into ideas and how the ideas may be related in a hierarchical outline. For example, in Chapter 8, Box 8–3 presented a passage about supertankers and Table 8–3 presented the "top-level structure" of the passage.

As an example, suppose that we took a typical story passage and broke it into idea units—sentences or phrases that convey one event or action. Then, suppose that we asked some skilled adult readers to point out one-fourth of the idea units as the least important (rated 1), one-fourth as the second least

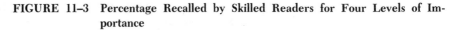

FIGURE 11–3   Percentage Recalled by Skilled Readers for Four Levels of Importance

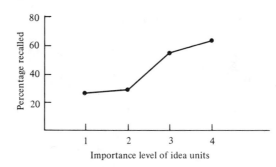

Adapted from Brown & Smiley (1978)

important (rated 2), one-fourth as the second most important (rated 3), and one-fourth as the most important (rated 4). Now, let's give this story in its normal form to some other skilled adult readers. We'll ask these adults to read and then recall the information in the passage. Do you think that the readers will show a preference for recalling the important information over the unimportant information? Figure 11–3 summarizes the results of just such a study carried out by Brown & Smiley (1978). As you can see, recall of important information is much better than recall of unimportant information. This pattern, obtained in many studies, can be called a "levels effect," because the level of importance of an idea unit influences its probability of being recalled.

Research on Differences in Children's Use of Prose Structure

Age-Related Differences in Using Prose Structure.   There is some evidence that more able and older readers have a better awareness of the structure of passages that they read as compared to less able or younger readers. Awareness of structure would be reflected in recognizing and paying attention to information that is important to the theme of the passage. For example, Brown & Smiley (1977) conducted a study using short stories called "The Dragon's Tears" and "How to Fool a Cat." First, they broke the story down into idea units and asked a group of skilled adult readers to identify one-quarter of the idea units as least important (rated 1), one-quarter as second least important (rated 2), one-quarter as second most important (rated 3), and one-quarter as most important (rated 4). Then, Brown & Smiley asked third graders, fifth graders, seventh graders, and college students to rate the importance of each idea unit in the stories, using a procedure similar to that just described. Figure 11–4 gives the average rating for each category of idea unit by age group. As you can see, the third and fifth graders do not seem to be able to recognize which of the idea units are important and which are unimportant—they tend to rate the most important idea units about the same as the least important ones. However, seventh graders, and to a greater extent, college students display an awareness of the relative importance of idea units—they tend to give high ratings to important idea units and low ratings to unimportant ones.

Ability-Related Differences in Using Prose Structure. Meyer (1975) has devised a technique for determining whether readers use the "top-level structure" of a passage, which is a sort of skeleton outline of the main topics (presented in Chapter 8). Using the top-level structure would be indicated by students recalling the main superordinate ideas before they recall the subordinate ideas. If more mature readers are more sensitive to top-level structure, their recall protocols should be organized around this top-level structure and recall should be enhanced mainly for the superordinate rather than the subordinate information in a passage.

Taylor (1980) asked good fourth grade readers, poor sixth grade readers, and good sixth grade readers to read and recall a short passage. As expected, on delayed recall, 59% of the good sixth grade readers used top-level structure in recalling the material compared to only 18% of the poor sixth grade readers and

FIGURE 11–4 Average Importance Ratings for Text Given by Students at Four Age Levels

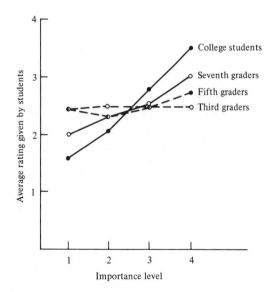

Adapted from Brown & Smiley (1977)

12% of the good fourth grade readers. If skilled readers focus more on top-level structure, we would expect them to excel particularly in recall of superordinate ideas. As expected, on delayed recall, the good readers in the sixth grade recalled about 75% more of the superordinate information than the poor readers in the sixth grade, but only 30% more of the subordinate information than the poor readers. These results are summarized in Figure 11–5.

Implications for Instruction

What can be done to help readers learn to pay attention to the top-level structure (or superordinate information) in a passage? Brown & Smiley (1978) provide some evidence concerning the potential trainability of structure-based reading strategies. For example, fifth, seventh/eighth, and eleventh/twelfth graders were asked to read along as the experimenter read a short story such as "The Dragon's Tears" or "How to Fool a Cat." Then subjects were asked to recall the passage, as summarized by the black line in Figure 11–6. The results in Figure 11–6 indicate that there was a levels effect for each age-group in which students performed better on recall of more important idea units. After the first recall test, students were given a 5-minute study period and told to undertake any activity that would improve recall. Paper, pens, and a copy of the passage (in primary type) were available. Then, a second recall test was

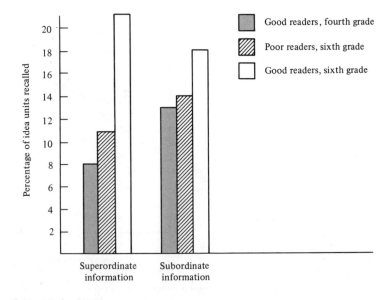

Adapted from Taylor (1980)

FIGURE 11–6   Percentage Correct Recall by Importance Level for Three Age Groups

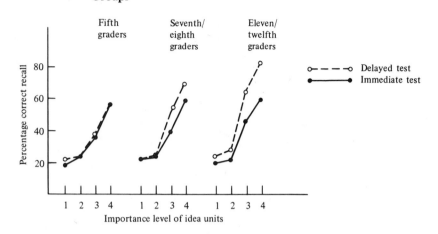

Adapted from Brown & Smiley (1978)

administered, as summarized by the dotted line in Figure 11–6. The results in Figure 11–6 show that the extra study time did not have much of an effect on the younger students but did improve the performance of the older students, particularly on recall of the more important idea units. Apparently, the older students knew to use study time in order to focus on important information while the younger students did not spontaneously use this strategy.

Can the younger students be induced to apply useful study strategies even if they would not use these strategies spontaneously? In order to investigate this question, Brown & Smiley continued the experiment for a second day. The procedure was identical except that during the 5-minute study interval students who did not show evidence of actively studying were prompted to engage in study activities such as underlining. Figure 11–7 shows the recall patterns for fifth graders who underlined spontaneously, fifth graders who were induced by the experimenter to underline, and fifth graders who could not be induced to underline during the 5-minute study period. Again, the solid line is the recall performance on the first test and the dotted line is the recall performance on the second test, after the 5-minute study period. As can be seen, the students who spontaneously underlined without having to be instructed to do so seem to have focused on important information; this is indicated by the improvement in recall of important idea units but not of other information. In contrast, inducing students to underline did not serve to focus their attention on important information, as is indicated by the improvement in recall of unimportant information only. Similar results were obtained for the seventh and eighth graders. Apparently, younger readers need practice in effective techniques for recognizing and using the hierarchical organization of a passage.

FIGURE 11–7   Percentage Correct Recall by Importance Level for Three Groups of Fifth Graders

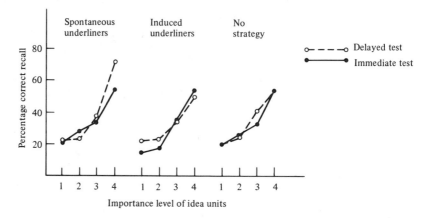

Adapted from Brown & Smiley (1978)

In a direct training study, Taylor & Beach (1984) taught seventh graders to use a hierarchical summary procedure for reading social studies texts. For each training passage, the student made a skeleton outline consisting of a thesis statement for the entire passage at the top of the page and a statement of the main idea of each section of the paper as indicated by headings. Then the student generated two or three important supporting details for each main idea statement, and students generated superordinate topic headings in the left margin connecting to sections of the text. Box 11–7 gives an example of a hierarchical summary of a three-page social studies text segment containing one heading and six subheadings. The trained students received seven 1-hour training sessions while the control students received no training. In order to test the effectiveness of the hierarchical summary procedure, students in both groups were given pretests and post-tests that involved reading passages and then recalling the passages and answering questions about the passages. As expected, the trained students showed greater pretest-to-post-test gains in recall and in answering questions than the control group. Similar results for adult readers are also described in the section on "schema training" in Chapter 8.

MAKING INFERENCES

What Is Inference Making?

The process of reading comprehension often requires that the reader make inferences. For example, consider the sentence, "Our neighbor unlocked

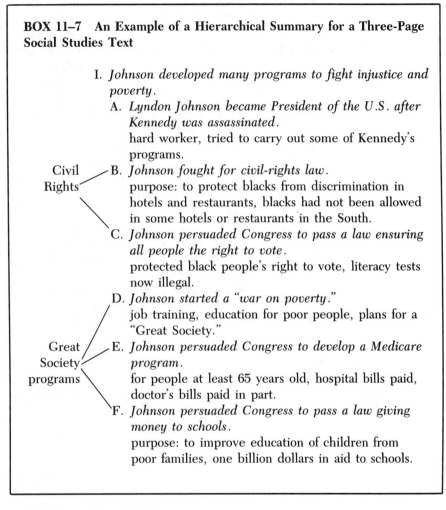

BOX 11-7   An Example of a Hierarchical Summary for a Three-Page Social Studies Text

I. *Johnson developed many programs to fight injustice and poverty.*

A. *Lyndon Johnson became President of the U.S. after Kennedy was assassinated.*
   hard worker, tried to carry out some of Kennedy's programs.

Civil Rights
B. *Johnson fought for civil-rights law.*
   purpose: to protect blacks from discrimination in hotels and restaurants, blacks had not been allowed in some hotels or restaurants in the South.

C. *Johnson persuaded Congress to pass a law ensuring all people the right to vote.*
   protected black people's right to vote, literacy tests now illegal.

D. *Johnson started a "war on poverty."*
   job training, education for poor people, plans for a "Great Society."

Great Society programs
E. *Johnson persuaded Congress to develop a Medicare program.*
   for people at least 65 years old, hospital bills paid, doctor's bills paid in part.

F. *Johnson persuaded Congress to pass a law giving money to schools.*
   purpose: to improve education of children from poor families, one billion dollars in aid to schools.

From Taylor & Beach (1984)

the door." An inference you might make is that the instrument used to unlock the door was a key (Paris & Lindauer, 1976). As another example, consider the sentence, "She slammed the door shut on her hand." An inference you might make is that she hurt her finger (Paris, Lindauer & Cox, 1977).

Research on the Development of Children's Inference Making

Paris and his colleagues (Myers & Paris, 1978; Paris & Lindauer, 1976; Paris, Lindauer & Cox, 1977; Paris & Upton, 1976) have found evidence of a de-

velopmental trend in which younger readers are less likely to make inferences
during reading than older readers. For example, kindergartners, second graders, and fourth graders listened to eight sentences. The sentences each suggested an implicit inference about the instrument used to carry out the action
stated in the sentence. For example, "Our neighbor unlocked the door" implies
that the instrument is a key. Students were given a cued recall test. For each
sentence the experimenter gave either an explicit cue—the subject, verb, or
object from the sentence—or an implicit cue—the implicit instrument. For
example, an explicit cue for the preceding sentence is "neighbor" or "unlocked"
or "door," whereas an implicit cue is "key." Figure 11–8 shows the percentage
of correctly recalled sentences when the cue was explicit versus implicit for
each age-group. For the kindergartners, performance was much better with the
explicit cue but for the second and fourth graders implicit cues were just about
as useful as explicit ones. Apparently, the younger children do not spontaneously go beyond the information given to make and use inferences as well
as the older children. Paris, Lindauer & Cox (1977) obtained a similar developmental trend, using inferences about consequences such as the "door
slamming" sentence given earlier.

In a related series of studies, Paris & Upton (1976) examined developmental
changes in children's inference making for short paragraphs. Students in each
grade K–5 listened to six stories such as the following:

FIGURE 11–8   Age-Related Differences in Children's Use of Inference

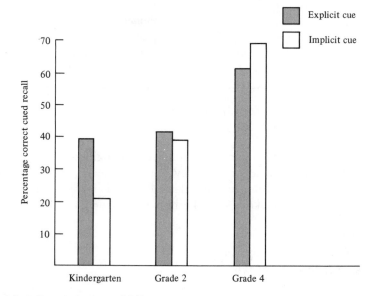

Adapted from Paris & Lindauer (1976)

Chris waited until he was alone in the house. The only sound he heard was his father chopping wood in the barn. Then he pushed the red chair over to the sink, which was full of dishes. Standing on the edge of the sink, he could just barely reach the heavy jar. The jar was behind the sugar and he stretched until his fingers could lift the lid. Just as he reached inside, the door swung open and there was his little sister.

Students were asked eight questions about each passage. Half of the questions concerned verbatim memory, such as, "Was the jar heavy?" or "Was the chair brown?" The other half of the questions concerned inferences, such as, "Was Chris's father using an ax?" or "Was Chris caught in the act of doing something he was not supposed to do?" Performance on both verbatim and inferential questions increased with age, but there was a larger increase for inference performance. In addition, ability to make inferences was highly correlated with overall amount recalled. These results suggest that as children develop, they become more able to make inferences that give meaning to the passage.

Implications for Instruction

Inference Training.   Inference training is a central feature of most basal reading programs (Rosenshine, 1980) and of many traditional reading programs (described later in this chapter). However, until recently there has been little empirical research concerning the effectiveness of inference training. For example, Hansen (1981) developed a 5-week classroom program for second graders. Some students were given practice in answering inference questions for each of several practice passages; other students used the same practice passages in class but followed the normal instructional program. On a post-test, students read passages and answered some "literal" and "inference" questions about the passages. The question-trained group performed 12% better than the control group on literal questions and 26% better on inference questions. However, a group that received training in the use of prereading strategies, such as trying to predict what would happen or relating the story to one's own experiences, did not show strong post-test advantages over the control group. Apparently, the best way to teach students how to answer inference questions is to give them direct instruction and practice in answering inference questions.

In a follow-up study, Hansen & Pearson (1983) provided 5 weeks of inference training to poor and good fourth grade readers. The training included prereading strategies such as discussing the reader's own experiences and making predictions about the story. For example, the script for prereading strategies was as follows:

TEACHER: What is it that we have been doing before we discuss each story?

DESIRED RESPONSE: We talk about our lives and we predict what will happen in the stories.

TEACHER: Why do we make these comparisons?

DESIRED RESPONSE: These comparisons will help us understand the stories.

TEACHER: Last week I asked you to think about a social studies lesson on Japan. Today, pretend that you are reading a science article about conservation. What might you be thinking about while you are reading the article?

DESIRED RESPONSE: Students relate personal experiences with conservation and explain how the experiences would be related to the text. For example, students talked about how their families heat with wood to conserve oil and stated that they wanted to find out how the Japanese conserve oil.

Then, the script for the upcoming story focused on understanding the main ideas:

TEACHER: Sometimes people are embarrassed by their personal appearance. Tell us about a time you were embarrassed about the way you looked.

TYPICAL RESPONSES: I got a short haircut. I wore some short pants. I'm too short.

TEACHER: In the next story there is an old man who is embarrassed about the way he looks. What do you think is the thing that embarrasses him?

TYPICAL ANSWERS: Ragged clothes. Cane. Gray hair. Wrinkles.

These prereading scripts led to discussions that lasted approximately 20 minutes. Then students read the passage independently. Students in the control group did not engage in the prereading activities. After reading the story, the class was asked to discuss ten questions. For the trained group, all the questions required inferences. For example, in a discussion of a basal version of *Charlotte's Web*, the teacher asked, "What kind of person do you think Templeton (the rat) would be if he were human?" The control group discussion involved questions using the ratio of four literal questions for each inference question. This ratio corresponds to the normal pattern of reading discussions. Following the training program, students were tested by asking them to read a passage appropriate for their reading level and to answer both literal and inference questions. Figure 11–9 shows that the training seems to have had no effect on the good readers, presumably because they already possessed good inference strategies. However, Figure 11–9 also shows that the training greatly enhanced the performance of the poor readers both on inference and literal questions.

Logical Reasoning Training.   In another study, fifth graders were given direct instruction logical reasoning skills relevant to making inferences during

FIGURE 11–9   Effects of Inference Training on Poor and Good Readers

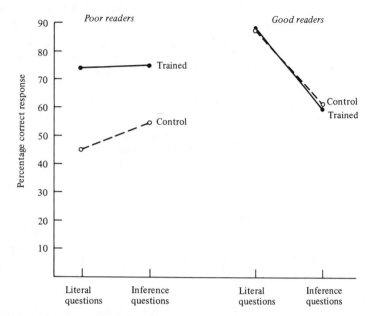

Adapted from Hansen & Pearson (1983)

reading (Patching, Kameenui, Carnine, Gersten & Colvin, 1983). The students' pretest scores indicated that they were good decoders but poor reasoners. The training involved three 30-minute sessions and focused on improving the reader's ability to detect three types of invalid arguments:

> *Faulty generalization*—Just because you know about a part doesn't mean you know about the whole thing. An example of faulty generalization is: "Sue has long legs. She must be a good runner."
>
> *False causality*—Just because two things happen together doesn't mean that one causes the other. An example is: "John opened a window in the house and that night his sister, Susie, became very sick. Opening the window must have done it."
>
> *Invalid testimony*—Just because an important person says something is good or bad doesn't make it so. An example is: "Dr. Smith is a very good doctor and everyone likes him. When I wanted to buy a lawn-mower, Dr. Smith told me that I should."

The instruction involved giving many practice problems to the reader with immediate feedback. Some students received individualized instruction from a teacher; others received the same kind of instruction using a workbook; and other students received no training.

In order to measure the effectiveness of instruction, students took a post-test consisting of short passages and questions concerning "which statements can you be sure of." For example, an item for faulty causality was:

Bob came to Grand Avenue School in December and started playing on the Room 101 basketball team. In January, they won every game.

Can you be sure that:

(1) The only reason Room 101 played so well in January and February is that Bob played on the team.   yes   no
(2) Bob must be a really good player.   yes   no
(3) The Room 101 team played well during January.   yes   no

Figure 11–10 shows the average percentage correct for each treatment group on detecting each type of invalid argument. As you can see, the individualized training tended to greatly enhance performance but the workbook did not. Apparently, intensive, individualized instruction on recognizing various kinds of valid and invalid inferences can improve test performance on recognizing valid and invalid inferences.

The foregoing studies provide some evidence that it is possible to improve

FIGURE 11–10   Effects of Inference Training on Ability to Make Correct Inferences

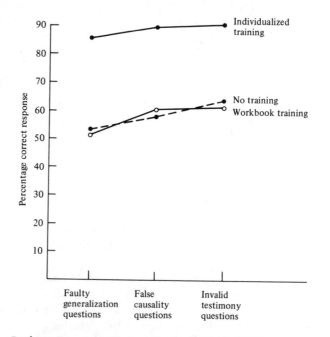

Adapted from Patching, Kameenui, Carnine, Gersten & Colvin (1983)

readers' performance on specific skills such as answering inference questions or recognizing invalid inferences. However, it is not clear whether the inference training produces the changes in overall reading comprehension or whether the changes in performance would have developed naturally.

USING METACOGNITIVE KNOWLEDGE

What Is Metacognition?

Metacognition refers to a knowledge and awareness of one's own cognitive processes. Brown, Campione & Day (1981) have pointed out that metacognitive skills are particularly difficult to teach to readers but are crucial for effective reading. For example, three kinds of metacognitive knowledge related to reading are comprehension monitoring, self-checking, and sensitivity to reading goals.

Research on Differences in Metacognitive Knowledge

Comprehension Monitoring. Comprehension monitoring refers to an awareness of whether you understand what you are reading. In essence, a reader with good comprehension monitoring skills is continually asking, Does this make sense? For example, Markman (1979) read three short essays to third, fifth, and sixth graders. Each story contained either an explicit or an implicit inconsistency as shown in Box 11–8. For example, the inconsistency in the fish essay is that there is not enough light at the bottom of the ocean to see colors and that fish see the color of their food at the bottom of the ocean. The experimenter told the children that she was trying to write a children's book and that she needed the children to serve as consultants. The children were asked to assess the understandability of the essays and to suggest ways of making the essays easier to understand. After reading the story twice, the experimenter prompted the student to point out any inconsistencies. The first seven prompts for the fish passage were: (1) Read essay. (2) Re-read essay. (3) "That's it. That's the information about fishes." (4) "What do you think?" (5) "Do you have any questions?" (6) "Did I forget to tell you anything?" (7) "Did everything make sense?"

Did children respond to these prompts by referring to the inconsistency in the passage? Box 11–8 lists the percentage of children at each grade level who recognized the inconsistencies in at least two out of three essays. As you can see, about half the students found the explicitly stated inconsistencies in at least two of the essays while almost none of the students did for implicitly stated inconsistencies. Apparently, it is very difficult for students to spontaneously recognize that the text they are reading is incomprehensible, especially when inconsistencies are implicit.

BOX 11–8   Do Young Readers Recognize Inconsistency in Prose Passages?

A Passage with an Explicit Inconsistency
   Many different kinds of fish live in the ocean. Some fish have heads that make them look like alligators, and some fish have heads that make them look like cats. Fish live in different parts of the ocean. Some fish live near the surface of the water, but some fish live way down at the bottom of the ocean. *Fish must have light in order to see. There is absolutely no light at the bottom of the ocean. It is pitch black down there. When it is that dark the fish cannot see anything. They cannot even see colors. Some fish that live at the bottom of the ocean can see the color of their food; that is how they know what to eat.*

A Passage with an Implicit Inconsistency
   Many different kinds of fish live in the ocean. Some fish have heads that make them look like alligators, and some fish have heads that make them look like cats. Fish live in different parts of the ocean. Some fish live near the surface of the water, but some fish live way down at the bottom of the ocean. *There is absolutely no light at the bottom of the ocean. Some fish that live at the bottom of the ocean know their food by its color. They will only eat red fungus.*

Percentage of Children Who Recognized Inconsistencies in at Least Two Out of Three Passages

Grade Level	Explicit Condition	Implicit Condition
Grade 3	50%	0%
Grade 5	60%	10%
Grade 6	60%	0%

Adapted from Markman (1979)

   Can children be induced to monitor their comprehension? In order to test this question, Markman (1979) conducted a follow-up study using third and sixth graders on the same task. However, half the children were told, "There is something tricky about each of the essays. Something which does not make any sense. Something which is confusing. I would like you to try and spot the problem with each essay and tell me what it was that did not make any sense." These instructions did not greatly influence the performance of the third graders on finding either implicit or explicit inconsistencies, but it did greatly improve the performance of sixth graders on finding both implicit and explicit inconsistencies. Apparently, the older children are capable of comprehension monitoring but do not engage in this activity spontaneously.

Myers & Paris (1978) interviewed second and sixth graders concerning their metacognitive knowledge about reading. Some of the questions focused on comprehension monitoring, such as, "Do you ever have to go back to the beginning of a paragraph or story to figure out what a sentence means? Why?" About 60% of the sixth graders were able to explain why they reread (e.g., to get context cues); in comparison, less than 10% of the second graders were able to explain why they reread. Apparently, younger readers are less aware of the role of comprehension monitoring in reading.

These results suggest that skilled readers are able to focus on inconsistencies in text. In order to examine this idea, Baker & Anderson (1982) asked college students to read short expository passages, some of which contained inconsistencies. The passages were presented on a computer terminal screen with only one sentence on the screen at a time. The reader pressed the NEXT button to see the next sentence, the BACK button to see the previous sentence, and the LAB button to start over at the beginning of the passage. The results indicated that readers spent much more time reading a sentence that conflicted with previously presented information as compared to reading the same sentence in a consistent passage. In addition, readers were far more likely to look back to an inconsistent sentence than to the same sentence when it was in a consistent passage. These results suggest that comprehension monitoring is a characteristic of skilled readers.

Self-checking. Another metacognitive skill, self-checking, may be displayed by an awareness of whether or not one has correctly decoded a passage. For example, Clay (1973; cited in Myers & Paris, 1978) asked good and poor young readers to read a passage aloud. The good young readers spontaneously corrected about one-third of their errors in oral reading whereas the poor readers spontaneously corrected about one-twentieth of their errors.

A related kind of self-checking involves awareness of whether one has learned enough from a passage to pass a test. In one study, performance in reading comprehension was improved by making children aware that they should study until they felt ready (Brown, Campione & Barclay, 1979). In another study, Andre & Anderson (1978) found that instruction in how to pose possible test questions to oneself improved reading comprehension performance.

Reading for a Goal. Finally, a third metacognitive skill involves adjusting one's study technique based on one's goals. For example, Rickards & Friedman (1978) found that skilled readers who expected an essay exam tended to recall more of the conceptual information from a lesson whereas those expecting a multiple choice exam tended to recall more low-level details. Myers & Paris (1978) found that second and sixth graders differed in their willingness to change how they study for different goals. For example, when asked "Would you do anything differently if you had to remember all the words?", 80% of the sixth graders and only 33% of the second graders said "yes." Related research on the development and training of metacognitive knowledge is presented in Chapter 3.

Implications for Instruction

What can be done to help students develop appropriate metacognitive skills? Based on existing research concerning children's comprehension monitoring, Markman (1985) makes the following suggestions:

1. Children should read a "variety of well-organized, tightly structured passages" that involve "simple logical, causal, and temporal relations." Unfortunately, textbooks written for young children often are unstructured, with many paragraphs consisting of lists of descriptive sentences. Thus, children are denied practice in determining whether the material they are reading makes sense, because the material has often been deliberately rewritten to minimize logical, causal, or temporal structure. In addition, children should be asked to predict what will happen next, to predict the actions of a character, to infer the order of events in a causal sequence, to guess the cause of an event, or to infer the motives of a character.

2. Children should be given a set of general questions to ask themselves during reading, such as, "Do I understand?", "What is the main point?", "What else do I know that is related?" Self-testing has been successfully used in improving the reading comprehension of educable retarded children (Brown, Campione & Barclay, 1979).

3. Children should be exposed to teachers who model appropriate comprehension monitoring techniques.

4. Children should practice evaluating explanations of a passage, such as choosing which of several possible explanations makes the most sense.

5. Children should practice detecting inconsistencies or problems in text.

In summary, children often fail to use appropriate comprehension monitoring and related skills even though they are capable of doing so. Instruction in using metacognitive knowledge may improve students' comprehension performance. Clearly, research work is needed to help determine how to apply these recommendations to the needs of individual children.

BUILDING A READING COMPREHENSION PROGRAM THAT WORKS

Research on reading comprehension has generally not been well coordinated with development of reading comprehension programs for schools. As we have seen in this chapter, there is a large body of scientific research on the role of readers' using their prior knowledge, making judgments of importance, making inferences, and monitoring their comprehension process. There is also a long tradition of developing reading comprehension programs that have been implemented in schools. Most of these programs—as well as the reading comprehension components of major basal reader series (Rosenshine, 1980)—have not been heavily studied or closely linked to research. Thus the failure to connect research and development means that programs are developed without benefit of the existing research on reading and the existing body of research continues to grow without being tested within the context of real school reading programs. This section briefly examines five reading comprehension programs: SQ3R, REAP, DRTA, ReQuest, and Chicago Master Learning Reading Program.

SQ3R

Robinson (1941) suggested that the learner be trained to use five steps in reading a new passage: *survey, question, read, recite,* and *review.* During the survey step, the reader skims the material to get an idea of what the passage is about. For example, in reading this chapter, you might read the beginning and concluding sentences and headings of each section. During the question step, the reader formulates a question for each subheading or unit of the passage. For example, for this section of the text you might ask, What are the procedures of SQ3R? In the read step, the student reads the passage with the goal of answering the question for each subheading or part of the passage. In the recite step, students answer each question in their own words. In the review step, students practice trying to recall as much information as they can from each section of the passage.

Adams, Carnine & Gersten (1982, p. 31) point out that during the past forty years SQ3R has been "widely reported in textbooks and teacher training manuals as being empirically based, though in fact the research literature does not support the claims." For example, Adams et al. (1982) were able to locate only six studies evaluating the effectiveness of SQ3R, but five had serious methodological flaws and the sixth did not use school-aged subjects. Similarly, Shepard (1978) has argued that some students fail to make use of this system because it appears to be too time-consuming.

Adams, Carnine & Gersten (1982) developed a 4-day training program similar to SQ3R, but with each step based on the current reading comprehension literature. Direct instruction was provided in each of the five skills listed above, using sample passages in social studies. Unlike previous studies, the subjects were elementary school children (i.e., fifth graders) who possessed adequate decoding skills but poor study skills. In order to assess the effectiveness of the training program, students were asked to read a passage and then to retell the passage and answer some factual questions about the passage. Students who were given the training scored 47% correct on the questions compared to only 28% correct for students who were not trained. The trained group also remembered more of the important information than the control group, but the difference failed to reach statistical significance. Apparently, students can be taught to read in ways that will enhance their ability to answer factual questions. However, more research is needed in order to understand when, why, where, and for whom SQ3R affects reading comprehension.

REAP

Eanet & Manzo (1976) and Eanet (1978) have argued that readers should be trained to translate the author's words into their own words. The four steps in REAP are: read, encode, annotate, and ponder. *Read* involves trying to read the author's words; *encode* involves trying to restate the author's words in one's own words; *annotate* involves writing a summary in one's own words; *ponder* involves reviewing and thinking about the summary. In a recent evaluation study, Eanet (1976) trained students to use REAP or SQ3R or a standard reading approach. Results showed that the control group performed best on subsequent tests of reading retention, presumably because students had difficulty in effectively using REAP and SQ3R systems with limited study time.

DRTA

Directed Reading and Thinking Activity (Stauffer, 1969) involves three steps: predict, read, prove. During the predict step, students are given a title or the first few sentences or a picture from the passage and are asked to predict what the passage is about. For example, readers might be asked to tell what they think a story called "War of the Ghosts" is about. In the read step, students silently read the passage looking for "proof" about their predictions. In the proving step, students are asked to state information that logically supports or negates their predictions. This procedure is repeated for each section of the passage. Stauffer (1969) has provided some evaluation data indicating that DRTA procedures enhance comprehension of passages, but useful independent evaluations of DRTA need to be carried out.

ReQuest

In the ReQuest procedure (Manzo, 1979) students and teachers silently read a passage and then take turns asking each other questions about the passage. This procedure gives students practice in formulating questions and in answering questions about the passage. As with the other programs, independent evaluations are needed.

Chicago Mastery Learning Reading Program

What would happen if a large metropolitan school district developed and implemented a comprehensive reading program that was inspired by research on reading? To answer this question, we can look at the results of the Chicago Master Learning Reading Program, which was recently implemented in the Chicago public schools (Jones, Amiran & Katims, 1985). The program consists of instructional materials for grades K–8 to be used in conjunction with stories from a basal reader. The program is broken into learning units, with one or more objectives addressed in each learning unit. For example, the objectives involve specific reading strategies such as recognizing different types of paragraph structures (as described in Chapter 8), using headings and subheadings, inferring topic sentences, and determining the question being addressed in a passage. Students must pass a mastery test before going on to the next unit; if they do not pass, they perform some corrective activities and retake the test until they succeed.

Does the Chicago Mastery Learning Reading Program work? In a series of evaluation studies, Jones, Amiran & Katims (1985) found evidence of systematic growth in the reading skills of students who participated in the program as compared to students who did not. These results have led to "probably the largest scale implementation ever conducted in the United States" (Jones, Amiran & Katims, 1985, p. 284). The Chicago Mastery Learning Reading Program is particularly exciting because of its close relation to educational research—it is a program that is inspired by existing research on reading and it is a program that is being scientifically evaluated. Although the final results are not yet in, the students of the Chicago public schools are participating in an important experiment.

In summary, although many interesting reading comprehension programs have been developed and implemented in schools, there has been little research assessing their effectiveness. The Chicago Mastery Learning Reading Program stands as a potentially important exception. Most programs seem to teach skills that are similar to the strategic and metacognitive skills described in this chapter. For example, the tactic of asking oneself questions is related to the metacognitive skill of self-checking. However, much more work is needed to bridge the gap between existing research on reading comprehension and the development of reading comprehension programs that work.

CONCLUSION

This chapter has briefly explored the processes by which a reader comes to understand a passage (i.e., the processes of reading comprehension). We began by examining Bartlett's concept of "effort after meaning"—that reading involves trying to assimilate what is presented with existing knowledge. Then, we explored three kinds of knowledge that are related to reading comprehension: content knowledge, such as prior knowledge; strategic knowledge, such as using prose structure and making inferences; and metacognitive knowledge, such as comprehension monitoring and reading for a purpose.

First, this chapter presented examples of the well-documented evidence concerning prior knowledge. For both adults and children, a reader who has appropriate background knowledge comprehends a passage differently from a reader who lacks appropriate background knowledge. In particular, a reader with rich background knowledge is more likely to make inferences that give coherence to the passage.

Second, this chapter presented examples of the well-documented evidence concerning prose structure. For adults and older children, readers are more likely to remember important information than unimportant information from a passage. However, younger readers are less likely to be able to distinguish between important and unimportant information in the text and are less likely to spend their study time focusing on the important information.

Third, this chapter examined examples of research concerning inference making during reading. Younger readers are much less likely to spontaneously make inferences. Although success in answering inference questions can be taught, the general effects of inference training on reading comprehension are not yet clear.

Fourth, this chapter examined the relatively new research on metacognitive processes such as comprehension monitoring. Again, there is some evidence that younger readers are less likely to monitor their performance or to alter their reading strategy for different task demands.

Finally, the chapter summarized procedures used in some of the traditional reading comprehension programs. What is needed, of course, is an understanding of how the reading comprehension processes of children can be influenced through training in content knowledge, strategic knowledge, or metacognitive knowledge. While this chapter cannot provide many definitive conclusions, it does point to the crucial contribution of the reader's existing knowledge—content, strategic, and metacognitive—in the reading process. Chapter 3 further explores issues in the development of learning strategies and Chapter 10 further explores issues in the training of learning strategies.

SUGGESTED READINGS

Bartlett, F. C. (1932). *Remembering*. London: Cambridge University Press. (Presents work that was the forerunner of modern cognitive research on learning from prose.)

Bransford, J. D. (1979). *Human cognition*. Belmont, Calif.: Wadsworth. (Cleverly written introduction to modern research on learning from prose.)

Pearson, P. D. (ed.) (1984). *Handbook of research on reading*. New York: Longman. (A collection of papers by leading researchers on reading.)

Spiro, R. J., Bruce, B. C. & Brewer, W. F. (eds.) (1980). *Theoretical issues in reading comprehension*. Hillsdale, N.J.: Erlbaum. (A collection of papers by leading researchers on reading comprehension.)

12 *Writing*

This chapter asks the question, What processes are involved in writing a composition? The answer to this question includes planning what to write, translating from the plan to words on the page, and reviewing what has been written. Students need training in each of these component processes in writing.

THE STORYTELLING PROBLEM

Read the story shown in Box 12–1. Now, put the paper aside and write the story in your own words. Assume that you are writing to a person who has never heard the story before. Your task is not to recall the story verbatim, but rather to tell the main events in the story to someone else.

Box 12–2 shows the main points in the story. Did your story contain all or most of these points? Did you clearly introduce the "lady" and the "fairy" (rather than just refer to them as "she")? Could someone else read your story and understand it? Did your story present the events in the proper order?

This story is taken from an early study by Piaget (1926). In the study, a child (between the ages of six and eight) was asked to listen to the story, and was given instructions like these:

Are you good at telling stories? Very well then,
we'll send your little friend out of the room, and

BOX 12–1   Can You Retell This Story?

Once upon a time, there was a lady who was called Niobe, and who had twelve sons and twelve daughters. She met a fairy who had only one son and no daughter. Then the lady laughed at the fairy because the fairy only had one boy. Then the fairy was very angry and fastened the lady to a rock. The lady cried for ten years. In the end she turned into a rock, and her tears made a stream which still runs today.

From Piaget (1926)

while he is gone, we'll tell you a story. You must listen carefully. When you have listened to it all, we'll make your friend come back, and then you will tell him the same story.

Some examples of the stories that children told are given in Box 12–3. As you can see, the children make many mistakes in their telling of the story. Some obvious problems are: children tend to leave out crucial pieces of information such as the reason that the fairy attacked the lady; refer to characters by pronouns that lack clear referents; or tell the story in a way that ignores

---

BOX 12–2   The Main Points in the Story

1. Once there was a lady (or Niobe, etc.)
2. She had children (provided they outnumber those of the other character).
3. She met a fairy (or a girl, etc.)
4. This fairy had few children (or none, provided their number is inferior to the first lot).
5. The lady laughed at the fairy.
6. Because the fairy had so few children.
7. The fairy was angry.
8. The fairy fastened the lady to a rock (or a tree, etc.)
9. The lady cried.
10. She turned into a rock.
11. Her tears made a stream.
12. Which flows to this day.

From Piaget (1926)

BOX 12–3   How Children Told the Story

Ri (age eight)
There was a lady once, she had twelve boys and twelve girls. She goes for a walk and she meets a fairy who had a boy and a girl and who didn't want to have twelve children. Twelve and twelve make twenty-four. She didn't want to have twenty-four children. She fastened N to a stone, she became a rock.

Gio (age eight)
Once upon a time there was a lady who had twelve boys and twelve girls, and then a fairy a boy and a girl. And then Niobe wanted to have some more sons. Then she was angry. She fastened her to a stone. He turned into a rock and then his tears made a stream which is still running today.

Met (age six)
The lady laughed at this fairy because she only had one boy. The lady had twelve sons and twelve daughters. One day she laughed at her. She was angry and she fastened her beside a stream. She cried for fifty months, and it made a great big stream.

Ce (age six)
There's a lady who was called Morel, and then she turned into a stream . . . then she had ten daughters and ten sons . . . and then after that the fairy fastened her to the bank of a stream and then she cried twenty months, and then after that she cried for twenty months and then her tears went into the stream, and then . . .

From Piaget (1926)

the order of events. Piaget (p. 16) summarizes the performance of his young storytellers as follows: "The words spoken are not thought of from the point of view of the person spoken to." In other words, young students seem to have trouble in taking the listener's point of view. Young children behave as if the listener already knows the story (i.e., young children assume that everyone else knows what they know). Piaget refers to this phenomenon as "egocentrism," as described in Chapter 2. Egocentrism does not mean that the children are selfish, but rather that the children tend to think that everyone views the world from the same perspective. In contrast, adults are often able to adjust their stories for different audiences (i.e., adults can often take the listener's perspective into account).

In this chapter, we will explore the nature of writing. What does Piaget's storytelling demonstration tell us about writing? His work suggests that one major aspect of speaking and of writing is to influence an audience. In speaking, the audience is physically present, but in writing, the audience is not physically present. Thus the requirement of keeping the "audience" in one's mind as one writes is particularly difficult; adult writing often shows some of the egocentric characteristics and disorganization of Piaget's young storytellers. This demonstration suggests that writing is a skill that depends partly on the writer's ability to take the perspective of the audience (i.e., of the potential readers).

What does a good writer need to know? In answer to this question, Applebee (1982) has identified three kinds of knowledge, each of which is exemplified in Piaget's storytelling study:

> *Knowledge of language*—such as the grammatical rules of English,
> *Knowledge of topic*—such as the specific information that should be conveyed, and
> *Knowledge of audience*—such as the perspective of the potential readers.

The remainder of this chapter explores how writers use these bodies of knowledge in the writing process, and how the writing process can be improved through instruction.

THE WRITING PROCESS

Analyzing Writing into Three Processes

Suppose that you were asked to write a short biographical story, write an essay on how a water faucet works, or write a business letter. What are the cognitive processes that occur as you write? In order to answer this question, Flower & Hayes (1981; Hayes & Flower, 1980) have given writing assignments to people and asked them to describe what they are thinking as they carry out the assignment. This procedure is called "thinking aloud" and the final transcript of everything that the writer says is called a "thinking aloud protocol."

Based on their analysis of writers' thinking aloud protocols, Hayes & Flower (1980) have identified three distinct processes in writing: planning, translating, and reviewing.

Planning. Planning involves searching for information from long-term memory, from the assignment and from what has been written so far, and using this information to establish a plan for producing text. Three subprocesses in planning are generating, organizing, and goal setting. Generating involves retrieving information relevant to the writing task from long-term memory; for example, in writing an essay on the "writing process" you might remember that the three major processes are planning, translating, and reviewing. Organizing involves selecting the most useful information that you have retrieved and structuring the information into a writing plan; for example, in writing an essay on the "writing process," you might devote one section to each of the three major processes in the order given earlier. Goal setting involves establishing general criteria for guiding the execution of the writing plan; for example, the writer may decide that since the audience is unfamiliar with the material, the essay should be kept simple and free of jargon terms.

Translating. Translating involves producing text that is consistent with the plan. For example, the produced text should consist of grammatically correct English sentences.

Reviewing. Reviewing involves improving the written text, using the subprocesses of reading and editing. In reading, the writer identifies problems in the text; in editing, the writer attempts to correct the problems. For example, if the first draft contains a sentence that is ungrammatical or that fails to convey the intended meaning the sentence will be rewritten as part of the reviewing process.

Figure 12–1 provides a simplified version of the general model of writing proposed by Hayes & Flower (1980). The three rectangles represent the three major processes in writing. The two parallelograms on the left represent the "input" into the writing process: the writing assignment (including an understanding of the topic and audience) and the writer's knowledge (including knowledge of topic, knowledge of audience, and knowledge of written English). The parallelogram on the right represents the "output" (i.e., the text that is produced). The arrows among the three writing processes represent the idea that the processes interact with one another rather than occur in a fixed order.

Similar analyses of the writing process have been proposed by other researchers. For example, Nold (1981) suggests three major processes: planning, transcribing, and reviewing. Similarly, Bruce, Collins, Rubin & Gentner (1982) suggest the following steps in their model of writing: production of ideas, production of text, editing. Gould (1980) lists four processes: planning, generat-

FIGURE 12–1   A Model of the Writing Process

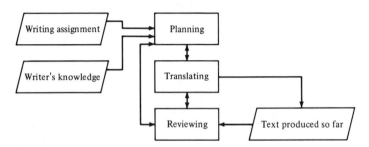

Adapted from Hayes & Flower (1980)

ing, reviewing, and accessing additional information. (Note that Hayes & Flower include "accessing additional information" as a subprocess within planning.) Apparently, there is some consensus on the major processes involved in writing. Furthermore, all the analyses assume that there is a great deal of interaction among the processes, rather than each process occurring separately.

Looking at Student Protocols

As evidence for their model of the writing process, Hayes & Flower (1980) presented an analysis of the thinking aloud protocol of a typical writer. The protocol contained fourteen pages covering 458 simple statements or comments made by the writer. The protocol could be divided into three sections. In the first section, consisting of the first 116 comments, the writer seemed to focus on the planning subprocess of generating information, with occasional interruptions to focus on reviewing. Some typical comments during this section of the protocol are: "And what I'll do now is simply jot down random thoughts. . . ." or "Other things to think about in this random search are . . ." In the second section, consisting of the next 154 comments, the writer seemed to focus on the planning subprocess of organizing the information, with occasional interruptions to focus on reviewing. Typical comments during this section of the protocol include: "Now I think it's time to go back and read over the material and elaborate on its organization." Finally, the third section of the protocol contained the final 188 comments and focused on the process of translating with occasional interruptions for generating and reviewing. Examples of typical comments include: "Let's try and write something," or "Oh, no. We need more organizing. . . ."

Figure 12–2 shows, for each section of the protocol, the proportion of comments directed toward generating, organizing, translating, and reviewing. These data are based on using only major comments from two different writers. As can be seen, the first section of the protocol is devoted mainly to generating ideas, the second is devoted mainly to organizing the ideas, and the final section is devoted mainly to translating the writing plan into acceptable sentences. In addition, the reviewing process (consisting mainly of editing) seems to play a small part in each of the three sections of the protocol.

Instructional Themes

As can be seen in the foregoing analysis, the study of writing is in its early stages of development. However, even in this early work on writing, several implications for writing instruction have emerged.

Process Versus Product.   Much of the emphasis in writing instruction is typically on the final *product*, including spelling, punctuation, and grammar. An additional focus suggested by the cognitive analysis of writing is that writing

FIGURE 12–2   What Writers Do During the Writing Process

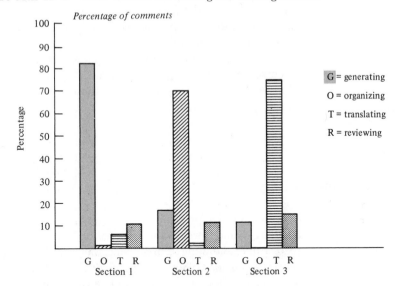

Adapted from Hayes & Flower (1980)

instruction should also focus on the *process* of writing. In particular, the foregoing analysis suggests that most of the time and effort in writing is devoted to planning rather than the actual production of acceptable text. Steinberg (1980, p. 156) summarizes this idea as follows: ". . . teaching of writing focuses too much on product, on the written paper that the student submits, and not enough on process, on how to write."

Problem Solving Versus Procedure Application.   Much of instruction in writing involves procedures for producing sentences properly, such as "Never begin a sentence with *because*" or "Each paragraph should have a topic sentence, a summary sentence, and approximately three core sentences." In addition to using such procedures, a writer must also engage in an act of problem solving. As in other types of problem solving (see Chapter 10), the writer must establish goals and work to achieve the goals. Thus instruction in writing may be viewed as instruction in problem solving. Flower & Hayes (1981, p. 40) make this argument as follows: "Writing is problem solving, and can be analyzed from a psychological view of problem-solving processes."

Communication Versus Composition.   Much of the instruction in writing involves learning to produce a composition that meets stylistic and grammatical requirements. Nystrand (1982a) points out there is an emphasis on "proper talk" and "standardized composition" rather than on writing in a way that influences the audience. In addition to teaching students how to write compositions that conform to "school English," writing instruction must also be sensitive to the idea that writing is an attempt to communicate with a reader. As

Frase (1982, p. 130) points out: "Effective writing is bringing one's own goals in line with the readers' constraints." Similarly, Nystrand (1982a) notes that writers need to develop a "notion of audience as person or persons whom . . . the writer hopes to influence."

In the remainder of this chapter, we examine each of the three major processes in writing—planning, translating, and reviewing—as well as the educational implications of work in these areas.

PLANNING

What Is Planning?

As noted in the previous section, planning is a major process in writing. Planning includes retrieving information from memory (what Hayes & Flower, 1980, call "generating"), organizing that information into a writing plan (what Hayes & Flower, 1980, call "organizing"), and establishing criteria for writing (what Hayes & Flower, 1980, call "goal setting").

Research on Planning

How Much Do Students Plan In Dictation? As an example of planning, let's suppose you were asked to dictate a one-page business letter. The dictation rate is potentially 200 words per minute (i.e., a person can speak comfortably at a rate of 200 words per minute). However, Gould (1980) reports that the normal dictation rate is approximately twenty-three words per minute. Similarly, suppose you were asked to write a one-page business letter. The writing rate is potentially forty words per minute, yet Gould (1980) reports that the normal writing rate for business letters is thirteen words per minute.

These results suggest that people's production of text is much slower than the limit imposed by the output device (writing or dictating). Why do people dictate (or write) at such slow rates? According to research summarized by Gould (1980), most of the writing time is devoted to planning. For example, by carefully recording pauses that are made during speaking or during writing, Gould (1978a, 1978b, 1980) was able to determine that pauses accounted for approximately two-thirds of total composition time in both writing and speaking. These results are summarized in Figure 12–3.

When Do Students Plan in Writing? Matsuhashi (1981, 1982) carefully observed the pauses made by high school students involved in writing essays. As in the Gould study, Matsuhashi found that planning time accounted for approximately one-half to two-thirds of total writing time. In addition, Matsuhashi found that pauses occurred mainly at the borders between ideas (e.g., at the end of sentences). Box 12–4 summarizes the essay written by a high

FIGURE 12–3   How Much Planning Time Is Used in Writing or Dictating a Letter?

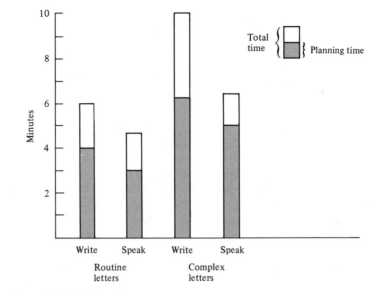

Adapted from Gould (1980)

school student; the numbers after each word indicate the length of the pause (in seconds) before going on to the next word. As can be seen, the long pauses are in line 5 (16.6 seconds after the sentence), line 8 (13.3 seconds before the new paragraph), line 11 (12.8 seconds after the sentence), and line 4 (9.7 seconds before going on to a new sentence). During some of the longer pauses, the writer removed his pen from the paper and shifted position in his seat. Matsuhashi suggests that the pauses allow the writer to organize the information and place that information within the appropriate context.

How Far Ahead Do Students Plan?   Additional evidence concerning the planning process is reported by Scardamalia, Bereiter & Goelman (1982). For example, in one study elementary school children were asked to write an essay. At various points during the writing process, the teacher would interrupt a student, asking what he or she was going to write. Usually students had the next five or six words in mind and had thought ahead to the end of the clause. Young children (in the primary grades) tended to dictate to themselves, mouthing each word during writing. In contrast, older children (grade 4 and above) rarely vocalized during writing but did vocalize during pauses. Apparently, young children rely on external memory (i.e., self-dictation) in order to keep the next few words in short-term memory, whereas older children behave as if a memory load of several words does not require external memory.

BOX 12–4   Pauses in Writing an Essay

1   Truly$\cdot^6$successful$^{1.1}$person$\cdot^5$-to$\cdot^8$-person$^{2.3}$communi-

2    $^{1.8}$cation$^{3.5}$is$^{1.9}$difficult$^{1.3}$because$^{6.9}$people$\cdot^6$in$\cdot^9$general$^{1.1}$are$\cdot^9$poor

3    $^{1.0}$listeners. $^{7.0}$They$^{1.0}$would$\cdot^7$rather$^{1.4}$listen$\cdot^5$to$\cdot^9$themselves$^{1.9}$speaking

4    $^{2.1}$than$\cdot^4$someone$\cdot^7$else$\cdot^5$. $^{4.7}$It$\cdot^9$is$\cdot^7$my$\cdot^7$feeling$^{1.9}$that$^{9.7}$this$\cdot^8$occurs

5    $^{1.6}$because$^{1.1}$of$^{1.2}$a$\cdot^8$basic$^{2.7}$self-centeredness.$^{16.6.}$ $^{5.5}$people$^{4.8}$tend$^{1.2}$to

6    $^{1.9}$be$\cdot^6$more$\cdot^5$interested$\cdot^7$in$\cdot^7$their$\cdot^9$own$\cdot^7$lives$^{1.5}$to$^{1.2}$bother$^{1.0}$exposing

7    $^{1.3}$themselves$\cdot^7$to$\cdot^5$how$\cdot^7$others$\cdot^8$live.

8        $^{13.3}$Communication$^{1.2}$is$\cdot^7$successful$\cdot^8$only$\cdot^8$when$^{2.9}$there

9    $^{2.2}$is$^{2.4}$"$\cdot^5$give$\cdot^6$and$\cdot^8$take"$^{1.1}$between$^{3.7}$the$\cdot^7$parties$^{1.1}$. $^{3.7}$Each$\cdot^7$one

10   $^{1.9}$should$\cdot^9$contribute$^{1.2}$equally$^{2.1}$, $^{1.0}$as$\cdot^8$well$\cdot^7$as$^{2.0}$accepting$\cdot^7$the

11   $^{2.2}$contributions$^{5.3}$of$\cdot^6$the$\cdot^7$others. $^{12.8}$The$\cdot^6$situation$\cdot^7$I$^{1.0}$have

12   $^{1.8}$described$^{6.6}$above$^{3.2}$leads$\cdot^6$to$\cdot^6$poor$\cdot^8$communication$^{1.7}$, $^{1.0}$since

13   $^{1.9}$everyone$\cdot^8$wants$\cdot^9$to$\cdot^6$"give"$^{1.2}$and$\cdot^8$no$^{1.0}$one$\cdot^6$wants$\cdot^9$to

14   $^{1.2}$"take."

(Numbers after words indicate pause times, in seconds.)

From Matsuhashi (1982)

Implications for Instruction

In summary, this section has presented three important findings concerning the planning process: planning is a time-consuming process accounting for most of writing time, planning seems to occur mainly at sentence and clause boundaries, local planning generally allows the writer to work on one clause or sentence at a time. Apparently, planning is a time-consuming process that occurs throughout the writing activity.

Yet, writing instruction does not normally teach students how to plan. The foregoing analysis of planning suggests that students need instruction and practice both in how to organize information and in how to select the content to fit into the organization.

Training students how to organize their compositions includes both global planning of the outline of the passage as well as local planning of each paragraph or sentence. Training in global planning includes breaking a passage into its main parts and then breaking each part into subparts and so on. Students need practice in developing an outline. Training in local planning includes practice in how to design a paragraph. For example, Chapter 8 presented several techniques for helping students to understand the organization of expository prose, including "networking" (Dansereau et al., 1979) and "schema training" (Cook, 1982). Complementary techniques could be used to help students to write paragraphs that correspond to basic formats such as generalization, enumeration, sequence, classification, and compare/contrast, as described in Chapter 8. The key foci of organization training are modularity—helping students break a composition into parts—and connectivity—helping students to build logical connections among the modules in the composition.

Training students in how to retrieve information is another important aspect of planning. Students need practice in how to search for needed information, including how to take (and use) notes from sources. A key finding in many writing studies is that students' knowledge of the domain is a crucial determinant of the quality of the writing (Voss & Bisanz, 1985). Similarly, Chapter 11 demonstrated the importance of specific knowledge in students' performance in comprehending passages. In short, students need to write about topics that they already know about or have researched.

TRANSLATING

What Is Translating?

The next component in the writing process is what Hayes & Flower (1980) call *translating*. This phase involves carrying out the writing plan by actually generating some written text. According to Hayes & Flower, translating is done interactively with planning; in other words, a writer generates a plan, translates a small part of it, then checks the next part of the plan, translates that part and so on. Research described in the previous section suggests that people may translate about one phrase (or simple sentence) at a time.

Constraints on Translating. Suppose that you write by checking your overall writing plan, sentence by sentence. In other words, you check your plan for the first main idea and then try to translate it into a sentence. Then you check your plan for the next main idea and try to translate it into a sentence, and so on. As you move from your writing plan (i.e., your idea of what you want to say) to the production of prose (i.e., the sentence that you actually write), you are constrained by several factors. As listed by Nystrand (1982b), these factors are:

Graphic—The sentences that you generate must be legible for the reader; the sentences must use lettering, penmanship, layout, spacing, indentation, and spelling that is familiar to the reader.

Syntactic—The sentences that you generate must be based on the rules of written English; grammar, punctuation, and sentence organization must be appropriate for the reader.

Semantic—The sentences that you generate must convey the meaning to the reader that you expected; assumptions about the "given information" that a reader brings to the reading task must be appropriate.

Textual—The sentences that you write must fit together into a cohesive paragraph and passage.

Contextual—The sentences must be written in the appropriate style, e.g., "sarcasm" or "understatement."

Each of these types of constraints involves trying to make sure that there is some correspondence between the writer's words and the reader's understanding of the words.

Examples of writers' failures to follow the constraints on writer-reader communication are suggested in Box 12–5. Nystrand (1982b) refers to these examples as "misconstraints" (i.e., cases in which the reader is either misled or misinterprets the information).

Research on Translating

Removing Constraints on Translating.   The translation process may require a great deal of attentional capacity on the part of young writers, because so much of the translation process is not yet automatic. One solution to this

---

BOX 12–5   Examples of Five Errors in Writer-Reader Communication

Graphic Misconstraint
"now here" for "nowhere"

Syntactic Misconstraint
"Your still going to get where your going with a seatbelt on."

Semantic Misconstraint
"The law against drinking is for your own safety." (Written to adults whereas the law against drinking applies only to minors.)

Textual Misconstraint
"I think that the snowmobilers will get used to these new laws, and people will see the laws the government put out are for our protection." (The previous sentences have discussed only automobile seatbelts so the reader has not been prepared to consider snowmobiles.)

Contextual Misconstraint
Asking high school students to read the state laws on drunk driving.

Adapted from Nystrand (1982)

problem is to ignore the normal constraints on writing, such as is demonstrated in the following writing from a six-year-old (Read, 1981, p. 106–7):

WONS A LITOL GIRL WOS WOKIG IN HR GARDIN INTIL SE GOT KOT BIY A ROBR AND TIN SE SKREMD AND TIN HR MON AND DAD KAM OUT AND HLPT HR OWT OV THE ROBRS HANDS AND TIN TAY KOLD THE POLES AND TIN THE POLES TOK KAR OV THE ROBR AND POT HIM IN THE GAOL

As can be seen, this young writer was able to tell a story without paying great attention to some of the basic rules of spelling, punctuation, grammar, and the like. By freeing herself from the tedious constraints on writing, the young writer was able to produce a story.

Read (1981, p. 114) suggests that "teachers and parents can look upon early writing in roughly the same way that they regard children's art, as an expression which is created with pleasure and which is not expected to be adult-like." In addition, Read provides some evidence that nonstandard spelling during writing does not adversely affect reading; for example, the little girl who wrote this story was able to sight read words such as "girl" even though she wrote "GROL."

In most school writing tasks, the graphic and syntactic constraints (as well as others) are enforced. If the rules of spelling, grammar, and even penmanship are not yet automatic, this means that the writer's full attentional capacity must be devoted to correct production of text rather than organizational planning. For example, Scardamalia, Bereiter & Goelman (1982) propose that since the information processing capacity of young writers is limited, and since the mechanical and syntactic aspects of writing are not automatic, emphasis on correctly formed sentences results in poorer overall writing quality. The low-level aspects of writing (such as correct spelling, punctuation, and penmanship) interfere with higher-level planning.

In order to test this idea, Scardamalia & Bereiter (as described in Scardamalia, Bereiter & Goelman, 1982), asked fourth and sixth grade children to write an essay, dictate an essay at a normal rate, or dictate an essay at a slow rate. The dictation modes were used because they presumably freed the young writer from some of the mechanical and syntactic demands of translating. As predicted, the dictation modes resulted in about twice as many words being produced and in small increases in judged quality, as compared to writing. However, Gould (1980) notes that dictation does not tend to increase the quality of prose in adults. Apparently, the mechanical processes of handwriting, proper spelling, and punctuation are not automatic in young writers but, for simple assignments, do eventually become automatic in adults. Thus the act of translating ideas into words may actually disrupt the flow of thinking in young writers.

Polished Versus Unpolished First Drafts. There is some potentially important evidence that the quality of adult writing is also hindered when attention must be focused on the mechanics of writing. For example, suppose that you were asked to write a formal business letter to your teacher in order to persuade your teacher to use a future class period for either a film that is related to the course or for a library reading session. First, you have 10 minutes to complete a preliminary draft. Then, after a 5-minute rest period, you have 10 minutes to produce the final draft.

Suppose your goal is to produce a high quality final draft, containing many persuasive arguments expressed in a coherent way. Would it be better to try to write a polished letter as your first draft—including proper sentence formation and compliance with the rules of punctuation and spelling—or would it be better to try to concentrate only on generating arguments in the preliminary draft—with revisions for organization, sentence formation, and mechanics handled in the final draft?

Glynn, Britton, Muth & Dogan (1982) investigated this question in a controlled experiment. Students were given writing assignments as just described. Some students were told to write a polished first draft:

> On this preliminary draft, you need to be concerned with content (i.e., the production of persuasive ideas), order (i.e., the logical sequence of these ideas), sentence formation (i.e., the incorporation of these ideas into sentences), and mechanics (i.e., compliance with punctuation and spelling rules). Communicate all the ideas that you think may be useful in persuading me to choose one alternative and not the other. More than one persuasive idea can be incorporated into each sentence.

Other students were told to write an unpolished first draft:

> On this preliminary draft you need to be concerned with content (i.e., the production of persuasive ideas). Communicate all the ideas that you think may be useful in persuading me to choose one alternative and not the other. Summarize each of these persuasive ideas using only three or four words, and write them in order. On this draft, do not attempt to work on order (i.e., the logical sequence of persuasive ideas), sentence formation (i.e. the incorporation of these ideas into sentences), or mechanics (i.e., compliance with punctuation and spelling rules). You will be permitted to work on order, sentence formation, and mechanics during the next draft.

For the final draft, all students were told to "produce the best letter you can" including consideration of content, order, sentence formation, and mechanics.

Table 12–1 summarizes the differences between the final drafts produced by the two groups of students. Students who wrote unpolished first drafts tended to write final drafts containing more persuasive arguments, more arguments per sentence, and fewer mechanical errors, as compared to students who wrote a polished first draft. Subsequent experiments determined that this pattern was most strongly pronounced for students with average verbal ability as compared to students with low verbal ability. These results suggest that

TABLE 12–1   Differences in the Final Drafts When Preliminary Drafts Were Polished Versus Unpolished

	Total Number of Arguments	Arguments per Sentence	Mechanical Errors per Sentence
Polished preliminary draft	2.9	.38	.43
Unpolished preliminary draft	8.0	.85	.23

Adapted from Glynn, Britton, Muth & Dogan (1982)

when good writers are forced to express early drafts in complete sentences, the quality of the final draft suffers. Apparently, the heavy load placed on attentional capacity limits the writers' ability to retrieve and organize information. This finding has practical significance concerning the use of word processors for writing of early drafts. By forcing ideas to be translated prematurely into polished sentences, without allowing time for planning, the result may be a final draft that lacks integrated content.

Individual Differences in Translating.   Another approach to the study of the translation process involves comparisons between older and younger writers, or between more skilled and less skilled writers. For example, in one study (Scardamalia, Bereiter & Goelman, 1982), fourth and sixth grade students were asked to write essays on topics such as "Is it better to be an only child or to have brothers and sisters?" or "Should boys and girls play sports together?" or "Should children be allowed to choose what subjects they study in school?" When students finished their essays, they were given cues to keep working such as, "You're doing fine. Now I know it's a bit tough, but you can write some more about this."

The results indicated that the cues to write more encouraged both fourth and sixth graders to add about 50% more to their essays. However, the judged quality of the essays improved only for the fourth graders. Apparently, the younger writers stopped before they were really finished whereas the sixth graders continued until they had written a good essay. One implication is that young children may be using the conventions of oral speech (e.g., needing someone to tell them to go on) while older writers can tell themselves to continue producing text.

When young writers were asked to dictate their essays, the students produced longer essays than when they were asked to write them. However, cues to produce more text resulted in more words being produced but did not result in increased quality ratings for the essays. Apparently young writers stop too soon when they must physically produce the sentences; however, when they are encouraged to continue or when they are allowed to dictate, they produce more complete, coherent essays.

There is clear evidence that as children grow, the quality and quantity of their writing increases. For example, an analysis of a national child development study revealed that older children write longer and more complex sentences than younger children (Richardson, Calnan, Essen & Lambert, 1975). In a typical research study, Bartlett & Scribner (1981) asked children in grades 3–6 to write a story using the idea, "A man leaves his house. His body is found the next morning." As expected, sixth graders produce longer stories than third graders (an average of 227 words versus 103 words, respectively); in addition, sixth graders produced more complex referring expressions (e.g., pronouns) as compared to third graders. Scardamalia, Bereiter & Goelman (1982) reported a study in which fourth and sixth graders were asked to write essays. The experimenters measured the length of the longest "coherent string," that is, the longest string of words with no nonfunctional units (such as "you know") and no incoherent orderings. For fourth graders the average was 4.1, and for sixth graders the average was 6.3, suggesting that older writers produce longer coherent strings.

Scardamalia (1981) has compared different levels of sophistication in sentence production. For example, writers using a low level of sophistication state single facts without any integration, such as:

> In the state of Michigan the climate is cool. In the state of Michigan the fruit crop is apples. In the state of California, the climate is warm. In the state of California the fruit crop is oranges.

In contrast, writers using a high level of sophistication integrate all of the information into a coherent sentence such as:

> In Michigan's cool climate they harvest apples, but with California's warm climate, oranges may be grown.

Scardamalia (1981) notes similar differences among levels of sophistication in writing an essay on "Should students be able to choose what things they study in school?" A low level of sophistication is exemplified in the following essay:

> Yes, I think we should. Because some subjects are hard like math. And because the teachers give us a page a day. I think the subjects that we should have is Reading. Because that is easyest one. I think we should't have math, science and social studies. Because in social studies and science we have to write up notes and do experiments. I think math is the worst subject. And I hate spelling to. Because in spelling there are so many words to write and they are all hard. And they waste my time. I think school shouldn't be to 3:45. I think it should be to 2:00. I think school is too long.

As can be seen, the writer simply expresses each idea that comes into her head in the order that the ideas occur to her. This type of writing is called *associative writing* by Bereiter (1980) and *writer-based prose* by Flower (1979).

In the following example, the writer uses a high level of sophistication in the production of sentences:

> Chose is an important thing but a very tricky thing to fool with. I feel that chose of school subjects should be something that is done carefully. A young child given a chose would pick the easiest subjects with no foresight into his future. But choose in his later years could be very important. To develop his leadership qualities. To follow and develop his interests and charictor to his fillest. So with these facts I come to the conclusion that chose of subjects should not be given until about the age of fifteen. You can not condem or praise what you know little about. Until the age of choise a full and general cericulum should be given. It is not up to the school board to decide your life and until you are old enough to decide it is not your dission either.

As can be seen, the writer is able to express conflicting points of view and weave them into a coherent solution. This type of writing requires holding many different ideas in mind at one time and seeing relationships among them. If a writer's attention is absorbed by the mechanics of writing, the writer will not be able to hold all of these relations in mind.

One implication of this work is that high-quality writing requires that the writer not have to use much attention for the mechanical aspects of sentence production. Good writing requires that the mechanics of penmanship, spelling, punctuation, and grammar be automatic. Thus, to be a good writer requires much more than having good ideas; it also requires a great deal of well-learned knowledge about the English language.

Stories Written by Computer Programs. Recent research in artificial intelligence demonstrates that good writing also requires a great deal of specific knowledge about the world. For example, Meehan (1976, 1977) developed a computer program, called TALE-SPIN, that could generate stories. Let's suppose we asked TALE-SPIN to write a story based on the theme, "Never trust flatterers." In order to write a story, TALE-SPIN has to know the rules of written English, so a great deal of the program included these rules. In addition, the program included information concerning the nature of stories (i.e., that there must be characters, a setting, and some events). Here is a story generated by an early version of TALE-SPIN:

> One day Joe Bear was hungry. He asked his friend Irving Bird where some honey was. Irving told him there was honey in the oak tree. Joe threatened to hit Irving if he didn't tell him where some honey was.

Here the program doesn't seem to know that bargaining can be stopped once the goal is attained.

A version of the story generated by a slightly more developed TALE-SPIN program still contained some problems:

> One day Henry Crow sat in his tree, holding a piece of cheese in his mouth, when up came Bill Fox. Bill saw the cheese and was hungry. He said, "Henry, I like your singing very much. Won't you please sing for me?" Henry, flattered by his compliment, began to sing. The cheese fell to the ground. Bill Fox saw the cheese on the ground and was very hungry. He became ill.

As can be seen, the program knew some information about the world, such as "if you get too hungry, you will become ill" and "a character cannot sing and hold something in its mouth at the same time." However, this version of TALE-SPIN still needed even more specific knowledge. A very well-developed version of TALE-SPIN produced the following story about a dishonest fox named Henry who lived in a cave and a trusting crow named Joe who lived in an elm tree:

> Joe had gotten a piece of cheese and was holding it in his mouth. One day, Henry . . . saw Joe Crow and the cheese and became hungry. He decided that he might get the cheese if Joe spoke, so he told Joe that he liked his singing very much and wanted to hear him sing. Joe was very pleased with Henry and began to sing. The cheese fell out of his mouth and down to the ground. Henry picked up the cheese and told Joe Crow that he was stupid. Joe was angry, and didn't trust Henry anymore. Henry returned to his cave.

In this example, the program was able to connect many facts into a coherent story. However, writing this story required that the program know a great deal about bargaining and about the world.

Implications for Instruction

The foregoing review of research on translation makes three points: First, the writer is constrained by many factors, including the mechanics of using proper grammar, spelling, and penmanship. Second, the mechanics of proper sentence writing may overload the writer's attentional capacity, thus interfering with high-level planning and organization. Third, there appears to be a developmental trend in which older writers, who presumably have automated much of the mechanics of writing, are able to write more complex sentences, to integrate the information, and to keep writing until finished.

Writing instruction that emphasizes correct spelling, punctuation, grammar, penmanship, and other mechanics may serve to reduce or eliminate the student's ability to plan. The result can be a mechanically correct composition that lacks coherence. Instead, students may also benefit from writing situations in which the mechanical constraints are removed or relaxed (e.g., students need to be free to write rough drafts that may not be mechanically perfect). The promising research on unpolished first drafts suggests that the quality of the final product may be higher if students are not forced to write polished first drafts. Even practice in oral expression—which certainly avoids constraints on spelling and penmanship—may provide needed practice in the translation process. These kinds of relaxations of mechanical constraints seem particularly important for young writers who have not yet automatized many of the mechanical aspects of writing.

Eventually, students need to develop automatic skills in the mechanics of writing such as penmanship (or typing), spelling, grammatical sentence construction, and punctuation. This will free their attentional capacity so that they can concentrate on the relations among ideas in the composition.

REVIEWING

What Is Reviewing?

The third major process in our model of writing is the reviewing process. As Bartlett (1982) points out, this process involves both detecting errors in the text and correcting the errors.

Research on Reviewing

How Many Changes Do Students Make?   Gould (1980) presents evidence that revision is almost totally absent from adult writing or dictating of simple assignments such as one-page business letters. Experienced dictators use less than 10% of dictation time on reviewing or revising what they have said. If reviewing is not used often in letter writing, then prohibiting writers from reviewing should not greatly affect writing performance. In order to test this idea, Gould (1978b) asked adults to engage in "invisible writing." This invisible writing involved writing with a wooden stylus on a sheet of paper that had carbon paper and another sheet of paper under it. Thus subjects could not see what they had written. Based on the writing of eight letters, invisible writers required about the same amount of time as normal writers (10 minutes for invisible writing versus 11 minutes for normal writing), achieved about the same quality ratings from judges (3.0 for invisible writing versus 3.2 for normal writing, with 1 being unacceptable and 5 being excellent), and required about the same amount of proof-editing changes (almost none for both groups). Apparently, adults do not review what they have written when the assignment is a fairly short and simple one.

What Kinds of Changes Do Students Make?   Bartlett (1982) has recently conducted an extensive series of studies of how children in grades 3–8 revise text. For example, in one study, fourth and fifth graders were asked to revise their own text and text provided by the teacher. Both texts contained syntax errors (such as failure of subject verb agreement or inconsistent use of verb tense), and referent errors (such as using a pronoun that has an unclear or ambiguous referent). Table 12–2 shows that students detected errors in someone else's text much more easily than errors in their own text; in addition, students detected syntax errors more easily than referent errors, especially in their own text. Apparently, detection of referent errors in one's own writing is a particularly difficult task for children.

TABLE 12–2   Detecting Errors in Text

	Percent of Errors That Were Detected	
	Referent Errors	Syntax Errors
In writer's own text	17%	53%
In other texts	73%	88%

Adapted from Bartlett (1982)

Children have difficulty not only in detecting referent errors, but also in making the appropriate correction. For example, Box 12–6 shows some original versions of text along with revised versions suggested by students. As can be seen, the correction strategies selected for the examples were not successful. Bartlett (1982) found that the most commonly used successful strategies for correcting referent errors are use of pronouns (such as, "One day a man went to the beach. The day was hot and *he* needed a cool swim.") and use of repetition

---

BOX 12–6   Some Unsuccessful Correction Strategies

Original Text
   One day a man left his house. Another man was standing outside. The man took out a letter and gave it to him. They talked for a while and then they got into a car. They were both policemen. They were going to catch a thief.

Attempts to Repeat an Antecedent (60% of Unsuccessful Corrections)
   The man took out a letter and gave it to the other man. . . .

Attempts to Differentiate Among Characters (25% of Unsuccessful Corrections)
   The man that was outside took a letter and gave it to the other man outside. . . .

Introduction of Nondiscriminating New Information (15% of Unsuccessful Corrections)
   Joe left his house. Another Joe was standing outside. Joe took out a letter and gave it to the other Joe. . . .

Adapted from Bartlett (1982)

(such as, "Shortly after Christmas, a young woman moved into the house. The *young woman* had few possessions and she settled in quickly."). However, in the examples in Box 12–6 these strategies are not appropriate.

Individual Differences in Reviewing. In another experiment reported by Bartlett (1982), children were given eight paragraphs to revise. Each paragraph included an unusual referent error that could not be corrected by the most common strategies of using pronouns or repetition. For example, one of the paragraphs involved what Bartlett called an "ambiguous referencing":

> One day two girls set out for the park.
> She had a bike. . . .

Figure 12–4 summarizes the revision performance of above-average and below-average writers in grades 5–7. As might be expected, above-average writers corrected about twice as many errors as below-average writers, and older writers corrected about twice as many errors as younger writers. However, even the oldest and most able writers successfully corrected only 36% of the referent errors.

Bartlett also found differences among the correction strategies used by above-average and below-average writers in grades 5–7. Box 12–7 lists five correction strategies, along with examples of each. Table 12–3 summarizes the proportion of solutions that involved each strategy for above-average writers and for below-average writers. As can be seen, above-average writers tend to rely most heavily on adding descriptive information about both referents or on

FIGURE 12–4 Detection and Correction of Referent Errors

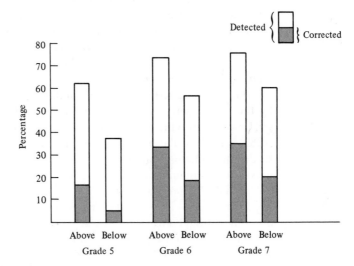

Adapted from Bartlett (1982)

BOX 12–7   Some Successful Corrections of a Referent Error

Original Text
One day two girls set out for the park. She had a bike. . . .

Adding Descriptive Information about Both Referents
One day two girls set out for the park. One was very athletic and the other hated sports. The athletic one had a bike. . . .

Adding Descriptive Information about One Referent
One day two girls set out for the park. One of the girls was athletic, and she had a bike. . . .

Naming Characters
One day two girls named Sandy and Karen went to the park. Sandy had a bike. . . .

Indefinite Referencing Using Plural Noun
One day two girls went to the park. They had a bike. . . .

Indefinite Referencing Using Singular Noun
One day two girls went to the park. One had a bike. . . .

Adapted from Bartlett (1982)

naming the characters; in contrast, the below-average writers rely on nondefinite reference or on adding descriptive information about only one referent. In a follow-up study, Bartlett found that the performance of adults closely paralleled the results with above-average fifth, sixth, and seventh graders. Apparently, good and poor writers differ with respect to both the quantity and quality of their corrections.

The foregoing task of correcting ambiguous referents is made more difficult by the lack of any disambiguating information in the text. For example, the writer must provide names or descriptions for the two characters. Bartlett (1982) compared the percentage of successful corrections of referent errors for text containing no disambiguating information (such as the foregoing examples) versus text containing disambiguating information. An example of a text without disambiguating information is: "A boy lived on Elm Street. Another boy lived next door. The boy had a new bike. . . ." An example of a text with disambiguating information is: "A girl named Linda lived on State Street. Another girl named Jane lived next door. The girl had a new sled. . . ." Figure 12–5 shows the proportion of successful corrections among sixth and seventh graders for the two types of text. As can be seen, both detection and correction

TABLE 12–3 Differences in Correction Strategies of Good and Poor Writers

Strategy Used	Percentage of Total Solutions	
	Above-Average Writers	Below-Average Writers
Adding descriptive information about both referents	33%	9%
Adding descriptive information about one referent	10%	41%
Naming characters	29%	5%
Indefinite referencing using plural noun	23%	27%
Indefinite referencing using singular noun	6%	18%

Adapted from Bartlett (1982)

of errors were much higher when the text contained the necessary disambiguating information. Apparently, generating appropriate disambiguating information is very difficult for young writers.

The foregoing research by Bartlett focused on how children revise text containing referent errors, including comparisons of the general revising behavior of skilled and less skilled writers. Using a similar approach, Stallard (1974) compared the writing performance of skilled twelfth graders versus a

FIGURE 12–5 Detection and Correction of Errors in Two Types of Text

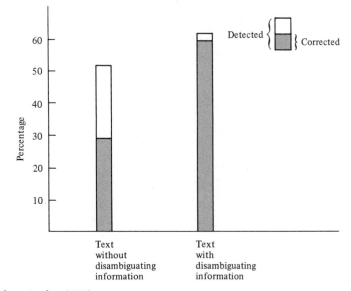

Adapted from Bartlett (1982)

randomly selected group of twelfth graders. As expected, the skilled writers took more time than the control writers (41 minutes versus 23 minutes) and produced more words (343 words versus 309) on the average. However, Stallard also noted that the skilled group conducted three times as many revisions (184 versus 64). In fact, less than half of the control group ever looked back to see what they had written, whereas most of the skilled writers did.

Research by Sommers (reported by Nold, 1981) suggests that skilled and less skilled adult writers differ with respect to the quality of their revisions. Skilled adult writers revise globally first and then revise locally; in other words, they added, deleted, or rearranged large chunks of prose first and then revised the specific wording. In contrast, less skilled writers focused on "finding the right word" and on correct grammar; they seldom added or deleted paragraphs or even changed the structure of sentences.

Additional information concerning the revision process is provided in an analysis of writing by the National Assessment of Educational Progress (1977). As reported by Nold (1981), the study included nine-year-olds and thirteen-year-olds who were asked to write a science report about the moon. Students were given 15 minutes to write the report in pencil; then, the students were given an additional 13 minutes to make revisions in pen. One startling finding is that 40% of the nine-year-olds and 22% of the thirteen-year-olds made no revisions during the 13-minute revision period. However, as Nold (1981) points out, many revisions were made during the initial 15-minute writing period.

Table 12–4 lists the types of revisions that were made during the revision period and the percentage of students within each age-group who used each type of revision. As can be seen, much attention is paid to the conventions of written English (e.g., cosmetic, mechanical, grammatical revisions) by both age-groups; however, the older writers also tend to show strong interest in making the writing accessible to the reader (e.g., stylistic, transitional, and organizational revisions). This finding is consistent with Scardamalia, Bereiter & Goelman's (1982) reporting that young children have difficulty in revising

TABLE 12–4 Types of Revisions Made by Two Age-Groups

Type of Revision	Percentage of Students Making Revision	
	Nine-Year-Olds	Thirteen-Year-Olds
Cosmetic	12%	12%
Mechanical	28%	49%
Grammatical	22%	37%
Continuational	20%	22%
Informational	25%	48%
Stylistic	26%	53%
Transitional	6%	24%
Organizational	7%	18%

Adapted from Nold (1981)

their writing for various audiences whereas fourteen-year-olds are more successful in altering their writing for specific audiences.

Implications for Instruction

In summary, the foregoing review of research makes several points concerning the review process. First, writers often do not review what they have written. Second, when writers are encouraged to review, they fail to detect most of the errors (especially referent errors), and even when they detect errors they often fail to correct them properly. Third, there appears to be a trend in which older or more skilled writers detect and correct far more errors and use more sophisticated review strategies than younger or less skilled writers. More skilled or older writers engage in more review than less skilled or younger writers.

These results suggest that students need to be encouraged to review what they have written. Some instruction may be needed in specific strategies for detecting and correcting errors. Checklists or questions can be used to guide a student's review, although the review process should eventually become internalized. The use of word processors may allow for easier review and revision, since students are freed from the need to handwrite each new draft. The difference between a good writer and poor writer is often not the quality of the first draft but the number of drafts that are generated. Students need to see how revision can turn a poor paper into an excellent one. Some of these ideas are examined more fully below in our examination of two instructional programs aimed at improving the revision process—revision training and writers' workbench.

Revision Training. Recently, de Beaugrande (1982) has developed an instructional program that emphasizes the teaching of revision strategies to high school students. In de Beaugrande's revision training, students are given essays written by other students and asked to revise them. Students are asked to detect errors, correct errors, and then to discuss the revision process with the instructor. During each session, the errors in the essay all require the same basic kind of revision. De Beaugrande focused on specific kinds of revision procedures such as:

Deletion—Removing fillers such as changing "happen to like" to "like."

Rearrangement—Matching the chronological order of events such as changing "there were eggs sitting on the table for me scrambled" to "a plate of scrambled eggs sitting on the table for me."

Differentiation—Expanding or adding to the text, such as changing "no matter what time I got up" into one of two distinct meanings: "no matter how early I awoke" and "by the time I was up and dressed."

Specification—Providing useful details, such as changing "they" to "my hostess."

Parallelism—Reusing the same surface structure for a new block of content, such as changing "there were eggs on the table for me" and "they brought out this big plate of grapes" to "a plate of scrambled eggs" and "a pile of purple seeded grapes."

Does revision training work? De Beaugrande (1982) does not provide an extensive evaluation of his instructional program. However, he does provide examples of the writing performance of students who graduated from his instructional program. For example, in one test a student is given 30 minutes to revise a short essay on the transition from high school to college. The samples presented by de Beaugrande show that the revised version is better than the original. However, more consistent and detailed evidence is required before de Beaugrande's program may be called a success.

The Computer As a Writer's Workbench.   Another way to provide instruction on how to revise prose comes from the use of intelligent computer coaches. For example, the writer's workbench (Macdonald, Frase, Gingrich & Keenan, 1982) is a collection of computer programs that analyze written prose and make suggestions for revisions. The writer's workbench is actually in use at Bell Laboratories, with over 1000 users. You can type your text into the computer, using a standard word processing system. Then, once you have finished your first draft, you can ask the program from the writer's workbench to suggest revisions in your manuscript.

The writer's workbench consists of three major parts: a proofreader, a style analyzer, and an on-line English reference guide. The proofreader consists of the following programs:

Spelling—lists all words that may be misspelled and allows the user to specify any new words (such as jargon or acronyms) to the list of acceptable words.
Punctuation—lists cases where punctuation may be needed or where existing punctuation may be incorrect.
Double words—lists all cases in which a word is repeated.
Faulty phrasing—lists phrases that may not be coherent.
Split infinitives—lists all instances of split infinitives.

An example of the output of the proofreading program is shown in Box 12–8. As can be seen, the program points out possible errors as well as making suggestions for how to correct the errors.

The style analyzer consists of the following programs:

Style—provides readability indices, measures of average word length and average sentence length, the percentage of verbs in the passive voice, the percentage of verbs in the passive voice, the percentage of nouns that are nominalizations, the number of sentences that begin with expletives, and other such information.
Prose—compares the style statistics listed above with some standard meas-

ures. If the text's measures are outside of the standards, then the program prints an explanation of why the text may be hard to read and prints suggestions of how to correct the problems.

Find—locates individual sentences that contain passive verbs, expletives, nominalizations, "to be" verb forms, and other potential problem sentences.

Box 12–9 gives a portion of the output from the prose program. As can be seen, this program tries to explain how to improve the text as well as pointing out problems.

The on-line reference programs include information on correct use of 300 commonly misused words and phrases, a computerized dictionary, and general information about the writer's workbench. Additional programs rate the words in the text for abstractness-concreteness, rate the paragraph organization, and detect possible instances of sexist language.

Although the authors do not report any controlled research studies concerning the effectiveness of the writer's workbench as a teaching tool, the authors do provide some encouraging observations. Informal studies of the writing of program users suggest that later drafts (as compared to first drafts) tended to include fewer abstract words, passive sentences, and wordy phrases. In addition, writers reported being able to detect more errors using the programs than if they did not use the programs. For example, in a study involving sixty-three users, the users reported that the programs found errors that would have otherwise gone undetected and that using the programs did not increase their writing time. These preliminary results seem to encourage the hope that writing instruction may someday make use of computer tutors to aid in the revision process. Other writer's helper systems include JOURNALISM, a proofreader that comments on the organization and style of news stories (Bishop, 1975) and CRES, a proofreader that identifies uncommon words, long sentences, and difficult phrases in NAVY documents (Kincaid, Aagard, O'Hara & Cottrell, 1981).

BUILDING A WRITING PROGRAM THAT WORKS

Instructional Method and Content of Writing Programs

This chapter has explored three important components in the writing process as well as some possible instructional techniques for improving each component. How could you put this information together into a writing program that works? To answer this question, Hillocks (1984) carefully analyzed every available experimental study on writing that was conducted during the last twenty years. In particular, Hillocks examined research on how to teach (i.e., instructional methods) and what to teach (i.e., instructional content).

From research on how to teach, Hillocks identified three general methods of instruction in writing programs:

Natural process mode—The student dominates by initiating most of the writing activity, working at her own pace, and seeking feedback, when needed, from other students or the teacher.

BOX 12–8   Input and Output from the Proofreader Program

INPUT: Our report, "The Basic Fundamentals of Computatonal Complexity", is enclosed. Please send any recommended changes at your earliest convenience. thanks.

PROOFER: *************** SPELLING ****************

OUTPUT: Possible spelling errors in examplefile are:

Computatonal   recomended

If any of these words are spelled correctly, later type
                spelladd word1 word2 . . . wordn
to have them added to your spelldict file.

************* PUNCTUATION *************

The punctuation in examplefile is first described.

2 double quotes and 0 single quotes
0 apostrophes
0 left parentheses and 0 right ones

The program next prints any sentence that it thinks is incorrectly punctuated and follows it by its correction.

line 1
OLD: Our report, "The Basic Fundamentals of Computatonal Complexity",
NEW: Our report, "The Basic Fundamentals of Computational Complexity,"
line 3
OLD: earliest convenience. thanks.
NEW: earliest convenience. Thanks.

For more information about punctuation rules, type:

punctrules

************* DOUBLE WORDS *************

For file examplefile:

No double words found

************* WORD CHOICE *************

Sentences with possibly wordy or misused phrases are listed next, followed by suggested revisions.

beginning line 1 examplefile
Our report, "The *[Basic Fundamentals]* of Computational Complexity",
is enclosed.

beginning line 2 examplefile
Please send any recommended changes *[at your earliest convenience]*.

file examplefile: number of lines 3, number of phrases found 2

------------------ Table of Substitutions ------------------

PHRASE   **SUBSTITUTION**

at your earliest convenience: use "soon" for " at your earliest convenience"
basic fundamentals: use "fundamentals" for " basic fundamentals"

*********** SPLIT INFINITIVES ***********

For file examplefile:

No split infinitives found

From Macdonald, Frase, Gingrich & Keenan (1982)

BOX 12–9   Some Output from the Prose Program

SENTENCE STRUCTURE

Passives

This text contains a much higher percentage of passive verbs (44%) than is common in good documents of this type (22%). A sentence is in the passive voice when its grammatical subject is the receiver of the action.

PASSIVE: The ball was hit by the boy.

When the doer of the action in a sentence is the subject, the sentence is in the active voice.

ACTIVE: The boy hit the ball.

The passive voice is sometimes needed

1. to emphasize the object of the sentence,
2. to vary the rhythm of the text, or
3. to avoid naming an unimportant actor.

EXAMPLE: The appropriations were approved.

Although passive sentences are sometimes needed, psychological research has shown that they are harder to comprehend than active sentences. Because of this, you should transform as many of your passives to actives as possible. You can use the *style* program to find all your sentences with passive verbs in them, by typing the following command when this program is finished.

style-p filename

Nominalizations

You have appropriately limited your nominalizations (nouns made from verbs, e.g., "description").

From Macdonald, Frase, Gingrich & Keenan (1982)

Presentational mode—The teacher dominates by providing traditional instruction and lectures on how to write, determining the writing topic, and providing extensive corrections of student writing.

Environmental mode—Student and teacher cooperate in discussing the goals and content and process of writing a composition. Instead of lecturing, the teacher works with small groups on specific writing projects, helping students to support assertions with evidence, predict and counter opposing arguments, generate appropriate assertions from available data, and so on. Instead of beginning with independent free writing, the student works on specific writing tasks under teacher supervision within small groups.

Which method of instruction is most effective? On the average, Hillocks (1984) found that the environmental mode resulted in three times more improvement than the natural process method and four times more improvement than the traditional presentational method. You may notice that these three methods—natural process, presentational, and environmental—correspond roughly to the discovery, rule, and guided discovery methods examined in Chapter 7. Like the results described in Chapter 7, the method that corresponds to guided discovery was the most effective. The environmental method allows students to come in contact with some specific skills needed for writing and at the same time keeps the learner actively involved in the learning process.

From research on what to teach, Hillocks (1984) noted differences in the content of instruction in various writing programs, including the following:

Grammar—The teacher focuses on the mechanics of writing including definitions of parts of speech, phrasing sentences, and so on. Usually, the teacher marks every error in a student's writing.

Models—Students are asked to study good pieces of writing as models for their own writing.

Free writing—The student is asked to write freely about anything she chooses.

Sentence combining—The student is asked to build more complex sentences out of simpler ones.

Scales—The student is given a list of questions or checklist to apply to her own composition or someone else's composition. Eventually the student should internalize this review process.

Inquiry—The student is asked to discuss her own writing process and to improve strategies for writing. For example, students might be asked to find details to describe a personal experience vividly.

Which kinds of content result in the most improvement in writing? Focusing on sentence combining, scales, and inquiry are the most effective, presumably because students acquire skills that are specifically related to composition writing. Focusing on models and free writing is less effective, presumably because the goal of instruction is unclear; focusing on grammar is the least effective of all the approaches, presumably because it draws attention away from the actual writing process. In fact, Hillocks' analysis of research shows that in some cases heavy emphasis on grammar in writing may actually decrease the quality of writing. This finding is consistent with research on translation cited in this chapter, which shows that mechanical constraints can interfere with students' attention to planning a coherent composition. Instead of focusing on grammar as a way of teaching writing, Hillocks suggests teaching grammar within the context of actually writing.

Hillocks (1984) reports the disturbing fact that the most popular writing programs currently favored in educational practice ignore the available educational research on writing. In spite of research to the contrary, many writing programs assume that the most effective method of instruction is natural process and the most effective content is free writing.

> For over a decade, authorities in the field have been caught up in the "writing as process" model, which calls for exploratory talk, followed by free writing, reading by or for an audience of peers, comments from peers, and revision. The teacher's role is simply to facilitate this process—not to make specific assignments, not to help students learn criteria for judging writing, not to structure classroom activities based on specific objectives as in environmental treatments, not to provide exercises in manipulating syntax, not to design activities that engage students in identifiable processes of examining data. In short, this mode . . . studiously avoids the approaches to writing instruction that this report demonstrates to be more effective. (Hillocks, 1984, p. 162)

The program that Hillocks describes seems too much like the "discovery" methods reviewed in Chapter 7. This kind of program may be a sort of reaction against the "rule" methods used in the past. In essence, Hillocks suggests a compromise of using "guided discovery" methods for teaching writing.

Graves' Writing Program

In contrast to Hillocks' research-based recommendations for the development of effective writing programs, Graves (1983) offers an exemplary writing program designed to be used in schools. Graves' (1983) classic book, *Writing: Teachers & Children at Work*, contains many recommendations for how to teach writing but provides no research support or rationale. In fact, Graves (1980, p. 914) rejects the usefulness of research on writing because: "It couldn't help teachers in classrooms."

What is Graves' writing program? Some of the key features of the program are:

1. Start to teach writing. Let students begin writing immediately without lengthy direction and instruction from the teacher. Integrate writing into the regular activities of the school day. Let students read and criticize each others' papers. Let students select compositions to be "published" as hardcover books and placed in the class library.

2. Make the writing conference work. Let students discuss their compositions with teachers and other students. Let the students present their ideas rather than imposing ideas on the students. Ask questions that help students improve their compositions rather than pointing out every error in the composition.

3. Help children learn the skills they need. Skills such as handwriting, grammar, spelling are not ends in themselves but rather are needed to enhance writing.

4. Understand how children develop as writers. Children begin by focusing on mechanics, such as spelling and being neat. Eventually, as these skills become more automatic in the primary school years, children focus more on content and organization of the composition. Finally, with more experience, revision becomes a major focus. Too much emphasis on mechanics can stifle development of higher-level skills, but ignoring mechanics can leave the child unsure of himself in writing.

5. Document children's writing development. Children should maintain a writing folder that keeps a record of their writing activity, including ideas as well as finished products. The teacher needs to monitor a student's progress by observing the student's writing folder, watching the child compose, and discussing writing with the student. Specific, individual records should be kept for each student concerning the quality and quantity of writing.

Does Graves' writing program work? There is often popular support among teachers for programs like that proposed by Graves; however, Graves (1983) does not present any evaluation of his program in his book. Thus we do not know whether Graves' writing program works.

Graves' writing program seems most closely related to what Hillocks calls the "natural process" method and "free writing" content, both of which are less effective than other methods and content. However, Graves' writing program can be implemented in ways that involve a more "environmental" method and more "inquiry" content. For example, the amount of direction given in writing conferences can be increased, and the teacher can focus more on teaching specific writing skills. In other words, although Graves' method is most like the "discovery" approach described in Chapter 7, it can be modified to be more like "guided discovery." Research cited by Hillocks, and in Chapter 7, suggests that such modifications could improve the effectiveness of the program.

CONCLUSION

The research on writing is just beginning to make sense of the writing process. However, even the preliminary research presented in this chapter invites implications for instruction.

First, planning, which includes the development of an organization and the generation of content information, is a major component in writing. Students need explicit and specific training in techniques for organizing compositions, paragraphs, and sentences. Similarly students need training and practice in how to generate and record information to be used in a composition.

Second, translation is a major writing component which involves converting ideas into words. The translation process relies on mechanical skills such as handwriting, spelling, punctuation, grammatical sentence construction, and so on. Students need to be freed from the mechanical constraints on translation so their attentional capacity can concentrate on planning a coherent composition. For older or more skilled students, the mechanical skills should become automatic; for younger or less skilled students, heavy emphasis on mechanics should not be required in the first draft.

Third, reviewing is a major writing component which involves the detection and correction of errors. The difference between a good composition and a poor composition may depend not on differences in the first draft, but on differences in how subsequent drafts are carried out. Students need explicit and detailed instruction in how to revise, with a final goal of having students internalize the revision procedures.

Finally, this chapter has explored the characteristics of effective writing programs. The more successful programs use instructional methods like "guided discovery," as described in Chapter 7.

SUGGESTED READINGS

Frederiksen, C. H. & Dominic, J. F. (ed.) (1981). *Writing: Volume 2*. Hillsdale, N.J.: Erlbaum. (A collection of papers by cognitive psychologists, linguists, and composition experts.)

Gregg, L. W. & Steinberg, E. R. (eds.) (1980). *Cognitive processes in writing*. Hillsdale, N.J.: Erlbaum. (A collection of papers by cognitive psychologists who are studying the writing process.)

Nystrand, M. *What writers know*. (ed.) (1982). New York: Academic. (Another collection of papers by cognitive psychologists, linguists, and composition experts.)

13 *Mathematics*

This chapter asks, "What does a student need to know in order to solve mathematics problems?" The answer to this question includes four components. Linguistic and factual knowledge are needed to help the student translate each sentence of the problem into some internal representation. Schematic knowledge is needed to help the student integrate the information into a coherent representation. Strategic knowledge is needed to help the student devise and monitor a solution plan. Procedural knowledge is needed to help the student carry out the computations required in the plan.

WHAT DO YOU NEED TO KNOW IN ORDER TO SOLVE MATH PROBLEMS?

Suppose I asked you to solve the following problem:

> Floor tiles are sold in squares 30 cm on each side. How much would it cost to tile a rectangular room 7.2 meters long and 5.4 meters wide if the tiles cost $.72 each?

What skills must you possess in order to solve this problem?

First, you need to be able to translate each statement of the problem into some internal representation. This translation process requires that you understand English sentences (i.e., you need linguistic knowledge). For example, you need to be able to recognize that the tile problem contains the following facts: each tile is a 30×30 centimeters square, the room is a 7.2×5.4 meter rectangle, each tile costs 72 cents, the unknown is the cost of tiling the room. This translation process also requires that you know certain facts, i.e., you need factual knowledge. For example, you need to know that all sides of a square are equal in length and that there are 100 centimeters in a meter. The top portion of Box 13–1 presents some examples of mathematical tasks that focus on problem translation. Go ahead and try these problems in order to exercise your problem translation skills.

Second, you need to be able to integrate each of the statements of the problem into a coherent problem representation. This problem integration process requires that you be able to recognize problem types (i.e., you need schematic knowledge). For example, you need to recognize that this problem is a rectangle problem requiring the formula, area = length $\times$ width. Problem integration also involves being able to distinguish between information that is relevant for solution and information that is not relevant for solution. The second portion of Box 13–1 presents some examples of mathematical tasks that focus on problem integration. Go ahead and try these problems in order to test your problem integration skills.

Third, you need to be able to devise and monitor a solution plan. This solution planning process requires knowledge of heuristics (i.e., strategic knowledge). For example, you need to break the problem down into sub-goals—such as finding the area of the room, finding the number of tiles needed, and finding the cost of those tiles. You also need to be able to monitor what you are doing—such as knowing that when you multiply 7.2×5.4 you are finding the area of the room in meters. The third portion of Box 13–1 presents some examples of mathematical tasks that focus on solution planning and monitoring. Go ahead and try some of these problems.

Finally, a fourth major component involved in answering the title problem is to be able to apply the rules of arithmetic. For example, you must be able to calculate the answer for $7.2 \times 5.4 = $ _____ or for $.72 \times 432 = $ _____. Accurate and automatic execution of arithmetic and algebraic procedures is based on procedural knowledge. The bottom of Box 13–1 presents some examples of mathematical tasks that focus on solution execution. Go ahead and select your answers.

As you can see from our examples, there is more to solving a problem than just getting the final answer. Our componential analysis of the tile problem suggests that there are at least four major components involved in mathematical problem solving. These four components are summarized in Table 13–1. In this chapter we will take a closer look at each of these four components of solving mathematics problems: being able to translate each statement of the problem, being able to integrate the information into a coherent problem representation, being able to devise and monitor a solution plan, and being able to accurately

TABLE 13–1 Four Components in Mathematical Problem Solving

Component	Type of Knowledge	Examples from the Tile Problem
Problem translation	Linguistic knowledge	The room is a rectangle with 7.2-meter width and 5.4-meter length.
	Factual knowledge	One meter equals 100 centimenters.
Problem integration	Schematic knowledge	Area = length × width
Solution planning & monitoring	Strategic knowledge	Find area of the room in meters by multiplying 7.2 × 5.4. Then, find the area of each tile in meters by multiplying 0.3 × 0.3. Then, find the number of needed tiles by dividing the area of the room by the area of each tile. Then, find total cost by multiplying the number of needed tiles by $.72.
Solution execution	Procedural knowledge	7.2 × 5.4 = 38.88 0.3 × 0.3 = 0.09 38.88/.09 = 432 432 × .72 = $311.04

and efficiently carry out the solution plan. (By the way, the correct final answer for the tile problem is $311.04. The correct answers for the items in Box 13–1 are: 1, b; 2, c; 3, a; 4, d; 5, a; 6, a; 7, a; 8, a; 9, d; 10, a; 11, c.)

PROBLEM TRANSLATION

What Is Problem Translation?

The first step in solving the tile problem is to translate each statement into an internal representation. For example, the major statements in the tile problem are: the tiles are squares measuring 30 centimeters by 30 centimeters; the tiles cost 72 cents each; the room is a rectangle measuring 7.2 meters by 5.4 meters, and the cost of tiling the room is unknown. In order to translate the statements of the tile problem, a problem solver needs some knowledge of the English language (i.e., linguistic knowledge) and some knowledge about the world (i.e., factual knowledge). For example, linguistic knowledge is required in order to determine that "floor tiles" and "the tiles" refer to the same thing. Similarly, factual knowledge is required in order to know that a "square" has four sides that are all equal in length, or in order to know that 100 centimeters equals 1 meter.

BOX 13–1   Some Skills Involved in Solving Math Problems

PROBLEM TRANSLATION

Restating the Problem Givens

1. Floor tiles are sold in squares 30 centimeters on each side. How much would it cost to tile a rectangular room 7.2 meters long and 5.4 meters wide if the tiles cost $.72 each?

Which of the following sentences is not true?

(a) the room is a rectangle measuring 7.2 meters by 5.4 meters
(b) each tile costs 30 cents
(c) each tile is a square measuring 30 centimeters by 30 centimenters
(d) the length of the long side of the room is 7.2 meters

Restating the Problem Goal

2. Floor tiles are sold in squares 30 centimeters on each side. How much would it cost to tile a rectangular room 7.2 meters long and 5.4 meters wide if the tiles cost $.72 each?

What are you being asked to find?

(a) the width and length of the room
(b) the cost of each tile
(c) the cost of tiling the room
(d) the size of each tile

PROBLEM INTEGRATION

Recognizing Problem Types

3. Melons were selling three for $1. How many could Larry buy for $4?

Which of the following problems can be solved in the same way as the preceding problem?

(a) There were three books for every four students. How many books were there in a class of twenty students?
(b) A car travels 25 miles per hour for 4 hours. How far will it travel?
(c) John has twenty-five marbles. Sue has twelve marbles. How many more marbles does John have than Sue?
(d) If balloons cost 10 cents each and pencils cost 5 cents each, how much do three balloons and two pencils cost?

Recognizing Relevant and Irrelevant Information

4. The manager bought 100 cameras for $3,578. The cameras sold for $6,024. How much was the profit?

Which numbers are needed to solve this problem?

(a) 100, 6024, 3578
(b) 100, 6024
(c) 100, 3578
(d) 3578, 6024

Determining Information That Is Needed for Solution

5. How much longer is the Mississippi River than the Yangtze River?

What information is needed to answer this question?

(a) the length of the Mississippi River and the length of the Yangtze River
(b) the location and length of the Mississippi River and the location and length of the Yangtze River
(c) the average rainfall for the Mississippi River and the average rainfall for the Yangtze River
(d) the length of the Yangtze River

Representing a Problem As a Diagram or Picture

6. Mary Jackson earns $215 a week. She pays 30% of this for housing. How much does she pay for housing each week?

Which diagram best represents the problem?

(a) <--HOUSING COSTS-->< ------ OTHER COSTS ------ >
< ------------------------ TOTAL COSTS ------------------------ >

(b) <--HOUSING COSTS-->< ------ TOTAL COSTS ------ >

(c) < -----TOTAL COSTS ----- >< ----- OTHER COSTS ----- >
     < --------------------- HOUSING COSTS --------------------- >

(d) < ---- TOTAL COSTS ---- >< ---- HOUSING COSTS ---- >
     < ------------------------ TOTAL COSTS ------------------------ >

SOLUTION PLANNING AND MONITORING

Representing the Problem As a Number Sentence or Equation or List of Necessary Operations

7. An insurance agent visited 585 customers. He sold 76 life insurance policies, 97 fire insurance policies, and 208 auto insurance policies. How many policies did he sell in all?

Which number sentence corresponds to this problem?

(a) $76 + 97 + 208 =$
(b) $585 - 76 - 97 - 208 =$
(c) $585 + 76 + 97 + 208 =$
(d) $208 - 97 - 76 =$

Establishing Subgoals

8. Floor tiles are sold in squares 30 centimeters on each side. How much would it cost to tile a rectangular room 7.2 meters long and 5.4 meters wide if the tiles cost $0.72 each?

To answer this question, you need to determine:

(a) how many tiles are needed
(b) how much longer one side of the room is than the other side
(c) how much 100 tiles would cost
(d) how much money will be left

Drawing Conclusions

9. The 130 students from Marie Curie School are going on a picnic. Each school bus holds fifty passengers. How many buses will they need?

Rose worked the following problem:

$$\begin{array}{r} 2 \\ 50\overline{)130} \\ \underline{100} \\ 30 \end{array}$$

Look back at the question in the problem. What is the answer?

(a) 2
(b) 2 R30
(c) 2 3/5
(d) 3

SOLUTION EXECUTION

Carrying Out Single Calculations

10. $7.2 \times 5.4 = $ _____

The correct answer is:

(a) 38.88
(b) 432
(c) 311.04
(d) 28

Carrying Out Chains of Calculations

11. $((7.2 \times 5.4)/(.3 \times .3)) \times .72 = $ _____

The correct answer is:

(a) 38.88
(b) 432
(c) 311.04
(d) 28

Research on Problem Translation

Comprehending Relational Sentences. Recent research has suggested that the translation process can be very difficult for students, especially when the problem contains relational statements (i.e., statements that express a quantitative relation between variables). For example, in an analysis of factors that contribute to problem difficulty, Loftus & Suppes (1972) found that the most difficult problems tend to contain relational statements, such as "Mary is twice as old as Betty was 2 years ago. Mary is 40 years old. How old is Betty?"

In another study (Riley, Greeno & Heller, 1982; Greeno, 1980), children were asked to listen to and then repeat word problems. For example, suppose that the following problem was presented: "Joe has three marbles. Tom has five more marbles than Joe. How many marbles does Tom have?" Children's errors included ignoring the relational statements, such as repeating the problem as follows: "Joe has three marbles. Tom has five marbles. How many marbles does Tom have?"

Adults also seem to have difficulty in translating relational statements. In one study (Soloway, Lochhead & Clement, 1982), college students were given statements and asked to translate them into equations. For example, suppose the statement was: "There are six times as many students as professors at this university." Approximately one-third of the students produced the wrong equation, such as $6S = P$.

Box 13–2 summarizes the approaches of two different students to the students and professors problem. One student takes a static approach by assuming that P stands for "a professor" and S stands for "the students of that professor." In contrast, another student takes a procedural approach by assuming that to determine the "number of students" one must perform an operation on the "number of professors." Thus errors in translation occur when students view the statement as a static description rather than a procedural instruction for how to convert one variable into another.

In a related study, Mayer (1982) asked college students to read and then recall eight algebra story problems. For example, one problem was: "The area occupied by an unframed rectangular picture is 64 square inches less than the area occupied by the picture mounted in a frame 2 inches wide. What are the dimensions of the picture if it is 4 inches longer than it is wide?" The problems contained three types of statements: assignments, which assigned a value to a variable, such as "the frame is 2 inches wide"; relations, which expressed a quantitative relation between two variables such as "the picture is 4 inches longer than it is wide"; and questions, which asked for the numerical value of an unknown such as, "What are the dimensions of the picture?" If students have difficulty in representing relational statements, then recall should be poor for relations. The results support this idea, since subjects made approximately three times as many errors in recalling relational statements (29% errors) as compared to assignment statements (9% errors).

Subsequent analyses revealed that students committed three kinds of recall errors: omission errors, in which the statement was not recalled at all; specifica-

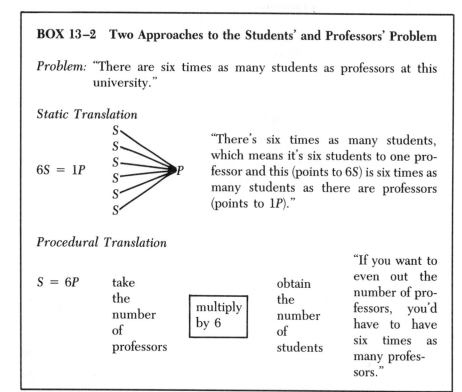

> **BOX 13–2** Two Approaches to the Students' and Professors' Problem
>
> *Problem:* "There are six times as many students as professors at this university."
>
> *Static Translation*
>
> $6S = 1P$
>
> "There's six times as many students, which means it's six students to one professor and this (points to 6S) is six times as many students as there are professors (points to 1P)."
>
> *Procedural Translation*
>
> $S = 6P$ take the number of professors   multiply by 6   obtain the number of students
>
> "If you want to even out the number of professors, you'd have to have six times as many professors."

tion errors, in which the variable in the statement was changed to another variable, such as changing "the frame is 2 inches wide" to "the frame is 2 inches long"; conversion errors, in which a statement is changed from a relation to an assignment or vice versa, such as changing "the picture is 4 inches longer than it is wide" into "the picture is 4 inches long." Figure 13–1 shows the proportions of each type of error for assignments and relations. As you can see, a substantial proportion of errors in recall of relational statement involve conversion into an assignment while almost none of the assignment statements were converted into relational statements. Apparently, some students lack the appropriate linguistic knowledge to represent relational statements in memory.

Using Factual Knowledge.   Factual knowledge is also a key component in problem translation. For example, Loftus & Suppes (1972) found that problems involving scale conversion were much more difficult than corresponding problems that did not. Scale conversions require factual knowledge; for example, converting 30 centimeters to .3 meters requires knowing that 100 centimeters equals 1 meter. Bobrow (1968) developed a computer program capable of solving algebra story problems. The program involved two major phases: translation of each statement into an equation and solution of the equations. In order for the program to translate, it required a large store of both linguistic

FIGURE 13–1   Conversion Errors Occur Often for Relational Propositions but Not for Assignments

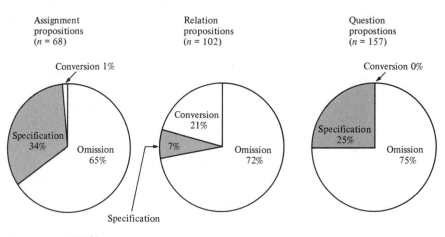

From Mayer (1982b)

and factual knowledge to be included in the program. For example, the program needed to know linguistic knowledge such as "pounds is the plural of pound" and factual knowledge such as "16 ounces equals 1 pound."

Implications for Instruction

The research summarized in this section suggests that problem translation may be a major source of difficulty in mathematical problem solving. Apparently, many students come to the problem-solving task lacking the prerequisite linguistic and factual knowledge. One implication of this research is that students may need practice in problem translation, such as paraphrasing statements from the problem. Another implication is that students need to have learned certain basic facts (such as the fact that all sides of a square are equal) prior to solving story problems.

Let's return to the tile problem described in the introduction to this chapter. The research presented in this section indicates that many students have difficulty in being able to comprehend each major statement in the problem, such as "Floor tiles are sold in squares 30 centimeters on each side." How can you provide translation training for a problem like the tile problem? Some activities that might encourage development of translation skills are: asking a student to restate the problem givens or the problem goal in his or her own words. In some cases students could be asked to draw a picture that corresponds to a sentence in the problem, such as the first sentence of the tile problem. Similarly, the first portion of Box 13–1 suggests multiple choice items that offer practice in recognizing problem givens and goals. These suggestions, of course, are tentative ones that require research verification.

PROBLEM INTEGRATION

What Is Problem Integration?

Accurate representation of a story problem often requires more than statement-by-statement translation. For example, Paige & Simon (1966) asked students to solve impossible problems such as: "The number of quarters a man has is seven times the number of dimes he has. The value of the dimes exceeds the value of the quarters by two dollars and fifty cents. How many has he of each coin?" Using factual and linguistic knowledge, a person could translate these statements into equations such as:

$$Q = 7D$$
$$D(.10) = 2.50 + Q(.25)$$

However, if you try to understand how the two statements fit together into a coherent problem, you might recognize an inconsistency. In Paige & Simon's study, both types of approaches were observed: some subjects translated each statement separately, while other subjects tried to understand how the statements related to one another.

The foregoing example shows that another important component in solving a story problem is to put the statements of the problem together into a coherent representation. In order to understand and integrate a problem, the problem solver needs to have some knowledge of problem types (i.e., schematic knowledge). For example, in the tile problem, you need to recognize that this is a "rectangle problem" that is based on the formula area = length × width. This knowledge will help you to understand how the statements in the problem fit together; for example, you know to expect certain information such as the length of the rectangle and the width of the rectangle.

Research on Problem Integration

Students' Schemas for Story Problems. Hinsley, Hayes & Simon (1977) have studied students' schemas (or categories) for story problems. Subjects were given a series of algebra story problems and asked to sort them into categories. Subjects were quite proficient at this task and reached high levels of agreement. Box 13–3 shows the eighteen different categories that subjects used. Apparently, students come to the problem-solving task with some knowledge of problem types.

Hinsley, Hayes & Simon (1977) also found that students were able to categorize problems almost immediately. For example, as soon as a student read the first few words of a problem, such as "The area occupied by an unframed rectangular picture," we would expect the student to say, "Oh, it's one of those picture frame problems." Follow-up studies (Hayes, Waterman & Robinson, 1977; Robinson & Hayes, 1978) found that students use their sche-

BOX 13–3   Examples of Eighteen Problem Types

Category Name	Example of Problem
1. Triangle	Jerry walks one block east along a vacant lot and then two blocks north to a friend's house. Phil starts at the same point and walks diagonally through the vacant lot coming out at the same point as Jerry. If Jerry walked 217 feet east and 400 feet north, how far did Phil walk?
2. DRT	In a sports car race, a Panther starts the course at 9:00 A.M. and averages 75 miles per hour. A Mallotti starts four minutes later and averages 85 miles per hour. If a lap is 15 miles, on which lap will the Panther be overtaken?
3. Averages	Flying east between two cities, a plane's speed is 380 miles per hour. On the return trip, it flies 420 miles per hour. Find the average speed for the round trip.
4. Scale conversion	Two temperature scales are established, one, the R scale where water under fixed conditions freezes at 15 and boils at 405, and the other, the S scale where water freezes at 5 and boils at 70. If the R and S scales are linearly related, find an expression for any temperature R in terms of a temperature S.
5. Ratio	If canned tomatoes come in two sizes and the radius of one is two-thirds the radius of the other, find the ratios of the capacities of the two cans.
6. Interest	A certain savings bank pays 3% interest compounded semiannually. How much will $2,500 amount to if left on deposit for 20 years?
7. Area	A box containing 180 cubic inches is constructed by cutting from each corner of a cardboard square a small square with side 5 inches, and then turning up the sides. Find the area of the original piece of cardboard.
8. Max-min	A real estate operator estimates that the monthly profit p in dollars from a building s stories high is given by $p = -2s^2 + 88s$. What height building would he consider most profitable?
9. Mixture	One vegetable oil contains 6% saturated fats and a second contains 26% saturated fats. In making a salad dressing how many ounces of the second may be added to 10 ounces of the first if the percent of saturated fats is not to exceed 16%?

10. River current	A river steamer travels 36 miles downstream in the same time that it travels 24 miles upstream. The steamer's engines drive in still water at a rate which is 12 miles an hour more than the rate of the current. Find the rate of the current.
11. Probability	In an extrasensory-perception experiment, a blindfolded subject has two rows of blocks before him. Each row has blocks numbered 1 to 10 arranged in random order. The subject is to place one hand on a block in the first row and then try to place his other hand on the block having the same numeral in the second row. If the subject has no ESP, what is the probability of his making a match on the first try?
12. Number	The units digit is 1 more than 3 times the tens digit. The number represented when the digits are interchanged is 8 times the sum of the digits.
13. Work	Mr. Russo takes 3 minutes less than Mr. Lloyd to pack a case when each works alone. One day, after Mr. Russo spent 6 minutes in packing a case, the boss called him away, and Mr. Lloyd finished packing in 4 more minutes. How many minutes would it take Mr. Russo alone to pack a case?
14. Navigation	A pilot leaves an aircraft carrier and flies south at 360 mph, while the carrier proceeds N30W at 30 mph. If the pilot has enough fuel to fly 4 hours, how far south can he fly before returning to his ship?
15. Progressions	From two towns 363 miles apart, Jack and Jill set out to meet each other. If Jill travels 1 mile the first day, 3 the second, 5 the third, and so on, and Jack travels 2 miles the first day, 6 the second, 10 the third, and so on, when will they meet?
16. Progression-2	Find the sum of the first 25 odd positive integers.
17. Physics	The speed of a body falling freely from rest is directly proportional to the length of time that it falls. If a body was falling at 144 ft per second $4\frac{1}{2}$ seconds after beginning its fall, how fast was it falling $3\frac{3}{4}$ seconds later?
18. Exponentials	The diameter of each successive layer of a wedding cake is two-thirds the previous layer. If the diameter of the first layer of a five-layer cake is 15 inches, find the sum of the circumferences of all the layers.

Adapted from Hinsley, Hayes & Simon (1977)

mas to make accurate judgments concerning what information is relevant in a problem and what is not. For example, the following "crop duster" problem was presented one phrase at a time (Robinson & Hayes, 1978):

> A crop-dusting plane carries 2,000 pounds of Rotenone dusting compound, 250 pounds of test fuel, a pilot highly skilled in low-altitude flying, and a duster-machinery operator, the pilot's younger brother. The plane must dust a rectangular tobacco field 0.5 miles wide by 0.6 miles long. The dusting compound must be spread with a density of 200 pounds per 0.001 square mile. Further, the compound must be spread between 6 A.M. and 9 A.M., when there is sufficient light and before the morning dew has evaporated, to assure the adherence of the compound to the plants. The plane flies the length of the field with 6 mph tailwind and back against the same headwind. With the wind, the plane uses fuel at the rate of 80 pounds per hour. The ratio of flying time against the wind to the time with the wind is 9:8. The duster operator must try to spread the compound uniformly on the ground despite varying speed.

As each phrase of the problem was presented, subjects were asked to judge whether the information was needed to solve the problem. The subjects correctly identified almost all of the relevant information and correctly rejected almost all of the irrelevant information. When subjects were told what the question was, 89% of the crucial factual information was judged relevant while only 46% of the unneeded factual information and 11% of the other irrelevant information was judged as relevant.

Many errors in problem integration occur when a person uses the wrong schema for determining which information is necessary. For example, the following problem, used by Hinsley et al. (1977), can be viewed as either a distance-rate-time problem or as a triangle problem:

> Because of their quiet ways, the inhabitants of Smalltown were especially upset by the terrible New Year's eve auto accident which claimed the life of one Smallville resident. The facts were these: Both Smith and Jones were New Year's babies and each had planned a surprise visit to the other on their mutual birthday. Jones had started out for Smith's house traveling due east on Route 210 just 2 minutes after Smith had left for Jones' house. Smith was traveling directly south on Route 140. Jones was traveling 30 miles per hour faster than Smith even though their houses were only five miles apart as the crow flies. Their cars crashed at the right-angle intersection of the two highways. Officer Franklin, who observed the crash, determined that Jones was traveling half again as fast as Smith at the time of the crash. Smith had been driving for just 4 minutes at the time of the crash. The crash occurred nearer to the house of the dead man than to the house of the survivor. What was the name of the dead man?

Some subjects interpreted this problem as a triangle problem. For example, they drew triangles and tried to determine the lengths of the two legs and the hypotenuse. One subject misread "4 minutes" as "4 miles" and assumed this was the length of one of the legs; another subject assumed "5 miles apart" referred to the length of the hypotenuse. In contrast, other subjects interpreted this problem as a time-rate-distance problem. For example, one subject said: "It looks like a distance problem. So Jones is going east two minutes after Smith is going west. So it might be an overtake problem." Subjects who interpreted the problem as a distance-rate-time problem initially assumed that one driver was going east and the other driver was going west. Apparently, students use either a triangle schema or a distance-rate-time schema as a template for understanding the problem. In all, Hinsley et al. identified 18 basic problem schemas and found that these schemas influence how a subject reads a problem.

In a recent follow-up study, Mayer (1981) analyzed the story problems given in some typical secondary school algebra textbooks. Approximately 100 problem types were found, including many varieties of the problems that Hinsley et al. had found. For example, there were at least 12 different kinds of distance-rate-time problems, including overtake, closure, round trip, speed change and opposite direction. Some problem types occurred frequently in the textbooks (e.g., more than 25 instances per 1000 problems) while other problem types were rarely observed (e.g., less than four instances per 1000 problems). Box 13–4 lists some problem types, with similar types grouped into families. The numbers in parentheses indicate the percentage of problems in books that belonged to the category.

In another study (Mayer, 1982), students were asked to read and then recall a series of eight story problems. The results of the study indicated that students were far more successful at recalling high-frequency problem types than low-frequency problems. Figure 13–2 shows the relationship between the frequency of the problem (i.e., how many times per 1000 problems this type of problem occurred in typical math books) and the probability of correct recall for the problem. As you can see, the probability that a student will correctly recall a problem is strongly correlated with the frequency with which the problem type is represented in typical math textbooks. In addition, an analysis of errors in recall revealed that there was a tendency for subjects to change a low-frequency problem into a similar problem that occurred with higher frequency; in contrast, no high-frequency problems were changed into low-frequency problems by subjects. Apparently, students possess "schemas" for some of the more typical problem types. When students are given a problem for which they do not possess an appropriate schema, representation of the problem is in jeopardy.

Developmental Differences Among Students' Schemas. Students' schematic knowledge may be related to prior experience with story problems. For example, Greeno and his colleagues (Greeno, 1982; Riley, Greeno & Heller, 1982) have identified three types of arithmetic word problems:

Cause/change problems, such as "Joe has two marbles. Tom gives him four more marbles. How many marbles does Joe have now?"
Combination problems, such as "Joe has two marbles. Tom has four marbles. How many marbles do they have altogether?"

BOX 13–4   Some Problem Types from Algebra Textbooks

Family	Category (Percent of Total)
Amount-per-time family	Motion (13%) Current (5%) Work (11%)
Cost-per-unit family	Unit cost (4%) Coins (7%) Dry mixture (6%)
Portion of total family	Interest/investment (12%) Profit/discount (2%)
Amount-per-amount family	Direct variation (16%) Inverse variation (3%) Wet mixture (6%)
Number story family	Part (4%) Age (3%) Consecutive interest (1%)
Geometry family	Rectangle/frame (3%) Circle (1%) Triangle (1%)

Adapted from Mayer (1981b)

Comparison problems, such as, "Joe has two marbles. Tom has four more marbles than Joe. How many marbles does Tom have?"

As you can see, all three of these problems involve the same underlying computations (2 + 4 = _____). However, Greeno and his colleagues found that the problems differed greatly in difficulty. Children in grades K–3 all performed well on cause/change problems. However, children in grades K and 1 performed poorly on combination and comparison problems, while children in grades 2 and 3 performed well on them. One way to interpret these data is to say that the younger children had only one schema for word problems (i.e., the cause/change schema) and that they try to apply this schema to all word problems. In contrast, the older children seem to have developed different schema for different problem types (i.e., they have added schemas for combination and comparison problems). Thus many errors on comparison problems

FIGURE 13-2   More Common Problem Types Are Easier to Recall

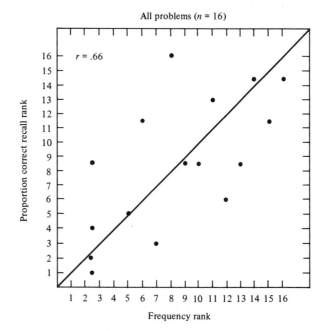

From Mayer (1982b)

seem to occur because students lack appropriate schemas rather than because students lack appropriate computational skill.

Similarly, Silver (1981) found that good problem solvers possess more useful problem schemas than poor problem solvers. In Silver's study, seventh graders were given sixteen story problems and asked to sort them into groups. Students who performed poorly in solving story problems tended to group the problems based on their cover stories, such as putting all "money" problems together. Students who performed well in solving story problems tended to group the problems based on their underlying mathematical structure. Apparently, learning to solve story problems successfully is related to the development of useful schemas for problem types.

Implications for Instruction

This section has provided some research evidence that errors occur when students lack a schema or use the wrong schema for organizing a problem. How could you provide schema training? Some textbooks organize practice problems so that all problems on a page are solvable by the same procedure. This homogeneous organization fails to give students practice in recognizing different problem types. A greater mixture of problems in each exercise would encourage students to learn how to discriminate among different types of problems.

Let's return to the tile problem. Some techniques for helping students learn about problem types include: asking students to draw an integrated diagram to represent the problem, asking students to sort the problems into categories, asking students to determine which information is irrelevant. The second portion of Box 13–1 gives some multiple-choice items aimed at fostering these skills. As with the suggestions given in the previous section, these suggestions require research verification.

Schema training is not the same as training students to recognize key words. For example, some students learn to categorize problems on basis of superficial key words, such as the following rules: if the problem says "more," then add the numbers in the problem and if the problem says "less," then subtract the second number from the first. This system is a poor one because it does not encourage the student to understand and represent the problem. It also can lead to errors, such as in the following problem: "Gasoline at Chevron costs $1.20. This is 5 cents less than the gas at Shell. How much per gallon is the gasoline at Shell?" Students who use key-word methods should be "entrapped" using problems such as the preceding one so that the students can see that key-word methods don't always work. Instead of relying on key words, students should be encouraged to represent the problem in their own words.

In summary, when students represent a problem, they must engage in problem translation and problem integration. The foregoing two sections have provided examples of how failures in problem solving may often be accounted for by students' lack of schematic, linguistic, or factual knowledge. Instructional techniques that help students acquire these kinds of knowledge must be recognized as a crucial aspect of mathematics instruction. One promising sign is that items testing problem representation are beginning to appear on standardized mathematics tests (California Assessment Program, 1982).

SOLUTION PLANNING
AND MONITORING

What Is Solution Planning and Monitoring?

The next component in solving a mathematics story problem is to devise and monitor a plan for solving the problem. For example, in the tile problem, the plan might involve breaking the problem into subproblems: First, find the area of the room by multiplying room length times room width; second, find the area of a single tile by multiplying tile length times tile width; third, find the number of tiles needed by dividing area of the room by the area of one tile; fourth, find the cost of the tiles by multiplying the number of tiles times the cost per tile. As you can see, this solution plan involves four parts; in solving the problem you must monitor where you are in the plan. In addition, you must be able to make scale conversions where needed, such as converting between meters and centimeters or between dollars and cents.

In Chapter 9, you learned about several programs aimed at teaching strategies for how to devise solution plans. For example, Schoenfeld (1979) taught five basic strategies to high school math students:

1. Draw a picture if at all possible.
2. If there is an integer parameter, look for an inductive argument.
3. Consider arguing by contradiction or contrapositive.
4. Consider a similar problem with fewer variables.
5. Try to establish subgoals.

Similarly, Wickelgren (1974) has suggested several strategies that may be used in mathematical problem solving:

Subgoals—breaking the problem into smaller problems;
Working backwards—starting with the goal and working towards the givens;
Finding a related problem—using the solution plan for a related problem;
Contradiction—showing that the goal cannot be achieved.

Polya (1957, 1965) offers a long list of strategies for devising solution plans. Some of his suggestions include:

Do you know a related problem?
Draw a figure.
Could you restate the problem?
Could you solve a part of the problem?
Could you think of other data appropriate to determine the unknown?
Can you work backwards?

As shown in Chapter 9, some basic strategies can be used in planning a solution.

Research on Solution Planning and Monitoring

Strategies for Solving Equations and Number Sentences. In recent experiments, Mayer and his colleagues (Mayer, 1982; Mayer, Larkin & Kadane, 1983) have found that the solution strategy a person uses depends on the characteristics of the problem and on the characteristics of the problem solver. For example, consider the following word problem:

Find a number such that if 8 more than 3 times the number is divided by 2, the result is the same as 11 less than 3 times the number.

One approach to this problem is the "reduce strategy" (i.e., trying to carry out any indicated operations as soon as possible). For example, in the preceding problem a first step would be to carry out the "divided by 2" operation, yielding:

> Find a number such that 4 more than $\frac{3}{2}$ of the number is the same as 11 less than 3 times the number.

This reduce strategy was preferred by 81% of the college students who solved problems that were presented in words. Presumably, the word format is so cluttered that subjects needed to reduce the information.

Now, consider a corresponding version of the problem, expressed in equation format:

$$(8 + 3X)/2 = 3X - 11.$$

The preferred solution strategy for this problem was not the reduce strategy. Instead, 95% of these subjects used an "isolate strategy" (i.e., trying to move all the X's to the left side and all the numbers to the right-hand side of the equality). Thus a first subgoal would be to move the $3X$ from the left so it can be combined with the $3X$ on the left; however, this cannot be carried out until the parentheses are cleared. Presumably, the equation format allowed subjects to rearrange the equation mentally.

In a follow-up study, four adult subjects were given a long series of very complicated equations to solve (Mayer, Larkin & Kadane, 1983). For two of the subjects, the pattern of response times could be accounted for by assuming that the subject used a reduce strategy; in contrast, the two other subjects used an isolate strategy. These results support the idea that there are individual differences in students' preferences for how to plan a solution. One instructional implication is that students could benefit from learning about alternative strategies for solving the same problem.

Attitudes for Mathematical Problem Solving.   Student attitudes about problem solving may also influence the strategy that is used. For example, Lester (1983) noted that poor problem solvers tend to believe problem difficulty depends on the size of the numbers and how many numbers are in a problem, that problems can be solved by directly applying an arithmetic operator to the numbers in the problem, that the key words in the problem determine which operator to apply. Branca (1983) noted some additional beliefs of poor problem solvers: there is only one correct answer and only one correct way to get the answer, it's important to get the answer in a short time, and so on. In contrast, good problem solvers are better able to discuss their solution process and are more aware that devising and monitoring a solution plan are crucial aspects of problem solving. Schoenfeld (1983) argues that students should be taught to monitor their solution progress by asking themselves: "Is this working or should we reconsider?"

Implications for Instruction

This section has shown that there are individual differences in solution plans. Thus it is important for students to recognize that there may be more than one right way to solve a problem. How can you provide strategy training? Students need to be able to describe their solution process, and compare their process with those used by other students. Some researchers, as summarized in Chapter 9, have been successful in explicitly teaching strategies—such as "use subgoals" or "work backwards" or "find a related problem." Other techniques for teaching strategic knowledge include asking the student to write a list of necessary operations (or a number sentence) for solving a problem, asking a student to list the subgoals needed in a multistep problem, asking a student to draw a conclusion based on the partial completion of a solution plan. Example multiple choice items are given in the third section of Box 13–1.

In summary, devising and monitoring a solution plan are crucial components in mathematical problem solving. Students differ greatly in their attitudes, their approaches, and in their ability to monitor plans. Students and teachers need to recognize that they should pay as much attention to process (i.e., to their solution strategy) as to product (i.e., to the final numerical answer). Research is needed to verify the preceding suggestions for improving students' strategic planning skills in mathematics.

SOLUTION EXECUTION

What Is Solution Execution?

Once you have understood the tile problem and devised a plan for how to solve it, the next major component is to carry out your plan. For a problem like the tile problem, you need to be able to carry out arithmetic operations such as: $7.2 \times 5.4 = $ _____ or $.72 \times 432 = $ _____. As you can see, problem execution requires procedural knowledge (i.e., knowledge about how to carry out a procedure such as addition, subtraction, division, or multiplication).

The acquisition of computational procedures involves a progression from naive procedures to more sophisticated procedures. Concurrently, the acquisition of computational procedures involves a progression from tedious application of procedures to automatic application. In summary, as children gain more experience, their procedures become more sophisticated and automatic.

Research on Solution Execution

Development of Expertise for Simple Addition. As an example of the development of expertise in computation, let's consider a child's procedure for solving single column addition problems. The form of the problem is:

$$m + n =$$

where m and n are single digit, positive integers whose sum is less than 10.

Fuson (1982) has identified four major stages in the development of computational expertise: counting-all, counting-on, derived facts, and known facts. Counting-all involves setting a counter to 0, incrementing it m times, and then incrementing it n times. For the problem, $2 + 4 = $ ___, the child might put out one finger and say "1," put out another finger and say "2," pause, put out a third finger and say "3," put out a fourth finger and say "4," put out a fifth finger and say "5," and put out a sixth finger and say "6."

Counting-on involves setting a counter to m (or n) and incrementing it n (or m) times. For the problem, $2 + 4 = $ ___, the child might put out two fingers and then say "3,4,5,6" as each of four additional fingers was put out. One version of this approach is what Groen & Parkman (1972) call the "min model"; this procedure involves setting a counter to the larger of m or n and then incrementing the counter by the smaller number. For the problem, $2 + 4 = $ ___, the child might put out four fingers and then say "5, 6" as each of two additional fingers was put out.

Derived facts involves using one's knowledge of number facts to figure out answers for related problems. For example, the first number facts that a child learns are usually the doubles, such as $1 + 1$, $2 + 2$, $3 + 3$, and so on. For the problem, $2 + 4 = $ ___, a student might say: "I can take 1 from the 4 and give it to the 2. That makes $3 + 3$, so the answer is 6." In this example, the child knew that the sum of 3 plus 3 is 6, but did not directly know the answer for 2 plus 4. Known facts involves having a ready answer for each number fact. For example, drill and practice with flash cards is generally aimed at helping students acquire rapid responses for a set of basic facts. For the problem, $2 + 4 = $ ___, the child would say: "6."

As you can see in this progression, the child's early procedures for single-digit addition are based on counting. The child can treat addition as if it were an extension of what the child already knows about counting. With more experience, the counting procedures can become more efficient—such as using a counting-on procedure instead of a counting-all procedure. With more experience, some of the facts become automatic and eventually all may become automatic. Figure 13–3 summarizes the counting-all procedure and two versions of the counting-on procedure. The boxes represent actions and the diamonds represent decisions.

What evidence is there for these four stages in the development of computational expertise? One method for studying students' solution procedures is to carefully observe what children do as they solve addition problems; in particular, we should listen to what they say and watch their fingers. Another method is to measure the time it takes to solve addition problems. For example, we could make the following predictions for each procedure: For the counting-all procedure, response time should be a function of the sum of $m +$ n. For the problem, $2 + 4 = $ ___, or the problem, $4 + 2 = $ ___, the child must increment a counter six times. For a simple version of the counting-on pro-

FIGURE 13–3   Counting-all and Counting-on Procedures for Simple Addition

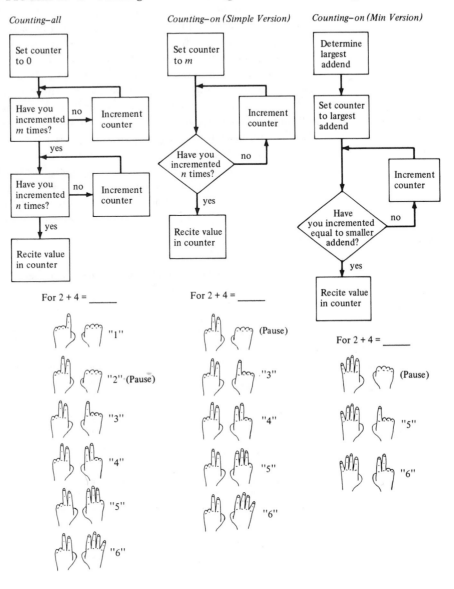

Counting–all

Counting–on (Simple Version)

Counting–on (Min Version)

For 2 + 4 = _____

For 2 + 4 = _____

For 2 + 4 = _____

cedure, response time should be a function of the second number, n. For the problem, $2 + 4 =$ ___, the child must increment a counter four times; for the problem $4 + 2 =$ ___, the child must increment two times. For the min-model version of the counting-on procedure, response time should be a function of the smaller number (m or n). For the problem, $2 + 4 =$ ___, the child must increment two times; similarly, for the problem, $4 + 2 =$ ___, the child must increment two times. For the derived facts procedure, response time should be fastest for the problems that are already known. Thus doubles (like 2 + 2 or 3 + 3) should yield the fastest response times when they become memorized. For the known facts procedure, response time should be the same for all problems since the child is simply "looking up" the answer in memory.

In order to determine which procedures children use as they begin formal instruction in computation, Groen & Parkman (1972) asked first graders to answer all single-column addition problems. The response time performance of the first graders could best be described by the min model version of the counting-on procedure. Figure 13–4 shows the response time for problems that the min model says require 0 increments (such as 1 + 0 = ___, or 5 + 0 = ___), 1 increment (such as 5 + 1 = ___, or 6 + 1 = ___), 2 increments (such as 5 + 2 = ___, or 6 + 2 = ___), 3 increments (such as 5 + 3 = ___, or 6 + 3 = ___), 4 increments (such as 5 + 4 = ___, or 4 + 5 = ___). As you can see, response time generally increases by about $\frac{1}{3}$ second for each additional increment in the value of the smaller number. Thus most of

FIGURE 13–4   Response Time Depends on the Number of Increments Required in the Min Model

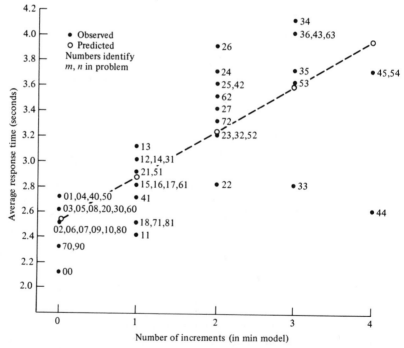

Note: Number pairs indicate addition problems; for example, 13 means 1 + 3 = ___.

From Groen & Parkman (1972)

setting a counter to the larger number and incrementing it by the smaller number. However, you might note that there is some evidence that doubles (0 + 0, 1 + 1, 2 + 2, 3 + 3, 4 + 4) were answered rapidly regardless of the number of increments; this suggests that the doubles might already be well-memorized number facts, while other problems require a counting procedure.

Parkman & Groen (1971) also found that a min model best fit the performance of adults. However, the time to make an increment for adults was $\frac{1}{50}$ second, compared to $\frac{1}{3}$ second for first graders. Since it is unlikely that a person can count silently at a rate of fifty increments per second, Parkman & Groen offered an alternative explanation: for almost all of the problems, adults have direct access to the answer in their memories (i.e., on most problems adults use a "known facts" approach), but on a few problems adults fall back to a counting procedure. Ashcraft & Stazyk (1981) have accounted for the performance of adults by assuming that answers must be "looked up" in a complicated network. Thus adults seem to be using some version of a "known facts" approach while first graders seem to be using some version of a counting approach.

Complex Computational Procedures. Once a child has achieved some level of automaticity in carrying out simple procedures (e.g., single column addition or subtraction), these procedures can become components in more complex computational procedures. For example, solving a three-column subtraction problem such as

$$456$$
$$-321$$

requires the ability to solve single-digit subtraction problems such as $6 - 1 =$ ___, $5 - 2 =$ ___, and $4 - 3 =$ ___. The procedure for three-column subtraction is summarized in Figure 13–5. In this flowchart, the boxes represent processes, the diamonds represent decisions, and the arrows show where to go next. As you can see, one of the skills required to use this procedure is the ability to carry out single-column subtraction (e.g., see step 2c).

The procedure shown in Figure 13–5 is a representation of the procedure that children are supposed to acquire; however, some students acquire a flawed version of it. For example, a student may have a procedure for three-column subtraction that contains one small "bug" (i.e., one of the steps in the student's procedure might be different from the corresponding step of the procedure in Figure 13–5). A student who uses a "buggy" procedure (i.e., a procedure with one or more bugs in it) may be able to correctly answer some problems but not others.

Consider the following five problems below:

564	722	821	954	349
−472	−519	−431	−233	−123
112	217	410	721	226

FIGURE 13–5   A Procedure for Three-Column Subtraction

Problem form

TTT   where T's are digits and B's are digits and computation begins on
– BBB   rightmost column.

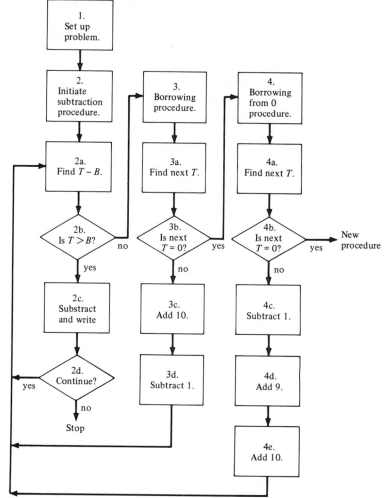

From Mayer (1981a)

As you can see, the student who solved these problems obtained correct answers for two out of the five. A more precise way of characterizing the student's performance is to say that the student is using a procedure that has a bug in it: at steps 2a, 2b, and 2c, the student subtracts the smaller number from the larger number regardless of which one is on top in the problem statement. Brown & Burton (1978) have argued that a student's knowledge of subtraction procedures can be described by listing the bugs (if any) that the student possesses. This example involves a very common bug, which Brown & Burton call "subtract smaller from larger."

According to Brown & Burton, errors in subtraction may be due to a student consistently using a procedure that is flawed, rather than due to a student not being able to apply a procedure. In order to test this idea, Brown & Burton gave a set of 15 subtraction problems to 1325 primary school children. Brown & Burton developed a computer program called BUGGY to analyze each student's subtraction procedure. If all the student's answers were correct, BUGGY would conclude that the student was using the correct procedure (such as shown in Figure 13–5). If there were errors, BUGGY would attempt to find one bug that could account for the errors. If no single bug could account for all the errors, BUGGY would evaluate all possible combinations of bugs in an attempt to find a combination that could account for the errors. Table 13–2

TABLE 13–2   Some Subtraction Bugs

Number of Occurrences in 1325 Students	*Name*	*Example*	*Description*
57	Borrow from zero	103 – 45 —— 158	When borrowing from a column whose top digit is 0, the student writes 9, but does not continue borrowing from the column to the left of zero.
54	Smaller from larger	253 –118 —— 145	The student subtracts the smaller digit in each column from the larger, regardless of which one is on top.
10	Diff $0 - N = N$	140 – 21 —— 121	Whenever the top digit in a column is 0, the student writes the bottom digit as the answer.
34	Diff $0 - N = N$ *and* move over zero	304 –75 —— 279	Whenever the top digit in a column is 0, the student writes the bottom digit as the answer. When the student needs to borrow from a column whose top digit is zero, he skips that column and borrows from the next one.

Adapted from Brown & Burton (1978)

shows some of the most common bugs: for example, 54 of the 1325 students behaved as if they had the "smaller from larger" bug.

Although the BUGGY program searched for hundreds of possible bugs and bug combinations, it still was not able to diagnose every student's subtraction procedure. The BUGGY program was able to find the subtraction procedure (including bugs) for about half of the students. The other students seemed to be making random errors, were inconsistent in their use of bugs, or may have been learning as they took the test. Thus Brown & Burton's work allows for a precise description of a student's procedural knowledge—even when that knowledge is flawed.

Implications for Instruction

What can you do to improve training in computational procedures? This question was addressed early in the history of educational psychology, by E. L. Thorndike (1925). Thorndike argued for the importance of practice with feedback, as exemplified in the last portion of Box 13–1 and as described in Chapter 5. Thus, to acquire skill in solving computation problems, students need practice in solving computation problems. In addition, students need feedback concerning whether or not their answers were correct. This advice has become very well accepted in educational psychology and is amply supported by research. However, more recent research has shown that complex procedures often develop out of more simple ones and that specific flaws (or bugs) in a procedure can be diagnosed. Thus one implication of more recent research is that the error patterns of students should be analyzed so that remediation can be directed towards the student's specific bugs. In addition, Resnick (1982) has argued that procedural knowledge should be tied to a learner's conceptual knowledge by making computation more concrete. This mapping of procedural and conceptual knowledge is examined in Chapter 7.

CONCLUSION

Let's return one final time to the tile problem described in the opening to this chapter. To solve that problem a person needs several kinds of knowledge: linguistic and factual knowledge for problem translation, schematic knowledge for problem integration, strategic knowledge for solution planning/monitoring, and procedural knowledge for solution execution.

A review of mathematics textbooks and mathematics achievement tests reveals that procedural knowledge is heavily emphasized in school curricula. For example, students are given drill and practice in carrying out computational procedures. In this chapter, we refer to this type of instruction as solution execution. However, systematic instruction in how to translate problems, how to make meaningful representations of problems, and how to devise solution plans is not always given.

Translation involves converting each statement into some internal representation, such a paraphrase or diagram. Students appear to have difficulty in comprehending simple sentences, especially when a relationship between variables is involved, and students often lack specific knowledge that is assumed in the problem (e.g., the knowledge that a square has four equal sides). Training in how to represent each sentence in a problem is an important and often neglected component of mathematics instruction.

Integration involves putting the information from the problem together into a coherent representation. Students appear to have trouble with unfamiliar problems for which they lack an appropriate schema. Training for schematic knowledge involves helping students to recognize differences among problem types.

Planning/monitoring involves devising and assessing a strategy for how to solve the problem. Students appear to have trouble in describing the solution procedure they are using, such as spelling out the subgoals in a multistep problem. In addition, students often harbor unproductive attitudes such as the idea that a problem has only one correct solution procedure. Strategy training is needed to help students focus on *process* in addition to product.

These three types of training complement the fourth component in mathematics instruction, solution training. All four components are needed for students to become productive mathematical problem solvers.

Although this chapter has focused on just one type of mathematics problem, many of the comments apply to other types of mathematics problems. The tile problem was selected because it is representative of the story problems that are found in secondary school mathematics courses. A major theme of this chapter has been that there is more to mathematics than learning to get the right answer (i.e., more than learning number facts and computational procedures). This chapter has provided examples of the important role played by linguistic and factual knowledge, schematic knowledge, and strategic knowledge, as well as procedural knowledge.

SUGGESTED READINGS

Carpenter, T. P., Moser, J. M. & Romberg, T. A. (eds.) (1982). *Addition and subtraction: A cognitive perspective*. Hillsdale, N.J.: Erlbaum. (A collection of papers on addition and subtraction by leading researchers in mathematics education.)

Resnick, L. B. & Ford, W. (1981). *The psychology of mathematics for instruction*. Hillsdale, N.J.: Erlbaum. (Provides an introduction to research on mathematical problem solving.)

Silver, E. A. (ed.) (1985). *Teaching and learning mathematical problem solving*. Philadelphia: Franklin Institute Press. (A collection of papers by leading researchers in mathematics education on how people solve story problems.)

14 Science

This chapter explores three aspects of how students learn science. First, students must overcome their misconceptions that conflict with school science. Second, students must develop skill in thinking scientifically. Third, students must acquire content knowledge that will allow them to begin to change from novices to experts.

THE INTUITIVE PHYSICS PROBLEM

Figure 14–1 shows a curved metal tube. In the figure, you are looking down on the tube. A metal ball is put into the end indicated by the arrow. The ball is then shot through the tube at a high speed, so that it comes out the other end of the tube. Your job is to use a pencil to draw the path that the ball will follow after it comes out of the tube. You can ignore air resistance.

Instructions and diagrams like these were used in a study by McCloskey, Caramazza & Green (1980). They found that college students tended to give two kinds of answers. Some students drew a curved line, such as in the left side of Figure 14–2. Other students drew a straight line, such as shown in the right-hand side of Figure 14–2. Does your answer correspond to either of these drawings?

Now, consider the two explanations shown in Box 14–1. The first explanation states that the ball acquires a "force" or "momentum" as it moves through the curved tube and that this force causes the ball to continue its curved path for some time after it emerges from the tube. In contrast, the second explana-

FIGURE 14–1 Where Will the Ball Go?
You are looking down on a curved metal tube. Assume that a metal ball is put in the end with the arrow, and that the ball is shot through the tube at a high rate of speed. Your task is to draw a line corresponding to the path that the ball will follow once it leaves the tube.

Adapted from McCloskey et al. (1980)

tion states that the ball will continue at a constant speed in a straight line until some force acts on the ball. Choose the explanation that corresponds most closely with your conception of motion.

If you drew a curved line, as shown in the left side of Figure 14–2, your answer is consistent with the majority of college students in the McCloskey et al. study. Similarly, if you selected the first explanation in Box 14–1, you are in agreement with a student who had completed one year of high school physics and one year of college physics. However, these answers are incorrect and seem to be based on a medieval conception of motion called the "theory of impetus"—the idea that when an object is set into motion it acquires a force or impetus that keeps it moving, at least until the impetus gradually dissipates. For example, this idea was popular in the fourteenth century writings of Buridan (cited in McCloskey, Caramazza & Green, 1980). In contrast, the correct answers, based on modern Newtonian conceptions of motion, are the straight path shown on the right-hand side of Figure 14–2 and the second explanation in Box 14–1. The Newtonian conception of motion is based on the idea that an object in motion will continue until some external force acts on the object.

FIGURE 14–2 Two Possible Answers for the Motion Problem

Curved Path   Straight Path

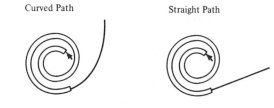

Adapted from McCloskey et al. (1980)

BOX 14–1   Two Possible Explanations for the Motion Problem

Student A
"The momentum that is acquired as it went around here (through the tube), well, the force holding it has given it angular momentum, so as it comes around here (out of the tube), it still has some momentum left, but it loses the momentum as the force disappears."

Student B
"The ball will continue to move in a line away from here (end of tube). It will keep going until some force acts on the ball. If no force acts on the ball, it will just continue."

Did you turn out to have a medieval conception of motion or a Newtonian conception of motion? If you are like many students, you may believe in medieval conceptions of physics, even if you have had coursework in physics. McCloskey et al. use the term "intuitive physics" to refer to people's conceptions of physical principles.

The point of this demonstration is not to show that people don't understand physics. Rather the point is that each person approaches learning and thinking in physics, or any science, with certain preexisting conceptions. An important educational implication of this demonstration is that instruction should take into account the fact that students already possess intuitions or conceptions about science. Thus, instruction cannot be viewed as providing knowledge about an entirely new topic; rather, instruction involves beginning with the learner's existing "intuitive physics" (or "intuitive science") and trying to change those conceptions.

This chapter explores three issues related to how students learn science: learners' misconceptions of scientific concepts (as in the preceding demonstration), the development of scientific thinking skills, and differences between experts and novices in science.

LEARNERS' MISCONCEPTIONS

What Are Learners' Misconceptions?

The foregoing demonstration suggests that students may enter the learning situation with certain preexisting conceptions (or misconceptions) of science. In this section, some additional examples of misconceptions of physics are presented, and educational implications are drawn.

Research on Learners' Misconceptions of Physics

Cliff Problem. Consider a typical cartoon character who runs over a cliff and falls into the valley below. Figure 14–3 presents such a situation. With a pencil, you should draw the path that the falling body will follow. Figure 14–4 shows four possible answers:

a. It will go on for some horizontal distance, and then fall straight down.
b. It will go on for some horizontal distance, and then gradually arc downward.
c. It will arc downward, maintaining its constant forward speed and an accelerating downward speed.
d. It will fall straight down as soon as it leaves the edge of the cliff.

Does your answer correspond to any of these four alternatives?

When high school and college students were asked to make predictions in a task similar to this one, 5% of the students opted for prediction a (these may have been fans of "Road Runner"), 35% opted for prediction b, 28% selected c, and 32% produced an answer like d (McCloskey, 1983).

The correct answer is c—the object will continue to move at the same rate horizontally since no force has changed its horizontal movement, and the object will move downward at an accelerating rate since gravity is acting on the object. This answer is based on the modern Newtonian conception of motion—an object will stay in motion unless some force acts on the object.

An alternative conception, similar to the medieval conception of motion, is that a moving object acquires some internal momentum or "impetus" that keeps it in motion until the momentum is dissipated. This view is consistent with answers a and b. The impetus conception is reflected in students' explana-

FIGURE 14–3   How Does a Moving Object Fall Over a Cliff?
Suppose that a cartoon character runs from point A to point B at a constant rate of speed. Draw a line corresponding to the path that the character will take on the way down from the edge of the cliff.

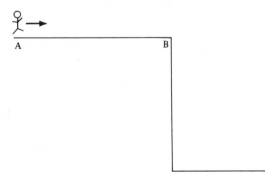

FIGURE 14–4   Four Paths for a Falling Body

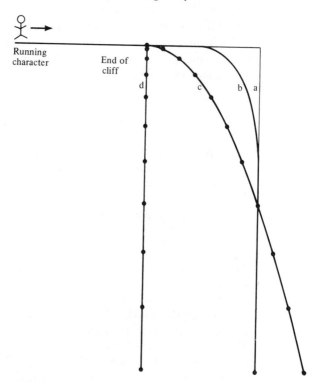

Adapted from McCloskey (1983)

tions: "It's something that carries an object along after a force on it has stopped. Let's call it the force of motion. It's something that keeps the body moving" (McCloskey, 1983, p. 125). Thus this student seems to believe that a moving object requires a force to keep it moving. Students also seem to believe that the ball will drop when the momentum is dissipated: "I understand that friction and air resistance adversely affect the speed of the ball, but not how. Whether they absorb some of the force that's in the ball . . ." (McCloskey, 1983, p. 126). As can be seen, students are expressing the medieval impetus theory that a moving object is kept moving by its own internal force and that movement is affected as the internal force dissipates. This view, while intuitively appealing, is inconsistent with the modern Newtonian view that objects do not require any force to continue moving at a constant speed (or to remain at rest). Instead, an external force is required to alter the velocity of a moving (or resting) body.

Ball Problem.   As another example of students' misconceptions of motion, consider the problem shown in Figure 14–5. In this problem, suppose that you are running forward at a constant speed with a heavy ball in your hand. As you are running, you drop the ball. Where will the ball land? Draw a line corresponding to the path that the ball will take once you drop it.

FIGURE 14-5   Where Will the Ball Fall?
Suppose you are running at a constant speed, holding a heavy ball. If you drop the ball at point X, where will the ball fall? Draw the path of the falling ball.

Point X
(drop ball)

Figure 14–6 lists three alternative answers:

a. The ball will land backwards from where you dropped it.
b. The ball will land directly below where you dropped it.
c. The ball will land forward from where you dropped it, reaching the ground at the same time you are running by.

Does your answer correspond to any of these three alternatives?

FIGURE 14-6   Three Possible Paths for a Falling Ball

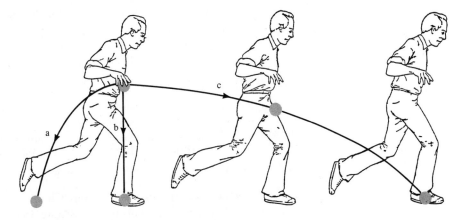

Adapted from McCloskey (1983)

As in the previously cited study, the most popular answer was consistent with impetus theory—49% of the students predicted that the ball would fall straight down. Six percent thought the ball would move backwards as it fell, and only 45% gave the Newtonian answer that the ball would move forward as it fell. In fact, the ball will continue to move forward at the same rate as the runner and will move downward at an accelerating rate.

You may be wondering whether training in physics helps to reduce learners' misconceptions of motion. In order to examine this question, McCloskey (1983) gave a modified version of this task to college students who had taken no physics courses and to college students who had taken at least one physics course. In this study, 80% of the nontrained students thought the ball would drop straight down, whereas only 27% of the physics trained group opted for this "impetus" view; alternatively, 13% of the nontrained students thought the ball would continue forward after being dropped compared to 73% of the trained group. Thus, while training in physics shows some positive effect, it should be noted that more than one-quarter of the trained students still held non-Newtonian conceptions of motion. In addition, McCloskey (1983) notes that some ideas are particularly resistant to instruction, such as the belief that impetus acquired when an object is set into motion serves to keep the object in motion. For example, 93% of the students held this belief prior to instruction in physics and 80% retained this belief even after instruction.

Coin Problem. Clement (1982) provides additional evidence concerning students' preconception that "motion implies a force." For example, a group of college engineering students, most with previous coursework in high school physics, was given the following "coin problem":

> A coin is tossed from point A straight up into the air and caught at point E. In the space to the left of the diagram, draw one or more arrows showing the direction of each force acting on the coin when it is at point B. Draw longer arrows for larger forces.

Figure 14–7 shows a diagram for this problem.

Figure 14–8 shows the correct answer on the left and the most typical incorrect answer on the right. The overwhelming majority of students (88%) gave incorrect answers based on the idea that if an object is moving upward, there must be some force acting on it. A typical description from a student is as follows (Clement, 1982, p. 68):

> So there's the force going up and there is the force of gravity pushing it down. And the gravity is less because the coin is still going up until it gets to C. (Draws upward arrow labeled "force of the throw" and shorter downward arrow labeled "gravity" at point B in the figure.) If the dot goes up, the force of the arrow gets less and less because gravity is pulling down on it, pulling down.

Rocket Problem. Another problem from Clement's study is shown in Figure 14–9. In this problem, you are to assume that a rocket is moving sideways in deep space, with its engine off from point A to point B. The rocket

FIGURE 14–7 Draw arrows corresponding to the forces acting on the coin at point B.

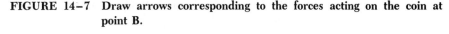

A coin is tossed from point A straight up into the air and caught at point E.

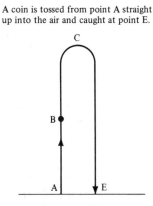

is far from any planets or other outside forces. Its engine is turned on at point B for 2 seconds while the rocket travels from point B to C. Your job is to draw the path of the rocket.

Figure 14–10 shows the correct answer, based on Newtonian physics, on the left, and the most common incorrect answer on the right. As in the coin problem, the overwhelming majority of students opted for incorrect answers. Apparently, students come to college with the preconception that "motion implies a force." This idea can be summarized as follows: If an object is moving, there is a force acting on the object; changes in speed or direction occur because the force dies out or builds up.

Does a college course in mechanics affect students' conceptions of motion? Table 14–1 shows the percentage of correct answers on the coin and the rocket

FIGURE 14–8 Two Answers to the Coin Problem

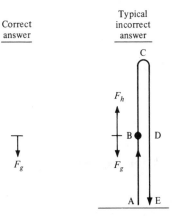

Adapted from Clement (1982)

FIGURE 14–9   What Is the Path of the Rocket?

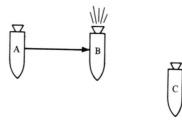

problems for students before and after a mechanics course. As can be seen, the course tends to double the number of correct responses; however, the error rates are still over 75%. Thus preconceptions built up over a lifetime seem resistant to schooling.

   Other Misconceptions.   Similarly, misconceptions have been observed in students' understanding of other scientific concepts, including gravity (Gunstone & White, 1981), acceleration (Trowbridge & McDermott, 1981), density (Novick & Nussbaum, 1978, 1981), living versus nonliving (Tamir, Gal-Choppin & Nussinovitz, 1981), chemical equilibrium (Wheeler & Kass, 1978), heat (Erickson, 1979), and the earth as a cosmic body (Nussbaum, 1979). For example, Nussbaum (1979) found evidence for a developmental progression in children's conception of the earth as a cosmic body. Fourth graders viewed the earth as flat, with down being toward the bottom of the cosmos. Sixth graders viewed the earth as round, but down still referred to a direction with respect to some cosmic "bottom." Eighth graders viewed the world as round and tended to view down as a direction with respect to the center of the earth. These were the dominant views at each age level, but there was also much variation among students within each age-group.

FIGURE 14–10   Two Answers to the Rocket Problem

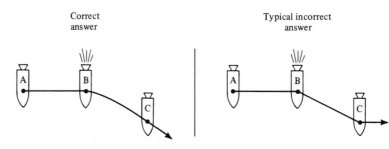

Adapted from Clement (1982)

TABLE 14-1 Correct Conceptions of Motion Before and After Instruction

	Percentage Correct on Coin Problem	Percentage Correct on Rocket Problem
Before instruction	12%	11%
After instruction	28%	23%

Adapted from Clement (1982)

In reviewing the research on misconceptions of elementary school children (ages eight to eleven), Osborne & Wittrock (1983) found the following examples: "light from a candle goes further at night," "friction only occurs between moving surfaces," "electric current is used up in a light bulb," "a worm is not an animal," "gravity requires the presence of air," "force is a quantity in a moving object in the direction of motion," and "the bubbles in boiling water are bubbles of air." In addition, Osborne & Wittrock reported that as children get older—and presumably learn more school science—some of their misconceptions actually increase before ultimately improving by age sixteen to eighteen.

Implications for Instruction

The research on students' misconceptions of scientific principles is both frustrating and challenging for science teachers. The results are frustrating because they suggest that students come to the science classroom with many preconceptions that are highly resistant to traditional instruction. However, the results are also challenging because they suggest a technique for teaching that is aimed specifically at helping students to revise their scientific intuitions and conceptions.

As Clement (1982) points out, it is not appropriate to assume that the student's mind is a blank slate. Instructional techniques must take students' beliefs into account. Much of science instruction involves helping students to change their preconceptions of science. Minstrell (cited in McCloskey, 1983) has developed a technique for directly challenging students' misconceptions of motion. Students are presented with problems such as the ones in the figures and are asked to verbalize their conceptions. The students' conceptions can then be compared to Newtonian conceptions, and differences can be explicitly pointed out. Minstrell has been successful in changing students' "intuitive physics" from the ancient impetus view to the modern Newtonian view.

When the student's conception of real world physical events conflicts with the conception underlying school science, students have several options. A common strategy used by students is to learn one set of rules for school science and another for the real world (West & Pines, 1985). In contrast, some students may discard their preexisting conceptions and replace them with concepts that are consistent with current scientific theories.

To induce this second kind of learning, Champagne, Gunstone & Klopfer (1985) have developed an instructional program called "ideational confrontation." Students are asked to make predictions about a common physical situation, such as the motion of an empty versus a loaded sled going downhill. Students develop theoretical explanations to support their predictions. Then the instructor demonstrates the physical situation and provides a scientific explanation. In ensuing discussions, students must reconcile their predictions with the actual results and must replace their ineffective conceptions with new ones. It is clear from Champagne et al.'s work that instructional procedures like ideational confrontation require a great deal of time and planning, but there is some evidence that the procedure can be effective (Champagne, Gunstone & Klopfer, 1985). Science instruction needs to make use of techniques that will help students discard misconceptions and replace them with correct conceptions of science.

This approach to teaching science is consistent with the general prescription proposed by Ausubel (1968, p. vi) in his classic book, *Educational Psychology:*

> If I had to reduce all of educational psychology to just one principle, I would say this: The most important single factor influencing learning is what the learner already knows. Ascertain this and teach him accordingly.

When the domain is science education, this approach means that the teacher must begin by assessing the students' preconceptions and then systematically work to revise these conceptions.

SCIENTIFIC THINKING

What Is Scientific Thinking?

Instruction in science may involve several goals. One goal, explored in the preceding section, is to help the student understand scientific principles. As noted in the preceding section, a major challenge to this goal is the fact that students are likely to enter the science classroom with certain preconceptions. A second goal of science instruction involves the "how" of science—teaching students to use the scientific method. This section explores students' dispositions to use scientific reasoning.

Several authors have noted that scientific reasoning requires what Piaget (1972; Inhelder & Piaget, 1958) calls "formal operations" or "formal thought." As summarized in Chapter 2, formal operations, expected to occur during adolescence, is the highest level of cognitive development. Formal operational thought involves thinking in terms of abstractions or symbols, being able to think about many variables or dimensions at the same time, and being able to think in terms of probabilities and proportions. Each of these skills is a crucial component in scientific tasks such as understanding the principles of motion in physics.

Research on Students' Scientific Thinking

Most science textbooks and instructional programs assume that high school and college science students are capable of scientific thinking (i.e., that the students are solidly in Piaget's formal operational period, described in Chapter 2). However, there is some startling evidence that some students may enter the science classroom without the prerequisite skills required for scientific thought. For example, many researchers have measured the proportion of college students consistently using formal thought for scientific tasks to be as low as 25% to 50% (Griffiths, 1976; Kolodiy, 1975; McKinnon & Renner, 1971; Lawson & Snitgen, 1982; Cohen, Hillman & Agne, 1978).

Proportional Reasoning in Adolescents. In a major study, Karplus and his colleagues (Karplus, Karplus, Formisano & Paulsen, 1979) developed two tasks to measure secondary school students' ability to engage in formal thinking—the proportional reasoning task and control-of-variables task. These tasks were administered to over 3000 secondary school students (generally thirteen to fifteen years old) in seven industrialized countries. Figure 14–11 shows an example of a proportional reasoning task, called the paper clip problem. Students are shown sheets of paper containing two stick figures, Mr. Tall and Mr. Small. When the heights of these two characters are measured using rows of large round buttons, it is found that Mr. Tall is 6 buttons tall and Mr. ~~Short~~ *Small* is 4 buttons tall. Then, students are given some standard paper clips. Students

FIGURE 14–11   What Is Mr. Tall's Height in Paper Clips?
Mr. Tall is 6 buttons tall. Mr. Small is 4 buttons tall. Now, measure Mr. Short with paper clips. He is 6 paper clips tall. What is Mr. Tall's height in paper clips?

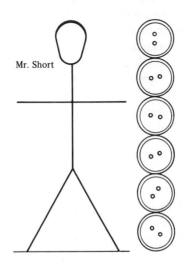

Adapted from Karplus et al. (1979)

are asked to measure the height of Mr. Short in paper clips (the answer is 6), and then to figure out the height of Mr. Tall in paper clips. In addition, students are asked to explain how they figured out the height of Mr. Tall.

The following major kinds of answers to the paper clip problem are given by students:

Intuitive—This approach does not fully use the available data, or uses the data in an illogical way. An example of a student's explanation is, "The way I got that Mr. Tall is 12 paper clips is I just doubled 6 buttons." Another example is, "I added 6 and 4 together."

Additive—This approach uses a single difference (such as the difference in buttons between Mr. Tall and Mr. Short) uncoordinated with other differences, and solves the problem by adding this difference to some number. For example, one student said, "If Mr. Tall is 6 buttons and Mr. Short is 4 buttons, that is a difference of 2. Now Mr. Short is 6 paper clips tall, so I took the 2 and added it to 6 and got 8."

Transitional—This approach partially uses proportional reasoning, but fails to generate a completely correct procedure. For example, one student said, "I divided 4 into 6; 4 is how many buttons Mr. Short is and 6 is the amount of paper clips, and I got $1\frac{1}{2}$. Then I added 6, the amount of buttons of Mr. Tall, to $1\frac{1}{2}$ and got $7\frac{1}{2}$."

Ratio—This is the correct procedure of deriving a proportion or ratio, and using the proportion to generate the answer. For example, "I got this by putting their height in buttons into a fraction (4/6) and by putting their height in paper clips into a fraction (6/X) and solved it. The result is 9." Another example is, "1 button = $1\frac{1}{2}$ paper clips, $1\frac{1}{2} \times 6 = 9$."

The results of the study are not encouraging. The left panel in Figure 14–12 shows the percentage of U.S. students using each of the four strategies (based on two proportional reasoning tasks). As can be seen, very few students use the ratio procedure (required for scientific thinking) and the most dominant procedure is the intuitive one. The right panel of Figure 14–12 shows the proportion of U.S. students using the ratio procedure, as a function of economic class and gender. As can be seen, upper- and middle-class students are far more likely than low-income students to engage in the ratio procedure, and there are no apparent sex differences.

The same general pattern of results was obtained in each of seven countries including Denmark, Sweden, Italy, United States, Austria, Germany, and Great Britain. However, students in selective schools in European countries scored much higher in ratio thinking (e.g., 75% consistently used ratio in a selective British school and 64% in a selective German school). In a pilot study, Karplus (1979) found that 92% of the students from a highly selective Chinese elementary school used proportional reasoning by applying ratios in tasks like the paper clip problem.

Control of Variables in Adolescents.   Another problem used by Karplus

FIGURE 14–12   Performance of U.S. Students on Proportional Reasoning Task

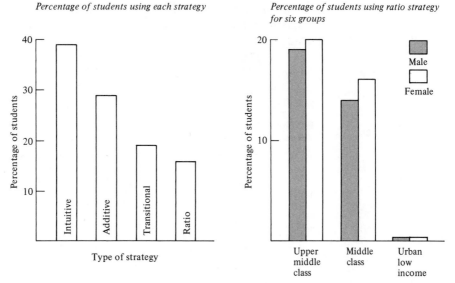

Adapted from Karplus et al. (1979)

and his colleagues (Karplus et al., 1979), is the control-of-variables task. In this problem, the student is shown a track, with a target ball in it, as shown in Figure 14–13. The student is told that if you roll another ball down the track, it will collide with the target and make it move some distance. The student has the option of using a heavy metal ball or a light glass ball (both of equal size) and of placing it either high, medium, or low in the track. The student is asked a series of questions in order to determine whether he or she understands how to control variables during experimentation. For example,

> Suppose you want to know how much difference the weight of the ball makes in how far the target goes. You are going to use two balls on the target. Where would you start the heavy ball? Where would you start the light ball? Please explain your answers carefully.

Karplus et al. discovered that students gave three types of answers to this question.

> *Intuitive*—This approach allows for any starting position. For example, "I would start the heavy sphere at medium to see if, even though the sphere is heavy, it will make a difference. I started the light one at high so it would pick up speed and knock the ball far."
> *Transitional*—This approach calls for starting the balls at the same position,

FIGURE 14–13   How Does the Weight of the Ball Affect the Movement of the Target?

A heavy- or lightweight ball may be placed either high, medium, or low on the track. How does the weight of the ball affect how far the target ball will move?

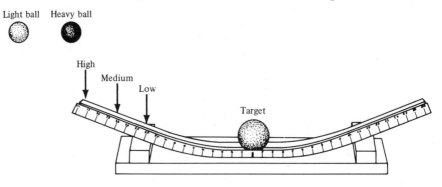

Adapted from Karplus et al. (1979)

but does not provide a complete rationale. For example, "Start them at the same place and give them the same speed, then measure how far the target goes up the other side."

Control—This approach calls for starting the balls at the same place, and stating that equality of conditions is crucial. For example, "The main reason of this experiment is the weight difference, so you would have to keep all other factors the same."

The results of this study, like those of the proportional reasoning study, are not encouraging. The left portion of Figure 14–14 shows the percentages of U.S. students who used each approach to a control-of-variables problem. In addition, the right of Figure 14–14 shows the corresponding percentages for upper-, middle- and lower-income boys and girls. As can be seen, there is a large effect due to economic level but no strong sex differences. Again, similar patterns were obtained in each of the industrialized countries studied.

These results, based on a large sample of students, clearly substantiate the findings of other researchers that the development of formal thought cannot be assumed to be complete in adolescents. Overall, Karplus et al. (1979) found 251 students (or about 7% of the sample) who consistently displayed use of ratios on the paper clip task and use of experimental control on the track task; in contrast, they identified 422 students (or about 14%) who consistently used intuitive reasoning on all clip task questions and all track task questions. Based on the total sample of 3300 students, Karplus et al. found that about 37% of eighth graders do not use formal thinking in both proportion reasoning and control of variables, and another 36% fail to use formal thinking on either of the two types of tasks. Thus the majority of eighth graders do not consistently show evidence of formal reasoning.

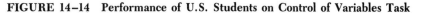

FIGURE 14–14   Performance of U.S. Students on Control of Variables Task

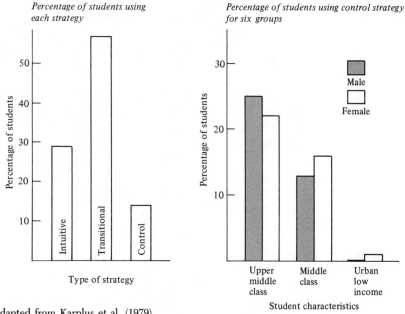

Adapted from Karplus et al. (1979)

The foregoing work suggests that many junior high school students enter the science classroom without adequate understanding of scientific reasoning. Recent work has also suggested that the problem is attenuated, but still present, in college students.

Proportional Reasoning in Adults.   Thornton & Fuller (1981) surveyed 8000 college students taking science courses. Students were asked to solve proportional reasoning problems such as the "shadows problem":

> Walking back to my room after class yesterday afternoon, I noticed my 6-foot frame cast a shadow 8 feet long. A rather small tree next to the sidewalk cast a shadow 18 feet long. My best guess of the height of the tree would be _____.

Students were also asked to explain "the reasoning you used to find your answer."

Students exhibited several different approaches to solving the problem, as listed below.

> *Intuitive*—Students either give no response or guess (e.g., "Can't tell. I'm not good at numbers").
> *Additive*—The student finds the difference between two numbers and adds this value to a number (e.g., "8 is to 6 as 18 is to 16").
> *Transitional*—The student attempts to use a ratio but fails for reasons other

than computational error (e.g., "6/8 is 3/4 but I didn't know how to find the height of the tree").

Ratio—The student uses a ratio to set up an equation or multiplies by a conversion factor based on a ratio (e.g., "6/8 = x/18 so x = (6/8)18 or $13\frac{1}{2}$ feet" or "The height is 6/8 or 75% of the shadow so the tree is 0.75 × 18 or 13.5 feet high").

Figure 14–15 shows the proportion of students who used each of these four strategies in solving the shadows problem. As can be seen, the majority of students taking college science courses used a ratio strategy to solve the problem; these students give evidence of formal thinking. However, more than one-quarter of the students do not use formal thinking strategies. Thus, even in college science courses, teachers should realize that students use a variety of problem-solving strategies, including many that are not useful in scientific thinking.

Implications for Instruction

An important educational question that emerges from this research is: Can scientific thinking be taught? In other words, if students come into the classroom without scientific thinking skills, can these prerequisite skills be directly taught? In order to address this question, Lawson & Snitgen (1982) used an inquiry-based approach to a college course, Biological Science for the Elementary Teacher. Students were given problems, asked to generate ex-

FIGURE 14–15   Percentage of Students Using Each of Four Strategies on the Shadows Problem

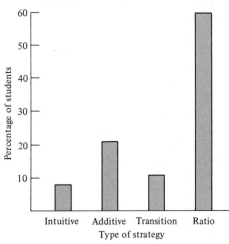

Adapted from Thornton & Fuller (1981)

periments, carry out experiments, and compare results with other students. For example, students were asked to determine the energy source(s) for developing plants. This required systematically varying variables such as watering, lighting, and soil composition, and noting the effects on various seed parts. Concepts relevant to "control of variables" were introduced during the discussion and applied in subsequent experiments. A similar procedure was used to introduce "proportional reasoning" and "statistical reasoning" examples.

Students were given pretests and post-tests. Figure 14–16 shows that there were substantial gains in performance on tests of proportional reasoning, control of variables, and statistical thinking—all of which were explicitly taught as part of the inquiry-based course; however, scores on tests of conservation of weight and volume were not affected by instruction and were not explicitly part of the instruction. These results are promising because they suggest that scientific reasoning can be taught through a carefully planned "inquiry-based" approach to science. However, the results must be viewed critically in light of the fact that no control group received a noninquiry training. The results are consistent with previous experiments that successfully increased scientific thinking (i.e., formal thinking) in science students (Lawson & Wollman, 1976; Wollman & Lawson, 1978; McKinnon & Renner, 1971). Inquiry-based methods are discussed further in Chapter 7.

Hands-on experience is sometimes viewed as a panacea that will foster creative students; similarly, the quality of a school's science program is often measured by the amount of lab experience given to students. Yet the research presented in this section implies that hands-on laboratory science experience

FIGURE 14–16   Changes in Scientific Thinking Following Training

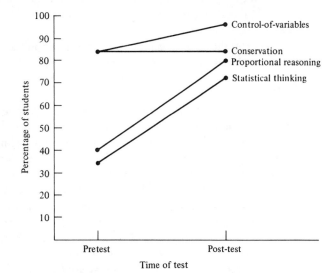

Adapted from Lawton & Snitgen (1982)

can be unproductive, especially when students do not approach problems scientifically. It is not lab activity per se that induces science learning; instead, students must be encouraged to think scientifically about situations, to control variables, to test hypotheses, and so on. Thus, while lab experience is an important component in school science programs, it must be administered in a way that fosters scientific thinking rather than blind activity.

EXPERT/NOVICE DIFFERENCES

What Are Expert/Novice Differences?

The foregoing sections have shown that students begin the study of science with certain preconceptions of the science and predispositions about scientific reasoning. Another approach to the study of science learning involves comparing novices—such as students in a beginning science course—to experts such as established scientists. The main question addressed in this approach is, What do experts know that novices do not know?

Research Comparing Novice and Expert Physicists

Let's explore the expert/novice issue by focusing on a domain of physics called "kinematics." Kinematics involves the study of motion, and the kinematics chapter in a physics textbook generally contains about a dozen formulas expressing relations among variables such as time, distance, average velocity, initial velocity, terminal velocity, and acceleration. For example, a typical kinematics problem (Larkin, McDermott, Simon & Simon, 1980) is:

> At the moment car A is starting from rest and accelerating at 4 meters per second car B passes it, moving at a constant speed of 28 meters per second. How long will it take car A to catch up with car B?

In order to study expert/novice differences, Larkin and her colleagues (Larkin et al., 1980) presented kinematics problems like this one to novices and experts. The subjects were asked to "think aloud" (i.e., to tell what was going on inside their heads as they solved the problem). An obvious difference between experts and novices was that novices required about four times as much time to solve the problems as experts. A deeper analysis of the thinking aloud protocols—the transcripts of what students said as they solved the problem—revealed two other major differences: differences in how physics knowledge is organized in memory and differences in the strategies that are used in problem solving. (Also see Chapter 9.)

Expert/Novice Differences in Organization of Knowledge. First, let's consider differences in the ways that experts and novices organize physics knowledge. In physics, most of the information can be expressed as formulas. For example, in the car problem shown above some of the relevant formulas are:

$$S = \tfrac{1}{2}at^2,$$
$$S = \bar{v}t,$$

where S is distance, a is acceleration, $\bar{v}$ is average velocity, and t is time. Novices seem to act as if they have knowledge in "small functional units" such as simple three-variable equations. To solve for t, they must substitute one equation into another and so on. However, experts seem to have the solution procedure available as one large equation, such as $\bar{v}t = \tfrac{1}{2}at^2$ or $t = 2\bar{v}/a$. Larkin (1979) calls this a large-scale functional unit. Thus, while novices have to go step by step with a lot of checking, experts are able to solve the problem all at once using a more automatic procedure.

Expert/Novice Differences in Solution Strategies. A second difference between experts and novices concerns the solution strategies. Larkin et al. (1980) found that novices tend to "work backwards" from the goal to the given. For example, the main unknown is to find the time it will take for car A to catch car B. One formula involving time is $S = \tfrac{1}{2}at^2$. The value of a is known (4 meters per second) but the values for t and S are not known. Thus the novice searches for an equation that contains S. One formula is $S = \bar{v}t$. Again, the value of $\bar{v}$ is given (28 meters per second), but S and t are not. The next step is to substitute the equations into each other, such as $\bar{v}t = \tfrac{1}{2}at^2$. Values for a and $\bar{v}$ are given, so the novice can solve for t, yielding an answer of 14. This strategy involves starting with the unknown, and asking: "What do I need in order to find the unknown?" Then, what do I need to find each of these variables, and so on. In contrast, the expert seems to "work forwards" from the givens to the goal. The expert simply plugs the values of the givens into the appropriate formula in order to generate the solution (i.e., $t = 2(28)/4 = 14$).

As a way of testing these observations, Larkin et al. (1980) produced a computer program that simulates the problem-solving performance of experts and novices. The expert program works forwards and uses large functional units while the novice program works backwards and uses small functional units. The main output of the program is a listing of the order in which formulas were used. The output of the expert program was fairly consistent with that of human experts, and the output of the novice program was fairly consistent with the human novices. Thus there is some reason to believe that the simulations correctly describe expert/novice differences.

Helping Novices Become Experts. Shavelson (1972, 1974) has provided an interesting analysis of changes in the way that students structure their knowledge of physics following instruction. In one study, high school students in the trained group read lessons about Newtonian physics over the course of 5 days while control students did not receive physics instruction. Students were given pretests and post-tests measuring achievement and knowledge structure.

BOX 14–2   Some Key Concepts in Physics

MOMENTUM
INERTIA
POWER
MASS
TIME
WORK
WEIGHT
ACCELERATION
FORCE
DISTANCE
VELOCITY
IMPULSE
SPEED
ENERGY

Based on Shavelson (1972)

The achievement test measured retention of material from the lesson, using a standard multiple choice format. As expected, the control group did not show a significant pretest to post-test gain (30 to 32%) but the trained group did show a significant pretest to post-test gain (33 to 54%).

The knowledge structure test listed fourteen key concepts; for each key concept, the subject was given 1 minute to write down all the words he or she could think of. The fourteen key concepts are shown in Box 14–2. Based on the word association responses given for the knowledge structure test, Shavelson was able to determine how strongly each of fourteen key words was related to each of the other words. For example, if a subject listed many of the same words for "force" and for "mass," then a "relatedness index" would indicate that these two concepts were highly related. As expected, the pretest results indicated that subjects entered the study with preexisting conceptions of Newtonian mechanics terms; clusters of terms were related by the students, although not in the way that Newtonian physics prescribes. However, the knowledge structure test was given after each of the five lessons. As can be seen in Figure 14–17, the relatedness index increased each day for the trained group but remained low throughout the study for the control group. In addition, Shavelson derived the "expert" word association responses based on the actual relations expressed in physics equations. As shown in Figure 14–17, the difference between the trained group and the ideal or expert knowledge structure decreases with each day of training; in contrast, the control group shows no change. These results are consistent with the idea that training in physics not only enhances general achievement, but also influences the way in which

FIGURE 14–17   **Changes in Knowledge Structure Following Physics Instruction**

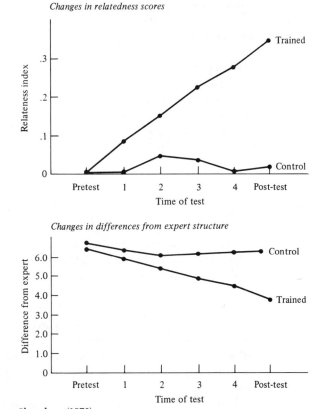

Adapted from Shavelson (1972)

knowledge is organized in memory. With training, the students are less likely to organize key concepts based on their everyday meanings and more likely to relate them based on the rules of physics (e.g., force = mass × acceleration).

Instructional Implications

What are the instructional implications of this line of research? Simon (1980) suggests that students in science need two important kinds of training: training to provide a rich knowledge base (e.g., lots of experience with the major formulas in kinematics), and training in general problem-solving strategies relevant to the science (e.g., how to recognize problem types and work forwards). Simon (1980) suggests that there is no substitute for experience; for example, Hayes (1985) estimates that to become an expert in a field requires approximately ten years of study. In addition, the road to expertise requires seeing worked out examples done by experts (Simon, 1980). Chapter 9 addresses these implications in more detail.

A major controversy in science education concerns the relative merits of teaching the fruits of scientific research (science facts) versus teaching how to do science (scientific thinking). The research on expertise suggests that facts and hands-on experience alone are not sufficient. Students need both a certain number of basic principles and facts as well as problem-solving skill in using this knowledge. Unfortunately, many science textbooks contain large numbers of relatively isolated facts about the physical world. Students' memorization of a large number of facts should not be the main goal of science instruction. Instead, the goal must be to help students understand the physical and natural events in the world. This goal requires well-organized knowledge as well as practice in scientific problem solving.

CONCLUSION

This chapter has explored three aspects of science learning. First, the learner enters the science classroom with many preexisting conceptions. Instruction is needed to help make the learner's conceptions consistent with modern conceptions.

Second, the learner enters the classroom with strategies for scientific thinking. Although some instruction may assume that the learner possesses adult scientific reasoning skills, there is much evidence that this assumption is dubious. Instead, instruction is needed in order to teach students how to think scientifically, including how to control variables and how to think in terms of proportions and probabilities.

Third, the learner who enters as a novice is qualitatively different from the expert. If we take a "snapshot" of the novice's knowledge structure before instruction and the expert's knowledge structure after extensive experience, we find that the information is organized differently. Thus acquisition of scientific knowledge involves more than adding information to memory; it also involves reorganizing the information in coherent and useful ways.

SUGGESTED READINGS

Karplus, R., Karplus, E., Formisano, M. & Paulsen, A. (1979). Proportional reasoning and control of variables in seven countries. In J. Lochhead & J. Clement (eds.), *Cognitive process instruction*. Philadelphia: Franklin Institute Press. (Presents an analysis of students' scientific reasoning strategies.)

Larkin, J., McDermott, J., Simon, D. P. & Simon, H. A. (1980). Expert and novice performance in solving physics problems. *Science, 208,* 1335–1342. (Summarizes recent research on differences between how experts and novices solve physics problems.)

McCloskey, M. (1983). Intuitive physics. *Scientific American, 248* (4), 122–130. (Summarizes recent research on students' misconceptions of Newtonian physics.)

West, L. H. T. & Pines, A. L. (eds.) (1985). *Cognitive structure and conceptual change*. New York: Academic. (Focuses on students' misconceptions of physics.)

PART IV

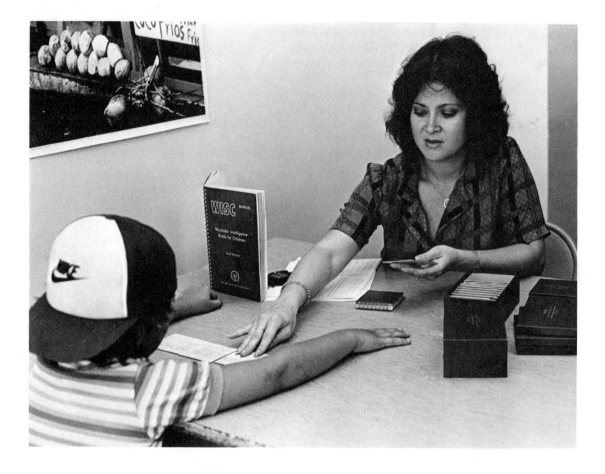

MEASUREMENT

What does measurement have to do with education? This is the question addressed in the next three chapters. In Chapter 15, you will learn about techniques for measuring the knowledge that a student has acquired through instruction. Such measurements can be useful both in diagnosing aspects of the student's knowledge that need further instruction and in assessing whether instructional efforts need to be modified. In Chapter 16, you will learn how to evaluate the characteristics of learners, including identification of students with special needs. Since effective instruction should be adjusted to the nature of the learner, it makes sense to understand the entering characteristics of students. In Chapter 17, you will learn about individual differences among students in general learning ability, domain-specific knowledge, motivation to learn, demographic characteristics, and cognitive style. In particular, this chapter explores the idea that not all children learn best under the same methods of instruction. In summary, this section focuses on what is in the learner's mind, including the knowledge acquired in learning or needed as prerequisites for subsequent learning.

The theme of this section is that measurement and instruction are complementary actitivies, much in the same way that the outcome of learning on one task serves as the entering characteristics for learning on the next task. The conditions of meaningful learning cited in Figure 1–3 emphasize the need for possessing and using prior knowledge in learning. Measurement is useful in determining whether the student has appropriate prior knowledge and in determining whether instruction has been successful in stimulating the growth of knowledge needed for subsequent learning.

15 Evaluation of Learning Outcomes

This chapter is concerned with evaluating student learning using teacher-made tests. The next chapter is concerned with evaluating student characteristics using commerical tests. In both chapters the focus is on understanding how the evaluation process can be used to guide and improve the instructional process.

THE EVALUATION PROBLEM

The report card has become a symbol of schools. The symbol is appropriate because report cards represent one of the most pervasive aspects of education—namely, measurement. Let's take a moment to consider the kinds of measurements that are generally included in report cards.

Box 15–1 shows a typical report card for a second grader. As you can see, the student is evaluated on several different kinds of factors, including academic performance in subject matter areas (e.g., reading, writing, language, arithmetic, science), participation in enrichment studies (e.g., art, music, physical education), and mastery of personal and social skills (e.g., completes tasks, cooperates with others, waits for turn, etc.). A multilevel grading scale (E for excellent, S+ for very good, S for satisfactory, and NI for needs improve-

BOX 15–1   A Report Card

Report Card
Valley View School
Green Valley School District

Student: SARAH KENNEY
Grade: 2
Room: 12
Teacher: Ms. Lite

	Fall	Winter	Spring
Subject Grades (E,S+,S,NI)			
Reading	S	S	S+
Written language	NI	S	S
Oral language	NI	S	S
Spelling	S	S+	S
Writing	E	S+	S+
Arithmetic	S+	E	E
Other Grades (S or NI)			
Science/Health	S	S	S
Social studies	S	S	S
Art	S	S	S
Music	S	S	S
Physical education	S	S	S
Work Habits (S+,S,NI)			
Completes classwork	S+	S+	S+
Works independently	S	S	S
Stays on task	S	S	S
Completes homework	NI	NI	S
Participates	NI	S	S
Social skills (S+,S,NI)			
Cooperates with others	NI	NI	NI
Respects others' property	NI	S	S
Waits to be called on	NI	S	NI
Controls temper	NI	S	S
Does not disrupt	NI	NI	NI
Grade Level			
Reading	1.5	2.0	2.2
Language	2.0	2.2	2.9
Arithmetic	2.5	3.0	3.3
Arithmetic Achievement			
Adds single-digit numbers without carrying	x	x	x
Adds single-digit numbers with carrying	x	x	x
Adds two-digit numbers without carrying	x	x	x

Adds two-digit numbers with carrying	—	x	x
Subtracts single-digit numbers without borrowing	x	x	x
Subtracts single-digit numbers with borrowing	—	x	x
Subtracts two-digit numbers without borrowing	—	x	x
Subtracts two-digit numbers with borrowing	—	—	x
Solves one-step word problems	—	—	x
Solves two-step word problems	—	—	—

Attendance	*Fall*	*Winter*	*Spring*
Days school open	60	60	60
Days attended	59	58	57
Days tardy	0	0	0
Excused absences	1	2	3
Unexcused absences	0	0	0

Comments:

Fall: Sarah is off to a fine start. She is doing very well in arithmetic; she needs to learn to control her temper when playing or working with other children.

Winter: Sarah continues to be doing well. We need to help her to verbalize what's bothering her instead of disrupting the class.

Spring: This has been a good year for Sarah!

Parents' Signature
Fall:
Winter:
Spring:

ment) is used to characterize performance in subject matter areas and personal/ social skills; only a two-level grading procedure (S or NI) is used for art, music, and PE participation. The academic grades are generally based on teacher observations of student behavior as well as on student performance on assignments, tests, and quizzes. The other grades are based largely on teacher observations.

In addition, the card provides information about whether the student is working at grade level in the major subject areas of reading, arithmetic, and language. This is a norm-referenced measurement because it tells where the student stands compared to other students of the same age. The card provides some detailed information about how far the student has progressed in acquiring the sequence of skills in the arithmetic curriculum. This is a criterion-referenced measurement because it tells us which objectives have been achieved and which have not.

Finally, the card contains a brief written evaluation, summarizing the student's strengths and weaknesses, and an attendance summary.

As you can see, the report card represents many different kinds of educational measurement. This chapter focuses on the evaluation of student learning, i.e., on determining what is learned.

Let's look a little more closely at the measurement of arithmetic computation. How can we evaluate a student's learning of computational skill in a way that would be useful in guiding future instruction? Suppose we gave a test and received the following answers:

$$3 + 5 = \underline{8}$$
$$4 + 2 = \underline{6}$$
$$5 + 6 = \underline{11}$$
$$7 + 8 = \underline{15}$$
$$11 + 3 = \underline{5}$$
$$4 + 13 = \underline{8}$$
$$15 + 6 = \underline{12}$$
$$7 + 23 = \underline{10}$$
$$22 + 49 = \underline{17}$$
$$55 + 35 = \underline{18}$$

We could evaluate the performance in several ways: a behavioral objectives approach, a task analysis approach, and a cognitive approach.

First, if we used a behavioral objectives approach, we might say that to get a satisfactory grade in second grade computation, a student must get at least 75% on this test. Since our student only got 40% correct, his grade would be NI—"needs improvement."

Second, if we used a task analysis approach, we would break the larger task of two-column-addition with carrying into a sequence of smaller skills. For example, to do two-column addition (such as in the ninth and tenth problems), a student must be able to do one-column addition with carrying (such as Problems 3 and 4) and two-column addition without carrying (as in Problems 5 and 6); to do these tasks a student must be able to do one-column addition without carrying (such as Problems 1 and 2). Our student seems to have mastered the two lowest skills in the hierarchy of skills—single-column addition with carrying and single-column addition without carrying—but none of the higher skills. Thus the task analysis approach allows us to determine how far a student has progressed in a sequence of skills.

Third, if we used a cognitive approach, we would try to characterize the student's knowledge—in this case, we would try to describe the procedure that the student is using. Our student seems to be using an addition procedure that has a slight bug in it: the student treats each digit as a separate number and adds all the numbers together. For example, $15 + 6$ is interpreted as $1 + 5 + 6$, so the answer is 12. As described earlier in Chapter 13, the cognitive approach allows us to describe bugs in the student's computational procedure.

In this chapter we explore the uses of tests in schools and the construction of "good" tests. Then we look at each of the three aforementioned approaches to evaluation of learning outcomes.

EVALUATION AND INSTRUCTION IN SCHOOLS

Types of Evaluation Used in Schools

Testing is a basic tool used in schools. Some of the common examples of evaluation of student learning include:

Report card grades—require teachers to make judgments of student learning based on tests, quizzes, homework, in-class assignments, and the systematic observation of student performance.

Unit mastery tests—are given at the end of a unit to determine whether the student has learned the material; these tests are often provided by publishers of graded series in reading, mathematics, and other subject areas or they may be provided by the school district.

Standardized achievement tests—measure the student's knowledge and skills in certain subject matter areas; these tests are often provided by commercial testing companies or government agencies and include norms for comparing a student with a peer group.

Proficiency tests—are district- or state-mandated tests to determine whether a student has learned enough to be allowed to graduate or move on to the next grade.

Placement tests—are pretests given to students in order to assess where they should be placed; for example, a teacher may want to group students for reading instruction based on a placement test that can be readministered whenever a student shows progress.

Standardized ability tests—such as IQ tests, are sometimes used as one criterion for admission into special classes.

As you can see from these examples, effective teaching requires knowing how to use tests as a way of enhancing instruction.

Role of Evaluation in Schools

In order for you to better understand the role of tests in schools it is helpful to make some basic distinctions. Table 15–1 summarizes four distinctions: teacher-made versus commercially made tests, achievement versus ability tests, criterion-referenced versus norm-referenced tests, and formative versus summative tests.

Teacher-Made Versus Commercially Made Tests. Tests may differ with respect to how they are created. Teacher-made tests are developed by an

TABLE 15–1   The Who, What, How, and Why of Testing

Question	Examples
Who makes the tests?	Teacher-made versus commerically-made tests
What is measured?	Achievement versus ability tests
How are tests scored?	Criterion-referenced versus norm-referenced tests
Why are tests used?	Formative versus summative tests

instructor for use in his or her class; exams, quizzes, and other assignments are graded by the teacher and may form the basis for the "report card" grade. Commercially made tests are developed by groups of experts for use in a wide variety of classes. Publishers of reading and math series often provide unit tests, for example, to evaluate students' mastery of the material; similarly, testing companies produce general tests of skills such as reading and mathematics used in diagnosing special needs of students; finally, some commerically made tests may be part of districtwide, statewide, or national assessments of educational progress or proficiency. (This chapter focuses mainly on teacher-made tests; the next chapter deals with commercial tests.)

Achievement Versus Ability Tests.   Tests also differ with respect to what they purport to measure. Some tests are aimed at measuring the specific knowledge that has been acquired through learning; these are tests of achievement. For example, a test of basic arithmetic facts is an achievement test because it tests something that a student must learn. In contrast, some tests are aimed at measuring a student's native aptitude in some area such as intelligence; these are tests of ability. For example, a test of general intelligence is supposed not to require any previous learning on the part of the student. As you may have detected, the distinction between achievement and ability is not a clear one. In any test of ability, a student's prior learning (i.e., achievement) may play a role; for example, most IQ tests used in the U.S. require that the student read English. In any test of achievement, a student's abilities may play a role; for example, most achievement test scores are related to tests of ability. (Achievement and ability tests are described more fully in the next chapter.)

Criterion-Referenced Versus Norm-Referenced Tests.   Tests also differ with respect to how you are supposed to score and interpret them. Some tests are set up so that you pass if your score exceeds a certain value; this is a criterion-referenced test. For example, a teacher may say that anyone scoring about 90% correct gets an A, anyone scoring about 80 to 90% gets a B, and so on. This is a criterion-referenced test because you have established certain criterion scores for each grade category. In contrast, other tests are interpreted by telling where a person stands in relation to a larger group who has taken the same test; this is a norm-referenced test. For example, a teacher may say that the top 20% of the class will get A's, the next 20% will get B's, and so on. If you are told you are in the upper 20% of of the class, you know that a norm-referenced test is being used. The norm is based on the distribution of scores of all the test takers. It should be noted that norm-referenced tests are often used in standardized testing such as districtwide or statewide assessments while criterion-referenced testing is used in proficiency exams and often in teachers' report card grading. In the former case, we want to know where a student stands with respect to his or her peers; in the latter, we want to know the degree to which a student has learned the material that was taught. (The next chapter focuses on norm-referenced tests; this chapter focuses on criterion-referenced tests.)

Summative Versus Formative Tests.   The purpose of testing is not always the same. Tests can be used to describe the learning that has taken place in a student; this type of testing is called *summative*. For example, at the end of a unit on parts of speech, a teacher might like to evaluate whether the students are capable of diagramming sentences. In contrast, tests can be used to describe the entering characteristics of a student so that the teacher can design an appropriate instructional environment; this type of testing is called *formative*. For example, a third grade teacher who is about to begin a unit on long division might like to pretest her students on prerequisite skills such as simple division, simple multiplication, and three-column subtraction. As you can see, formative testing occurs during or before instruction while summative testing is a more formal evaluation at the conclusion of instruction. It should be noted that the same test can serve as a summative test for instruction that has just been completed and as a formative test for the next unit of instruction. (This chapter focuses mainly on summative evaluation; the next chapter focuses on formative evaluation.)

HOW TO CONSTRUCT A GOOD TEST

What makes a good test? Box 15–2 lists four main characteristics: validity, reliability, objectivity, and standardization.

Validity

A test should measure what it is supposed to measure. If you want to measure a student's learning of American history, it is not valid to include test items on some other topic such as chemistry. In an ideal world, the test would measure each of the main concepts or facts or skills that was taught; however, since testing time is limited, the test should contain a representative sample of the taught information. Thus, in a math course covering addition and subtraction of integers, solving word problems, and fractions, the test should include typical items from each category.

Face Validity.   One type of validity is *face validity*; this means that the test items should be identical or very similar to the actual task being taught. For example, if students given a spelling lesson were taught by dictation (i.e., to write the word that the teacher speaks), then the test should approximate this

---

BOX 15–2   Characteristics of a Good Test

Validity   Does the test measure what it is supposed to measure?
Reliability   Are the scores that a person obtains consistent?
Objectivity   Is the test administered and scored the same way for each person?
Referencing   Can you translate the raw score into a meaningful description of
              performance?

---

situation. In contrast, some tests require that the student correctly use the word in a sentence or that the student select the word from a list of four spellings (e.g., calander, calendar, calender, calandar). These tests seem to violate the requirement of face validity.

Predictive Validity.   Another type of validity is *predictive validity;* in this case, performance on the test should serve to predict performance on some "real world" task. For example, mastery of a basic mathematics test might serve to predict performance on a next course in mathematics. Performance on a test of basic English skills in spelling, punctuation, and grammar may be predictive of performance in higher-level courses in English composition. If a test is valid, it should be usable for predicting how a student will behave in a certain learning task.

Construct Validity.   Another type of validity is *construct validity;* this means that the test items should be related to the concept that is being tested. For example, intelligence is a concept that may be tested in many ways. However, the test items should be related to a theory of intelligence.

In order to be valid, a test does not have to possess each of these types of validity. However, you should be able to justify the test on the basis of at least one of these types of validity.

Reliability

A test should provide consistent results for a student. For example, suppose you took an intelligence test that told you that your IQ was 100, and then you took another version of the test that told you that your IQ was 150, and then you took another version that told you your IQ was 80. This test seems to violate the criterion of reliability! As another example, suppose that you are given a two-part test on mathematical achievement; the first and second parts are designed to measure the same skills but you score very high on test 1 while you fail test 2. This test also seems to be unreliable. One way of testing for reliability is to have at least two test items for each concept, skill, or fact that you evaluate; this is like having two tests in one. The scores on each "half" should correspond.

Objectivity

The test should be administered and scored in the same way for each student. For example, if you are more lenient with some students than others, you have failed to meet the criterion of objectivity. It is easier to be objective when you have a clear scoring key for each answer on the test. Open-ended essay questions can be used objectively, of course; however, they require that the procedure for scoring be spelled out precisely and used identically for all students. Adherence to objectivity can sometimes violate the requirement for validity; for example, recently some students taking the SATs solved a problem in a way that the test makers had not thought of, yielding an answer that was correct but was scored as wrong.

Referencing

The score on the test must be translated into a number that tells where the learner stands. One way to do this is through norm referencing, as discussed in the previous section. For example, if a student gets a raw score of 85 out of 100 on the exam, a norm-referenced procedure might tell the student that he or she was in the upper 10% of the class. Another way to provide referencing (or standardization) is criterion referencing, as discussed in the previous section. For example, if a student gets a raw score of 85 out of 100, this is a B if the grading criterion is 80 to 90 is B. Standards help the learner and teacher translate a raw score, such as percentage correct, into a more useful measure of learning.

In the remainder of this chapter, we focus on three techniques for measuring student learning. Each technique involves an attempt to integrate the processes of measurement and instruction rather than keeping them separate. As briefly summarized in the introduction to this chapter, the three major ways of describing what a student has learned are: behavioral objectives, which describe the learner's behavior; task analysis, which describes the instructional task (or stimulus); and cognitive analysis, which describes the learner's knowledge.

USING BEHAVIORAL OBJECTIVES TO EVALUATE STUDENT LEARNING

What Are Behavioral Objectives?

Behavioral objectives are clear statements of what a learner should be able *to do* at the end of instruction. Mager (1962) states that an objective is a "description of a pattern of behavior." Furthermore, Mager (1962) asserts that an objective should (1) define the behavior in a way that includes the conditions imposed on the learner, and (2) state the criterion level of minimal acceptable performance. For example, consider the objectives:

> "The student will develop an appreciation of the role of numbers in our society."
> "Given ten minutes to solve 10 three-column subtraction problems that do not involve borrowing, the student will get at least 7 correct."

The first objective is too vague: it does not clearly describe the behavior that the student is expected to perform, and it does not clearly state the criterion of success. The second objective better matches Mager's definition; it is stated clearly enough for someone else to be able to implement it.

Bloom's Taxonomy of Objectives

You may have noticed that instructional objectives are not all alike. For example, "being able to recite, without error, the last names of the U.S. presidents in order, starting with Washington" requires rote memorization while "being able to sort whole numbers into even numbers and odd numbers" requires the application of a rule. Several taxonomies of instructional objectives have been developed for use in schools. One of the most widely used sets of objectives is Bloom's taxonomy (Bloom, Engelhart, Furst, Hill & Krathwohl, 1956).

Box 15–3 summarizes Bloom's taxonomy of objectives that may be relevant to the "cognitive domain" of learning; other taxonomies have been developed for the "affective domain" (Krathwohl, Bloom & Masia, 1964) and the "psychomotor domain" (Simpson, 1966). As you can see in the box, the taxonomy consists of six major categories of objectives with subcategories listed under each. Each category or subcategory can contain many different objectives; examples are provided in Box 15–3. It should also be noted that each instructional objective can be expressed more precisely as a behavioral objective. For example, "The ability to read musical scores" is an instructional objective that fits under the "translation" subcategory and "comprehension" category. A corresponding behavioral objective could be: "When given a musical score for 'Pop Goes The Weasel,' the student will be able to play the song without errors."

Mastery Learning as a Guide to Instructional Evaluation

Principles of Mastery Learning.   Behavioral objectives can be used in a way that integrates both the evaluation and the instructional process. For example, several authors have suggested the use of mastery learning in schools

---

BOX 15–3   Some Categories and Subcategories of Instructional Objectives in the Cognitive Domain

1.00 Knowledge
    1.10 Knowledge of specifics
    1.20 Knowledge of ways and means of dealing with specifics
    1.30 Knowledge of the universals and abstractions in a field

2.00 Comprehension
    2.10 Translation
    2.20 Interpretation
    2.30 Extrapolation

3.00 Application

4.00 Analysis
    4.10 Analysis of elements
    4.20 Analysis of relationships
    4.30 Analysis of organizational principles

5.00 Synthesis
    5.10 Production of a unique communication
    5.20 Production of a plan, or proposed set of operations
    5.30 Derivation of a set of abstract relations

6.00 Evaluation
    6.10 Judgments in terms of internal evidence
    6.20 Judgments in terms of external criteria

From Bloom et al. (1956)

(Block, 1971, 1974; Bloom, 1976; Carroll, 1963). In mastery learning, behavioral objectives are established for each unit of material and these objectives are communicated to the learners. Learners may study until they feel that they have mastered the material; then they are given a test on the material. If they pass the test, they go on to the next section of material; if they do not pass, they study the material again, and take another version of the test with this process being repeated until they pass. This procedure is summarized in Figure 15–1.

Mastery learning is based on Carroll's (1963) model of school learning. Two main ideas in this model are: (1) If all students are given the same instruction, then learning aptitude and achievement measured at the end of instruction will be highly related. (2) If each student is given appropriate instruction and

FIGURE 15–1 Mastery Learning

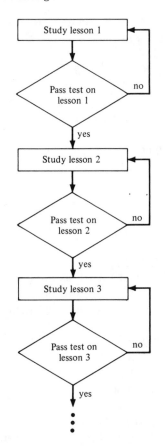

learning time, then the majority of students will master the material, and the relation between incoming aptitude and achievement will become close to zero.

In his classic book, *Human Characteristics and School Learning*, Bloom (1976) argued that mastery learning can be used as a way of eliminating individual differences among students in their ability to learn. Bloom's (1976, p. 1) idea is based on the premise that "most students can learn what the schools have to teach—if the problem is approached sensitively and systematically." Bloom recognizes that initially students may differ with respect to *how long* it takes them to learn; however, given appropriate amounts of instruction, nearly all students can master any school learning task. Since school learning tasks often build on previous learning, it is extremely important that students master prerequisite skills before moving on to new learning. In fact, differences in the amount of prerequisite knowledge may be responsible for most of the differences in learner's time to learn.

Critique of Mastery Learning.   Does mastery learning work? One major prediction is that mastery approaches should result in more achievement than nonmastery approaches used in traditional classrooms. Several reviews of classroom studies have tended to support this prediction (Block, 1971, 1974; Block & Burns, 1976; Johnson & Ruskin, 1977; Robin, 1978). However, these results may be interpreted as saying that the more time students spend on a task, the more they will learn.

A second, more crucial, prediction is that as instruction progresses, mastery students should become less variable on measures of achievement and learning time. As students acquire the required prerequisite knowledge, the time required to learn the next piece of knowledge will be reduced. Cariello (1980) has reviewed the results of five dissertations by Bloom's students (Block, 1970; Arlin, 1973; Anderson, 1973; Binor, 1974; Levin, 1975) which tend to support these predictions. For example, Arlin (1973) asked students to learn an eight-lesson sequence on an imaginary science. The mastery group was required to reach 85% correct on a test before going on to the next lesson; the control group was required to score 85% on a mastery test only on the last chapter. The results showed that the average learning time for lesson 8 was half as long for the mastery students as for the control students. In addition, the mastery students became less variable across the eight lessons and were far less variable than the control group on the eighth lesson.

The mastery approach has been criticized on both empirical and methodological grounds. First, Resnick (1977) has pointed out that the data do not perfectly support the predictions. In some cases, the differences among students' learning times did not decrease across lessons, and the differences between the best and poorest learners were not eliminated through mastery learning. For example, in some studies, the poor learners took twice as long to learn as the good learners even on the last lesson in the series.

Greeno (1978, p. 71) has criticized the method used in mastery learning studies:

> . . . when Bloom's tests of learning achievement fail to show substantial differences among the large majority of students, I am inclined to suspect that the tests failed to make contact with the differences that may have been there. By restricting himself to a narrowly conceived idea of what was learned, based on a first order analysis of the subject matter alone, Bloom failed to provide a convincing test of his assertion that most students achieved a common learning outcome.

This criticism is based on the idea that mastery tests usually cover material that is very similar to that presented during instruction. Greeno suggests that if students were also tested on transfer to different material, huge individual differences would reappear.

A recent study by Cariello (1980) provides some support for Greeno's argument. Students learned a five-lesson sequence on computer programming under a mastery or nonmastery treatment. Although the mastery group tended to perform well on test items like those used throughout instruction, the nonmastery group performed relatively better on transfer test items. Thus there is a danger that mastery learning may restrict the learner's attention to a narrow set of information, whereas nonmastery students may retain a broader learning perspective.

USING TASK ANALYSIS TO EVALUATE STUDENT LEARNING

What Are Learning Hierarchies?

Task analysis involves breaking a task down into its component subtasks, breaking each subtask into its components, and so on. The product of task analysis is a clear specification of the component tasks that are prerequisites for the main task. Gagne (1968, 1970; Gagne, Mayor, Garstens, & Paradise, 1962) has used the term *learning hierarchy* to refer to some of the task analyses that he has performed. Gagne & Briggs (1974, p. 109) have defined a learning hierarchy as "an arrangement of intellectual skill objectives into a pattern which shows the prerequisite relationships among them."

Figure 15–2 shows a learning hierarchy for a subtraction task. As you can see, to be able to carry out the main task (XI) requires knowledge of four subtasks (IV, VIII, IX and X); tasks VIII, IX and X each depend on a subtask (VII) which in turn can be broken down into two subtasks (V and VI); task V requires two subtasks (II and III) and tasks VI, II and III each require the subtask of knowing simple subtraction facts (I). Gagne, Mayor, Garstens & Paradise (1962, p. 1) summarize the procedure for generating a learning hierarchy as follows:

> Such an analysis is executed by asking the question of the final task, "What would the individual have to know how to do in order to perform this task, after being given only instructions?" and successively asking the same question of the learning sets so defined, until one describes a "hierarchy of knowledge" containing very simple and general learning sets at its lowest level.

Validation of Learning Hierarchies

How can you tell whether a learning hierarchy, such as shown in Figure 15–2, is correct? One way to validate a learning hierarchy is to observe the number of cases in which a learner passes a test for a higher-level skill but fails a test for a prerequisite, lower-level skill. If this happens frequently, then the learning hierarchy is not valid. In order to test the validity of the learning hierarchy in Figure 15–2, Gagne et al. (1962) evaluated the performance of a large sample of

FIGURE 15–2   Learning Hierarchy for Subtraction

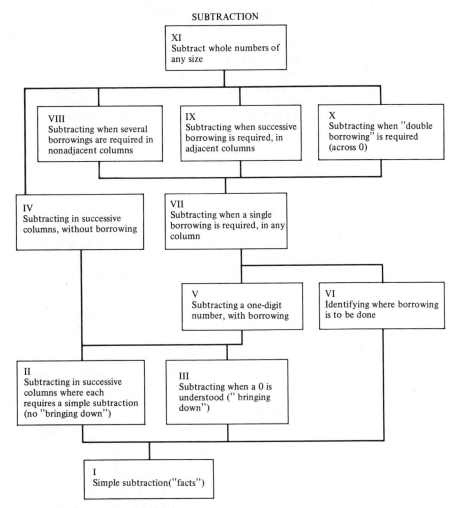

From Gagne, Mayor, Garstens, and Paradise (1962)

students on each of the subskills in the hierarchy. Table 15–2 shows that there are relatively few cases in which a student fails a prerequisite skill test but passes a higher-level test; thus there is no strong evidence that the learning hierarchy is not valid.

More recently, White (1974) has shown how to validate a learning hierarchy for determining velocity from a position-time graph. An example of the task is shown in Figure 15–3. Based on a logical analysis of the task, White identified twenty-three subtasks, organized into seven levels. However, when he tested students on each of the subtasks he found some cases in which the hierarchy did

TABLE 15–2 Can a Person Pass a Test for a Higher Skill Without Passing a Test for a Prerequisite Lower Skill?

	Number of Cases	Proportion of Cases
Pass higher, pass lower	746	.69
Fail higher, fail lower	143	.13
Fail higher, pass lower	186	.17
Pass higher, fail lower	13	.01

Adapted from Gagne, Mayor, Garstens & Paradise (1962)

not seem correct; for example, a substantial number of students passed a test for a higher skill but failed a test for a lower skill. The hierarchy was revised to eliminate these connections, and to ensure that all relevant prerequisite skills were included. For example, in the original hierarchy skill 19 (Given several lines of different lengths and slopes on a pair of axes marked with positive direction, subject places lines in order of their slopes) was listed as a prerequisite for skill 15 (Given several lines of different lengths and slopes passing through the origin of a pair of positive-time axes that have no scales, subject

FIGURE 15–3 What is the velocity at point A?

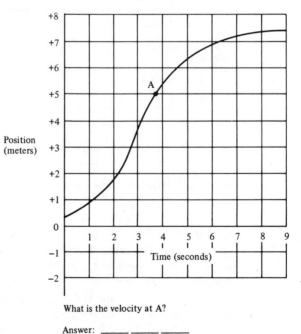

What is the velocity at A?

Answer: _____ _____ _____
        + or –   no.   unit

From White (1974)

grades the lines in order of the velocities they represent) which in turn was listed as a prerequisite for skill 14 (When asked what property of an object is represented by the slope of its position-time graph, subject answers velocity). However, many students were able to pass a test on skill 14 without passing a test on skill 15, while almost no cases were observed of a student passing a test on skill 15 without passing skill 19. Therefore, part of the hierarchy was amended so that skills 15 and 19 were prerequisites for skill 14.

Learning Hierarchies As Guides to Instruction and Evaluation

Learning hierarchies, like behavioral objectives, can be used in a way that unites learning and evaluation. For example, Gagne (Gagne, Mayor, Garstens & Paradise, 1962; Gagne, 1968) argues that learning hierarchies can serve as prescriptions for teaching. Specifically, a teacher should determine the lowest-level skills that a learner does not yet possess and build up from there; thus instruction should proceed from the bottom to the top of the hierarchy.

Once a learning hierarchy has been developed and empirically validated, it can be used to guide instruction. Resnick (1976; Resnick, Siegel & Kresh, 1971) has provided some support for this idea. In her experiments, students were taught a skill by moving from the bottom to top of a hierarchy or from the top to bottom. The results indicated that the hierarchical bottom-to-top sequence was most effective for most children. However, for some of the students, learning higher-level objectives first was faster. Apparently, these students possessed the ability to learn the lower-level skills at the same time they learned the higher-level skill.

Learning hierarchies provide an extension of the behavioral objectives approach. For example, objectives may be placed in a hierarchy that prescribes a sequence of teaching. However, the learning hierarchy approach also serves as a bridge to the cognitive analysis of learning. The success of the task analysis approach (such as learning hierarchies) suggests that the same kind of analyses could be performed on the intellectual processes that a person uses to achieve a correct answer. Resnick (1976, p. 58) summarizes the role of learning hierarchies as follows:

> Gagne's hierarchy analyses appear to flirt with information processing conceptions of psychology, but not come to grips with them. There is a kind of implicit process analysis involved in the method of hierarchy generation.

Thus Gagne's work was a breakthrough in applying task analysis to evaluation and instruction of school tasks; his work stimulated new developments in cognitive psychology that have provided the "next generation" in analytic techniques.

USING COGNITIVE ANALYSIS TO EVALUATE STUDENT LEARNING

What Are the Types of Knowledge?

Cognitive analysis of learning refers to a description of the knowledge acquired by the learner. Three types of knowledge are:

Semantic knowledge—Factual and conceptual knowledge about the world, such as knowing about the nitrogen cycle or knowing the definition of a square.

Procedural knowledge—Knowledge of how to carry out some procedure, such as how to engage in long division.

Strategic knowledge—Knowledge of how to establish goals, select appropriate procedures, and monitor progress towards achieving goals.

The analytic tools of cognitive psychology have been applied to each of these kinds of knowledge (Mayer, 1981).

Semantic Knowledge

A person's semantic knowledge may be analyzed and represented as a set of nodes (corresponding to ideas) and arrows (corresponding to connections among ideas). In Chapter 7, Figure 7–13 shows a simplified representation of knowledge about growing of rice (Collins & Stevens, 1982). As you can see, the figure shows some of the conditions involved in growing rice (indicated as nodes) as well as relations among the conditions (indicated as arrows). According to this representation, the growing of rice depends on flooding a flat area, fertile soil, and warm temperature; flooding a flat area depends on a supply of fresh water and a flat area; a supply of fresh water depends on heavy rainfall or a body of land water; a flat area depends on a flat terrain or terracing.

In order to evaluate whether a person possesses a knowledge structure such as shown in Figure 7–13 you can ask the student a series of questions. Collins & Stevens (1982, p. 81) have devised some "entrapment strategies" for evaluating a student's knowledge, as exemplified in the following dialogue:

TEACHER: Why do they grow rice in Louisana?
STUDENT: Places where there is a lot of water. I think rice requires the ability to selectively flood fields.
TEACHER: O.K. Do you think there's a lot of rice in, say, Washington and Oregon?

This dialogue, presented more fully in Box 7–4, is investigating whether the student's knowledge of rice growing contains all of the conditions organized in Figure 7–13. As you can also see, this dialogue may serve to help the student learn, as well as to provide an evaluation. According to Collins & Stevens (1982), the use of tutoring strategies such as entrapment is based on cognitive analysis of the knowledge that you want the student to acquire. This instructional procedure is described more fully in Chapter 7.

Procedural Knowledge

Procedural knowledge may be analyzed and represented as a flow chart (or process model). In Chapter 13, Figure 13–3 shows some process models for simple addition; the rectangles indicate processes, the diamonds represent decisions that are made, and the arrows indicate the order in which operations occur. As noted in Chapter 13, these models represent a developmental sequence in which children move from a counting-all to a counting-on procedure as they get more experience.

Similarly, Figure 13–5 shows a process model for three-column subtraction. As described in the chapter, Brown & Burton (1978) developed a computer program called BUGGY, which locates student's "bugs" in procedures for three-column subtraction. The program begins with the idea that a student consistently uses some procedure for solving subtraction problems and then tries to find the appropriate bugs or combination of bugs that will describe the student's performance on a test. Thus a student's knowledge of subtraction can be represented as a procedure, with some bugs in it.

Strategic Knowledge

Problem Space.   Strategic knowledge may be represented using a problem space and a production system. The problem space is a description of the given state of the problem, the goal state, and all possible intervening states that result from applying legal moves in the problem (Newell & Simon, 1972). For example, Figure 15–4 shows the problem space for the algebraic equation,

$$5(2x) = 2 + 8x$$

The rectangles indicate the states of the problem, with 1 as the given state and 6 as the goal state. The arrows represent legal moves, including moving a variable from one side to the other (MV), moving a number from one side to the other (MC), combining variables (CV), combining numbers (CC) and clearing parentheses (CP).

Production System.   A production system represents a strategy for how to move through a problem space (Newell & Simon, 1972). A production system consists of a list of productions, with each production consisting of a condition and an action. For example, a production for algebra equation solving may be:

FIGURE 15–4 A Problem Space for 5(2x) = 2 + 8x

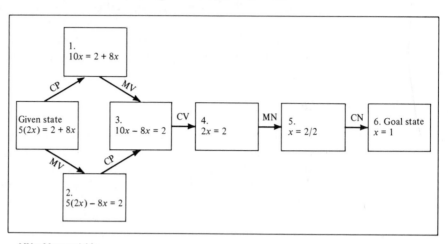

MV = Move variable
MN = Move number
CV = Combine Variables
CN = Combine numbers
CP = Clear parentheses

IF there are two instances of *x* on one side of the equation,
THEN combine them.

The condition part of the production (i.e., the IF clause) says to look for a situation such as the two instances of *x* in the equation, $3x + 2x = 10$. The action part of the production (i.e., the THEN clause) says to carry out the operation, yielding the equation, $5x = 10$. As you can see, a production is simply a condition-action pair; if the condition is met, then the action is carried out.

Box 15–4 shows a production system for solving algebra equations (Mayer, 1981, 1982). In using a production system, you start with the first production and work your way down the list. Whenever a condition is met, you carry out the corresponding action and then return to the top of the production list.

Let's see how this production system would be used to solve an equation such as

$$5(2x) = 2 + 8x$$

As you go down the list of the productions, the conditions for production 1 are met (i.e., there are *x*'s on both sides of the equation). When you carry out the action, the equation is changed into

$$5(2x) - 8x = 2$$

BOX 15–4   A Production System for $5(2x) = 2 + 8x$

1. IF there is an x on the right of the equality,
   THEN move the x to the left of the equality (MV).
2. IF there is a number on the left of the equality,
   THEN move the number to the right of the equality (MN).
3. IF there are two instances of x on one side of the equality,
   THEN combine them (CV).
4. IF there are two instances of numbers on one side of the equality,
   THEN combine them (CN).
5. IF your goal is to combine two numbers or two x's and there is a
   parenthesis blocking your compuatation,
   THEN clear the parenthesis (CP).

We now go to the top of the list, and go down again: productions 1 and 2 do not
fire but production 3 does. However, it is not possible to directly carry out the
action of combining the x terms because of the parentheses. Thus production 5
fires and the action is carried out, yielding

$$10x - 8x = 2$$

Then, we can execute the action for production 3, yielding

$$2x = 2$$

Going down the production system again, production 2 now fires, and the
action yields an equation:

$$x = 2/2$$

Finally, production 4 now fires and yields

$$x = 1$$

As you can see, the production system guides your movement through the
problem space (see Newell & Simon, 1972 for a more detailed description).

The problem space and production system techniques allow us to evaluate a
person's solution strategy in great detail. For example, as described in Chapter
13, Mayer (1982) and Mayer, Larkin & Kadane (1983) found that some people
used a production system that emphasized combining variables or numbers
(reduce strategy) while other subjects used a production system that empha-

sized isolating x on one side of the equation (isolate strategy). Thus individual differences in problem-solving strategies can be described by listing the production system being used by different problem solvers.

As you can see, the cognitive approach to evaluating student learning is based on precise descriptions of the student's semantic, procedural, and strategic knowledge. This approach to describing "what is learned" is an advance over earlier techniques such as describing objectives, because it allows for a more precise description. In the future, teachers may be able to more clearly specify their "cognitive objectives of instruction" such as saying that "Sally needs to correct the bug she has in step 2a of the subtraction algorithm" or "Johnny needs to add some nodes concerning flat land to his understanding of rice growing" or "Bill needs to see how to replace production 4 with a more efficient one."

CONCLUSION

This chapter began by looking at the ways in which evaluation has traditionally been used in schools—including report card grades, unit mastery tests, standardized achievement tests, proficiency tests, placement tests, standardized ability tests. Then we looked at four basic distinctions: teacher versus commercial tests; achievement versus ability tests; criterion-referenced versus norm-referenced tests; and summative versus formative tests. Then this chapter described the four characteristics of a good test—validity, reliability, objectivity, and referencing.

A main theme of this chapter has been that the evaluation of student learning can be integrated with the instructional program. Evaluation can be used to enrich the instructional program by providing information that guides instruction. Three exemplary approaches were described. In the first, behavioral objectives can be used to describe learning outcomes and mastery learning can be used to guide instruction. In the second, task analysis can be used to break a large set of materials to be learned into a sequence of smaller ones, and this sequence can be used as a prescription for instruction. In the third approach, the semantic, procedural, and strategic knowledge of the learner can be described, and tests can be aimed at measuring specific changes in a learner's knowledge.

The promise of the cognitive approach is that it provides a level of detail not previously available. It allows us to pinpoint exactly which aspect of a student's knowledge is incorrect or incomplete. While this approach is still in its infancy, some of the techniques may ultimately find a place in school measurement. For example, versions of BUGGY programs are beginning to appear in schools as a way of diagnosing errors in arithmetic computational procedures.

This chapter deals mainly with evaluating student learning using teacher-made, criterion-referenced tests, although it is also possible to evaluate student learning using commerical, norm-referenced tests (as described in the next chapter). In summary, a theme of this chapter and the next is that evaluation can be used both to assess where the student currently "is" and to help shape an instructional program so that the student will move forward.

SUGGESTED READINGS

Bloom, B. (1976). *Human characteristics and school learning*. New York: McGraw-Hill. (A theoretical defense of mastery learning.)

Mayer, R. E. (1981). *The promise of cognitive psychology*. New York: Freeman. (Provides examples from cognitive psychology that can be used to describe people's semantic, procedural, and strategic knowledge.)

16 Evaluation of Learner Characteristics

Chapter 16 examines how the evaluation of student achievement and ability can be used to improve an instructional program. The chapter examines both psychometric and cognitive approaches to the evaluation of learner characteristics. The chapter also focuses on how the psychometric and cognitive approaches can be applied to special education.

WHAT'S NORMAL? WHO'S NORMAL?

Suppose that we want a test that will measure a student's creative ability, so that we can determine who will benefit from special "giftedness" instruction. Box 16–1 presents a simple two-part test that might be used. Go ahead and try either or both parts of the test. Give yourself 2 minutes for each part.

Once you have finished, you must score your answer. Count up the number of uses you invented for part 1. (Typical answers are: paperweight, doorstop, bookends, weapon, and so on.) Count up the number of correctly solved

---

BOX 16–1   A Test for Creativity

Part 1
Time limit: 2 minutes
List all the possible uses for a brick.
1.
2.
3.
4.
5.
6.
7.
8.

Part 2
Time limit: 2 minutes
Rearrange the letters in each group to form a word.
RTHAE
OESHR
IERDT
AEPHS
AECRT
HROAC
TANOG
OBRAC

---

anagrams in part 2. (The answers are, respectively: HEART, SHORE, TRIED, SHAPE, CRATE, ROACH, TANGO, COBRA.) Write down you scores:

Score for part 1: _____
Score for part 2: _____

Now that we have your scores, how can we tell how you did on the test? One procedure would be to set some criterion score, such as saying: "You must get a score of 4 or more on each test in order to be called gifted." This is called a criterion referenced measurement. Alternatively, we could compare your score to that of other people who took the test to see where you fit in. This is called a norm-referenced measurement and is the basis for "standardized" tests of achievement and ability—the focus of this chapter.

To get a better idea of standardized testing, suppose we gave our creativity test to 100 college students. Further, suppose that we obtained the same results for each part of the test such as shown in Box 16–2. The left side of Box 16–2 gives possible scores on the *x* axis and number of people achieving each score on the *y* axis; for the right side of Box 16–2 the *x* axis lists the possible scores and the *y* axis lists the percentage of people who obtained each score. As you can see, the average score for each part of the test is 3.5. Most (68%) of the students obtained scores between 3 and 4, the overwhelming majority (95%) obtained scores between 2 and 5, and 99% obtained scores between 1 and 6. The curve shown in Box 16–2 is a normal curve because its shape meets the following conditions: half the people score above the average and half score below; the curve is symmetrical; the curve is bell-shaped. As you will see later in this chapter, many tests produce normal curves (i.e., symmetrical, bell-shaped curves).

To simplify matters, use Table 16–1 to convert your "raw" score to a "percentile" score. Write your percentile scores below:

Percentile for part 1: _____
Percentile for part 2: _____

A percentile score tells the percentage of people who received your score or poorer on the test. Thus, if you scored at the fiftieth percentile, this means that your score is the same or better than 50% of the people who took the test; if you scored at the ninetieth percentile, your score is the same or better than 90% of the people taking the test, and so on.

Are your scores normal, according to the percentile tables? Even if your scores are below normal, don't be concerned, because there are many problems with our creativity test. In the previous chapter, you learned about the four characteristics of a good test: reliability, validity, objectivity, referencing. The test's reliability can be questioned because by changing the raw score by just 1 point you can change the percentile rank greatly. The test's validity can be questioned because there is not a strong relation between one's score on this test and the probability that a person will invent or discover something new.

TABLE 16–1   Table for Converting Raw Score on Creativity Test to Percentile Score

Raw Score	Percentile Score
0	1
1	3
2	16
3	50
4	84
5	97
6	99
7	99
8	99

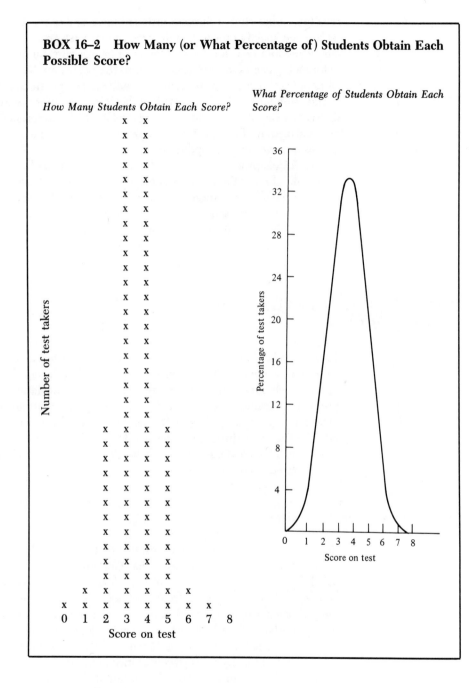

BOX 16–2 How Many (or What Percentage of) Students Obtain Each Possible Score?

The test's objectivity can be questioned because the scoring procedure for Part 1 does not specify how to handle very similar answers or "wrong" answers, and not all people take the test under the same circumstances. Finally, the test's referencing can be questioned, because the norms are based on a small sample of people who may not be typical of all test takers. In contrast, a technically "good" standardized test meets all of these criteria; however, the distinguishing characteristic of a *standardized* test is that the reference norms (such as summarized in Box 16–2 and Table 16–1) are based on a very large and representative group of people.

In this chapter, we examine standardized tests, including tests of achievement and ability. First, we examine the role of standardized testing in education and the interpretation of standardized test results. Second, we explore the psychometric approach to testing and the cognitive approach to testing. Finally, we see how these two approaches have been applied to the measurement of cognitive abilities in special students.

INTERPRETING STANDARDIZED TEST RESULTS

Two major kinds of standardized tests commonly used in schools are standardized achievement tests and standardized ability tests. As described in the previous chapter, achievement tests measure knowledge acquired through previous learning (e.g., a test of arithmetic computation) while ability tests measure a person's potential to learn or to perform on some task (e.g., an intelligence test). In this section, we focus on how to interpret the results of standardized achievement tests, although the same general principles apply to standardized ability tests.

Evaluating A Student's Achievement

Box 16–3 lists some test items similar to those found on a commonly used standardized achievement test, the Comprehensive Tests of Basic Skills (CTBS). These items are for third graders, although forms are available for grades K–12. It is a "standardized" test because it has been given to a very large sample of children so it is possible to compare any student's score with the scores of others of the same age. It is an "achievement" test because it attempts to measure what a student has learned in certain subject matter areas.

These items focus on word recognition, but other items test different factors such as spelling or mathematics computation or reading comprehension. Scores on test factors, such as measured by the CTBS, can be used to help teachers make decisions about how to provide instruction for a student. In fact, the theme of this chapter is that measurement—of which standardized testing is

---

BOX 16–3   Sample Test Items from a Standardized Test

Read the word with the underlined part. Now look at the other words. Find the word that has the same *vowel* sound as the underlined part. Mark your answer.

Sample A

r<u>a</u>g	day	coat	rain	glad
	○	○	○	○

Read the underlined word. Find the root word of the underlined word. Mark your answer.

Sample B

<u>called</u>	all	alled	call	led
	○	○	○	○

Look at the underlined word. Find the *suffix* of the underlined word. Mark your answer.

Sample C

<u>painted</u>	ted	painte	ed	pain
	○	○	○	○

Look at the words. Find the word that is a compound word. Mark your answer.

Sample D

neighbor	together	waterfall	wonderful
○	○	○	○

From Comprehensive Tests of Basic Skills (1982)

one example—can be viewed as an aid to instruction. In short, educational measurement and instruction should be closely related endeavors.

Let's suppose that you are given test results such as shown in Table 16–2, for a fifth grader named John. These results, let's suppose, are from a standardized achievement test such as the Comprehensive Test of Basic Skills (CTBS) described earlier. What do these results mean? In order for you to be able to interpret the results you need to understand some of the basic terms: factor, raw score, percentile, confidence interval, stanine, grade-equivalents.

Factor. A factor is a basic unit of achievement or ability, such as spelling, vocabulary, reading comprehension, mathematics computation. Each factor may be further broken down into subfactors; for example, fourth grade mathematics computation can be broken down into add whole numbers, add decimals and fractions, subtract whole numbers, subtract decimals and fractions, multiply whole numbers or fractions, divide whole numbers. Box 16–4 lists the major factors and subfactors in the fourth grade level of the CTBS. As you can see, an achievement test can provide evaluations of knowledge in broad areas as well as specific skills. However, since the subfactors are based on just a few test items (e.g., ranging from 4 to 10 in the fourth grade test), measurement may not be as accurate as for main factors that are based on many items (e.g., usually more than twenty items).

Raw Score. The raw score is the actual score that a student obtained based on the scoring key. For example, John got a raw score of 607 on the vocabulary factor.

TABLE 16–2 Example of Standardized Test Results

NAME:	Doe John D	DISTRICT:	Goleta USD	FORM:	U/G
CLASS:	Jones	CITY/STATE:	Goleta CA	GRADE:	5.1
SCHOOL:	Oceanview	RUN DATE:	11/01/85	TEST DATE:	10/01/85

Factor	Raw Score	National Percentile	Confidence Interval	National Stanine	Grade Equivalent
VOCABULARY	607	15	10–30	3	3.2
COMPREHENSION	517	6	0–30	2	2.1
TOTAL READING	562	8	2–22	2	2.5
SPELLING	630	20	15–30	3	4.0
LANGUAGE MECHANICS	676	50	40–65	5	5.1
LANGUAGE EXPRESSION	651	29	20–40	4	4.3
TOTAL LANGUAGE	664	37	32–44	4	4.6
MATH COMPUTATION	689	43	32–63	5	4.9
MATH CONCEPTS	689	76	70–85	6	6.5
TOTAL MATH	689	63	58–72	6	5.7
TOTAL BATTERY	638	22	16–31	3	4.0

Modified from Comprehensive Tests of Basic Skills (1982)

Percentile. Unfortunately, a raw score does not tell you much about the student's performance. However, John's raw score can be converted to a percentile score, based on identifying how his score compares with other fifth graders' scores. A percentile score tells you how many students scored the same or lower than that score. For example, if John is at the 8th percentile in reading, this means that his score was the same or better than 8% of the other students at his grade level and that 92% of the students scored higher than he did. If John is at the 63rd percentile in math, he did as well or better than 63% of the children at his grade level, but 37% of the children performed better than he did. Percentile is not the same as percentage correct; for example, a score of 80% on a very difficult test might put you in the 99th percentile.

Confidence Interval. Tests cannot precisely determine a student's percentile because tests have only a limited number of items. However, a given test can be accurate within a certain range. For example, if John scores at the 15th percentile in vocabulary, the confidence interval may be 10 to 30. This means that we are fairly sure that John's knowledge of vocabulary places him somewhere between the 10th and 30th percentile. If there are more items on the test, then the confidence interval can usually be smaller.

Stanine. A raw score can be converted into a percentile score and a percentile score can be converted into a stanine score. A stanine score is simply a number from 1 to 9, with 1 as the lowest and 9 as the highest. Table 16–3 shows how to convert a percentile score into a stanine score. For example, if John scores at the 43rd percentile that would put him in the fifth stanine; if he scored at the 20th percentile, he'd be in the 3rd stanine.

Grade Equivalent. A student's score on certain tests can also be converted into a grade-equivalent (i.e., a statement of the grade level at which the student is operating). If we say that Billy is at the grade level of 5.7 in mathematics, this means that his score would put him as an average student among students who have been in the fifth grade for 7 months. Thus the first number corresponds to the grade level and the second number to the months at that grade level.

TABLE 16–3 Comparison of Stanines and Percentiles

Stanines	Approximate Percentiles	Percentage of Students
9 Highest level	96–99	4%
8 High level	90–95	7%
7 Well above average	78–89	12%
6 Slightly above average	60–77	17%
5 Average	41–59	20%
4 Slightly below average	23–40	17%
3 Well below average	11–22	12%
2 Low level	5–10	7%
1 Lowest level	1–4	4%

BOX 16–4   Some Tests and Subtests for Fourth Graders

Test	Category Objective	No. of Items
1	Vocabulary	
	24 Same Meaning	20
	25 Unfamiliar Words in Context	5
	26 Multimeaning Words	5
	27 Missing Words in Context	10
	28 Meaning of Affixes	5
2	Reading Comprehension	
	30 Passage Details	7
	31 Character Analysis	6
	32 Main Idea	5
	33 Generalizations	13
	34 Written Forms	6
	35 Writing Techniques	8
3	Spelling	
	36 Consonants	9
	37 Vowels	11
	38 Structural Units	10
4	Language Mechanics	
	Capitalization	
	39 Pronoun I, Nouns, Adjectives	6
	40 Beginning Words, Titles	4
	Punctuation	
	41 Period, Question Mark, Exclamation Point, Comma	8
	42 Quotation Marks	4
	Capitalization and Punctuation	
	44 Editing Skills	6
5	Language Expression	
	Usage	
	45 Nouns	4
	46 Pronouns	4
	47 Verbs	5
	48 Adjectives, Adverbs	4
	Sentence Structure	
	50 Sentence Formation	4
	51 Sentence Recognition	4
	Paragraph Development	
	52 Sentence Combining	10
	53 Topic Sentence	5
	54 Sequence	5

6	Mathematics Computation	
	57 Add Whole Numbers	6
	58 Add Decimals or Fractions	4
	59 Subtract Whole Numbers	6
	60 Subtract Decimals or Fractions	4
	61 Multiply Whole Numbers or Fractions	8
	63 Divide Whole Numbers	9
7	Mathematics Concepts and Applications	
	68 Numeration	10
	69 Number Sentences	7
	70 Number Theory	6
	71 Problem Solving	9
	72 Measurement	9
	73 Geometry	4

Adapted from Comprehensive Test of Basic Skills (1982)

Evaluating a Group's Achievement

Now, let's consider Box 16–5, which summarizes the reading scores of twenty-five students on an achievement test. In order to interpret these results you need to understand the following terms: frequency distribution, median, mean, standard deviation.

Frequency Distribution.   A frequency distribution is a list, table, or figure that tells each possible score and how many people obtained that score. For example, Box 16–5 shows how many students received each score on a test of reading comprehension: most scored around 40 with fewer scoring less than 20 or more than 60.

Median.   The median is a measure of central tendency of scores in the frequency distribution. In particular, half of the scores are greater than the median and half of the scores are less. In order to find the median, you must place the scores of all students in order—for lowest to highest—and then find the exact middle of the list. Half of the scores will be lower than this score and half will be higher. As you can see, the median is also the 50th percentile.

Mean.   The mean is another measure of central tendency. It is the average score, as determined by adding up all the scores and dividing by the number of scores.

Standard Deviation.   The standard deviation is a measure of variability; it tells how different the scores are from one another. If the scores are spread out, then the standard deviation will be large; if the scores all fall within a very narrow range, then the standard deviation will be smaller. You can think of the

BOX 16–5   Reading Scores for Twenty-five Students in a Class

Frequency Distribution

Score	Number of Students	Score	Number of Students	Score	Number of Students	Score	Number of Students
1	0	21	0	41	2	61	1
2	0	22	0	42	1	62	0
3	0	23	0	43	1	63	0
4	0	24	0	44	2	64	0
5	0	25	1	45	1	65	0
6	0	26	0	46	0	66	0
7	0	27	0	47	1	67	0
8	0	28	0	48	0	68	0
9	0	29	1	49	0	69	1
10	0	30	0	50	1	70	0
11	0	31	0	51	0	71	0
12	0	32	1	52	1	72	0
13	0	33	0	53	0	73	1
14	0	34	0	54	0	74	0
15	0	35	0	55	0	75	0
16	0	36	1	56	1	76	0
17	0	37	0	57	1	77	0
18	0	38	2	58	0	78	0
19	1	39	2	59	0	79	0
20	0	40	1	60	0	80	0

Summary Frequency Distribution

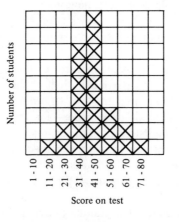

Number of students

1 - 10   11 - 20   21 - 30   31 - 40   41 - 50   51 - 60   61 - 70   71 - 80

Score on test

Median

19 25 29 32 36 38 38 39 39 40 41 41 ⟨42⟩ 43 44 44 45 47 50 52 56 57 61 69 73

Half the scores below   Median   Half the scores above

Mean

$19 + 25 + 29 + 32 + 36 + 38 + 38 + 39 + 39 + 40 + 41 + 41 + 42 + 43$
$+ 44 + 44 + 45 + 47 + 50 + 52 + 56 + 57 + 61 + 69 + 73 = 1100$

Mean = sum of scores/number of scores = 1100/25 = 44

Standard Deviation

Score	Mean	Difference	Square of Difference
19	44	25	625
25	44	19	361
29	44	15	225
32	44	12	144
36	44	8	64
38	44	6	36
38	44	6	36
39	44	5	25
39	44	5	25
40	44	4	16
41	44	3	9
41	44	3	9
42	44	2	4
43	44	1	1
44	44	0	0
44	44	0	0
45	44	1	1
47	44	3	9
50	44	6	36
52	44	8	64
56	44	12	144
57	44	13	169
61	44	17	289
69	44	25	625
73	44	29	841
			3758

$$\text{standard deviation} = \sqrt{\frac{\text{sum of differences}}{\text{number of scores}}} = \sqrt{\frac{3758}{25}} = \sqrt{150.32} = 12.26$$

standard deviation as a measure of the difference between each score and the mean score. To compute the standard deviation for a distribution of scores, you subtract each score from the mean, square each of these deviations, add these squared deviations together, divide by the number of scores, and take the square root.

As you can see, the frequency distribution is one way of describing how a group performed on a test, whereas the mean (or median) and standard deviation allow for a briefer summary of group performance on a test.

Evaluating a Student's Ability

We have used the CTBS as an example of an achievement test although we could have used any of a large number of available achievement tests (see Buros, 1972). Let's briefly look at the Wechsler Intelligence Test for Children, Revised Form (WISC-R) as an example of an intelligence test. Unlike the CTBS, the WISC-R is administered individually to the student by a trained psychologist. Like the CTBS, the WISC-R consists of several subscales, including the following:

> *Information*—The student is asked to answer factual questions such as "What is the month after March?"
>
> *Picture Completion*—A child is shown a picture, and then is tested on memory for a specific detail in the picture.
>
> *Similarities*—The child is asked to describe how two objects are similar (e.g., two things can both be eaten).
>
> *Picture Arrangement*—The child is given some pictures and asked to put them in order (e.g., so that they tell a story in the proper temporal order).
>
> *Arithmetic*—The student is tested on basic skills such as addition and subtraction.
>
> *Block Design*—This tests the child's ability to visualize in space.
>
> *Vocabulary*—This tests the child's ability to express ideas in words.
>
> *Object Assembly*—The child is asked to put parts together into a whole object.
>
> *Comprehension*—Verbal listening comprehension is tested.
>
> *Coding*—This test involves translating a sequence of geometric symbols into other symbols, using a code.
>
> *Digit Span*—This is a test of short-term memory, described in Chapter 4.

Kaufman's (1979) *Intelligent Testing with the WISC-R* provides a more complete description of how to use the WISC-R.

As with any standardized test, a student's raw score can be converted into a more standardized measure such as percentile. For intelligence tests, the standardized measure is often IQ—in which 100 is average (i.e., 50th percentile). An IQ score that is one standard deviation below the mean (e.g., IQ = 85) represents approximately the 16th percentile; an IQ score that is one standard deviation above the mean (e.g., IQ = 115) represents approximately the 84th percentile. Intelligence tests are discussed more fully in the next section, including tests that can be administered to large groups rather than individuals.

UNDERSTANDING STANDARDIZED
ABILITY AND ACHIEVEMENT TESTING

Let's suppose that we want to plan a program of instruction in reading and mathematics for a beginning class of twenty-five third graders. Would it be useful to know the entering characteristics of each child? For example, we could obtain achievement scores in reading and mathematics for each student; this would give us an indication of what each child has already learned. We could obtain ability scores such as measures of intelligence; this gives us an indication of whether each child is achieving at a level corresponding to his or her ability.

How seriously should we take our collection of achievement and ability scores for each student? There is strong agreement among test makers and users that a single test score, by itself, should not be taken too seriously. The score needs to be checked against other measures, including scores on other similar standardized tests, evaluations from previous teachers, and your own observations or information about the student. In addition, since ability and achievement are so difficult to separate, it may be possible for a person to show large changes in ability or achievement due to educational experiences. Thus a test score is not a scientifically perfect description of some unchangeable characteristic of a child. However, a test score (when properly used) can help describe (within some margin of error) the current characteristics of the child; without this information we are left only with our own biases and selective observations in describing the child.

In the next two sections of this chapter, we explore two approaches to the measurement of learner characteristics (including achievement and ability): the psychometric approach and the cognitive approach.

PSYCHOMETRIC APPROACH TO
ABILITY AND ACHIEVEMENT TESTING

What Is the Psychometric Approach?

Very early in the development of public schooling, an important observation was made: students differ from one another. They differ with respect to how fast they learn, for example. Educational testing developed out of a desire to make instruction more sensitive to the differences among students.

The traditional approach to testing could be called the *psychometric approach*. The psychometric approach is based on the idea that a number of traits or factors underlie human behavior. The goal of the psychometric approach is to identify the major traits and to determine how to measure them. For example, Figure 16–1 shows that a person's responses to a test of verbal ability may be based on several underlying factors such as English usage, spelling, reading comprehension, and vocabulary.

FIGURE 16–1   A Factor Theory Approach to Verbal Ability

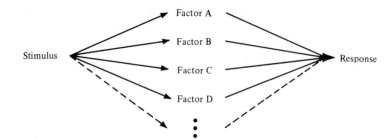

Analysis of Verbal Ability

Verbal ability score = .22 English usage
.33 Spelling
.29 Reading comprehension
.33 Vocabulary

Note: Numbers indicate weights of each factor; for example, spelling (.33) is
more important than English usage (.22), and so forth.

From Mayer (1981)

Binet's Intelligence Test

The first major breakthrough came in the early 1900s when Alfred Binet was
asked by the French government to design a test that would predict students'
success in the French schools. Binet approached this problem in a very
straightforward way: he observed students at each age level in order to determine the kinds of things that a typical student could do. Box 16–6 lists some
of the skills that an average child at each age level should be able to do, based
on an American version of Binet's test.

After Binet collected a list of tasks for each age level, he then proceeded to
test children. If a student could do all of the tasks appropriate for his or her age
level, but could not perform those above his age level, that student was
considered to have normal intelligence (i.e., had an IQ of about 100). If a
student could do tasks of younger students but could not do some of the tasks
for children of his or her age level, that student was considered to be below
average intelligence (i.e., had an IQ of less than 100). If a student could do the
things that his or her peers could do as well as some of the things that older
children could do, that student was above average intelligence (i.e., had an IQ
above 100).

There are three interesting implications of Binet's work. First, you should
note that intelligence was defined as the ability to succeed in school and that
the goal of the original intelligence tests was to predict school performance.
Many skills are required for success in school, including being able to conform,
being able to generate answers to factual questions, and so on. These may not

BOX 16–6 Some Test Items from the Stanford-Binet Test of Intelligence

Age two

1. Three-hole Form Board. Placing three geometric objects in form board.
2. Delayed Response. Identifying placement of hidden object after 10-second delay.
3. Identifying Parts of the Body. Pointing out features on paper doll.
4. Block Building Tower. Building four-block tower by imitating examiner's procedure.
5. Picture Vocabulary. Naming common objects from pictures.
6. Word Combinations. Spontaneous combination of two words.

Age six

1. Vocabulary. Correctly defining 6 words on 45-word list.
2. Differences. Telling difference between two objects.
3. Mutilated Pictures. Pointing out missing part of pictured object.
4. Number Concepts. Counting number of blocks in a pile.
5. Opposite Analogies II. Items of form "Summer is hot; winter is _____."
6. Maze Tracing. Finding shortest path in simple maze.

Age ten

1. Vocabulary. Correctly defining 11 words on same list.
2. Block Counting. Counting number of cubes in three-dimensional picture, some cubes hidden.
3. Abstract Words I. Definition of abstract adverbs.
4. Finding Reasons I. Giving reasons for laws or preferences.
5. Word Naming. Naming as many words as possible in one minute.
6. Repeating Six Digits. Repeating six digits in order.

Average adult

1. Vocabulary. Correctly defining 20 words.
2. Ingenuity I. Algebraic word problems involving mental manipulation of volumes.
3. Differences between Abstract Words. Differentiating between two related abstract words.
4. Arithmetical Reasoning. Word problems involving simple computations.
5. Proverbs I. Giving meaning of proverbs.
6. Orientation: Direction II. Finding orientation after a verbal series of changes in directions.
7. Essential Differences. Giving principal difference between two related concepts.
8. Abstract Words III. Meanings of abstract adverbs.

Source: Adapted from *Principles of Educational and Psychological Testing,* second edition, by Frederick G. Brown. Copyright © 1970 by the Dryden Press Inc. Copyright © by Holt, Rinehart and Winston. Used by permission of CBS College Publishing.

correspond to your conception of intelligence. Second, note that the test is partly based on the students' knowledge (or achievement); the test assumes equality among students in the culture that they share. Thus the test would not be appropriate for children from different cultural backgrounds because the tests measure how much has been learned, *assuming* equal access to learning situations. Third, the test revealed large individual differences among students and was at least partially successful in its goal of predicting school success. Thus, Binet encouraged optimism that the science (or technology) of testing could be developed. In fact, Binet's test was so successful that by the 1920s it became the basis for intelligence tests used in America and around the world.

Measuring Mental Factors

Spearman's G-Factor.   The history of the psychometric approach involves attempts to identify the factors involved in general abilities such as intelligence. Spearman (1904, 1927) used factor analysis techniques to determine the relation among tests. For example, he gave a large number of mental tests to people; he found that all the tests correlated with one another (i.e., if you scored high on one, you tended to score high on the other), but these correlations were not perfect. Based on his analysis, Spearman developed a "two-factor" theory of intelligence—the idea that there is a general intellectual factor (called the g-factor) and many specific factors (called s-factors) such as visual, verbal, and numerical ability. A person's score on an intelligence test was based on the combination of g and s factors.

Thurstone's Primary Mental Abilities.   Later, Thurstone (1938) revised the statistical procedures used in factor analysis and found that all tests of mental ability seemed to fall into seven categories: verbal comprehension, number, memory, perceptual speed, space, verbal fluency, and inductive reasoning. Thus, where Spearman found one general mental ability, Thurstone found seven primary mental abilities.

Guilford's Structure of the Intellect.   Finally, Guilford (1959, 1967) developed a theory, called *structure of the intellect,* which generated 120 basic mental abilities. This theory was based on a logical analysis of mental tasks rather than on statistical analyses of test scores. Box 16–7 shows that all mental tasks can be viewed as requiring some operation, applied to some content, to generate some product; since there are 5 operations, 4 contents, and 6 products, there are a total of $5 \times 4 \times 6$ or 120 possible mental abilities. Examples are shown in Box 16–7.

Critique of the Psychometric Approach to Testing

The theories of Spearman, Thurstone and Guilford demonstrate the problems involved in the psychometric approach. As you can see, the psychometricians

BOX 16-7 Guilford's Structure-of-Intellect Theory

Structure of the Intellect

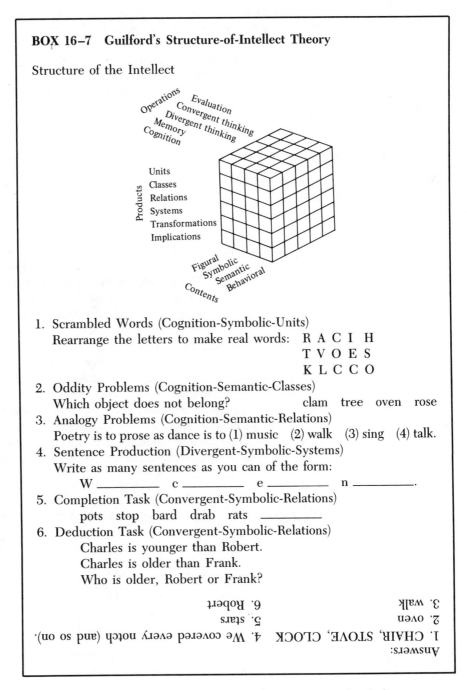

1. Scrambled Words (Cognition-Symbolic-Units)
   Rearrange the letters to make real words: R A C I H
   T V O E S
   K L C C O

2. Oddity Problems (Cognition-Semantic-Classes)
   Which object does not belong?   clam tree oven rose

3. Analogy Problems (Cognition-Semantic-Relations)
   Poetry is to prose as dance is to (1) music (2) walk (3) sing (4) talk.

4. Sentence Production (Divergent-Symbolic-Systems)
   Write as many sentences as you can of the form:
   W _____ c _____ e _____ n _____.

5. Completion Task (Convergent-Symbolic-Relations)
   pots stop bard drab rats _____

6. Deduction Task (Convergent-Symbolic-Relations)
   Charles is younger than Robert.
   Charles is older than Frank.
   Who is older, Robert or Frank?

Answers:
1. CHAIR, STOVE, CLOCK 4. We covered every notch (and so on).
2. oven 5. stars 6. Robert
3. walk

Source: Diagram adapted from J. P. Guilford, "Three Faces of Intellect," *The American Psychologist*, vol. 14, 1959, pp. 469–479. Copyright 1959 by the American Psychological Association. Reprinted by permission.

were able to develop tests to measure almost any mental factor you can name, but the psychometricians had a much tougher time trying to define the main mental factors. In short, they were successful in the technology of test development but unsuccessful in the science of analyzing human intellectual ability. Today's ability tests still reflect this dilemma: there are many tests of mental ability but it is hard to know exactly what they are measuring.

COGNITIVE APPROACH TO ABILITY AND ACHIEVEMENT TESTING

What Is the Cognitive Approach?

The psychometric approach focused on developing tests for measuring individual differences in human mental ability, but did not build an accepted theory of intelligence. In contrast, cognitive psychologists worked on developing a theory of human cognitive processes, but did not focus on individual differences. The existence of these two separate approaches led Cronbach (1957) to conclude that there were two separate disciplines of scientific psychology. However, during the past decade there has been a promising merger of the psychometrician's interest in measurement of individual differences and the cognitive psychologist's interest in a theory of human intelligence.

Hunt and his colleagues (Hunt, 1976, 1978; Hunt, Frost & Lenneborg, 1973; Hunt, Lenneborg & Lewis, 1975) provide an example of the cognitive approach to the measurement of individual differences. Hunt begins by assuming that each learner comes equipped with a memory system (or information-processing system). Figure 16–2 presents a summary of the components in a

FIGURE 16–2   Some Cognitive Components That May Be Related to Verbal Ability

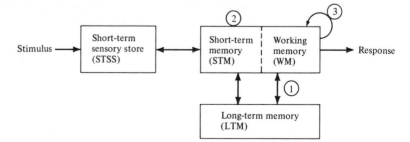

Component 1: Speed of retrieval of information from LTM
Component 2: Holding capacity of STM
Component 3: Speed of mental manipulation in WM

memory system. As described for Box 1–5 in Chapter 1, these components include four memory stores indicated as boxes (short-term sensory store, short-term memory, working memory, long-term memory) and four memory processes indicated as arrows (attention, rehearsal, encoding, retrieval). Figure 16–2 focuses on three components that may be related to individual differences in verbal ability: the time required to search and find the name of a specific symbol in long-term memory, the amount of information that can be held in short-term memory (similar to the digit span test on the WISC-R), and the time required to make a mental comparison between two symbols held in working memory.

While this model of the memory system is superficial and possibly even incorrect (Klatzky, 1980), it can serve as a useful framework for describing individual differences. The main idea is that people may differ with respect to the characteristics of their memory stores and processes; for example, one person's retrieval time from long-term memory (LTM) may be shorter than another person's, or the capacity of one person's short-term memory may be greater than another person's. In order to test this idea, Hunt and his colleagues investigated individual differences among students' information-processing components related to verbal ability, including the three components highlighted in Figure 16–2. Let's look at each of these three components, in turn, beginning with the idea that people may differ in their speed of retrieval of information from LTM.

Measuring Cognitive Processes and Capacities

Retrieval Speed from Long-term Memory.   How can you measure the time it takes to retrieve the name of a letter from memory? Box 16–8 summarizes a letter-matching task based on the work of Posner (Posner, Boies, Eichelman & Taylor, 1969; Posner & Mitchell, 1967). A student is seated in front of a computer terminal screen, and two letters are presented. On some trials (called *physical match*), the student's job is to determine whether or not the two letters are physically identical; for example, for AA or aa or BB the student would press the "same" button but for Aa or aA or AB the student would press the "different" button. On other trials (called *name match*), the student's job is to determine whether or not the two letters have the same name; for example, the student should press the button labeled "same" for Aa or AA or bB, but should press the button labeled "different" for AB or ab or Ba.

What are the cognitive processes involved in the physical match task and the name match task? The physical match task requires three main steps: (1) get the stimuli into short-term memory, (2) make a decision, (3) execute a response. The name match task requires the same three steps, plus one more step: (1) get the stimuli into short term memory, (2) look up the name of each letter in long-term memory, (3) make a decision, and (4) execute a response. As you can see, the name match task requires one more step than the physical

---

BOX 16–8   Measurement of Decoding Time Using a Posner Task

A a

yes   no

Present letter pair.
Subject presses *yes* (same) or *no*
(different) button.

Physical match: Are these letter pairs physically identical?

AA	yes
Aa	no
aA	no
aa	yes
AB	no
Ab	no
BB	yes
bb	yes

Name match: Are these letter pairs the same letter?

AA	yes
Aa	yes
aA	yes
aa	yes
AB	no
Ab	no
BB	yes
bb	yes

From Mayer (1981)

match task that a student retrieve the names of letters from long-term memory.
Posner and his colleagues used the formula: letter retrieval time = time for a
name match − time for physical match.

   Hunt and his colleagues gave these kinds of tasks to students who scored
very high on a test of verbal ability and to students who scored very low on a
test of verbal ability. In one experiment, the difference between a name match
and physical match was 33 milliseconds for the high verbal ability students
compared to 86 milliseconds for the low verbal ability students. In another
experiment, the difference was 64 milliseconds for the high verbal ability

students and 89 milliseconds for the low verbal ability students. Apparently, the high verbal students are faster in searching long-term memory for letters. Although the high verbals are just a fraction of a second faster than low verbals (e.g., 25–50 milliseconds), these differences add up when a reader must carry out this retrieval process repeatedly in the course of reading even a short passage. It is interesting to point out that high verbals are *not* faster on all decision tests (Perfetti, 1983).

Holding Capacity of Short-term Memory. The holding capacity of short-term memory is another aspect of the memory system that might be related to verbal ability. Readers with larger storage capacities could more easily deal with long phrases or sentences, for example. Figure 16–3 summarizes a short-term memory task, adapted from the work of Peterson & Peterson (1959). The student is seated in front of a computer terminal screen and watches as four letters are presented in order. Then the student is asked to count backwards by threes from some number, in order to prevent rehearsal. Then, after a few seconds, the student is asked to recall the four letters in order.

Hunt and his colleagues gave this task to students who scored high or low in verbal ability. The results showed that high verbals performed much better than low verbals on this test of short-term memory capacity; for example, when

FIGURE 16–3 Measurement of STM Capacity Using a Peterson Task

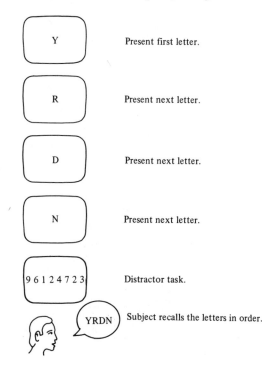

the retention interval was short, the low verbals made three times as many errors as the high verbals. Apparently, high verbals were better able to retain strings of letters in active short-term memory as compared to low verbals.

Mental Comparison Speed in Working Memory.   Finally, let's consider another aspect of the memory system that may be related to verbal ability. Reading comprehension requires that a person be able to manipulate information in working memory, such as assigning parts of speech to words being held. Figure 16–4 shows a simplified version of a mental comparison task, suggested by Sternberg (1969), in which a person must carry out a simple operation in working memory. In the task, a person is seated in front of a computer terminal screen; then a series of target letters is presented, followed by a probe letter. If the probe letter corresponds to any of the target letters, the subject is supposed to press the "yes" button; otherwise, the "no" button should be pressed.

This task requires that the subject make a series of mental comparisons (i.e., compare the probe to each of the letters being held in memory). When there is

FIGURE 16–4   Measurement of Mental Comparison Time Using a Sternberg Task

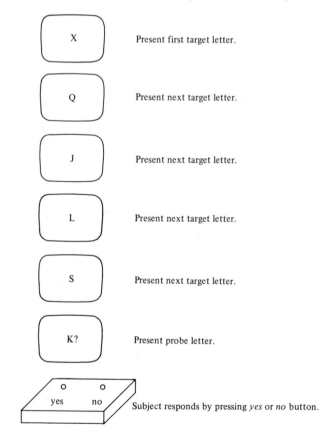

X   Present first target letter.

Q   Present next target letter.

J   Present next target letter.

L   Present next target letter.

S   Present next target letter.

K?   Present probe letter.

yes   no   Subject responds by pressing *yes* or *no* button.

just one target letter, only one comparison is needed; when there are two target letters, two comparisons are needed, and so on. The results indicated that the extra time required for each additional comparison was about 80 milliseconds for low verbals and 60 milliseconds for high verbals. Apparently, high verbals are about 20 milliseconds faster in making a simple mental comparison.

Critique of the Cognitive Approach to Testing

Hunt's work is interesting because it suggests that individual differences in ability, such as verbal ability, may ultimately be describable in terms of individual differences in the capacity and speed of a person's memory system. For example, instead of saying that John scored high in a test of reading comprehension, we may be able to say that John has a short-term memory capacity of 4.7, a retrieval rate of 55 milliseconds, and a mental comparison rate of 65 milliseconds. While this information-processing description of a student's ability may seem less glamorous than the factor names used by psychometric tests, the information-processing descriptions may be more useful. For example, if a student's short-term memory capacity is small, reading assignments can be tailored to meet this need. Unfortunately, however, cognitive psychologists have not yet devised reliable tests of higher-level cognitive strategies such as those described in Chapter 11 on reading comprehension.

UNDERSTANDING SPECIAL STUDENTS

Special Education for Special Students

Rationale for Special Education. Special students possess learner characteristics which are different from other students' learner characteristics. Because they possess special characteristics, these students may require specially designed instruction that is different from regular instruction (i.e., special education). These are the premises underlying the concept of special education for special students. The concept can be summarized by saying that exceptional students have special instructional needs.

The concept of special education has a long history. For example, as early as 1905 the French minister of public education, recognizing the limitations of a "one size fits all" approach to public education, asked Alfred Binet to design some tests for use in schools. The purpose of the tests was to locate "mentally deficient" students who might need special instruction. In essence, Binet was asked to design a test to predict who would not succeed in a regular school environment.

Public Law 94-142. More recently, new emphasis has been placed on special education through a series of U.S. federal laws enacted during the 1960s and 1970s. The most influential of these laws is Public Law 94-142, also known as the Education for All Handicapped Children Act of 1975. The law requires the following: (a) "free and appropriate education" for all special students, (b) "placement in the least restrictive environment" for all special students, (c) "access to due process," and (d) "tailoring of an Individualized Educational Program (IEP)" for each special student. According to a recent review, "the legislative process has not only been affirmative but has been almost all-inclusive in accommodating the needs of the handicapped" (Meyer & Altman, 1982, p. 1739). Similarly, the Bilingual Educational Act of 1968, also known as Title VII of the Elementary and Secondary Education Act, calls for special instruction for students whose native language is not English (Gunderson, 1982). Dejnozka & Kapel (1982) estimate that 5 million American school children speak languages other than English and that 8 million can be classified as handicapped.

Classifying Special Students

There are, of course, many ways of classifying special students, and the names of the categories seem to change every few years. However, some of the currently important categories of special students (also called *exceptional students*) include the following:

Learning Disabled (LD).   LD students have trouble in learning within a specific domain or context. The disability is related to a specific psychological process (perhaps affecting the students' learning to read or write or calculate) rather than general intellectual ability. A learning disability occurs when there is a discrepancy between a student's ability to learn and the student's demonstrated achievement within some specific domain. The typical special education for learning disabled students is intensive tutoring with specific academic goals; usually the learning disabled student remains in the regular classroom except when "pulled out" to work with a resource specialist.

Mentally Retarded (MR).   MR students have a general deficit in intellectual ability. Mental retardation can range from mildly retarded learners (e.g., sometimes called "slow learners"), who may remain in the regular classroom, to more severely retarded learners who require training in functional living skills within a residential school setting. Thus the typical special education for MR students ranges from separate classes in a day school site to a residential school devoted entirely to special education.

Emotionally Disturbed (ED).   ED students exhibit grossly inappropriate behaviors or cognitions or feelings that interfere with the instructional process. The typical special education ranges from "pull-out" meetings with a counselor to a segregated classroom.

Physically Handicapped.   This category includes hard of hearing, deaf, speech impaired, visually handicapped, blind, orthopedically impaired, and motor impaired. The typical special education formats are like those described for MR students, although the specific content differs.

Limited English Proficiency or No English Proficiency (LEP/NEP). This category includes students whose native language is not English. Bilingual education can be based on either a "transition" approach or an "immersion" approach. The transition approach involves teaching the child to read and write in his/her native language and then transferring the student gradually into English-based classes. The immersion approach involves teaching mainly in English, with special instruction in "English as a second language" (ESL).

Gifted or Talented. While not part of Public Law 94-142, this category refers to students who excel in general intellectual ability or in specific abilities (such as artistic or musical or mathematical skills). Special education for gifted and talented students ranges from pull-out programs in which students spend a few hours per week with their gifted cohorts to special "advanced" classes within a normal school to special magnet schools for gifted students.

Special education depends on adequate ways of defining special learner characteristics and of evaluating these characteristics. Unfortunately, there are serious problems both in defining and in evaluating each type of special student. In the next two sections, we explore two categories of special students in more detail: learning disabled (LD) students and mentally retarded (MR) students. First, we examine how the psychometric approach attempts to define and evaluate LD and MR students. Second, we examine how the cognitive approach offers an alternative way of defining and evaluating LD and MR students.

PSYCHOMETRIC APPROACH TO SPECIAL STUDENTS

Learning disabilities are generally identified using standardized achievement tests; mental retardation is generally identified using standardized intelligence tests. According to a psychometric approach, an LD student would score low on achievement tests for some skill but normal or near normal on intelligence tests related to that skill; in contrast, an MR student would score low on a standardized intelligence test.

Uses of Psychometric Tests for Special Students

According to the psychometric approach (as well as Public Law 94-172), tests should be used in the following ways:

a. Problem specification.   There should be a clear and concise definition of the abilities or characteristics to be identified so that appropriate tests may be selected or devised.

b. Referral.   There should be a clear and concise set of criteria used by regular classroom teachers for referring potential special students.

    c. Determination of eligibility.   A team of experts should collect reliable
       and valid data (not necessarily just test data) about the student in order to
       determine whether the student meets the criteria for special education
       placement.
    d. Special instruction.   The goals and methods of the special instructional
       program should be coordinated with the student's assessed needs.
    e. Evaluation.   The student's progress toward goals should be evaluated in
       reliable and valid ways on a regular basis in order to determine whether
       to change the child's special placement.

According to this scenario, standardized, objective, reliable, and valid
measurement is a key element at each of the five stages. However, as you will
see, there are many measurement problems at each of the stages: problem
specification, referral, determination of eligibility, special instruction, evaluation.

    Problem Specification.   Let's examine some of the problems involved in
identifying achievement and intelligence tests that correspond to specific learning disabilities. We begin with the problem of definition. Kirk (1962, p. 263)
claims to have issued the first definition of "learning disability":

> A learning disability refers to a retardation, disorder, or related development in one
> or more of the processes of speech, language, reading, spelling, writing, or arithme-
> tic resulting from possible cerebral dysfunction and/or emotional or behavioral
> disturbance and not from mental retardation, sensory deprivation, or cultural or
> instructional factors.

The following definition was developed in 1969 by the National Advisory
Committee on Handicapped Children and was eventually included in Public
Law 94-142 in 1975:

> The term "children with specific learning disabilities" means those children who
> have disorders in one or more of the basic psychological processes involved in
> understanding or in using language, spoken or written, which may manifest itself in
> imperfect ability to listen, think, speak, read, write, spell, or do mathematical
> calculations. Such disorders include such conditions as perceptual handicaps, brain
> injury, minimal brain dysfunction, dyslexia, and developmental aphasia. Such a
> term does not include children who have learning problems which are primarily the
> result of visual, hearing, or motor handicaps, of mental retardation, of emotional
> disturbance, or environmental, cultural or economic disadvantage.

Kirk & Kirk (1983) have compiled a summary of the various definitions of
learning disabilities, from which the preceding two definitions have been
taken.

    Although definitions exist, there is much confusion concerning how to
measure learning disabilities. For example, in a recent review of how experts

evaluate students for one of the most "famous" learning disabilities, dyslexia, White & Miller (1983) concluded that dyslexia remains "a term in search of a definition." White & Miller examined the measurement techniques for dyslexia reported in articles published in the *Journal of Learning Disabilities*. There was almost no agreement among the articles concerning how to define dyslexia: many used standardized reading tests such as the reading subscale of the Wide Range Achievement Test or even standardized intelligence tests such as verbal or perceptual subscales of the Wechsler Intelligence Scale for Children-Revised (WISC-R); some used more idiosyncratic measures such as "student in the low reading group" or "student receiving failing grades in reading" or "student assigned to remedial reading clinic." In summary, White & Miller reaffirmed Applebee's (1971) earlier warning that dyslexia is not a single disability caused by one factor. Rather, it seems to be an "artifact of our lack of knowledge." Every reading or perceptual problem seems to be called dyslexia because we do not yet have a good understanding of the reading process. As our understanding of reading processes increases, our definitional problems will decrease.

A recent report examined the criteria used by educational institutions to identify LD children (Mann, Davis, Boyer, Metz & Wolford, 1983). Public Law 94-142 included three criteria:

a. The LD child could not be MR (i.e., could not score more than one standard deviation below the mean in intelligence).
b. The LD child could not have any other handicap or cultural deprivation.
c. The LD child has some specific psychological processing disorder.

Mann et al. found almost none of the educational institutions they studied complied with the criteria. Instead, Mann et al. (1983, p. 16) concluded that "any consensus on the definition of LD [learning disability] if indeed one ever existed, has, of course dissipated since 1971." Apparently, learning disability was interpreted to mean "children doing poorly in school."

The definitional problems have led Ysseldyke & Algozzine (1983, p. 29) to argue that "our fishing for the definition of LD has been largely unproductive and the entire field is suffering." Their paper, amusingly entitled, "LD or not LD: That's Not the Question," points out that some students are failing in school, these students need special help, and what we call them matters little.

Referral.   If there are no clearly established criteria for defining LD and MR, how do teachers decide who to refer for potential placement in special education programs? A national survey of directors of special education found that most students are placed in special education classes based on teachers' referrals (Ysseldyke & Algozzine, 1983; Ysseldyke & Thurlow, 1984). Approximately 3 to 5% of students are referred; of these 92% are evaluated and 73% are placed in special education classes. There are problems with the validity, reliability, and objectivity of referrals.

First, Ysseldyke and his colleagues have found that teachers often do not use valid criteria for making decisions (Ysseldyke & Algozzine, 1983; Ysseldyke & Thurlow, 1984). These researchers found that teachers tend to refer students whose classroom behavior is disruptive; in many cases, low achieving students with behaviors that are acceptable to the teacher are not referred. In short, teachers may refer "students whose behaviors in the classroom bother them" with hopes that the student will be removed from the regular classroom. Students' problems are attributed to "factors within the classroom or the student's home situation" rather than any problem in the teacher's program of instruction. A survey of teachers revealed that appropriate behavior (e.g., being alert, completing tasks on time) versus inappropriate behavior (e.g., defiance, aggression, hostility) is a more important dimension than academic ability.

Second, teachers do not seem to be reliable or objective in their assessments. For example, in an observational study of teacher decision making, Borko & Cadwell (1982) concluded that teachers' referral decisions were "idiosyncratic." Apparently, a student referred by one teacher would not be referred by another. In another study of teachers' referral decisions, Gerber & Simmel (1984) found that different teachers refer at different rates; even the same teacher uses different criteria for different students. (Teacher decision making is discussed in Chapter 18.)

It is not surprising that teachers' referral decisions often lack reliability, validity, and objectivity, since teachers are not trained in assessment techniques. In essence, teachers are being asked to serve as evaluators without being given clear definitions of what or how to evaluate.

Determination of Eligibility.   Once a student is referred by a teacher, a multidisciplinary team is formed to obtain data required in order to determine the student's eligibility for special education. Ysseldyke and his colleagues (Ysseldyke & Algozzine, 1983; Ysseldyke & Thurlow, 1984) found that the majority of evaluation measures used were not technically adequate (i.e., they were either not reliable, not valid, not objective, or not standardized). In simulated decision-making studies, the multidisciplinary team was more influenced by the teacher's recommendation than by objective standardized test data (Ysseldyke & Algozzine, 1983).

Should we eliminate psychometric tests from the decision process? For example, Gerber & Semmel (1984) argue that we should view the "teacher as an imperfect test" rather than rely on "psychometry-based procedures." Gerber & Semmel seem to be arguing that the teacher is in the best position to recognize when there is a mismatch between a student's needs and the teacher's skills. In fact, Gerber & Semmel (p. 137) accuse the schools of creating learning disabilities: "it is the failure of social institutions, such as schools, to tolerate and accommodate individual differences which creates handicaps."

What's wrong with letting teacher's recommendations serve as the main vehicle for determining eligibility for special education? Unfortunately, teachers fail to meet the criteria of a good test (as described in Chapter 15). For example, Silverstein, Brownlee, Legutki & MacMillan (1983) compared the reliability over 3 years of teacher ratings of students' disabilities in reading, math, and general versus standardized test scores in these three areas. Figure 16–5 shows the correlations between the teacher rating in year 1 to year 3, as well as the correlations between standardized test scores in year 1 to year 3, for each of the three domains. As you can see, the standardized tests tend to give reliable results (i.e., a student's diagnosis is consistent from year to year). However, teachers' ratings are not reliable, indicating quite different diagnoses from year to year. Similarly, Reynolds (1984) has found that a student's race is often a major influence in eligibility decisions.

In rebuttal, Gerber & Simmel (1984) argue that teacher ratings are based on the teacher's assessment of whether the student can learn in the context of his/her classroom (i.e., the interaction between teacher and student) rather than the specific ability of the learner. In addition, with training, a teacher's referral decisions may become more reliable. However, the present data seem to suggest that a teacher's decisions alone do not yet meet the criteria of a good test. Thus something more than teacher recommendations are needed for determining the eligibility of a student for special education.

Special Instruction. Once students are determined to be eligible, they are placed in some sort of special education environment ranging from "pull-out" programs to segregated classes. Figure 16–6 shows the special education placement options as an eight-level cascade (Dejnozka & Kapel, 1982).

FIGURE 16–5 Are Teachers More Reliable Evaluators Than Standardized Tests?

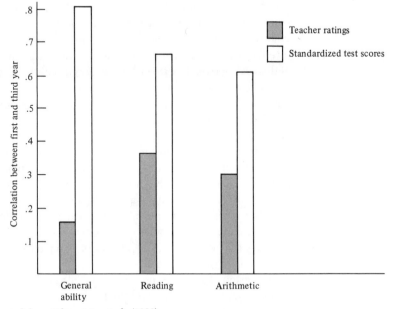

Adapted from Silverstein et al. (1983)

FIGURE 16–6   Placement Options for Special Students

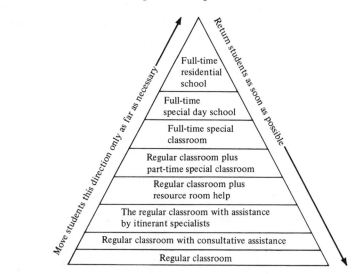

From Dejnozka & Kapel (1982)

Since federal law calls for placing students in the "least restrictive environment," there has been a keen interest in determining whether special students show more academic achievement and social/personal growth in mainstreamed environments (i.e., when placed in regular classrooms) or segregated classrooms. In a recent review of research, Carlberg & Kavale (1980) looked at fifty studies comparing the academic or social/personal growth of mainstreamed versus segregated special students. For students who scored low in general intellectual ability (called slow learners or mildly mentally retarded), academic and social/personal performance averaged about .3 standard deviations better in regular classes than in special classes. For students who were diagnosed as learning disabled or emotionally/behaviorally disturbed, academic and social/personal performance averaged about .3 standard deviations better in special classes than in regular classes. Carlberg & Kavale (1980, p. 304) conclude that there is "no justification for placing low IQ children in special classes . . . [but there is] some justification . . . for special class placement of LD and BD/ED children." Unfortunately, however, it is difficult to draw strong conclusions since many research studies are methodologically flawed. For example, the MR students assigned to special classes may be quite different from the MR students assigned to regular classrooms. Therefore, comparisons in their rate of learning are not valid. (The effects of mainstreaming on regular students are discussed in Chapter 18.)

For each student assigned to special education, an Individualized Educational Program (IEP) is developed. The IEP is supposed to specify the goals of instruction as well as ways of evaluating when the student will be ready for placement back in regular classrooms. However, teachers have much difficulty in preparing a useful IEP, often stating very broad goals such as "improve student's reading ability" or producing pages of very detailed behavioral goals (McLoughlin & Kelley, 1982; Tymitz, 1981; Ysseldyke & Thurlow, 1984). In spite of the available data about each student, special education teachers tend to make instructional decisions based on subjective impressions of the students or on the curriculum materials used (Ysseldyke & Thurlow, 1984). In summary, Ysseldyke & Thurlow (1984, p. 127) point out that "placement of a student in special education does not ensure that the student will receive instruction based on the collection of information about the student. Nor does it ensure that the student necessarily receives instruction different from that received by regular education students."

Evaluation.   Finally, special students are evaluated regularly (e.g., at least once a year) in order to determine the extent to which special placement should be changed. The annual evaluation generally involves giving the student an assessment test. However, Thurlow & Ysseldyke (1979) reviewed the assessment tests used in model LD programs and found that tests were used mainly for program evaluation rather than assessment of individual student progress. Instead, the opinions of the regular classroom teacher and the special education teacher are the main determinants of a special student's future in special education. Thus evaluation of students' progress is typically based on "subjective information about how the student is doing" rather than reliable or valid measurement data.

Critique of the Psychometric Approach to Special Students

In summary, there is a vast discrepancy between the psychometric view of how measurement should be involved in special education and how measurement is actually involved. Most decisions are based on subjective impressions rather than on measurements that are objective, reliable, and valid. Although standardized tests are administered, they do not seem to be used effectively in making decisions about school children. Standardized psychometric tests are, of course, not the only measurements that could be used. For example, Swanson (1984) argues for the use of "process assessment" (i.e., measurement of the student's specific cognitive processes, including strategies for learning). This approach is discussed in the next section.

COGNITIVE APPROACH TO SPECIAL STUDENTS

The preceding section has summarized the fact that the psychometric scenerio for special education has not often taken place in the way it was supposed to. Why has the psychometric approach failed? There are many "good" standardized achievement and ability tests (i.e., the tests are technically valid, reliable, objective, and referenced). However, the tests do not seem to be used effectively in special education. One major problem, of course, is our lack of understanding of the nature of intellectual abilities. This problem is reflected in our inability to adequately define LD or MR. In this section, we explore a cognitive approach to learning disability and mental retardation. This approach attempts to define and understand intellectual abilities rather than only to measure them.

Uses of Cognitive Tests for Special Students

According to the cognitive approach, learning disabilities and mental retardation can be understood in terms of information-processing capacities and processes. A learning disability refers to a lack of specific kinds of strategies for acquiring, storing, or using knowledge. Mental retardation refers to a developmental process in which strategies for acquiring, storing, or using knowledge develop at a slower rate and ultimately reach lower levels than for normal students. Rather than saying that a student does poorly in reading or arithmetic or some other subject, the cognitive approach focuses on the cognitive processes and capacities that underlie performance. The advantages of this approach are that it gives a clearer specification of the nature of an individual's deficits and it provides implications for instruction.

For example, Sternberg (1981) has suggested that intelligent behavior can be analyzed in terms of components of the information-processing system as described earlier in this chapter. A component is a basic cognitive process that operates on knowledge within the learner's memory system. For example, some of the best studied cognitive processes include translating sensory information into an internal representation, searching for a target in long-term memory, rehearsing information for storage into long-term memory, and organizing information in working memory. In particular, three basic kinds of information-processing components are:

> *Acquisition components*—Processes involved in learning new information.
> *Retention components*—Processes involved in remembering information that has been learned.
> *Application components*—Processes involved in applying learned information in problem-solving contexts.

In addition to these three basic components, Sternberg adds metacomponents—higher-order control strategies for selecting, combining, and monitoring the basic components.

In this section, we explore some examples of how the cognitive approach can be used to identify deficits in cognitive processing and for training in cognitive processing. (Chapter 3 also examines the development of some cognitive processing strategies in children, and Chapters 9 and 10 examine the teaching of cognitive processing strategies to students.)

Identifying Cognitive Processing Deficits in LD and MR Students

Do LD or MR children exhibit information-processing deficits that can be clearly related to the information-processing model described earlier in this chapter? Cermak (1983) has presented an interesting summary of research that assesses cognitive processes used by LD children to acquire, retain, and use verbal information.

Rehearsal Deficits.   First, let's examine a simple task to measure rehearsal processes during short-term retention of information. In a typical short-term memory experiment, three monosyllabic words are read to the child, then the child engages in some distractor task for a period of 3 or 9 or 18 seconds, and then the student is asked to recall the three words. This procedure is repeated for many different sets of three words. Several different types of distractor tasks can be used, including nonverbal tasks and semantic tasks. For example, in a nonverbal distractor task children are required to listen to recorded pairs of tones and raise their hands if the tones sounded identical, or children are required to view pairs of shapes on a screen and raise their hands if the shapes were identical. In contrast, in a semantic distractor task, children view or listen to pairs of words and raise their hands if the words belong to the same category (e.g., both are animals).

Cermak (1980) summarizes his findings by noting that LD and normal students performed at about the same level of short-term retention when there was no distractor task (i.e., students could do anything they wanted during the retention interval) or when the distractor task was very different from the material to be remembered (e.g., nonverbal tasks when the stimuli were words). However, when the distractor task was similar to the material to be remembered (e.g., semantic tasks when the stimuli were three words), the LD children performed much worse than the normal children. Apparently, the retention processes used by LD students are far more susceptible to interference than the processes used by normal children.

Encoding Deficits.   Next, Cermak (1980) investigated the idea that LD students do not process each word as deeply as normal children. He used a standard running list learning method in which children listened to a list of words presented one at a time. In one treatment group (repetition condition), the child's job was to raise his/her hand whenever the current word was the same as an earlier word; other children were asked to raise their hands whenever a word rhymed with an earlier word (rhyme condition); finally, other children were asked to raise their hands whenever a word was from the same category as an earlier word (category condition). As you can see, the repetition treatment requires only a shallow level of processing (i.e., focusing on the acoustic properties of the words); in contrast, the category treatment requires the deepest level of processing (i.e., focusing on the semantic meaning of the word). If verbal memory deficits in LD children are due mainly to failures in the semantic level of processing, then we would expect the LDs and normals to perform at about the same level on repetition questions but LDs to perform more poorly than normals on semantic questions. This prediction was confirmed for all LD students except older LD students who scored high in verbal ability.

Can LD students be encouraged to control their level of processing for words to be learned? Suppose we asked a student to listen to a list of words, answering a question for each word. The question can focus on shallow levels of processing including the physical appearance of the word, such as "Is this word written in capital letters?" Slightly more processing is required to focus on the sound of the word, such as "Does this word rhyme with *bring*?" Finally, the question can focus on deeper, semantic levels of processing, such as "Does this word fit into the sentence, "The man picked up the _____?" Cermak (1980) summarized a study in which LD and normal children learned a list of words with one of these three kinds of questions asked for each word. Figure 16–7 shows the percentage of correctly remembered words when the questions required physical processing, rhyme processing, and semantic processing. As

FIGURE 16–7   Deeper Levels of Processing of Words Lead to Better Retention for LD and Normal Children

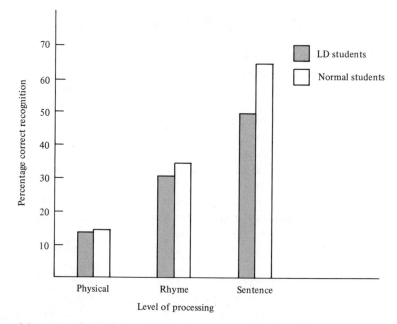

Adapted from Cermak (1983)

you can see, forcing students to use shallow levels of processing reduced LDs and normals to the same low level of retention. Forcing students to use deeper processing increased retention for both LD and normal students, although the normals still showed an advantage. These results show that LD children can exert control over their learning processes and that forcing the use of semantic processing results in substantial increases in retention. However, Cermak (1980) points out that the LD children required much more time to answer questions than normals, suggesting that their encoding processing is not yet automatic.

Retrieval Deficits. The foregoing results suggest that LD and normal students may not differ in their speed and accuracy in performing low-level cognitive tasks, but may differ for tasks requiring higher levels of processing. As described earlier in this chapter (e.g., Box 16–8), the Posner letter-matching task provides a measure of the speed of retrieval of semantic information from long-term memory. Using a revised version of this task, Cermak presented two symbols that were either both the same number or letter (such as 55 or AA), two different numbers or two different letters (such as 56 or AB), or one letter and one number (such as A5 or 6B). For "physical match" questions, the student's job is to press the "yes" button if the symbols are identical (e.g., AA or 55) and press the "no" button if the symbols are not identical (e.g., 56, AB, A5, or 6B). This task requires only low-level processing of the stimuli, including perception, decision, and response phases (as described earlier in this chapter). For "category match" questions, the student's job is to press the "yes" button if the symbols are both letters or both numbers (e.g., AA, AB, 56, or 55) and press the "no" button if the symbols are from different categories (e.g., A6, 5B). This task requires the same processes as the name match task, but also requires another process—looking up the category membership of each symbol in long-term memory.

Figure 16–8 shows the average response time to say "yes" for LD and normal students on physical and category match questions. As you can see, the LD students are only slightly slower than the normals for physical matches but much slower on the more semantically demanding category questions. The difference between time for physical match and time for category match—a rough estimate of the semantic processing time—is six times longer for LD than for normal students. Again, while LD and normal students do not seem to differ greatly in response time to questions involving a low level of perceptual processing, they do differ greatly in the time to engage in deeper, semantic processing.

Strategy Deficits. Finally, Cermak (1980) examined the strategies used by students in learning a list of twenty words. Suppose that we present a list of twenty words (including five words from each of four categories) at a slow rate of one word every 5 seconds. Further, suppose we encourage the learner to rehearse aloud during the 5 seconds after each word. A simple strategy would be to simply name the current word over and over again; a more sophisticated strategy would be to say the current word as well as some of the earlier words, and to organize the words into categories. You might recall that in Chapter 3,

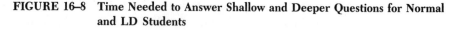

FIGURE 16–8   Time Needed to Answer Shallow and Deeper Questions for Normal
and LD Students

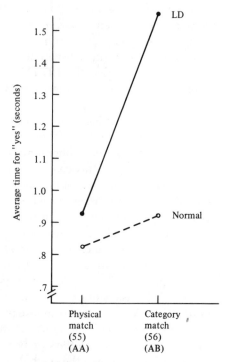

Adapted from Cermak (1983)

we found a developmental trend in which younger children used the naming
strategy while older children used more sophisticated strategies for organizing
and rehearsing a list of items. In comparing LD and normal children of various
ages, Cermak found a similar developmental trend for the normal children;
however, the older and younger LD children (ages eight to fourteen) performed like the younger normal children (ages eight to ten) by using mainly the
strategy of repeating only the presented word. The LD children rehearsed just
as much as the normals, but their rehearsal did not take advantage of the
semantic features (i.e., category organization) of the words.

In summary, Cermak's comparisons of LD and normal students on traditional information processing tasks revealed:

1. LD–normal differences on short-term retention were great for semantic
    interfering tasks but not for lower-level interfering tasks.
2. LD–normal differences in long-term retention were great for memory of
    semantic features of words but not for lower level features.
3. LD–normal differences in the speed of processing were great for seman-

tic processes such as finding the name or category of a symbol in long-term memory but not for lower-level processes such as matching and responding.

4. LD–normal differences in strategies for free recall list learning were great for qualitative aspects of rehearsal (such as using a simple naming strategy versus a more sophisticated strategy) but not for quantitative aspects of rehearsal (such as how many times each word was repeated by the learner).

In addition, Cermak's research provides some indication that LD students can be encouraged to engage in deeper levels of processing—such as answering semantic questions—and that deeper processing leads to better retention. This brief look has suggested that it might be profitable to describe students' learning disabilities in terms of specific kinds of processing deficits—such as lack of automatic and effective semantic processing. The next section examines attempts to take this approach one step further by providing specific process training for LD and MR students.

Training Cognitive Processes in LD and MR Students

Rehearsal Strategies. Once tests have identified an information-processing deficit in a student, the next step might be to develop a program of training to help the student overcome the deficit. For example, Belmont & Butterfield (1971) assessed learning strategies in mildly mentally retarded teenagers, and then provided training in learning strategies. To assess learning strategies, Belmont & Butterfield asked students to use a panel such as shown in Figure 16–9. Along the bottom was a row of translucent screens; when the student pressed a button, a projector from behind the panel caused a letter to appear in the first screen for $\frac{1}{2}$ second. Then, when the student pressed the button, a letter appeared in the next screen for $\frac{1}{2}$ second, and so on. After seeing six letters, at a rate that the student controlled, the student saw a probe letter in the top screen. The student's job was to touch the screen corresponding to where the probe letter had appeared in the original sequence of six letters. Both mildly MR and normal teenagers engaged in this task for eighteen different trials, with a different sequence of six letters on each trial.

The results of this assessment revealed quite different learning strategies for MR and normal students. As discussed in Chapter 3 and in the preceding section, a sophisticated learning strategy for list learning is to rehearse all or part of the list each time a new item is added. If a student were using this learning strategy in Belmont & Butterfield's assessment, then the pause time should increase as the length of the list grows from one to six. For example, when the first letter is presented, the student may press the button to see what's next fairly rapidly, but when the fifth or sixth letter is presented more time is needed to rehearse the earlier items in the list. The top of Figure 16–10 shows that normal students seem to have used this sophisticated learning

FIGURE 16–9   A Serial Learning Task

strategy because their pause time increases for each added item to the list. However, the MR students show the reverse trend—spending less time as the list gets longer. Apparently, the normal students spend time rehearsing the earlier items when the items are no longer present and thus encode these items into long-term memory; in contrast, the MR students do not rehearse the earlier items when the items are no longer present and thus fail to encode many of these items into long-term memory. If this hypothesis is correct, then we could predict that the normal students would recall the earlier items on the list better than the MR students, but that there would be no differences for the last one or two items. As you can see in the bottom of Figure 16–10, our prediction is upheld. From this assessment, Belmont & Butterfield concluded that MR students may not be effectively rehearsing the list during the pauses.

To provide learning strategy training, Belmont & Butterfield asked students to participate in eighteen more trials. The trained students were asked to simply say the letter and then press the button to go on to the next letter for letters 1, 2, 3, 5, and 6; however, on letter 4, the students were supposed to say the four letters aloud as a sequence three times. This could be called an active strategy because the student must actively rehearse the list (after the fourth letter is presented). In contrast, other students were asked to simply name each letter and then immediately press the button for the next letter. This could be called a passive strategy, because students were prevented from actively

FIGURE 16–10   Assessment of Learning Strategies for Serial Learning in Normal and Mentally Retarded Students

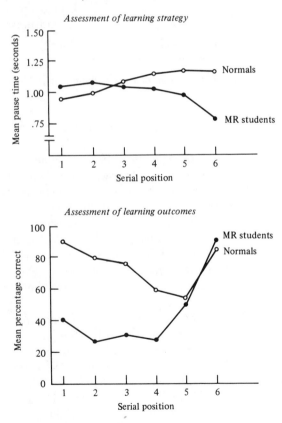

Adapted from Belmont & Butterfield (1971)

BOX 16–9   An Active and Passive Strategy for Learning a Short List

Active Strategy

The screen shows:	The student says:
A _ _ _ _ _	A (and press button)
_ H _ _ _ _	H (and press button)
_ _ P _ _ _	P (and press button)
_ _ _ L _ _	AHPL, AHPL, AHPL (and press button)
_ _ _ _ E _	E (and press button)
_ _ _ _ _ X	X (and press button)

Passive Strategy

The screen shows:	The student says:
A _ _ _ _ _	A (and press button)
_ H _ _ _ _	H (and press button)
_ _ P _ _ _	P (and press button)
_ _ _ L _ _	L (and press button)
_ _ _ _ E _	E (and press button)
_ _ _ _ _ X	X (and press button)

Adapted from Belmont & Butterfield (1971)

rehearsing the list. The active and passive strategies are summarized in Box 16–9.

   Could MR students learn to use the active strategy? The top of Figure 16–11 shows the average pause time for MR and normal students under the active and passive strategies. As you can see, for the passive strategy, the pause time is about the same for each letter in the sequence, for both MRs and normals. This suggests that we can encourage the normals to use a strategy like that used spontaneously by the MR students. As you can also see, for the active strategy, both normals and MR students show a large increase in pause time on the fourth letter in the sequence. This suggests that the MR students can be encouraged to behave more like the normals (i.e., to spend time rehearsing earlier items in the list).

   Since the active strategy encourages MR students to actively rehearse earlier items in the list but the passive strategy does not, we can predict that the active strategy will increase recall of the earlier items in the list as compared to the passive strategy. The bottom of Figure 16–11 shows the percentage recalled by serial position for MR students and normal students using the active and passive strategies. As can be seen, the MR students show the predicted pattern, in which recall of earlier items is greatly enhanced by active rehearsal.

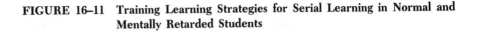

FIGURE 16–11   Training Learning Strategies for Serial Learning in Normal and Mentally Retarded Students

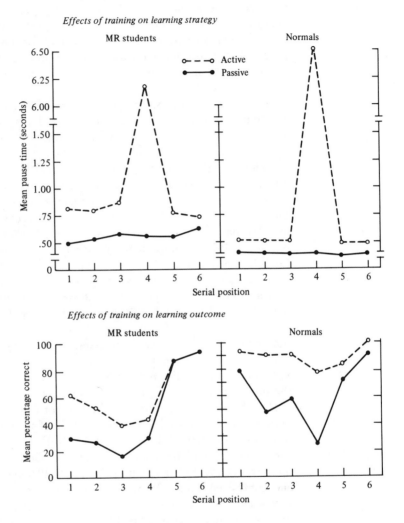

Effects of training on learning strategy

Adapted from Belmont & Butterfield (1971)

Since the passive strategy encourages normal students not to actively rehearse earlier items in the list, we can predict that the passive strategy will decrease recall of earlier items in the list as compared to the active strategy. The bottom right-hand panel of Figure 16–11 shows the predicted pattern, although it should be noted that the normals using the active strategy scored at almost 100% for each item.

These results seem to show that MR students can be taught to use learning strategies that make them perform more like normals. Although the task used by Belmont & Butterfield is a very simple one (i.e., learning a list of six letters), the results are encouraging. These results suggest that assessment of learning handicaps (such as mental retardation and learning disabilities) can be made in terms of information-processing deficits and that an instructional program can be developed to train needed learning strategies. This study holds out hope that deficits in information-processing strategies can be detected and, to some extent, remediated.

Learning Strategies.   Let's consider another example of the assessment and training of learning strategies in MR students (Brown & Campione, 1977). The subjects were mildly mentally retarded children selected from the top special education classes in an elementary school. To assess their learning strategies, students were given a set of twelve pictures of common objects, asked to name each picture, and then given 60 seconds to study the pictures. Then subjects were asked to recall as many of the names as possible. Following the recall test, subjects were allowed to select six of the twelve pictures to study for 60 seconds. This was repeated four times. Earlier work by Masur, McIntyre & Flavell (1973) found that the most efficient strategy is to select the missed items for further study. However, an analysis of the performance of mildly MR students indicated that this strategy was not widely used.

Can students be taught to use the strategy of studying the items that they missed? In order to study this question, Brown & Campione (1977) gave some of the students practice in using the "missed-item" learning strategy. The training trials were similar to the assessment trials (i.e., the student was given twelve pictures to remember and had to select six to study after each recall test). For the trained group, after each recall attempt, the student was given the missed items (up to a total of six items) for further study. For the control group, after each recall attempt, the student was given a random collection of both correct and missed items (up to a total of six items) for further study. This procedure was repeated for several lists so that students could get practice in using the "trained" or "control" strategy. Following training, another assessment was conducted. The left of Figure 16–12 shows the proportion of trained and control children who were classified as using the missed-item strategy before and after training. As you can see, the training greatly increased the number of students using the effective strategy, but the control students show no improvement. The right of Figure 16–12 shows the recall scores before and after training for the two training groups. As you can see, the strategy training seems to have greatly increased the recall performance of the trained group as compared to the control group. However, it should be pointed out that this missed-item strategy was not effective for lower-level MR students, although a simpler strategy was effective. These results again show that information-processing deficits can be assessed and remediated, but that students must be taught strategies that are appropriate for their level of cognitive functioning.

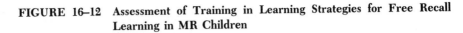

FIGURE 16–12   Assessment of Training in Learning Strategies for Free Recall
Learning in MR Children

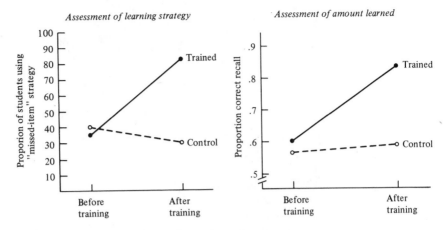

Adapted from Brown & Campione (1977)

Critique of the Cognitive Approach to Special Students

In summary, we have seen examples of how cognitive deficits can be assessed and remediated. Research on the cognitive analysis of learning strategies is just beginning, but already there is some promise. As additional work investigates the teachable aspects of information processing, we will have a clearer picture of how to assess and instruct students who have special learning needs.

CONCLUSION

Each student enters the classroom with a unique set of entering characteristics, including prior knowledge based on earlier learning as well as intellectual and personal/social attributes. This chapter has introduced standardized tests as devices for measuring the entering characteristics of learners.

First, we examined the features of standardized tests—including factors, raw scores, percentiles, confidence intervals, stanines, grade equivalents, frequency distributions, medians, means, and standard deviations. All standardized tests are based on "norm-referenced" measurements, in which a student's score is compared to the scores of other similar students.

Second, we examined the use of standardized ability and achievement tests in schools. According to a psychometric approach, tests can be used to evaluate individual differences in specific or general factors. According to a cognitive approach, tests can be used to evaluate individual differences in how people process information, including differences in specific processes or memory capacities. One of the major strengths of the psychometric approach is its high level of technical sophistication (i.e., the psychometric approach tells us *how* to measure). One of the major strengths of the cognitive approach is its high level of theoretical sophistication (i.e., the cognitive approach tells us *what* to measure). Of course, what is needed is an integration of the technical contribution of the psychometric approach with the theoretical contribution of the cognitive approach.

Third, we examined the use of standardized tests in special education. After defining some of the key terms—such as learning disability, mental retardation, emotionally disturbed, physically handicapped, limited English proficiency, gifted and talented—we explored the psychometric and cognitive approaches. The psychometric approach calls for the use of tests in each of five phases of special education: disability specification, referral, determination of eligibility, special instruction, and evaluation of student progress. The cognitive approach calls for the identification of deficits in specific learning strategies and for training in these needed learning strategies. A major problem with the psychometric approach is the lack of clear criteria for how to use standardized tests in teacher decision making. A major problem with the cognitive approach is the lack of proven track record, owing to the newness of the approach. A useful future trend would be to define, measure, and teach specific learning or memory processes.

SUGGESTED READINGS

Resnick, L. B. (1976). *The nature of intelligence*. Hillsdale, N.J.: Erlbaum. (Contains many useful papers describing how cognitive psychologists study individual differences.)

Sternberg, R. J. (1977). *Intelligence, information processing, and analogical reasoning*. Hillsdale, N.J.: Erlbaum. (Provides a history of psychometric work on intelligence as well as an extensive study using the cognitive approach to intelligence.)

Sternberg, R. J. (1985). *Human abilities: An information processing approach*. New York: Freeman. (Chapters by leading cognitive psychologists concerned with how to understand various kinds of human abilities.)

17 *Individual Differences*

This chapter explores the idea that students may differ in the ways that they learn. In particular, five kinds of learner characteristics are examined: the student's general learning ability, the student's existing knowledge, the student's motivation to learn, the student's demographic characteristics (such as gender), and the student's cognitive style. Each section also discusses the instructional implications of individual differences.

ARE THERE TWO KINDS OF PEOPLE?

In a moment, you will answer some questions. Please find a friend who is willing to read two questions to you and who will observe your eyes as you answer. OK, have your friend read the following questions to you:

1. Which way does George Washington face on a one-dollar bill?
2. What does it mean to say, "Haste makes waste"?

The scoring key is as follows. For question 1, did the answerer's eyes initially gaze more to the left or to the right? For question 2, did the answerer's eyes initially gaze more to the right or to the left?

These items are similar to those in a larger test used by Kinsbourne (1972) and by Kocel, Galin, Ornstein & Merrin (1974). These items are used to measure "laterality of gaze"—the direction in which your eyes move when you answer a question. According to Kinsbourne (1972), the direction of the gaze can indicate which side of your brain you are using to answer the question. A gaze to the right indicates that you are using the left side of your brain, an area that might be specialized for verbal thinking and learning; a gaze to the left indicates that you are using the right side of your brain, an area that might be specialized for spatial thinking and learning. However, for some subjects, such as most left-handed subjects, the brain functions are specialized in the reverse order, with left for spatial and right for verbal (Wittrock, 1980).

In the example, according to Kinsbourne's theory, you would be more likely to gaze to the left for the George Washington question since it requires spatial (right-brain) processing, and you would be more likely to gaze right for the proverb question since it requires verbal (left-brain) processing. In addition, there are individual differences among people, with some preferring to gaze right (or left) regardless of the type of question (Bakan, 1969). If you gazed right on both questions, you could be classified as left-brained; if you gazed left on both questions, you could be classified as right-brained.

The media have popularized the distinction between two types of people: left-brained and right-brained. Similarly, the educational community has been presented with the proposition that left-brained people learn best from verbal-based instruction while right-brained people learn best from visual-based instruction. This proposition is summarized in Figure 17–1 as an attribute treatment interaction (ATI). As you can see, the x axis gives some measure of individual differences (such as left- versus right-brained-ness) and the y axis gives some measure of success in schooling (such as how much is learned from a given set of lessons). The two lines correspond to two different methods of instruction or treatments (such as treatment 1 being a visually-based in-

FIGURE 17–1   An Attribute Treatment Interaction

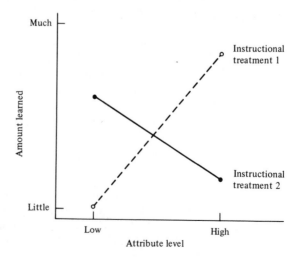

structional program versus treatment 2 being a verbally-based instructional program).

Should you be critical of the foregoing example about brain lateralization? Yes! This example contains several of the classic problems in interpreting attribute treatment interactions. Let's examine three such problems: measurement, reliability, and validity.

First, you could question the eye gaze measure. Does it really tell us about individual differences in people's tendency to favor spatial or verbal types of processing? One serious problem with the measure is that the gaze can be influenced by whether the questioner stands in front rather than behind the answerer, or whether the questions are easy rather than difficult. Events that seem to increase the anxiety of the subject tend to ruin the usefulness of the measure (Ehrlichman, Weiner & Baker, 1974; Gur, Gur & Harris, 1975). Since seemingly minor variations in the testing situation can elicit very different responses, the eye gaze measure seems to be a problematic one. In short, under sloppy "real-world" testing conditions, we cannot be sure that eye gaze is really measuring a person's preference for verbal versus visual kinds of processing.

Second, even if we could find a foolproof method for classifying people into visual versus verbal processors, there might not be consistent evidence of ATIs. For example, we might sometimes obtain ATIs like the one shown in Figure 17–1, sometimes obtain the reverse pattern, and sometimes get no interaction at all. Since the evidence for ATIs involving the left-brain/right-brain distinction is not consistent, we would not want to apply the results to the classroom.

Third, even if we could accurately measure brain hemispheric dominance and even if we obtain consistent ATIs, we would still have a problem in understanding what the ATIs mean. The distinction between left-brain and right-brain dominance is a dubious one, since both sides of the brain are involved in cognitive functioning. The sides of the brain are not separate entities without connections to one another. Thus there is insufficient physiological basis for dividing people into two groups—right- versus left-brained. More recently, cognitive psychologists have attempted to analyze the processes and skills involved in learning and remembering. A more valid approach to the verbal/visual distinction might be to examine individual differences in these "cognitive components," as described in the previous chapter. Similarly, it is extremely naive to think that there are two kinds of people, unless your distinction is between people who think there are two kinds of people and people who don't. In fact, there are many dimensions upon which people may differ and by focusing on just one dimension we miss the multivariate nature of real classroom learning. Thus it is not enough to obtain ATIs; we must also be able to understand them within the context of a theory of human learning and memory.

Finally, even if the eye-gaze research allowed for perfect measurement, consistency of ATI results, and validity of concepts, we would not be finished. The instructional implications of ATIs are far from clear. A straightforward response might be to give different methods of instruction to students with differing attributes. An alternative is to provide the weaker students with appropriate prerequisite experiences and then give all learners the same method of instruction. Thus two ways of individualizing instruction involve, respectively, varying the quality of the instructional method or varying the amount of pretraining.

The present chapter explores five kinds of individual differences and their relation to instruction: general ability to learn, domain-specific knowledge, motivation to learn, demographic characteristics such as gender, and cognitive style. Further, this chapter explores whether each of these kinds of differences is related to school performance, whether each interacts with instructional method, and what the implications are for instruction.

GENERAL ABILITY TO LEARN

We begin with a simple fact: students differ in their ability to learn from instruction. In a recent review of research on individual differences, Snow & Lohman (1984, p. 347) recognized general ability to learn as the best understood individual differences variable: "The existence of individual differences in cognitive aptitude for learning from instruction is the most longstanding, well-established fact in educational psychology." For purposes of their review, general cognitive ability was evaluated using a variety of tests, including IQ and achievement tests, as described in Chapter 16. This section explores some of the best established points concerning the relationship between a student's general cognitive ability and school learning.

Overall Relation between Cognitive Ability and Amount Learned

Snow & Lohman (1984, p. 354) note that "the first fact about cognitive aptitude for learning is that measures [of general cognitive ability] virtually always predict [cognitive learning] in . . . conventional instructional treatments." This relationship has been consistently found over the course of this century in all academic subjects and educational levels. For example, the correlation between measures of general cognitive ability and amount learned is most commonly between .6 and .7 for elementary school, .5 to .6 for high school, and .4 to .5 for college (Jensen, 1980).

It should be pointed out, however, that not all cognitive ability tests are equally predictive of academic success for all kinds of students. For example, using a form of test that is for much older or much younger students may result in nonpredictive measures of academic performance. Also, some general cognitive abilities tests may not be predictive for certain minority groups. As pointed out in the previous chapters, a test should be proven to be valid before it is used. Also, you should note that even in the best possible circumstances, general ability is only partially related to school success.

Attribute × *Treatment Interactions*

A second key finding is that the relationship between cognitive ability and amount learned is stronger for instruction that demands complex cognitive information processing on the part of learners than for less demanding instruction. Another way to state this pattern is to say that the effects of cognitive ability can be reduced by using instructional methods that minimize the demands on learners' active information processing.

Guided Versus Conventional Methods. For example, Figure 17–2 gives the results of a study involving conventional instruction and individually prescribed instruction (IPI) for reading comprehension in the fifth grade (Sharps, 1974; reported in Snow & Lohman, 1984). The conventional instruction is more cognitively demanding because it requires students' monitoring and guiding their own learning. The *x* axis gives the level of cognitive ability as measured by a standardized test, and the *y* axis gives the level of performance on tests of reading comprehension. As you can see, there is the predicted pattern of ATI, with low ability students doing better under IPI and high ability students doing better under conventional instruction. Similar results are reported in Chapter 6, in which making prose more coherent (e.g., through adding advance organizers) helps low ability students but not high ability students (Mayer, 1975).

FIGURE 17–2 Interaction between General Cognitive Ability and Method of Instruction

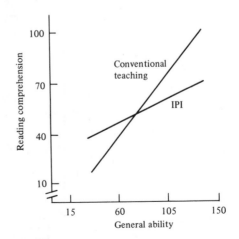

Adapted from Snow and Lohman (1984)

Direct Training in Skills Versus Conventional Methods.   A related ATI concerns the finding that training in learning strategies seems to help low ability students more than high ability students. Another way to express this finding is to say that the effects of ability are weakened when students are given direct training in relevant learning strategies. For example, Figure 17–3 summarizes a study in which high and low ability students were taught a networking strategy for transforming text into a coherent outline (as described in Chapter 8). The *x* axis gives the students' academic ability as measured by grade point average (GPA) while the *y* axis gives the students' performance on a reading retention test (Dansereau et al., 1979). As you can see, the low ability students perform better when given pretraining in networking, while high ability students do better without the pretraining. Apparently, high ability learners already possessed effective learning strategies and the externally imposed networking strategy may have interfered; in contrast, low ability learners presumably lacked appropriate learning strategies, so the pretraining provided them with techniques that they would not have normally used.

Implications for Instruction

There are many examples of ATIs similar to those just given. The main theme in these ATIs is that cognitive abilities tend to predict learning in conventional instructional situations—where the learner is responsible for maintaining a high level of active information processing. The positive relationship between ability and learning can be reduced or even reversed by instructional treat-

FIGURE 17–3   Interaction between General Cognitive Ability and Strategy Training Treatment

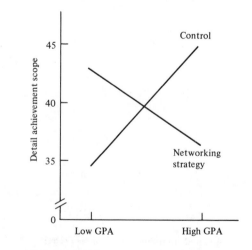

Adapted from Snow and Lohman (1984)

ments that reduce the demands on the information processing system—by not requiring students to monitor their own learning (as in IPI) or by direct instruction in prerequisite skills and strategies. Providing these "improvements" to high ability students can interfere with the idiosyncratic information-processing strategies already well established in the student. Apparently, for high ability students an intellectually demanding environment results in better learning; in contrast, low ability students excel in a less demanding, more controlled environment with more direct instruction.

One interpretation of these results suggests providing different kinds of instruction to different ability groups. Snow & Lohman (1984, p. 372–3) make the following suggestion, based on their review of existing ATI research:

> For lower [ability] learners, the instructional treatment should be made more explicit, direct, and structured . . . it should provide guided . . . learning.

Thus direct, guided instruction is recommended for lower ability learners.

Another interpretation of these results suggests providing appropriate pretraining to low ability learners. Snow & Lohman (1984, p. 373) summarize this point as follows:

> Direct training for low [ability] learners . . . should aim at the development of specified learning strategies and skills and their flexible adaptation to real learning programs.

The teaching of learning and thinking strategies is the main theme of Chapters 8 and 9. Also, the next section of this chapter explores the idea that some differences in aptitude for learning may be caused by differences in teachable aspects of the learners' prerequisite knowledge; thus, instead of using different instructional methods for low and high aptitude students, we can provide pretraining that equips low aptitude students with the prerequisite knowledge they need to benefit from meaningful instruction.

A related implication of the foregoing two points is that low ability learners may become high ability learners by acquiring expertise in relevant skills, strategy, and knowledge. Instructional programs should involve frequent testing so that students may appropriately be moved from structured, direct instruction to less structured instruction. Snow & Lohman (1984, p. 373) summarize this recommendation as follows:

> A measurement system is needed to accompany the instructional and training treatments that would monitor progress in each treatment . . . [and] indicate when any given lower [ability] learner might be shifted from relatively complete structured instruction to relatively incomplete, unstructured instruction or when direct training might be discontinued for that person.

Thus it is important to be sensitive to changes in the general cognitive ability of the learner.

DOMAIN-SPECIFIC KNOWLEDGE

Learners also differ with respect to the specific knowledge they bring to the learning task. There may not be a firm dividing line between general ability to learn (as examined in the previous section) and domain-specific knowledge (as examined in this section). However, domain-specific knowledge refers to knowledge that is specifically related to the material to be learned and (presumably) is teachable.

Overall Relation between Specific Knowledge and Amount Learned

One of the most common findings in the individual differences literature is that past achievement in a particular subject matter domain is a very strong predictor of future achievement in that subject matter domain (Cronbach & Snow, 1977). Apparently, success in learning new material can be predicted somewhat by a student's past success in learning related kinds of school material. This pattern was suggested in Chapter 11, which examined the effects of prior knowledge on readers' comprehension of text. A key finding is that students who possess appropriate prerequisite knowledge learn more from an ambiguous or difficult passage than students who lack specific prerequisite knowledge. For example, knowing the rules of baseball increases one's comprehension and retention of material from a passage about a baseball game (Chiesi, Spilich & Voss, 1979).

Attribute × Treatment Interactions

In this section we examine a related prediction concerning the relationship between instructional methods and students' existing domain-specific knowledge: Instructional methods that require active integration of new and old information by the learner (such as the discovery and inductive methods described in Chapter 7) will be more successful for learners who possess relevant prerequisite knowledge than for students who do not; instructional methods that do not require active integration of knowledge by the learner (such as direct instruction in the rules to be learned) will not be strongly affected by the prior knowledge of the learner.

Rule Versus Active Methods. In order to test this prediction, Mayer, Stiehl & Greeno (1975) asked college students to learn the concept of binomial probability from a programmed text. Some students studied from a deductive (or rule-based) text that began with the formula and gave practice in how to use the formula; other students were given an inductive text that began with familiar situations and tried to build up to the rule slowly. Both texts presented the same basic information and example problems; only the sequencing and emphasis differed. Before reading the text, students were given pretests that measured students' familiarity with and intuitions about the concept of probability (i.e., with information that was specifically relevant to the material in the text) and general mathematical aptitude (i.e., SAT—Mathematics). None of the students had any knowledge of the binomial probability concept to be taught.

Figure 17–4 shows the proportion correct on a post-test of solving binomial probability problems for students who scored low, medium, and high in specif-

FIGURE 17–4 Interaction between Specific (or General) Knowledge and Inductive Versus Deductive Methods of Instruction

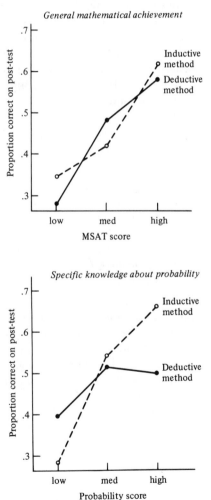

Adapted from Mayer, Sthiel & Greeno (1975)

ic knowledge about probability, and for students who scored low, medium, and high in general mathematical achievement. As you can see, general mathematical competence is related to performance under both methods of instruction. This is not surprising, of course, since general measures—by definition—are supposed to predict success under a wide variety of instructional methods. However, there is an interesting pattern of attribute × treatment interaction (ATI) for measures of specific knowledge about probability. As you can see, specific knowledge of probability is not strongly related to performance under the deductive method, but is strongly related to performance under the inductive method.

Mastery Versus Conventional Methods. Stinard & Dolphin (1981) examined the role of students' prior domain-specific knowledge and general achievement within the context of a college course on anatomy and physiology. Some students took the course in its traditional format while others took a self-paced mastery version of the course. The self-paced mastery format provided a structure that allowed students to assess their learning through mastery tests, to devote additional study to areas that gave them trouble in the tests, and to retake the tests after appropriate study. The traditional format was less structured, and thus required that students actively monitor their studying on their own.

The main results of the study were similar to those obtained by Mayer, Stiehl, & Greeno (1975) in the aforementioned studies:

1. General school achievement, as measured by standardized achievement tests, was positively related to student's final exam grade for both traditional and mastery methods. There was no ATI for general achievement and method of instruction.
2. Domain-specific knowledge, as measured by the number of previous science courses taken, was much more strongly related to performance when the traditional method rather than the mastery method was used.

This ATI produced a pattern in which students with little previous experience performed better under mastery than under the traditional method, but students with more experience performed better under the traditional method than mastery. For the mastery group, there was almost no correlation between prior knowledge of science and final exam score ($r = .08$); for the traditional group, there was a strong correlation between prior knowledge and final course grade ($r = .44$).

Implications for Instruction

The foregoing studies provide some exemplary support for our predictions concerning interactions between specific knowledge and method of instruction.

In particular, the results suggest that using active teaching methods such as discovery and induction on students who lack appropriate specific knowledge will not result in discovery or inductive learning and may result in no learning at all. Similarly, methods that require much self-study and self-assessment (e.g., in traditional college classrooms) seem to be strongly dependent on students having rich prior experience in similar courses. Does this mean that we should use rule (or mastery) methods for students who lack prerequisite concepts and discovery (or unstructured) methods for students who possess prerequisite concepts? Mayer, Stiehl & Greeno (1975, p. 350) argue that a better recommendation might be to provide appropriate pretraining to students who lack prerequisite concepts:

> On the basis of the ATI results . . . it could be argued that students with low aptitudes should be given instruction emphasizing algorithmic computation, since overall test scores will probably be higher if that is done. However, the fact that relevant aptitudes appear to involve relatively specific knowledge and skills argues that subjects lacking the necessary background can probably be provided with that background and then given instruction that leads to understanding as well as skillful performance. The desirability of this policy seems indicated by considering the consequences of algorithmic emphasis for later learning. If students are taught by a method that leaves minimal understanding of what they have learned, then their conceptual preparation for later learning will be more deficient that it was previously.

Thus ATIs do not always imply that different kinds of students should be given different kinds of instructional methods.

In summary, there is some evidence of an overall effect due to prior knowledge (i.e., more is learned by students who possess more relevant domain-specific knowledge) and of an attribute × treatment interaction (ATI) (i.e., the effect of prior knowledge is stronger for methods of instruction involving active participation than for more structured methods). Although the foregoing results suggest that some individual differences may be reduced through extensive pretraining or highly structured instructional methods, far more research is needed in order to clarify this distinction between domain-specific knowledge and general ability to learn.

MOTIVATION TO LEARN

A student's classroom performance may also be affected by personality or motivational variables. For example, some of the most potentially important personality variables involve the learner's motivation for schooling. Cronbach & Snow (1977) have distinguished between two kinds of motivational variables: "defensive motivation" refers to the learner's level of anxiety as reflected in the learner's sensitivity to threats; "constructive motivation" refers to the learner's desire to seek success as reflected in the learner's response to academically demanding tasks. In this section, we briefly explore "anxiety" as an example of defensive motivation and "achievement motivation" as an example of constructive motivation.

Anxiety

What Is Anxiety? An anxious person is someone who is prone to nervous states, who expects to fail, who sees the world as threatening, and who lacks confidence in his own abilities. Many tests have been developed to measure anxiety-related factors, including the Taylor Manifest Anxiety Scale (Taylor, 1953) and the Spielberger State-Trait Anxiety Scale (Spielberger, Gorsuch & Lushene, 1970). Many theorists (Spielberger, 1966; Spielberger, 1972; Lamb, 1978) make a distinction between measuring a person's current level of anxiety—called "state anxiety"—and a person's general level of anxiety—called "trait anxiety." For example, an item from a state anxiety questionnaire could be: "I am tense." An item from trait anxiety questionnaire could be: "I feel disappointments so keenly that I can't put them out of my mind." The subject must respond by circling: 1—almost never, 2—sometimes, 3—often, or 4—almost always.

Spielberger (1972) and Sarason (1960) characterize a highly anxious person (i.e., trait anxiety) as someone who responds to a stressful situation with high amounts of state anxiety; in contrast, a low anxiety person responds to stress without high amounts of state anxiety. Stressful situations threaten a

---

BOX 17–1   Two Students Who Differ in Anxiety

Susan
Susan never raises her hand in response to a teacher's question because she fears that she will "make a fool of herself." She gets terribly tense whenever the teacher calls on her. She does her homework, but thinks that she hasn't done what the teacher wanted her to do. She calls herself a "nerd" and avoids facing any difficult problems or crises.

Linda
Linda likes to participate in class discussions because it gives her a chance to show that she "knows her stuff." She generally thinks she will do well on any questions the teacher asks her. She does her homework, but likes to add additional answers that go beyond the assignment. When a problem or crisis confronts her, she likes to attack it head-on.

person's self-esteem and include the possibility of failure. Sarason (1960, p. 402) describes the high anxiety person as "more self-depreciating, more self-preoccupied, and generally less content." Spielberger (1972) describes the high anxiety person as someone who is "more self-depreciatory . . . fearing failure . . . and will manifest higher levels of A-state [state anxiety] in situations that involve psychological threats to self-esteem."

For example, consider the descriptions of two students shown in Box 17–1. Susan fits the pattern of a high anxious person—fearing failure, depreciating herself, responding to stress in inefficient ways. In contrast, Linda fits the pattern of a low anxious person—showing the opposite traits. An important educational question concerns how a person's anxiety level influences their performance in school learning tasks.

Anxiety and Learning.   What is the relationship between anxiety and performance? Figure 17–5 shows the inverted U-shaped relationship that was originally known as the Yerkes–Dodson law (Yerkes & Dodson, 1908; Spence & Spence, 1966). As you can see, for low levels of arousal, performance is poor—presumably because the learner is not sufficiently motivated. For high arousal, performance is poor—presumably because the learner is too motivated to perform adequately. However, at intermediate levels of arousal, the learner performs best. The problem, of course, is that finding the "intermediate level of arousal" is a difficult task because each student may respond to stress differently.

Based on the Yerkes–Dodson law, we can make the following prediction concerning ATIs. First, for highly anxious students, stressful instructional or

FIGURE 17–5   The Proposed Relationship between Arousal and Performance

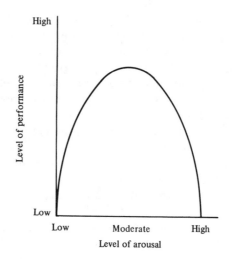

testing conditions should reduce performance; this is so because high anxiety students may begin a school task already with a moderate-to-high level of arousal so the stressful situation pushes them to the extreme right end of the curve. In contrast, for low anxious students, stressful instructional or testing conditions could enhance performance; this is so because low anxiety students begin at the extreme left end of the curve—with a low level of arousal—so the stress helps to push them rightward into the middle range of the curve.

In order to test this prediction, let's examine an exemplary research study by Gross & Mastenbrook (1980). College students took an anxiety questionnaire ("trait-anxiety"); based on their responses, students were classified as high or low in anxiety. Then, students were asked to engage in a concept learning task. Students were presented with cards that had geometric objects varying in shape (circle or square), size (large or small), color (red or blue), and pattern (striped or dotted). The experimenter presented the cards one at a time; for each card, the student was asked to guess whether it belonged to the target category or not, and then the experimenter told the correct answer. For example, a rule might be, "Blue is yes; red is no." Students engaged in the concept learning task under one of two learning conditions. Some students (memory aid group) were given eight cards corresponding to each of possible values of each dimension used—circle, square, large, small, red, blue, striped, dotted. Subjects were trained on how to use these cards to help focus on the correct answer. For example, if the first card showed a large dotted red circle and this was a "no," then the learner could take away the cards for large, red, dotted, and circle. Other students did not receive the memory aid (no memory aid group).

Let's try to arrange the four groups—high anxiety/memory aid, high anxiety/no memory aid, low anxiety/memory aid, low anxiety/no memory aid—on the basis of amount of arousal or motivation. Let's assume that the no memory aid treatment is more stressful than the memory aid condition. Thus the least aroused group is the low anxiety/memory aid condition. Based on the U-shaped Yerkes–Dodson curve, we might expect these subjects to perform poorly because they are undermotivated. The most aroused group is the high anxiety/no memory aid condition. We might expect these subjects to perform poorly because they are overmotivated. In between these two extremes are the low anxiety/no memory aid group and the high anxiety/memory aid group. These groups might perform relatively better than the others because they involve intermediate levels of arousal or motivation (i.e., they are in the middle of the inverted U-shaped curve).

Figure 17–6 shows the performance of the four groups on the number of problems correctly solved and on the percentage of subjects using an efficient strategy in learning. As you can see, there is a strong evidence of an interaction between anxiety and learning treatment: for low anxiety subjects, performance is better with a more demanding learning situation (no memory aid); for high anxiety subjects, performance is better with a less demanding learning situation (memory aid). Figure 17–7 shows the same data plotted in a different way: the

FIGURE 17–6   Interaction between Anxiety and Difficulty of Learning Situation

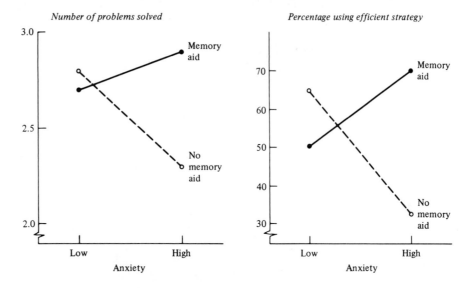

Adapted from Gross & Mastenbrook (1980)

FIGURE 17–7   U-Shaped Relation between Level of Arousal and Quantity Performance

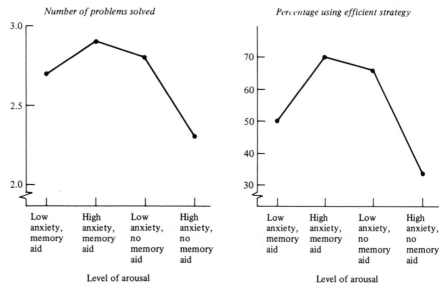

Adapted from Gross & Mastenbrook (1980)

x axis gives the level of arousal ranging from undermotivated (low anxiety/ memory aid) to overmotivated (high anxiety/no memory aid). As you can see, there is some evidence of the inverted U-shaped curve relationship between level of arousal and quality of performance.

Another prediction derived from the Yerkes–Dodson law is that high anxiety people will perform better on easy or rote tasks while low anxiety people will perform better on difficult or conceptual tasks. High anxiety people begin with moderate levels of arousal; easy tasks don't add much to that level but difficult tasks produce stress that pushes the level of arousal to the right side of the curve. Low anxiety people begin with low levels of arousal at the left side of the curve; easy tasks keep the arousal level at the left end, but difficult tasks help push the level rightward to the moderate zone.

In order to test for this predicted ATI, Mayer (1977) conducted a study in which college students who scored high or low in state anxiety were asked to solve cognitively demanding problems that required novel responses (such as anagrams and creative thinking problems) and rote problems that required overlearned responses (such as circling all the letter *a*'s on a sheet of paper or carrying out simple computation problems). Both high and low anxiety groups were equivalent on tests of general intellectual ability. In addition, there were time limits for solving each type of problem, so all students were under moderate test stress.

Let's try to order the four situations—high anxiety students working on rote problems, high anxiety students working on cognitive problems, low anxiety students working on rote problems, low anxiety students working on cognitive problems—in terms of the students' levels of arousal. The lowest level of arousal—perhaps corresponding to the left side of the Yerkes–Dodson curve— is for low anxiety students solving rote problems; the highest level of arousal— perhaps corresponding to the right side of the curve—is for high anxiety students solving cognitive problems. These two groups would be expected to perform relatively poorly because they elicit either too much or not enough motivational arousal. In contrast, the other two groups—low anxiety solving cognitive problems or high anxiety solving rote problems—correspond to moderate levels of arousal and hence should show the highest performance on the Yerkes–Dodson curve.

Figure 17–8 shows the proportion correct response for low and high anxious students on rote and cognitive problems. As you can see, there is an ATI in which low anxiety students perform better on cognitive tasks than high anxiety students, while high anxiety students perform better on rote tasks than low anxiety students. Figure 17–9 presents the same data in the form of a curve with amount of arousal on the *x* axis and level of performance on the *y* axis. As you can see, there is some evidence of an inverted U-shaped curve in which performance is best at moderate levels of arousal. These results are consistent with the idea that high anxiety enables students to excel on well-learned responses but not on producing creative or novel answers.

FIGURE 17–8   Interaction between Anxiety and Difficulty of Test Item

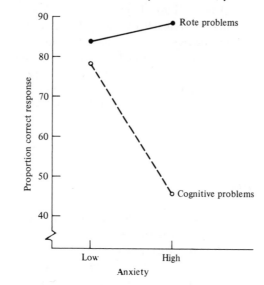

Adapted from Mayer (1977)

FIGURE 17–9   U-Shaped Relation between Level of Arousal and Test-Taking Performance

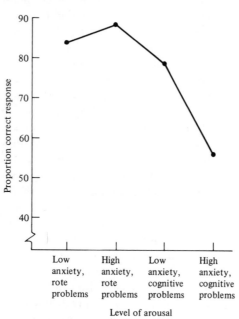

Adapted from Mayer (1977)

The research on anxiety and instruction does not always produce ATIs as clear as those described. In reviewing the somewhat complex research findings, Cronbach & Snow (1977, p. 430) concluded: "The data imply that the interactive affects of anxiety and instruction are complex and that no single generalization about the treatment contrasts accounts for them." One problem in anxiety research is to produce situations that correspond to low, moderate, and high levels of arousal. Another problem is that different students interpret and respond to stress differently. Measures of anxiety are essentially attempts to determine whether or not a person will respond to stress in an unproductive way.

Achievement Motivation

What Is Achievement Motivation? A person with high achievement motivation is someone who is prone to choose tasks that will lead to success, who will work persistently for a long-term goal of success, who is concerned about performing well and who sees himself/herself as competent. In contrast to the high anxious person who is "fear-oriented," the high need for achievement person is "hope-oriented." For example, in early research on risk-taking by Atkinson and his colleagues (1958, 1964; Atkinson & Feather, 1966; McClelland, Atkinson, Clark & Lowell, 1953), students who scored high and low in achievement motivation were asked to choose tasks to perform. Students with high need to achieve preferred moderately difficult tasks (i.e., tasks that were challenging but that could ultimately lead to success). Students with a low need for achievement were less likely to choose moderately difficult tasks. Weiner (1978) points out that selecting a moderately difficult task and monitoring one's success provides the student with information about his or her ability. Thus one characteristic of students who display a high need for achievement may be a desire to realistically gauge their abilities.

Achievement motivation (or need to achieve) refers to the degree to which a student desires to be successful (Atkinson & Feather, 1966; McClelland, Atkinson, Clark & Lowell, 1953). Within the context of schooling, achievement motivation refers to the degree to which a student desires to perform well on school tasks. Achievement motivation can be thought of as a personality characteristic, but it also can be thought of as an interpretive process in which a student attempts to monitor his or her abilities (Weiner, 1978).

Achievement motivation was originally measured using projective tests such as the Thematic Apperception Test (TAT). For example, one picture shows a young and old woman standing near each other. The subject's job is to tell a story about the picture, in response to questions such as, "What is happening? What led up to this situation? What is being thought? What will happen?" If the story involves achievement-oriented themes, then the subject would be scored as high in need for achievement. Box 17–2 gives examples of two possible responses to the picture described. As you can see, Jane's story

---

BOX 17–2   Responses to Projective Test by Two Students

Jane
The older woman is the mother and the younger woman is the daughter. The mother is very proud of her daughter, because her daughter has worked her way through college and graduate school. The younger woman is about to become a doctor.

Nancy
These two woman are tired. The older woman is thinking about going home and going to sleep. The younger woman wishes that the older woman would not stand so close to her. Soon they will each go their own way.

---

shows strong achievement themes but Nancy's story does not. Unfortunately, the TAT is very difficult to score and questions have been raised concerning its reliability (Weiner, 1978). More recently, many objective questionnaires have been developed (Hermans, 1970; Mehbrabian, 1969). For example, Mehbrabian (1969) developed a reliable need-for-achievement questionnaire that contains items such as "I think I love winning more than I hate losing."

Achievement Motivation and Learning.   How does achievement motivation affect students' academic performance? In a review of achievement research related to education, Atkinson (1965) found evidence that students with a high need for achievement tended to get higher grades. In addition, high need for achievement students responded to failure differently from high fear of failure (i.e., highly anxious) students. For example, Feather (1961) found that high need for achievement students are far more likely than low need for achievement students to respond to repeated failure by persisting and working harder on a task. In contrast, highly anxious students are far more likely than low anxiety students to respond to repeated failure by quitting the task.

How does achievement motivation interact with teachers' instructional styles? Domino (1968, 1971) provides some evidence that the effects of achievement motivation may depend on the teaching styles of the teachers. For example, in one study, college students were asked to fill out questionnaires measuring achievement through independence (Ai) and achievement through conformity (Ac). Achievement through independence refers to the need to achieve on one's own terms; high Ai students describe themselves as mature, demanding, and self-reliant. Achievement through conformity refers to the need to achieve by complying with the requirements of the teacher; high Ac students describe themselves as capable, efficient, and responsive. Four groups of students were identified, with the groups matched for sex and general intelligence: high Ai/high Ac, high Ai/low Ac, low Ai/high Ac, low Ai/low Ac. Then, the experimenter interviewed the teachers of these students, and classified the teachers either as "encouraging independence" or "requiring conformity." Teachers who encouraged independence tended to give students many options, whereas teachers who required conformity expected students to carry out very specific assignments.

Figure 17–10 gives the mean Grade Point Average (GPA) of students in the four need for achievement groups for classes in which teachers encouraged independence and classes in which teachers encouraged conformity. As you can see by comparing the high Ai/high Ac group versus the low Ai/low Ac group, students who are high in need for achievement as measured by both Ai and Ac tended to get much better grades than students who were low in both Ai and Ac. Apparently, getting good grades is related to the personality characteristic of needing to achieve. In addition, there is an interesting attribute by treatment interaction (ATI) in which high Ai/low Ac students get better grades from teachers who encourage independence than from teachers who require conformity while low Ai/high Ac students get better grades from teachers who require conformity than from teachers who encourage independence. Apparently, in the Domino study, independent achievers perform better with teachers who encourage independence while conforming achievers perform better with teachers who require conformity.

FIGURE 17–10   **Interactions between Achievement Motivation and Teaching Style—Course Grade**

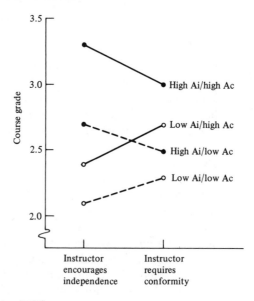

Adapted from Domino (1968)

In order to examine this interesting ATI more carefully, Domino (1971) conducted a follow-up study using college students taking a psychology course. Based on their responses to a personality questionnaire, students were classified either as high Ai/low Ac or as low Ai/high Ac. Half the students in each personality group took the course from a teacher who required conformity and half took the course from a teacher who encouraged independence. Figure 17–11 shows the students' scores on a multiple-choice final exam, essay final exam, and overall course performance. As you can see, independent achievers (high Ai/low Ac) get higher scores when the teacher encourages independence while conforming achievers (low Ai/high Ac) get higher scores when the teacher requires conformity.

Cronbach & Snow (1977) have reviewed much of the research on how students' achievement motivation and the instructors' teaching styles interact. Unfortunately, studies involving elementary and secondary school children generate inconsistent results. One reason for the lack of consistency is that teaching style and student personality involve many factors—these are often hard to define and measure, and in any well-running classroom more than just one teaching style factor and one personality factor are involved. Yet, Cronbach & Snow suggest that there is enough initial evidence to warrant further study of the idea that students with high achievement motivation perform better when the instructor's teaching style exploits their level of achievement motivation.

FIGURE 17–11 **Interactions between Achievement Motivation and Teaching Style— Final Exam**

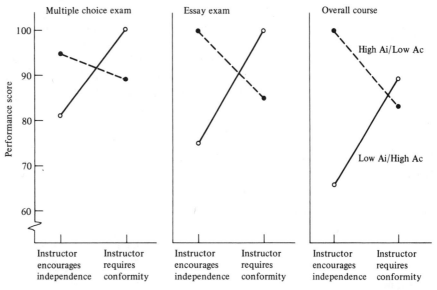

Adapted from Domino (1971)

Implications for Instruction

The relevance of motivational variables is obvious for educational settings. Performance on educational tasks depends both on the students' ability and effort. This section has shown that students differ in their motivations. Some students are more strongly motivated by fear of failure than other students; these highly anxious students respond to stressful learning or testing situations in inefficient ways. Hence instructional situations that are not stressful will result in the best performance for these students. Some students are more strongly motivated by need for success than other students; these high need achievement students respond to stressful learning or teaching situations by working harder. Hence long-term challenging tasks may be more appropriate for students with high needs for achievement. In short, instructional programs should be sensitive to the possibility that stress has different effects for different students—such as sometimes helping high need for achievement students but hurting highly anxious students.

Although anxiety and need for achievement may be characterized as personality variables, they also imply something about the way people interpret information. Table 17–1 gives a summary of an attributional model of achievement strivings suggested by Weiner (1978). As you can see, a student can attribute success or failure to many different causes, including his/her ability, the amount of effort put into the task, the difficulty of the task, or luck. Attributions may reflect stable causes (e.g., ability or difficulty) or unstable causes (e.g., effort or luck). If a person's attributions are stable, this will lead to consistent expectancies. For example, if success is attributed to high ability or ease of the task, then the student will expect to succeed again when confronted with a similar task. Similarly, attributions may reflect an internal locus of control—such as ability or effort—or an external locus of control—such as luck or difficulty. Affect is related to locus of control: If success is attributed to ability or effort, a person will feel more pride than if success is attributed to luck or ease of task; if failure is attributed to ability or effort, a person will feel more shame than if failure is attributed to luck or difficulty of task. Finally, a person's

TABLE 17–1   An Attributional Model of Achievement Strivings

Causal attributions	Causal dimensions		Internal Consequences		Behavioral Consequences
	Stability	Locus of control	Expectancy	Affect	Persistence & Intensity
Ability	high	high	high	high	low
Effort	low	high	low	high	high
Task difficulty	high	low	high	low	low
Luck	low	low	low	low	high

Adapted from Weiner (1978)

affect and expectations concerning a task influence the person's academic behavior, such as choice of tasks, persistence, and intensity of effort. For example, if a student attributes failure to bad luck, he may keep trying since his luck could change; similarly, if failure is attributed to difficulty, the student may give up since task difficulty will not change.

Weiner (1978) points out that high and low need for achievement students may differ in the way they interpret success and failure. Students who score high in need for achievement tend to attribute success to their own effort and ability to a greater extent than students who score low in need for achievement. Students who score high in need for achievement are more likely to attribute failure to lack of effort, hence they respond with persistence; while students who score low in need for achievement are more likely to attribute failure to lack of ability, hence they respond by quitting. Students who score high in need for achievement tend to have higher self-concepts because they attribute success to ability and failure to effort; students who score low in need for achievement have lower self-concepts because they more often attribute failure to lack of ability and success to luck or task ease.

DEMOGRAPHIC CHARACTERISTICS

What Are Demographic Characteristics?

The demographic characteristics of a student involve another widely studied class of individual difference variables. Demographics refer to descriptions of the student's gender, age, name, socioeconomic status, ethnicity, religion, and so on. For example, socioeconomic status can be evaluated by classifying the level of education of a student's parents or by the parents' occupational level. Recent results of a large-scale achievement testing of schoolchildren in California are summarized in Figure 17–12. As you can see, students whose parents were professionals or highly educated performed much better than students whose parents were less educated or nonprofessionals.

Even a person's first name may be related to school learning. For example, Garwood (1976) found that teachers rated some boy's names desirable—such as Craig, Gregory, James, Jeffrey, John, Jonathan, Patrick, Richard, and Thomas—and rated other boy's names as undesirable—such as Bernard, Curtis, Darrell, Donald, Gerald, Horace, Maurice, Roderick, and Samuel. Sixth grade boys with desirable names performed better on many measures of educational performance including tests of achievement—even when the "desirable" and "undesirable" name groups were matched for ethnic composition. Similarly, teachers gave higher grades to essays written by students named Lisa or David than equivalent essays written by students named Bertha or Elmer (Harari & McDavid, 1973).

FIGURE 17–12   Some Factors That Are Related to Students' Mathematics Test Scores

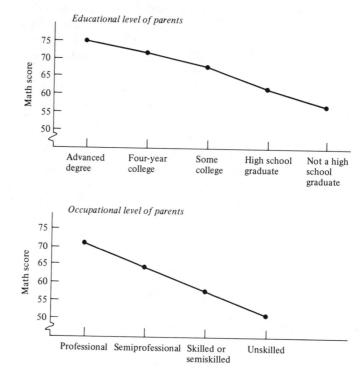

Adapted from the California Assessment Program (1980)

Unfortunately, research on demographic characteristics of learners offers very few insights into why certain characteristics seem to be related to school performance. Since there are so many possible characteristics, it is difficult to isolate one as the cause of differences in academic achievement. For example, we might find that one ethnic group performs more poorly on tests of achievement than another group. However, this could be due to one group receiving a better quality and quantity of education, on the average, as compared to the other group. Thus, if we look only at well-educated members of the two groups, differences in achievement might disappear. Even when we find a variable that seems to be related to school performance in a fairly systematic way, the underlying processes are not often clear. Thus making educational decisions based on differences in demographic characteristics can be hazardous. Instead, we need to understand how a particular variable interacts with others to affect school performance. In this section we focus on just one characteristic—sex differences—with hopes of trying to determine whether a person's gender is related to learning and if so, why.

Gender Differences

One of the most salient dimensions on which students differ is gender. For example, with regard to elementary and secondary schooling, there is strong evidence that girls get better grades than boys, girls are more interested in school-related skills from an earlier age than boys, and girls are less likely to quit before completing high school than boys (Maccoby & Jacklin, 1974).

Founded and Unfounded Claims. There is, of course, a massive "folklore" about intellectual and personality differences between boys and girls. In an extensive review of scientific research on sex differences, Maccoby & Jacklin (1974) were able to list eight common beliefs that are clearly unfounded:

1. Girls are more social than boys.
2. Girls are more suggestible than boys.
3. Girls have lower self-esteem.
4. Girls are better at rote learning; boys are better at conceptual learning.
5. Boys are more analytic.
6. Girls are more affected by heredity; boys are more affected by environment.
7. Girls lack achievement motivation.
8. Girls are more auditory; boys are more visual.

However, Maccoby & Jacklin also found four sex differences that are fairly well established:

1. Girls have greater verbal ability than boys. For example, in a review of twenty-six large-scale comparisons, girls outperformed boys on twenty-two of the comparisons; the average difference was about .2 standard deviations. Girls tended to outperform boys beginning at very young ages.

2. Boys have greater mathematical ability than girls (beginning in the teenage years). For example, in a review of 11 large scale comparisons using teenagers, boys outperformed girls on eight of the comparisons; the average difference was about .2 standard deviations. Although boys did not outperform girls at early ages, the differences were strong by the teenage years.

3. Boys have greater visual-spatial ability than girls (beginning in the teenage years). For example, of thirty-one studies involving teenagers or older students, boys outperformed girls in eighteen but girls outperformed boys in none of the comparisons; the average difference was about .4 standard deviations. As with mathematical ability, boys did not tend to consistently outperform girls during the early years.

4. Males are more agressive than females. This trend can be observed as early as two years of age.

Gender Differences in Mathematical Ability. As an example, let's take a closer look at one of the "well-established" sex differences (e.g., that boys outperform girls in mathematical ability). At the outset, it should be pointed out that the difference in test scores is "on the average" (i.e., some girls perform better than some boys). Certainly, one's gender is not the only factor related to one's mathematical competence.

Maccoby & Jacklin (1974) reviewed twenty-seven studies that involved thirty-five comparisons between boys and girls for scores on standardized mathematics tests. The results of the review indicated that sex differences depended on the students' ages: for ages three to eight, there is a tendency for girls to outperform boys; for ages nine to twelve, no sex differences are observed; for ages thirteen and above, there is a strong advantage for boys. Similar results have been obtained from standardized mathematics tests given to all third, sixth, and twelfth graders in California public schools (California Assessment Program, 1980). Figure 17–13 shows that in the third grade girls outperform boys, but by the twelfth grade boys outperform girls. Similar age trends have been obtained in other studies (Fennema, 1974; Hilton & Berglund, 1974).

Theories of Gender Differences.   The foregoing results provide fairly consistent evidence that by adolescence, boys average higher scores than girls on tests of mathematical ability or achievement. However, the really difficult question is why such results are obtained. Three major theories of sex differences in mathematical ability attribute differences to experience, socialization, or biology.

First, let's examine the idea that boys and girls receive different math-related experiences. For example, in primary grades, students generally have no choice about which courses they take, so boys and girls receive similar exposures to school mathematics. However, beginning in high school, students have more options concerning whether to take more math courses, and boys are more likely to opt for taking more mathematics courses than girls (Fennema & Sherman, 1977). Thus, teenage boys may perform better than teenage girls

FIGURE 17–13   Math Test Results by Age and Sex

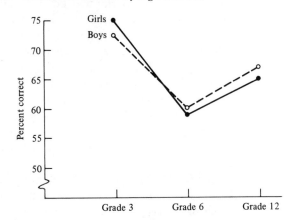

Adapted from California Assessment Program (1980)

because boys, on the average, have taken more school mathematics courses.

In order to test this idea, Fennema & Sherman (1977) surveyed approximately 1200 high school students concerning their experience in math, attitudes towards math, parents' attitudes, and so on. In addition, all students took math achievement tests. As expected, the average achievement score for boys was higher than for girls. However, when a statistical analysis took into account the number of math-related courses taken by each student, the differences were reduced or disappeared. We could stop at this point, content that the sex differences problem has been explained, if it weren't for several troublesome problems. One problem is that Fennema and Sherman seem to have analyzed the data in a way that reduces the sample size and thus reduces the chances of getting statistically significant results. A second problem is that other researchers have not yet substantiated this finding.

More recently, Benbow & Stanley (1980) surveyed 9927 "intellectually gifted" junior high school students selected from five states and the District of Columbia for Project Talent. The goal of Project Talent is to identify the most talented students (e.g., upper 5%) early in their lives so they can be educated appropriately. Benbow & Stanley argue that if Fennema & Sherman (1974, 1977) are right concerning the importance of the number of math courses taken, then there should be no sex differences among junior high school students. This is so because junior high students generally have not yet had options to take additional math courses. However, boys in the sample averaged higher than girls on the Mathematics scale of the Scholastic Aptitude Test (SAT), the brighest boys tended to score higher than the brightest girls, and a higher percentage of boys scored above 600. Based on these findings, Benbow & Stanley concluded (1980, p. 1263): "The sex difference in mathematical reasoning ability we found was observed before girls and boys started to differ significantly in the number and type of mathematics courses taken."

Although the results of the Benbow & Stanley study are inconsistent with the theory that sex differences are caused by differences in the number of mathematics courses taken, the results do not disprove the experience theory and do not provide definitive support for an alternative theory. For example, boys and girls may receive different math-related experiences outside of school, including playing with different kinds of toys and hobbies (Fennema, 1974; Fennema & Sherman, 1977). Maccoby & Jacklin (1974) point out that parents may tend to praise boys for engaging in math-related activities but discourage girls from doing so. Furthermore, the Benbow & Stanley study can be criticized on the grounds that Project Talent may have been more successful in searching for talented boys than for talented girls. Thus, before we can accept or reject the experience theory, we need some large-scale studies that include measures of in-school math-related experiences, out-of-school math-related experiences, and mathematics achievement.

Second, another theory of sex differences is based on the idea that boys and girls are socialized differently. For example, Maccoby & Jacklin (1974) point out that boys may tend to imitate male role models (who presumably emphasize math) and girls may tend to imitate female role models (who presumably do not emphasize math). Similarly, boys' self-concepts may tend to include performing well in mathematics while girls' self-concepts may not emphasize excellence in math. For example, Fennema and her colleagues (Fennema, 1974; Fennema & Sherman, 1977, 1978) conducted surveys of schoolchildren's attitudes and found that girls have lower expectations for themselves in mathematics, girls believed that math was for boys, and girls tended to receive less encouragement to engage in math-related activities than boys. Fennema & Sherman (1978, p. 202) summarize their findings as follows:

> At younger ages, girls did not see mathematics as any less useful than did boys, nor did they perceive any less attitudes toward them as students of mathematics from parents and teachers. However, as early as sixth grade, girls expressed less confidence than boys in their ability to do mathematics, and the subject was clearly sex-typed male, especially by boys. In the high school years these differential attitudinal influences continued and were joined by a host of other negative attitudinal influences.

Fennema & Sherman (1974) found that when statistical analyses took into account the students' attitudes and math-socialization experiences, sex differences in math achievement were reduced or disappeared. Unfortunately, such statistical adjustments are not as convincing as a "real-life" experiment would be. If social attitudes were changed so that math (and computers) were no longer perceived as a "male domain," we would expect to see a reduction or elimination of sex differences in math achievement. Until this kind of attitude change is complete in our society or until we have much more definitive statistical data, we cannot accept or reject the socialization theory.

Finally, let's examine the theory that sex differences are due, at least in part, to biological (or genetic) differences between boys and girls. For example, Benbow & Stanley (1980, p. 1264) argue that both biological and environmental (e.g., experiences and socialization) factors underlie the sex differences in mathematical ability: "This male superiority is probably an expression of a combination of both endogenous and exogenous variables. . . . Putting one's faith in the boy-versus-girl socialization processes as the only permissible explanation of the sex differences in mathematics is premature." Although Benbow & Stanley seem to argue for a biological theory of sex differences, they fail to present any positive evidence to support this theory. Although magazines may stir readers with headlines about "math genes" in males, there is at present no solid evidence to support such a hypothesis. In addition, it is not clear how a biological theory could account for the fact that sex differences change with age. However, in spite of how unpleasant or just plain silly the biological theory may seem, we should remember that the test of a theory lies in careful study and empirical data rather than in our own biases.

In summary, although the pattern of sex differences in math ability is well-documented, we do not yet have a clear explanation of why the differences exist. At the present time, the most reasonable hypothesis seems to be the socialization theory.

Implications for Instruction

What are the instructional implications of the foregoing research on sex differences? If one is interested in reducing sex differences, it is important to seriously address girls' attitudes and expectations concerning mathematics and to not let math become sex-typed as a male domain.

Being realists for a moment, we might recognize that for the present, "boys and girls on the average do seem to have different areas of intellectual strength and weakness" (Maccoby & Jacklin, 1974, p. 366). Does this mean that they should be taught in different ways? In a thoughtful analysis of this kind of question, Glaser (1972) has argued against separate instructional programs. Instead, if some students seem to lack certain prerequisite spatial or quantitative skills, they should be given training to improve these skill. At the present time, there does not seem to be any compelling evidence for providing separate math instruction to the two sexes.

In addition, it should be pointed out that the observed sex differences in mathematical ability are relatively small. For example, in the California Assessment Program data shown in Figure 17–13, high school boys outperform high school girls by only two points. In contrast, Figure 17–12 shows that other factors, such as the parents' educational or professional level are much more strongly related to mathematics scores. Even the number of hours of TV viewing is more strongly related to math achievement than gender. For example, the difference between the children who watch the most TV and those who watch the least is 16 points. Viewed in this light, the gender of the student seems to be a relatively minor factor in relation to one's mathematical achievement.

COGNITIVE STYLE

What Is Cognitive Style?

Cognitive style refers to a learner's preferred mode of processing information. Examples of some major distinctions include: using visual versus verbal modes of representing knowledge, degree of reliance on context in processing of information, and level of complexity and abstraction in processing information. The most obvious instructional prediction concerning cognitive style is that students will learn better when the instructional method corresponds to their preferred cognitive style. Let's examine this prediction within the context of the following examples of cognitive style variables.

Verbal Versus Visual Processors

Some students tend to score better on tests of visual ability than verbal ability; these students could be classified as visual processors. Other students tend to score better on tests of verbal ability than on tests of visual ability; these students could be called verbal processors. Do visual processors perform better when given visual kinds of instruction—such as figures and diagrams—while verbal processors do better when given verbal kinds of instruction? Unfortunately, the question cannot be answered with a simple "yes." After reviewing the research literature, Cronbach & Snow (1977, p. 291) concluded: "Rarely were the original hypotheses confirmed in even one study."

Does it help some students to convert instruction from its traditionally verbal mode into a more visual presentation—such as using films and pictures? Cronbach & Snow (1977) report that both verbal and visual ability are related to performance under visual methods of instruction. Thus we can reject the idea that visual-based methods of instruction depend only on visual ability. These findings suggest that the search for ATIs must take many variables into account, including the student's general ability to learn and the student's prior knowledge of the material.

Field Independence Versus Dependence

Field independence/dependence refers to the degree to which a person can work on tasks by himself. A field independent person has internal frames of reference for deciding how to work on a task. In contrast, a field dependent person relies on the environmental context for deciding how to work on a problem. Witkin and his colleagues (Witkin, Moore, Goodenough & Cox, 1977) argued that a field independent person would be better able to find an embedded or degraded figure in a complex context. For example, Figure 17–14 gives an item from the Gestalt Completion Test. Your job is to figure out what object is represented in the picture. According to Witkin's theory, a field independent person should be able to see that this is a picture of a hammer faster than a field dependent person.

One instructional implication is that field independent students will perform better under methods of instruction that do not emphasize sensitivity to social demands or structure while field dependent students will prefer more structured methods. Witkin et al. (1977) provide some modest support for this hypothesis by noting that field independent students tend to outperform field dependent students in mathematics and science courses. Presumably, science and math require independent thought and do not rely on sensitivity to social context. However, Witkin et al. (1977) also point out that there is no strong difference in overall academic achievement between field independent and field dependent students. In a recent review, Goodenough (1978) noted that

FIGURE 17–14   What Do You See in This Picture?

career choices may be related to field independence/dependence, although the matter is still not resolved.

High Versus Low Conceptual Level

Conceptual level refers to the degree to which a person perceives concepts as complex and differentiated rather than as one-dimensional. A high conceptual person can see many sides of an argument or issue, avoids using stereotypes, can tolerate ambiguity, and can think abstractly. Hunt and his colleagues (Tomlinson & Hunt, 1971; Noy & Hunt, 1972) have measured conceptual level by asking students to write sentence completions on topics such as "following directions," "uncertainty," "rules," "criticism," "parents," and "disagreements." The written answers are scored for degree of conceptual complexity and abstractness.

An instructional implication is that high conceptual level students would perform better under unstructured methods (such as induction or discovery) while low conceptual level students would perform better under structured methods (such as deduction and rule). In order to test this idea, Tomlinson & Hunt compared low and high conceptual level students learning under rule/example methods (i.e., much guidance and structure) or example/rule methods (i.e., less guidance and structure). The overall academic ability of the highs and lows was statistically balanced so that ability would be a factor in the study, and the high and low conceptual level students were selected from the extremes. The post-test was a delayed essay test covering the material. As predicted, the high conceptual level students performed much better than lows when given example/rule methods but lows outperformed highs for rule/example methods.

Siegel & Siegel (1965) used a questionnaire to determine college students' preferences for "fact"-oriented instruction versus "concept"-oriented instruction. This distinction seems similar to Hunt's distinction between low and high conceptual level. In a college biology course, fact-oriented students and concept-oriented students were given study sessions that included quizzes on factual information or on conceptual information. The final exam contained both types of questions. The results were complicated, but if we look only at the students with high general ability or prior knowledge, the expected ATI was obtained. Conceptually oriented students did better on the final exam if the study sessions were conceptual while factually oriented students did better on the exam if the study sessions were factual.

Pask & Scott (1972, 1973) classified students as either "serialist" or "wholist" based on their performance on a learning task. The serialists tended to remember information in lists and focus only on "low order relations." The "wholists" tended to logically organize information as a whole and focus on "high order relations." The wholist students seem to share many of the characteristics of high conceptual level students while the serialists tend to share characteristics of the low conceptual level students. In Pask & Scott's studies, students learned science material using either a wholist or serialist method of instruction. As predicted, students learned more when the method of instruction matched their cognitive style than when it did not match.

These kinds of results suggest that conceptual level may be an important individual differences dimension. However, more research is needed in order to determine whether the various measures described above are related to one another. More importantly, since general ability and prior knowledge may be far more potent variables, more research is needed to see how cognitive style variables interact with ability and knowledge.

Implications for Instruction

As you can see from the examples, there have been many attempts to understand the role of a student's cognitive style in school learning. Unfortunately, as Cronbach & Snow (1977) point out, the results have not been encouraging. First is the problem of measurement; for example, as we have seen, there are many problems in scoring of projective tests. Second is the problem of research methodology; for example, many of the studies use flawed designs (e.g., making multiple tests for the same ATI, or failing to control for important variables such as ability and knowledge). Third, there is the problem of research results; the findings often are contradictory. In light of these problems, Cronbach & Snow (1977, p. 385) conclude: "A few findings suggest that it helps to make the treatment similar in style to that of the learner. This is a reasonable hypothesis . . . but there are enough inconsistencies to make generalization impossible for the present." Further research that carefully examines the role of multiple attributes within real instructional settings is needed.

From these results, it seems premature to advocate the development of separate instructional programs for students with different learning styles. In short, the current results do not warrant the development of one comprehensive program for one type of student and a different comprehensive program for another type of student. Instead, teachers should be sensitive to the idea that, for a given instructional domain, not all students learn in the same way. One solution to this problem is to provide small scale individualization of instructional method to fit each student's cognitive style within a specific situation, especially when conventional methods do not succeed.

CONCLUSION

We began this chapter with several questions concerning the relevance to instruction of individual differences among learners. Let's see what kinds of answers we found.

Question 1: What are the major dimensions upon which learners differ? In this chapter we explored five major categories of individual differences: general ability to learn, prior knowledge in a specific domain, motivation to learn, demographic characteristics such as gender, and cognitive style such as conceptual level. We found strong evidence for the importance of ability, knowledge, and motivation; we also found examples of demographic characteristics and cognitive style variables that seem to be related in sometimes complex ways to academic performance. There are, of course, many other dimensions on which people differ, including introversion-extroversion, emotional stability, specific skills (such as artistic or musical ability), and interests. However, the five dimensions described in this chapter present a representative sample of the role of individual differences in school learning.

Question 2: Do these differences affect academic performance? We found consistent relations between overall achievement and ability or knowledge. Motivation, demographics, and cognitive style tended to be related to achievement mainly under certain situations (i.e., within interactions).

Question 3: Are there attribute treatment interactions (ATIs)? Here we are asking, "Do some kinds of students learn better under one method while other kinds of students learn better under other methods?" We did find some evidence for ATIs involving each of the five types of variables. For ability, there is some evidence that unstructured instructional methods depend more heavily on general ability than do tightly guided or structured methods. For knowledge, there is corresponding evidence that active instructional methods that require students to integrate old and new information depend more on prior knowledge than do more passive, direct instructional methods. For motivation, there is some evidence that highly anxious students learn better under stress-free conditions while low anxiety students might perform better under more stressful conditions. Also, students who score high in need for achievement tend to respond to failure by working harder on a task while students who score low in need for achievement respond by quitting. Although the ATIs involving motivational variables are not as consistent as we might like, there does appear to be evidence that differences in students' motivation are related to their learning and test-taking performance. The results concerning demographics and cognitive style are less clear, with far more empirical and theoretical work needed.

Question 4: What are the implications of ATIs? Finally, let's assume that there is strong and consistent evidence for at least some ATIs. How can we individualize instruction in light of these findings? There are two major approaches to the problem: to provide qualitatively different methods of instruction to different kinds of learners or to provide pretraining in prerequisite skills to students who lack the skills. For prerequisite skills that are easily teachable (e.g., some of the skills discussed in the section on domain-specific knowledge), the second alternative seems warranted. For prerequisite skills that cannot be easily taught (e.g., general ability to learn), the first alternative may be warranted.

SUGGESTED READINGS

Cronbach, L. J. & Snow, R. E. (1977). *Aptitudes and instructional methods*. New York: Irvington. (A critical review of ATI research.)

Glaser, R. (1972). Individuals and learning: The new aptitudes. *Educational Researcher*, *1*(6), 5–13. (A call to analyze individual differences in terms of information processing components.)

Snow, R. E., Federico, P. & Montague, W. E. (eds.) (1980). *Aptitude, learning, and instruction*, Volumes 1 and 2. Hillsdale, N.J.: Erlbaum. (A two-volume collection of "state-of-the-art" papers by leading individual-differences researchers.)

Snow, R. E. & Lohman, D. F. (1984). Toward a theory of cognitive aptitude for learning from instruction. *Journal of Educational Psychology, 76,* 347–376. (An integrative summary of individual differences research.)

PART V

CLASSROOM PROCESSES

How does learning and instruction occur within the classroom? How does the social context of the classroom affect how children learn? How can we describe the interactions between teacher and students in the course of real classroom instruction? These are the kinds of questions addressed in this section of the book.

In this section, you are asked to consider all of the processes that go on in a classroom. Remembering the general framework from Figure 1–3, you should ask yourself the following questions: How does the teachers approach affect learning? and How do children affect the learning of each other? Are there classroom activities that help to satisfy the requirements of meaningful learning (i.e., activities that stimulate relevant prior knowledge within learners and encourage them to use this knowledge in learning of new material)? In a sense, this section puts together in one place all of the actors in the teaching/learning process—learner, teacher, and subject matter all meet in the classroom. Although research is just beginning to unravel the processes involved in classroom learning and instruction, this section helps you to see how answers to some of these questions are emerging.

18 Classroom Processes

All the phenomena described so far in this book—development, instruction, learning, curriculum, measurement—occur within the context of the school classroom. This chapter examines how all these elements come together within the classroom.

A classroom is more than a physical setting; it is a social environment that shapes the way that students and teachers think and behave. The classroom culture, which is an important part of the child's life, affects the way that teachers and students interpret the process of education. This chapter examines how classroom processes affect, and are affected by, the educational process.

In examining these classroom processes, we begin by looking at how time is spent and how students are grouped in school classrooms. Then, we examine how teachers' expectations and decision making affect the nature of student-teacher interactions in the classroom. Our goal, of course, is to understand how classroom processes can be improved to foster student learning and development.

A CLASSROOM SCENE

Suppose that we looked into a second grade classroom. We see a teacher seated at a round table with five students. She is showing them a flash card that says, $14 - 5 = \underline{\quad}$. There are also some bundles of sticks on the table. As we listen in, this is what we hear:

TEACHER: Who can tell me the answer to this problem?

CLIFF: Zero. Four and one makes five. Five take away five is zero.

TEACHER: No. Remember that the one in the tens column is equal to one bundle of ten sticks.

KATHY: I can't do it. I don't know how to take five from four.

TEACHER: Use your bundles of sticks and the individual sticks if you need to.

MARTHA: Yo no comprendo.

(Teacher turns to help Martha by showing her how to use the sticks to solve the problem.)

PHILLIP: The answer is nine.

TEACHER: That's right, Phillip. Show us how you figured it out.

PHILLIP: I needed one more one so I took one stick from the bundle of ten sticks and that left nine.

TEACHER: Very good. Now let's try thirteen minus seven.

CLIFF: I still don't get it.

(The teacher walks around to help Cliff. Martha gets up and goes to the drinking fountain without permission.)

KATHY: The answer is sixty.

TEACHER: How did you get sixty?

KATHY: I took three away from this three and that left zero. Then I took four away from the ten and that left six.

(The teacher walks over to help Kathy.)

MICHAEL: Cliff has one of my sticks.

TEACHER: Cliff, did you take one of Michael's sticks?

CLIFF: Well, he was teasing me.

TEACHER: Please give it back and keep your hands off other people's property.

(The teacher continues to help Kathy. Suddenly students throughout the room begin to laugh. The teacher looks over to Phillip who has used two of the sticks to make fangs and is pretending to be a monster.)

TEACHER: Phillip! OK, everyone, get back to work. Michael, did you get the answer?

MICHAEL: I don't know how to do it.

You may be detecting that the students are losing interest. If you were the teacher, which of the following plans would you adopt? Plan A is to continue until the end of your planned lesson, which means to go on showing flash cards for another 10 minutes. Plan B is give a worksheet on subtraction facts. In this plan, the teacher hands out worksheets and says: "OK, everyone, put your sticks in the box. Then take these worksheets. I want you to work alone on these problems. If you have trouble, raise your hand, and I'll come around and help you. When you finish, raise your hand, and I'll correct your work." Plan C is to try to make the task more enjoyable by turning it into a game. In this plan the teacher goes to the closet and takes out some play money. Then she says:

"Let's put away our sticks and papers and play a game. Let's pretend that this is a grocery store and I am the clerk. Everybody gets fifteen dollars to start with." She gives each child, except Phillip, a ten and five ones. "Now, Phillip is a banker. When you buy something, I will only take the correct amount; I don't keep change because I'm afraid of burglars. When you pay me, I drop the money into this closed safe. If you don't have the right amount of change, you'll have to get change from Phillip. Whenever you buy something, write down how much money you are starting with, how much your bill is, and how much you have left over when you have paid your bill." After each child has had several successful turns, the teacher changes the rules slightly, "Now, let's see if you can work these problems in your head."

The preceding dialogue comes from the work of Borko, Cone, Russo & Shavelson (1979, p. 136–37). Even though we have only looked into a classroom for a brief time, it is clear that the process of teaching involves active cognitive processing on the part of the teacher. For example, the teacher must be sensitive to the pattern of teacher-student interaction in order to detect that the lesson is not going as planned. In addition, the teacher must decide whether to change the plan and, if so, how to change the plan. The need to make observations and decisions is not an isolated event but rather a continuing feature of classroom teaching. In this chapter we will explore classroom processes, with special interest in the role of the teacher's cognitions such as planning, expectations, and decision making.

TIME TO LEARN

How Much School Time Is Available?

One of the most obvious planning decisions involves how to best use the limited resource of classroom instructional time. Table 18–1 lists the average number of daily instructional minutes in grades K–12 for a national sample of U.S. schools (Anton, 1981). As you can see, in grades 1 through 12 the allocated time for instruction ranges from 310–333 minutes, with a mean of about 325 minutes per day. It should be noted that there are large differences from school to school, and even from state to state, in allocated instructional time per day. For example, California schools averaged only 296 minutes per day in grades 1–12, or about $\frac{1}{2}$ hour less per day than the national average (California Assessment Program, 1982).

A typical school year consists of approximately 180 days (Berliner, 1979). For example, in a recent national survey (Anton, 1981) the average school year consisted of 178.5 days. However, as Berliner (1979) has pointed out, approximately 30 days per year may be lost due to absences, standardized testing, special days close to vacations, and teacher strikes.

If we assume that the average instructional day contains 325 minutes and

TABLE 18–1   Average Daily Minutes of Instructional
             Time for U.S. Schools

Grade	Daily Minutes of Instruction
K	191
1	310
2	311
3	314
4	322
5	323
6	326
7	332
8	333
9	331
10	332
11	331
12	331

Adapted from Anton (1981)

the average school year contains 180 days, this yields slightly less than 1000 hours of potential instructional time per year or 12,000 hours over the course of grades 1–12. To gain some perspective on this figure, a recent survey of sixth graders attending California schools found that approximately one-third of the students watched 3 or more hours of television per day (California Assessment Program, 1980). Thus these students actually spent more time per year in front of a TV set than in a school classroom.

How Is Time Spent in School Classrooms?

Looking into Classrooms. In order to help answer this question, the Beginning Teacher Evaluation Study (BTES) was conducted (Berliner, 1979; Denham & Lieberman, 1980). The study involved twenty-five second grade classrooms and twenty-five fifth grade classrooms in California. As part of the study, teachers were taught how to keep logs for selected students, of the time allocated to each classroom activity in each content area. In addition, trained observers visited the classroom throughout the year, including a visit at least one day per week for 20 weeks. The observers kept track of the amount of time that selected students were engaged in learning, and the observers noted the level of difficulty of the instructional materials or activities.

Berliner (1979) points out that three measures of time were used:

Allocated time—refers to the amount of time provided by the teacher for a given instructional activity.

Engaged time—refers to the amount of time that a student is paying attention to the instructional activity or materials during the allocated time. Thus the engagement rate is the percentage of allocated time during which the learner is working "on-task." For example, if a teacher allocated 20 minutes for seatwork in math, and if a student was actively engaged in that work for 15 minutes (and was sharpening pencils, doodling, and waiting for help during 5 minutes) then the engagement rate would be 15/20 or 75%.

Academic learning time (ALT)—refers to the amount of time that a student is engaged in working on academically appropriate materials and activities. "Appropriate" instruction consists of material that is easy for the student to master (i.e., materials that generate error rates of less than 20%). For example, if a student was actively engaged in working in a math workbook for 15 minutes, but one-third of the material was so difficult that the student made mostly errors, then ALT would consist of only 10 minutes.

In a recent review of the BTES data, Rosenshine (1980) summarized several interesting findings concerning allocated time, engaged time, classroom settings, and differences among classrooms.

How Much Time Is Allocated to Academic Learning?   First, the survey indicated that second and fifth grade students receive academic instruction during about 58% of the instructional school day or about 45% of the total school day (including recess and lunch). Figure 18–1 summarizes the amount of time devoted to: (1) academic instruction in reading, mathematics, and other topics; (2) nonacademic instruction, such as art, music, and physical education (PE); and (3) noninstruction, such as transitions between activities and clean up. For purposes of the survey, instruction in science or social studies that involved reading was counted as reading instruction, and science or social studies work that involved math was counted as math instruction. As you can see, an average of 131 minutes (or 42% of the total school day) is allocated to academic instruction in the second grade and approximately 175 minutes (or about 48% of the school day) is allocated to academic instruction in the fifth grade.

How Often Are Students Engaged in Academic Learning?   Second, the survey showed that the average student is actively engaged in relevant instructional work during about one-third of the school day. Figure 18–2 summarizes the engagement rates for second and fifth graders when they are presented with reading, mathematics, and other academic instruction. As you can see, students are actively engaged in learning during about 73% of their allocated instructional time. Figure 18–2 also shows that students spend their nonengaged time in a variety of activities including (1) interim activities such as sharpening pencils or passing papers, (2) waiting for help such as waiting for a teacher to grade a worksheet, and (3) off-task activities such as daydreaming, socializing, or misbehaving. Thus during the average school day second graders

FIGURE 18–1   Less Than Half of School Day Is Allocated to Academic Learning

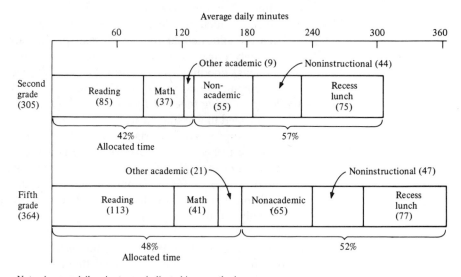

Note: Average daily minutes are indicated in parenthesis.

Adapted from Berliner (1979)

spend only about 95 minutes engaged in academic learning, and fifth graders spend only about 130 minutes engaged in academic learning. When we take absences and other losses of school days into account, this yields less than 300 hours per year during which elementary school students are actively engaged in relevant academic learning.

Is There More Seatwork or Teacher-Led Activity?   Third, the survey showed that students spend almost twice as much time in individual seatwork as in teacher-led groups, but that students are less engaged in academic learning during seatwork than in teacher-led groups. Figure 18–3 summarizes the amount of time and engagement rates for individual seatwork and teacher-led learning. As you can see, students spend about two-thirds of their instructional time working alone at their seats and are engaged in that work about 70% of the time; in contrast, students spend about one-third of their time in teacher-led instruction and are engaged in learning during about 84% of the time.

How Do Effective Teachers Use Class Time?   Fourth, the survey found that effective teachers (i.e., teachers who were most successful in increasing student achievement) allocated more time for academic instruction and elicited higher engagement rates. Figure 18–4 compares the three most effective and three least effective teachers on allocated time and engagement rates. As you can see, second grade students in the classrooms of effective teachers spend 50 more minutes per day engaged in academic learning than students

FIGURE 18–2 During Allocated Instruction Students Are Engaged in the Task about 73% of the Time

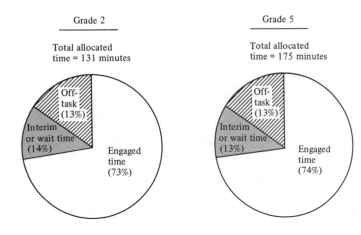

Adapted from Rosenshine (1980)

FIGURE 18–3 About 70% of Allocated Learning Time Involves Seatwork but Students Are More Likely to Be Engaged in Learning during Teacher-Led Instruction

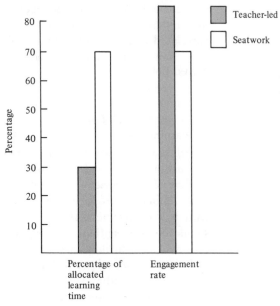

Adapted from Rosenshine (1980)

FIGURE 18–4   Effective Teachers Allot More Time to Academic Learning But Also Elicit Higher Engagement Rates Than Less Effective Teachers

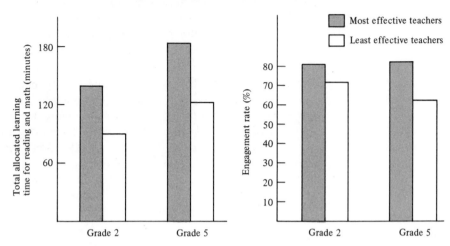

Adapted from Rosenshine (1980)

in ineffective teachers' classrooms; fifth grader students in effective classrooms spend 60 more minutes per day engaged in academic learning as compared to ineffective classrooms. It is interesting to note that effective teachers are able to allocate more time to academic learning without adversely affecting the students' engagement in learning; in fact, more allocated learning time and higher engagement rates seem to go together. For example, in a correlational analysis, the amount of time spent in breaks (such as recess and play) was negatively correlated with engagement rates. Thus there is no evidence that giving lots of break time helps students to concentrate more completely on their academic work.

Implications of Research on School Time

Based on studies like these it is tempting to conclude that increasing allocated instructional time will serve to increase student achievement. For example, Stallings & Kaskowitz (1974) found that school programs with high engagement rates tended to produce larger gains in student achievement than programs with low engagement rates. However, there are several reasons why one should be very cautious concerning the prediction that increased instructional time will lead to increased achievement. First, most studies of class time— including the ones described in this section—are correlational studies. In other words, these studies show only that there is a relation between time and achievement; we cannot assume a causal relationship. We cannot conclude that lower engaged time leads to less achievement; it is also possible that lower achievement leads to disruptive classroom behavior, which leads to less engaged learning time. Second, studies of class time provide too gross a level of analysis. It is not time per se that affects achievement but rather how the teacher plans to use the time and how students interpret instruction. This issue is what has motivated Berliner to distinguish among allocated time (i.e., the amount of time a teacher has planned for a particular instructional activity), engaged time (i.e., the amount of time the student is paying attention to an instructional activity), and academic learning time (i.e., the amount of engaged time that is productive for the learner). Thus it is not surprising that in a review, Karweit (1976) was unable to find a strong relationship between quantity of instruction and student achievement. An accurate understanding of the relation between time and achievement requires a deeper understanding of the cognitive processes of the teacher and the student during classroom instruction. These cognitive processes are discussed in subsequent sections of this chapter.

CLASS SIZE AND COMPOSITION

Another global decision concerns the size and composition of the class or instructional groups within the class. First, we will explore the issue of how class size affects classroom processes and student achievement. Second, we will explore how homogeneous versus heterogeneous groupings of students affects classroom processes and student achievement.

Class Size

Does Class Size Affect Student Achievement? In a well-known analysis of the results of eighty studies of class size, Glass & Smith (1979) found consistent evidence for the proposition that "as class size increases, achievement decreases." This finding is summarized graphically in Figure 18–5. As you can see, as class size increases from 1 to 70, achievement percentile rank drops from about the 80th percentile to about the 50th percentile. Hedges & Stock (1983) reanalyzed Smith & Glass's data using different statistical procedures, but arrived at similar conclusions. One interesting aspect of the analysis is that class size effects were obtained both in controlled experiments (where students were randomly assigned to varying sized classrooms) and in field studies (where actual classrooms were observed).

How Does Class Size Affect Student Achievement? A recent study by Smith & Glass (1980) helps to provide an answer. They used the same studies as in the original analysis, but focused on the relationship between class size and variables such as teacher attitudes, student attitudes, and classroom processes. Teacher attitudes included "attitude towards students," "job satisfaction," and

FIGURE 18–5 Is Class Size Related to Student Achievement?

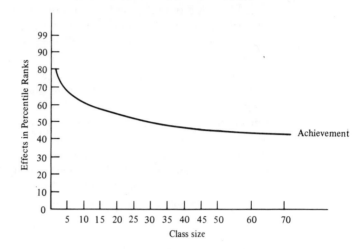

Adapted from Smith & Glass (1980)

"expectations for student performance." Student attitudes included "attitude toward teachers," "attitude towards school or class," "self-concept," "interest and enthusiasm for classwork," and "on-task behavior." Classroom processes included: "amount of teacher-student interaction," "number and variety of activities," "general climate," and "innovations and adaptations." Figure 18–6 shows that class size adversely affects teacher attitude most strongly; in addi-

FIGURE 18–6 Is Class Size Related to Teacher Attitudes, Student Attitudes, and Classroom Processes?

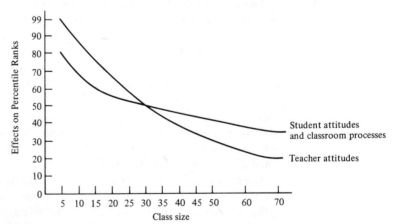

From Smith & Glass (1980)

tion, class size adversely affects student attitude and classroom processes. Apparently, class size affects student achievement indirectly, because class size affects how teachers and students think about the class and because class size limits the opportunities for student-teacher interaction, student participation, and individualization of instruction.

Class Composition

Does Class Composition Affect Student Achievement? A related issue concerns the role of classroom heterogeneity. In particular, a classic issue in educational psychology is whether or not grouping students by ability affects student achievement and attitude. In a recent analysis of data from fifty-two studies on grouping effects, Kulik & Kulik (1982) found a small positive relationship between ability grouping and achievement. On the average, students achieved about $\frac{1}{10}$ standard deviation better when grouped than when not grouped by ability. For average and low ability students, ability grouping had no significant effects on achievement; however, for high ability students, ability grouping produced a large increase in achievement, averaging $\frac{1}{3}$ standard deviation. In addition, ability grouping tended to raise interest in subject matter for all students, averaging about $\frac{1}{3}$ standard deviation. In summary, grouping appears to have positive effects on both achievement and attitudes, with no negative effects for low, average, or high ability students.

In a more detailed study, Beckerman & Good (1981) examined the consequences of various mixtures of high and low ability students in a classroom. They defined "more favorable" classroom composition as having more than one-third high aptitude students but less than one-third low aptitude students in a class; they defined "less favorable" classroom composition as having more than one-third low aptitude students but less than one-third high aptitude students in a class. An examination of over one hundred third and fourth grade math classes revealed that achievement gains were greatest in more favorable classrooms than in less favorable classrooms. Of particular interest is the fact that low aptitude and high aptitude students each gained more in favorable classrooms than their respective colleagues in less favorable classrooms. These results help to provide some details concerning how heterogeneity can adversely affect classroom learning. Apparently, when the classroom consists of a wide range of students (as in the present study), the hetereogeneity causes more difficulty when there is a large number of low aptitude students than when there are fewer lower aptitude students.

How Does Heterogeneous Grouping Affect Student Achievement? A recent study by Everston, Sanford & Emmer (1981) provides some information concerning how class heterogeneity affects classroom processes as well as achievement. The authors systematically observed junior high school English classrooms that contained a wide range of student abilities (e.g., up to ten grade levels difference among students) and classrooms with a narrow range of student abilities (e.g., less than three grade levels difference). "Special" classes consisting mainly of low ability or high ability students were not included; instead, the study focused on "average" level English classes with wide versus narrow ranges of student ability. Results of the observations revealed many significant differences in the classroom processes of the two types of classrooms. For example, the more heterogeneous grouping of students resulted in fewer instances of content being related to students' interest, fewer instances of adaptation of lessons to students' ability levels, less positive reinforcement, fewer instances of the teacher being receptive to student input, and lower engagement rates (i.e., less time "on-task"). Overall, the heterogeneous and homogeneous classrooms did not differ significantly in achievement. However, a closer examination revealed that while high ability students were not adversely affected by heterogeneous grouping, low ability students achieved significantly less when placed in heterogeneous versus homogeneous classrooms. Apparently, heterogeneous classes place many burdens on teachers, some of which are resolved by a lowering in the quality of classroom processes, especially for low ability students. Everston et al. (p. 230) conclude:

> If . . . school systems feel impelled to abandon ability grouping and "special" classes for some students, then they must recognize that the extremely heterogeneous classes that result are also "special." They place extraordinary demands on the teachers' time, attention, and classroom management skills.

In summary, teachers may need training in how to manage highly heterogeneous classes.

Implications of Research on Class Size and Composition

Although research suggests that smaller class size is related to better student achievement, the reason for this effect is not straightforward. Apparently, teachers and students in smaller classes may have more productive attitudes towards learning and more opportunities for individualized student-teacher interaction. When smaller class size is not economically feasible, it becomes increasingly important to develop ways of fostering good expectations in both teachers and students. In addition, creative ways of allowing student participation, individualized instruction, and student-teacher interaction become more important. Possible solutions include using parent or community volunteers, using peer tutoring, using classroom teaching aides, developing a split schedule so all students are not in the classroom all the time, and using computers.

Like an extremely large class, an extremely heterogeneous class is also related to lower student achievement. The reasons for this effect are similar to those for class size: students and teachers may have lower expectations, there may be less time for teaching that is appropriate for each child, there may be less student participation. Some of these problems can be reduced by grouping students by ability; however, the groups should still allow for some diversity and students should be allowed to move from one group to another with ease. When ability grouping is not used, a heavy burden is put on the teacher. The teacher of an extremely heterogeneous class must make sure that the instructional activity is appropriate for each student. The logistics of carefully monitoring the achievement of each student and productively individualizing instruction requires both time and resources, which must be provided. For example, resource specialists are needed to help suggest materials appropriate for students who are achieving on different levels, and additional tutoring may be needed for some students.

TEACHER EXPECTATIONS

Teachers may form attitudes and expectations concerning the academic, social, and personality characteristics of their students. In this section, we will examine two aspects of teacher expectations: (1) the effects of giving teachers external information about the academic ability of their students; (2) teachers' natural process of developing attitudes and expectations about their students.

Effects of Experimenter-Induced Teacher Expectations on Student Achievement

The Pygmalion Effect. Suppose that at the beginning of the school year, we provide some information to a first grade teacher. We give all twenty-five children in the class a test, which we call the Harvard Test. Furthermore, we tell the teacher that the test has identified five students—Billy, Sue, Amanda, Phil, and Tikino—as "late bloomers." These children, according to the test results, will "show unusual intellectual gains" over the year.

However, let's suppose that the test is really just a standard IQ test and that it is administered at the beginning and the end of the school year. Furthermore, let's suppose that what we told the teacher is really a lie; in fact we just picked five students at random to label "late bloomers." What will happen to these students? Will the label that we have given them turn into a self-fulfilling prophecy (i.e., will these students actually show greater gains in IQ over the year than the rest of the students in the class)?

In order to help answer these questions, Rosenthal & Jacobson (1968) conducted a well-known experiment similar to the one just outlined. The study took place in a real school, and involved three classrooms at each grade level from 1–6. Figure 18–7 shows the average gain in IQ over the school year (i.e., as measured by tests given at the beginning and end of the year) for the control group (i.e., children not labeled as "late bloomers") and experimental group (i.e., children labeled as "late bloomers") at each grade level. As you can see,

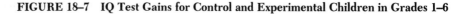

FIGURE 18–7   IQ Test Gains for Control and Experimental Children in Grades 1–6

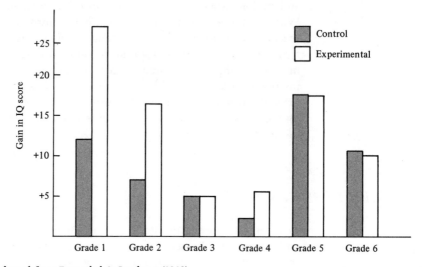

Adapted from Rosenthal & Jacobson (1968)

there is a tendency for the experimental students (i.e., the labeled students) to gain more IQ points than the control students, although this effect is most clear in grades 1 and 2. This "Pygmalion effect" seems to demonstrate that the labels that teachers are given for each student's intellectual ability can become self-fulfilling.

Critique of the Pygmalion Effect.   Although the Rosenthal & Jacobson study has received great publicity, it has not been possible to convincingly replicate the results in other similar studies (Brophy & Good, 1974). Even when all types of expectancy studies are reviewed, only about one-third of them produced significant effects (Rosenthal, 1976). There are several possible explanations for the lack of success in replicating the original Rosenthal & Jacobson results. First, there may be individual differences among teachers in their susceptibility to labeling effects. For example, in one study (Fleming & Anttonen, 1971) teachers were given false information about the IQs of some of their students; in particular, the IQ scores for some students were (falsely) increased by 16 points. However, this manipulation had no consistent effect on student achievement (i.e., the "over-rated" students did not show greater achievement gains that the rest of the class). In a post-experimental interview, teachers reported that they did not believe the IQ scores and thus ignored them.

You may also note in Figure 18–7 that the Rosenthal & Jacobson study obtained strong effects only for the youngest children; perhaps teachers had many other sources of information for the older students. Also, in follow-up studies (Conn, Edwards, Rosenthal & Crowne, 1968), consistent expectancy effects were not obtained when the bogus information was not given until the start of second semester—presumably after the teacher had already formed some expectations. Apparently, teachers are more susceptible to labeling when the labels are consistent with their existing expectations or when there is not another reliable source of information.

A related explanation for the failure to find consistent expectancy effects is that the fame of the original study may have sensitized teachers about blindly accepting test scores as the only source of information about children. Finally, Elashoff & Snow (1971) have severely criticized the Rosenthal & Jacobson study on the grounds that the conclusions are not supported by the data and methodology. Thus, research since the original Pygmalion study seems to indicate that giving a teacher grossly inaccurate information about a student's academic ability is not a guarantee that the information will become a self-fulfilling prophecy.

Effects of Teachers' Natural Expectations on Classroom Processes and Student Achievement

Amount of Student-Teacher Interaction. Although experimenter-induced teacher expectations (such as in the Pygmalion study) may not have consistent effects on student achievement, there is some research evidence that teacher's naturally developed expectations about students influence the pattern of classroom interactions. For example, Good (1970) observed first grade classes; he looked specifically at the amount of attention given to students who the teacher perceived as "high," "medium," and "low" achievers. Figure 18–8

FIGURE 18–8   Effects of Teacher Expectations on Students' Opportunities to Respond in Class

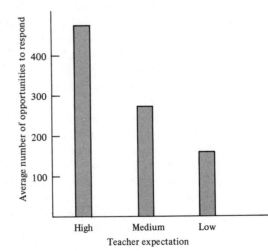

Adapted from Good (1970)

shows the mean number of times that the teacher called on students to respond to a teacher-initiated question. As can be seen, high achievers are called upon almost three times more often than low achievers. In another study, Rist (1970) periodically observed the classroom processes for low SES ghetto children as they progressed from grades K–2. Rist observed that in kindergarten the low SES tended to be placed in a group, seated further from the teacher, and given less frequent and less positive interaction than the children that the teacher perceived as "fast learners." The same observations were made as the children progressed through first and second grade. Thus, expectations that were formed based on the students' registration forms tended to exert a strong influence on children's school lives, in spite of their actual performance and ability. These results, and others like them (Brophy & Good, 1974) suggest that teachers' expectations about students influence the nature of classroom interaction patterns. In particular, students who the teacher perceives as fast learners may receive more positive communications from the teacher than students who the teacher perceives as slower learners.

Quality of Student-Teacher Interaction. Further research on classroom process shows that teacher expectations can influence the quality of student-teacher interactions. For example, Brophy & Good (1970) observed student-teacher interactions in a first-grade classroom. Teachers were asked to rank their students in order of expected achievement. For purposes of the study, the top three boys and the top three girls were counted as "highs" and the bottom three boys and three girls were counted as "lows." Figure 18–9 shows some of the differences in classroom interactions for students who the teacher perceived as "high" versus "low" in achievement ability. As can be seen, the highs and lows receive equivalent amounts of attention, but the quality of the interactions varies greatly—in particular, highs obtain more praise, lows obtain more criticism, highs participate in student-initiated interactions more often, lows participate in teacher-initiated interactions more often. Brophy & Good (1974) reconcile the data in Figure 18–8 with the data in Figure 18–9 by noting that the latter study took place in a school that used tracking and thus the differences between highs and lows would be less than in the previously reported studies. Brophy & Good (1974) also found evidence that teachers communicate their expectations to students. Figure 18–10 shows that teachers tend to give relatively more attention to the correct answers of highs than the correct answers of lows, and more attention to the wrong answers of lows as compared to the wrong answers of highs. Also teachers tend to follow through to help highs find the right answer much more often than for lows. These student-teacher interactions could help students develop their own low or high expectations. This process of communicating teacher expectations to students may be the mechanism through which teacher expectations influence student achievement.

How Teacher Expectations Affect Student Achievement. Teachers' natural expectations may influence student achievement as well as classroom processes. For example, Palardy (1969) used a general interview consisting of

FIGURE 18–9   Differences in Classroom Interactions for Low and High Expectation Students

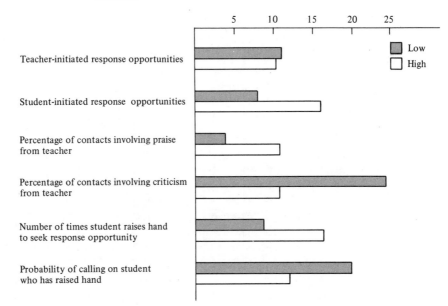

Adapted from Brophy and Good (1974)

many different kinds of questions in order to identify five first grade teachers who believed girls were generally better readers than boys and five teachers who believed that there were no sex differences in reading ability. Next, Palardy examined the reading achievement scores for the students of these ten teachers, adjusting the scores for students' IQ. In classes where teachers did not expect sex differences, no sex differences in reading achievement were obtained; in classes where teachers expected girls to read better than boys, girls performed better than boys in reading achievemen..

More recently, Firestone & Brody (1975) carefully observed student-teacher classroom interactions at various times during children's progression through kindergarten and first grade. The observations included noting the number of times: a student was encouraged or praised, a student was directed to do something, a student's idea was accepted or used by the teacher, a student was chosen to demonstrate something to the class, a student was criticized, and so on. In addition, students were given a standardized test of reading and math achievement. Using only information about classroom interaction and some demographic information, Firestone & Brody (1975) were able to predict performance on the achievement test with moderate success. For example, IQ correlated with reading achievement at $r = .47$ but a combination of classroom interaction and demographic variables correlated with

FIGURE 18–10   **Differential Communication of Teacher Expectations to High and Low Expectation Students**

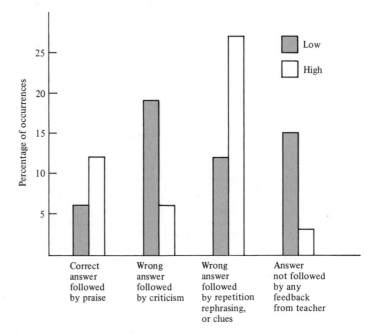

Adapted from Brophy & Good (1970)

reading achievement at $r = .62$. Apparently, the pattern of classroom interaction and the student's achievement are related; however, in the Firestone & Brody study it is not clear whether classroom interactions cause differences in achievement or whether differences in achievement cause different patterns of classroom interaction. Cooper (1979) has suggested that achievement and classroom interaction patterns may serve to support and maintain each other, although the specific mechanisms are not yet understood.

In summary, Figure 18–11 shows a preliminary model of the relation between teacher expectations, classroom processes, and student achievement. As can be seen, the teacher uses external sources of information such as test score data (i.e., "labels") as well as his/her own observations in order to form an expectation about a student. These teacher expectations, then, influence the quality of the student-teacher interactions in the classroom. In turn, these interactions serve to communicate expectations about academic achievement to the student. Finally, these student expectations influence student achievement. The circle is closed—and the system maintained—by arrows from student achievement back to test data and teacher observations; in other words, the student's level of achievement may be detected in tests

FIGURE 18–11 A Model of the Relationships among Teacher Expectations, Classroom Processes, and Student Achievement

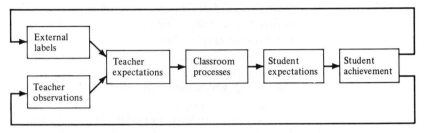

and observations that the teacher uses to make his/her own expectations for
the student.

Implications of Research on Teacher Expectations

It may be tempting to conclude from the foregoing discussion that labels and
expectations are "bad"; however, a more accurate conclusion would be that
teachers will naturally form attitudes and expectations about their students.
Thus it is important that teachers develop expectations that are most likely to
help each child and that can be modified as warranted. For example,
Shavelson, Cadwell & Izu (1977) found that teachers are able to change their
expectations of students when given new information. Labels per se may not be
the culprits that Rosenthal & Jacobson's study suggested; for example, objective data about a student's academic ability may serve to increase teacher
expectations that would otherwise be formed solely on the basis of a student's
social class or ethnic background. If objective tests are eliminated from schools,
this will leave teachers with more subjective information (e.g., prejudices that
are not relevant) to use in forming expectations. Furthermore, it is clear that
most teachers do not accept "labels" from standardized tests as the only source
of information in building expectations.

TEACHER DECISION MAKING

What happens in the classroom often involves a social interaction between the
teacher and the students. The nature of the interaction depends partly on how
the teacher processes information, including the teacher's thinking, judgment,
and planning. Let's refer to these cognitive processes as teacher decision
making, and in this section we will explore the view of the "teacher as a decision
maker" (Clark & Yinger, 1979).

Describing Episodes of Teacher Decision Making

Shavelson (1973, 1976) has analyzed classroom videotapes in order to provide examples of teacher decision making. For example, one videotape presented the following teacher behaviors:

1. The teacher initiated a discussion with a question.
2. When several students raised their hands, the teacher called on one of them.
3. After the student answered, the teacher was dissatisfied with the answer.
4. The teacher asked the student a second question.
5. Since the student did not respond, the teacher asked a third question.
6. The teacher mumbled something and eventually redirected the questions to other students.

A straightforward analysis of teacher and student behavior would find that the teacher asked three questions of which one was answered by a student. However, Shavelson argues that much more is going on in this segment than question asking and answering; the teacher is making many decisions throughout even this short segment. Shavelson suggests that the teacher makes the following decisions (corresponding to the six behavior descriptions listed):

1. The teacher decided to begin by asking a question rather than using some other instructional act.
2. The teacher decided to call on a particular student rather than some other student.
3. The teacher decided that the student's answer was inadequate.
4. The teacher decided on a technique for how to deal with the inadequate answer (i.e., to ask another question).
5. The teacher decided on a technique for how to deal with the student's inability to answer the second question (i.e., to ask a third question).
6. The teacher decided that the technique of asking additional questions was not working, so the teacher decided to adopt a new plan (i.e., to call on a different student).

The traditional method of evaluating the teacher's "effectiveness" would be to count the number of questions that were asked. However, as Shavelson points out, the asking of questions probably had little positive effect on the student. Instead, Shavelson points out that the critical measure of the teacher's effectiveness was the decision to continue questioning the student when other techiques (such as explaining or refocusing) might have been better for the student's learning. Shavelson summarizes (1976, p. 374) his analysis: "In considering teaching as decision making, then, one focuses on when a particular act is used and which act among other alternative acts is used, rather than on how often it is used."

Cognitive Analysis of Teacher Decision Making

Steps in Teacher Decision Making.   Suppose that we were able to know what was going on inside a teacher's head as he/she taught a lesson to a class of students. What are some of the ongoing decisions that a teacher makes during the lesson? Peterson & Clark (1978) have suggested a cyclical process involving the following steps:

1. The teacher provides instruction.
2. As part of the classroom instructional process, the teacher observes student behavior.
3. The teacher decides whether the behavior is tolerable. If so, the teacher continues teaching (i.e., goes to step 1); if not, the teacher must make another decision, in step 4.
4. The teacher decides whether it is possible to change the instruction (i.e., to change his/her teaching behavior). If not, the teacher continues with the current instruction (i.e., goes to step 1); if so, the teacher makes another decision, in step 5.
5. The teacher, having decided that there is intolerable student behavior and that the teacher knows a plan of action for responding, now decides whether or not to engage in the alternative plan of action. If not, the teacher continues in current instruction (i.e., goes to step 1); if so, the teacher initiates new classroom instructional behavior to replace the existing sequence (i.e., step 6).
6. The teacher initiates a new instructional sequence (and goes to step 1).

This description of ongoing classroom teacher decision making is summarized in Figure 18–12. As you can see, there are four major paths that a teacher may take in making decisions about how to respond to student behavior:

1. Path 1. Decide at step 3 that the student behavior is tolerable.
2. Path 2. Decide at step 3 that the student behavior is intolerable; decide at step 4 that there is not an acceptable alternative teacher behavior.
3. Path 3. Decide at step 2 that the student behavior is intolerable; decide at step 4 that there is an alternative teacher behavior available; decide at step 5 not to use that alternative behavior.
4. Path 4. Decide at step 3 that the student behavior is intolerable; decide at step 4 that an alternative teacher behavior is available; decide at step 5 to initiate that alternative instructional behavior.

Changes in Decision Making Due to Experience.   In order to study the occurrence of these four decision paths, Peterson & Clark (1978) made videotapes of twelve experienced teachers who were giving a 3-hour social studies lesson to eight students. Later, parts of the tapes were played for the teachers and they were asked to tell what they were doing and thinking about

FIGURE 18–12 A Model of Teacher Decision Making

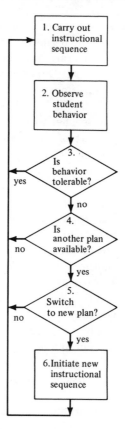

Adapted from Peterson & Clark (1978)

during each segment. In particular, the teachers were interviewed in a way that would reveal whether the teacher was attending to student behavior (i.e., step 2), whether a decision was made about the acceptability of the student behavior (step 3), whether the teacher considered changing the course of instruction (step 4), whether the teacher actually did change his/her behavior (step 5).

Table 18–2 summarizes the average number of times that the teachers seemed to be following each of the four paths. Table 18–2 shows these statistics for each of three days; on each day, the teachers taught the same lesson to different students. As you can see, on the first day, most of the student behaviors are judged to be tolerable by the teacher and there are very few instances of a teacher deciding to change his/her behavior during the lesson (i.e., opting for path 4). In contrast, by the third day, there is less of a tendency to judge student behaviors as tolerable (path 1) and more of a tendency to change teacher behavior in response to intolerable student behavior (path 4).

TABLE 18–2 How Many Times Does a Teacher Follow Each of Four Major Kinds of Decision Paths during a Social Studies Lesson?

	Path 1	Path 2	Path 3	Path 4
Day 1	2.8	.4	.3	.4
Day 2	2.6	.5	.2	.7
Day 3	2.4	.3	.2	1.0

Adapted from Peterson & Clark (1978)

Apparently, as the teachers gain more experience in teaching the lesson assigned to them, they are able to deviate from their plan in response to their interactions with students during instruction.

Teachers' Planning of Classroom Instruction

Types of Planning. Another crucial aspect of teacher decision making may be the teacher's planning of instruction. In order to investigate teachers' planning, Peterson, Marx & Clark (1978) asked twelve experienced teachers to plan and present a 3-hour social studies lesson to a group of junior high school students. (In fact, teachers were asked to repeat this process for 3 days, but we will look only at the first day here.) Each teacher was given 90 minutes to plan a lesson, and during this time the teacher was asked to "think aloud" as he or she planned. In looking over the teachers' planning statements, Peterson et al. identified eight different kinds of statements, summarized below:

Subject matter—Statements dealing with information found in the text or information clearly derived from material in the text.

Lower-order subject matter—Subject matter statements in which the material is used as given.

Higher-order subject matter—Subject matter statements in which material is interpreted, compared/contrasted, conceptualized, applied in problem solving.

Instructional processes—Statements about instructional activities or strategies that the teacher intends to use.

Objectives—Statements about the intended learning outcomes or products of instruction.

Materials—Statements about the physical materials or physical environment of learning.

Learner—Statements about the cognitive or affective characteristics of students.

Miscellaneous—Statements that do not fit into any other category.

Table 18–3 shows the average number of statements made during planning for each of eight categories. As can be seen, the teachers spent a lot of effort in

TABLE 18–3 Average Number of Planning Statements Made Corresponding to Each of Eight Categories

Planning Category	
Subject matter	79.7
Lower-order	55.5
Higher-order	19.0
Instructional process	48.7
Objectives	7.8
Materials	12.8
Learner	10.4
Miscellaneous	40.3
Total	199.7

Adapted from Peterson, Marx & Clark (1978)

planning the subject matter. Within this category, teachers produced almost three times as many statements about low-order aspects of the subject matter (such as facts) as about high-order aspects of the subject matter (such as application of principles). The next most active category was the instructional process, suggesting that teachers were also concerned with planning specific activities. Relatively little attention was paid to materials, learners, or objectives. In short, this study indicates that teachers tended to focus their planning on the curriculum (i.e., subject matter) that was given to them, rather than beginning by trying to set objectives or ascertain student needs.

The teachers differed from one another in how they spent their planning time. Teachers who scored high on a test of "conceptual level" (Hunt, Greenwood, Noy & Watson, 1973) tended to make more statements about instructional processes and objectives (i.e., they tended to focus on what they want to happen and how to make it happen). In contrast, teachers who scored low on a test of "conceptual level" tended to make more statements about lower-level aspects of the subject matter (i.e., they tended to focus on the material given to them).

Effects of Planning on Teaching. Does teacher planning affect teacher behaviors during instruction? Peterson et al. (1978) observed that teachers who made many planning statements about subject matter also tended to focus on subject matter during the lesson; teachers who made many planning statements about lower-order subject matter tended to focus on lower-order cognitive processes during instruction; teachers who made many planning statements about higher-order subject matter tended to focus on higher-order cognitive processes during instruction. Interestingly, teachers who made many planning statements about objectives did not seem to focus on goals during instruction. However, this may be due to the way that the experimenter described the nature of the lesson to the teachers. In general, there does seem to be a sensible relationship between teachers' planning statements and their in-class behaviors.

Effects of Planning on Learning. Finally, we might want to ask, Are teachers' planning statements related to student achievement and attitude? Table 18–4 shows the correlations between each of the planning statement categories and performance on a 63-item multiple choice exam covering both facts and concepts. As can be seen, focus on subject matter, including both lower-order and higher-order material, tended to be positively related to student achievement. Table 18–4 also shows that focus on instructional process and objectives was positively related to students' attitude toward the teacher and subject. In summary, there does seem to be a relationship between the teacher's decision making (e.g., decisions made during planning) and student achievement and attitude.

Implications of Research on Teacher Decision Making

Teachers' decision making affects what happens in classrooms and hence what students learn. Two types of decision making explored in this section were decisions during instruction and decisions during planning for instruction. Decisions during instruction include deciding whether a lesson is working and deciding how to change the lesson if it is not working. More experience with teaching a lesson seems to allow teachers more flexibility in adapting the lesson to the needs of the students. This finding suggests that frequently changing teaching assignments may serve to reduce the the flexibility of teachers' decision making during instruction.

Planning decisions may focus on questions such as what to teach, what the goal of instruction should be, and how to accomplish the goal. One interesting aspect of the research presented in this section is that teachers who spend much time planning subject matter tend to devote more instruction to the subject matter and students tend to learn more. The role of planning is a crucial

TABLE 18–4   Is Teacher Planning Related to Student Achievement and Attitude?

Planning Category	Achievement Test	Attitude Test
Subject Matter	.59	−.35
Lower-order	.38	−.30
Higher-order	.64	−.32
Instructional process	−.48	.35
Objectives	−.34	.61
Materials	.11	.15
Learner	−.35	.31
Miscellaneous	−.40	−.11

Adapted from Peterson et al. (1978)

one that affects student learning. Thus teachers should be given adequate time and support to plan classroom activities.

In a recent review, Shavelson & Stern (1981) summarized some of the decisions that teachers had to make in planning and carrying out a reading program. For example, teachers made decisions about whether to group by ability, use whole class instruction, or group heterogeneously. Since most teachers decide to group by ability, another decision concerns the rate of instruction for different ability groups. In some cases, for example, the high group is paced fifteen times faster than the slow group (Shavelson & Stern, 1981). Furthermore, Shavelson & Stern argue that we need a comprehensive taxonomy of the kinds of decisions that teachers make, including planning decisions and in-class decisions.

CONCLUSION

Research on classroom processes is in its childhood. For example, in a recent review, Good (1983, p. 128) pointed out that fifteen years ago "we simply had no idea about what took place in American classrooms," but today we can say "classroom research has made considerable progress." Early research on classroom processes was at a very gross level of inquiry, asking questions like, "Does time (or class size, or some other global variable) affect student achievement?" However, as Good (1983, p. 142) points out, in order to understand and improve the process of classroom instruction, we need to describe the subject matter that is being examined and we need to focus on "how teachers and students think and behave" during the classroom instructional process.

In this chapter we have examined four representative topics concerning classroom processes: the roles of instructional time, class size and composition, teacher expectations, and teacher decision making. In examining the role of time and class size variables, we found that we needed to also examine the role of teacher and student cognitive processes during instruction. In examining teacher decision making and teacher expectations, we found that classroom instructional processes are heavily influenced by the cognitive processes of the teacher.

This final chapter takes us full circle. This chapter has shown that an understanding of classroom instruction requires an understanding of how children develop and think (Chapters 2–4), how instruction affects children's processing of information (Chapters 5–9), how to describe and analyze learning of different subject matters (Chapters 10–14), and how individual differences among students affect instruction (Chapters 15–17). As you can see, the theme of this chapter also represents the theme of this book: a fuller understanding of classroom processes requires an understanding of the cognitive processes of teachers and students.

SUGGESTED READINGS

Berliner, D. C. (ed.) (1983). *Special Issue: Research on Teaching*. Published in *Educational Psychologist, 1*(3). (A collection of papers by leading researchers of classroom processes.)

Cooper, H. & Good, T. L. (1983). *Pygmalion grows up*. New York: Academic. (A review of the current status of the "Pygmalion effect.")

Peterson, P. & Walberg, H. J. (eds.) (1979). *Research on teaching*. Berkeley: McCutchan. (A collection of papers on classroom processes.)

Wittrock, M. C. (ed.) (1985). *Handbook of research on teaching*. New York: Macmillan. (A collection of articles concerned with research on classroom teaching.)

References

Adams, A., Carnine, D. & Gersten, R. (1982). Instructional strategies for studying content area texts in the intermediate grades. *Reading Research Quarterly, 18,* 27–55.

Adams, J. A. (1976). *Learning and memory.* Homewood, IL: Dorsey Press.

Aiken, E. G., Thomas, G. S. & Shennum, W. Memory for a lecture: Effects of notes, lecture rate, and information density. (1975). *Journal of Educational Psychology, 67,* 439–444.

Anastasiow, N. J., Bibly, S. A., Leonhardt, T. M. & Borish, G. D. (1970). A comparison of guided discovery, discovery and didactic teaching of math to kindergarten poverty children. *American Educational Research Journal, 7,* 493–510.

Anderson, L. W. (1973). *Time and school learning.* Unpublished doctoral dissertation, University of Chicago.

Anderson, R. C. & Biddle, W. B. (1975). On asking people questions about what they are reading. *Psychology of Learning and Motivation, 9,* 90–132.

Anderson, R. C. & Freebody, P. (1981). Vocabulary knowledge. In J. T. Guthrie (Ed.), *Comprehension and teaching: Research Reviews.* Newark, DE: International Reading Association.

Andre, M. D. A. & Anderson, T. H. (1979). The development and evaluation of a self-questioning study technique. *Reading Research Quarterly, 14,* 605–623.

Anton, T. A. (1981). *Length of school day and school year: A comparison of California with other states.* Stockton, CA: Lincoln Unified School District.

Appel, L. F., Cooper, R. G., McCarrell, N., Sims-Knight, J., Yussen, S. R. & Flavell, J. H. (1972). The development of the distinction between perceiving and memorizing. *Child Development, 43,* 1365–1381.

Applebee, A. N. (1971). Research in reading retardation: Two critical problems. *Journal of Child Psychology and Psychiatry, 12,* 91–113.

Applebee, A. N. (1982). Writing and learning in school settings. In M. Nystrant (Ed.), *What writers know.* New York: Academic Press.

Armbruster, B. B. & Anderson, T. H. (1984). Mapping: representing informative text diagrammatically. In C. D. Holley & D. F. Dansereau (Eds.), *Spatial learning strategies.* Orlando, FL: Academic Press.

Arlin, M. N. (1973). *Learning rate and learning rate variance under mastery learning conditions.* Unpublished doctoral dissertation, University of Chicago.

Ashcraft, M. H. & Stazyk, E. H. (1981). Mental addition: A test of three verification models. *Memory & Cognition, 9,* 185–196.

Atkinson, J. W. (1958). *Motives in fantasy, action, and society.* Princeton, NJ: Van Nostrand.

Atkinson, J. W. (1964). *An introduction to motivation.* Princeton, NJ: Van Nostrand.

Atkinson, J. W. (1965). The mainsprings of achievement-oriented activity. In J. D. Krumboltz (Ed.), *Learning and the educational process*. Chicago: Rand-McNally.

Atkinson, J. W. & Feather, N. T. (1966). *A theory of achievement motivation*. New York: Wiley.

Atkinson, R. C. (1975). Mnemotechnics in second-language learning. *American Psychologist, 30*, 821–828.

Atkinson, R. C. & Raugh, M. R. (1975). An application of the mnemonic keyword method to the acquisition of a Russian vocabulary. *Journal of Experimental Psychology: Human Learning and Memory, 104*, 126–133.

Ausubel, D. P. (1960). The use of advance organizers in the learning and retention of meaningful verbal material. *Journal of Educational Psychology, 51*, 267–272.

Ausubel, D. P. (1968). *Educational psychology: A cognitive view*. New York: Holt, Rinehart & Winston.

Ausubel, D. P. & Youssef, M. (1963). The role of discriminability in meaningful parallel learning. *Journal of Educational Psychology, 54*, 331–336.

Bakan, P. (1969). Hypnotizability, laterality of eye movements, and functional brain asymmetry. *Perceptual and Motor Skills, 28*, 927–932.

Baker, L. & Anderson, R. C. (1982). Effects of inconsistent information on text processing: Evidence for comprehension monitoring. *Reading Research Quarterly, 17*, 281–293.

Bandura, A. & Walters, R. H. (1963). *Social learning and personality development*. New York: Holt, Rinehart & Winston.

Barnes, B. R. & Clawson, E. U. (1975). Do advance organizers facilitate learning? Recommendations for further research based on an analysis of 32 studies. *Review of Educational Research, 45*, 637–659.

Barnett, J. E., DiVesta, F. J. & Rogozinski, J. T. (1981). What is learned in note taking? *Journal of Educational Psychology, 73*, 181–192.

Baron, J. (1977). What we might know about orthographic rules. In S. Dornic (Ed.), *Attention and performance VI*. Hillsdale, NJ: Erlbaum.

Baron, J. (1978). The word-superiority effect: Perceptual learning from reading. In W. K. Estes (Ed.), *Handbook of learning and cognitive processes. Vol. 6*. Hillsdale, NJ: Erlbaum.

Bartlett, B. J. (1978). *Top-level structure as an organizational strategy for recall of classroom text*. Unpublished doctoral dissertation, Arizona State University.

Bartlett, E. J. (1982). Learning to revise: Some component processes. In M. Nystrand (Ed.), *What writers know*. New York: Academic Press.

Bartlett, E. J. & Scribner, S. (1981). Text and content: An investigation of referential organization in children's written narratives. In C. H. Frederiksen & J. F. Dominic (Eds.), *Writing. Vol. 2*. Hillsdale, NJ: Erlbaum.

Bartlett, F. C. (1932). *Remembering: A study in experimental and social psychology*. Cambridge, UK: Cambridge University Press.

Bayman, P. and Mayer, R. E. (1983). Diagnosis of beginning programmers' misconceptions of BASIC programming statements. *Communications of the ACM, 26*, 519–521.

Beck, I. L., Perfetti, C. A. & McKeown, M. G. (1982). Effects of long-term vocabulary instruction on lexical access and reading comprehension. *Journal of Educational Psychology, 74*, 506–521.

Beckerman, T. M. & Good, T. L. (1981). The classroom ratio of high and low aptitude students and its effects on achievement. *American Educational Research Journal, 18,* 317–327.

Beilin, H. (1971). The training and acquisition of logical operations. In M. F. Rosskopf, L. P. Steffe, and S. Tabach (Eds.), *Piagetian cognitive-developmental research and mathematical education.* Washington, D.C.: National Council of Teachers of Mathematics.

Belmont, J. M. & Butterfield, E. C. (1971). Learning strategies as determinants of memory deficiencies. *Cognitive Psychology, 2,* 411–420.

Benbow, C. & Stanley, J. (1980). Sex differences in mathematics ability: Fact or artifact? *Science, 210,* 1262–1264.

Bereiter, C. (1980). Development in writing. In L. W. Gregg & E. R. Sternberg (Eds.), *Cognitive processes in writing.* Hillsdale, NJ: Erlbaum.

Berliner, D. C. (1979). Tempus educare. In P. L. Peterson & H. J. Walberg (Eds.), *Research on teaching.* Berkeley, CA: McCutchan.

Binet, A. (1962). The nature and measurement of intelligence. In L. Postman (Ed.), *Psychology in the making: Histories of selected research programs.* New York: Knopf. (Originally published, Paris: Flammarion, 1911).

Binor, S. (1974). *The relative effectiveness of mastery learning strategies in second language acquisition.* Unpublished masters thesis, University of Chicago.

Bishop, R. L. (1975). The JOURNALISM programs: Help for the weary writer. *Creative Computing, 1,* 28–30.

Block, J. H. (1970). *The effects of various levels of performance on selected cognitive, affective, and time variables.* Unpublished doctoral dissertation, University of Chicago.

Block, J. H. & Anderson, L. W. (1975). *Mastery learning in classroom instruction.* New York: Macmillan.

Block, J. H. & Burns, R. B. (1976). Mastery learning. In L. S. Shulman (Ed.), *Review of Research in Education, Vol. 4.* Itasca, IL: Peacock.

Bloom, B. S. (1976). *Human characteristics and school learning.* New York: McGraw-Hill.

Bloom, B. S. and Broder, L. J. (1950). *Problem-solving processes of college students.* Chicago: University of Chicago Press.

Bloom, B. S., Englehart, M. D., Furst, E. J., Hill, W. H. & Krathwohl, D. R. (1956). *Taxonomy of educational objectives: The classification of educational goals. Handbook 1: Cognitive domain.* New York: McKay.

Bobrow, D. G. (1968). Natural language input for a computer problem solving system. In M. Minsky, (Ed.), *Semantic Information Processing.* Cambridge, MA: M.I.T. Press.

Boker, J. (1974). Immediate and delayed retention effects of interspersing questions in written instructional passages. *Journal of Educational Psychology, 66,* 96–98.

Borko, H. & Cadwell, J. (1982). Individual differences in teachers' decision strategies: An investigation of classroom organization and management decisions. *Journal of Educational Psychology, 74,* 598–610.

Borko, H., Cone, R., Russo, N. A., & Shavelson, R. J. (1979). Teachers' decision making. In P. L. Peterson & H. J. Walberg (Eds.), *Research on Teaching.* Berkeley, CA: McCutchan.

Bower, G. H. & Trabasso, T. R. (1963). Reversals prior to solution in concept identification. *Journal of Experimental Psychology, 66,* 409–418.

Brainerd, C. J. (1974). *Neo-Piagetian training programs revisited: Is there any support for the cognitive developmental stage hypothesis?* Cognition, 2, 349–370.

Branca, N. (1983). *Problem solving processes of upper elementary school children*. Report FED-79-19617. Washington: National Science Foundation.

Bransford, J. D., Arbitman-Stein, R., Stein, B. S. & Vye, N. J. (1985). Improving thinking and learning skills: An analysis of three approaches. In J. W. Segal, S. F. Chipman, & R. Glaser (Eds.), *Thinking and learning skills: Volume 1, Relating instruction to research*. Hillsdale, NJ: Erlbaum.

Bransford, J. D. & Johnson, M. K. (1972). Contextual prerequisites for understanding: Some investigations of comprehension and recall. *Journal of Verbal Learning and Verbal Behavior, 11,* 717–726.

Bransford, J. D. & Stein, B. (1984). *The IDEAL problem solver*. New York: Freeman.

Bretzing, B. H. & Kulhavy, R. W. (1981). Note-taking and passage style. *Journal of Educational Psychology, 73,* 242–250.

Brophy, J. & Good, T. (1970). Teachers' communication of different expectations for children's classroom performance: Some behavioral data. *Journal of Educational Psychology, 61,* 365–374.

Brophy, J. E. & Good, T. L. (1974). *Teacher-student relationships: Causes and consequences*. New York: Holt, Rinehart & Winston.

Brown, A. L. & Campione, J. C. (1977). Training strategic study time apportionment in educable retarded children. *Intelligence, 1,* 94–107.

Brown, A. L., Campione, J. C. & Barclay, C. R. (1979). Training self-checking routines for estimating test readiness: Generalization from list learning to prose recall. *Child Development, 50,* 501–512.

Brown, A. L., Campione, J. C. & Day, J. D. (1981). *Learning to learn: On training students to learn from texts*. Educational Researcher, 10, 14–21.

Brown, A. L. & Smiley, S. S. (1977). Rating the importance of structural units of prose passages: A problem of metacognitive development. *Child Development, 48,* 1–8.

Brown, A. L. & Smiley, S. S. (1978). The development of strategies for studying texts. *Child Development, 49,* 1076–1088.

Brown, F. G. (1970). *Principles of educational and psychological testing*. New York: Holt, Rinehart and Winston.

Brown, J. S. and R. R. Burton. (1978). Diagnostic models for procedural bugs in basic mathematical skills. *Cognitive Science, 2,* 155–192.

Brownell, W. A. (1935). Psychological considerations in the learning and teaching of arithmetic. In *The teaching of arithmetic: Tenth yearbook of the National Council of Teachers of Mathematics*. New York: Columbia University Press

Brownell, W. A. and Moser, H. E. (1949). Meaningful vs. mechanical learning: A study on grade 3 subtraction. In *Duke University Research Studies in Education, No. 8.* Durham, NC: Duke University Press.

Bruce, B., Collins, A., Rubin, A. & Gentner, D. (1982). Three perspectives on writing. *Educational Psychologist, 17,* 131–145.

Bruner, J. S. (1960). *The process of education*. Cambridge, MA: Harvard University Press.

Bruner, J. S. (1961). The act of discovery. *Harvard Educational Review, 31,* 21–32.

Bruner, J. S. (1964). The course of cognitive growth. *American Psychologist, 19,* 1–15.

Bruner, J. S. & Kenney, H. (1966). Multiple ordering. In J. S. Bruner, R. R. Oliver, & P. M. Greenfield (Eds.), *Studies in cognitive growth*. New York: Wiley.

Buros, O. K. (1978). *Eighth mental measurement yearbook*. Highland Park, NJ: Gryphon.

Calfee, R., Chapman, R. & Venezky, R. (1972). How a child needs to think to learn to read. In L. W. Gregg (Ed.), *Cognition in learning and memory*. New York: Wiley.

California Assessment Program. (1980). *Student achievement in California schools: 1979–80 annual report*. Sacramento, CA: California State Department of Education.

California Assessment Program. (1982). *Student achievement in California schools: 1981–82 annual report*. Sacramento, CA: California State Department of Education.

Camstra, B. & Van Bruggen, J. (1984). Schematizing: The empirical evidence. In C. D. Holley & D. F. Dansereau (Eds.), *Spatial learning strategies*. Orlando, FL: Academic Press.

Cariello, R. P. (1980). *The selective effects of questions in mastery and nonmastery instruction*. Unpublished doctoral dissertation, University of California, Santa Barbara.

Carlberg, C. & Kavale, K. (1980). The efficacy of special versus regular placement for exceptional children: A meta-analysis. *Journal of Special Education, 14*, 295–309.

Carpenter, P. A. & Just, M. A. (1981). Cognitive processes in reading: Models based on readers' eye fixations. In A. M. Lesgold & C. A. Perfetti (Eds.), *Interactive processes in reading*. Hillsdale, NJ: Erlbaum.

Carrell, J. & Tiffany, W. R. (1960). *Phonetics: Theory and application to speech improvement*. New York: McGraw-Hill.

Carrier, C. A. & Titus, A. (1981). Effects of notetaking pretaining and test mode expectations on learning from lecture. *American Educational Research Journal, 18*, 385–397.

Carroll, J. B. (1963). A model of school learning. *Teachers College Record, 64*, 723–733.

Carter, J. F. & Van Matre, N. H. (1975). Notetaking versus note having. *Journal of Educational Psychology, 67*, 900–904.

Carter, L. F. (1984). The sustaining effects study of compensatory and elementary education. *Educational Researcher, 13*, 4–13.

Caruso, D. R., Taylor, J. J. & Detterman, D. K. (1982). Intelligence research and intelligent policy. In D. K. Detterman & R. J. Sternberg (Eds.), *How and how much can intelligence be increased?* Norwood, NJ: ABLEX.

Carver, R. P. (1971). *Sense and nonsense in speed reading*. Silver Springs, MD: Revrac.

Carver, R. P. (1973). Reading as reasoning: Implications for measurement. In W. H. MacGinitie (Ed.), *Assessment problems in reading*. Newark, DE: International Reading Association.

Case, R. (1972). Validation of a neo-Piagetian mental capacity construct. *Journal of Experimental Child Psychology, 14*, 287–302.

Case, R. (1978a). Intellectual development from birth to adulthood: A neo-Piagetian interpretation. In R. S. Siegler (Ed.), *Children's thinking: What develops?* Hillsdale, NJ: Erlbaum.

Case, R. (1978b). Implications of developmental psychology for the design of effective instruction. In A. M. Lesgold, J. W. Pellegrino, S. D. Fokkema & R. Glaser (Eds.), *Cognitive psychology and instruction*. New York: Plenum Press.

Case, R. (1985). A developmentally based approach to the problem of instructional design. In S. F. Chipman, J. W. Segal & R. Glaser (Eds.), *Thinking and learning skills, Volume 2. Research and open questions*. Hillsdale, NJ: Erlbaum.

Cattell, J. M. (1886). The time taken up by cerebral operations. *Mind, 11*, 220–242.

Cermak, L. S. (1983). Information processing deficits in children with learning disabilities. *Journal of Learning Disabilities, 16*, 599–605.

Chall, J. S. (1967). *Learning to read: The great debate*. New York: McGraw-Hill.

Chall, J. S. (1979). The great debate: Ten years later, with a modest proposal for reading stages. In L. B. Resnick & P. A. Weaver (Eds.), *Theory and practice of early reading*. Hillsdale, NJ: Erlbaum.

Champagne, A. B., Gunstone, R. F. & Klopfer, L. E. (1985). Effecting changes in cognitive structures among physics students. In H. T. West & A. L. Pines (Eds.), *Cognitive structure and conceptual change*. Orlando, FL: Academic Press.

Chi, M. T. H. (1978). Knowledge structures and memory development. In R. S. Siegler (Ed.), *Children's thinking: What develops?* Hillsdale, NJ: Erlbaum.

Chiesi, H. L., Spilich, G. J. & Voss, J. F. (1979). Acquisition of domain-related information in relation to high and low domain knowledge. *Journal of Learning and Verbal Behavior, 18,* 257–273.

Clark, C. M. & Yinger, R. J. (1979). Teachers' thinking. In P. L. Peterson & H. J. Walbert (Eds.), *Research on teaching*. Berkeley, CA: McCutchan.

Clark, H. H. & Clark, E. V. (1977). *Psychology and language*. New York: Harcourt, Brace, Jovanovich.

Clarke, A. (1977). *The encyclopedia of how it works*. New York: A&W.

Clay, M. M. (1973). *Reading: The patterning of complex behavior*. Auckland, NZ: Heinemann.

Clement, J. (1982). Students' preconceptions in introductory mechanics. *American Journal of Physics, 50,* 66–71.

Cohen, H., Hillman, D. & Agne, R. (1978). Cognitive level and college physics achievement. *American Journal of Physics, 46,* 1026.

Collins, A. (1977). Processes in acquiring knowledge. In R. C. Spiro & W. E. Montague (Eds.), *Schooling and the acquisition of knowledge*. Hillsdale, NJ: Erlbaum.

Collins, A. and Stevens, A. L. (1982). Goals and strategies of inquiry teachers. In R. Glaser (Ed.), *Advances in instructional psychology, Vol. 2*. Hillsdale, NJ: Erlbaum.

Collins, A., Warnock, E. H., Aiello, N. & Miller, M. L. (1975). Reasoning from incomplete information. In D. G. Bobrow & A. Collins (Eds.), *Representation and understanding: Studies in cognitive science*. Orlando, FL: Academic Press.

Comprehensive Tests of Basic Skills. (1982). *CTBS: Forms U and V test review kit*. Monterey, CA: CTB/McGraw-Hill.

Conn, L., Edwards, C., Rosenthal, R. & Crowne, D. (1968). Perception of emotion and response to teachers' expectancy by elementary school children. *Psychological Reports, 22,* 27–34.

Cooper, H. M. (1979). Pygmalion grows up: A model for teacher expectation communication and performance influence. *Review of Educational Research, 49,* 389–410.

Cook, L. K. (1982). The effects of text structure on the comprehension of scientific prose. Unpublished doctoral dissertation, University of California, Santa Barbara.

Covington, M. V. & Crutchfield, R. S. (1965). Facilitation of creative problem solving. *Programmed Instruction, 4,* 3–5, 10.

Covington, M. V., Crutchfield, R. S. & Davies, L. B. (1966). *The productive thinking program*. Berkeley, CA: Brazelton.

Covington, M. V., Crutchfield, R. S., Davies, L. B. & Olton, R. M. (1974). *The productive thinking program*. Columbus, OH: Merrill.

Craig, R. C. (1956). Directed versus independent discovery of established relations. *Journal of Educational Psychology, 47,* 223–234.

Crawford, C. (1925). Some experimental studies of the results of college notetaking. *Journal of Educational Research, 12,* 379–386.

Cronbach, L. J. (1957). The two disciplines of scientific psychology. *American Psychologist, 12,* 671–684.

Cronbach, L. J. & Snow, R. E. (1977). *Aptitudes and instructional methods*. New York: Irvington.

Crowder, R. G. (1982). *The psychology of reading*. New York: Oxford University Press.

Dalbey, J. & Linn, M. C. (1985). The demands and requirements of computer programming: A literature review. *Journal of Educational Computing Research, 1,* 253–274.

Dansereau, D. F. (1978). The development of a learning strategies curriculum. In H. F. O'Neill, Jr. (Ed.), *Learning strategies*. New York: Academic Press.

Dansereau, D. F., Collins, K. W., McDonald, B. A., Holley, C. D., Garland, J. C., Diekhoff, G. & Evans, S. H. (1979). Development and evaluation of an effective learning strategy program. *Journal of Educational Psychology, 71,* 64–73.

Davis, G. A. (1973). *Psychology of problem solving: Theory and practice*. New York: Basic Books.

Davis, G. A. & Houtman, S. E. (1968). *Thinking creatively: A guide to training imagination*. Madison, WI: Wisconsin Research and Development Center.

de Beaugrande, R. (1982). Psychology and composition: Past, present, and future. In M. Nystrand (Ed.), *What writers know*. New York: Academic Press.

de Bono, E. (1976). *Teaching thinking*. London: Temple Smith.

de Bono, E. (1985). The CoRT thinking program. In J. W. Segal, S. F. Chipman & R. Glaser (Eds.), *Thinking and learning skills: Volume 1, Relating instruction to research*. Hillsdale, NJ: Erlbaum.

Deci, E. L. (1971). Effects of externally mediated rewards on intrinsic motivation. *Journal of Personality and Social Psychology, 18,* 105–115.

Dejnozka, E. L. & Kapel, D. E. (1982). *American Educators' Encyclopedia*. Westport, CT: Greenwood Press.

Denham, C. & Lieberman, A. (1980). *Time to learn*. Washington, DC: National Institute of Education.

Dewey, J. (1902). *The child and the curriculum*. Chicago: University of Chicago Press.

Dewey, J. (1913) *Interest and effort in education*. Cambridge MA: The Riverside Press.

Dewey, J. (1938). *Experience & education*. New York: Collier.

Dienes, Z. P. (1960). *Building up mathematics*. New York: Hutchinson Educational Ltd.

Dienes, Z. P. (1967). *Fractions: An operational approach*. New York: Herder & Herder.

DiVesta, F. J. & Gray, G. S. (1973). Listening and note taking: II. Immediate and delayed recall as functions of variations in thematic continuity, note taking, and length of listening review intervals. *Journal of Educational Psychology, 64,* 278–287.

DiVesta, F., Schultz, C. B. & Dangel, I. R. (1973). *Passage organization and composed learning strategies in comprehension and recall of connected discourse*. Memory & Cognition, 6, 471–476.

Doctorow, M., Wittrock, M. C. & Marks, C. (1978). Generative processes in reading comprehension. *Journal of Educational Psychology, 70,* 109–118.

Dominguez, J. (1985). The development of human intelligence: The Venezuelan case. In J. W. Segal, S. F. Chipman & R. Glaser (Eds.), *Thinking and learning skills: Volume 1, Relating instruction to research*. Hillsdale, NJ: Erlbaum.

Domino, G. (1968). Differential predictions of academic achievement in conforming and independent settings. *Journal of Educational Psychology, 59,* 256–260.

Domino, G. (1971). Interactive effects of achievement orientation and teaching style on academic achievement. *Journal of Educational Psychology, 62,* 427–431.

Eanet, M. (1978). An investigation of the REAP reading/study procedure: Its rationale and efficacy. In P. E. Pearson & J. Hansen (Eds.), *Reading: Disciplined inquiry in process and practice*. Clemson, SC: National Reading Conference.

Eanet, M. & Manzo, A. V. (1976). REAP: A strategy for improving reading, writing, study skills. *Journal of Reading, 19,* 647–652.

Ehri, L. C. & Roberts, K. T. (1979). Do beginners learn printed words better in context or in isolation? *Child Development, 50,* 675–685.

Ehrlichman, H., Weiner, S. & Baker, A. (1974). Effects of verbal and spatial questions on initial gaze shifts. *Neuropsychologia, 12,* 265–277.

Elashoff, J. & Snow, R. (1971). *Pygmalion reconsidered*. Worthington, OH: Charles A. Jones.

Elkind, D. (1967). Introduction. In J. Piaget, *Six psychological studies*. New York: Random House.

Entwistle, D. R., Forsyth, D. F. & Muuss, R. (1964). The syntactic-paradigmatic shift in children's word associations. *Journal of Verbal Learning and Verbal Behavior, 3,* 19–29.

Erickson, G. L. (1979). Children's conception of heat and temperature. *Science Education, 63,* (2), 222–230.

Everstson, C. M., Sanford, J. P. & Emmer, E. T. (1981). Effects of class heterogeneity in junior high school. *American Educational Research Journal,* 219–232.

Faw, H. W. & Waller, T. G. (1976). Mathemagenic behaviors and efficiency in learning from prose. *Review of Educational Research, 46,* 691–720.

Feather, N. T. (1961). The relationship of persistence at a task to expectation of success and achievement related motives. *Journal of Abnormal and Social Psychology, 63,* 552–561.

Fennema, E. L. (1974). Mathematics learning and the sexes: A review. *Journal for Research in Mathematics Education, 5,* 126–139.

Fennema, E. L. & Sherman, J. A. (1977). Sex-related differences in mathematics achievement, spatial visualization and affective factors. *American Educational Research Journal, 14,* 51–71.

Fennema, E. L. & Sherman, J. A. (1978). Sex-related differences in mathematical achievement and related factors: A further study. *Journal for Research in Mathematics Education, 9,* 189–203.

Feuerstein, R. (1979). The *dynamic assessment of retarded performers. The learning potential assessment device: Theory, instruments and techniques*. Baltimore: University Park Press.

Feuerstein, R. (1980). *Instrumental enrichment: An intervention program for cognitive modifiability*. Baltimore: University Park Press.

Feuerstein, R., Jensen, M., Hoffman, M. B. & Rand, Y. (1985). Instructional enrichment, An intervention program for structural cognitive modifiability: Theory and practice. In J. W. Segal, S. F. Chipman & R. Glaser (Eds.), *Thinking and learning skills: Volume 1, Relating instruction to research*. Hillsdale, NJ: Erlbaum.

Firestone, G. & Brody, N. (1975). Longitudinal investigation of teacher-student interactions and their relationship to academic performance. *Journal of Educational Psychology, 67,* 544–550.

Fisher, J. L. & Harris, M. B. (1973). Effect of note taking and review on recall. *Journal of Educational Psychology, 65,* 321–325.

Flavell, J. H. (1963). *The developmental psychology of Jean Piaget*. Princeton, NJ: Van Nostrand.

Flavell, J. H. (1970). Developmental studies of mediated memory. In H. W. Reese &

L. P. Lipsitt (Eds.), *Advances in child development and behavior* (Vol. 5). New York: Academic Press.

Flavell, J. H. (1971). First discussant's comments: What is memory development the development of? *Human Development, 14,* 272–278.

Flavell, J. H., Beach, D. R. & Chinsky, J. M. (1966). Spontaneous verbal rehearsal in a memory task as a function of age. *Child Development, 37,* 283–299.

Flavell, J. H., Friedrichs, A. G. & Hoyt, J. D. (1970). Developmental changes in memorization processes. *Cognitive Psychology, 1,* 324–340.

Flavell, J. H. & Wellman, H. M. (1977). Metamemory. In R. V. Kail & J. W. Hagen (Eds.), *Perspectives on the development of memory and cognition*. Hillsdale, NJ: Erlbaum.

Fleisher, L. S., Jenkins, J. R., & Pany, D. (1979). Effects on poor readers' comprehension of training in rapid decoding. *Reading Research Quarterly, 15,* 30–48.

Fleming, E. & Anttonen, R. (1971). Teacher expectancy or My Fair Lady. *American Educational Research Journal, 8,* 241–252.

Flesch, R. P. (1955). *Why Johnny can't read*. New York: Harper.

Flower, L. (1979). Writer-based prose: A cognitive basis for problems in writing. *College English, 41,* 13–18.

Flower, L. & Hayes, J. R. (1981). Plans that guide the composing process. In C. H. Frederiksen & J. F. Dominic (Eds.), *Writing: Volume 2*. Hillsdale, NJ: Erlbaum.

Frase, L. T. (1982). Introduction to special issue on the psychology of writing. *Educational Psychologist, 17,* 129–130.

Furth, H. G. & Wachs, H. (1975). *Thinking goes to school: Piaget's theory in practice*. New York: Oxford University Press.

Fuson, K. C. (1982). An analysis of the counting-on solution procedure in addition. In Carpenter et al. (1982).

Gagne, E. D. (1985). *The cognitive psychology of school learning*. Boston: Little, Brown.

Gagne, R. M. (1968). Learning hierarchies. *Educational Psychologist, 6,* 1–9.

Gagne, R. M. (1974). *Essentials of learning for instruction*. Hinsdale, IL: Dryden Press.

Gagne, R. M. (1977). *The conditions of learning, third edition*. New York: Holt, Rinehart and Winston.

Gagne, R. M. & Briggs, L. J. (1974). *Principles of instructional design*. New York: Holt, Rinehart and Winston.

Gagne, R. M. and Brown, L. T. (1961). Some factors in the programming of conceptual learning. *Journal of Experimental Psychology, 62,* 313–321.

Gagne, R. M., Mayor, J. R., Garstens, H. L. & Paradise, N. E. (1962). Factors in acquiring knowledge in a mathematics task. *Psychological Monographs, 76,* No. 7 (Whole No. 526).

Garwood, S. G. (1976). First-name stereotypes as a factor in self-concept and school achievement. *Journal of Educational Psychology, 68,* 482–487.

Gelman, R. (1969). Conservation acquisition: A problem of learning to attend to the relevant attributes. *Journal of Experimental Child Psychology, 7,* 67–87.

Gelman, R. & Gallistel, C. R. (1978). *The child's understanding of number*. Cambridge, MA: Harvard University Press.

Gerber, M. M. & Semmel, M. I. (1984). Teacher as imperfect test: Reconceptualizing the referral process. *Educational Psychologist, 19,* 137–148.

Getzels, J. W. & Jackson, P. W. (1963). The highly intelligent and the highly creative adolescent: A summary of some research findings. In C. W. Taylor and F. Barron (Eds.), *Scientific creativity: Its recognition and development*. New York: Wiley.

Glaser, R. (1972). Individuals and learning: The new aptitudes. *Educational Researcher, 1*(6), 5–13.

Glass, G. V. & Smith, M. L. (1979). Meta-analysis of research on class size and achievement. *Educational Evaluation and Policy Analysis, 1,* 2–16.

Glynn, S. M., Britton, B. K., Muth, D. & Dogan, N. (1982). Writing and revising persuasive documents: Cognitive demands. *Journal of Educational Psychology, 74,* 557–567.

Goldschmidt, M. (1971). The role of experience in the rate and sequence of cognitive development. In D. R. Green, M. Ford, and G. Flammer (Eds.), *Measurement and Piaget.* New York: McGraw-Hill.

Good, T. L. (1970). Which pupils do teachers call on. *Elementary School Journal, 70,* 190–198.

Good, T. L. (1983). Classroom research: A decade of progress. *Educational Psychologist, 18,* 127–144.

Goodenough, D. R. (1978). Field dependence. In H. London & J. E. Exner (Eds.), *Dimensions of personality.* New York: Wiley.

Gould, J. D. (1978a). How experts dictate. *Journal of Experimental Psychology: Human Perception and Performance, 4,* 648–661.

Gould, J. D. (1978b). An experimental study of writing, dictating, and speaking. In J. Requien (Ed.), *Attention and performance, VII.* Hillsdale, NJ: Erlbaum.

Gould, J. D. (1980). Experiments on composing letters: Some facts, some myths, and some observations. In L. W. Gregg & E. R. Steinberg (Eds.), *Cognitive processes in writing.* Hillsdale, NJ: Erlbaum.

Graesser, A. C. (1981). *Prose comprehension beyond the word.* New York: Springer-Verlag.

Graesser, A. C., Hauft-Smith, K., Cohen, A. D. & Pyles, L. D. (1980). Advanced outlines, familiarity, text genre, and retention of prose. *Journal of Experimental Education, 48,* 209–221.

Graves, D. H. (1980). Research update. A new look at writing research. *Language Arts, 57,* 913–918.

Graves, D. H. (1983). *Writing: Teachers and children at work.* Exeter, NH: Heinemann.

Green, D., Sternberg, B. & Lepper, M. R. (1976). Overjustification in a token economy. *Journal of Personality and Social Psychology, 34,* 1219–1234.

Greeno, J. G. (1978a). A study of problem solving. In R. Glaser (Ed.), *Advances in instructional psychology. Vol. 1.* Hillsdale, NJ: Erlbaum.

Greeno, J. G. (1978b). Book review of *Human Characteristics and School Learning. Journal of Educational Measurement, 15,* 67–76.

Greeno, J. G. (1980). Some examples of cognitive task analysis with instructional implications. In R. E. Snow, P. Frederico, and W. E. Montague (Eds.), *Aptitude, learning, and instruction, Vol. 2.* Hillsdale, NJ: Erlbaum.

Gregg, L. W. (1978). Spatial concepts, spatial names, and the development of exocentric representations. In R. Siegler (Ed.), *Children's thinking: What develops?* Hillsdale, NJ: Erlbaum.

Griffiths, D. (1976). Physics teaching: Does it hinder intellectual development? *American Journal of Physics, 44,* 81–85.

Groen, G. J. and Parkman, J. M. (1972). A chronometric analysis of simple addition. *Psychological Review, 97,* 329–343.

Gross, T. F. & Mastenbrook, M. (1980). Examination of the effects of state anxiety on problem-solving efficiency under high and low memory conditions. *Journal of Educational Psychology, 72,* 605–609.

Guilford, J. P. (1959). The three faces of intellect. *American Psychologist, 14,* 469–479.

Guilford, J. P. (1967). *The nature of human intelligence.* New York: McGraw-Hill.

Gunderson, D. V. (1982). Bilingual education. In H. E. Mitzel (Ed.), *Encyclopedia of Educational Research, Fifth Edition.* New York: Macmillan.

Gunstone, R. F. & White, R. T. (1981). Understanding of gravity. *Science Education, 65,* 291–300.

Gur, R. E., Gur, R. C. & Harris, L. (1975). Cerebral activation as measured by subjects' lateral eye movements is influenced by experimenter location. *Neuropsychologia, 15,* 35–44.

Hagen, J. W. & Kail, R. V. (1973). Facilitation and distraction in short-term memory. *Child Development, 44,* 831–836.

Hansen, J. (1981). The effects of inference training and practice on young children's comprehension. *Reading Research Quarterly, 16,* 391–417.

Hansen, J. & Pearson, P. D. (1983). An instructional study: Improving the inferential comprehension of good and poor fourth-grade readers. *Journal of Educational Psychology, 75,* 821–829.

Harari, H. & McDavid, J. (1973). Name stereotypes and teachers' expectations. *Journal of Educational Psychology, 65,* 222–225.

Hasher, L. & Clifton, D. A. (1974). A developmental study of attribute encoding in free recall. *Journal of Experimental Child Psychology, 17,* 332–346.

Hayes, J. R. (1980). Teaching problem-solving mechanisms. In D. T. Tuma & F. Reif (Eds.), *Problem solving and education: Issues in teaching and research.* Hillsdale, NJ: Erlbaum.

Hayes, J. R. (1981). *The complete problem solver.* Philadelphia: Franklin Institute Press.

Hayes, J. R. (1985). Three problems in teaching general skills. In S. F. Chipman, J. W. Segal & R. Glaser (Eds.), *Thinking and learning skills: Volume 2, Research and open questions.* Hillsdale, NJ: Erlbaum.

Hayes, J. R. & Flower, L. S. (1980). Identifying the organization of writing processes. In L. W. Gregg & E. R. Steinberg (Eds.), *Cognitive processes in writing.* Hillsdale, NJ: Erlbaum.

Hayes, J. R., Waterman, D. A. & Robinson, C. S. (1977). Identifying relevant aspects of a problem text. *Cognitive Science, 1,* 297–313.

Hedges, L. V. & Stock, W. (1983). The effects of class size: An examination of rival hypotheses. *American Educational Research Journal, 20,* 63–85.

Hendrix, G. (1947). A new clue to transfer of training. *Elementary School Journal, 48,* 197–208.

Hendrix, G. (1961). Learning by discovery. *Mathematics Teacher, 54,* 290–299.

Hermann, G. (1969). Learning by discovery: A critical review studies. *Journal of Experimental Education, 38,* 58–72.

Hermans, H. J. (1970). A questionnaire measure of achievement motivation. *Journal of Applied Psychology, 54,* 353–363.

Higbee, K. L. (1977). *Your memory: How it works and how to improve it.* Englewood Cliffs, NJ: Prentice-Hall.

Higbee, K. L. (1979). Recent research on visual mnemonics: Historical roots and educational fruits. *Review of Educational Research, 49,* 611–629.

Hillocks, G. (1984). What works in teaching composition: A meta-analysis of experimental treatment studies. *American Journal of Education, 93,* 133–170.

Hilton, T. L. & Berglund, G. W. (1974). Sex differences in mathematics achievement: A longitudinal study. *Journal of Educational Research, 67,* 231–237.

Hinsley, D., Hayes, J. R., & Simon, H. A. (1977). From words to equations. In P. Carpenter & M. Just (Eds.), *Cognitive Processes in Comprehension.* Hillsdale, NJ: Erlbaum.

Holley, C. D. & Dansereau, D. F. (1984). The development of spatial learning strategies. In C. D. Holley & D. F. Dansereau (Eds.), *Spatial learning strategies.* Orlando, FL: Academic Press.

Holley, C. D., Dansereau, D. F., McDonald, B. A., Garland, J. C. & Collins, K. W. (1979). Evaluation of a hierarchical mapping technique as an aid to prose processing. *Contemporary Educational Psychology, 4,* 227–237.

Holzman, T. G., Glaser, R. & Pellegrino, J. W. (1976). Process training derived from a computer simulation theory. *Memory & Cognition, 4,* 349–356.

Hooper, J. H. & Defrain, J. D. (1980). On delineating distinctly Piagetian contributions to education. *Genetic Psychology Monographs, 101,* 151–181.

Howe, M. J. A. (1970). Note taking strategy, review, and long-term retention of verbal information. *Journal of Educational Research, 63,* 285.

Huey, E. B. (1908). *The psychology and pedagogy of reading.* New York: Macmillan. (Reprinted by M.I.T. Press in 1968).

Hunt, D. E., Greenwood, J., Noy, J. & Watson, N. (1973). *Assessment of conceptual level: Paragraph completion test method.* Toronto: Institute for Studies in Education.

Hunt, E. (1976). Varieties of cognitive power. In L. B. Resnick (Ed.), *The nature of intelligence.* Hillsdale, NJ: Erlbaum.

Hunt, E. (1978). Mechanisms of verbal ability. *Psychological Review, 85,* 109–130.

Hunt, E., Frost, N. & Lunneborg, C. (1973). Individual differences in cognition: A new approach to intelligence. *Psychology of Learning and Motivation, 7,* 87–122.

Hunt, E., Lunneborg, C. & Lewis, J. (1975). What does it mean to be high verbal? *Cognitive Psychology, 7,* 194–227.

Inhelder, B. & Piaget, J. (1958). *The growth of logical thinking from childhood to adolescence.* New York: Basic Books.

Inhelder, B. & Piaget, J. (1964). *The early growth of logic in the child.* London: Routledge and Kegan Paul.

Jensen, A. R. (1980). *Bias in mental testing.* New York: Free Press.

Johnson, K. R. & Ruskin, R. S. (1977). *Behavioral instruction: An evaluative review.* Washington, DC: American Psychological Association.

Johnson, R. E. (1970). Recall of prose as a function of the structural importance of linguistic units. *Journal of Verbal Learning and Verbal Behavior, 9,* 12–20.

Johnson-Laird, P. N. & Wason, P. C. (1977). A theoretical analysis of insight into a reasoning task. In P. N. Johnson-Laird & P. C. Watson (Eds.), *Thinking: Readings in cognitive science.* Cambridge, UK: Cambridge University Press.

Johnston, J. C. (1978). A test of the sophisticated guessing theory of word perception. *Cognitive Psychology, 10,* 123–153.

Johnston, J. C. (1981). Understanding word perception: Clues from studying the word-superiority effect. In O. J. L. Tzeng & H. Singer (Eds.), *Perception of Print.* Hillsdale, NJ: Erlbaum.

Johnston, J. C. & McClelland, J. L. (1980). Experimental tests of a hierarchical model of word identification. *Journal of Verbal Learning and Verbal Behavior, 19,* 503–524.

Jones, B. F., Amiran, M. R. & Katims, M. (1985). Teaching cognitive strategies and text structures within language arts programs. In J. W. Segal, S. F. Chipman &

R. Glaser (Eds.), *Thinking and learning skills: Volume 1, Relating instruction to research*. Hillsdale, NJ: Erlbaum.

Jones, B. F. & Hall, J. W. (1982). School applications of the mnemonic keyword method as a study strategy by eighth graders. *Journal of Educational Psychology, 74,* 230–237.

Just, M. A. & Carpenter, P. A. (1978). Inference processes during reading: Reflections from eye fixations. In J. W. Senders, D. F. Fisher & R. A. Monty (Eds.), *Eye movements and the higher psychological functions*. Hillsdale, NJ: Erlbaum.

Just, M. A. & Carpenter, P. A. (1980). A theory of reading: From eye fixations to comprehension. *Psychological Review, 87,* 329–354.

Kameenui, E. J., Carnine, D. W. & Freschi, R. (1982). Effects of text construction and instructional procedures for teaching word meanings on comprehension and recall. *Reading Research Quarterly, 17,* 367–388.

Kamii, C. & DeVries, R. (1977). Piaget for early education. In M. C. Day & R. K. Parker (eds.), *The preschool in action: Exploring early childhood programs (2nd ed)*. Boston: Allyn & Bacon.

Karplus, R. (1979). Proportional reasoning in the People's Republic of China. In J. Lochhead & J. Clement (Eds.), *Cognitive process instruction: Research on teaching thinking skills*. Philadelphia: Franklin Institute Press.

Karplus, R., Karplus, E., Formisano, M. & Paulsen, A. (1979). Proportional reasoning and control of variables in seven countries. In J. Lochhead & J. Clement (Eds.), *Cognitive process instruction: Research on teaching thinking skills*. Philadelphia: Franklin Institute Press.

Karweit, N. (1976). *A reanalysis of the effect of quantity of schooling on achievement*. Sociology of Education, 49, 236–246.

Kaufman, A. S. (1979). *Intelligent testing with the WISC-R*. New York: Wiley.

Katona, G. (1940). *Organizing and memorizing*. New York: Columbia University Press.

Kenney, T. J., Cannizzo, S. R., & Flavell, J. H. (1967). Spontaneous and induced verbal rehearsal in a recall task. *Child Development, 38,* 953–966.

Kendler, H. H. & Kendler, T. S. (1962). Vertical and horizontal processes in problem solving. *Psychological Review, 69,* 1–16.

Kendler, H. H. & Kendler, T. S. (1975). From discrimination learning to cognitive development: A neobehavioristic odyssey. In W. K. Estes (Ed.), *Handbook of learning and cognitive processes. Vol. 1*. Hillsdale, NJ: Erlbaum.

Kincaid, J. P., Aagard, J. A., O'Hara, J. W. & Cottrell, L. K. (1981). Computer readability editing system. *IEEE Transactions on Professional Communication, PC-24,* 38–41.

Kinsbourne, M. (1974). Direction of gaze and distribution of cerebral thought processes. *Neuropsychologia, 12,* 279–281.

Kintsch, W. (1976). Memory for prose. In C. N. Cofer (Ed.), *The structure of human memory*. New York: Freeman.

Kirk, S. A. (1962). *Educating exceptional children*. Boston: Houghton Mifflin.

Kirk, S. A. & Kirk, W. D. (1983). On defining learning disabilities. *Journal of Learning Disabilities, 16,* 20–21.

Kittell, J. E. (1957). An experimental study of the effect of external direction during learning on transfer and retention of principles. *Journal of Educational Psychology, 48,* 391–405.

Klatzky, R. L. (1980). *Human memory: Second edition*. New York: Freeman.

Kocel, K., Galin, D., Ornstein, R. & Merrin, R. (1972). Lateral eye movement and cognitive mode. *Psychonomic Science, 27,* 223–224.

Kohler, W. (1925). *The mentality of apes*. New York: Harcourt, Brace, Jovanovich.

Kolers, P. A. (1968). Introduction. In E. B. Huey, *The psychology and pedagogy of reading*. Cambridge, MA: MIT Press.

Kolodiy, G. (1975). The cognitive development of high school and college science students. *Journal of College Science Teaching, 5*(1), 20–22.

Kotovsky, K. & Simon, H. A. (1973). Empirical tests of a theory of human acquisition of concepts for sequential patterns. *Cognitive Psychology, 4*, 399–424.

Krathwohl, D. R., Bloom, B. S. & Masia, B. B. (1964). Taxonomy of educational objectives: The classification of educational goals. *Handbook 2: Affective domain*. New York: McKay.

Kreiger, L. E. (1975). Familiarity effects in visual information processing. *Psychological Bulletin, 82*, 949–974.

Kuhn, D. (1974). *Inducing development experimentally: Components on a research paradigm*. Developmental Psychology, 10, 590–600.

Kulhavy, R. W., Dyer, J. W. & Silver, L. (1975). The effects of notetaking and test expectancy on the learning of text material. *Journal of Educational Research, 68*, 363–365.

Kulik, C. C. & Kulik, J. A. (1982). Effects of ability grouping on secondary school students: A meta-analysis of evaluation findings. *American Educational Research Journal, 19*, 415–428.

Kurland, D. M. & Pea, R. D. (1985). Children's mental models for recursive Logo programs. *Journal of Educational Computing Research, 2*, 235–244.

LaBerge, D. & Samuels, S. J. (1974). Toward a theory of automatic information processing in reading. *Cognitive Psychology, 6*, 293–323.

Lamb, D. (1978). Anxiety. In H. London & J. E. Exner (Eds.), *Dimensions of personality*. New York: Wiley.

Lane, H. (1976). *The wild boy of Aveyron*. Cambridge, MA: Harvard University Press.

Larkin, J. H. (1979). Information processing models and science instruction. In J. Lochhead & J. Clement (Eds.), *Cognitive process instruction: Research on teaching thinking skills*. Philadelphia: Franklin Institute Press.

Larkin, J. H. (1981). Enriching formal knowledge: A model for learning to solve textbook physics problems. In J. R. Anderson (Ed.), *Cognitive skills and their acquisition*. Hillsdale, NJ: Erlbaum.

Larkin, J., McDermott, J., Simon, D. P. & Simon, H. A. (1980). Expert and novice performance in solving physics problems. *Science, 208*, 1335–1342.

Lavatelli, C. (1970). *Early childhood curriculum—A Piaget program*. Boston: American Science & Engineering.

Lawson, A. E. (1983). Predicting science achievement: The role of developmental level, disembedding ability, mental capacity, prior knowledge and beliefs. *Journal of Research in Science Teaching, 20*, 117–129.

Lawson, A. E. & Snitgen, D. A. (1982). Teaching formal reasoning in a college biology course for preservice teachers. *Journal of Research in Science Teaching, 19*, 233–248.

Lawson, A. E. & Wollman, W. T. (1976). Encouraging the transition from concrete to formal operative functioning: An experiment. *Journal of Research in Science Teaching, 13*, 413–430.

Lepper, M. R. & Greene, D. (1975). Turning play into work: Effects of adult surveillance and extrinsic rewards on children's intrinsic motivation. *Journal of Personality and Social Psychology, 31*, 479–486.

Lepper, M. R. & Greene, D. (1978). *The hidden costs of reward*. Hillsdale, NJ: Erlbaum.

Lepper, M. R., Greene, D. & Nisbett, R. E. (1973). Undermining children's intrinsic interest with external rewards: A test of the overjustification hypothesis. *Journal of Personality and Social Psychology, 28,* 129–137.

Lester, F. K. (1983). Trends and issues in mathematical problem solving research. In R. Lesh & M. Landau (Eds.), *Acquisition of mathematics concepts and processes*. New York: Academic Press.

Levin, J. R. (1976). What have we learned about maximizing what children learn? In J. R. Levin & V. L. Allen (Eds.), *Cognitive learning in children*. New York: Academic Press.

Levin, J. R. (1981). The mnemonic '80s: Keywords in the classroom. *Educational Psychologist, 16,* 65–82.

Levin, J. R. & Kaplan, S. A. (1972). Imaginal facilitation of paired-associate learning: A limited generalization. *Journal of Educational Psychology, 63,* 429–432.

Levin, J. R., McCormick, C. B., Miller, G. E., Berry, J. K. & Pressley, M. (1982). Mnemonic versus nonmnemonic vocabulary learning strategies for children. *American Educational Research Journal, 19,* 121–136.

Levin, T. (1975). The effect of content prerequisite process-oriented experiences on application ability in the learning of probability. Unpublished doctoral dissertation, University of Chicago.

Liddle, W. (1977). *Reading for concepts*. New York: McGraw-Hill.

Linn, M. C. (1985). The cognitive consequences of programming instruction in classrooms. *Educational Researcher, 14,* 14–16, 25–29.

Lipson, M. Y. (1983). The influence of religious affiliation on children's memory for text information. *Reading Research Quarterly, 18,* 448–457.

Loftus, E. F. & Suppes, P. (1972). Structural variables that determine problem-solving difficulty in computer assisted instruction. *Journal of Educational Psychology, 63,* 531–542.

Loman, N. L. & Mayer, R. E. (1983). Signaling techniques that increase the understandability of expository prose. *Journal of Educational Psychology, 75,* 402–412.

Lorayne, H. & Lucas, J. (1974). *The memory book*. New York: Ballantine.

Maccoby, E. E. & Jacklin, C. N. (1974). *The psychology of sex differences*. Stanford, CA: Stanford University Press.

Macdonald, N. H., Frase, L. T., Gingrich, P. S., & Keenan, S. A. (1982). The writer's workbench: Computer aids for text analysis. *Educational Psychologist, 17,* 172–179.

Machado, L. A. (1981). The development of intelligence: A political outlook. *Intelligence, 5,* 2–4.

Madsen, C. H., Becker, W. C. & Thomas, D. R. (1968). Rules, praise, and ignoring: Elements of elementary classroom control. *Journal of Applied Behavioral Analysis, 1,* 139–150.

Mager, R. F. (1962). *Preparing instructional objectives*. Belmont, CA: Fearon.

Main, G. C. & Munro, B. C. (1977). A token reinforcement program in a public junior-high school. *Journal of Applied Behavior Analysis, 10,* 93–94.

Mandler, J. M. A. (1978). A code in the node: The use of story schema in retrieval. *Discourse Processes, 1,* 14–35.

Mandler, J. M. & Johnson, N. S. (1977). Remembrance of things passed: Story structure and recall. *Cognitive Psychology, 9,* 111–151.

Mann, L., Davis, C. H., Boyer, C. W., Metz, C. M., & Wolford, B. (1983). LD or not

LD, that was the question: A retrospective analysis of child service demonstration centers' compliance with the federal definition of learning disabilities. *Journal of Learning Disabilities, 16,* 14–17.

Mansfield, R. S., Busse, T. V. & Krepelka, E. J. (1978). The effectiveness of creativity training. *Review of Educational Research, 48,* 517–536.

Manzo, A. V. (1969). The ReQuest procedure. *Journal of Reading, 13,* 123–126.

Markman, E. (1973). *Factors affecting the young child's ability to monitor his memory.* Unpublished doctoral dissertation. University of Pennsylvania.

Markman, E. (1979). Realizing that you don't understand: Elementary school children's awareness of inconsistencies. *Child Development, 50,* 643–655.

Markman, E. M. (1981). Comprehension monitoring. In P. Dickson (Ed.), *Children's oral communication skills.* New York: Academic Press.

Markman, E. M. (1985). Comprehension monitoring: Developmental and educational issues. In S. F. Chipman, J. W. Segal & R. Glaser (Eds.), *Thinking and learning skills: Volume 2, Research and open questions.* Hillsdale, NJ: Erlbaum.

Marks, C. B., Doctorow, M. J. & Wittrock, M. C. (1974). Word frequency in reading comprehension. *Journal of Educational Research, 67,* 259–262.

Marr, M. B. & Gorley, K. (1982). *Children's recall of familiar and unfamiliar text.* Reading Research Quarterly, 18, 89–104.

Marshall, H. H. (1981). Open classrooms: Has the term outlived its usefulness? *Review of Educational Research, 51,* 181–192.

Masur, F. E., McIntyre, C. W. & Flavell, J. H. (1973). Developmental changes in apportionment of study time among items in a multitrial free recall test. *Journal of Experimental Child Psychology, 15,* 237–246.

Matsuhashi, A. (1981). Pausing and planning: The tempo of written discourse production. *Research in the Teaching of English, 15,* 113–134.

Matsuhashi, A. (1982). Explorations in the real-time production of written discourse. In M. Nystrand (Ed.), *What writers know.* New York: Academic Press.

Mayer, R. E. (1975a). Information processing variables in learning to solve problems. *Review of Educational Research, 45,* 525–541.

Mayer, R. E. (1975b). Different problem solving competencies established in learning computer programming with and without meaningful models. *Journal of Educational Psychology, 67,* 725–734.

Mayer, R. E. (1975c). Forward transfer of different reading strategies evoked by test-like events in mathematics text. *Journal of Educational Psychology, 67,* 165–169.

Mayer, R. E. (1976). Some conditions of meaningful learning for computer programming: Advance organizers and subject control of frame sequencing. *Journal of Educational Psychology, 68,* 143–150.

Mayer, R. E. (1977). Problem-solving performance with task overload: Effects of self-pacing and trait anxiety. *Bulletin of the Psychonomic Society, 9,* 283–286.

Mayer, R. E. (1978). Qualitatively different encoding strategies for linear reasoning: Evidence for single association and distance theories. *Journal of Experimental Psychology: Human Learning and Memory, 4,* 5–18.

Mayer, R. E. (1979). Twenty years of research on advance organizers: Assimilation theory is still the best predictor of results. *Instructional Science, 8,* 133–167.

Mayer, R. E. (1980). Elaboration techniques that increase the meaningfulness of technical text: An experimental test of the learning strategy hypothesis. *Journal of Educational Psychology, 72,* 770–784.

Mayer, R. E. (1981a). *The promise of cognitive psychology*. New York: Freeman.

Mayer, R. E. (1981b). Frequency norms and structural analysis of algebra story problems into families, categories, and templates. *Instructional Science, 10,* 135–175.

Mayer, R. E. (1982a). Learning. In H. E. Mitzel (Ed.), *Encyclopedia of educational research: Fifth edition*. Washington, DC: American Educational Research Association.

Mayer, R. E. (1982b). Memory for algebra story problems. *Journal of Educational Psychology, 74,* 199–216.

Mayer, R. E. (1982c). Different problem solving strategies for algebra word and equation problems. *Journal of Experimental Psychology: Learning, Memory and Cognition, 8,* 448–462.

Mayer, R. E. (1983a). *Thinking, problem solving, cognition*. New York: Freeman.

Mayer, R. E. (1983b). Can you repeat that? Qualitative and quantitative effects of repetition and advance organizers on learning from science prose. *Journal of Educational Psychology, 75,* 40–49.

Mayer, R. E. (1984). Aids to prose comprehension. *Educational Psychologist, 19,* 30–42.

Mayer, R. E. (1985). Learning in complex domains: A cognitive analysis of computer programming. *Psychology of Learning and Motivation, 19,* 89–130.

Mayer, R. E. & Cook, L. K. (1980). Effects of shadowing on prose comprehension and problem solving. *Memory & Cognition, 8,* 101–109.

Mayer, R. E. & Greeno, J. G. (1972). Structural differences between learning outcomes produced by different instructional methods. *Journal of Educational Psychology, 63,* 165–173.

Mayer, R. E., Larkin, J. H. & Kadane, J. (1984). A cognitive analysis of mathematical problem solving ability. In R. Sternberg (Ed.), *Advances in the psychology of human intelligence* (pp. 231–273). Hillsdale, NJ: Lawrence Erlbaum Associates.

Mayer, R. E., Stiehl, C. C. & Greeno, J. G. (1975). Acquisition of understanding and skill in relation to subjects' preparation and meaningfulness of instruction. *Journal of Educational Psychology, 67,* 331–350.

McClelland, D. C., Atkinson, J. W., Clark, R. W. & Lowell, E. L. (1953). *The achievement motive*. New York: Appleton-Century-Crofts.

McCloskey, M. (1983). Intuitive physics. *Scientific American, 248*(4), 122–130.

McCloskey, M., Caramazza, A. & Green, B. (1980). Curvilinear motion in the absence of external forces: Naive beliefs about the motion of objects. *Science, 210*(No. 4474), 1139–114.

McConkie, G. W. (1976). The use of eye-movement data in determining the perceptual span in reading. In R. A. Monty & J. W. Senders (eds.), *Eye movements and psychological processes*. Hillsdale, NJ: Erlbaum.

McConkie, G. W. & Rayner, K. (1975). The span of the effective stimulus during a fixation in reading. *Perception & Psychophysics, 17,* 578–586.

McConkie, G. W., Rayner, K. & Wilson, S. J. (1973). Experimental manipulation of reading strategies. *Journal of Educational Psychology, 65,* 1–8.

McKeown, M. G., Beck, I. L., Omanson, R. C. & Perfetti, C. A. (1983). The effects of long-term vocabulary instruction on reading comprehension: A replication. *Journal of Reading Behavior, 15,* 3–18.

McKinnon, J. W. & Renner, J. W. (1971). Are colleges concerned with intellectual development? *American Journal of Physics, 39,* 1047–1052.

McLoughlin, J. A. & Kelly, D. (1982). *Issues facing the resource teacher*. Learning Disabilities Quarterly, 5, 58–64.

Meehan, J. R. (1976). The metanovel: Writing stories by computer. Unpublished doctoral dissertation, Yale University.

Meehan, J. R. (1977). TALESPIN: An interactive program that writes stories. *Proceedings of the Fifth International Joint Conference on Artificial Intelligence,* 91–98.

Meyer, B. J. F. (1975). *The organization of prose and its effects on memory.* Amsterdam: North-Holland.

Meyer, B. J. F. (1977). The structure of prose: Effects on learning and memory and implications for educational practice. In R. C. Anderson, R. J. Spiro, & W. E. Montague (Eds.), *Schooling and the acquisition of knowledge.* New York: Wiley.

Meyer, B. J. F. (1981). Basic research on prose comprehension: A critical review. In D. F. Fisher & C. W. Peters (Eds.), *Comprehension and the competent reader: Inter-spaciality perspectives.* New York: Praeger.

Meyer, B. J. F. (1985). Prose analysis: Purposes, procedures, and problems. In B. K. Britton & J. B. Black (Eds.), *Understanding expository prose.* Hillsdale, NJ: Erlbaum.

Meyer, B. J. F., Brandt, D. H. & Bluth, G. J. (1980). Use of top-level structure in text: Key for reading comprehension of ninth-grade students. *Reading Research Quarterly, 16,* 72–103.

Meyer, B. J. F. & McConkie, G. W. (1973). What is recalled after hearing a passage? *Journal of Educational Psychology, 65,* 109–117.

Meyer, B. J. F. & Rice, G. E. (1981). Information recalled from prose by young, middle, and old adults. *Experimental Aging Research, 7,* 253–268.

Meyer, E. L. & Altman, R. (1982). Special education. In H. E. Mitzel (Ed.), *Encyclopedia of educational research: Fifth edition.* New York: Macmillan.

Mhrabian, A. (1969). Measures of achieving tendency. *Educational and Psychological Measurement, 29,* 493–502.

Miller, G. A. (1956). The magic number seven plus or minus two: some limits on our capacity for processing information. *Psychological Review, 63,* 81–97.

Mirande, M. (1984). Schematizing: Techniques and applications. In C. D. Holley & D. F. Dansereau (Eds.), *Spatial Learning Strategies.* Orlando: Academic Press.

Moely, B. E., Olson, F. A., Halwes, T. G. & Flavell, J. H. (1969). Production deficiency in young children's clustered recall. *Developmental Psychology, 1,* 26–34.

Montessouri, M. (1964). *Advanced Montessouri method.* Cambridge, MA: Bentley.

Murray, F. B. (1978). Teaching strategies and conservation training. In A. M. Lesgold, J. W. Pellegrino, S. D. Fokkema & R. Glaser (Eds.), *Cognitive psychology and instruction.* New York: Plenum Press.

Myers, M. & Paris, S. B. (1978). Children's metacognitive knowledge about reading. *Journal of Educational Psychology, 70,* 680–690.

Myers, R. E. & Torrance, E. P. (1964). *Invitations to thinking and doing.* Boston: Ginn.

Nagy, W. E. & Anderson, R. C. (1984). How many words are there in printed school English? *Reading Research Quarterly, 19,* 304–330.

Nagy, W. E. & Herman, P. A. (1984). *Limitations of vocabulary instruction.* (Technical Report No. 326). Center for the Study of Reading. Champaign, IL: University of Illinois.

Nagy, W. E. Herman, P. A. & Anderson, R. C. (1985). Learning words from context. *Reading Research Quarterly, 20,* 233–253.

National Advisory Committee on Handicapped Children. (1968). *Special education for handicapped children: First annual report.* Washington, DC: Department of Health, Education and Welfare.

National assessment of educational progress write/rewrite: An assessment of writing skills. (1977). Writing Report No. 05-W-04. Denver: U.S. Government Printing Office.

Nemko, B. (1984). Context versus isolation: Another look at beginning readers. *Reading Research Quarterly, 19,* 461–467.

Neves, D. M. & Anderson, J. R. (1981). Knowledge compilation: Mechanisms for the automatization of cognitive skills. In J. R. Anderson (Ed.), *Cognitive skills and their acquisition*. Hillsdale, NJ: Erlbaum.

Newell, A. & Simon, H. A. (1972). *Human problem solving*. Englewood Cliffs, NJ: Prentice-Hall.

Newell, K. M. (1974). Knowledge of results and motor learning. *Journal of Motor Behavior, 6,* 235–244.

Nold, E. W. (1981). Revising. In C. H. Frederiksen & J. F. Dominic (Eds.), *Writing: Volume 2*. Hillsdale, NJ: Erlbaum.

Norman, D. A. (1980). Cognitive engineering and education. In D. T. Tuma & F. Reif (Eds.), *Problem solving and education: Issues in teaching and research*. Hillsdale, NJ: Erlbaum.

Novick, S. & Nussbaum, J. (1978). Junior high school pupils' understanding of the particle nature of matter: An interview study. *Science Education, 62,* 273–281.

Novick, S. & Nussbaum, J. (1981). Pupil's understanding of the particulate nature of matter: A cross-age study. *Science Education, 65,* 187–196.

Noy, J. E. & Hunt, D. E. (1972). Student-directed learning from biographical information systems. *Canadian Journal of Behavioral Science, 4,* 54–63.

Nurss, J. R. & Hodges, W. L. (1982). Early childhood development. In H. E. Mitzel (Ed.), *Encyclopedia of Educational Research*. New York: Macmillan.

Nussbaum, J. (1979). Children's conception of the earth as a cosmic body: A cross-age study. *Science Education, 63,* 83–93.

Nystrand, M. (1982a). Rhetoric's "audience" and linguistic's "speech community": Implications for understanding writing, reading, and text. In M. Nystrand (Ed.), *What writers know*. New York: Academic Press.

Nystrand, M. (1982b). An analysis of errors in written communication. In M. Nystrand (Ed.), *What writers know*. New York: Academic Press.

Olton, R. M. & Crutchfield, R. S. (1969). Developing the skills of productive thinking. In P. Mussen, J. Langer & M. V. Covington (Eds.), *New directions in developmental psychology*. New York: Holt, Rinehart and Winston.

Open Court Phonics Kit. La Salle, IL: Open Court.

O'Leary, K. D., Becker, W. C., Evans, M. B. & Saudargas, R. A. (1969). A token reinforcement program in a public school: A replication and systematic analysis. *Journal of Applied Behavior Analysis, 2,* 3–13.

O'Leary, K. D. & Drabman, R. S. (1971). Token reinforcement programs in the classroom: A review. *Psychological Bulletin, 75,* 379–398.

O'Leary, K. D., Poulos, R. W. & Devine, V. T. (1972). Tangible reinforcers: Bonuses or bribes? *Journal of Consulting and Clinical Psychology, 38,* 1–8.

Osborne, R. J. & Wittrock, M. C. (1983). Learning science: A generative process. *Science Education, 67,* 489–508.

O'Shea, T. & Self, J. (1983). *Learning and teaching with computers: Artificial intelligence in education*. Brighton, UK: Harvester Press.

Paige, J. M., & Simon, H. A. (1966). Cognitive processes in solving algebra word problems. In B. Kleinmuntz (Ed.), *Problem Solving: Research, Method, and Theory*. New York: Wiley.

Paivio, A. (1971). *Imagery and verbal processes*. New York: Holt, Rinehart & Winston.

Palardy, J. (1969). What teachers believe—what children achieve. *Elementary School Journal, 69,* 370–374.

Papert, S. (1980). *Mindstorms.* New York: Basic Books.

Paris, S. G. & Lindauer, B. K. (1976). The role of inference in children's comprehension and memory for sentences. *Cognitive Psychology, 8,* 217–227.

Paris, S. G., Lindauer, B. K. & Cox, G. L. (1977). The development of inferential comprehension. *Child Development, 48,* 1728–1733.

Paris, S. G. & Upton, L. R. (1976). Children's memory for inferential relationships in prose. *Child Development, 47,* 660–668.

Parkman, J. M. & Groen, G. J. (1971). Temporal aspects of simple addition and comparison. *Journal of Experimental Psychology, 89,* 333–342.

Pascual-Leone, J. (1970). A mathematical model for the transition rule in Piaget's developmental states. *Acta Psychologica, 63,* 301–345.

Pask, G. & Scott, B. C. E. (1972). Learning strategies and individual competence. *International Journal of Man-Machine Studies, 4,* 217–253.

Pask, G. & Scott, B. C. E. (1973). CASTE: A system for exhibiting learning strategies and regulating uncertainties. *International Journal of Man-Machine Studies, 5,* 17–52.

Patching, W., Kameenui, E., Carnine, D., Gersten, R. & Colvin, G. (1983). Direct instruction in critical reading skills. *Reading Research Quarterly, 18,* 406–418.

Pea, R. D. & Kurland, D. M. (1984). On the cognitive effects of learning computer programming. *New Directions in Psychology, 2,* 137–168.

Pearsons, P. D. & Gallagher, M. (1983). The instruction of reading comprehension. *Contemporary Educational Psychology, 8,* 317–344.

Pearson, P. D., Hanson, J. & Gordon, C. (1979). The effect of background knowledge on young children's comprehension of explicit and implicit information. *Journal of Reading Behavior, 11,* 201–209.

Peper, R. & Mayer, R. E. (1978). Note taking as a generative activity. *Journal of Educational Psychology, 70,* 514–522.

Perfetti, C. A. & Hogaboam, T. (1975). The relationship between single word decoding and reading comprehension skill. *Journal of Educational Psychology, 67,* 461–469.

Perfetti, C. A. & Lesgold, A. M. (1979). Coding and comprehension in skilled reading and implications for reading instruction. In L. B. Resnick & P. A. Weaver (Eds.), *Theory and practice of early reading.* Hillsdale, NJ: Erlbaum.

Perkins, D. N. (1985). The fingertip effect: How information processing technology shapes thinking. *Educational Researcher, 14,* 11–14.

Peters, D. L. (1972). Effects of note taking and rate of presentation on short-term objective test performance. *Journal of Educational Psychology, 63,* 276–280.

Peterson, L. R. & Peterson, M. J. (1959). Short-term retention of individual verbal items. *Journal of Experimental Psychology, 58,* 193–198.

Peterson, P. L. & Clark, C. M. (1978). Teachers' reports of their cognitive processes during teaching. *American Educational Research Journal, 15,* 555–565.

Peterson, P. L., Marx, R. W. & Clark, C. M. (1978). Teacher planning, teacher behavior, and student achievement, *American Educational Research Journal, 15,* 417–432.

Phillips, J. L. (1969). *The origins of intellect: Piaget's theory.* New York: Freeman.

Piaget, J. (1926). *The language and thought of the child.* London: Kegan Paul, Trench, Trubner & Co.

Piaget, J. (1951). *Plays, dreams and imitation in childhood.* New York: Norton.

Piaget, J. (1952). *The child's conception of number.* London: Routledge & Kegan Paul.

Piaget, J. (1954). *The construction of reality in the child.* New York: Basic Books.

Piaget, J. (1965a). *The child's conception of number.* New York: Norton.

Piaget, J. (1965b). *The moral judgment of the child.* New York: Free Press.

Piaget, J. (1971). *Science of education and the psychology of the child.* New York: Viking Press.

Piaget, J. (1972). Intellectual evolution from adolescent to adulthood. *Human Development, 15,* 1–12.

Piaget, J. & Inhelder, B. (1971). *Mental imagery in the child.* New York: Basic Books.

Pichert, J. & Anderson, R. C. (1977). Taking different perspectives on a story. *Journal of Educational Psychology, 69,* 309–315.

Plato. (1924). *Laches, Protagoras, Meno, and Euthydemus.* Cambridge, MA: Harvard University Press.

Pressley, M. (1977). Children's use of the keyword method to learn simple Spanish vocabulary words. *Journal of Educational Psychology, 69,* 465–472.

Pressley, M. & Dennis-Rounds, J. (1980). Transfer of a mnemonic keyword strategy at two age levels. *Journal of Educational Psychology, 72,* 575–582.

Pressley, M. & Levin, J. R. (1978). Developmental constraints associated with children's use of the keyword method of foreign language vocabulary learning. *Journal of Experimental Child Psychology, 26,* 359–372.

Pressley, M., Levin, J. R. & McCormick, C. B. (1980). Young children's learning of foreign language vocabulary: A sentence variation of the keyword method. *Contemporary Educational Psychology, 5,* 22–29.

Polson, P. G. & Jeffries, R. (1985). Instruction in general problem-solving skills: An analysis of four approaches. In J. W. Segal, S. F. Chipman & R. Glaser (Eds.), *Thinking and learning skills: Volume 1, Relating instruction to research.* Hillsdale, NJ: Erlbaum.

Polya, G. (1945). *How to solve it.* Princeton, NJ: Princeton University Press.

Polya, G. (1965). *Mathematical discovery.* New York: Wiley.

Posner, M. I., Boies, S. J., Eichelman, W. & Taylor, R. (1969). Retention of visual and name codes of single letters. *Journal of Experimental Psychology Monographs, 79,* (1, Pt. 2).

Posner, M. I. & Mitchell, R. F. (1967). Chronometric analysis of classification. *Psychological Review, 74,* 392–409.

Pople, H. (1977). Problem-solving: An exercise in synthetic reasoning. *Proceedings of the fifth international joint conference on artificial intelligence.* Pittsburgh: Carnegie-Mellon University.

Raugh, M. R. & Atkinson, R. C. (1975). A mnemonic method for learning a second-language vocabulary. *Journal of Educational Psychology, 67,* 1–16.

Rayner, K. & McConkie, G. W. (1976). What guides a reader's eye movements? *Vision Research, 16,* 829–837.

Rayner, K., Well, A. D. & Pollatsek, A. (1980). Asymmetry of the effective visual field in reading. *Perception and Psychophysics, 27,* 537–544.

Read, C. (1981). Writing is not the inverse of reading for young children. In C. H. Frederiksen & J. F. Dominic (Eds.), *Writing: Volume 2.* Hillsdale, NJ: Erlbaum.

Reese, H. W. (1977). Imagery and associative memory. In R. V. Kail & J. W. Hagen (Eds.), *Perspectives on the development of memory and cognition.* Hillsdale, NJ: Erlbaum.

Reicher, G. M. (1969). Perceptual recognition as a function of the meaningfulness of stimulus material. *Journal of Experimental Psychology, 81,* 275–280.

Resnick, L. B. (1973). Hierarchies in children's learning: A symposium. *Instructional Science, 2,* 311–362.

Resnick, L. B. (1976). Task analysis in instructional design: Some cases from mathematics. In D. Klahr (Ed.), *Cognition and instruction*. Hillsdale, NJ: Erlbaum.

Resnick, L. B. (1977). Assuming that everyone can learn everything, will some learn less? *School Review, 85*, 445–452.

Resnick, L. B. (1982). Syntax and semantics in learning to subtract. In T. Carpenter, J. Moser & T. Romberg (Eds.), *Addition and subtraction: A cognitive perspective*. Hillsdale, NJ: Erlbaum.

Resnick, L. B. & Ford, W. W. (1981). *The psychology of mathematics for instruction*. Hillsdale, NJ: Erlbaum.

Resnick, L. B., Siegel, A. W. & Kresh, E. (1971). Transfer and sequence in learning double classification skills. *Journal of Experimental Child Psychology, 11*, 139–149.

Reynolds, C. R. (1983). Test bias: In God we trust, All others must have data. *Journal of Special Education, 17*, 241–260.

Richardson, K., Calnan, M., Essen, J. & Lambert, M. (1975). Linguistic maturity of 11-year olds: Some analysis of the written compositions of children in the National Child Development Study, *Journal of Child Language, 3*, 99–116.

Rickards, J. P. & DiVesta, F. J. (1974). Type and frequency of questions in processing textual material. *Journal of Educational Psychology, 66*, 354–362.

Rickards, J. P. & Friedman, F. (1978). The encoding versus the external storage hypothesis in note-taking. *Contemporary Educational Psychology, 3*, 136–143.

Riley, M., Greeno, J. G. & Heller, J. (1982). The development of children's problem solving ability in arithmetic. In H. Ginsburg (Ed.), *The development of mathematical thinking*. New York: Academic Press.

Rippa, S. A. (1967). *Education in a free society: An American history*. New York: Longman.

Rist, R. (1970). Student social class and teacher expectations. The self-fulfilling prophecy in ghetto education. *Harvard Educational Review, 40*, 411–451.

Robin, A. L. (1976). Behavioral instruction in the college classroom: A review. *Review of Educational Research, 46*, 313–354.

Robinson, C. S. & Hayes, J. R. (1978). Making inferences about relevance in understanding problems. In R. Revlin & R. E. Mayer (Eds.), *Human Reasoning*. Washington: Winston.

Robinson, F. P. (1964). *Effective study*. New York: Harper & Row.

Rosenshine, B. V. (1980a). Skill hierarchies in reading comprehension. In R. J. Spiro, B. C. Bruce & W. F. Brewer (Eds.), *Theoretical Issues in Reading Comprehension*. Hillsdale, NJ: Erlbaum.

Rosenshine, B. V. (1980b). How time is spent in elementary classrooms. In C. Denham & A. Lieberman (Eds.), *Time to learn*. Washington, DC: National Institute of Education.

Rosenthal, R. (1976). *Experimenter effects in behavioral research. Second edition*. New York: Irvington.

Rosenthal, R. & Jacobson, L. (1968). *Pygmalion in the classroom: Teacher expectation and pupils' intellectual development*. New York: Holt, Rinehart & Winston.

Ross, M. (1975). Salience of reward and intrinsic motivation. *Journal of Personality and Social Psychology, 32*, 245–254.

Rossi, S. & Wittrock, M. C. (1971). Developmental shifts in verbal recall between mental ages two and five. *Child Development, 42*, 333–338.

Rothkopf, E. Z. (1966). Learning from written materials: An exploration of the control of inspection by test-like events. *American Educational Research Journal, 3*, 241–249.

Rothkopf, E. Z. (1970). The concept of mathemagenic activities. *Review of Educational Research, 40,* 325–336.

Rothkopf, E. Z. & Bisbicos, E. (1967). Selective facilitative effects of interspersed questions on learning from written material. *Journal of Educational Psychology, 58,* 56–61.

Roughhead, W. G. & Scandura, J. M. (1968). What is learned in mathematical discovery. *Journal of Educational Psychology, 59,* 283–289.

Royer, J. M. & Cable, G. W. (1975). Facilitated learning in connected discourse. *Journal of Educational Psychology, 67,* 116–123.

Royer, J. M. & Cable, G. W. (1976). Illustrations, analogies, and facilitative transfer in prose learning. *Journal of Educational Psychology, 68,* 205–209.

Rubinstein, M. F. (1975). *Patterns of problem-solving.* Englewood Cliffs, NJ: Prentice-Hall.

Rubinstein, M. F. (1980). A decade of experience in teaching an interdisciplinary problem-solving course. In D. T. Tuma & F. Reif (Eds.), *Problem solving and education: Issues in teaching and research.* Hillsdale, NJ: Erlbaum.

Rumelhart, D. E. (1975). Notes on a schema for stories. In D. G. Bobrow & A. Collins (Eds.), *Representation and understanding.* New York: Academic Press.

Rumelhart, D. E. (1977). Toward an interactive model of reading. In S. Dornic (Ed.), *Attention and performance: VI.* Hillsdale, NJ: Erlbaum.

Samuels, S. J. (1967). Attentional processes in reading: The effect of pictures in the acquisition of reading responses. *Journal of Educational Psychology, 58,* 337–342.

Samuels, S. J. (1979). The method of repeated readings. *The Reading Teacher, 32,* 403–408.

Sarason, I. G. (1960). Empirical findings and theoretical problems in the use of anxiety scales. *Psychological Bulletin, 57,* 403–415.

Scardamalia, M. (1981). How children cope with the cognitive demands of writing. In C. H. Frederiksen & J. F. Dominic (Eds.), *Writing: Volume 2.* Hillsdale, NJ: Erlbaum.

Scardamalia, M., Bereiter, C. & Goelman, H. (1982). The role of production factors in writing ability. In M. Nystrant (Ed.), *What writers know.* New York: Academic Press.

Schoenfeld, A. H. (1979). Explicit heuristic training as a variable in problem solving performance. *Journal for Research in Mathematics Education, 10,* 173–187.

Schoenfeld, A. H. (1985). *Mathematical problem solving.* Orlando, FL: Academic Press.

Schonberg, H. (1970). *The lives of the great composers.* New York: Norton.

Schvaneveldt, R., Ackerman, B. P., Semelar, T. (1977). The effect of semantic context on children's word recognition. *Child Development, 48,* 612–616.

Segal, J. W., Chipman, S. F. & Glaser, R. (Eds.), (1985). *Thinking and learning skills: Volume 1, Relating instruction to research.* Hillsdale, NJ: Erlbaum.

Shapiro, B. J. & O'Brien, T. C. (1970). Logical thinking in children ages six through thirteen. *Child Development, 41,* 823–829.

Sharp, E. (1969). *Thinking is child's play.* New York: Avon Books.

Sharps, R. (1973). A study of interactions between fluid and crystallized abilities and two methods of teaching reading and arithmetic. (Doctoral dissertation. Pennsylvania State University). *Dissertation Abstracts International, 35,* 1432A.

Shavelson, R. J. (1972). Some aspects of the correspondence between content structure and cognitive structure in physics instruction. *Journal of Educational Psychology, 63,* 225–234.

Shavelson, R. J. (1973). What is the basic teaching skill? *Journal of Teacher Education, 14,* 144–151.

Shavelson, R. J. (1974). Some methods for examining content structure and cognitive structure in instruction. *Educational Psychologist, 11,* 110–122.

Shavelson, R. J. (1976). Teachers' decision making. In N. L. Gage (Ed.), *The Psychology of Teaching Methods.* Yearbook of the National Society for the Study of Education. Chicago: University of Chicago Press.

Shavelson, R. J., Cadwell, J. & Izu, T. (1977). Teachers' sensitivity to the reliability of information in making pedagogic decisions. *American Educational Research Journal, 14,* 83–97.

Shavelson, R. J. & Stern, P. (1981). Research on teachers' pedagogical thoughts, decisions, and behavior. *Review of Educational Research, 51,* 455–498.

Shepherd, D. L. (1978). *Comprehensive high school reading methods.* Columbus, OH: Merrill.

Shimmerlick, S. M. & Nolan, J. D. (1976). Organization and recall of prose. *Journal of Educational Psychology, 68,* 779–786.

Shortliffe, E. (1976). *Computer-based medical consultations: MYCIN.* New York: Elsevier.

Shulman, L. S. & Keisler, E. R. (1966). *Learning by discovery.* Chicago: Rand McNally.

Siegel, L. & Siegel, L. C. (1965). Educational set: A determinant of acquisition. *Journal of Educational Psychology, 56,* 1–12.

Siegler, R. S. (1978). The origins of scientific reasoning. In R. S. Siegler (Ed.), *Children's thinking: What develops?* Hillsdale, NJ: Erlbaum.

Silver, E. A. (1979). Student perceptions of relatedness among mathematical verbal problems. *Journal for Research in Mathematics Education, 10,* 195–210.

Silver, E. A. (1981). Recall of mathematical problem information: Solving related problems. *Journal for Research in Mathematics Education, 12,* 54–64.

Silverstein, A. B., Brownlee, L., Legutki, G. & MacMillan, D. L. (1983). Convergent and discriminant validation of two methods of assessing three academic traits. *Journal of Special Education, 17,* 63–68.

Simon, H. A. (1974). How big is a chunk? *Science, 183,* 482–488.

Simon, H. A. (1980). Problem solving and education. In D. T. Tuma & F. Reif (Eds.), *Problem solving and education: Issues in teaching and research.* Hillsdale, NJ: Erlbaum.

Simon, H. A. & Kotovsky, J. (1963). Human acquisition of concepts for sequential patterns. *Psychological Review, 70,* 534–546.

Simpson, E. J. (1966). The classification of educational objectives, psychomotor domain. *Illinois Teacher of Home Economics, 10,* 110–144.

Singer, H. (1981). Teaching the acquisition phase of reading development: An historical perspective. In O. J. L. Tzeng & H. Singer (Eds.), *Perception of print.* Hillsdale, NJ: Erlbaum.

Skinner, B. F. (1938). *The behavior of organisms: An experimental analysis.* Englewood Cliffs, NJ: Prentice-Hall.

Skinner, B. F. (1953). *Science and human behavior.* New York: Macmillan.

Skinner, B. F. (1957). *Verbal behavior.* Englewood Cliffs, NJ: Prentice-Hall.

Skinner, B. F. (1968). *The technology of teaching.* Englewood Cliffs, NJ: Prentice-Hall.

Skinner, B. F. (1969). *Contingencies of reinforcement: A theoretical analysis.* Englewood Cliffs, NJ: Prentice-Hall.

Sleeman, D. & Brown, J. S. (Eds.). (1982). *Intelligent tutoring systems.* Orlando, FL: Academic Press.

Smith, E. E. & Spoehr, K. T. (1974). The perception of printed English: A theoretical perspective. In B. H. Kantowitz (Ed.), *Human information processing: Tutorials in performance and cognition*. Hillsdale, NJ: Erlbaum.

Smith, M. L. & Glass, G. V. (1980). Meta-analysis of research on class size and its relationship to attitudes and instruction. *American Educational Research Journal, 17*, 419–433.

Snow, R. E. & Lohman, D. F. (1984). Toward a theory of cognitive aptitude for learning from instruction. *Journal of Educational Psychology, 76*, 347–376.

Soloway, E., Lochhead, J. & Clement, J. (1982). Does computer programming enhance problem solving ability? Some positive evidence on algebra word problems. In R. J. Seidel, R. E. Anderson, & B. Hunter (Eds.), *Computer Literacy*. New York: Academic Press.

Spache, G. G. (1965). *Toward better reading*. Champaign, IL: Garrard Press.

Spearman, C. (1904). The proof and measurement of association between two things. *American Journal of Psychology, 15*, 72–101.

Spearman, C. (1927). *The abilities of man*. New York: Macmillan.

Spence, J. A. & Spence, K. W. (1966). The motivational components of manifest anxiety: Drive and drive stimuli. In C. D. Spielberger (Ed.), *Anxiety and Behavior*. New York: Academic Press.

Spielberger, C. D. (1966). *Anxiety and behavior*. New York: Academic Press.

Spielberger, C. D. (1972). *Anxiety: Current trends in theory and research*. New York: Academic Press.

Spielberger, C. D., Gorsuch, R. L. & Lushene, R. E. (1970). *The state-trait anxiety inventory*. Palo Alto, CA: Consulting Psychologists Press.

Spoehr, K. T. & Schuberth, R. E. (1981). Processing words in context. In O. J. L. Tzeng & H. Singer (Eds.), *Perception of print*. Hillsdale, NJ: Erlbaum.

Stahl, S. A. & Fairbanks, M. M. (1986). The effects of vocabulary instruction: A model-based meta-analysis. *Review of Educational Research, 56*, 72–110.

Stallard, C. K. (1974). An analysis of the writing behavior of good student writers. *Research in the Teaching of English, 8*, 206–218.

Stallings, J. A. & Kaskowitz, D. H. (1974). *Follow Through Classroom Evaluation, 1972–73*. Menlo Park, CA: Stanford Research Institute.

Stanley, J. C. (1973). *Compensatory education for children ages two to eight: Recent studies of educational intervention*. Baltimore: Johns Hopkins University Press.

Stanovich, K. E. (1980). Toward an interactive-compensatory model of individual differences in the development of reading fluency. *Reading Research Quarterly, 16*, 32–65.

Stauffer, R. G. (1975). *Directing the reading-thinking process*. New York: Harper & Row.

Stein, J. (Ed.). (1966). *The Random House Dictionary of the English Language*. New York: Random House.

Steinberg, E. R. (1980). A garden of opportunities and a thicket of dangers. In L. W. Gregg & E. R. Steinberg (Eds.), *Cognitive processes in writing*. Hillsdale, NJ: Erlbaum.

Sternberg, R. J. (1977). *Intelligence, information processing, and analogical reasoning: The componential analysis of human abilities*. Hillsdale, NJ: Erlbaum.

Sternberg, R. J. (1981). Cognitive-behavioral approaches to the training of intelligence in the retarded. *Journal of Special Education, 15*, 165–183.

Sternberg, R. J. & Ketron, J. L. (1982). Selection and implementation of strategies in reasoning by analogy. *Journal of Educational Psychology, 74*, 399–413.

Sternberg, S. (1969). The discovery of processing stages: Extensions of Donders' method. *Acta Psychologica, 30,* 276–315.

Stevens, A., Collins, A. & Goldin, S. E. (1982). Misconceptions in students' understanding. In D. Sleeman & J. S. Brown (Eds.), *Intelligent tutoring systems.* Orlando, FL: Academic Press.

Stinard, T. A. & Dolphin, W. D. (1981). Which students benefit from self-paced mastery instruction and why. *Journal of Educational Psychology, 73,* 754–763.

Suchman, J. R. (1960). Inquiry training in the elementary school. *Science Teacher, 27,* 42–47.

Suchman, J. R. (1966). *Inquiry development program in physical science.* Chicago: Science Research Associates.

Sulzbacher, S. I. & Houser, J. E. (1968). A tactic to eliminate disruptive behaviors in the classroom: Group contingent consequences. *American Journal of Mental Deficiency, 73,* 88–90.

Strauss, S. (1972). *Inducing cognitive development and learning: A review of short-term training experiments.* Cognition, 1, 329–357.

Swanson, H. L. (1984). Process assessment of intelligence in learning disabled and mentally retarded children: A multidirectional model. *Educational Psychologist, 19,* 149–162.

Tamir, P., Gal-Choppin, R., & Nussinovitz, R. (1981). How do intermediate and junior high school students conceptualize living and nonliving? *Journal of Research in Science Teaching, 18,* 241–248.

Taylor, B. (1980). Children's memory for expository text after reading. *Reading Research Quarterly, 15,* 399–411.

Taylor, B. M. & Beach, R. W. (1984). The effects of text structure instruction on middle-grade students' comprehension and production of expository text. *Reading Research Quarterly, 19,* 134–146.

Taylor, J. A. (1953). A personality test of manifest anxiety. *Journal of Abnormal and Social Psychology, 48,* 285–290.

Thorndike, E. L. (1898). Animal intelligence: An experimental study of the associative processes in animals. *Psychological Review, Monograph Supplement, 2*(8).

Thorndike, E. L. (1911). *Animal intelligence.* New York: Macmillan.

Thorndike, E. L. (1913a). *Educational psychology.* New York: Columbia University Press.

Thorndike, E. L. (1913b). *The principles of teaching: Based on psychology.* New York: Seiler.

Thorndike, E. L. (1931). *Human learning.* New York: Century.

Thorndike, E. L. (1932). *The fundamentals of learning.* New York: Teachers College Press.

Thorndyke, P. W. (1977). Cognitive structures in comprehension and memory for narrative discourse. *Cognitive Psychology, 9,* 77–110.

Thornton, M. C. & Fuller, R. G. (1981). How do college students solve proportion problems? *Journal of Research in Science Teaching, 18*(4), 335–340.

Thurstone, L. L. (1924). *The nature of intelligence.* New York: Harcourt, Brace.

Thurstone, L. L. (1938). *Primary mental abilities.* Chicago: University of Chicago Press.

Thurstone, L. L. & Thurstone, T. G. (1941). *Factorial studies of intelligence.* Chicago: University of Chicago Press.

Tomlinson, P. D. & Hunt, D. E. (1971). Differential effects of rule-example order as a function of learner conceptual level. *Canadian Journal of Behavioral Science, 3,* 237–245.

Trowbridge, D. E. & McDermott, L. C. (1981). Investigation of student understanding of the concept of acceleration in one dimension. *American Journal of Physics, 49*(3), 242–253.

Trowbridge, M. H. & Cason, H. (1932). An experimental study of Thorndike's theory of learning. *Journal of General Psychology, 7,* 245–258.

Tulving, E. & Gold, C. (1963). Stimulus information and contextual information as determinants of tachistoscopic recognition of words. *Journal of Experimental Psychology, 66,* 319–327.

Tymitz, B. L. (1981). Teacher performance on IEP instructional planning tasks. *Exceptional Children, 48,* 258–260.

Tzeng, O. J. L. (1981). Relevancy of experimental psychology to reading instruction. In O. J. L. Tzeng & H. Singer (Eds.), *Perception of print.* Hillsdale, NJ: Erlbaum.

Vaugh, J. L. (1984). Concept structuring: The technique and empirical evidence. In C. D. Holley & D. F. Dansereau (Eds.), *Spatial learning strategies.* Orlando, FL: Academic Press.

Voss, J. F. & Bisanz, G. L. (1985). Knowledge and processing of narrative and expository texts. In B. K. Britton & J. B. Black (Eds.), *Understanding expository text.* Hillsdale, NJ: Erlbaum.

Wargo, M. J., Tallmadge, G. K., Michaels, D. D., Lipe, D. & Morris, S. J. (1972). *ESEA Title 1: A reanalysis and synthesis of evaluation data from fiscal year 1965 through 1970.* Palo Alto, CA: American Institute for Research.

Wason, P. C. (1968). Reason about a rule. *Quarterly Journal of Experimental Psychology, 20,* 273–281.

Watts, G. H. & Anderson, R. C. (1971). Effects of three types of inserted questions on learning from prose. *Journal of Educational Psychology, 62,* 387–394.

Weaver, P. A. (1979). Improving reading comprehension: Effects of sentence organization instruction. *Reading Research Quarterly, 15,* 129–146.

Weaver, P. A. & Resnick, L. B. (1979). The theory and practice of early reading: An introduction. In L. B. Resnick & P. A. Weaver (Eds.), *Theory and practice of early reading.* Hillsdale, NJ: Erlbaum.

Webb, N. M. (1984). Microcomputer learning in small groups: Cognitive requirements and group processes. *Journal of Educational Psychology, 6,* 1076–1088.

Wechsler, D. (1974). *Manual for the Wechsler intelligence scale for children: Revised.* New York: Psychological Corporation.

Weil, M. L. and Murphy, J. (1982). Instructional processes. In H. E. Mitzel (Ed.), *Encyclopedia of Educational Research* Fifth Edition. New York: Macmillan.

Weinstein, C. E. & Mayer, R. E. (1985). The teaching of learning strategies. In M. C. Wittrock (Ed.), *Handbook of Research and Teaching,* Third Edition. New York: Macmillan.

Wiekart, D., Epstein, A., Schweinhant, L. & Bond, J. (1978). *The Ypsilanti preschool curriculum demonstration project: Preschool years and longitudinal results.* Ypsilanti, MI: High Scoped Educational Research Foundation.

Weiner, B. (1978). Achievement strivings. In H. London & J. E. Exner (Eds.), *Dimensions of personality.* New York: Wiley.

Wertheimer, M. (1959). *Productive thinking.* New York: Harper & Row.

West, L. H. T. & Fensham, P. J. (1976). Prior knowledge or advance organizers affective variables in chemical learning. *Journal of Research in Science Teaching, 13,* 297–306.

West, L. H. T. & Pines, A. L. (Eds.). (1985). *Cognitive structure and conceptual change.* Orlando, FL: Academic Press.

West, R. F. & Stanovich, K. E. (1978). Automatic contextual facilitation in readers of three ages. *Child Development, 49,* 717–727.

Whaley, J. F. (1981). Readers' expectations for story structures. *Reading Research Quarterly, 17,* 90–114.

Wheeler, A. E. & Kass, H. (1978). Student misconceptions in chemical equilibrium. *Science Education, 62*(2), 223–232.

Whimbey, A. & Lochhead, J. (1979). *Problem solving and comprehension: A short course in analytic reasoning.* Philadelphia: Franklin Institute Press.

White, B. Y. (1984). Designing computer games to help physics students understand Newton's laws of motion. *Cognition and Instruction, 1,* 69–108.

White, M. & Miller, S. R. (1983). Dyslexia: A term in search of a definition. *Journal of Special Education, 17,* 5–10.

White, R. T. (1974). The validation of a learning hierarchy. *American Educational Research Journal, 11,* 121–236.

White, R. T. & Mayer, R. E. (1980). Understanding intellectual skills. *Instructional Science, 9,* 101–127.

Wickelgren, W. A. (1974). *How to solve problems.* New York: Freeman.

Winch, W. A. (1913). *Inductive versus deductive methods of teaching.* Baltimore: Warwick & York.

Witkin, H. A., Moore, C. A., Goodenough, D. R. & Cox, P. W. (1977). Field-dependent and field-independent cognitive styles and their educational implications. *Review of Educational Research, 47,* 1–64.

Wittrock, M. C. (1974). Learning as a generative activity. *Educational Psychologist, 11,* 87–95.

Wittrock, M. C. (1980). *The brain and psychology.* New York: Academic Press.

Wittrock, M. C., Marks, C. & Doctorow, W. (1975). Reading as a generative process. *Journal of Educational Psychology, 67,* 484–489.

Wolff, P. & Levin, J. R. (1972). The role of overt activity in children's imagery production. *Child Development, 43,* 537–547.

Wollman, W. T. & Lawson, A. E. (1978). The influence of instruction on proportional reasoning in seventh graders. *Journal of Research in Science Teaching, 15*(3), 227–232.

Woodworth, R. S. & Schlosberg, H. (1965). *Experimental psychology.* New York: Holt, Rinehart & Winston.

Worthen, B. R. (1968). Discovery and expository task presentation in elementary mathematics. *Journal of Educational Psychology Monographs Supplement, 59,* (1, Pt. 2).

Yates, F. A. (1966). *The art of memory.* London: Routledge and Kegan Paul.

Yerkes, R. M. & Dodson, J. D. (1908). The relation of strength of stimulus to rapidity of habit formation. *Journal of Comparative Neurology and Psychology, 18,* 459–482.

Yesseldyke, J. E. & Algozzine, B. (1983). LD or not LD: That's not the question! *Journal of Learning Disabilities, 16,* 29–21.

Yesseldyke, J. E. & Thurlow, M. L. (1984). Assessment practices in special education: Adequacy and appropriateness. *Educational Psychologist, 19,* 123–136.

Yussen, S. R. & Levy, V. M., Jr. (1975). Developmental changes in predicting one's own span of short-term memory. *Journal of Experimental Child Psychology, 19,* 502–508.

Zeaman, D. & House, B. J. (1963). The role of attention in retardate discrimination learning. In N. R. Ellis (Ed.), *Handbook of mental deficiency.* New York: McGraw-Hill.

Credits and Acknowledgments *(continued from page iv)*

Box 4–1: From Moely, Olson, Halwes, & Flavel, "Production deficiency in young children's recall" *Developmental Psychology*, 1. Copyright 1969 by the American Psychological Association. Adapted by permission of the publisher.

Figure 4–7: Adapted from S. I. Rossi & M. C. Wittrock, "Developmental shifts in verbal recall between mental ages 2 and 5" *Child Development*, 42, 1971. © The Society for Research in Child Development, Inc. Used by permission.

Figure 4–8: Adapted from P. Wolff & J. R. Levin, "The role of overt activity in children's imagery production" *Child Development*, 43, 1972. © The Society for Research in Child Development, Inc. Used by permission.

Figure 5–5: Adapted from B. F. Skinner, *The Behavior of Organisms*, Prentice-Hall, 1938. Used by permission of the author.

Figure 5–6: From S. I. Sulzbacher & J. E. Houser, "A tactic to eliminate disruptive behaviors in the classroom: Group contingent consequences" *American Journal of Mental Deficiency*, 73, 88–90, 1968. Reprinted by permission of the American Association on Mental Deficiency.

Figures 5–7 and 5–8: From K. D. O'Leary, W. C. Becker, M. B. Evans & R. A. Saudargas, (1969), *Journal of Applied Behavior Analysis*, 2, pp. 3–13. Copyright 1969 by the Society for the Experimental Analysis of Behavior, Inc.

Figure 5–10: From M. H. Trowbridge & H. Cason, "An experimental study of Thorndike's theory of learning" *Journal of General Psychology*, 7, 245–258, 1932. Reprinted with permission of the Helen Dwight Reid Educational Foundation. Published by Heldref Publications, 4000 Albemarle Street, N.W., Washington, D.C. 20016. Copyright © 1932.

Figure 5–11: From K. M. Newell, "Knowledge of results and motor learning" *Journal of Motor Behavior*, 16, 235–244, 1974. Reprinted with permission of the Helen Dwight Reid Educational Foundation. Published by Heldref Publications, 4000 Albemarle Street, N.W., Washington, D.C. 20016. Copyright © 1974.

Box 6–1: From D. Clarke, *The Encyclopedia of How It Works*, © Marshall Cavendish Ltd. 1977. Reprinted by permission.

Figure 6–2: From R. E. Mayer, "Aids to text comprehension" *Educational Psychologist*, copyright © 1984 by Division 15 of the American Psychological Association. Reprinted by permission of publisher and author.

Box 6–5: From W. Liddle, *Reading For Concepts, Book G*. Copyright © 1977. McGraw-Hill Book Company. Reprinted by permission of McGraw-Hill Book Company.

Figure 7–13: From "Processes in acquiring knowledge" by A. Collins, 1977, in R. C. Anderson, R. J. Spiro & W. E. Montague, (Eds.), *School and the Acquisition of Knowledge*, p. 341. Copyright 1977 by Lawrence Erlbaum Associates, Inc. Reprinted by permission of the publisher.

Box 8–1: From *Student Achievement In California Schools: 1979–80 Annual Report*, California Assessment Program 1980. Published by California State Department of Education. Used by permission.

Figure 8–1: From M. Pressley & J. R. Levin, "Developmental constraints associated with children's use of the keyword method of foreign language vocabulary learning" *Journal of Experimental Child Psychology*, 28. (1978) Art created by M. Pressley. Reprinted by permission of Academic Press and M. Pressley.

Figures 8–2 and 8–3: From J. R. Levin, C. B. McCormick, G. E. Miller & J. K. Berry, "Mnemonic versus nonmnemonic vocabulary-learning strategies for children" *American Educational Research Journal*, 19, 121–136, (1982). Reprinted by permission of American Educational Research Association.

Table 8–1: From B. F. Jones and J. W. Hall, "School applications of the mnemonic keyword method as a study strategy for eighth graders" *Journal of Educational Psychology*, 74, 230–237. Copyright 1982 by American Psychological Association. Reprinted by permission of the publisher and J. W. Hall.

Figure 8–4: From A. Paivio. (1971), *Imagery and Verbal Processes*, New York, Holt, Rinehart & Winston. (Reprinted in 1979 by Lawrence Erlbaum Associates, Hillsdale, New Jersey). Reprinted by permission of the author.

Table 8–2 and Figure 8–5: From C. D. Holley, D. F. Dansereau, B. A. McDonald, J. C. Garland & K. W. Collins. "Evaluation of a hierarchical mapping technique as an aid to prose processing" *Contemporary Educational Psychology*, 4, 227–237, (1979). Academic Press. Used by permission.

Box 8–3, Figure 8–7, and Table 8–4: From B. Meyer, D. H. Brandt and G. J. Bluth, "Use of Top-Level Structure In Text: Key for Reading Comprehension of Ninth-Grade Students" *Reading Research Quarterly*, Vol. 16, No. 1, pp. 72–103. Reprinted with permission of B. Meyer and the International Reading Association.

Boxes 8–4 and 8–5: From L. Cook, 1982 PhD Thesis, "Reading Strategies Training for Scientific Text," Appendix I (p. 113–5) and Appendix III (p. 124–6). Reprinted by permission of L. Cook.

Boxes 9–3 and 9–4: From B. S. Bloom & L. J. Broder, *Problem-Solving Processes of College Students: An Exploratory Investigation*. Copyright © 1950. University of Chicago Press. Reprinted by permission of the University of Chicago Press.

Boxes 9–5 and 9–6: From M. Covington, R. Crutchfield, L. Davies and Olton, "The Productive Thinking Program" (1974), Charles E. Merrill Publishing Company. Used by permission.

Figure 9–2: Adapted from Feuerstein et al, *Instructional Enrichment: An Intervention Program For Cognitive Modifiability*. Copyright © 1980. Published by University Park Press, Baltimore.

Box 9–9: From Moshe F. Rubinstein, *Patterns of Problem Solving*, © 1975, p. 65. Reprinted by permission of Prentice-Hall, Englewood Cliffs, New Jersey.

Figure 9–4: From R. J. Sternberg and J. L. Ketron, "Selection and implementation of strategies in reasoning by analogy" *Journal of Educational Psychology*, 74, 399–413. Copyright 1982 by the American Psychological Association. Reprinted by permission of the publisher and R. J. Sternberg.

Figure 9–5: From J. H. Larkin et al, "Expert and Novice Performance in Solving Physics Problems", Vol. 208, pp. 1335–1342, Fig. 20, July 1980 *Science*, Copyright 1980 by The American Association for the Advancement of Science. Reprinted by permission of the AAAS and J. H. Larkin.

Figure 9–6: From "Three problems in teaching general skills" by J. R. Hayes, 1985, in S. F. Chipman, J. W. Segal & R. Glaser (Eds.), *Thinking and Learning Skills*, Volume 2, p. 395. Copyright 1985 by Lawrence Erlbaum Associates, Inc. Reprinted by permission of the publisher.

Box 10–6: Adapted from the Open Court Wall Sound Cards used in the first grade Foundation Program and Phonics Kits 2 and 3. Copyright © 1979 Open Court Publishing Company. Reprinted by permission.

Table 10–1: Adapted from "Understanding word perception" by J. C. Johnston, 1981, in O. J. L. Tzeng & H. Singer (Eds), *Perception of Print*. Copyright 1981 by Lawrence Erlbaum Associates, Inc. Reprinted by permission.

Figure 10–3: From S. Jay Samuels, "The Method of Repeated Readings," *The Reading Teacher*, January 1979. Reprinted with permission of S. Jay Samuels and the International Reading Association.

Figure 10–4: From E. Tulving and C. Gold, "Stimulus information and contextual information as determinants of tachistoscopic recognition of words" *Journal of Experimental Psychology*, 66,

319–327. Copyright 1963 by the American Psychological Association. Reprinted with permission of the publisher and E. Tulving.

Figure 10–5: From R. F. West and K. E. Stanovich, "Automatic contextual facilitation in readers of three ages" *Child Development*, 49, 717–727, copyright © The Society for Research in Child Development, Inc. Reprinted by permission.

Box 10–7 and Figure 10–7: Adapted from G. W. McConkie and K. Rayner, "The span of effective stimulus during a fixation in reading" *Perception and Psychophysics*, 17, 578–586, (1975). Reprinted by permission of Psychonomic Society Publications and G. W. McConkie.

Box 10–8: From "Cognitive processes in reading: Models based on readers' eye fixations" by P. A. Carpenter and M. A. Just, 1981, in A. M. Lesgold and C. A. Perfetti (Eds.), *Interactive Processes in Reading*, p. 177–213. Copyright 1981 by Lawrence Erlbaum Associates, Inc. Reprinted by permission.

Boxes 11–1 and 11–2: From F. C. Bartlett, *Remembering*, published by Cambridge University Press. Copyright © 1932 by Cambridge University Press. Reprinted by permission of Cambridge University Press.

Box 11–4: From J. D. Bransford and M. K. Johnson, "Contextual prerequisites for understanding: Some investigations of comprehension and recall" *Journal of Verbal Learning and Verbal Behavior*, 61, 717–726, (1972). Reprinted with permission of Academic Press and J. D. Bransford.

Box 11–5: From J. Pichert and R. C. Anderson, "Taking different perspectives on a story" *Journal of Educational Psychology*, 69, 309–315. Copyright 1977 by American Psychological Association.

Figures 11–3, 11–4, 11–6, and 11–7: From A. L. Brown and S. S. Smiley, "The development of strategies for studying texts" *Child Development*, 49, 1076–1088, copyright © 1978 The Society for Research in Child Development, Inc. Reprinted by permission.

Box 11–7: From Barbara M. Taylor and Richard W. Beach, "The Effects of Text Structure Instruction on Middle-Grade Students' Comprehension and Production of Expository Text" *Reading Research Quarterly*, Vol. 19, No. 2, p. 139. Reprinted with permission of Barbara Taylor and the International Reading Association.

Box 12–1, 12–2, and 12–3: From *The Language and Thought of the Child* by J. Piaget, 1955. Reprinted by permission of Routledge and Kegan Paul.

Box 12–4: From A. Matsuhashi, "Explorations in the real-time production of written discourse", *What Writers Know*, edited by M. Nystrand, copyright 1982. Reprinted with permission of Academic Press and A. Matsuhashi.

Figures 13–1 and 13–2: From R. E. Mayer, "Memory for algebra story problems" *Journal of Educational Psychology*, 74, 199–218. Copyright 1982 by American Psychological Association. Reprinted with permission of the publisher and author.

Box 13–3: From "From words to equations: Meaning and representation in algebra word problems" by D. A. Hinsley, J. R. Hayes, and H. A. Simon, 1977, in M. A. Just and P. A. Carpenter (Eds.), *Cognitive Processes in Comprehension*, p. 93–4. Copyright 1977 by Lawrence Erlbaum Associates, Inc. Reprinted by permission.

Box 13–4: From Richard E. Mayer, *Thinking, Problem Solving, Cognition*. Copyright © 1983 W. H. Freeman and Company. Used by permission.

Figure 13–4: From G. Groen and J. M. Parkman, "A chronometric analysis of simple addition" *Psychological Review*, 79, 329–343. Copyright 1972 by American Psychological Association. Reprinted by permission of the publisher.

Figure 13–5: From Richard E. Mayer, *The Promise of Cognitive Psychology*. Copyright © 1981 W. H. Freeman and Company. Used by permission.

Figures 14–1 and 14–2: From M. McCloskey, et al, "Curvilinear Motion in the Absence of External Forces: Naive Beliefs About the Motion of Objects," Vol. 210, pp. 1139–1141, 5 December 1980, *Science*. Copyright 1980 by the American Association for the Advancement of Science. Reprinted by permission of the AAAS and M. McCloskey.

Figures 14–4, 14–5, and 14–6: From "Intuitive Physics" by M. McCloskey. Copyright © 1983 by Scientific American, Inc. All rights reserved.

Figures 14–7, 14–8, 14–10 and Table 14–1: From J. Clement, "Students' preconceptions in introductory mechanics" *American Journal of Physics*, 50 (1), 66–71. Copyright © 1982 by the American Association of Physics Teachers. Reprinted by permission of the AAPT and J. Clement.

Figures 14–11 and 14–13: From "Proportional reasoning and control of variables in seven countries" by R. Karplus, E. Karplus, M. Formisano and A. Paulsen, 1979, in J. Lochhead and J. Clement (Eds.), *Cognitive Process Instruction*, p. 100, Appendix A1 and p. 56. Copyright 1979 by Lawrence Erlbaum Associates, Inc. Reprinted by permission.

Figure 15–2: From R. M. Gagne, J. R. Mayor, H. L. Garstens and N. E. Paradise, "Factors in acquiring knowledge of a mathematical task" *Psychological Monographs*, Vol. 76, no. 7, Whole No. 526. Copyright 1962 by the American Psychological Association. Reprinted by permission of the publisher and R. M. Gagne.

Figure 15–3: From R. T. White, "The validation of a learning hierarchy" *American Educational Research Journal*, 11, 121–136, (1974). Reprinted by permission.

Boxes 16–3, 16–4, and Table 16–2: From *Comprehensive Test of Basic Skills* (1982), CTBS Examinational Materials, CTBS/McGraw-Hill. Reprinted by permission.

Box 16–8 and Figure 16–1: From Richard E. Mayer, *The Promise of Cognitive Psychology*. Copyright © 1981 W. H. Freeman and Company. Used by permission.

Box 16–6: From *Principles of Educational and Psychological Testing*, Second Edition, by Frederick G. Brown. Copyright © 1970 by the Dryden Press Inc. Used by permission of CBS College Publishing.

Box 16–7: From J. P. Guilford, "Three faces of intellect" *American Psychologist*, 14, 469–479. Copyright 1959 by the American Psychological Association. Reprinted by permission of the publisher and author.

Figure 16–6: From Edward L. Dejnozka and David E. Kapel, *American Educators' Encyclopedia* (Greenwood Press, Westport, CT, 1982), p. 488. Copyright © 1982 by Edward L. Dejnozka and David E. Kapel. Used by permission of the publisher.

Figures 16–10 and 16–11: From J. M. Belmont and E. C. Butterfield, "Learning strategies as determinants of memory deficiencies" *Cognitive Psychology*, 2, 411–420, (1971). Reprinted by permission of Academic Press and E. C. Butterfield.

Figures 17–2, 17–3, and 17–4: From R. E. Snow, and D. F. Lohman, Figures 2a, 3a, and 4a, *Journal of Educational Psychology*, 76, 347–376. Copyright 1984 by American Psychological Association. Reprinted by permission of the publisher and R. E. Snow.

Figure 17–4: From R. E. Mayer, C. C. Stiehl and J. G. Greeno, "Acquisition of understanding and skill in relation to subjects' preparation and meaningfulness of instruction" *Journal of Educational Psychology*, 67, 331–350. Copyright 1975 by the American Psychological Association. Reprinted by permission of publisher and R. E. Mayer.

Figure 17–14: From Gestalt Completion Test (CS-1) from "Kit of Factor-Referenced Cognitive Tests." Copyright © 1962, 1975 by Educational Testing Service. All rights reserved. Reprinted by permission.

Figures 18–5 and 18–6: From M. L. Smith and G. V. Glass, "Meta-analysis of research on class size

Credits and Acknowledgments

and its relation to attitudes and instruction" *American Educational Research Journal*, 17, 419–433, (1980). Reprinted by permission of the American Educational Research Association.

Pages 328–329: Writing samples (data) from "How children cope with the cognitive demands of writing" by M. Scardamalia, 1981, in C. H. Frederiksen and J. F. Dominic (Eds.), *Writing*, Vol. 2, pp. 89–94. Copyright 1981 by Lawrence Erlbaum Associates, Inc. Reprinted by permission.

Page 508: Dialogue reprinted by permission of McCutchan Publishing Corporation from Penelope L. Peterson and Herbert J. Walberg, editors, *Research on Teaching: Concepts, Findings, and Implications*, pp. 136–137. © 1979 by McCutchan Publishing Corporation.

Part I Opener: © 1980 Will McIntyre. Used by permission of Photo Researchers Inc.

Part II Opener: © 1980 Sybil Shelton. Used by permission of Monkmeyer Press Photo Service.

Part III Opener: © 1980 Barbara Rios. Used by permission of Photo Researchers Inc.

Part IV Opener: © 1980 Barbara Rios. Used by permission of Photo Researchers Inc.

Part V Opener: © 1984 Karen Preuss. Used by permission of Taurus Photos.

SUBJECT INDEX

Author Index